To
Marg

Merry X mas 2015
Enjoy

From
Jim + Becky

Family Cookbook

Family Cookbook

Caroline Bretherton

DK

LONDON, NEW YORK,
MUNICH, MELBOURNE, DELHI

Senior Editor Scarlett O'Hara
Senior Art Editor Sara Robin
Editor Lucy Bannell
US Senior Editor Rebecca Warren
US Editor Christy Lusiak
US Consultant Kate Curnes Ramos
Managing Editor Dawn Henderson
Managing Art Editor Christine Keilty
Senior Jacket Creative Nicola Powling
Jackets Assistant Rosie Levine
Producer, Pre-Production Sarah Isle
Senior Producer Oliver Jeffreys
Creative Technical Support Sonia Charbonnier
Art Director Peter Luff
Publishing Manager Anna Davidson
Publisher Peggy Vance

DK INDIA
Senior Editor Dorothy Kikon
Senior Art Editor Ivy Roy
Editor Arani Sinha
Art Editor Simran Kaur
Assistant Art Editors Karan Chaudhary, Gazal Roongta
Managing Editor Alicia Ingty
Managing Art Editor Navidita Thapa
Pre-Production Manager Sunil Sharma
DTP Designers Sourabh Challariya, Umesh Singh Rawat

This edition first published in Canada in 2013
DK is represented in Canada by
Tourmaline Editions Inc., 662 King Street West, Suite 304,
Toronto, ON CANADA M5V 1M7

13 14 15 16 17 10 9 8 7 6 5 4 3 2
192157 – Oct/2013

ISBN 978-1-55363-225-2

DK books are available at special discounts when purchased in bulk for sales promotions, premiums, fundraising, or educational use. For details, contact:
DK Publishing Special Markets, 345 Hudson Street,
New York 10014 or SpecialSales@dk.com.

Color reproduction by Alta Image Ltd
Printed and bound in China by South China

Discover more at **www.dk.com**

Contents

How to use this book

This family cookbook has six chapters of recipes: purées and food for **Babies and Toddlers**, options for healthy **Family Meals**, **Easy Entertaining** ideas for when you need to produce something special, suggestions for **Food to Go** for packed lunches or family picnics, much-loved and easy-to-achieve cookies, cakes, and breads in **Baking**, and a **Cooking with Kids** section, with step-by-step recipes children can cook for themselves. There are also useful features tackling subjects such as Kids' Parties, Picky Kids and Teenagers, and Batching and Freezing. **Recipe Choosers** give an inspiring selection of dishes from the book on themes such as Pantry Meals, Quick Breads and Desserts, and Cheap Eats.

The Chapters

Babies and Toddlers

This section has been specially compiled to provide a range of healthy recipes to take your baby from simple first tastes through to more complex meals and finger foods. All the choices here are healthy and balanced and the texture of all of them can be adjusted to suit the weaning stage of your baby.

Family Meals

This chapter is subdivided into sections including fish, poultry, meat, vegetables, pasta, rice, and eggs and cheese. Each section begins with appetizers, soups, and salads before

Delicious dishes such as Braised lamb with spring vegetables (p135) fill the Family Meals chapter, many with variations, tips on how to prepare ahead, or suggestions for making the most of leftovers.

If you're entertaining you will want to create something special. This Mediterranean chicken (p106) makes an impressive dish that tends to go over well with adults and children alike.

progressing into suggestions for main courses. The vegetable section includes main course vegetarian options, as well as soups, salads, and sides. All the meals are designed to appeal to a growing family with plenty of new twists on family favorites as well as recipes that give more economical items such as pasta, rice, eggs, and cheese a starring role.

Easy Entertaining

Entertaining another family for lunch, friends for dinner, or catering for a larger number of people at a celebration, demands a little more from your culinary skills. Catering for all ages and tastes can be demanding, but with some planning and preparation it needn't be stressful. In this chapter you will find brunch options, barbecue recipes, a mouthwatering array of desserts, and lots of inspiration for hot and cold fun snacks and treats for kids' parties, including birthday cakes.

Food to Go

Whether you are preparing a summer picnic with the family, or simply looking for inspiration for the children's lunchboxes, this chapter will help. Everyday sandwiches are turned into interesting and tasty fare to eat on the go, and there are recipes for delicious wraps, salads, side dishes, and baked goods that are all easy to transport.

Baking

Baking is probably the most family-friendly activity you can try in the kitchen, so here you will find many simple recipes that are easy to prepare. As well as the familiar cakes and cookies, there are delicious recipes for savory bakes and simple breads to extend your baking repertoire. Seasoned bakers will find some fresh and exciting ideas here with inspiration from around the world, as well as some tried-and-tested classics.

Cooking with Kids

We all want our children to grow up eating well, so it's a good idea to introduce them to cooking as soon as possible. Children who have helped to prepare a meal are far more likely to eat it, after all. All the recipes included here are ideal for children to cook and most are accompanied by helpful step-by-step photography to guide you while you supervise your young chefs. There are recipes for children to make for their own parties, healthy meals they could serve to the family, and items that they could make and give as gifts.

Feature pages

Scattered throughout the book are feature pages that include handy tips for common situations that arise in the family kitchen. So, there is a feature on coping with Picky Eaters, managing After School, and feeding Picky Kids and Teenagers. There is advice on Smart Shopping, and The Hardworking Fridge, suggestions for being Smart with Leftovers, providing Meals for a Week, and Batching and Freezing. There are also tips on feeding Vegetarian Kids, Cooking for Allergies, dealing with Unexpected Guests, and hosting Kids' Parties.

The Recipes

Information boxes A really helpful feature of this book is the extra guidance given after many recipes on how to freeze or batch cooking, with suggestions on what to prepare ahead, and tips on being clever with leftovers. There is also advice on adapting meals for fussy eaters, or highlighting meals that might appeal to them, plus notes on cooking for a crowd, as well as many other handy cook's tips.

Icons These appear at the top of every recipe and advise on preparation and cooking times, and highlight recipes that are vegetarian or freezable.

Special equipment Any special equipment you will need for a specific recipe, such as a food processor or hand-held blender, will be listed at the beginning of the recipe. Check if any items are listed so that you can gather together your equipment before you start cooking.

Nutrition boxes All recipes have a breakdown of the amounts of key nutrients, including saturated fat, contained in one serving. If the recipe says that it serves six, then the breakdown is for one sixth of the total recipe. Nutrition boxes in the Babies and Toddlers chapter give amounts of iron and calcium rather than saturated fat.

Variations Many recipes have suggestions for a variation to provide a new twist on the recipe or ideas on how to alter the ingredients to satisfy different palates.

Cook smart

Feeding a family can be challenging when you are trying to cater to different tastes and various schedules, while providing well-balanced, tasty meals. As well as offering fresh ideas for family meals alongside some tried-and-trusted favorites, this book aims to make this process more streamlined so that your time in the kitchen is spent wisely, producing, where possible, one meal for all and making good use of leftovers, as well as batching and freezing, and preparing ahead.

One meal for all

All too often home cooks end up preparing more than one meal every night—either because each family member likes different things or because they come home at various times. Cooking just one meal for everyone to share means less time spent in the kitchen and more with the family—and this ideal is not impossible to achieve. Throughout this book, there are suggestions for preparing parts of meals ahead, adapting recipes to suit different tastes (from adding spices to producing a vegetarian option), as well as recipes that are ideal for reheating as and when family members make their way through the door. Don't ditch the leftovers before reading the ideas on how to rework them into the next day's meal, and many recipes also include a variation, so that you can try a new twist on an old favorite—an easy way to change things up.

Spanish tortilla (p248) makes a nutritious meal with green beans or broccoli. Save the leftovers to eat the following day packed in lunch boxes or with a tomato salad.

Spicy sausage casserole (p147) is easy to adapt for different tastes. Adjust the spiciness or add vegetables to make the dish go further. Serve with plenty of mashed potatoes for hungry teens.

Plan ahead

To save time, trouble, and money, it makes sense to be smart about the amount of time you spend in the kitchen. Planning weekly meals, or at least weekly shopping lists, means you make the most of the food you have in the fridge and freezer, and avoid getting stuck with nothing to eat on a busy day. When you know the family's schedule for the week, you can plan around it. It's easier when everyone will be at home and eating together, but there will also be days when people will require meals at different times. Try to plan ahead by cooking extra food one day so there is more for another day, or making sure that, when schedules differ, you have an easy one-pot dish simmering away that you can reheat as needed. Don't forget your leftovers—roasted meats can be included in another dish such as a curry or pilaf, enjoyed again as part of a tasty wrap in a packed lunch, or as part of a children's party.

Batch and freeze

Multiplying the quantities of ingredients to cook twice or three times the amount of a recipe is an easy way to get ahead in the kitchen. Certain foods really lend themselves to cooking in bulk and freezing in portions; any recipe using chicken leg or thigh portions, for example, is easier to freeze than one using a whole chicken, while dishes with plenty of liquid, such as soups or stews, tend to freeze better than drier ones. All the recipes in this book that are suitable for freezing are labeled with freezer symbols, so look out for those to make planning ahead even easier.

Freezing food is a safe and easy way to preserve it for another day, but do make sure the food is properly stored in heavy-duty freezer bags or airtight, lidded, freezerproof containers. If food is badly wrapped and exposed to the air in the freezer, it can become dry and discolored due to "freezer burn" and will have to be discarded. Remember to label containers clearly, with the contents and the date on which it was frozen, to help you use frozen food in rotation and ensure it is not left in the freezer too long. Defrosting frozen food is best done slowly, overnight, in the fridge, and once defrosted the food should never be refrozen.

Store food safely

Few of us have time to go shopping every day, so it is important to think carefully about how you store food as well as how you cook it. To avoid possible contamination, check the temperatures of your fridge and freezer; the fridge should be set to between 37°F (3°C) and 41°F (5°C), and the freezer to at least 0°F (-18°C). A build-up of ice can affect the temperature of either appliance, so be sure to defrost them regularly.

Wrap well all produce that is to be stored in the fridge, especially meats, fish, dairy, and liquids, to prevent leaking or spillages. Always store raw and cooked products on separate shelves, with raw meats on the bottom shelf, to prevent cross-contamination. Don't leave cooked rice standing at room temperature for too long, serve it immediately. If you are storing leftover cooked rice or pasta, make sure it has been cooked and then cooled as quickly as possible before being placed in an airtight container in the fridge. Don't keep it for more than one day before reheating. Don't reheat it again. Eat other pre-cooked food within two days of placing it in the fridge. If you are leaving meat to marinate, always put it in a non-reactive (non-metal) dish, to avoid a chemical reaction with the food that will taint its flavor and make it inedible.

Freezing times

Although most foods can be frozen, the appearance, texture, and quality of some foods deteriorates more quickly than others, even in the freezer. Label items with the date they were frozen and stick to these simple guidelines for safe freezing.

Raw poultry, fish, and meat (in small pieces) – up to 6 months

Raw ground beef or poultry – up to 3 months

Soups – up to 3 months

Stocks – up to 6 months

Stews and casseroles – up to 3 months

Pies and pastries, uncooked – up to 3 months

Pies and pastries, cooked – up to 6 months

Fruit, raw – up to 1 year *

Fruit, cooked – up to 9 months*

Vegetables, blanched – up to 9 months*

Vegetables, cooked – up to 9 months*

Butter – up to 3 months

Cheese, grated – up to 4 months

Bread – up to 3 months

* The exact length of time for which these can be frozen depends on the fruit or vegetable itself, and how it is prepared. Those with a lower water content tend to freeze better and last longer, too.

Get the kids involved

Encouraging your children to help out in the kitchen from an early age not only gives them the skills to cook for themselves, but it also helps to expand their culinary horizons and makes it more likely that they will experiment with food and try new ingredients. Trying out the recipes here will help them learn more about what goes into a healthy balanced meal made with fresh ingredients. Get small children involved with everything from setting the table to helping with simple baking, while older children and teenagers can be let loose in the kitchen to create dinner from scratch with only a little help from their parents. If you can overlook the mess and offer plenty of praise (along with only a little constructive criticism!) you may see them return to cook again another day.

Eat well

Ensuring that each member of your family has a varied, nutritious diet is not always easy. With the different ages and stages of a family, from growing babies and toddlers to less-active adults, there are different nutritional needs to consider. Young children benefit from the calcium richness of full-fat dairy products, for example, whereas most older children and adults would be advised to consume the low-fat equivalents.

Keep it balanced

A balanced diet for the whole family should include protein, carbohydrate, and healthy fats, as well as a full array of vitamins and minerals. Protein, a nutrient needed for growth and repair, is found in meat, poultry, fish, and seafood, as well as nuts, beans, seeds, and eggs. Vegetarian sources also include tofu and quinoa. Some cuts of meat can be high in saturated fat, so you might want to vary the sources of protein in your diet.

Carbohydrates are nutrients that provide energy. They are found in many sources, from wholegrain bread to sugar and fruit, so choose the sources that are better for you. Complex carbohydrates, such as whole grains, beans, and starchy vegetables, release sugar more slowly into the bloodstream, providing energy but avoiding the highs and lows that are associated with consuming simple carbohydrates, such as refined white flour and sugar.

A balanced meal includes a lean source of protein, carbohydrate, and lots of colorful, tasty vegetables. Baked fish with cherry tomatoes (p75) is a great example of a healthy family meal.

A healthy breakfast such as Granola (p268) makes an excellent start to the day, and keeps you and your family feeling full for longer. A breakfast like this means you are less likely to reach for sugary snacks.

A healthy breakfast of homemade oatmeal, granola, or whole wheat cereal, for example, will release its energy over a longer period and leave you and your family less hungry than grabbing a slice of white toast, a sugary breakfast cereal, or a sweet drink would do.

It's sometimes easy to think that fats are the enemy but this is not the case. In fact, our bodies need a source of healthy fat to provide energy and protect the heart, among other things. Good fats, such as monosaturated or polyunsaturated fat, are found in olive oil, sunflower oil, nuts, seeds, avocados, and fatty fish such as salmon or tuna. The types of fats to be avoided are saturated fats—found in some cuts of red meat, poultry skin, and full-fat dairy products—and also trans fats, which are found in many commercially made baked goods, snack foods, and fried foods.

Make it colorful

Our bodies need a vast array of vitamins and minerals to flourish, some in tiny quantities, some in greater ones. One of the easiest ways to ensure that your family's diet is vitamin- and mineral-rich is to include vegetables in a wide variety of colors. Red, orange, and green fruits and vegetables, tend to be rich in vitamins. Vitamin C, which boosts your immune system and helps your body fight off viruses, can be found in kiwis, strawberries, and bell peppers as well as oranges. Dark green, leafy vegetables such as spinach, greens, and kale are rich in many vitamins and minerals including vitamin C, iron for the healthy function of red blood cells, and calcium for the formation of strong bones and teeth.

Different needs

Cooking for the diverse nutritional needs in a family can be tricky, but it does not have to be impossible. Buying both whole- and low-fat milk for example, is an easy way to ensure both young children and adults are catered for. Growing teenagers will often need extra energy, so stock up on whole grain muffins, breads, and bananas and allow them to snack between meals on these healthy complex carbohydrates, which will release sugars more slowly into the bloodstream and keep them fuller for longer.

If you are trying to lose weight, avoid "finishing off" the children's party food—snacking on leftovers often means you have no real idea how many calories you have consumed. The whole family will benefit from a diet rich in fruits and vegetables, so start making breakfast smoothies on the weekend and check the vegetable section of the Family Meals chapter for vegetable-based recipes that the whole family will enjoy. Too much salt is not good for anyone, so try using powdered stocks and spices instead to add flavor to a meal and use good quality sea salt sparingly at the table, where it will have the most impact.

There are a few recipes, such as Quick chocolate mousse (p360) or Hollandaise sauce for the Eggs Benedict (p254) that contain raw or undercooked eggs. For these recipes, only the freshest eggs should be used, and pregnant women, young children, and the elderly should avoid these dishes altogether.

Portion caution

From the time children first move on to solid foods, it is easy to overestimate how much they will eat. When your child is very small, be led by them, and if you are concerned that they are not eating enough, cut back on snacks between meals and make sure they are not consuming sugary fruit juices that fill them up. It is often better to offer small children a few different things on their plate than expect them to make their way through a pile of pasta, which can leave them feeling overwhelmed. Try dishing up a small serving of protein, one of carbohydrate, and a couple of vegetable choices instead. By contrast, older teenagers, especially active ones, will often need second helpings (or even thirds) as they continue to grow. Toast or cereal can often be a good filler here, but make sure that the choices available are from healthy, complex carbohydrates such as whole grains or pulses.

When serving adult portions, a good rule of thumb is to choose a medium-sized plate. Don't load up the plate and make sure that half your serving is made up of fruit or vegetables, a quarter with a low-fat source of protein, and a quarter with some complex carbohydrate.

Choose good food

Beyond the basics of making sure that your family gets a balanced diet, there is the issue of the sources of that diet to consider. If you want to use organic ingredients but are limited by the cost, choose organic meat, eggs, and milk. Factory-farmed eggs and chicken are cheaper, but may not be as nutrient-rich as free-range or organic equivalents. If you choose to shop for free range or organic products, eat either cheaper cuts of meat (chicken legs or thighs rather than breasts, for example) or eat meat less often. In this case, you may need to expand your repertoire of dishes to come up with the best recipe for that cheaper cut, cook dishes that include protein in different forms such as beans and eggs, and start thinking about how to make the most of your leftovers.

Over-fishing has led to a marked decrease in the populations of a variety of fish and seafood, and it is wise to choose to eat only sustainable varieties. Check the labels of what you buy and speak to your fishmonger. There are new varieties of fish available that make a good alternative to old favorites.

Stay healthy

Picky children or teenagers whose diets are restricted due to choice may benefit from a specially formulated multivitamin. If you are concerned that someone in your family isn't getting the full array of nutrients they need for a healthy diet, it would be wise to consult a health professional.

Recipe choosers

Pantry meals

A well-stocked pantry containing canned beans or fish can be the source of balanced, nutritious meals for the family, with the addition of only a few fresh items from the fridge or freezer.

Cheesy soufflé omelet page 248

5 mins   5-10 mins, plus resting

Cheese croquettes page 244

25 mins, plus chilling   20 mins

Baked gnocchi with cheese sauce page 212

10 mins   25 mins

Cheesy potato-topped tuna pie page 87

15 mins   40 mins

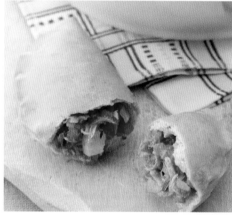

Tuna empanadas page 397

45 mins, plus chilling   40-50 mins

Sausage and butterbean goulash page 149

10 mins   35 mins

Cannellini bean, tuna, and red onion salad
page 390

10 mins

Tuna, tomato, and black olive pasta sauce
page 199

15 mins   1 hr 10 mins

Dan dan noodles page 214

10 mins   10 mins

Quick tomato, bacon, and garlic pasta page 205

10 mins   15 mins

Vegetable biryani
page 232

20-30 mins   40-45 mins

Mushroom and spinach curry page 184

15 mins   30 mins

Tomato, bean, and pasta soup page 190

15 mins   45-50 mins

Quick meals

Family life can be very busy and there will often be times when you need to put together a satisfying meal quickly. Try fish and seafood dishes as well as stir fries and pasta classics.

Thai beef salad page 122

10 mins   10 mins

Steak glazed with mustard and brown sugar page 128

5 mins   10 mins

Butternut squash soup
page 156

5 mins   20 mins

Easy carbonara page 197

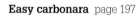

10 mins   10 mins

Egg salad page 237

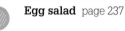

10 mins,   10 mins
plus cooling

Grilled salmon and salsa verde page 72

5 mins · 5 mins

Pork steaks with fried apples page 128

5 mins · 15 mins

Broiled red mullet with rosemary and chile page 90

5 mins · 10 mins

Thai-style stir-fried ground beef page 126

5 mins · 10 mins

Sweet chile shrimp skewers page 66

15 mins, plus soaking and cooling · 5 mins

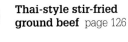

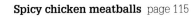

Spicy chicken meatballs page 115

10 mins · 10 mins

Quick rice with tomatoes, shrimp, and peas page 227

5 mins · 10 mins

Quick breads and desserts

Baking shouldn't take all day. These simple breads and desserts will only take 20 minutes or less to prepare and pop in the oven. There are sweet and savory items here to have for snacks or an impromptu party.

Apricot and almond bars page 432

20 mins | 35-40 mins

Blueberry muffins with streusel topping page 412

20 mins | 15-20 mins

Southern-style cornbread page 448

10-15 mins | 25-35 mins

Three-cheese scones page 440

5 mins | 10-15 mins, plus cooling

Oat and raisin cookies page 404

10 mins | 15 mins

Orange and marmalade loaf cake page 435

15 mins | 45-50 mins

Strawberry shortcakes page 411

  15 mins 15-17 mins

Easy crust apple pies
page 478

15 mins 25 mins

Buttermilk biscuits
page 271

 10 mins 10-12 mins

Savory breakfast muffins
page 442

  10 mins 25 mins

Madeleines
page 412

  15-20 mins 10 mins

Quick cheese pastries
page 442

  15 mins 10-15 mins, plus cooling

Double chocolate chip muffins page 410

  10 mins 15 mins

Cheap eats

Feeding a growing family can be expensive. Hearty stews and pasta dishes can be made with inexpensive cuts or leftovers, herbs, and spices. Omelets and soups also make economical and filling meals.

Classic buttermilk pancakes page 263

15 mins   10-12 mins

Chicken and barley stew page 104

10 mins   1hr 15 mins

Harvest vegetable soup page 157

10 mins   30 mins

Leftover pork chili page 146

15 mins   1 hr

New potato, sweet potato, and tarragon salad page 160

10 mins   10-15 mins

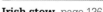

Spicy sausage casserole page 147

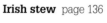

15 mins   1 hr 15 mins

Irish stew page 136

25 mins   3 hrs

Angel hair pasta with arugula pesto page 194

10 mins, plus resting 10 mins

Crispy risotto cakes page 221

5 mins 30 mins

Ham and cheese family omelet page 249

5 mins 5-10 mins

Penne with creamy butternut squash and bacon page 204

15 mins 30 mins

Lemon, garlic, and herb barbecued chicken page 284

10 mins, plus marinating 30-40 mins

Pasta with peas and pancetta page 205

10 mins 15 mins

Picky eaters

Throughout this book we have highlighted dishes that often appeal to fussy eaters or recipes that can be adapted to suit different tastes. Here are some of those, plus some tried and tested children's favorites.

Sausage and sweet potatoes page 302

10 mins   45 mins

Tomato and mascarpone pasta page 192

10 mins   10-15 mins

Mini-pizzas page 363

20 mins, plus rising   10 mins

Zucchini and feta loaf
page 453

20 mins   40-45 mins

Zucchini fritters
page 163

20 mins, plus draining   10 mins

Blueberry pancakes
page 265

10 mins   10 mins

Crispy southern-baked chicken page 113

 10 mins, plus chilling 45 mins - 1 hr

Spicy chicken fajitas
page 114

15 mins, plus marinating 15 mins

Swedish sausage casserole
page 147

10 mins 35-45 mins

"Mac and cheese"
page 210

 10 mins 15 mins

Salmon in foil page 73

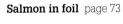   10 mins 20-25 mins

Blanquette de veau
page 138

   15 mins 1 hr 40 mins

Quick tuna pâté
page 68

  10 mins 1 min

Babies and toddlers

Babies and toddlers

Introducing a baby to solid food can seem daunting, especially for a first-time mom. However, with some simple guidelines, helping a child learn to eat and enjoy a wide variety of foods can be fairly stress free. The goal is to get to the point where a toddler can happily enjoy a nutritionally balanced meal alongside the rest of the family, providing it is not salted and is cut into manageable pieces.

What is weaning?

Weaning is really nothing more complicated than gradually introducing a baby to the tastes and textures of the kinds of foods we eat every day. To do this it makes sense to start with simple tastes and soft textures (remember that they have only had breast or formula milk up to this point) before moving on to more complex tastes and lumpier textures. It is currently recommended by the World Health Organization that a baby should start with weaning foods around six months (26 weeks). Your baby might be ready for solids earlier than this, but note that weaning should **never** occur before the age of 17 weeks.

First tastes

A baby's first tastes will be simple purées of individual fruit and vegetables and then combinations. Although store-bought baby food is quick and convenient, it can also be expensive. Making your own purée is easy; the only equipment you need is a hand-held blender, ice-cube trays, and freezer bags. Once the cubes of food are frozen, you can decant them into freezer bags, label, and store in the freezer until you need them. Babies will only eat tiny portions at first, so cooking in batches and then freezing means you can defrost one or two cubes of purée at a time to prevent waste.

Cooked peas or juicy segments of canned peaches make excellent finger foods for older babies.

Fruit and yogurt smoothies such as this Banana, mango, and yogurt smoothie (p32) can be adapted to include different fruits for your baby to try.

Your baby's milk

Breast milk remains the ideal source of nutrition for your baby and should be continued if possible during the weaning stage, as it contributes essential nutrients. Babies who aren't breastfeeding should be given formula until at least one year of age. A healthcare professional can advise you on this. Both expressed breast milk and formula can be used in recipes for your baby (referred to in this chapter as "your baby's usual milk"), for thinning purées and adding nutrients. From six months of age, you can use full-fat cow's milk for cooking for your baby, but this should not replace breast or formula as the main milk source.

Watching out for allergies

Certain foods are more likely than others to cause an allergic reaction in babies. These include cow's milk, egg, soy, wheat, nuts, and seafood. These foods add essential nutrients for normal growth and development, so do not avoid them in your baby's diet beyond six months of age, unless you have been advised to do so by a healthcare professional. Introducing new foods one at a time may not only help your baby get used to these new tastes, but also identify any possible culprits should an allergic reaction occur.

Finger foods

It is an important part of oral motor skill development and progress in self-feeding to try finger foods. Even young babies can be encouraged to pick up and try easy finger foods, such as well cooked carrots, broccoli florets, or rice cakes. It is important to remember never to leave your baby alone when he is eating in case of choking.

A balanced diet

For your baby to grow into a healthy, active toddler and child, he needs to eat a well-balanced diet. Babies need plenty of good fats, as well as a variety of fresh fruits and vegetables, good quality protein including red meat, poultry, fish, beans, egg and milk products, and some carbohydrates.

Toddlers

You should aim to introduce most food into your baby's diet when they are between six months and one year of age, as they are receptive to new tastes and textures at this age and this will ensure you don't have a toddler who is picky with food. Once your baby reaches the important milestone of his or her first birthday, they become more independent in their feeding and sometimes more specific with their likes and dislikes. Don't give up if they reject some new recipes the first time. Allow them to self-feed as much as possible, even though it might be messy. All the recipes in this chapter are suitable for toddlers as well as babies (with varying textures) but you can branch out and cook from the rest of the book as long as you are careful about the addition of salt.

Vegetable couscous (p37) is a great way to introduce lots of vitamin-rich vegetables as well as some texture into your baby's diet.

Weaning guide

Once you have decided that your baby is ready for solid food (talk to your healthcare provider if you are not sure) you can start introducing him or her to the first tastes in this chapter. Once your baby tolerates a variety of tastes and textures from the first tastes, you can move to first meals, which should be puréed, mashed, or chopped as appropriate to your child's age and oral motor skills.

First tastes

Make your baby's first tastes runny in texture, thinning out purées with your baby's usual milk or the cooking water. Start by introducing rice cereal, and single vegetable and fruit purées, then combine different flavors, making the purées less runny as he or she gets used to them.

First meals

Gradually begin making the textures thicker and lumpier until by the age of one, your child can cope with chopped up family meals. Once you have introduced vegetables, fruit, and baby rice, try out the following:

Any meat protein – beef, lamb, chicken, turkey	Well-cooked eggs
Any fish – such as well-cooked salmon, cod, tuna	Pulses – including lentils and chickpeas
Pasteurized cows' milk and its derivatives – milk for cooking, pasteurized cheese, full-fat yogurt	Gluten containing foods – such as wheat, oats, rye, and barley, and baby cereals, pasta, and bread

Drinks

While your baby is under one, he or she should continue to have his or her usual milk to drink (breast milk or formula) but may require a small amount of water in a cup with meals. Toddlers aged one year and over can drink whole milk cow's milk as their main drink. At age two, children can switch to low-fat milk (but discuss this with your healthcare provider).

Foods to avoid

You should not give your baby salt, honey, or lightly cooked or raw eggs while they are under one, nor should you give them sugary foods, which are bad for their teeth. Toddlers over one should continue to eat a diet that is low in salt and sugar.

Baby rice

Your baby's first solid food should be a smooth, milky powdered rice made with their usual milk.

2 mins

MAKES 1 PORTION

1 tbsp baby rice

3 tbsp breast or baby's usual milk, cold or warm, or more to taste

1 Using a sterilized spoon, put the baby rice into a sterilized, dried plastic baby bowl.

2 Add the milk and stir well to break up any lumps until the mixture is smooth. If it seems a little thick, add more milk until the texture is right for your baby.

3 Check the temperature of the cereal if using warm milk, in case it is too warm, then serve. Use it up within 30 minutes.

MOM'S TIP

This is merely a general guide; make up your baby rice according to the package instructions. Vary the texture with more or less milk as required, and remember that older babies will have bigger appetites and need a larger portion.

CALORIES: 89kcals/376kJ	
SUGAR: 4g	
FAT: 2.6g saturated: 0.9g	
SALT: trace	
CALCIUM: 146mg	
IRON: 3mg	

Pea purée

This simple, sweet purée can be made in minutes as long as you have some peas in the freezer.

2–3 mins   5–6 mins

SPECIAL EQUIPMENT
hand-held blender

MAKES 8–12 ICE CUBES

7oz (200g) frozen peas

a little of baby's usual milk (optional)

1 Put the peas into a small saucepan and cover them with boiling water.

2 Return to a boil over high heat, then reduce the heat and simmer for 5–6 minutes.

3 Drain, reserving the water. Use a hand-held blender to purée the peas in the saucepan, adding enough cooking water or formula milk to make a purée. Cool. Serve, or freeze in ice-cube trays.

VARIATION

For a broccoli purée, simmer 7oz (200g) small florets for 8–10 minutes. Purée as above, with enough cooking water to make a purée. Makes 12 ice cubes.

CALORIES: 16kcals/69kJ	
SUGAR: 0.4g	
FAT: 0.4g saturated: 0.2g	
SALT: trace	
CALCIUM: 6mg	
IRON: 0.5mg	

Sweet potato purée

Sweet potatoes are a good source of vitamins, and add a lovely, sweet taste to other purées, too.

5 mins   10 mins

SPECIAL EQUIPMENT
hand-held blender

MAKES 8–10 ICE CUBES

7oz (200g) sweet potatoes, cut into ½in (1cm) cubes

a little of baby's usual milk (optional)

1 Put the sweet potatoes into a small saucepan and cover them with boiling water.

2 Return to a boil over high heat, then reduce the heat and simmer for 10 minutes, until tender when pierced with a sharp knife.

3 Drain and purée as for Pea purée (see left). Cool. Serve, or freeze in ice-cube trays.

VARIATION

Normal potatoes can't be puréed with a blender, as they turn gluey. For potato purée, follow the recipe above, but mash or "rice" them instead.

CALORIES: 21kcals/88kJ	
SUGAR: 1g	
FAT: 0.2g saturated: 0.1g	
SALT: trace	
CALCIUM: 7mg	
IRON: 0.16mg	

Butternut squash purée

A sweet purée that babies love. It's a great bright color too. Mix with other purées to add sweetness.

5 mins   15 mins

SPECIAL EQUIPMENT
hand-held blender

MAKES 8 ICE CUBES

7oz (200g) butternut squash, cut into ½in (1cm) cubes

a little of baby's usual milk (optional)

1 Put the squash into a small saucepan and cover it with boiling water.

2 Return to a boil over high heat, then reduce the heat and simmer for 15 minutes, until tender when pierced with a sharp knife.

3 Drain and purée as for Pea purée (see left). Cool. Serve, or freeze in ice-cube trays.

CALORIES: 13kcals/56kJ	
SUGAR: 1g	
FAT: 0.2g saturated: 0.1g	
SALT: trace	
CALCIUM: 15mg	
IRON: 0.21mg	

Carrot purée

The soft texture and sweet taste of carrots make them an ideal first food for a weaning baby.

5 mins   15 mins

SPECIAL EQUIPMENT
hand-held blender

MAKES 8 ICE CUBES

7oz (200g) carrots, cut into ½in (1cm) cubes

a little of baby's usual milk (optional)

1 Put the carrots into a small saucepan and cover them with boiling water.

2 Return to a boil over high heat, then reduce the heat and simmer for 15 minutes, until tender when pierced with a sharp knife.

3 Drain and purée as for Pea purée (see left). Cool. Serve, or freeze in ice-cube trays.

VARIATION

Parsnips have a sweet taste and are good mixed half and half with potato purée. Prepare 7oz (200g) parsnips, and cook for just 10 minutes, then purée and store as above. Makes 8 ice cubes.

CALORIES: 13kcals/53kJ
SUGAR: 1.8g
FAT: 0.3g
    saturated: 0.1g
SALT: trace
CALCIUM: 10mg
IRON: 0.11mg

Apple purée

This versatile purée is great on its own, or used to sweeten stronger tasting vegetable purées.

5 mins   15 mins

SPECIAL EQUIPMENT
hand-held blender (optional)

MAKES 10 ICE CUBES

4 small apples

1 Peel, core, and chop the apples. This should give about 9oz (250g) of peeled fruit.

2 Put the apples in a small saucepan with 2 tbsp of water. Cover, bring to a boil, then reduce to a low simmer for 15 minutes, stirring occasionally, or until tender.

3 Mash, or purée with a hand-held blender. If too thick, stir in a little cooled, boiled water. Cool. Serve, or freeze in ice-cube trays.

VARIATION

For a quick canned peach purée, use a hand-held blender to purée 2 drained peach halves. If the mixture is too liquid, add a little Baby rice (see far left), 1 tsp at a time. Makes 4 ice cubes.

CALORIES: 18kcals/78kJ
SUGAR: 4g
FAT: 0g
    saturated: 0g
SALT: 0.0–0.0g
CALCIUM: 2mg
IRON: 0.08mg

Pear purée

Pears are a delicious versatile fruit to use for a purée. It can be blended with other purées too.

5 mins   10-12 mins

SPECIAL EQUIPMENT
hand-held blender (optional)

MAKES 8 ICE CUBES

2 large pears, organic if possible

1 Peel, core, and chop the pears. This should give you about 7oz (200g) of peeled fruit.

2 Prepare as for Apple purée (see left) but cook for 10–12 minutes. Mash or purée as for Apple purée. If the mixture is too liquid for your baby, add a little Baby rice (see far left), 1 tsp at a time, until it reaches the desired consistency. Cool. Serve, or freeze in ice-cube trays.

VARIATION

For an avocado purée, use ½ a small, ripe avocado. (Keep the other half with the pit in, to keep it from discoloring, for later use.) Use a fork to mash the avocado before serving immediately. If it seems a little thick, stir in cooled, boiled water. Avocado can't be frozen.

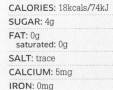

CALORIES: 18kcals/74kJ
SUGAR: 4g
FAT: 0g
    saturated: 0g
SALT: trace
CALCIUM: 5mg
IRON: 0mg

Mango purée

High in essential vitamins, mangoes are an excellent weaning food, although they can be expensive.

5 mins

SPECIAL EQUIPMENT
hand-held blender

MAKES 8 ICE CUBES

1 large, very ripe mango
Baby rice (optional, see far left)

1 Slice the mango through on either side of the large, flat pit, so that you are left with two discs of fruit. Take a small, sharp knife and score the flesh of each half into ½in (1cm) squares, cutting down to, but not through, the skin. Now push the skin from underneath to "flip" the mango inside out, revealing the cubed mango, which is now easy to separate from the skin.

2 Cut the flesh from the skin and purée using a hand-held blender. If the mixture is too liquid, add a little Baby rice, 1 tsp at a time, until it reaches a consistency that suits your baby. Freeze any excess mango in an ice-cube tray.

CALORIES: 12kcals/54kJ
SUGAR: 3g
FAT: 0g
    saturated: 0g
SALT: trace
CALCIUM: 3mg
IRON: 0.1mg

Apple and pear purée

Full of essential nutrients for your baby, apple and pear is almost always a favorite.

5 mins   10-15 mins

SPECIAL EQUIPMENT
hand-held blender (optional)

MAKES 8 ICE CUBES

2 small apples

1 ripe pear

1 Peel, core, and chop the apples and pear into ½in (1cm) pieces, keeping them separate.

2 Put the apples in a small saucepan with 1 tbsp of cooled, boiled water. Cover, bring to a boil, then reduce the heat to a low simmer for 5 minutes. Halfway through, stir and add a splash more water if the pan looks dry.

3 Add the pear and cook for 5–10 minutes, or until all the fruit is tender when pierced with a knife. Mash or purée in the pan with a hand-held blender. Cool. Serve, or freeze in ice-cube trays.

CALORIES: 19kcals/81kJ	
SUGAR: 4.5g	
FAT: 0g	saturated: 0g
SALT: trace	
CALCIUM: 3mg	
IRON: 0mg	

Banana and apricot purée

Naturally canned fruit in unsweetened juice make quick purées, here thickened with banana.

5 mins

MAKES 1 PORTION

1 apricot half, in natural unsweetened juice, drained

½ small, ripe banana

1 Chop the apricot into small pieces and place in a small bowl. Use a fork to mash it well.

2 Slice the banana into the bowl in small pieces and mash it well into the apricot. Serve immediately.

CALORIES: 45kcals/191kJ	
SUGAR: 10g	
FAT: 0g	saturated: 0g
SALT: trace	
CALCIUM: 7mg	
IRON: 0.2mg	

Avocado and banana purée

For a quick lunch on the go, pack a banana and a ripe avocado for this no-cook combination.

5 mins

MAKES 1 PORTION

½ small, ripe banana

½ small, ripe avocado

1 Peel and chop the banana into small pieces and do the same with the avocado.

2 Place in a small bowl and mash well with a fork. Serve the purée immediately.

CALORIES: 153kcals/633kJ	
SUGAR: 8g	
FAT: 12g	saturated: 3g
SALT: trace	
CALCIUM: 9mg	
IRON: 0.36mg	

Carrot and pea purée

This simple, sweet mixture is perfect for when your baby starts moving on to combination purées.

5 mins   15 mins

SPECIAL EQUIPMENT
hand-held blender (optional)

MAKES 8 ICE CUBES

3½oz (100g) carrots, cut into ½in (1cm) cubes

3½oz (100g) frozen petits pois or garden peas

a little of baby's usual milk (optional)

1 Put the carrots into a small saucepan and cover them with boiling water.

2 Return to a boil over high heat, then reduce the heat and simmer for 10 minutes. Add the peas for 5 minutes until everything is tender when pierced with a knife.

3 Drain, reserving the water. Use a hand-held blender to purée it in the pan, adding enough water or milk to make a purée. Cool. Serve, or freeze in ice-cube trays.

CALORIES: 19kcals/78kJ	
SUGAR: 1.2g	
FAT: 0.5g	saturated: 0.2g
SALT: trace	
CALCIUM: 9mg	
IRON: 0.4mg	

Cauliflower and potato purée

Cauliflower has a strong taste alone, but added to creamy mashed potato it makes a delightful purée.

5 mins   12 mins

SPECIAL EQUIPMENT
hand-held blender

MAKES 8 ICE CUBES

3½oz (100g) Russet potatoes, peeled and cut into ¾in (2cm) cubes

3½oz (100g) cauliflower, cut into small florets

a little of baby's usual milk (optional)

1 Put the potatoes into a small saucepan and cover them with boiling water.

2 Return to a boil over high heat, then reduce the heat and simmer for 7 minutes. Add the cauliflower for 5 minutes, until both are tender when pierced with a knife.

3 Drain, reserving the cooking water. Purée as for Carrot and pea purée (see left), or mash for a more textured purée. Cool. Serve, or freeze in ice-cube trays.

CALORIES: 18kcals/74kJ
SUGAR: 0.4g
FAT: 0.4g
  saturated: 0.1g
SALT: trace
CALCIUM: 6mg
IRON: 0.17mg

Carrot, parsnip, and apple purée

Parsnips and apples make a classic combination, and carrots add sweetness and color.

5–10 mins   15 mins

SPECIAL EQUIPMENT
hand-held blender

MAKES 6–8 ICE CUBES

1¾oz (50g) carrots, cut into ½in (1cm) cubes

1¾oz (50g) parsnips, cut into ½in (1cm) cubes

3½oz (100g) apples, peeled, cored, and cut into ½in (1cm) cubes

a little of baby's usual milk (optional)

1 Put the carrots into a small saucepan and cover them with boiling water.

2 Return to a boil over high heat, then reduce the heat and simmer for 5 minutes. Add the parsnips and apples for 10 minutes, until tender when pierced with a knife.

3 Drain and purée as for Carrot and pea purée (see left). Cool. Serve, or freeze in ice-cube trays.

CALORIES: 16kcals/67kJ
SUGAR: 2g
FAT: 0.3g
  saturated: 0.1g
SALT: trace
CALCIUM: 8mg
IRON: 0.11mg

Sweet potato and broccoli purée

Broccoli is high in vitamins and contains calcium and iron. Sweet potato is very high in vitamin A.

5 mins   10 mins

SPECIAL EQUIPMENT
hand-held blender

MAKES 8 ICE CUBES

3½oz (100g) sweet potatoes, cut into ½in (1cm) cubes

3½oz (100g) broccoli florets, cut into small pieces

a little of baby's usual milk (optional)

1 Put the sweet potatoes into a small saucepan and cover them with boiling water.

2 Return to a boil over high heat, then reduce the heat and simmer for 5 minutes. Add the broccoli for 5 minutes, until tender when pierced with a knife.

3 Drain and purée as for Carrot and pea purée (see left). Cool. Serve, or freeze in ice-cube trays.

CALORIES: 15kcals/64kJ
SUGAR: 0.9g
FAT: 0.1g
  saturated: 0g
SALT: trace
CALCIUM: 10mg
IRON: 0.3mg

Butternut squash and zucchini purée

Zucchini is a vegetable with a milky flavor that is readily accepted by most infants.

5 mins   10–12 mins

SPECIAL EQUIPMENT
hand-held blender

MAKES 8 ICE CUBES

3½oz (100g) butternut squash, cut into ½in (1cm) cubes

3½oz (100g) zucchini, cut into ½in (1cm) pieces

a little of baby's usual milk (optional)

1 Put the squash into a small saucepan and cover it with boiling water.

2 Return to a boil over high heat, then reduce the heat and simmer for 5–7 minutes. Add the zucchini for 5 minutes, until tender when pierced with a knife.

3 Drain and purée as for Carrot and pea purée (see left). Cool. Serve, or freeze in ice-cube trays.

CALORIES: 11kcals/45kJ
SUGAR: 0.8g
FAT: 0.3g
  saturated: 0.1g
SALT: trace
CALCIUM: 12mg
IRON: 0.22mg

Banana porridge

A great breakfast for your baby—easy to digest and healthy. It can be puréed for younger babies.

5 mins   5 mins

SPECIAL EQUIPMENT
hand-held blender (optional)

MAKES 1 PORTION

1 tbsp old-fashioned oats

¼ cup whole milk or baby's usual milk, plus extra if needed

¼ small, ripe banana

1 Put the oats and milk into a small, heavy-bottomed saucepan and bring to a boil.

2 Reduce the heat to a low simmer and cook for about 5 minutes, stirring frequently, until the porridge has thickened and the oats are soft.

3 Peel and mash the small chunk of banana into a serving bowl, then add the cooked porridge and stir together.

4 The texture can be loosened with a little more milk. The porridge can also be made smoother, if necessary, by puréeing it briefly with a hand-held blender.

VARIATION
To cook banana porridge in a microwave, put the oats and milk into a small microwave-proof bowl. Cook in a microwave on a high setting for 30 seconds, stir, and if necessary cook for another 10 seconds. Mash the banana into the bottom of the bowl, then stir together. The texture can be loosened or made smoother, if necessary, as in step 4.

MOM'S TIP
When cooking with a microwave, look out for "hot spots" in cooked or heated food. Make sure you stir the heated food thoroughly and cool slightly before giving anything to your baby.

CALORIES: 90kcals/380kJ

SUGAR: 5.8g

FAT: 2g
    saturated: 0.6g

SALT: trace

CALCIUM: 27mg

IRON: 0.65mg

Banana, mango, and yogurt smoothie

Making this thick enough to be spooned up helps a baby eat it easily, and it makes a quick, healthy breakfast.

5 mins

SPECIAL EQUIPMENT
hand-held blender

MAKES 1 PORTION

1¼oz (40g) frozen mango chunks, defrosted, or 1¼oz (40g) fresh mango chunks

½ small, ripe banana

2 tbsp thick, whole milk Greek yogurt

1 Put the mango chunks into a small bowl and purée with a hand-held blender until smooth.

2 Mash the banana into the puréed mango, then add the yogurt and mix until smooth.

VARIATION

This recipe is very adaptable and a great way of introducing your baby to the flavors of different fruits. Keeping to the same weight of fruit, and always adding the banana, replace the mango with peaches, nectarines, blueberries, raspberries, or strawberries, or a mixture of whatever soft fruits you have available. (If using berries containing seeds, push the fruit through a sieve first to remove them.)

CALORIES: 88kcals/374kJ

SUGAR: 14.6g

FAT: 2g
    saturated: 1.3g

SALT: 0.11g

CALCIUM: 52mg

IRON: 0.65mg

Peachy cottage cheese spread

This simple dish can be spoon fed or spread on fingers of toast if your baby can manage finger food.

5 mins

SPECIAL EQUIPMENT
hand-held blender (optional)

MAKES 2 PORTIONS

2 canned peach halves, in natural juice, drained

¼ cup full-fat cottage cheese

fingers of whole wheat bread, to serve (optional)

1 Depending on the age of your child, either purée the peaches with a hand-held blender until smooth, or semi-smooth, or just chop finely into small pieces.

2 Put the peaches into a serving bowl and mash the cottage cheese into them.

3 Serve on its own or spread on fingers of whole wheat bread, toasted, with the crusts removed.

VARIATION

Substitute any canned fruit for the peaches in this recipe, to get your baby used to different flavors. Try 2 apricot halves, or pear halves.

CALORIES: 53kcals/224kJ
SUGAR: 5.8g
FAT: 2.4g
 saturated: 1.7g
SALT: trace
CALCIUM: 35mg
IRON: 0.22mg

Banana and strawberry smoothie pops

Fruit and yogurt freeze really well to make delicious popsicles for little ones.

10 mins, plus freezing

SPECIAL EQUIPMENT
blender

popsicle mold

MAKES 4–6

1 ripe banana, roughly chopped

5½oz (150g) ripe strawberries, hulled and roughly chopped

¼ cup (2oz) plain whole milk yogurt

1 Place all the ingredients in a blender and blend until completely smooth. Push through a nylon sieve to remove the seeds.

2 Pour into a popsicle mold and freeze until frozen solid. Remove from the freezer for at least 15 minutes before serving, to soften slightly.

VARIATION

Any soft fruit, when it's in season and cheap, is great to use here. You can try any berry instead of strawberries. Try blueberries for a dramatic dark color, or raspberries, or even try the same weight of pitted, chopped peaches or apricots for orange-colored popsicles. They can be frozen for up to 12 weeks.

COOK'S TIP

When making popsicles, use a silicone mold, if possible. It is much easier to extract the popsicles from these. You could also try freezing this dessert in ice-cube trays, then defrosting a little at a time to serve as a healthy dessert.

CALORIES: 30kcals/129kJ
SUGAR: 5.5g
FAT: 0.4g
 saturated: 0.2g
SALT: trace
CALCIUM: 25mg
IRON: 0.16mg

Basic tomato sauce

Having some frozen cubes of this sauce gives an almost instant meal and adds color and flavor to other dishes.

10 mins 20 mins

SPECIAL EQUIPMENT
hand-held blender

MAKES 1½ CUPS

2 tsp olive oil

1 small onion, finely chopped

1 x 14oz (400g) can of chopped tomatoes

1 tbsp tomato paste

¼ tsp dried basil or oregano

1 Heat the oil in a small, heavy-bottomed saucepan. Add the onion and cook it over low heat for 5 minutes, until soft, but not brown.

2 Add the tomatoes, tomato paste, and dried herbs. Bring to a boil, then reduce the heat to a low simmer and cook, uncovered, for 10 minutes, stirring occasionally, until the sauce has reduced and thickened.

3 Purée the sauce in the pan using a hand-held blender before serving over pasta, or freeze in an ice-cube tray for later use.

VARIATION

This sauce is an excellent place to "hide" extra vegetables. Try adding finely diced carrot and celery to the onions before cooking. Zucchini, butternut squash, and sweet potato also work really well here.

CALORIES: 17kcals/73kJ	
SUGAR: 2.2g	
FAT: 0.5g saturated: 0.1g	
SALT: Trace	
CALCIUM: 9mg	
IRON: 0.3mg	

Easy cheesy sauce

This recipe comes in handy for many dishes. Add a cube to any dish for a smooth, creamy texture that babies love.

5 mins 10 mins

MAKES 1¼ CUPS

2 tbsp butter

2 tbsp all-purpose flour

1¼ cups whole milk

1¼oz (40g) coarsely grated mild Cheddar cheese

1 Melt the butter in a small, heavy-bottomed saucepan. Whisk in the flour over low heat. Continue to cook the flour and butter mixture over low heat for 2 minutes, whisking constantly, until the mixture bubbles and separates under the whisk.

2 Take the pan off the heat and slowly whisk in the milk, a little at a time, whisking it well between each addition until it is smooth. Return the pan to the heat and cook the sauce over medium heat, stirring constantly, until it comes to a boil and thickens.

3 Reduce the heat to low and continue to cook, stirring frequently, for 5 minutes. Be sure to whisk right into the edges of the saucepan, as this is where the sauce can burn if left undisturbed. Add the cheese and cook until it has melted and the sauce is smooth, thick, and creamy. Transfer to ice-cube trays, cool, and freeze.

CALORIES: 106kcals/440kJ	
SUGAR: 2.2g	
FAT: 7.8g saturated: 4.9g	
SALT: 0.24g	
CALCIUM: 115mg	
IRON: 0.12mg	

Lentils with carrots and spinach

Lentils are a good source of protein and iron. This recipe provides both protein and vitamins and minerals.

5 mins   20-25 mins

SPECIAL EQUIPMENT
hand-held blender (optional)

MAKES 4 PORTIONS

3½oz (100g) red lentils

1 large or 2 small carrots, cut into ½in (1cm) cubes

1 tbsp butter

1¼oz (40g) baby spinach leaves, finely chopped

2 tbsp finely grated Parmesan cheese

1 Rinse the lentils well under running water and check them over for any small rocks. Put them in a pan of boiling water with the carrots and cook for 15–20 minutes until they are soft. Drain them well.

2 Put the butter into the pan and cook the spinach over medium heat for 2–3 minutes, stirring constantly, until it has completely wilted.

3 Return the lentils and carrots to the pan and add the Parmesan. Mash or purée the mixture together, depending on the age of your child. For best results after freezing, reheat the cubes in a microwave.

CALORIES: 152kcals/639kJ	
SUGAR: 3g	
FAT: 6g	
saturated: 3.5g	
SALT: 0.28g	
CALCIUM: 115mg	
IRON: 2.2mg	

MOM'S TIP

Don't worry if your child's diapers change color after eating spinach for the first time; certain brightly colored foods such as spinach and blueberries will have this effect, but it is not harmful to the baby, only potentially alarming to the parent or caregiver!

Potato and cauliflower cheese bake

Turn cauliflower and cheese into a nutritionally complete meal with carbohydrates, protein, and vegetables.

5 mins   12-15 mins

SPECIAL EQUIPMENT
hand-held blender (optional)

MAKES 1 PORTION

3½oz (100g) Yukon Gold potato, cut into small chunks

2oz (60g) cauliflower, in small florets

2–3 cubes Easy cheesy sauce (see left), defrosted

1–2 tbsp whole milk or baby's usual milk (optional)

1 tbsp grated mild cheese, such as Cheddar

1 Put the potato and cauliflower into a small pan of boiling water. Cook for 5–8 minutes until tender. Drain. Purée with a hand-held blender, or mash, or chop the vegetables into small pieces, suitable for your child's age.

2 Place the cheesy sauce in the pan and reheat it gently, adding a little extra milk to loosen the mixture. Stir in the chopped vegetables. Preheat the broiler to its highest setting.

3 Put the cheesy vegetable mixture into a very small flame- and ovenproof dish and top with the cheese. Broil the dish for 2 minutes, or until the cheese has melted and the top is starting to brown a little. Cool before serving.

Vegetables are often more appealing in a cheese sauce. Add chunks of carrot, (cook for 10 minutes, or until tender), or replace potato with parsnip or squash, (cook for 5 minutes, or until tender).

Fussy eaters!

CALORIES: 200kcals/840kJ	
SUGAR: 4.2g	
FAT: 8.5g	
saturated: 5g	
SALT: 0.3g	
CALCIUM: 133mg	
IRON: 0.92mg	

Harvest vegetable bake

This is a recipe that combines vegetables rich in vitamins and protein. Select the vegetables that your baby enjoys.

5 mins   10 mins

SPECIAL EQUIPMENT
hand-held blender (optional)

MAKES 2 PORTIONS

5½oz (150g) finely diced vegetables, such as carrots, potatoes, butternut squash, parsnips, sweet potatoes, cauliflower, or green beans

2–3 cubes of Easy cheesy sauce (see p34), defrosted

1–2 tbsp whole milk or baby's usual milk (optional)

2 tbsp finely grated mild cheese, such as Cheddar

CALORIES: 215kcals/893kJ
SUGAR: 3.2g
FAT: 13.5g
  saturated: 8.4g
SALT: 0.54g
CALCIUM: 246mg
IRON: 0.42mg

1 Bring a large pan of water to a boil. Add the vegetables to the water in order of their length of cooking time. For example, for the vegetables listed, first add carrots, then a couple of minutes later add potatoes, then squash, parsnips, sweet potatoes, cauliflower, and green beans. Cook the vegetables together until they are soft, then drain well. Purée the vegetables with a hand-held blender, or mash, or chop, according to what your child can manage.

2 Gently reheat the cheesy sauce in a pan over low heat, adding a little extra milk to loosen it, if necessary, then stir in all of the vegetables. Preheat the broiler to its highest setting.

3 Put the cheesy vegetable mixture into a small, heatproof dish, or a ramekin, and top with the grated cheese. Broil the dish until the cheese has melted and the top is starting to brown a little. Cool before serving.

Sweet potato, broccoli, and rice

This mixture of purée and small pieces is a good way to introduce texture. This meal contains vitamins A and C.

5 mins   15 mins

MAKES 1 PORTION

¼oz (10g) white rice

1oz (30g) broccoli, broken into small florets

2 cubes of Sweet potato purée (see p28), defrosted

1 Cook the rice in a small pan of boiling water according to the package instructions, adding the broccoli for the last 5 minutes until the florets are quite soft.

2 Drain, return to the pan, and mash or chop the broccoli into pieces your child can manage.

3 Add the sweet potato purée to the pan and reheat it gently over low heat. Cook for 2–3 minutes, until everything is piping hot throughout. Cool before serving.

VARIATION

Swap in the same weight of any other vegetable purée, such as squash, in place of the sweet potato used here.

MOM'S TIP

You can also add small strips of chicken to create a nutritionally complete meal. Some children may prefer a meal like this where the meat can be hidden.

CALORIES: 50kcals/210kJ
SUGAR: 210g
FAT: 0.34g
  saturated: 0.12g
SALT: trace
CALCIUM: 20.4mg
IRON: 0.63mg

Vegetable couscous

An easy way to help your child get five portions of fruit and vegetables per day. Rich in vitamins and carbohydrates.

10 mins   10 mins

MAKES 2 PORTIONS

scant 1oz (25g) couscous

½ tbsp olive oil

1 small carrot, finely chopped

¾in (2cm) piece of zucchini,
  finely chopped

2 cubes of Butternut squash purée
  (see p28), defrosted

1 Put the couscous in a small bowl and rub the oil into it well, so each piece is coated in oil. Now pour enough boiling water over the couscous so that it is covered by ¼in (5mm), and cover the bowl with plastic wrap, making sure no air escapes.

2 Set aside for 5 minutes, then remove the plastic wrap. All the water should be absorbed and the couscous soft. Fluff it up with a fork to ensure the grains do not stick together.

3 Meanwhile, cook the carrot in a small pan of boiling water for 5 minutes, then add the zucchini and cook for another 3–4 minutes until all the vegetables are quite soft. Drain them well.

4 Put the Butternut squash purée in the pan and reheat it gently over low heat. Add the couscous and vegetables and mix well, adding a little extra water if necessary to get the required texture. Cool before serving. If freezing, reheat in a microwave for best results.

VARIATION

If your baby is not yet able to manage diced vegetables, purée the vegetables with a hand-held blender before mixing with the couscous.

CALORIES: 76kcals/317kJ

SUGAR: 3.25g

FAT: 3g
  saturated: 0.5g

SALT: trace

CALCIUM: 24mg

IRON: 0.35mg

Pasta with cheesy broccoli sauce

Another quick and nutritious meal for your growing child, pasta is a great food for older babies.

5 mins   5-8 mins

SPECIAL EQUIPMENT
hand-held blender (optional)

MAKES 1 PORTION

1oz (30g) small pasta shapes

1¼oz (40g) broccoli, broken into small florets

2 cubes of Easy cheesy sauce (see p34), defrosted

1-2 tbsp whole milk or baby's usual milk (optional)

CALORIES: 243kcals/1022kJ

SUGAR: 4.7g

FAT: 10g
   saturated: 6g

SALT: 0.3g

CALCIUM: 180mg

IRON: 1.12mg

---

1 Place the pasta shapes and broccoli in a small pan of boiling water and cook them according to the pasta package instructions (but don't add salt).

2 Drain the pasta and broccoli, then remove the broccoli and chop it, mash it, or purée it until smooth with a hand-held blender, according to the age of your child.

3 Gently heat the Easy cheesy sauce (see p34) over low heat in the saucepan, adding a little milk if necessary. Stir in the pasta and broccoli and mix it together well before serving.

VARIATION

Any greens can be used instead of the broccoli here (but keep to the same prepared weight). Try curly kale, spring greens, or chard, or whatever is in season and available.

Pasta with quick tomato and tuna sauce

Produce a tasty and wholesome meal in minutes from the pantry and freezer.

2 mins   10 mins

MAKES 1 PORTION

scant 1oz (25g) small pasta shapes

2-3 cubes of Basic tomato sauce (see p34), defrosted

1 x 2oz (40g) canned tuna, drained and mashed

finely grated Parmesan cheese, to serve (optional)

1 Cook the pasta in boiling water in a small saucepan according to the package instructions (but don't add salt). Drain them well.

2 Add the Basic tomato sauce (see p34) and tuna to the pan and cook together over low heat for 2–3 minutes until heated through.

3 Add the drained pasta and stir to combine before serving with a little Parmesan (if using).

VARIATION

Any canned oily fish would be good here, but stick to the same weight. Try canned mackerel.

CALORIES: 180kcals/761kJ

SUGAR: 2.7g

FAT: 4.5g
   saturated: 0.8g

SALT: 0.3g

CALCIUM: 20mg

IRON: 1.3mg

Quick macaroni cheese

All children love macaroni cheese, and babies are no exception. Add bacon bits for older children.

5 mins   20 mins

MAKES 2 PORTIONS

1¼oz (40g) small macaroni or similar pasta shapes

⅓ cup (2¼oz) full-fat cream cheese or soft cheese

2 tsp all-purpose flour

2–3 tbsp whole milk or baby's usual milk

2 tbsp grated mild cheese, such as Cheddar (do not use mold-ripened soft cheeses when feeding babies)

1 Cook the pasta in plenty of boiling water according to the package instructions, until it is soft (but don't add salt). Drain it well.

2 Preheat the broiler to its highest setting. Add the cream cheese to a saucepan and cook it over low heat until it melts. Sprinkle in the flour and whisk it in well, so that there are no lumps. Continue to cook over low heat for 2–3 minutes, then stir in enough milk to make a thick, creamy sauce. Add 1 tbsp of the cheese and stir until melted.

3 Add the cooked pasta to the sauce and stir it well. Place in a very small, flame- and ovenproof dish, sprinkle the top with the remaining cheese, and broil for 3–5 minutes, until the cheese has melted and the top is golden brown. Cool before serving.

VARIATION

A little canned tuna, or chopped cooked chicken can be added to the pasta before it is grilled to add extra protein, if you wish.

CALORIES: 313kcals/1301kJ

SUGAR: 1g

FAT: 23g
  saturated: 14g

SALT: 0.6g

CALCIUM: 175mg

IRON: 0.5mg

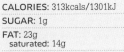

Orzo with creamy butternut squash

This small rice-shaped pasta is very easy for children to eat. If you can't find it, just use any tiny pasta shape.

5 mins   10 mins

MAKES 1 PORTION

scant 1oz (25g) orzo, or other small shaped pasta

2 cubes of Butternut squash purée (see p28), defrosted

1 tbsp full-fat cream cheese or other soft cheese (do not use mold-ripened soft cheeses when feeding babies)

1 Cook the pasta in boiling water in a small saucepan according to the package instructions (but don't add salt). Drain it well.

2 Mix the Butternut squash purée (see p28) and the cream cheese together in the saucepan and heat it over low heat, stirring it well, until it is heated through.

3 Add the pasta to the sauce and stir well to combine evenly before serving.

MOM'S TIP

Most babies prefer soft textures in their first foods. It is best to cook pasta for a little longer than stated on the package, until truly soft (and definitely not *al dente*), before serving.

CALORIES: 179kcals/754kJ

SUGAR: 2.5g

FAT: 8.4g
  saturated: 4.7g

SALT: 0.1g

CALCIUM: 51mg

IRON: 0.8mg

Hidden vegetable pasta sauce

Try this tasty sauce to ensure your kids get vegetables in their diet—they'll be eating lots without realizing it!

10 mins 1 hr 10 mins

SPECIAL EQUIPMENT
hand-held blender

MAKES 6–8 PORTIONS

2 tbsp olive oil

1 onion, finely chopped

1 small carrot, finely chopped

½ celery stalk, finely chopped

¼ red bell pepper, finely chopped

¼ yellow bell pepper, finely chopped

2in (5cm) piece of zucchini,
    finely chopped

1 garlic clove, crushed

1 x 14oz (400g) can of chopped
    tomatoes

1 tbsp tomato paste

freshly ground black pepper (optional)

CALORIES: 47kcals/197kJ
SUGAR: 4g
FAT: 3g
    saturated: 0.4g
SALT: Trace
CALCIUM: 16mg
IRON: 0.4mg

1 Heat the oil in a heavy-bottomed saucepan and cook the onion, carrot, and celery over medium heat for 5 minutes, until softened, but not browned. Add the peppers and zucchini and cook for 2–3 minutes, then add the garlic and cook for a final minute.

2 Now add the tomatoes. Half-fill the empty can with water and add that too, with the tomato paste. Bring to a boil, then reduce to a low simmer. Cook, partially covered, for about 1 hour, until the sauce has reduced. If it boils down too quickly, add a little more water. Taste the sauce and season lightly with pepper (if using).

3 Purée the sauce with a hand-held blender until the required consistency is reached, or the vegetables are completely unnoticeable! Serve with any pasta you like, over meatballs, or even as a sauce for grilled chicken.

VARIATION

The nature of this sauce makes it the perfect vehicle for accommodating any vegetables you need to use up. Try using parsnips, chard stalks, or leeks.

Quick fried rice

This simple stir-fry uses a few staple ingredients to make a quick and tasty meal for your growing baby.

5 mins 8–10 mins

MAKES 1 PORTION

1 tsp unsalted butter

1 tbsp olive oil

2in (5cm) piece of zucchini, very finely
    chopped

1 ripe tomato, peeled, seeded, and
    finely chopped

scant 1oz (25g) frozen or canned corn,
    or frozen peas

½ small garlic clove, crushed

1¾oz (50g) cooked, cold white rice
    (see food safety note, below right)

freshly ground black pepper (optional)

1 Melt the butter and oil in a wok or small frying pan. Add the zucchini and cook over medium heat for 2–3 minutes until golden brown.

2 Add the tomato and corn to the pan. Cook for a couple more minutes until the tomato starts to go soft, but not mushy. Add the garlic and cook for another minute.

3 Finally add the rice. Increase the heat to the highest setting and cook for a couple more minutes until the rice is hot right through. Lightly season with pepper (if using), and serve.

COOK'S TIP

Always cool cooked rice as quickly as possible, and within 1 hour, and always store in the fridge, never leave at room temperature. Reheat thoroughly and eat within 2 days. Add small pieces of turkey to this dish to create a meal containing carbohydrate, protein, and vegetables.

CALORIES: 262kcals/1093kJ
SUGAR: 6g
FAT: 16.5g
    saturated: 4.5g
SALT: 0.27g
CALCIUM: 30mg
IRON: 1.1mg

Stir-fried noodles with ribbon vegetables

A colorful stir-fry like this with broccoli pieces is a great way to encourage children to experiment with finger foods.

10 mins | 8–12 mins

MAKES 1 PORTION

scant 1oz (25g) fine or medium dried egg noodles

1oz (30g) broccoli, broken into small florets

1 small carrot

½ small zucchini

2 tbsp sunflower oil

reduced-salt soy sauce, to taste (optional)

1 Cook the dried noodles in a medium pan of boiling water according to the package instructions. Break them up, if necessary, with a fork as they start to cook, so that the strands separate. Two minutes before the end of the cooking time, add the broccoli florets and cook until both the broccoli and the noodles are soft. Drain well.

2 Use a potato peeler to peel the carrot and zucchini into thin ribbons, saving the last pieces that are too difficult to peel to make vegetable stock (see p156), or to add to stews, or soups.

3 Heat 1 tbsp of the oil in a wok or non-stick frying pan. Add the vegetable ribbons and cook over medium heat for 2–3 minutes, until they soften and start to color at the edges. For very young babies, reduce the heat, cover, and cook until the vegetables are very soft.

4 Add the remaining oil to the pan and increase the heat to high. Add the noodles and broccoli and stir fry for 2–3 minutes, or until everything is heated right through. Season lightly with a little reduced-salt soy sauce, to taste (if using), then serve.

COOK'S TIP

If the drained noodles start to stick together before you are ready to stir-fry, rinse under a cold tap to separate them again. Rubbing cold cooked noodles with light oil will keep them separated, and is a good idea if you want to chill some for later use.

CALORIES: 341kcals/1415kJ
SUGAR: 7g
FAT: 25g
  saturated: 3.5g
SALT: 0.17g
CALCIUM: 55mg
IRON: 16mg

Salmon with rice and pumpkin

Salmon is a sweet, tasty fish and full of super-healthy omega-3 fatty acids—excellent food for your growing child.

10 mins   15 mins

MAKES 2–4 PORTIONS

1¾oz (50g) white rice, such as basmati

2oz (60g) pumpkin or squash, cut into ½in (1cm) cubes (prepared weight)

1 x 3oz (105g) can boneless, skinless salmon, drained and mashed

1 tsp unsalted butter

1 tbsp finely grated Parmesan cheese

1 Cover the rice with plenty of boiling water and cook for 5 minutes. Add the pumpkin and cook for another 10 minutes, or until both the rice and the pumpkin are well cooked.

2 Drain the rice and pumpkin and put back into the pan. Add the mashed salmon, butter, and Parmesan cheese and mix it through until they are all evenly blended together.

3 Use a potato masher to mash the pumpkin gently. This will help the ingredients to bind together and make it easier to eat. Purée the mixture with an electric hand-held blender. You may need to moisten it with a splash of boiled water before serving.

VARIATION

Try making this dish with the same weight of fresh poached salmon fillet, checked carefully for bones.

MOM'S TIP

Adapt this recipe to suit older babies or toddlers by omitting the puréeing at the end of step 3.

CALORIES: 112kcals/468kJ

SUGAR: 0.3g

FAT: 4g
    saturated: 2g

SALT: 0.2g

CALCIUM: 69mg

IRON: 0.4mg

Butternut squash and pea risotto

Small children will love the mild, sweet flavors and creamy texture of this delicious, easy-to-eat risotto.

5 mins   25-30 mins

MAKES 4 PORTIONS

1 tbsp olive oil

½ onion, finely chopped

1 small garlic clove, crushed (optional)

5½oz (150g) risotto rice, such as arborio or carnaroli

3-4 cubes of Butternut squash purée (see p28), defrosted

1¾oz (50g) frozen peas

2 heaping tbsp finely grated Parmesan cheese

1 Heat ½ tbsp of the oil in a large, heavy-bottomed frying pan with deep sides. Cook the onion over low heat for 5 minutes, until it softens, but does not brown. Add the garlic (if using) and cook for another minute.

2 Keep 1½ cups of boiled water gently simmering on the stove near the risotto pan, with a ladle at the ready.

3 Add the remaining ½ tbsp of the oil to the pan with the rice. Turn the rice through the oil and onions so it is well coated.

4 When the rice begins to sizzle, add the simmering water, a ladleful at a time, stirring constantly, for 20–25 minutes (this will depend on the type of rice used), allowing the liquid to evaporate between ladlefuls. Add more boiling water if needed.

5 When the rice is cooked, but still al dente, add the Butternut squash purée and the frozen peas to the pan. Continue to cook the risotto for 5 minutes, until the peas are cooked and the rice is tender. Take the risotto off the heat and stir in the Parmesan to serve.

HOW TO FREEZE

This risotto freezes quite well, although the texture of the rice changes. Reheat it in a microwave, not in a saucepan, for the best results.

CALORIES: 219kcals/914kJ

SUGAR: 2.5g

FAT: 5.4g
  saturated: 2g

SALT: 0.2g

CALCIUM: 108mg

IRON: 1mg

Picky babies and toddlers

When a child moves from breast milk or formula onto solid foods, they can often show distinct preferences for certain foods. However, it's sometimes too easy to label a small child a "fussy eater" when perhaps they aren't hungry or have not developed the palate to enjoy the same things as the rest of the family. Additionally, for many young children, texture is a challenge, and not just at the weaning stage. Toddlers are also beginning to exert their independence at mealtimes, too. When your child doesn't eat, or doesn't eat as much as you think she should, it's easy to worry that she isn't getting the nourishment she needs. These few tips and ideas should help make mealtimes easier.

New tastes and textures

As soon as your child is developmentally ready (see the Weaning Guide, p27), introduce new tastes and textures into her diet. This will help to prevent picky eating later on and make it easier to include her in family meals. Children are far more likely to try new foods if they are joining in with an adult meal. Begin by mixing new foods with tried and tested ones (such as adding new vegetables into a stir-fry or pasta sauce), and remember that some children will have to be offered new foods several times before they accept them. For children who have difficulty with texture, try blending any of the recipes in this chapter to a texture they like and gradually adjusting the texture until they get used to it.

Plate politics

Some children like to eat each item thing on the plate individually, and some go further and don't want the separate food items to touch. Serving food on toddler plates that have divided areas can help here.

child-friendly food

If a child is happy and relaxed around food he is far more likely to end up with a wide and varied diet. If your child is struggling, keep it fun, try presenting food in different ways, mix new tastes with old favorites, and involve children in the cooking process.

Mix it up Try combining old favorites with new flavors such as yogurt with mashed or grated fruit. Spreading fruity cottage cheese (p33) on toasted fingers makes an easy and nutritious finger food. You can even try presenting the ingredients in a new form, such as creating fruit pops by freezing yogurt and fruit smoothies (p33).

Get toddlers involved Young children can start to help out in the kitchen, under your careful supervision, of course. Even if they only arrange their lunch on a plate they can begin to see food as fun. Getting kids involved in the kitchen is a great way to encourage them to try new things. They are far more likely to eat something they have made themselves.

Hide it Tempt your children into eating a more varied diet by disguising vegetables in a pasta sauce such as this Hidden vegetable pasta sauce (p40). You can adjust the texture of the sauce with a blender. They will be trying different flavors here without realizing it, and you can vary the vegetables in the sauce to suit what you have available.

Fun food Children often enjoy eating from an amusingly presented plate. If children are picky around food, try making faces or shapes with their food to encourage them to try something. Create faces on the Mini-pizzas (p363), for example, or get kids to make up their own. Make up a story about the ingredients while they eat, to turn it all into a game.

Tried-and-tested ways to get your child eating

⭐ **Change of scenery** If the dinner table has become a battleground, try making a picnic of easy-to-eat finger foods and eating on a rug on the floor.

⭐ **Eat with older children** If you have older children, encourage them to eat at the table with your toddler. This can often persuade young children to eat.

⭐ **Offer manageable portions** Don't overwhelm your child. Offer a few small servings of different foods on a plate, so that they have the satisfaction of finishing a meal.

⭐ **Keep it calm** Try not to turn mealtimes into a daily struggle—it will be so unenjoyable for both you and your child. Food is one of the few things small children have any control over, so allow them a certain amount of choice, and try to make mealtimes fun. Don't let the meal drag on for more than 30 minutes if they are not eating.

⭐ **Don't give up** Keep offering different flavors to your child—even though they have rejected them, they may end up liking them after three or four attempts.

⭐ **Eat together** Set your children a good example by eating as a family as often as possible, and showing your appreciation of your food.

⭐ **Adjust the texture** Try grating fruits and vegetables and adding them to smoother textures such as mashed potatoes or yogurt. If your child continues to struggle with texture, seek help from a health professional.

Two spoons trick

Some babies, when confronted with solid food for the first time, want to feed themselves, but can't. Giving them one spoon to hold, while you feed them a few mouthfuls with a second spoon, is an easy way to avoid an unnecessary battle.

Spinach and potato soup

This soup has vitamins, carbohydrates, and protein for a growing child. Use frozen spinach if you wish.

10 mins　　25 mins

SPECIAL EQUIPMENT
hand-held blender

MAKES 4 PORTIONS

1 tbsp olive oil

1 onion, finely chopped

1 garlic clove, crushed

3½oz (100g) baby spinach leaves

1 large Russet potato, chopped into small cubes

2 tbsp full-fat cream cheese or soft cheese, or more (optional)

whole wheat bread, to serve

1 Heat the oil over medium heat in a small, heavy-bottomed saucepan. Cook the onion in the oil for 5 minutes, until softened, but not browned. Add the garlic and cook for another minute.

2 Add the spinach, potato, and ¾ cup of boiling water.

3 Return to a boil and add a few tablespoons of boiling water if it looks thick. Reduce the heat, cover, and simmer for 15 minutes, or until the potato is soft.

4 Use a hand-held blender to purée the soup. Stir in the cheese until it melts, adding more for a creamier consistency, and serve with whole wheat bread.

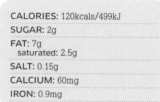

CALORIES: 120kcals/499kJ

SUGAR: 2g

FAT: 7g
　saturated: 2.5g

SALT: 0.15g

CALCIUM: 60mg

IRON: 0.9mg

MOM'S TIP

Some children may like to float bread in their soup. This helps in two ways: it works like a sponge soaking up the soup so they eat more and there's less mess. Also, bread "boats" that float in a soup "sea" before being eaten by giant "sea monsters" (children) makes a good game!

Mini minestrone

Pasta shapes add texture and volume to this hearty Italian-style soup. The vegetables bring lots of vitamins.

10 mins　　35-40 mins

MAKES 4-6 PORTIONS

2 tbsp olive oil

½ onion, finely chopped

1 leek, finely chopped

1 carrot, finely chopped

1 celery stalk, finely chopped

1 garlic clove, crushed

1 x 14oz (400g) can of chopped tomatoes

1 tsp dried Italian herbs

1¾oz (50g) green beans, chopped into ½in (1cm) pieces

1¾oz (50g) small pasta shapes

freshly ground black pepper (optional)

finely grated Parmesan cheese, to serve

CALORIES: 87kcals/367kJ

SUGAR: 4g

FAT: 4g
　saturated: 0.5g

SALT: Trace

CALCIUM: 25mg

IRON: 0.9mg

1 Heat the oil in a heavy-bottomed saucepan and cook the onion, leek, carrot, and celery over medium heat for 8–10 minutes, until softened, but not browned. Add the garlic and cook for another minute.

2 Add the chopped tomatoes, herbs, and ⅔ cup of cold water and bring to a boil. Reduce to a simmer and cook, partially covered, for 10 minutes until the vegetables are nearly soft. Use a potato masher to crush the tomatoes lightly. Add the beans, partially cover, and cook for 5 minutes.

3 Add the pasta, with ⅓ cup of boiling water if the soup is quite thick. Stir, partially cover, and cook for 10 minutes, stirring occasionally to prevent the pasta from sticking, or until the pasta and vegetables are cooked. Taste, season lightly with pepper if you want, then serve with Parmesan.

HOW TO FREEZE

Cool the soup completely at the end of step 2, then freeze it for up to 12 weeks. Defrost and reheat, then add the pasta and cook as in step 3.

Vegetable and barley soup

This thick, nourishing soup is a meal in one and freezes well, too, so it's excellent for batch cooking in advance.

10 mins   45 mins

SPECIAL EQUIPMENT
food processor

MAKES 4 PORTIONS

1oz (30g) pearl barley

1 onion, roughly chopped

1 celery stalk, roughly chopped

1 large carrot, roughly chopped

1¾oz (50g) butternut squash, roughly chopped

1 tbsp olive oil

freshly ground black pepper (optional)

1 Rinse the pearl barley, then put it in a small, heavy-bottomed saucepan with plenty of cold water. Bring to a boil, reduce to a simmer, and cook for 20 minutes, until partially cooked. Drain well.

2 Put the roughly chopped vegetables in a food processor and process them until they are finely chopped, but not mushy.

3 Heat the oil in a heavy-bottomed saucepan. Add the vegetables and cook over medium heat for 5 minutes, stirring occasionally, until they are soft, but not brown. Add the barley and 1¼ cups of boiling water.

4 Reduce the heat to a simmer and cook for another 20 minutes until the vegetables and barley are soft. Taste the soup and season lightly with a little pepper (if using).

VARIATION

For toddlers, add 1 tsp or ½ cube of reduced-salt vegetable stock, to give a stronger flavor to the soup.

CALORIES: 81kcals/340kJ

SUGAR: 5g

FAT: 3g
saturated: 2.5g

SALT: Trace

CALCIUM: 28mg

IRON: 0.6mg

Chicken soup and rice

A great way to utilize the goodness of a leftover chicken carcass, and loved by children.

20 mins   1¼–2¼ hrs

SERVES 4

FOR THE STOCK

1 cooked chicken carcass

a few leek tops, green part only

1 carrot, roughly chopped

1 celery stalk, roughly chopped

1 onion, quartered

½ tsp black peppercorns

1 bouquet garni

FOR THE SOUP

2 tbsp olive oil

1 onion, finely chopped

1 leek, white part only, finely chopped

2 carrots, finely chopped

1 celery stalk, finely chopped

1 garlic clove, crushed

1oz (30g) white rice

1 Put the chicken carcass in a large saucepan. Add the vegetables, peppercorns, and bouquet garni. Top with boiling water to cover the chicken, 5½–7 cups depending on the size of the pan.

2 Bring to a boil and simmer, uncovered, for 1–2 hours. At the end of cooking the stock should taste concentrated and delicious.

3 Strain into a bowl and cool the contents of the strainer. Once they are cool enough to handle, strip out all the chicken flesh. Chop any large pieces.

4 Meanwhile, heat the oil and cook the onion, leek, carrots, and celery over medium heat for 5 minutes, until softened, but not browned. Add the garlic and cook for another minute.

5 Add the stock and chicken to the vegetables. If there is too little liquid, add a little more from the kettle. Simmer for 15 minutes until all the vegetables are soft. Meanwhile, cook the rice according to the package instructions, then drain thoroughly. Add the rice to the soup and heat through for 2–3 minutes before serving.

CALORIES: 224kcals/936kJ

SUGAR: 5g

FAT: 9g
saturated: 1.5g

SALT: 0.16g

CALCIUM: 34mg

IRON: 0.9mg

Chicken and vegetable stew

This has protein and iron in the chicken and vitamins in the vegetables, especially vitamin A in the carrots.

10 mins   30 mins

MAKES 4 PORTIONS

1 tbsp sunflower or vegetable oil

½ small onion, finely chopped

½ celery stalk, finely chopped

1 small carrot, finely chopped

1 small potato, finely chopped

½ parsnip, finely chopped

1 boneless, skinless chicken breast, finely chopped

1 Heat the oil in a heavy-bottomed saucepan and cook the onion and celery over low heat for 5 minutes, until softened, but not browned.

2 Add 1 cup of boiling water. Add the carrot, reduce the heat to a simmer, and cook for 5 minutes.

3 Add the potato and parsnip to the pan and cook for another 15 minutes. Stir in the chicken, cover, and cook for a final 5 minutes, until the chicken is cooked and all the vegetables are tender.

4 Serve the stew as it is, or use a potato masher to gently crush some of the vegetables, and mix this into the stew. This will thicken the sauce and make it easier for a baby to eat.

MOM'S TIP

To cut up the vegetables small enough, use a food processor to do the job in no time and with minimum effort.

CALORIES: 108kcals/454kJ

SUGAR: 2.5g

FAT: 3.5g
  saturated: 0.5g

SALT: trace

CALCIUM: 38mg

IRON: 1.4mg

Cod with lentils and vegetables

Fish is a good source of protein for children, and along with lentils and vegetables makes a wholesome meal.

15 mins   25 mins

SPECIAL EQUIPMENT

food processor

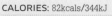

MAKES 4–6 PORTIONS

½ onion, roughly chopped

½ celery stalk, roughly chopped

2 carrots, roughly chopped

2 tbsp sunflower or vegetable oil

1¼oz (40g) red lentils, rinsed

3½oz (100g) skinless cod fillet, or other firm white fish fillet, cut into ½in (1cm) cubes

1 Use a food processor to chop all the vegetables finely. These will be irregularly sized, but it doesn't matter. Just fish out any large pieces and cut them by hand.

2 Heat the oil in a heavy-bottomed saucepan over low heat. Add the vegetables and cook them for 5 minutes, until softened, but not browned.

3 Add the lentils to the pan, then cover with 1 cup of boiling water. Cover and cook the lentils for 15 minutes, until softened, but not browned.

4 Finally add the fish and cook for another 5 minutes, until it is well cooked and the liquid has reduced.

5 Remove the lentils from the heat and use a fork to gently break up the fish and mix it into the vegetables and lentils. The lentils can also be made creamier by mashing them gently with a potato masher before serving.

CALORIES: 82kcals/344kJ

SUGAR: 3g

FAT: 4g
  saturated: 0.5g

SALT: trace

CALCIUM: 16mg

IRON: 0.66mg

Cheesy fish and peas

This recipe is not only easy but also introduces your baby to a variety of textures.

5 mins   5-7 mins

MAKES 1 PORTION

2 good-quality chunky fish fingers, defrosted

1oz (30g) frozen peas

2-3 cubes Easy cheesy sauce (see p34), defrosted

1 Carefully peel the fish fingers of their breaded coating, to give 2 small fillets of white fish.

2 Pour some boiling water into a small saucepan. Add the frozen peas and cook, uncovered, for 2–3 minutes.

3 Add the fish fillets, reduce to a simmer, and cook for another 2–3 minutes, uncovered, until the fish is well cooked and starts to flake when tested with a fork. Drain well.

4 Put the cheesy sauce into the pan and reheat it gently. Flake or mash the fish into the sauce, add the peas, stir it all together well, and serve.

VARIATION

Finely chopped carrots or red and yellow bell peppers can be added along with the peas, for more exciting colors, textures, and flavors.

CALORIES: 230kcals/957kJ
SUGAR: 3g
FAT: 14g
  saturated: 6.5g
SALT: 1g
CALCIUM: 172mg
IRON: 1.12mg

Ground beef and vegetables

When your baby is ready for red meat, nutritious ground beef allows your baby to try a more advanced texture.

10 mins   45-50 mins

MAKES 4 PORTIONS

2 tbsp sunflower or vegetable oil

½ onion, finely chopped

½ celery stalk, finely chopped

3½oz (100g) lean ground beef, organic if possible

1 tsp all-purpose flour

1 tsp tomato paste

1 small carrot, finely chopped

1 small sweet potato, finely chopped

1oz (30g) frozen peas

2 cubes Potato purée (see p31), defrosted

CALORIES: 148kcals/620kJ
SUGAR: 4g
FAT: 8g
  saturated: 2g
SALT: 0.15g
CALCIUM: 25mg
IRON: 1mg

1 Heat 1 tbsp of the oil in a heavy-bottomed saucepan and cook the onion and celery over low heat for 5 minutes, until softened, but not browned.

2 Add the remaining oil to the pan, increase the heat to medium, and cook the ground beef for 3–5 minutes, until it is well browned. Sprinkle the flour over the meat and cook it for another minute or two, stirring occasionally.

3 Add the tomato paste and 1 cup boiling water, reduce the heat to a low simmer, and cook for 15 minutes.

4 Add the carrot and sweet potato and cook for another 15 minutes. Add the frozen peas and cook for a final 5 minutes until they are cooked through and all the other vegetables are soft. Cover the pan if it seems to be drying out. The liquid should have reduced.

5 Add the potato purée and stir in to thicken the gravy, to make it easier for a baby to eat. (Or serve the potato purée on the side.)

Root vegetable chips

These delicious, healthy roasted root veggies are perfect for when your baby is ready to start finger foods.

5 mins   30 mins

SERVES 4 (as an accompaniment)

1 parsnip

1 sweet potato

1 carrot

1 tbsp sunflower or vegetable oil

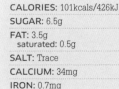

When you roast root vegetables, their natural sugars caramelize, turning them brown and sweet. These are popular even with children who are not keen on vegetables.

Fussy eaters!

1 Preheat the oven to 400°F (200°C). Peel all the vegetables and cut them into similar-sized wedges or fingers so they cook evenly.

2 Toss the vegetable chips in the oil and spread out in a single layer on a baking sheet.

3 Cook for 25–30 minutes, turning them halfway, until they are well cooked and browning at the edges.

VARIATION

Exactly the same method can be used with potato, to make lower-fat oven fries (1 large potato serves 2 toddlers).

CALORIES: 101kcals/426kJ	
SUGAR: 6.5g	
FAT: 3.5g saturated: 0.5g	
SALT: Trace	
CALCIUM: 34mg	
IRON: 0.7mg	

Spinach and cream cheese spread

Spread strips of whole wheat toast with this tasty dip as a finger food to ensure children have a varied diet.

5 mins   5 mins

MAKES 2 PORTIONS

1 tsp butter

½oz (15g) baby spinach

2 tbsp full-fat cream cheese or soft cheese

2 slices of thick-cut whole wheat bread

1 Heat the butter in a small saucepan and add the spinach. Cook over medium heat for 3–4 minutes, until it wilts completely and is well cooked.

2 Place the cooked spinach into a sieve and press out all the moisture. Transfer it to a cutting board and chop it as finely as possible. Place the cream cheese in a bowl and stir in the spinach.

3 Lightly toast the bread, spread it with the spinach and cream cheese spread, and cut into fingers before serving. (If you need only 1 portion, toast just 1 piece of toast and cover and chill the remaining dip for up to 1 day.)

VARIATION

Use other soft-leaved greens instead of spinach, though keep to the same weight. Chard is inexpensive and plentiful in summer and autumn, while spring greens make a nutritious substitute in the spring.

CALORIES: 173kcals/724kJ	
SUGAR: 1g	
FAT: 10g saturated: 6g	
SALT: 0.6g	
CALCIUM: 70mg	
IRON: 1mg	

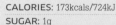

Smoked salmon and cream cheese pinwheel sandwiches

Children will like the mild taste and fun shapes of these, and salmon is a great source of omega-3 fatty acids.

5 mins

MAKES 6

1 slice of thin-cut whole wheat bread, crusts cut off

1 tbsp full-fat cream cheese or soft cheese

scant 1oz (25g) smoked salmon trimmings

cucumber and carrot sticks, to serve

1 Use a rolling pin to roll out the bread as thinly as possible. Spread the bread evenly with a layer of cream cheese, then top with a layer of smoked salmon.

2 Now roll the bread up tightly and slice it into 6 even pieces with a serrated knife.

3 Serve it cut-side up, so that you can see the spiral pattern inside, along with some cucumber and carrot sticks.

VARIATION

These are great made with soft lettuce leaves instead of smoked salmon, for a vegetarian option. Add 1 tsp chopped dill fronds for an aromatic version.

MOM'S TIP

Keeping a pre-sliced loaf of soft bread in the freezer means you can simply remove and defrost as many slices as you need. Take them out 1 hour before mealtime to make these pinwheel sandwiches.

CALORIES: 32kcals/133kJ

SUGAR: 0.2g

FAT: 2g
saturated: 1g

SALT: 0.2g

CALCIUM: 9mg

IRON: 0.1mg

Toasted cheese fingers

Serve this quick dish with cherry tomatoes, sliced cucumber, or cooked broccoli for a full finger food meal.

5 mins   5 mins

MAKES 1 PORTION

1 slice of thick-cut whole wheat bread

1–2 cubes of Easy cheesy sauce (see p34), defrosted

2 tbsp finely grated mild cheese, such as Cheddar

cherry tomatoes, or sliced tomatoes, to serve

1 Preheat the broiler to its highest setting. Lightly toast the bread on both sides. Meanwhile, mash together the cheesy sauce and the grated cheese.

2 Spread the toast with the creamy cheese mixture and broil for 2–3 minutes, until the mixture has melted and is golden brown on top.

3 Allow the cheese to cool and set a little before cutting into fingers to serve, with tomatoes.

VARIATION

For toddlers, add a slice of ham and a light smear of Dijon mustard under the cheese for an extra layer of flavor.

CLEVER WITH LEFTOVERS

Odds and ends of leftover cheese can be used to make this snack. Remember that mold-ripened soft cheeses should not be given to babies.

CALORIES: 314kcals/1312kJ

SUGAR: 3.2g

FAT: 18.8g
saturated: 11.4g

SALT: 1.24g

CALCIUM: 367mg

IRON: 1.12mg

Crispy fish fingers

Making your own fish fingers takes only minutes and provides an easy source of protein for babies.

15 mins, plus chilling 4-6 mins

MAKES 8

7oz (200g) skinless firm-fleshed white fish fillet

2 tbsp all-purpose flour

1 large egg, lightly beaten

½ cup panko bread crumbs or day-old bread crumbs

2 tbsp sunflower or vegetable oil

1 Cut the fish into 8 strips, about ½in- (1.5cm-) thick. Pat them dry with paper towels. Place the flour, beaten egg, and bread crumbs in 3 wide, shallow bowls.

2 Coat the fish fingers by dusting them first with the flour, then dipping them in the egg, then rolling them in the bread crumbs, until they are well covered. Put the coated fish on a plate, cover with plastic wrap, and chill for 30 minutes. (This will help the coating to stick when they are fried.) At this stage you can also freeze them.

3 Heat the oil in a large, heavy-bottomed frying pan and cook the fish fingers over medium heat for 2–3 minutes each side, until golden brown and crispy all over. Drain them on paper towels before serving with Sweet potato wedges (see p366).

CALORIES: 88kcals/371kJ

SUGAR: 0.2g

FAT: 4g
saturated: 0.6g

SALT: 0.2g

CALCIUM: 19mg

IRON: 0.4mg

HOW TO FREEZE

Open-freeze the uncooked fish fingers on a baking sheet, spaced a little apart. Once they are frozen, pack them into an airtight container in the freezer for up to 8 weeks. Defrost, covered, on a plate in the fridge before cooking as usual.

Crispy cornflake salmon nuggets

A good finger food for independent eaters, as well as an excellent source of protein and omega-3 fatty acids.

15 mins, plus chilling 4-6 mins

SPECIAL EQUIPMENT
food processor (optional)

MAKES 16–20

1 cup cornflakes

2 tbsp finely grated Parmesan cheese

2 tbsp all-purpose flour

1 large egg, lightly beaten

7oz (200g) skinless salmon fillet, cut into ¾in (2cm) cubes

2 tbsp sunflower or vegetable oil

1 Put the cornflakes and Parmesan into a food processor and reduce to rough crumbs. Alternatively, crush them together in a sealed plastic bag with a rolling pin. Pour the mixture into a shallow bowl. Place the flour and egg in 2 wide, shallow bowls.

2 Coat the salmon nuggets by dusting them first with the flour, then dipping them in the egg, and finally rolling them in the cornflake mix, until they are well covered.

Put them on a plate, cover with plastic wrap, and chill for 30 minutes. This will help the coating to stick during frying. (At this stage you can also freeze any you will not need.)

3 Heat the oil in a large, heavy-bottomed, non-stick frying pan and cook the nuggets over medium heat for 2–3 minutes on each side, until they are golden brown and crispy all over. Drain on paper towels before serving.

CALORIES: 51kcals/214kJ

SUGAR: 0.2g

FAT: 3g
saturated: 0.7g

SALT: 0.1g

CALCIUM: 21mg

IRON: 0.3mg

Veggie burgers

These delicious burgers are a great alternative to meat, and contain protein and lots of vitamins and iron.

15 mins   12–15 mins

MAKES 8

2 tbsp olive oil

1 onion, finely chopped

½ celery stalk, finely chopped

1 small carrot, grated

½ small zucchini, grated, excess moisture squeezed out

1 garlic clove, crushed

1 x 14oz (400g) can of mixed beans, drained and rinsed

½ cup fresh bread crumbs

1 tsp dried mixed herbs

2 tbsp sunflower or vegetable oil

1 Heat the oil in a heavy-bottomed saucepan. Cook the onion, celery, carrot, and zucchini for 5 minutes over medium heat until softened. Add the garlic and cook for another minute. Cool.

2 Put the beans in a bowl and mash with a potato masher to a texture that suits your child. Add the vegetables, bread crumbs, and herbs, and mix.

3 Use damp hands to form eight 2½in (6cm) patties, pressing them lightly between your palms. Cover and chill for 30 minutes.

4 Heat the oil in a frying pan and cook the burgers for 3–4 minutes on each side, turning carefully, until browned and crispy. Serve with ketchup for older children.

MOM'S TIP

These can be made large or small. Try bite-sized patties for small fingers, and adult-sized traditional burgers, to be served in a soft bun with salad. (Add 1 tsp reduced-salt vegetable bouillon powder for adults or older children.)

HOW TO FREEZE

The uncooked burgers can be open-frozen, then packed into a freezer bag for up to 12 weeks.

CALORIES: 113kcals/472kJ
SUGAR: 3g
FAT: 6g
    saturated: 0.8g
SALT: 0.4g
CALCIUM: 39mg
IRON: 0.9mg

Mini fishcakes

These are handy to make with a little leftover mashed potato. They are another great source of protein.

15 mins, plus chilling   6–8 mins

MAKES 8

1 x 3oz (80g) can of tuna, well drained

5½oz (150g) cold mashed potatoes

2 scallions, white part only, finely chopped

1 tbsp melted butter

2 tbsp all-purpose flour

1 large egg, lightly beaten

½ cup day-old white bread crumbs

sunflower or vegetable oil, for shallow frying

1 Pour the tuna into a bowl and mash it well. Mix in the potato and scallions. Stir in the butter to bring the mixture together. Shape into 8 equal-sized fishcakes and chill, covered, for 30 minutes.

2 Have 3 shallow bowls ready, one with flour, one with egg, and one with bread crumbs.

3 Dip the fishcakes in flour, then coat in egg, and finally coat in bread crumbs. Cover and chill for 30 minutes, to help the coating stick.

4 Heat a little oil in a non-stick frying pan. Cook the fishcakes over medium heat for 3–4 minutes each side, until heated through. Drain on paper towels.

VARIATION

Canned salmon can be substituted for the tuna here. For toddlers, add 1 tbsp of ketchup to the mix, too.

HOW TO FREEZE

These can be open-frozen, uncooked, then packed into an airtight container in the freezer for up to 8 weeks.

CALORIES: 148kcals/618kJ
SUGAR: 0.6g
FAT: 10g
    saturated: 2.5g
SALT: 0.3g
CALCIUM: 25mg
IRON: 0.6mg

Baked pasta squares

Bind leftover pasta with some egg and cheese and make these easy pasta bites that are high in protein and iron.

10 mins   30 mins, plus cooling

MAKES 8

2 large eggs, lightly beaten

⅓ cup whole milk

7oz (200g) cooked, cooled small pasta shapes, such as macaroni

1¾oz (50g) grated mild cheese

freshly ground black pepper (optional)

butter, for greasing

1 Preheat the oven to 375°F (190°C). In a mixing bowl, whisk together the eggs and milk. Add the pasta and cheese (reserving 1 tbsp), and stir. Season lightly with pepper, if you want.

2 Lightly grease a non-stick loaf pan, pour in the pasta, and press it down well. Scatter with the reserved cheese and bake in the center of the hot oven for 30 minutes, until golden brown and just set.

3 Remove the pasta cake from the oven and allow it to cool for at least 15–20 minutes before turning it onto a cutting board. Cut up into chunks before serving. These bites are also tasty served cold.

VARIATION

These squares are also good when mixed with 1¾oz (50g) of drained canned tuna in oil, or for toddlers, 1¾oz (50g) of chopped ham.

CALORIES: 140kcals/592kJ

SUGAR: 1g

FAT: 4.5g
   saturated: 2g

SALT: 0.2g

CALCIUM: 70mg

IRON: 0.7mg

Chicken nuggets with a basil and Parmesan crust

Make your own children's favorite—chicken nuggets. Chicken has a lot of protein and iron.

20 mins, plus chilling   6 mins

SPECIAL EQUIPMENT
food processsor

MAKES 12

1 boneless, skinless chicken breast

1 slice of white bread, crusts cut off

4 basil leaves, or a pinch of dried basil

2 tbsp finely grated Parmesan cheese

freshly ground black pepper

2 heaping tbsp all-purpose flour

1 large egg, lightly beaten

sunflower or vegetable oil, for cooking

1 Put the chicken breast between 2 sheets of plastic wrap and gently pound it out with a rolling pin to an even thickness of about ½in (1.5cm).

2 Tear the bread and put it into a food processor with the basil and Parmesan. Season lightly with pepper and process to fine crumbs.

3 Cut the chicken into 12 bite-sized pieces. Place the flour in a plastic food bag and add the chicken. Holding the top of the bag securely closed, shake the bag until the chicken is well coated. Pour it into a sieve to shake off excess flour, then place on a plate.

4 Put the beaten egg and the bread crumbs in 2 shallow bowls. Dip the floured chicken pieces into the egg, shake off any excess, then roll them in the bread crumbs until well coated. Lay them on a plate, cover with plastic wrap, and chill for 30 minutes to help the coating to stick. (Or freeze them at this point.)

5 Heat a thin layer of oil in a heavy-bottomed frying pan. Cook the chicken pieces over medium heat for about 3 minutes each side, until golden brown and springy to the touch. Drain on paper towels before serving with Root vegetable chips (see p50).

CALORIES: 80kcals/338kJ

SUGAR: 0.1g

FAT: 3.5g
   saturated: 1g

SALT: 0.15g

CALCIUM: 37mg

IRON: 0.35mg

Mini falafel

These tasty little falafel are an excellent way to get protein and iron into your child's diet.

10 mins, plus chilling 30 mins, plus cooling

SPECIAL EQUIPMENT
food processor

MAKES 10–12

1 x 14oz (400g) can of chickpeas, drained and rinsed

¼ cup fresh bread crumbs

1 large egg yolk

½ onion, finely chopped

1 garlic clove, crushed

2 tbsp all-purpose flour

2 tbsp finely chopped flat-leaf parsley

1 tbsp sunflower or vegetable oil

Hummus (see p388), cucumber and carrot sticks, to serve

1 Place all the ingredients except the oil into a food processor and process it to a rough paste. Roll the mixture into 10–12 walnut-sized balls, cover, and chill for 30 minutes.

2 Preheat the oven to 400°F (200°C). Grease a heavy baking sheet with the oil and heat in the oven for a couple of minutes. Lay the falafel on the pan, spaced apart, and cook for 15 minutes, until they start to brown underneath.

3 Turn carefully and cook for another 15 minutes, until brown and crispy all over. Press down lightly as you turn them, to make them flatter and easier to eat with little fingers.

4 Cool on paper towels for 5 minutes. Serve with hummus and cucumber and carrot sticks.

VARIATION
For toddlers, add 1 tsp (or ½ cube) reduced-salt vegetable stock, for a stronger flavor.

CALORIES: 65kcals/274kJ
SUGAR: 0.5g
FAT: 2g
saturated: 0.3g
SALT: 0.2g
CALCIUM: 22mg
IRON: 0.6mg

Rice balls

These delicious rice balls are good for the whole family, containing protein as well as vegetables and rice.

10 mins, plus cooling, and chilling 12–13 mins

MAKES 4

¼oz (10g) white rice

2–3 cubes of Butternut squash purée (see p28), defrosted

2 tbsp finely grated Parmesan cheese

1 heaping tbsp all-purpose flour

1 large egg, lightly beaten

½oz (15g) panko bread crumbs or day-old bread crumbs

sunflower or vegetable oil, for deep-frying

CALORIES: 205kcals/853kJ
SUGAR: 2.4g
FAT: 15g
saturated: 3g
SALT: 0.3g
CALCIUM: 120mg
IRON: 0.9mg

1 Place the rice in a small saucepan, cover with water, and bring to a boil. Boil for 10 minutes, until tender, then drain. Cover and put in the fridge to cool quickly.

2 As soon as the rice is cool, mix it with the Butternut squash purée and grated Parmesan. Form the rice mixture into 4 even-sized balls. Cover and chill for 30 minutes.

3 Put the flour, egg, and bread crumbs into 3 shallow bowls. Roll the rice balls in the flour and shake off any excess. Roll them in the egg, then roll them in the bread crumbs so they are well covered.

4 Heat 1in (3cm) of the oil in a small, heavy-bottomed saucepan. The oil is ready to use when a piece of bread dropped into it starts sizzling immediately. Carefully lower the rice balls into the oil and cook them for 2–3 minutes, turning once, until golden brown and crispy. Remove from the oil with a slotted spoon and allow to drain for 5 minutes on paper towels before serving.

Chicken patties

These small patties are a nutritious food for your baby, containing protein and vegetables for vitamins and minerals.

15 mins, plus cooling | 4–8 mins

SERVES 4

3 tbsp sunflower or vegetable oil

¾in (2cm) piece of zucchini, finely grated

¾in (2cm) piece of carrot, finely grated

2 scallions, white part only, finely chopped

½ cup fresh white bread crumbs

2 tbsp finely grated Parmesan cheese

5½oz (150g) good-quality ground chicken or ground turkey

freshly ground black pepper

1 Heat 1 tbsp of the oil in a small, heavy-bottomed frying pan. Cook the zucchini, carrot, and scallions, stirring frequently, for 5 minutes over medium heat, until they have softened, but not browned. Remove the pan from the heat and allow the vegetables to cool completely.

2 Stir the bread crumbs and cheese into the cooled vegetables. Add the chicken and a little black pepper to the pan and mix until well combined.

3 Form the mixture into 4 large or 8 small equal-sized balls. Flatten them gently between your palms, cover, and chill in the fridge for 30 minutes.

4 Heat the remaining oil in a large, non-stick frying pan over medium heat. Cook the chicken patties for 2–4 minutes on each side, depending on their size, until they are golden brown and springy to the touch.

VARIATION

If your baby has moved on to red meat, try substituting the chicken or turkey here for ground beef, or pork.

MOM'S TIP

These patties can be served small as a finger food or larger and stuffed into a soft roll as a slider.

This is a great dish for fussy eaters because you can sneak in some vegetables, and it's a great finger food for babies who like to feed independently.

Fussy eaters!

CALORIES: 120kcals/499kJ

SUGAR: 1g

FAT: 7.5g
    saturated: 1.7g

SALT: 0.2g

CALCIUM: 64mg

IRON: 0.5mg

Mini pasties

These are a complete meal for your baby containing carbohydrates and protein, as well as vegetables.

15 mins, plus cooling

20 mins, plus resting

MAKES 6

1 tbsp sunflower or vegetable oil

1 small onion, finely chopped

1 small carrot, finely grated

3½oz (100g) good-quality ground beef or lamb

1 heaping tsp all-purpose flour, plus extra for dusting

1 x 14oz (320g) pack of good-quality ready-rolled puff pastry

1 large egg, lightly beaten

1 Heat the oil in a small, heavy-bottomed saucepan. Cook the onion and carrot over medium heat for 5 minutes, until softened, but not browned.

2 Add the meat to the pan and cook it over high heat, stirring frequently, until it is browned all over. Sprinkle in the flour and cook for another 2 minutes, stirring frequently to keep it from sticking.

3 Pour ⅓ cup of boiling water over the meat. Bring to a boil, reduce to a low simmer, and cook, uncovered, for 10 minutes until the liquid has evaporated. Let the meat cool completely.

4 Preheat the oven to 400°F (200°C). Unroll the pastry on a lightly floured work surface and cut out six 4in (10cm) circles.

5 Place 2 tsp of the cooled meat mixture on one half of each pastry circle, leaving a ½in (1.5cm) border. Brush this border with a little beaten egg, then fold the pastry over and crimp the edges to seal the filling inside. Use a sharp knife to make a small slit in the pastry to allow the steam to escape.

6 Place the pasties on a baking sheet and brush the surfaces with a little more beaten egg. Cook in the middle of the oven for 20 minutes, until puffed up and

golden brown. Let rest and cool for at least 5 minutes before serving. They can be served hot or cold.

HOW TO FREEZE

The uncooked pasties can be open-frozen, then packed into an airtight container to freeze for up to 8 weeks. Defrost as many as you need, covered, on a plate in the fridge, before baking as usual.

CALORIES:	288kcals/1201kJ
SUGAR:	2.8g
FAT:	18g
	saturated: 7.7g
SALT:	0.5g
CALCIUM:	50mg
IRON:	1mg

Banana and date mini muffins

These delicious little cakes are sweetened with banana and dates to make a healthier treat.

15 mins 12-15 mins

SPECIAL EQUIPMENT

24 mini paper liners

24-hole mini muffin pan

MAKES 20–24

⅔ cup all-purpose flour

⅓ cup whole wheat flour

½ tsp baking soda

½ tsp baking powder

½ tsp ground cinnamon

1¾oz (50g) pitted soft dates, finely chopped

¼ cup light brown sugar

1 small egg, lightly beaten

2 tbsp sunflower or vegetable oil

1 ripe banana, mashed with a fork

CALORIES: 40kcals/170kJ

SUGAR: 4g

FAT: 1g
    saturated: 0.2g

SALT: 0.2g

CALCIUM: 34mg

IRON: 0.7mg

1 Preheat the oven to 350°F (180°C). Place 24 mini paper paper liners into a 24-hole mini muffin pan.

2 Sift the flours, baking soda, baking powder, and cinnamon into a large mixing bowl. Add the dates and sugar and stir to mix well.

3 Stir together the egg and oil with a fork, and stir in the mashed banana. Pour the wet mixture into the dry and stir well to combine. Divide the batter evenly between the liners.

4 Bake in the center of the oven for 12–15 minutes, or until a toothpick inserted into the center of a muffin comes out clean. Transfer to a wire rack to cool.

VARIATION

Use raisins instead of dates if you prefer, or substitute half the dates with finely chopped walnuts, if your child likes them, for added protein. Note, though, that childen under the age of three should not be given large nuts.

Oat and apple pancakes

Versatile for your baby's weekday or weekend healthy breakfast, dessert, or snack.

15 mins 10 mins

SPECIAL EQUIPMENT

food processor

MAKES 8

⅔ cup whole wheat flour

½ cup instant oats

1 tbsp light brown sugar

1 tsp baking powder

½ tsp ground cinnamon

1 large egg, lightly beaten

½ cup whole milk or formula

½ tsp vanilla extract

1 large apple peeled, cored, and grated, approx. 3½oz (100g) in total

butter, for cooking

1 Put the flour, oats, and sugar into a food processor and process until the oats have broken down to a fine powder. Pour them into a large mixing bowl. Add the remaining dry ingredients.

2 Whisk together the egg, milk, and vanilla extract. Make a well in the center of the dry ingredients and whisk in the liquid to make a smooth batter. Fold in the apple.

3 Melt a pat of butter in a large, non-stick frying pan. Ladle out the pancake batter in 2¾in (7cm) rounds and cook them for 2–3 minutes over medium heat, until the edges of the pancake start to set, and bubbles appear and burst on the top. Turn them over and cook for another 1–2 minutes, until slightly risen and golden brown.

These are good for smuggling some fruit into your child's diet. They are also an ideal recipe for children to help prepare. Getting children involved can encourage them to try new tastes.

Fussy eaters!

CALORIES: 93kcals/390kJ

SUGAR: 4g

FAT: 3.7g
    saturated: 1.6g

SALT: 0.2g

CALCIUM: 34mg

IRON: 0.7mg

Carrot cake cookies

These soft cookies will become a real favorite; they have all the goodness of carrot cake in a bite-sized snack.

15 mins　　12–15 mins

SPECIAL EQUIPMENT
electric hand-held mixer

MAKES 20

7 tbsp, softened

½ cup light brown sugar

½ cup granulated sugar

1 large egg, lightly beaten

¾ cup all-purpose flour

⅔ cup whole wheat flour

½ tsp baking powder

½ tsp ground cinnamon

3½oz (100g) finely grated carrot

1¾oz (50g) raisins

CALORIES: 115kcals/485kJ

CARBOHYDRATE: 12g

FAT: 5g
　saturated: 3g

SALT: 0.1g

FIBER: 18mg

IRON: 0.33mg

1 Preheat the oven to 350°F (180°C). In a large mixing bowl, cream together the butter and sugars with an electric hand-held mixer until light and fluffy. Add the egg and beat well to combine.

2 Sift the flours, baking powder, and cinnamon into the cookie mixture, pouring in any bran that is left in the sieve. Add the carrot and raisins and stir well.

3 Put heaping teaspoons of the cookie batter, spaced well apart, onto 2 baking sheets lined with parchment paper.

4 Bake in the middle of the oven for 12–15 minutes, until golden brown and risen slightly.

5 Remove from the oven and cool for 5 minutes on the baking sheets before transferring to a wire rack to cool completely.

Fruity ice pops

Make these simple fruit pops as a way to get some vitamin-rich fruit into your child's diet.

15 mins,
plus freezing

SPECIAL EQUIPMENT
blender

popsicle mold

MAKES 4–6

2½oz (75g) frozen mixed berries

¾ cup apple juice

1 Place the frozen berries and the apple juice in a blender and blend until completely smooth.

2 Press the fruit mixture through a nylon sieve to remove any seeds or small pieces of skin. Pour the fruit juice into an popsicle mold, cover, and freeze until solid (or for up to 12 weeks).

3 Remove the ice pops from the freezer at least 15 minutes before serving, to soften slightly.

CLEVER WITH LEFTOVERS

You can substitute any juice your child prefers for the apple juice here. You can use up a carton that is approaching its use-by date.

MOM'S TIP

Babies find it hard to regulate their body temperature in hot weather. These ice pops are an effective—and nutritious—way to cool them down.

CALORIES: 16kcals/69kJ

SUGAR: 4g

FAT: 0g
　saturated: 0g

SALT: 0g

CALCIUM: 4mg

IRON: 0mg

Family meals

Family meals

Finding time to eat together has become harder for many people, with long working hours and busy family timetables getting in the way. Yet time spent around the table is time well spent—it helps family relationships, communication, and can encourage healthy eating, too. Working out how to please everyone can be a dilemma, but there are plenty of recipe suggestions here that will make that decision easier. There's nothing better than pulling out a pre-prepared meal on a busy weeknight, but you don't need to buy one, as there are lots of tips on how you can get ahead on homemade meals in this chapter.

Catering for all tastes

To feed a family without fuss you need to choose a dish that everyone likes—or at least that they will all eat without requiring too much persuasion! In this chapter you will find plenty of failsafe classics, such as Ham and cheese family omelet (p249) or Chili con carne (p143), which are real weekday winners, but also exciting new dishes to try using a variety of ingredients in mouthwatering combinations, such as Lamb, apricot, and chickpea tagine (p137), Chicken and coconut curry (p99), or Smoked haddock and spinach crumble (p89). Don't be put off trying new recipes if you have a picky eater. Start with variations on favorites and work up to completely new taste and texture experiences (see Sources of inspiration, opposite).

Cooked slow and steady this Rosemary and garlic leg of lamb makes for an easy Sunday dinner (p296). It can be left to roast in the oven while you spend time with your family.

Spicy chicken meatballs (p115) are a real family favorite. Making your own meatballs means you know exactly what's gone into them. Add extra noodles if you need to fill hungry teens.

Eating for less

Rising food prices and a growing family to feed can easily stretch your weekly budget, so many of the recipes in this chapter are designed to help your cash go further either by using good value ingredients in mouthwatering ways or by leaving you with tasty leftovers that you can use for another meal. For example, replace the Friday-night take-out with cheaper, and healthier, homemade versions, such as Crispy southern-baked chicken (p113), Homemade fish and chips (p81), Indian lamb kebabs with cucumber and mango (p123), or Thai-style stir-fried ground beef (p126) with Thai coconut rice (p226). Remember you can accompany everyday meals with carbohydrate-heavy side dishes such as potatoes, rice, and pasta for economical ways to fill up your growing family, and add plenty of fresh vegetables to bulk up stews and one-pots, making the meat stretch a little further.

Sources of inspiration

There are times in the lives of most parents when they find themselves staring into the fridge with no enthusiasm for what they see there. Perhaps it seems like you've been cooking the same few dishes for your family, week in, week out, or perhaps you just lack the energy or inspiration to put together something different. If so, you'll be pleased to know that with a few changes, old classics can be given a new lease on life, try Crispy polenta fish fingers with easy tartar sauce (p80), Ricotta-stuffed chicken breasts (p110), Swedish meatballs with gravy (p127), or a Quick paella (p223). There are also great ideas to add interest to everyday ingredients such as rice, fish, or meat.

Tasty vegetable dishes such as firm favorite Creamy cauliflower cheese (p172) always goes down well, and not just with vegetarians. Serve as a main dish or a side with Roast chicken (p294).

Change things up with dishes such as Lamb, apricot, and chickpea tagine (p137) or try some new ways with familiar ingredients such as Sausage and butterbean goulash (p149).

Fuss-free family meals

Family life is hectic enough, so make your life easier with a few simple tricks. With a bit of planning, you can spend less time in the kitchen and have more fun with your family.

Kids' corner

If what you serve up has become a source of tension at every mealtime, why not ask the children to choose what the family eats one day a week? If they are old enough, get them to help you prepare it too (see Cooking with kids, p458). This will encourage them and help them feel that their opinion has been heard—and it makes one less decision for you!

Plan ahead

Time spent planning ahead will save you time later. Once a week, decide what you will cook for the next few days, then you don't have to make that decision each evening, plus you will save money and waste less by buying only the ingredients you need.

Here's one I prepared earlier...

When you cook a favorite meal, increase the quantities and freeze a few portions for another day, then you always have something on hand for that last-minute dinner. When reheating previously cooked foods that have been chilled or frozen, make sure you heat them all the way through, to kill off any potentially unhealthy bacteria. The food should reach a temperature of around 175°F (80°C) for at least two minutes before serving. All recipes marked with the freezer symbol are suitable for freezing, just make sure they are completely cool before you put them in the freezer (see Batching and freezing, p120).

Good recipes for freezing include:

Smoked fish chowder (p69)

Chicken cacciatore (p108)

Spanish chicken, chorizo, and pepper stew (p105)

Chili con carne (p143)

Chinese braised beef with ginger and soy sauce (p133)

Cheese and onion pie (p247)

Fish cakes (p82)

Spicy coconut shrimp

These delectable little morsels are addictively good, so cook plenty, as you tend to need more than you think.

10 mins, plus resting   5 mins

SPECIAL EQUIPMENT
food processor

SERVES 4 (as an appetizer)

1¾oz (50g) unsweetened shredded coconut

3½oz (100g) panko bread crumbs or day-old bread crumbs

1 tsp chile powder

2-3 tbsp all-purpose flour

salt and freshly ground black pepper

1 large egg, beaten

14oz (400g) raw large shrimp, shelled and deveined

sunflower or vegetable oil, for frying

sweet chili sauce, to serve

CALORIES: 389kcals/1629kJ
CARBOHYDRATE: 24g
  sugar: 1.5g
FAT: 22g
  saturated: 8.5g
SALT: 1g
FIBER: 3g

1 Put the coconut, bread crumbs, and chile powder in a food processor and purée to fine crumbs. Place in a shallow bowl. Put the flour in a second bowl and season well, and the egg into a third.

2 Dust each shrimp with the flour, shaking off excess. Dip each briefly into the egg, then roll it in the bread crumbs, making sure it is well covered. Place on a plate. Repeat to coat all the shrimp. Cover and rest in the fridge for 30 minutes. This will help the coating to stick.

3 Fill a large, heavy-bottomed saucepan with a 2in (5cm) depth of oil. It is ready when a cube of bread thrown in sizzles and starts to turn golden brown. Fry the shrimp, a few at a time, in the hot oil for a minute or two until golden brown all over. Be careful not to overcrowd the pan or they will stick together. Remove them with a slotted spoon and rest on a plate lined with paper towels while you fry the rest. Serve hot, with sweet chilli sauce for dipping.

Chinese shrimp toasts

These fabulous snacks are always far better when homemade, and are a real children's favorite.

10 mins   10 mins

SPECIAL EQUIPMENT
food processor

SERVES 4 (as an appetizer)

6oz (175g) raw large shrimp, shelled, deveined, and roughly chopped

1 tsp cornstarch

2 scallions, finely chopped

½ tsp finely grated fresh ginger

1 tsp soy sauce

1 tsp sesame oil

1 large egg white

4 large slices of day-old white bread, crusts removed

sunflower or vegetable oil, for frying

1oz (30g) white sesame seeds

CALORIES: 287kcals/1200kJ
CARBOHYDRATE: 20g
  sugar: 1.5g
FAT: 17g
  saturated: 2.5g
SALT: 1g
FIBER: 1.5g

1 Put the shrimp, cornstarch, spring onions, ginger, soy sauce, sesame oil, and egg white into a food processor, and process to a fairly smooth paste.

2 Cut each piece of bread into quarters and spread with a little of the shrimp paste, being sure to go right up to the edges and mounding it up slightly so that all the paste is used up.

3 Heat a 2in (5cm) depth of oil in a large, heavy-bottomed frying pan or deep fryer. It is ready when a crust of spare bread, dropped in, sizzles and starts to turn golden brown. Spread the sesame seeds out on a plate. Press each piece of bread, shrimp-side down, into the sesame seeds, so each is topped with a thin layer.

4 Fry the shrimp toasts in small batches, sesame seed-side down, for 1–2 minutes, until becoming golden brown, then carefully turn them over and fry for another minute. Drain the cooked toasts on a plate lined with paper towels while you fry the remaining pieces. Serve hot.

Salt and pepper squid

Squid is an economical source of low-fat protein. Try this spicy Asian treatment as part of a family feast.

10 mins | 6–8 mins

SERVES 4 (as an appetizer)

1 tbsp sea salt flakes

1 tbsp black peppercorns

¼ cup all-purpose flour

¼ cup cornstarch

¼–½ tsp chile flakes (optional)

4 squid tubes, cleaned, approx. 10oz (300g) in total

1¼ cups vegetable oil, for frying

lemon wedges, to serve

1 Using a mortar and pestle, crush the sea salt and peppercorns until fine. Place the flour and cornstarch in a bowl and stir in the sea salt, pepper, and the chile flakes (if using).

2 Make a slit down one edge of each squid pouch and open it out flat. Using a sharp knife, score a diamond pattern on the inside of each pouch. Cut each into eight pieces. Dust the pieces in the seasoned flour.

3 Heat the vegetable oil to 350°F (180°C) in a medium, heavy-bottomed pan. To check the temperature of the oil without a thermometer, carefully lower a cube of bread into the oil. The oil is hot enough when a piece of bread, dropped in, sizzles and starts to turn golden brown after 1 minute.

4 Cook the squid, in four batches, for 1½–2 minutes, or until golden brown, returning the oil to 350°F (180°C) between batches. Transfer to a plate lined with paper towels to drain, then place in a warm oven to keep warm. Repeat, working quickly, to cook all the squid. Serve piping hot, with lemon wedges.

Many children who profess to hate fish will eat deep-fried squid. Try the spicy version for a homemade equivalent to take-out food, but omit the chile flakes for very young children.

Fussy eaters!

CALORIES: 264kcals/1108kJ

CARBOHYDRATE: 24.5g
  sugar: 0.5g

FAT: 12.5g
  saturated: 2g

SALT: 3.9g

FIBER: 0.5g

Sweet chile shrimp skewers

Broil these sweet, sour, spicy skewers and serve as a delicious appetizer, or as part of a larger Asian feast.

15 mins, plus soaking and cooling   5 mins

SPECIAL EQUIPMENT
8 bamboo skewers

SERVES 4 (as an appetizer)

¼ cup granulated sugar

1 red chile, seeded and finely chopped

finely grated zest of ½ lime

½ cup rice vinegar or white wine vinegar

½ tsp salt

32 raw large shrimp, shelled and deveined

CALORIES: 141kcals/597kJ
CARBOHYDRATE: 13g
  sugar: 13g
FAT: 0.7g
  saturated: 0.1g
SALT: 1g
FIBER: 0g

1 Before you start, soak the bamboo skewers in water for at least 30 minutes. This will help keep them from burning when you broil the shrimp.

2 Meanwhile, in a small saucepan, mix together all the ingredients except the shrimp. Bring them to a boil, then reduce the heat to a low simmer and cook, uncovered, for 7–10 minutes, until the sauce has thickened to a sweet, sticky syrup. Set it aside to cool (it will thicken further as it cools).

3 Preheat the broiler to its highest setting. Thread 4 shrimp on to each skewer. Brush both sides of the shrimp with the syrup and place them on a baking sheet or broiler pan that has been lined with foil. Grill the skewers for 2–3 minutes on each side, brushing once more with syrup as you turn them.

HOW TO FREEZE

Freeze the shrimp (make sure they have not been previously frozen) in the sweet chile syrup, but uncooked. Defrost thoroughly before broiling.

Asian-style soy and sesame fish bites

A great way to get children to eat fish, these sweet and sticky fish bites both look and taste utterly delicious.

10 mins, plus cooling and marinating   10 mins

SERVES 4 (as a light meal)

¼ cup soy sauce

¼ cup rice wine or dry sherry

2 tbsp rice vinegar or white wine vinegar

1 tbsp light brown sugar

1 tbsp honey

2 tsp sesame oil

1lb 2oz (500g) firm white-fleshed fish fillets, cut into ¾in (2cm) cubes

2 tbsp sesame seeds

1 Combine the soy sauce, rice wine, vinegar, sugar, honey, and oil in a small, heavy-bottomed saucepan and bring it to a boil.

2 Reduce the heat to a simmer and cook, uncovered, for 5 minutes, until the sauce has reduced. Allow it to cool.

3 Turn the fish in the cooled sauce to coat, cover, and marinate in the fridge for 1 hour.

4 Preheat the broiler to its highest setting. Line a baking sheet or broiler pan with foil and spread out the marinated fish in a single layer. Sprinkle half the sesame seeds evenly over the fish.

5 Broil the fish for 3–4 minutes, until it is beginning to turn crispy at the edges, then turn it over carefully, sprinkle with the remaining sesame seeds, and broil for another 3–4 minutes.

VARIATION

Try this marinade with salmon, or even chicken pieces. Or reheat the leftover marinade until boiling, then use as a sauce for the fish bites.

CALORIES: 210kcals/881kJ
CARBOHYDRATE: 8.5g
  sugar: 8.5g
FAT: 7g
  saturated: 1g
SALT: 2.9g
FIBER: 1g

Smoked mackerel pâté

This easy, quick pâté is a tasty and inexpensive way to get healthy, oily fish into the family diet.

10 mins

SPECIAL EQUIPMENT
food processor (optional)

SERVES 4

7oz (200g) hot-smoked mackerel fillets, skinned

¾ cup (7oz) low-fat créme fraîche

2 tsp horseradish sauce (optional)

2 tbsp roughly chopped dill

finely grated zest of 1 lime, plus juice of ½ lime

freshly ground black pepper

whole grain toast, to serve

CALORIES: 254kcals/1054kJ

CARBOHYDRATE: 0.5g
  sugar: 0.5g

FAT: 22g
  saturated: 7g

SALT: 1g

FIBER: 0g

1 Break the mackerel into pieces and place in a food processor (if using). Add the crème fraîche, horseradish sauce (if using), dill, and lime zest and juice. Process to a smooth paste. Or, for a chunkier pâté, combine all the ingredients in a large bowl, mashing with a fork.

2 Season to taste with pepper and transfer to a serving dish. Cover and chill until ready to serve.

3 Serve with hot, buttered whole grain toast.

VARIATION

Use peppered smoked mackerel fillets, or even smoked mackerel fillets with added chile, or honey, for a stronger flavored pâté.

CLEVER WITH LEFTOVERS

Once opened, smoked mackerel does not have a very long shelf life. If you have the odd fillet nearing use-by date, skin it, pop it in a freezer bag, and freeze until you have enough to make this recipe.

Smoked salmon pâté

Smoked salmon can be expensive, but cheaper packages of salmon trimmings work well for this recipe.

10 mins

SERVES 4

7oz (200g) low-fat cream cheese, at room temperature

7oz (200g) smoked salmon trimmings, very finely chopped

finely grated zest and juice of ½ lemon

2 tbsp chopped chives

freshly ground black pepper

crackers and cucumber sticks, to serve

CALORIES: 149kcals/623kJ

CARBOHYDRATE: 2g
  sugar: 2g

FAT: 8g
  saturated: 4g

SALT: 2.3g

FIBER: 0g

1 Place the cream cheese in a mixing bowl and break it up with a fork until smooth. Stir in the salmon, lemon zest and juice, chives, and plenty of pepper.

2 Transfer to a serving dish, cover with plastic wrap, and chill until ready to serve.

3 Spread the pâté on crackers and serve with cucumber sticks.

VARIATION

Use the zest and juice of ½ lime and 2 tbsp chopped dill instead of the lemon and chives.

COOK'S TIP

Smoked salmon freezes wonderfully, so pop a few packages of cheap trimmings in the freezer as a standby. They defrost in minutes and can be whipped into this delicious pâté or mixed with crème fraîche and tossed through hot pasta for an instant sauce.

Quick tuna pâté

This simple pâté can be ready in minutes, and makes an almost instant appetizer or light lunch.

10 mins   1 min

SPECIAL EQUIPMENT
food processor
4 x 5fl oz (150ml) ramekins

SERVES 4

4 tbsp butter

2 x 7oz (200g) cans tuna in spring water, drained

1 tbsp olive oil

finely grated zest and juice of ½ lemon

2 tbsp chopped flat-leaf parsley leaves

½ cup fresh white bread crumbs

salt and freshly ground black pepper

crudités and toast, to serve

1 Place the butter in a small microwave-proof bowl and heat it in a microwave on medium heat for 30 seconds to 1 minute, or until melted. (Or melt it in a small saucepan over very low heat.)

2 Put the tuna, melted butter, and oil in a food processor and blend until smooth. Add the lemon zest and juice, parsley, and bread crumbs. Season and pulse-blend to combine.

3 Spoon into four 5fl oz (150ml) ramekins, cover, and chill until ready to serve. Serve with crudités and toast.

Most children who don't like fish can be won over by the mild flavor and firm texture of canned tuna. Try making little servings of this pâté for lunch boxes, adding some cucumber or carrot sticks. *Fussy eaters!*

CALORIES: 246kcals/1024kJ
CARBOHYDRATE: 5g
  sugar: 0.2g
FAT: 14g
  saturated: 7g
SALT: 0.6g
FIBER: 0.5g

Moules marinière

Discard any mussels that do not close firmly when sharply tapped on the sink.

25 mins   10 mins

SERVES 4 (as an appetizer)

1 tbsp olive oil

2 tbsp butter

1 onion, roughly chopped

2 celery stalks, finely chopped

1 carrot, finely chopped

2 garlic cloves, finely chopped

½ cup dry white wine

3lb 3oz (1.5kg) live mussels, scrubbed and beards removed

freshly ground black pepper

½ cup heavy cream

leaves from 1 bunch of flat-leaf parsley, finely chopped

baguette, to serve

1 Heat the oil and butter in a large pan, big enough easily to hold all the mussels, over medium heat, and gently cook the onion, celery, carrot, and garlic for 5 minutes, stirring occasionally.

2 Add the wine and mussels and season with pepper. Increase the heat and bring to a boil. Cover and cook for 5 minutes, shaking the pan occasionally. Discard any mussels that do not open, and warn your guests to do the same.

3 Stir in the cream and parsley. Serve immediately with chunks of baguette.

CLEVER WITH LEFTOVERS

Any leftover mussels that have opened on cooking can be taken from their shells and open-frozen on a baking sheet. Once frozen, transfer to a freezer bag and add up to 10 at a time to enrich dishes such as fish pies and fish crumbles.

CALORIES: 373kcals/1551kJ
CARBOHYDRATE: 8g
  sugar: 4g
FAT: 28g
  saturated: 15g
SALT: 1g
FIBER: 1.5g

Smoked fish chowder

This soup is like a stew, full of nourishing fish, potatoes, and corn. Omit the bacon if you do not eat meat.

25 mins   **30 mins**

SERVES 4-6

½ tbsp olive oil

1 onion, finely chopped

1 leek, finely sliced

2 garlic cloves, finely chopped

4 strips bacon, chopped

2 celery stalks, finely sliced

1¼lb (550g) floury potatoes, such as Russets, cut into 1in (3cm) cubes

2½ cups fish stock

freshly ground black pepper

1 x 7oz (195g) can corn (no added salt or sugar), drained

1lb (450g) undyed smoked haddock fillet, skinned and chopped into bite-sized pieces

2 tbsp chopped flat-leaf parsley leaves

whole wheat bread, to serve

1 Heat the oil in a large pan over medium heat. Cook the onion and leek for 5 minutes, until soft, but not browned. Add the garlic, bacon, and celery. Cook for 2 minutes.

2 Add the potatoes and stock, season well with pepper, and bring to a boil. Reduce the heat, cover, and simmer for 15 minutes, or until the potatoes are tender when pierced with a sharp knife.

3 Stir in the corn and haddock, cover, and cook for 3–5 minutes, or until the fish just starts to flake. Be careful not to overcook the fish. Gently stir in the parsley.

4 Ladle into warmed bowls and serve with thickly sliced whole grain bread.

VARIATION

Make this extra special by adding cooked shrimp, shelled and deveined, with the haddock, heating them through thoroughly.

CALORIES: 348kcals/1472kJ

CARBOHYDRATE: 36g
  sugar: 8g

FAT: 5g
  saturated: 1g

SALT: 2.6g

FIBER: 7g

Seared tuna Niçoise

Although traditionally served without potatoes, the addition of small, warm new potatoes makes this a complete meal.

10 mins 30 mins

SERVES 4

10oz (300g) small new potatoes, halved

salt and freshly ground black pepper

3½oz (100g) thin green beans, halved

4 skinless tuna steaks, approx. 3½oz (100g) each

16 cherry tomatoes, halved

bag of mixed leaf salad, approx. 4oz (120g)

4 hard-boiled eggs, peeled and quartered

1¾oz (50g) pitted black olives

FOR THE DRESSING

3 tbsp olive oil, plus extra for brushing

1½ tbsp red wine vinegar

1 tsp granulated sugar

1 heaping tsp Dijon mustard

1 Cook the potatoes in a large pan of boiling salted water until tender (about 20 minutes). Drain.

2 Meanwhile, make the dressing in a large bowl. Whisk together the oil, vinegar, sugar, and mustard, and season well. Cook the green beans in a pan of boiling salted water for 2–3 minutes until just tender, then drain them, refresh under cold water, and drain again.

3 When the potatoes are ready, heat a grill pan or large frying pan. Brush the tuna with a little oil and season well. Cook over high heat for 2–3 minutes each side for medium-rare, or longer for well done. Rest the fish while you finish the salad.

4 Put the still-warm potatoes into the dressing and turn them through to coat. Add the green beans, tomatoes, and salad leaves and toss them all together.

5 Serve the salad on a platter, or individual plates. Place the egg around, scatter with the olives, and top with tuna, sliced into pieces.

FEEDING A CROWD

If you are having a summer lunch party or buffet, make double or triple quantities of this salad. Fresh tuna can be expensive, so don't double up on that, just cut it into strips and sear it for a minute on each side before scattering on top of the salad.

CALORIES: 432kcals/1805kJ

CARBOHYDRATE: 15g
  sugar: 4g

FAT: 27g
  saturated: 5g

SALT: 0.7g

FIBER: 3g

Warm herring, new potato, and beet salad

A modern version of a Swedish main course salad, this is even more delicious served while the potatoes are warm.

10 mins 20 mins

SERVES 4

14oz (400g) small new potatoes, peeled and halved

salt and freshly ground black pepper

12oz (300g) tub of marinated herrings

2 tbsp light olive oil

2 tbsp finely chopped dill

2 heaping tsp Dijon mustard

2 Little Gem lettuces, leaves separated (larger ones halved lengthwise)

7oz (200g) cooked baby beets (not in vinegar)

3 hard-boiled eggs, peeled and quartered

1 Cook the potatoes in a large pan of boiling salted water until they are tender (about 20 minutes, depending on the potato type). Drain and set aside.

2 Meanwhile, make the dressing in a large salad bowl. Whisk together ¼ cup of the herring marinade, the oil, dill, and mustard, and season well. Reserve 1 tbsp of the dressing.

3 While the potatoes are warm, toss them in the dressing. Gently toss through the fish and lettuce leaves. In a separate bowl, toss the beets with the reserved dressing, then decorate the salad with the eggs and beets.

COOK'S TIP

Marinated herrings and beets store, chilled, for weeks. Keep some in your fridge to have the basis of this dish.

CALORIES: 372kcals/1558kJ

CARBOHYDRATE: 27g
 sugar: 13g

FAT: 19g
 saturated: 2.5g

SALT: 2.1g

FIBER: 3g

Grilled salmon and salsa verde

A simple, tasty meal that takes just minutes to prepare but tastes piquant and sophisticated.

5 mins   5 mins

SPECIAL EQUIPMENT

small food processor

SERVES 4

4 salmon fillets, approx. 5½oz (150g) each

⅔ cup extra virgin olive oil, plus extra for rubbing

salt and freshly ground black pepper

2 tbsp chopped basil leaves

2 tbsp chopped flat-leaf parsley leaves

2 tbsp chopped mint leaves

3 tbsp lemon juice

6 anchovy fillets

1 tbsp capers, rinsed

2 tsp Dijon mustard

1 garlic clove, crushed

1 Preheat the broiler to its highest setting. Rub the salmon with a little oil and season it well on both sides. Broil for 3–5 minutes on each side (depending on thickness), until crispy outside and moist within.

2 Meanwhile, to make the salsa verde, put all the remaining ingredients except the oil into the bowl of a small food processor. Purée to a rough paste, then pour in the oil in a thin stream, still processing, until you have a thick, vibrant, green sauce (you may not need all the oil). Season to taste.

3 Serve the fish over mashed potatoes with the salsa verde on the side.

BATCHING AND FREEZING

Buying herbs can be expensive and you may not need to use the whole bunch. Try doubling or tripling this salsa verde recipe, to use as many of the herbs as possible. The sauce will store in a jar in the fridge for up to 1 week, and can be used on grilled meats, in sandwiches, or even mixed into mayonnaise for an instant dip for crudités or dressing for a warm potato salad.

CALORIES: 541kcals/2242kJ
CARBOHYDRATE: 0.5g
  sugar: 0.5g
FAT: 46g
  saturated: 7g
SALT: 1g
FIBER: 0g

Smoked mackerel salad

A package of smoked mackerel is a great fridge standby, and this healthy salad is a simple way of using it.

15 mins   10-15 mins

SERVES 4

salt and freshly ground black pepper

1¼lb (550g) new potatoes, well scrubbed and chopped into bite-sized chunks

7oz (200g) hot-smoked mackerel fillets, skinned

2oz (60g) baby salad leaves

2 tbsp chopped dill

2 tbsp chopped chives

7oz (200g) cooked beets (not in vinegar), roughly chopped

baguette, to serve

FOR THE DRESSING

¼ cup extra virgin olive oil

juice of 1 lemon

1 tsp whole grain mustard

1 tsp honey

1 garlic clove, finely chopped

1 Bring a large pan of salted water to a boil, add the potato chunks, and cook for 10–15 minutes, or until tender. Drain and set aside.

2 Meanwhile, break the mackerel into bite-sized pieces, removing any bones you find as you go, and place in a large serving bowl. Add the salad leaves and herbs, and gently toss together.

3 Place the dressing ingredients in a small bowl, season, and whisk together with a fork.

4 Add the warm potatoes to the serving bowl, pour in the dressing, and stir gently. Add the beets and serve immediately with the baguette.

CALORIES: 405kcals/1687kJ
CARBOHYDRATE: 27g
  sugar: 7.5g
FAT: 27g
  saturated: 5g
SALT: 1.2g
FIBER: 3.5g

Salmon in foil

Baking in foil keeps the flavors in the fish and the smells out of the kitchen, and saves on the cleaning up too!

10 mins   20–25 mins

SERVES 4

1 tbsp olive oil

4 salmon fillets, approx. 3½oz (100g) each

salt and freshly ground black pepper

2 lemons

4 tbsp butter, cut into cubes

bunch of chives

new potatoes and steamed green vegetables, to serve

1 Preheat the oven to 350°F (180°C). Line a shallow ovenproof dish, large enough to hold all the salmon fillets, with a piece of foil big enough to completely wrap over the top of the dish. Brush the foil with the oil.

2 Place the salmon on the foil, skin-side down, and season well. Squeeze the juice from one lemon and drizzle it over the fish. Slice the second lemon into four and place a slice centrally on each fillet, to release juice and baste the fish as it bakes.

3 Arrange the butter over and around the salmon and place the whole chives over the fish. Bring the edges of the foil together to make a sealed parcel.

4 Bake in the oven for 20–25 minutes, depending on the size of the fillets. Remove the lemon slices and chives from the foil and discard.

5 Transfer the fish to warmed serving plates. Drizzle the lemon butter from the foil over the salmon and serve with new potatoes and steamed green vegetables.

Cooking in individual foil parcels allows you to vary the seasonings within each. This way you can spice up your own portion, and keep others completely plain for those who prefer it that way.

Fussy eaters!

CALORIES: 300kcals/1234kJ

CARBOHYDRATE: 0g
  sugar: 0g

FAT: 24g
  saturated: 9g

SALT: 0.3g

FIBER: 0g

Spice-rubbed salmon

This simple Cajun-inspired rub instantly livens up any fish, and is ideal for those who can find fish dull.

5 mins, plus resting   5–10 mins

SPECIAL EQUIPMENT
spice grinder (optional)

SERVES 4

1 tsp smoked paprika

1 tsp cayenne pepper

½ tsp dried thyme

1 tsp light brown sugar

½ tsp salt

4 skinless salmon fillets, approx. 5½oz (150g) each

2 tbsp olive oil

CALORIES: 324kcals/1384kJ

CARBOHYDRATE: 1g
  sugar: 1g

FAT: 22g
  saturated: 3.5g

SALT: 0.6g

FIBER: 0g

1 Combine the spices, thyme, sugar, and salt in a mortar and pestle or a spice grinder and grind to a fine powder.

2 Rub the mixture over both sides of the fish, cover with plastic wrap, and let rest in the fridge for 1 hour, so the flavors can sink into the fish.

3 Preheat the broiler to its highest setting and line a broiler pan with foil. Brush the fish with a little oil on both sides, being careful not to dislodge the spice rub, and broil for 3–4 minutes on each side, depending on thickness.

HOW TO FREEZE
The salmon can be marinated in the rub and frozen, uncooked. Defrost thoroughly before cooking from the start of step 3.

Salmon and potato gratin

This rich, creamy dish would convert anyone to the joys of eating oily fish. It's immensely comforting, too.

15 mins   1 hr

SPECIAL EQUIPMENT
10in (25cm) ovenproof dish

SERVES 4

1¾lb (800g) potatoes, peeled weight

salt and freshly ground black pepper

butter, softened, for greasing

2 heaping tbsp finely chopped dill

12oz (350g) skinless salmon fillets, cut into ¾in (2cm) chunks

¾ cup half-and-half

⅔ cup fish or vegetable stock (see p156)

CALORIES: 423kcals/1769kJ

CARBOHYDRATE: 33g
  sugar: 2g

FAT: 22g
  saturated: 9g

SALT: 0.6g

FIBER: 3.5g

1 Preheat the oven to 375°F (190°C). Cut the potatoes into ¼in- (5mm-) thick slices. Bring them to a boil in a large pan of boiling salted water and simmer for five minutes, until part-cooked. Drain well. Rub a 10in (25cm) ovenproof dish with the butter.

2 Layer half the potato slices in the dish. Sprinkle the dill on the potatoes, lay the salmon over in a single layer, and season well. Top with the rest of the potatoes, making sure that the final layer looks neat.

3 Whisk the half-and-half and stock together, pour it over the potatoes, and cook for 50 minutes to 1 hour, until the top is crispy and the potatoes cooked through.

COOK'S TIP
Salmon can be expensive, but should be part of a family's diet as it is rich in healthy omega-3 fatty acids. Try buying the more inexpensive tail fillets, which are perfect for this dish.

Baked fish with cherry tomatoes

Use really ripe tomatoes for this dish and they will partially break down to make an instant sauce.

10 mins   25–30 mins

SERVES 4

4 tuna steaks, approx. 5½oz (150g) each

salt and freshly ground black pepper

finely grated zest of 1 lime, plus juice of ½ lime

2 garlic cloves, finely chopped

7oz (200g) cherry tomatoes, halved

⅔ cup dry white wine

¾ cup (7oz) plain yogurt

3 tbsp chopped cilantro leaves

roast new potatoes and green beans, to serve

CALORIES: 277kcals/1167kJ

CARBOHYDRATE: 5g
   sugar: 5g

FAT: 9g
   saturated: 3g

SALT: 0.3g

FIBER: 0.7g

1 Preheat the oven to 350°F (180°C). Place the tuna steaks in a single layer in a shallow ovenproof dish. Season well and sprinkle with the lime zest.

2 Arrange the chopped garlic and tomatoes over and around the fish. Pour the wine into the dish and cover tightly with foil. Bake for 20–25 minutes.

3 Meanwhile, put the yogurt, lime juice, and cilantro in a small serving dish, season generously with pepper, and stir well.

4 Remove the tuna steaks from the dish and place on warmed serving plates. Arrange a few tomatoes on each plate and spoon over some of the cooking juices. Serve with the cilantro and lime sauce, and with roast new potatoes and green beans.

VARIATION

Instead of tuna, this also works well with haddock or cod fillet, or any sustainable fish with a firm texture.

Baked fish with a herby crust

This easy fish recipe looks amazing with its vivid green crust, and is an aromatic crowd-pleaser.

5 mins   10 mins

SPECIAL EQUIPMENT
small food processor

SERVES 4

1 cup fresh white bread crumbs

2 tbsp roughly chopped basil leaves

2 tbsp roughly chopped flat-leaf parsley leaves

2 tbsp roughly chopped chives

finely grated zest of ½ lemon

salt and freshly ground black pepper

¼ cup olive oil, plus extra for brushing

4 fillets firm-fleshed, white, sustainable fish, such as cod or haddock, approx. 5½ oz (150g) each

CALORIES: 290kcals/1214kJ

CARBOHYDRATE: 9g
   sugar: 0g

FAT: 15g
   saturated: 2g

SALT: 0.5g

FIBER: 0.5g

1 Preheat the oven to 425°F (220°C). In a small food processor, pulse the bread crumbs, herbs, lemon zest, and seasoning, until the bread crumbs are bright green.

2 Add the oil in a slow stream, with the food processor running, until it forms a thick, bright green paste.

3 Brush the fish fillets with a little oil on both sides and season them well. Press the herby crust onto the top (or skinless side) of the fillets, packing it down well. Place on a non-stick baking sheet and bake in the top of the oven for 10 minutes, or until cooked through and turning crispy on top.

HOW TO FREEZE

Use up extra herbs by making larger quantities of this bread crumb mix, and simply freeze in a sturdy freezer bag until needed. The bread crumbs can be used straight from the freezer.

Hake in green sauce

Add extra vegetables, such as lightly cooked peas or asparagus tips, to the sauce in keeping with its green theme.

10 mins 14-16 mins

SERVES 4

2 tbsp olive oil

2 garlic cloves, finely chopped

2 tbsp plain flour

⅔ cup dry white wine

¾ cup fish stock

¼ cup chopped flat-leaf parsley leaves

salt and freshly ground black pepper

4 skin-on hake fillets, approx. 5½oz (150g) each

sautéed potatoes and green beans, to serve

1 Heat the oil in a large, non-stick frying pan over medium heat. Gently cook the garlic for 1 minute.

2 Sprinkle the flour into the pan and stir thoroughly with a wooden spoon. Cook for 2 minutes, stirring until smooth. Gradually add the wine, followed by the stock, stirring constantly.

3 Stir in the parsley and simmer very gently over low heat for about 5 minutes.

4 Season the fish and add to the pan, skin-side down. Spoon some sauce over the top and cook for 2–3 minutes. Turn and cook for another 2–3 minutes, or until cooked through.

5 Transfer to warmed plates and serve immediately with sautéed potatoes and green beans.

CALORIES: 238kcals/998kJ

CARBOHYDRATE: 6g
  sugar: 0.3g

FAT: 9g
  saturated: 1.5g

SALT: 0.8g

FIBER: 0.3g

Keralan fish curry

The flavor and aroma of this exotic curry is beautifully subtle and fragrant, so try it with any firm white fish.

10 mins   15 mins

SERVES 4

1¾lb (800g) skinless haddock fillets, cut into bite-sized pieces

2 tsp ground turmeric

salt and freshly ground black pepper

1 tbsp vegetable oil

1 large onion, finely sliced

1 tsp black mustard seeds

5 curry leaves

1½in (4cm) fresh ginger, finely chopped

2 tbsp tamarind paste

¾ cup coconut milk

⅔ cup fish stock

2 scallions, finely sliced

1 red chile, seeded and finely chopped (optional)

basmati rice and chopped cilantro leaves, to serve

1 Place the haddock in a bowl, sprinkle with the turmeric, season, and stir to coat. Set aside.

2 Heat the oil in a large, non-stick frying pan over medium heat, and add the onion, black mustard seeds, and curry leaves. Cook gently for 10 minutes, stirring occasionally, until the onion is lightly brown.

3 Add the ginger and cook for 1 or 2 minutes, then add the tamarind paste, coconut milk, and stock, and stir well. Heat the sauce to a low simmer.

4 Add the fish and simmer gently for 3–4 minutes or until it is just cooked. Stir in the scallions and chile (if using).

5 Serve the curry with basmati rice, sprinkled with chopped cilantro leaves.

PREPARE AHEAD

Make the sauce (following steps 2 and 3) up to 2 days in advance. You can then reheat the sauce gently (do not boil or it may split, because of the coconut milk), and season and cook the fish just before you are ready to serve.

CALORIES: 213kcals/905kJ

CARBOHYDRATE: 5.5g
  sugar: 5g

FAT: 4.5g
  saturated: 0.5g

SALT: 0.8g

FIBER: 0.8g

Spinach and coconut shrimp curry

This mild, creamy curry flavored with coconut makes a light and fragrant supper dish that is easy to prepare.

15 mins   20 mins

SERVES 4

2 tbsp sunflower or vegetable oil

2 red onions, finely chopped

4 garlic cloves, finely chopped

2in (5cm) piece of fresh ginger, finely grated

¼–½ tsp chile powder

½ tsp turmeric

2 tsp ground cumin

1 tsp ground coriander

4 large tomatoes, peeled and finely chopped (see p191)

1 x 14fl oz (400ml) can coconut milk

10 fresh or dried curry leaves (optional)

5½oz (150g) spinach, shredded

14oz (400g) raw large shrimp, shelled and deveined

½ tsp granulated sugar

salt

basmati rice, warmed naan bread, and lime wedges, to serve

1 Heat the oil in a large, deep-sided frying pan or wok. Add the onions, garlic, and ginger and cook for 2–3 minutes over low heat until softened, but not browned. Add the spices and cook for another 1 or 2 minutes to release the flavors.

2 Add the tomatoes and continue to cook over low heat for another 2 minutes, until the tomato flesh starts to break down. Add the coconut milk and curry leaves (if using), and bring to a boil. Mix in the spinach and reduce the heat, continuing to cook until the spinach has wilted. Baby spinach will take 1 or 2 minutes, bigger leaves up to 4 minutes.

3 Add the shrimp, sugar, and a pinch of salt, and cook for another 2 minutes over high heat, or until the shrimp turns a bright pink color. Serve with basmati rice, warmed naan bread, and lime wedges on the side.

COOK'S TIP

A bag of shrimp in the freezer can be a life saver. To defrost them quickly, put them in a bowl of cold water for a few minutes, rubbing occasionally, until the ice starts to melt. Drain, put in one layer on a plate, and cover; they will be ready to cook in 30 minutes.

CALORIES: 204kcals/859kJ
CARBOHYDRATE: 14g
  sugar: 13g
FAT: 7g
  saturated: 1g
SALT: 0.9g
FIBER: 4g

Mackerel teriyaki

This Japanese-style mackerel is an affordable, tasty way to enjoy a fish high in healthy omega-3 fatty acids.

5 mins   15 mins

SERVES 4

2 garlic cloves, finely chopped

¾in (2cm) piece of fresh ginger, finely chopped

2 tbsp granulated sugar

¼ cup rice vinegar

¼ cup mirin

¼ cup sake

¼ cup soy sauce

salt and freshly ground black pepper

4 mackerel fillets, approx. 3½oz (100g) each

1 tbsp vegetable oil

chopped scallions, to garnish

noodles and stir-fried vegetables, to serve

1 Place the garlic, ginger, sugar, vinegar, mirin, sake, and soy sauce in a small pan and bring to a boil. Reduce the heat and simmer for about 10 minutes, until the mixture has thickened to a coating consistency.

2 Season the fish on both sides. Heat the oil in a large, non-stick frying pan over medium heat, add the mackerel skin-side down, and cook for 2 minutes until crisp.

3 Turn the fish over and cook for 1 minute. Add the sauce to the pan and cook for 2 minutes more.

4 Place the mackerel on serving plates, drizzle with a little of the sauce, and garnish with the scallions. Serve with noodles and stir-fried vegetables.

CALORIES: 317kcals/1320kJ
CARBOHYDRATE: 9g
  sugar: 9g
FAT: 19g
  saturated: 3.5g
SALT: 2.8g
FIBER: 0g

The strong taste of spinach means that children often don't like it. Try this creamy treatment of the iron-rich vegetable alongside chicken or fish.

Fussy eaters!

Spanish fish stew

Give everyday white fish a piquant, hearty Spanish twist with chorizo and olives to liven up a midweek meal.

15 mins   1 hr 15 mins

SPECIAL EQUIPMENT
large, heavy-bottomed Dutch oven

SERVES 4

1 x 7oz (280g) jar roasted peppers in oil, drained and chopped (oil reserved)

2 red onions, cut into chunks

1 garlic clove, finely chopped

¾ cup dry white wine

1lb 2oz (500g) new potatoes, scrubbed, unpeeled, and chopped into large chunks

6oz (175g) dry Spanish style chorizo, roughly chopped

1 x 15oz (500g) can tomato sauce

salt and freshly ground black pepper

1lb (450g) white fish fillets, such as pollock, skinned and cut into chunks

1¼oz (40g) pitted green olives

crusty bread, to serve

1 Preheat the oven to 325°F (160°C). Heat 1 tbsp of oil from the roasted pepper jar in a large, Dutch oven over medium heat.

2 Cook the onions for 10 minutes, until softened, but not browned, then add the garlic for 1 minute.

3 Pour in the wine, increase the heat, and allow to simmer until the liquid is reduced to about one-half of its original volume. Stir occasionally to prevent the onions from sticking to the bottom.

4 Add the potatoes, chorizo, tomato sauce, and chopped peppers. Stir in 1 more tbsp of the reserved oil from the peppers and season well. Bring to a boil, cover, and cook in the oven for 1 hour.

5 Remove from the oven and stir the fish and olives into the dish. Return to the oven for 15 minutes. Serve in warmed bowls with crusty bread.

FEEDING A CROWD

This kind of recipe is easy to adapt to feed larger numbers, and can suit whatever the fishmonger has in stock and your wallet can afford. Just vary the amounts and type of fish according to the season, and be sure you are buying sustainable fish.

CALORIES: 443kcals/1860kJ

CARBOHYDRATE: 33g
  sugar: 5.5g

FAT: 16.5g
  saturated: 4g

SALT: 0.9g

FIBER: 7g

Crispy cornmeal fish fingers with easy tartar sauce

Homemade fish fingers are fun and healthy, and a light cornmeal coating gives them a lovely crunchy finish.

10 mins, plus chilling   5 mins

SERVES 4

14oz (400g) skinless firm-fleshed white fish fillets, such as catfish

2 tbsp all-purpose flour

1 large egg, lightly beaten

¾ cup fine cornmeal

salt and freshly ground black pepper

sunflower or vegetable oil, for frying

FOR THE TARTAR SAUCE

2 cornichons, coarsely grated

6 heaping tbsp good-quality mayonnaise, preferably Homemade mayonnaise (see p395)

1 tbsp white wine vinegar

1 tbsp capers, very finely chopped

finely grated zest of ½ lemon

1 heaping tbsp finely chopped dill

1 Cut the fish into ¾in- (2cm-) thick strips. Pat it dry with paper towels. Lay the flour, egg, and cornmeal out in 3 shallow bowls. Season the flour well.

2 Coat the fish fingers by dusting them first with the flour, then dipping them in the egg, then rolling them in the cornmeal, until they are well covered. Put them on a plate, cover with plastic wrap, and chill for 30 minutes. This helps the coating to stick.

3 Meanwhile, make the tartar sauce. First, put the grated cornichons on to a cutting board and chop again, finely, with a sharp knife. Mix the cornichons, mayonnaise, vinegar, capers, lemon zest, and dill, and season well. Cover and chill until needed.

4 Heat a large, deep-sided frying pan and add enough oil to cover the bottom. Fry the fish fingers for 2 minutes on each side, turning carefully, until golden and crisp all over. Rest them on a plate lined with paper towels while you cook the rest. Serve with homemade chunky oven fries or Cajun-spiced potato wedges (see p170) and the tartar sauce.

COOK'S TIP

Using cornmeal is a good alternative to bread crumbs when it comes to frying fish. The dry texture of cornmeal gives you a far crisper finish. You can also add seasonings, such as ½ tsp onion powder or 1 tsp smoked paprika, to the cornmeal, if you like.

CALORIES: 478kcals/1988kJ

CARBOHYDRATE: 23g
  sugar: 0.5g

FAT: 32g
  saturated: 4.5g

SALT: 0.8g

FIBER: 1g

Homemade fish and chips

One of the best-loved British meals of all time. Making it at home ensures you use only the freshest ingredients.

15 mins · 40 mins

SERVES 4

4 baking potatoes, scrubbed well and cut into thin wedges

3½ cups sunflower or vegetable oil for deep-frying, plus extra for the chips

salt and freshly ground black pepper

1½ cups all-purpose flour

1 tsp baking powder

½ tsp salt

1¼ cups cold beer

4 skinless firm-fleshed, white fish fillets, such as pollock, approx. 4½oz (125g) each

lemon wedges or Tartar sauce (see left), to serve

1 Preheat the oven to 400°F (200°C). Toss the potato wedges in a little oil, season them well, and lay them in a single layer on a large baking sheet. Cook for 40 minutes, turning halfway, until golden brown and crispy.

2 After 30 minutes, prepare the fish. Heat the oil for deep-frying in a large, heavy-bottomed saucepan or deep fryer until a cube of bread, dropped in, sizzles and starts to turn golden brown. When the oil is hot, turn the heat off momentarily (this will stop the temperature from rising any further).

3 Meanwhile, sift the flour, baking powder, and salt into a wide bowl and mix them well.

4 Whisk the beer into the flour to make a thick batter. Turn the heat back on under the oil.

5 Dip each piece of fish into the batter so it is well coated, and lower it gently into the hot oil. Be careful, as it may spit, and let it go only at the last minute, to keep it from sticking. You will be able to cook 1 or 2 pieces of fish at a time.

6 Cook the fish for 2 minutes on each side, turning carefully halfway, until golden brown and crispy. Remove to a baking sheet lined with paper towels with a slotted spoon and keep warm while you finish cooking the rest. Serve with lemon wedges or Tartar sauce (see left).

COOK'S TIP

Frying oil can easily be recycled. If you have used it to fry fish, just cool it, then filter it through a fine sieve before pouring it back into the bottle. Label the bottle clearly, and re-use it only for fish.

CALORIES: 632kcals/2655kJ

CARBOHYDRATE: 70g
  sugar: 3.5g

FAT: 24g
  saturated: 3g

SALT: 1.1g

FIBER: 5.5g

Fish tacos

Anything served in a wrap is a sure family favorite, as it enables everyone to assemble their own as they like.

5 mins,
plus resting

10 mins

SERVES 4

14oz (400g) firm-fleshed white fish, cut into ¾in (2cm) cubes

¼ cup all-purpose flour

2 eggs, lightly beaten

¾ cup fine cornmeal

1 tsp smoked paprika

salt and freshly ground black pepper

sunflower or vegetable oil, for frying

TO SERVE

8 tortillas or wraps, warmed

lettuce leaves or green salad

finely sliced red onion or scallions

salsa, such as Classic tomato salsa (see p288), or Mango salsa (see p288)

Guacamole (see p290)

Greek yogurt or sour cream

hot sauce

lime wedges

1 Pat the fish dry with paper towels. Lay the flour, eggs, and cornmeal out in 3 wide, shallow bowls. Toss the flour with the smoked paprika and season it well.

2 Coat the fish pieces by dusting them first with the seasoned flour, then dipping them in the eggs, then rolling in the cornmeal, until they are well covered. Put

them on a plate, cover with plastic wrap, and rest in the fridge for 30 minutes. This helps the coating to stick.

3 Heat a ½in (1cm) depth of oil in a large, deep-sided frying pan. Fry the fish chunks for 2 minutes on each side, turning them carefully, until golden brown and crispy all over. Do not crowd the pan; you may need to cook in 2 batches. Rest on a plate lined with paper towels while you cook the rest.

4 Serve the fish with the warmed tortillas and a selection of accompaniments for everyone to assemble their own wraps.

VARIATION

For a healthier, though less crispy, option, season the fish well with salt, pepper, and paprika, toss it in a little olive oil, and broil it under a preheated broiler until cooked through, instead of coating with cornmeal and cooking.

CALORIES: 656kcals/2769kJ

CARBOHYDRATE: 99g
  sugar: 1.5g

FAT: 12g
  saturated: 2g

SALT: 1.2g

FIBER: 5.5g

Thai fishcakes

Give your fishcakes a Thai twist with this easy recipe, and serve with some easy noodles or Pad thai (see p214).

15 mins   15 mins

SPECIAL EQUIPMENT
food processor

SERVES 4

10oz (300g) cooked, shelled, and deveined shrimp

3 garlic cloves, peeled but left whole

small handful of cilantro leaves

2 hot red chiles, seeded

splash of Thai fish sauce, such as *nam pla*

splash of dark soy sauce

small handful of basil leaves

juice of 2 limes

1 large egg

salt and freshly ground black pepper

3–4 tbsp vegetable or sunflower oil

sweet chili sauce, to serve

wild arugula leaves, to serve

1 Put the ingredients except the egg, seasoning, and oil in a food processor and process to a rough paste, scraping down the sides once or twice. Add the egg and plenty of salt and pepper, and process again.

2 Heat a little of the oil in a frying pan over medium-high heat. Scoop up 1 tbsp of the mixture, then carefully slide it into the pan and flatten slightly; it should be about ¾in (2cm) thick. Repeat until all the mixture has been used, but do not crowd the pan (you may need to cook in batches, adding more oil as needed).

3 Shallow-fry for 1 or 2 minutes on each side until golden, turning carefully. Transfer to a plate lined with paper towels. Serve hot with a drizzle of sweet chili sauce and wild arugula leaves.

VARIATION

Try making miniature versions of these for an easy canapé. Make them 1 day in advance, store them in an airtight container in the fridge, and reheat in a hot oven until piping hot before serving with a bowl of sweet chili dipping sauce.

CALORIES: 156kcals/647kJ
CARBOHYDRATE: 0.7g
  sugar: 0.5g
FAT: 10.5g
  saturated: 1.5g
SALT: 2g
FIBER: 0g

Smoked haddock fishcakes

Try to find Japanese panko bread crumbs if you can. They give a wonderfully extra-crispy finish to any fried food.

40 mins, plus chilling

10 mins

SERVES 4

14oz (400g) potatoes, peeled weight

salt and freshly ground black pepper

2 tbsp butter

1 tbsp olive oil

1 leek, finely chopped

14oz (400g) skinless smoked haddock, undyed if possible

¼ cup finely chopped flat-leaf parsley leaves

finely grated zest of 1 lemon

1 heaping tbsp capers, rinsed, dried, and roughly chopped

⅓ cup all-purpose flour

1 large egg, lightly beaten

¾ cup panko bread crumbs or day-old bread crumbs

sunflower or vegetable oil, for frying

1 Chop the potatoes into large cubes and put them in a large pan of cold salted water. Bring them to a boil, reduce the heat to a simmer, and cook for 20–25 minutes until soft. (The time will vary depending on the type of potato you use.) When they are cooked, drain and mash them with the butter and plenty of salt and pepper until smooth, but still quite dry and stiff.

2 Meanwhile, heat the oil in a frying pan and gently cook the leek for 5 minutes until softened but not browned. Work it into the potato. Set aside to cool completely.

3 At the same time, bring a large saucepan of water to a boil, then add the smoked haddock and reduce the heat to a simmer. Cook gently for 5–7 minutes (depending on thickness), until the fish flakes easily with a fork. Drain the fish

and, when it is cool enough to handle, break it into large flakes with your fingers, removing any bones at the same time. Set aside to cool completely.

4 Once the potato and fish have cooled, combine them in a large bowl and add the parsley, lemon zest, and capers. Mix well, being careful not to break up the fish too much, and taste for seasoning. Shape the mixture into eight fishcakes, cover, and rest for 30 minutes in the fridge.

5 Prepare 3 shallow bowls, the first with the flour, seasoned well, the next with the egg, and the last with the bread crumbs. Dip the fishcakes in the flour, patting off excess, then in the egg, then in the bread crumbs, being sure they are well coated. Cover and rest again in the fridge for another 30 minutes.

6 Heat 2 large frying pans and add enough sunflower oil to cover the bottom of each. Fry over medium heat for 4–5 minutes on each side, until crisp, golden, and heated through.

VARIATION

Try using smoked mackerel, or any leftover cooked fish instead of the haddock. The piquant capers and lemon zest will lift the flavors even of unsmoked fish.

CALORIES: 423kcals/1779kJ

CARBOHYDRATE: 39.5g
  sugar: 2g

FAT: 17.5g
  saturated: 5.5g

SALT: 2.7g

FIBER: 3.5g

Salmon fishcakes

These are ideal as a main course, or you can form the mixture into small fishcakes to make bite-sized canapés.

20 mins, plus chilling — 30 mins

SERVES 6

1lb (450g) potatoes, peeled and chopped into cubes

2lb (900g) skinless salmon fillets

1 onion, halved

2–3 bay leaves

1 tsp black peppercorns

4 scallions, finely chopped

2 tbsp horseradish cream

salt and freshly ground black pepper

juice and finely grated zest of 1 lemon

large handful of dill, chopped

pinch of cayenne pepper

FOR THE COATING

2 cups fresh bread crumbs

2 tbsp chopped chives (optional)

2 tbsp chopped parsley leaves (optional)

all-purpose flour, for coating

2 large eggs, lightly beaten

sunflower or vegetable oil, for frying

1 Place the potatoes in water and boil for 20 minutes, or until very tender. Drain and mash. Set aside.

2 Place the salmon in cold water with the onion, bay leaves, and peppercorns. Bring to a boil, simmer for 2 minutes, then turn off the heat and let cool for 20 minutes. Drain well, discarding the cooking liquid, and cool.

3 Flake the salmon into a large bowl. Fold in the cooled mashed potatoes and all the other fishcake ingredients. Mix well and shape into 12 round cakes. Cover with plastic wrap and chill for 1 hour before coating.

4 Mix the bread crumbs well with the herbs (if using). Season the flour, then put the flour, eggs, and bread crumbs in separate shallow bowls. Roll the salmon cakes in flour, dusting off excess, then in egg, then in bread crumbs.

5 Heat enough oil to cover the bottom of a frying pan and cook the fishcakes for 3–4 minutes on each side, or until crisp and hot. Drain on paper towels and serve.

CALORIES: 546kcals/2289kJ

CARBOHYDRATE: 43g
sugar: 3.5g

FAT: 24g
saturated: 4g

SALT: 1.1g

FIBER: 3g

Crispy trout with sweet tomato relish

This is a simple dish of fried fish made special with a homemade sweet-sour "ketchup."

10 mins, plus chilling — 40 mins

SERVES 4

¼ cup all-purpose flour

1 tsp paprika

salt and freshly ground black pepper

2 large eggs, lightly beaten

1 cup panko bread crumbs or day-old bread crumbs

4 skinless trout fillets

sunflower or vegetable oil, for frying

Warm new potato salad (see p159), to serve

FOR THE TOMATO RELISH

¼ cup olive oil

½ red onion, finely chopped

2 large ripe tomatoes, peeled and roughly chopped (see p191)

2 tsp granulated sugar

2 tbsp balsamic vinegar

1 Sift the flour with the paprika and season well. Lay the flour, eggs, and bread crumbs out in 3 wide, shallow bowls.

2 Dust the fish fillets first with the flour, then coat them in egg, then in bread crumbs. Put them on a large plate, cover in plastic wrap, and rest in the fridge for 30 minutes. This helps the coating to stick.

3 Meanwhile, make the relish. Heat the olive oil in a heavy-bottomed saucepan. Cook the onion, covered, over low heat for up to 15 minutes, until soft and sweet but not brown. Add the tomatoes and cook for 10 minutes, until they break down. Add the sugar, vinegar, and 2 tbsp of water and cook over low heat for 5 minutes, until reduced to a thick relish. Season.

4 After the fish has rested, heat a ½in (1cm) depth of sunflower oil in a large frying pan. When it is hot, fry the fish for 2–3 minutes on each side, turning carefully, until golden brown and crispy. You will need to do this in two batches, so keep the first warm while you cook the rest. Serve with the relish and Warm new potato salad (see p159).

CALORIES: 536kcals/2244kJ

CARBOHYDRATE: 36g
sugar: 8g

FAT: 26g
saturated: 3g

SALT: 0.8g

FIBER: 2.5g

Fish pie

Try to use small, Gulf shrimp in this dish, which are tastier and also less likely to have been farmed.

20 mins | 30–35 mins, plus resting

SPECIAL EQUIPMENT

7in (18cm) baking dish

SERVES 4

10oz (300g) skinless salmon fillet

7oz (200g) skinless smoked haddock fillet

4 tbsp unsalted butter

5 tbsp all-purpose flour, plus extra for dusting

1½ cups whole milk

salt and freshly ground black pepper

pinch of grated nutmeg

7oz (200g) cooked shrimp, shelled and deveined

3½oz (100g) baby spinach

9oz (250g) store-bought puff pastry, preferably all-butter

1 large egg, lightly beaten, for glazing

1 Preheat the oven to 400°F (200°C). Poach the salmon and haddock in simmering water for 5 minutes. Drain and cool.

2 Melt the butter in a pan. Remove from the heat and whisk in the flour until a paste is formed. Gradually add the milk, whisking to avoid any lumps. Season well and add the nutmeg. Bring the sauce to a boil, reduce the heat, and cook for 5 minutes, stirring.

3 Flake the fish into a bowl and add the shrimp. Spread the uncooked spinach over the top and pour the hot sauce over it. Season to taste. When the spinach has wilted, mix the filling together and transfer to a 7in (18cm) baking dish.

4 On a floured surface, roll out the pastry to a shape bigger than the baking dish, ⅛–¼in (3–5mm) thick. Cut a shape to fit the pie. Roll some of the trimmings out into long strips. Brush the rim of the dish with some egg and press the pastry strips around the rim.

5 Brush the edging with egg and top with the pastry lid. Press down to seal the lid and trim off any overhang. Brush the top with

egg and cut two slits in it. Bake in the top of the oven for 20–25 minutes until golden, and let rest for 5 minutes before serving.

PREPARE AHEAD

Leave the pie until cold, then cover, chill overnight, and reheat the next day. Make sure it is piping hot in the center, and cover the top with foil if the pastry is becoming too dark.

CALORIES: 694kcals/2908kJ

CARBOHYDRATE: 40g
  sugar: 5g

FAT: 39g
  saturated: 17g

SALT: 2.5g

FIBER: 2.8g

Cheesy potato-topped tuna pie

An all-time kids' favorite: leave out the scallions for fussy eaters, or add more veggies for the adventurous child.

15 mins   35-40 mins

SPECIAL EQUIPMENT
2-quart (2-liter) ovenproof dish

SERVES 4

FOR THE TOPPING
2¼lb (1kg) floury potatoes, such as Russet, peeled and chopped into small chunks

salt and freshly ground black pepper

4 tbsp butter

¼ cup whole milk

FOR THE FILLING
4 tbsp butter

⅓ cup all-purpose flour

1¼ cups whole milk

4oz (115g) aged Cheddar cheese, coarsely grated

2 x 7oz (185g) cans tuna in spring water, drained well

1 x 7oz (195g) can corn, drained

5½oz (150g) frozen peas

4 scallions, finely chopped

2 tbsp finely chopped parsley leaves

3½oz (100g) firm mozzarella cheese, grated (or pre-grated mozzarella)

1 Cook the potatoes in a large saucepan of boiling salted water for 15 minutes, or until tender. Drain the potatoes, return to the pan, and mash. Stir in the butter and the milk, season to taste, and mix well. Set aside. Preheat the oven to 400°F (200°C).

2 For the filling, melt the butter in a medium pan. Stir in the flour and cook for 2–3 minutes over medium heat, stirring constantly with a wooden spoon, until a smooth paste is formed and the flour has lost its raw taste. Gradually add the milk, stirring, to make a white sauce.

3 Stir in the Cheddar cheese, tuna, corn, peas, scallions, and parsley, and season well. Transfer to a 2-quart ovenproof dish. Top with the mash, spreading it out in an even layer, and sprinkle evenly with the grated mozzarella.

4 Place the dish on a baking sheet and bake for 15–20 minutes, or until bubbling and golden brown.

VARIATION

If you prefer, use the same amount of Cheddar cheese for the topping, instead of the mozzarella. The flavor will be more pronounced; and this is probably a more economical choice.

CALORIES: 845kcals/3530kJ
CARBOHYDRATE: 67g
  sugar: 10.5g
FAT: 41g
  saturated: 25g
SALT: 1.8g
FIBER: 8g

Fisherman's pie

Haddock is the fish of choice in this traditional family dish, though you can use other sustainable white fish too.

20 mins, plus infusing   50 mins–1 hr

SPECIAL EQUIPMENT
2-quart (2-liter) baking dish

SERVES 6

FOR THE TOPPING
1lb 5oz (625g) potatoes, peeled and cut into chunks

salt and freshly ground black pepper

¼ cup whole milk

4 tbsp butter

FOR THE FILLING
3 large eggs

3½ cups whole milk

10 peppercorns

2 bay leaves

1 small onion, quartered

1lb 10oz (750g) skinless haddock fillets, cut into pieces

6 tbsp butter

½ cup all-purpose flour

handful of parsley leaves, chopped

4½oz (125g) cooked shrimp, shelled and deveined

1 Cook the potatoes in a saucepan of boiling salted water for 15–20 minutes until tender, adding the eggs for the filling for the last 10 minutes. Drain thoroughly. Cool the eggs, then peel, quarter, and set aside. Return the potato to the pan and mash. Heat the milk in a small pan, add the butter, salt, and pepper, and stir. Pour the milk mixture into the potatoes and beat over medium heat for 2 minutes, until fluffy. Taste for seasoning. Set aside.

2 For the filling, pour the milk into a frying pan, then add the peppercorns, bay leaves, and onion. Bring to a boil, then remove from the heat, cover, and leave to infuse for 10 minutes.

3 Return the infused milk to a boil, then reduce the heat to low. Add the fish, cover, and simmer for 5–10 minutes, depending on thickness: it should flake easily. Transfer the fish to a large plate, using a slotted spoon; strain and reserve the liquid. Flake the fish.

4 Melt the butter in a pan over medium heat. Whisk in the flour and cook for 1 minute. Off the heat, gradually add the fish cooking liquid, whisking. Return to the heat and whisk until the sauce boils and thickens. Season and simmer for 2 minutes, then add the parsley.

5 Preheat the oven to 350°F (180°C). Ladle one-third of the sauce into a 2-quart (2-liter) baking dish. Spoon the flaked fish on top, in an even layer. Cover with the remaining sauce, then scatter with the shrimp and quartered eggs, pushing them into the sauce.

6 Spread the mashed potatoes on top to cover the filling, forking it to make an attractive pattern. Bake for 20–30 minutes until brown and bubbling.

CALORIES: 543kcals/2269kJ

CARBOHYDRATE: 32.5g
  sugar: 9g

FAT: 30g
  saturated: 16g

SALT: 1.1g

FIBER: 2.5g

Smoked haddock and spinach crumble

A deliciously different fish pie, deeply soothing on a cold autumnal night. The leek crumble is an excellent topping.

20-30 mins   35-40 mins

SPECIAL EQUIPMENT

food processor

wide, deep, 2-quart (2-liter)
  flameproof dish or Dutch oven

SERVES 4–6

FOR THE CRUMBLE

2 tbsp butter

2 leeks, roughly chopped

2 cups fresh white bread,
  roughly torn

3 tbsp chopped parsley leaves

2oz (60g) grated Parmesan cheese

¾ cup oats

freshly ground black pepper

FOR THE FILLING

4 tbsp butter

⅓ cup all-purpose flour

2 cups whole milk

juice of ½ lemon

½ tsp ground nutmeg

2¼oz (70g) grated aged
  Cheddar cheese

3½oz (100g) spinach, roughly chopped

1lb 5oz (600g) smoked haddock
  fillet, skinned and chopped into
  bite-sized pieces

peas, to serve

1 Preheat the oven to 350°F
(180°C). For the crumble, melt
the butter in a large, non-stick
frying pan and cook the leeks over
medium-low heat for 10 minutes.

2 Place the bread, parsley, and
Parmesan in a food processor
and process to even-sized crumbs.
Add the leeks and pulse until
combined, retaining some texture.
Stir in the oats and plenty of pepper.

3 For the filling, melt the butter
in a wide, deep, 2-quart (2-liter)
flame- and ovenproof dish. Stir in
the flour and cook for 2–3 minutes
over medium heat, stirring with a
wooden spoon. Then gradually add
the milk, stirring.

4 Stir in the lemon juice, nutmeg,
and Cheddar. Season with
pepper and stir until the cheese
melts. Stir in the spinach, a handful
at a time, until wilted. Carefully fold
in the fish.

5 Sprinkle the crumble over
the top and place on a baking
sheet. Bake, uncovered, for 20
minutes. Serve with buttered peas.

This is a
great recipe for
smuggling some healthy
spinach into your children's
diet, smothered as it is
in a creamy sauce and
hidden under a
crispy topping.

Fussy eaters!

CALORIES: 696kcals/2917kJ

CARBOHYDRATE: 45g
  sugar: 8g

FAT: 35g
  saturated: 21g

SALT: 4.6g

FIBER: 5g

Pan-fried fish in a lemon and chive sauce

A simple, deeply comforting 10-minute supper dish. Serve with mashed potatoes and creamed spinach.

5 mins   10 mins

SERVES 4

salt and freshly ground black pepper

1 tbsp all-purpose flour, for dusting

4 sustainable, flat fish fillets, such as tilapia, approx. 3½oz (100g) each

1 tbsp olive oil

2 tbsp butter

5–6 tbsp white wine

5–6 tbsp fish stock

1 tbsp lemon juice

2 heaping tbsp crème fraîche

1 tbsp finely chopped chives

CALORIES: 213kcals/890kJ
CARBOHYDRATE: 3g
  sugar: 0.5g
FAT: 13.5g
  saturated: 6.5g
SALT: 0.6g
FIBER: 0.2g

---

1 Preheat the oven to 300°F (150°C). Season the flour and dust the fish with seasoned flour on both sides.

2 Heat the oil and 1 tbsp of the butter in a large frying pan and cook 2 of the fish fillets for 2 minutes on each side, until golden brown and crispy. Keep them warm in the oven on a baking sheet, loosely covered with foil, while you cook the rest.

3 When all the fish is cooked and keeping warm in the oven, make the sauce. Add the remaining 1 tbsp of butter to the pan and allow it to melt. Over high heat add the wine and stock, and allow them to reduce by half, then add the lemon juice and whisk in the crème fraîche, continuing to cook until it reduces and thickens slightly. Take it off the heat, season well, mix in the chives, and pour a little sauce over each fish fillet to serve.

Broiled red mullet with rosemary and chile

If you can't find red mullet, substitute whole rainbow trout. Both are able to stand up to these robust flavors.

5 mins   10 mins

SERVES 4

4 whole red mullet or rainbow trout, each portion-sized (choose smaller fish for children)

2 tbsp olive oil

1 tbsp finely chopped rosemary leaves, plus 4 sprigs of rosemary

1 red chile, seeded and finely chopped

½ tsp sea salt

1 lemon, quartered

couscous salad, to serve

CALORIES: 213kcals/892kJ
CARBOHYDRATE: 0g
  sugar: 0g
FAT: 11g
  saturated: 0.8g
SALT: 0.8g
FIBER: 0g

---

1 Preheat the broiler to its highest setting. Cut 3 deep, diagonal slashes on each side of each fish, making sure the knife goes right down to the bone with each slash. This will help the fish cook evenly.

2 Mix together the oil, rosemary, chile, and sea salt, and rub it into the fish, making sure to get it right down into all the slashes on both sides.

3 Tuck a sprig of rosemary inside each fish and place on a foil-lined baking sheet or broiler pan, to make cleaning-up easier later. Broil them for 4–5 minutes on each side, depending on size, or until the skin starts to char and the fish is cooked through. Turn very carefully, using a metal spatula. Serve with a lemon wedge and a couscous salad (see pp392–393 for couscous salad recipes).

COOK'S TIP

Red mullet has large bones, so the fish is fairly simple for older children to dissect by themselves, though an adult should always be on hand to help. For children who won't want to try this, fillet the fish just before serving.

Cod in parsley and mustard sauce

This soothing white sauce is enlivened with the use of ample amounts of parsley and some piquant mustard.

10 mins   30 mins

SERVES 4

3 tbsp butter

¼ cup all-purpose flour

1½ cups whole milk

6 tbsp chopped flat-leaf parsley leaves

2–3 tsp Dijon mustard

finely grated zest of 1 lemon

salt and freshly ground black pepper

4 skinless cod fillets, approx. 5½oz (150g) each

mashed potatoes and broccoli, to serve

1 Preheat the oven to 350°F (180°C). Melt the butter in a small, non-stick pan over low heat and whisk in the flour.

2 Cook, whisking constantly, for 2 minutes, until the mixture bubbles and separates.

3 Remove the pan from the heat and whisk in the milk, a little at a time, whisking well between each addition, until it has all been added and the sauce is smooth.

4 Return the pan to the heat and cook, stirring constantly, until the sauce thickens. Reduce the heat to low and cook, stirring occasionally, for 5 minutes. Whisk right into the edges of the sauce, as this is where it can burn.

5 Remove from the heat and add the parsley, mustard, lemon zest, and seasoning.

6 Place the cod fillets in a single layer in a shallow ovenproof dish. Pour the sauce over the top and cook in the oven for 20–25 minutes. Serve the cod with mashed potatoes and broccoli.

CALORIES: 290kcals/1211kJ

CARBOHYDRATE: 11g
  sugar: 4g

FAT: 13g
  saturated: 7.5g

SALT: 0.7g

FIBER: 0.4g

Sole with butter sauce

This sauce is perfect with flat fish or salmon steaks. Change it up by using tarragon or dill instead of parsley.

15 mins   10 mins

SERVES 4

4 small whole sole, fins and tails trimmed

2 tbsp butter, melted

salt and freshly ground black pepper

1 small onion, finely chopped

2 tbsp cider vinegar

8 tbsp butter, cut into cubes

2 tbsp chopped parsley leaves

baby carrots and steamed new potatoes, to serve

1 Preheat the broiler. Line the broiler pan with foil. Lay the fish on the broiler pan and brush all over with butter. Season lightly on both sides. Broil for about 5 minutes on each side, turning carefully, until lightly golden and cooked through.

2 Meanwhile, put the onion in a small pan with 2 tbsp of water and the cider vinegar. Bring to a boil, reduce the heat, and simmer until the onion is soft and the liquid is reduced by one-half.

3 Whisk in the butter, a piece at a time, until the sauce is thickened. Stir in the parsley and season to taste.

4 Transfer the cooked fish to warmed plates, spoon over the sauce, and serve with baby carrots and steamed new potatoes.

CLEVER WITH LEFTOVERS

Fresh herbs can be expensive and sometimes they do not get used up before going bad. Finely chop leftover herbs and freeze them in ice cube trays with a little water, then transfer into freezer bags until needed. The flavor is not as aromatic as fresh herbs, but they are well suited to adding to sauces.

CALORIES: 500kcals/2079kJ

CARBOHYDRATE: 1.5g
  sugar: 1.5g

FAT: 34g
  saturated: 19g

SALT: 1.2g

FIBER: 0.3g

Smart shopping

You can save yourself and your family a lot of time, money, and effort with some smart shopping. This could mean shopping online to save time and fuel costs, or combing the shelves for in-store offers, last-minute discounts, and culinary inspiration. Buying in bulk can be effective, but only if you know you are going to use the items you are buying. Don't be attracted by supposed "offers" to buy things you don't need. For all smart shoppers, eating seasonally, planning ahead, and making a list can prevent waste and save money.

Cupboard love

A well-stocked pantry is a wonderful thing. It doesn't really matter whether you have a walk-in pantry or a few shelves in the kitchen, as long as you know where to find your culinary basics whenever you need them. Rotate the items in the cupboard regularly so that you move older items to the front and use them first. Throw out anything that's past its use-by-date, especially anything that's been opened. Simple, cheap plastic fasteners are great for keeping open packages airtight and spill free.

shopping on a budget

Grocery bills can be expensive for a growing family, so look carefully at items that are on sale. Break out of your usual routine and think about shopping in different places or buying store-brand alternatives.

Bulk buying This can be economical, as long as you have adequate storage. If you don't, consider buying commonly used items in larger, more cost-effective quantities and splitting the costs with friends or family.

shopping list

Keep your shopping list somewhere accessible—hanging up in the kitchen perhaps—so that all the family can add to it when they notice that something has run out.

Decant

Decanting bulk purchases into airtight storage containers makes them easier to store and to serve. For picky kids, try decanting store-brand cereal into clear containers and see if anyone detects the difference!

Eat seasonally and locally
Seasonal shopping isn't just good for the planet, it's also good for your health and your wallet. Food that has traveled shorter distances will be fresher, and seasonal gluts of fruit and vegetables bring prices down.

Check the sell-by dates before you buy. Make sure you choose items with the latest date—not only will they be fresher, but they will keep longer, too.

Special offers A good rule of thumb for a tempting offer is only to buy something if it is genuinely cheaper than usual, you use it regularly, or you've always wanted to try it but it was too expensive.

Store-brand products Some brands are iconic for a reason—we love them because they taste good. Others are simply the result of good advertising. Experiment with store-brand products to find the ones that suit your family.

Shop around If you live close to an ethnic shop or supermarket, why not use it? Many Asian supermarkets sell dried herbs and spices at a fraction of the cost of big superstores, as well as bags of rice, dried beans, and an array of authentic ingredients at rock-bottom prices.

Keep in stock...

Stock up on these great pantry favorites—some are excellent bulk buys.

⭐ Dried pasta – various shapes and sizes

⭐ Dried beans – suitable for quick soups and stews

⭐ Rice – Arborio, basmati, white, and brown rice

⭐ Baking essentials – flours, rising agents, fast-acting dried yeast packages, dried fruits

⭐ Sugars – granulated, light brown, dark brown, and confectioners' sugar

⭐ Tomato products – canned tomatoes, tomato sauce, tomato paste

⭐ Oils – olive oil, extra virgin olive oil, sunflower oil, and vegetable oil

⭐ Vinegars – balsamic, cider, red, and white wine vinegars

⭐ Asian products – soy sauce, oyster sauce, sesame oil, chili oil, rice wine

⭐ Stocks – good quality chicken, beef, and vegetable stocks and stock powders

⭐ Canned fish – tuna, salmon, sardines, anchovies

shop online

Shopping online can be a life saver for busy parents. Using a basic weekly list that you add extras to can prevent unnecessary purchases. Choose late-night delivery slots, which are sometimes cheaper or even free.

Chicken noodle soup

Make this with chicken stock (see right) to get a second delicious meal from a simple roast chicken.

20 mins   20 mins

SERVES 4

2 tbsp olive oil

1 onion, finely chopped

1 leek, white part only, finely chopped

1 celery stalk, finely chopped

2 carrots, finely chopped

4 cups chicken stock (see right)

7oz (200g) cooked chicken, shredded, or the meat from making chicken stock (see right)

5½oz (150g) soup noodles, such as vermicelli

salt and freshly ground black pepper

2 tbsp finely chopped flat-leaf parsley leaves, to serve (optional)

1 Heat the oil in a large stock pot. Add the vegetables and cook over medium heat for 5–7 minutes until softened, but not browned.

2 Add the stock and bring to a boil. Reduce the heat to a gentle simmer and cook for about 10 minutes, until the vegetables are soft.

3 Add the chicken and noodles and continue to cook until the noodles are ready (follow the package instructions). Check the seasoning, add the parsley (if using), and serve.

CLEVER WITH LEFTOVERS

Save the green part of the leeks, wash them well, and store in the freezer. They have a more bitter taste than the white part, so are not good in this soup, but are excellent added to chicken stock (see right).

BATCHING AND FREEZING

If you have a lot of stock, double the recipe and cook it up to step 3. Add the chicken but leave out the noodles. Freeze it in portions. Defrost, bring to a boil, add the noodles, and cook until tender.

CALORIES: 359kcal/1503kJ
CARBOHYDRATE: 35g
  sugar: 5.5g
FAT: 8g
  saturated: 1.5g
SALT: 0.9g
FIBER: 3g

Chicken stock

Never throw away a chicken carcass. The bones make fantastic stock, which is the basis of many meals.

5 mins   1 hr 10 mins

MAKES 5½ CUPS

1 leftover cooked chicken carcass

1 celery stalk, roughly chopped

1 onion, quartered

1 large carrot, roughly chopped

1 leek, green part only

sprig of thyme, or some parsley sprigs, or both

1 bay leaf

½ tsp salt

1 heaping tbsp black peppercorns

1 Put the chicken, vegetables, herbs, and seasoning into a large stock pot. Cover with 7 cups of water.

2 Bring to a boil, then reduce the heat to a simmer and cook, uncovered, for 1 hour, until reduced to a bit more than half the original volume. Skim off any impurities from the surface as necessary.

3 Strain the stock, cool completely, and chill or freeze. The stock can either be used as it is, or the meat can be picked from the carcass and used to make chicken noodle soup (see left).

COOK'S TIP

Use a raw chicken carcass to make a lighter, more refined stock suitable for sauces and Asian recipes. The darker stock recipe above, made from a cooked carcass, is more suitable for using in stews and soups.

CALORIES: 7kcals/27kJ
CARBOHYDRATE: 0g
  sugar: 0g
FAT: 0.7g
  saturated: 0.1g
SALT: 0.2g
FIBER: 0g

Ribollita

Meaning "reboiled" in Italian, ribollita is a tasty and economical dish that is based on a traditional Tuscan soup.

10 mins, plus soaking   2 hrs

SERVES 4

3½oz (100g) dried navy beans, soaked overnight

2 tbsp extra virgin olive oil

1¾oz (50g) chopped pancetta

1 celery stalk, finely chopped

1 carrot, finely chopped

1 small onion, finely chopped

2 garlic cloves, crushed

2 sprigs of thyme

1 quantity chicken stock (see left)

2 handfuls or 3½oz (100g) kale, shredded

sea salt and freshly ground black pepper

scant 1oz (25g) finely grated Parmesan cheese

1 Rinse the soaked beans and place in a pan with plenty of cold water. Bring to a boil, skim off any foam, and reduce the heat to a simmer. Cook the beans for about 1 hour, until softened. Drain and set aside.

2 Heat the olive oil in a separate large saucepan and add the pancetta. Cook for 2–3 minutes over medium heat until crispy. Add the celery, carrot, and onion, then add the garlic and thyme. Continue to cook for another 2–3 minutes, until the vegetables are softened. Pour in the stock and add the drained beans. Simmer the stew for 30–40 minutes, uncovered, until the beans are very soft.

3 Add the kale, cover, and cook for 5 minutes until the leaves have wilted. Season to taste,

sprinkle with the Parmesan cheese, and serve with lots of chunks of crusty bread for dipping.

CALORIES: 206kcals/860kJ

CARBOHYDRATE: 15g
  sugar: 4g

FAT: 11g
  saturated: 3g

SALT: 1.3g

FIBER: 8g

Smoked chicken, bacon, and apple salad

This main course has a great smoky flavor, and plenty of crunch from the apple and walnuts.

20 mins   5 mins

SERVES 4

4 strips thick-cut bacon

1 crisp apple, such as Granny Smith

juice of ½ lemon

½ cup walnut pieces

7oz (200g) arugula or watercress

2 skinless smoked chicken breasts, approx. 10oz (300g) in total, sliced

FOR THE DRESSING

2 tbsp cider vinegar

¼ cup extra virgin olive oil

1 tsp Dijon mustard

2 tsp maple syrup

salt and freshly ground black pepper

1 Preheat the broiler to its highest setting. Broil the bacon until crisp, then drain on paper towels. When cold, break into large pieces.

2 Peel, core, quarter, and thinly slice the apple and drop into a bowl of water mixed with the lemon juice. Place a heavy-bottomed frying pan over medium heat, add the nuts, and stir to toast. Let cool.

3 Whisk together the dressing ingredients in a salad bowl until emulsified.

4 Put the arugula or watercress in the bowl and toss with the dressing. Drain and dry the apple and add to the salad with the chicken and three-quarters each of the walnuts and bacon. Gently toss the salad, then sprinkle with the remaining walnuts and bacon.

CLEVER WITH LEFTOVERS

Any leftover salad can be chopped up and mixed with good-quality mayonnaise to make an instant sandwich or wrap filling for a lunch box the following day.

CALORIES: 370kcals/1534kJ

CARBOHYDRATE: 7g
  sugar: 7g

FAT: 27g
  saturated: 5g

SALT: 1.1g

FIBER: 2g

Spicy Asian chicken salad

This vibrant salad is tasty as well as healthy, and a great dish to serve at a summer buffet.

25-30 mins   15 mins

SERVES 4-6

14oz (400g) boneless, skinless chicken breasts

salt

¼ cup lime juice (approx. 2 limes)

4 tsp Thai fish sauce

1 tbsp granulated sugar

pinch of chile flakes (optional)

1 Little Gem lettuce, shredded

3½oz (100g) beansprouts

1 large carrot, shaved using a vegetable peeler

6in (15cm) piece of cucumber, seeded and finely sliced

½ red bell pepper, finely sliced

½ yellow bell pepper, finely sliced

approx. 15 cherry tomatoes, halved

small handful of mint leaves, chopped

small handful of cilantro leaves, chopped

1¾oz (50g) salted peanuts, chopped (optional)

1 Poach the chicken in a large saucepan in plenty of simmering salted water or chicken stock (see p94) for 7–10 minutes, depending on thickness, until cooked through. Let cool, then thinly slice.

2 Whisk the lime juice, fish sauce, sugar, a pinch of salt, and the chile flakes (if using) together, until the sugar dissolves.

3 Mix together the salad vegetables, most of the herbs, and the chicken. Mix in the dressing and scatter with the remaining herbs and the peanuts (if using), to serve.

CALORIES: 245kcals/1031kJ

CARBOHYDRATE: 13g
  sugar: 12g

FAT: 8g
  saturated: 1.5g

SALT: 1.3g

FIBER: 4.5g

Grilled chicken Caesar salad

This has an easy version of the classic Caesar dressing, replacing the traditional recipe made with raw egg.

20 mins   20 mins

SPECIAL EQUIPMENT
mini food processor or
  hand-held blender

SERVES 4

3½oz (100g) day-old baguette,
  or other rustic white bread

4 tbsp olive oil

salt and freshly ground black
  pepper

14oz (400g) boneless, skinless
  chicken breasts

1 large Romaine lettuce, leaves
  broken into bite-sized pieces

1oz (30g) Parmesan cheese shavings

FOR THE DRESSING
½ cup extra virgin olive oil

1 tbsp Dijon mustard

3 tbsp good-quality mayonnaise

4 anchovy fillets, chopped

½ tsp Worcestershire sauce

1 garlic clove, crushed

2 tbsp finely grated Parmesan
  cheese

pinch of granulated sugar

1 Preheat the oven to 400°F (200°C). Trim the bread of any crusts and cut into ¾in (2cm) cubes. Toss them with 3 tbsp of the olive oil, season well, and spread them out on a large baking sheet, in a single layer if possible. Cook them at the top of the oven for 6–8 minutes, turning occasionally, until they are golden brown on all sides. Watch carefully so that they do not burn. Set aside to cool. If you do not have a grill pan, preheat the broiler to its highest setting.

2 Meanwhile, rub the chicken breasts with the remaining olive oil, season well, and either grill in a grill pan or broil them for 5 minutes on each side, or until cooked through and nicely charred. Set aside to cool, then slice.

3 To make the dressing, put all the ingredients into the bowl of a mini food processor, or into a suitable container for a hand-held blender, and process or blend until they have emulsified into a thick, creamy dressing. Season with pepper. To serve, put the lettuce in a large bowl and toss it in the dressing. Scatter with the croutons and Parmesan shavings and arrange the warm chicken slices on top.

CALORIES: 593kcals/2467kJ

CARBOHYDRATE: 15g
  sugar: 2.5g

FAT: 45g
  saturated: 9g

SALT: 1.5g

FIBER: 1.5g

Mild creamy chicken curry

Introducing children to more adventurous tastes can be hard, so start them off with this gently spiced curry.

15 mins   35-40 mins

SERVES 4

2 tbsp sunflower or vegetable oil

1 onion, finely chopped

2 garlic cloves, finely chopped

2–3 tbsp medium curry powder

1 tsp ground cumin

4 boneless, skinless chicken breasts, sliced lengthwise into 4–5 strips

2 cups chicken stock (see p94)

5½oz (150g) red lentils

⅔ cup (5oz) plain yogurt

salt and freshly ground black pepper

½ cup toasted sliced almonds

2 tbsp chopped cilantro leaves

basmati rice or naan breads, to serve

1 Heat half the oil in a large, non-stick frying pan that has a lid, and cook the onion for 5 minutes, or until softened, but not browned. Add the garlic and spices and cook for 2 minutes.

2 Add the remaining oil and the chicken and cook for 5–7 minutes, turning to coat the chicken in the spices and to seal it on all sides. Add the stock and lentils and bring to a boil. Cover, reduce the heat, and simmer for 20 minutes or until the chicken and lentils are cooked.

3 Stir in the yogurt, season to taste, and heat through for 2 minutes until piping hot once more. Do not return to a boil after adding the yogurt, or there is a risk that the curry sauce might separate.

4 Sprinkle the curry with the almonds and cilantro and serve with basmati rice or warmed naan bread.

CALORIES: 475kcals/1996kJ

CARBOHYDRATE: 26g
  sugar: 5.5g

FAT: 16g
  saturated: 2.5g

SALT: 0.7g

FIBER: 4g

Spicy chicken and tomato curry

Try making double or triple amounts of this fresh, zingy curry paste and freezing leftovers for another time.

20 mins   30-35 mins

SPECIAL EQUIPMENT
food processor

SERVES 4

FOR THE CURRY PASTE

1 onion, chopped

1in (2.5cm) fresh ginger, chopped

2 garlic cloves

juice of ½ lemon

2 tsp ground coriander

2 tsp ground cumin

½–1 tsp medium chili powder

1 tsp ground allspice

2 tsp garam masala

FOR THE CURRY

1 tbsp vegetable oil

1 onion, sliced

8 boneless, skinless chicken thighs

salt and freshly ground black pepper

2 tbsp tomato paste

2 potatoes, cut into ¾in (2cm) cubes

1 green bell pepper, sliced

1 red bell pepper, sliced

4 tomatoes, peeled, seeded, and chopped

1¼–1½ cups chicken stock (see p94)

rice and mini naan bread, to serve

1 Put the curry paste ingredients in a food processor. Blend to a paste. Set aside until needed.

2 For the curry, heat the oil in a large pan over medium heat and cook the onion for 5 minutes. Add the curry paste and chicken, season, and cook for 5 minutes.

3 Stir in the tomato paste, vegetables, and stock to cover. Cover. Simmer for 20–25 minutes. Serve with rice and warmed naan.

CALORIES: 344kcals/1450kJ

CARBOHYDRATE: 28g
  sugar: 11.5g

FAT: 8g
  saturated: 2g

SALT: 0.6g

FIBER: 6g

Chicken and coconut curry

This Thai-inspired curry is delicious. You can omit the eggplant and add cooked broccoli at the end instead.

20 mins, plus marinating 25–30 mins

SPECIAL EQUIPMENT
mini food processor

SERVES 4

FOR THE MARINADE

2 lemongrass stalks

3 garlic cloves, finely chopped

1 red chile, seeded and chopped

2 tbsp Madras curry paste

1 tbsp dark brown sugar

3 tbsp soy sauce

FOR THE CURRY

1lb (450g) boneless, skinless chicken thighs, cut into strips

½ tbsp vegetable oil

1 red onion, finely chopped

⅔ cup chicken stock (see p94)

1 x 14fl oz (400ml) can coconut milk

1 eggplant, cut into ¾in (2cm) cubes

2 zucchini, cut into ¾in (2cm) cubes

salt and freshly ground black pepper

Thai or regular basil leaves, to garnish

jasmine rice, to serve

1 Peel the lemongrass stalks to reveal the soft white centers; discard the tough outer layers and trim the ends of the stalks. Roughly chop the tender white inner layers of the lemongrass and place in a mini food processor with the garlic, chile, curry paste, sugar, and soy sauce. Blend well to a smooth paste, trying to remove all lumps as much as possible.

2 Place the chicken strips in a shallow dish and spoon over the marinade, stirring to coat thoroughly. Cover and set aside to marinate for 1 hour at room temperature. (You may marinate the chicken for up to 1 day if it is more convenient, but refrigerate if you plan to do so.)

3 Heat a large, non-stick frying pan that has a lid over high heat, add the oil, and reduce the temperature to medium. Add the onion and cook for 5 minutes, stirring occasionally, until softened, but not browned. Add the chicken and its marinade and cook for another 5 minutes, stirring occasionally to color the chicken on all sides.

4 Pour in the stock and coconut milk, then add the eggplant and zucchini. Season well, bring to a boil, cover, then reduce the heat and simmer gently for 15–20 minutes. Scatter with the Thai basil and serve with jasmine rice.

PREPARE AHEAD

Blend the marinade up to 2 days in advance, cover, and refrigerate. The flavors will deepen—especially the strengths of the chile and garlic tastes—the longer you leave it.

CALORIES: 387kcals/1623kJ

CARBOHYDRATE: 12g
 sugar: 8g

FAT: 24g
 saturated: 16g

SALT: 2.7g

FIBER: 2.5g

Easy chicken tikka skewers with cucumber and mint raita

This easy-to-make Indian dipping sauce can be a staple accompaniment to so many grilled or broiled dishes.

20 mins
plus marinating   10 mins

SPECIAL EQUIPMENT
8 bamboo skewers

SERVES 4

FOR THE MARINADE

6 tbsp plain low-fat yogurt

1 tbsp lemon juice

1 tsp ground cumin

1 tsp ground coriander

½ tsp turmeric

2 tsp cayenne pepper or chili powder

½ tsp salt

1 garlic clove, crushed

1in (3cm) fresh ginger, grated

1lb 5oz (600g) boneless, skinless chicken breast or thigh, cut into 1in (3cm) cubes

FOR THE RAITA

4in (10cm) piece of cucumber, seeded and grated

¾ cup (7oz) Greek-style yogurt

handful of mint leaves, finely chopped

1 small garlic clove, crushed

salt and freshly ground black pepper

1 Mix the marinade ingredients, except the chicken, in a bowl. Add the chicken, turning to coat. Cover and refrigerate for 1 hour.

2 Meanwhile, place 8 bamboo skewers in a large, shallow bowl of water, to keep them from burning.

3 Put the cucumber in a clean kitchen towel and squeeze well. Mix with the remaining raita ingredients and season to taste. Cover and chill.

4 Thread the chicken onto the soaked, drained skewers, distributing it evenly. Preheat the broiler and broil the chicken for 3–5 minutes on each side, or until starting to char. Serve with the raita.

VARIATION

For an even easier recipe, mix 2 tbsp of store-bought tikka paste with the yogurt and use that as the marinade.

CALORIES 242kcals/1019kJ

CARBOHYDRATE: 4.5g
sugar: 4g

FAT: 7g
saturated: 4g

SALT: 0.8g

FIBER: 0.5g

Easy General Tso's chicken

A healthier version of a take-out classic, try making this recipe as part of a weekend family feast.

15 mins
plus marinating   10 mins

SERVES 4

FOR THE MARINADE

1 tbsp soy sauce

1 tbsp rice wine or dry sherry

1 tsp granulated sugar

FOR THE CHICKEN

1lb 2oz (500g) boneless, skinless chicken thighs, cut into ¾in (2cm) cubes

2 heaping tbsp cornstarch

½ cup sunflower or vegetable oil, plus 1 tbsp

2 garlic cloves, finely chopped

1in (3cm) fresh ginger, finely chopped

shredded scallions, to serve

jasmine rice, to serve

FOR THE SAUCE

⅔ cup chicken stock (see p94)

1 tbsp tomato paste

2 tbsp soy sauce

1 tbsp hoisin sauce

1 tsp crushed chile flakes

1 tsp granulated sugar

1 Mix the marinade ingredients in a bowl, add the chicken, and turn to coat. Cover and refrigerate for 30 minutes. Whisk together the sauce ingredients. Set aside.

2 Put the cornstarch in a freezer bag. Add the chicken and shake to coat. Pour into a sieve to remove excess cornstarch.

3 Heat the ½ cup of oil in a wok. It's ready when an oil thermometer reads 350°F (180°C), or a cube of bread sizzles immediately. Fry the chicken in batches for 2–3 minutes each side, until crispy. Remove with a slotted spoon and drain on paper towels. Repeat to cook all the chicken.

4 Pour the oil from the wok and wipe it with paper towels. Heat another 1 tbsp of oil in the wok and cook the garlic and ginger for a minute. Mix the sauce ingredients, then pour into the wok and bring to a simmer. Return the chicken and cook for 2 minutes. Scatter with scallions and serve with rice.

CALORIES: 386kcals/1609kJ

CARBOHYDRATE: 10g
sugar: 4.5g

FAT: 24.5g
saturated: 3.5g

SALT: 2.5g

FIBER: 0.1g

Spicy stir-fried chicken with vegetables

This dish is quite spicy so, to reduce the heat for young or sensitive palates, cut down the amount of chile used.

15 mins plus marinating **10 mins**

SERVES 4

3 tbsp soy sauce

2 tbsp rice wine or dry sherry

1 tsp sugar

2½ tbsp sunflower or vegetable oil

14oz (400g) boneless, skinless chicken thighs, cut into ½in (1cm) strips

1¾oz (50g) thin green beans, halved

salt

1¾oz (50g) broccoli florets

2 garlic cloves, crushed

1in (3cm) fresh ginger, finely chopped

1 red chile, seeded and finely chopped

bunch of scallions, cut into ¾in (2cm) pieces

3½oz (100g) sugarsnap peas, halved on the diagonal

1 tbsp oyster sauce

1 Mix 1 tbsp of the soy sauce, 1 tbsp of the rice wine, the sugar, and ½ tbsp of the oil in a bowl. Stir in the chicken, cover, and refrigerate for 30 minutes.

2 Cook the green beans in a pan of boiling salted water for 1 minute. Add the broccoli and cook for another minute. Drain and refresh under cold water. Set aside.

3 Heat the remaining oil in a wok, add the garlic, ginger, and chile, and cook for 1 minute. Now add the chicken and stir for 2–3 minutes. Add the scallions and peas and stir-fry for another 2–3 minutes. Pour in the remaining soy sauce, rice wine, and the oyster sauce, and bubble up. Add in the blanched vegetables and heat through to serve.

CALORIES:	216kcals/904kJ
CARBOHYDRATE:	6g
sugar:	5g
FAT:	10g
saturated:	1.5g
SALT:	2.6g
FIBER:	2g

Stir-fried chicken and asparagus

The mild spicing in this dish complements the delicate flavor of the asparagus.

15 mins plus marinating **10 mins**

SERVES 4

2 tsp cornstarch

3 tbsp soy sauce

2 tbsp rice wine or dry sherry

2 tsp granulated sugar

1lb 2oz (500g) boneless, skinless chicken thighs, finely sliced

bunch of asparagus, woody ends removed, cut into 1in (3cm) pieces, stalks and tips separated

salt

2 tbsp sunflower or vegetable oil

2 garlic cloves, finely chopped

1½in (4cm) fresh ginger, finely chopped

bunch of scallions, cut into 1in (3cm) pieces

rice, to serve

1 Mix together 1 tsp of the cornstarch, 1 tbsp of the soy sauce, 1 tbsp of the rice wine, and 1 tsp of the sugar in a large bowl. Toss through the chicken, cover, and refrigerate for 30 minutes.

2 Meanwhile, cook the asparagus stalks in a pan of boiling salted water for 1 minute, then add the tips and blanch for another minute. Drain and refresh under cold water. Mix the remaining cornstarch with 1 tbsp of cold water. Set aside.

3 Heat the oil in a wok and, when it is hot, add the garlic and ginger and cook for 1 minute. Add the chicken and stir-fry for 3–4 minutes. Add the scallions and cook for another 2 minutes.

4 Add the remaining soy sauce, rice wine, sugar, and 2 tbsp of water, and bring to a boil.

5 Stir and add the cornstarch mixture, then the asparagus. Cook for another 2 minutes until the mixture thickens and the asparagus is hot. Serve over rice.

CALORIES:	241kcals/1008kJ
CARBOHYDRATE:	8g
sugar:	6g
FAT:	9.5g
saturated:	1.5g
SALT:	2.3g
FIBER:	2g

Sweet and sour chicken

Removing the pineapple chunks of the take-out version makes this a more sophisticated alternative.

15 mins, plus marinating | 10 mins

SERVES 4

FOR THE MARINADE

1 tsp cornstarch

1 tbsp soy sauce

1 tbsp rice wine or dry sherry

1 tsp granulated sugar

FOR THE CHICKEN

1lb 2oz (500g) boneless, skinless chicken breast, cut into ½in (1cm) slices

2 tbsp sunflower or vegetable oil

2 garlic cloves, finely chopped

1in (3cm) fresh ginger, finely chopped

3½oz (100g) raw, unsalted cashews, roughly chopped

FOR THE SAUCE

2 tbsp rice wine vinegar or white wine vinegar

2 tbsp rice wine or dry sherry

3 tbsp ketchup

2 tbsp soy sauce

½ cup chicken stock (see p94)

1 tbsp granulated sugar

1 Mix the marinade ingredients in a bowl and turn the chicken to coat. Cover and refrigerate for at least 30 minutes.

2 Whisk together all the sauce ingredients and set aside.

3 Heat the oil in a wok, add the garlic and ginger, and stir-fry for 1 minute. Add the chicken and stir-fry until it turns pale.

4 Add the sauce and bring to a boil. Add the cashews and cook for 2–3 minutes until the mixture has thickened and the chicken is coated in a glossy sauce. Serve.

PREPARE AHEAD

If you want to get ahead, make this recipe without the cashews and freeze it. Defrost the chicken thoroughly, then reheat quickly until piping hot, stirring in the nuts just before serving.

CALORIES: 386kcals/1616kJ
CARBOHYDRATE: 14g
  sugar: 10g
FAT: 19g
  saturated: 3.5g
SALT: 2.7g
FIBER: 1g

Chicken and broccoli simmered in soy sauce and star anise

Deeply aromatic, this is a great recipe to cook for minimum fuss and easy clean-up.

10 mins | 20–25 mins

SERVES 4

½ cup rice wine or dry sherry

¼ cup soy sauce

1¾ cups chicken stock (see p94)

1½in (4cm) fresh ginger, cut into matchsticks

2 garlic cloves, sliced

4 star anise

3 tbsp light brown sugar

4 boneless, skinless chicken breasts

1 tbsp cornstarch

5½oz (150g) broccoli rabe or broccoli florets

1 In a large, deep-sided frying pan or wok, mix the rice wine, soy sauce, stock, ginger, garlic, star anise, and sugar and bring to a boil over medium heat. Reduce the heat and simmer for 5 minutes.

2 Add the chicken in a single layer, making sure it is submerged as much as possible, and poach for 7–10 minutes, turning occasionally, until firm. Remove with a slotted spoon, cover, and keep warm.

3 Strain the liquid through a sieve and return it to the pan. Return it to a boil over medium heat, then reduce the heat to a simmer. Mix the cornstarch with 1 tbsp of water and add, whisking until it thickens. Add the broccoli and cook for 3–5 minutes until tender.

4 Pour the sauce over the chicken and arrange the broccoli around to serve.

VARIATION

Use quartered bok choy, Napa cabbage cut into wedges, or lengths of scallions instead of broccoli.

CALORIES: 282kcals/1192kJ
CARBOHYDRATE: 16g
  sugar: 12.5g
FAT: 2g
  saturated: 0.5g
SALT: 2.8g
FIBER: 1.5g

Pot-roast chicken

A simple one-pot, succulent, and tender variation of the traditional roast chicken loved by all.

10 mins   1 hr 45 mins

SPECIAL EQUIPMENT
large Dutch oven

SERVES 4

2 tbsp olive oil

1 large onion, cut into 8 wedges

1 leek, cut into 1in (3cm) pieces

1 celery stalk, cut into 1in (3cm) pieces

4 carrots, cut into 1in (3cm) pieces

2 garlic cloves, roughly chopped

8 new potatoes, skin on, halved

1½ cups chicken stock (see p94)

sprig of thyme

1 bay leaf

salt and freshly ground black pepper

1 chicken, approx. 3lb 3oz (1.5kg)

pat of butter

1 Preheat the oven to 350°F (180°C). Heat the oil in a large Dutch oven. Cook the onion, leek, celery, and carrots for 5 minutes until softened and browning. Stir in the garlic and potatoes and cook for 2 minutes.

2 Add the stock, herbs, black pepper, and a little salt. Rub the chicken with the butter and season the breast with salt and pepper.

3 Place the chicken on the vegetables. If it is close to the lid of the pan, cover it loosely with parchment paper to prevent it from sticking. Cover and cook in the oven for 1 hour.

4 Remove the lid, increase the oven temperature to 400°F (200°C), and cook for another 30 minutes, until the breast is golden brown and the sauce reduced. Remove the herbs before serving.

COOK'S TIP

Remove the chicken and vegetables and reduce the cooking liquid over high heat for 5 minutes to thicken.

HOW TO FREEZE

Remove the chicken from the bone in the largest pieces possible before freezing. (Smaller pieces can dry out in the freezer.)

CALORIES: 495kcals/2082kJ

CARBOHYDRATE: 27g
  sugar: 11.5g

FAT: 13.5g
  saturated: 3.5g

SALT: 0.7g

FIBER: 6g

Chicken with pancetta, peas, and mint

This delicious dish can be prepared in minutes and left in the oven to cook, with no extra attention needed.

15 mins   1 hr 45 mins

SPECIAL EQUIPMENT
large Dutch oven

SERVES 4

2 tbsp olive oil

4 large or 8 small skin-on bone-in chicken pieces

2 onions, finely chopped

7oz (200g) chopped pancetta or bacon

2 garlic cloves, grated or finely chopped

1 cup dry white wine

2 cups hot chicken stock (see p94)

salt and freshly ground black pepper

handful of flat-leaf parsley leaves, finely chopped

handful of mint leaves, finely chopped

8oz (225g) frozen peas

crusty bread and sautéed potatoes, to serve

1 Preheat the oven to 300°F (150°C). Heat 1 tbsp of the oil in a large Dutch oven over medium heat. Add the chicken and cook for about 8 minutes, turning, until golden all over. Remove from the Dutch oven and set aside.

2 Reduce the heat to low and add the remaining oil and onions to the Dutch oven. Cook gently for 5 minutes until soft and translucent, then add the pancetta. Increase the heat and cook for 5 minutes until the pancetta is golden. Stir in the garlic, then pour in the wine. Increase the heat to high and simmer for a few minutes until the alcohol has evaporated.

3 Add the stock and return to a boil. Season with salt and pepper and stir through. Return the chicken. Stir in half the parsley and mint, cover, and cook in the oven for 1½ hours. Check the level of liquid occasionally—it needs to be fairly dry, but if it needs more, add a little hot water. Stir in the peas and remaining chopped herbs 5 minutes before the end of cooking time. Serve hot with crusty bread or sautéed potatoes.

CALORIES: 510kcals/2125kJ

CARBOHYDRATE: 10g
  sugar: 4g

FAT: 26g
  saturated: 7g

SALT: 2.1g

FIBER: 4.5g

Chicken and barley stew

A nutritious, warming, and comforting one-pot dish that needs nothing more than mashed potatoes on the side.

10 mins   1 hr 15 mins

SPECIAL EQUIPMENT
large Dutch oven (optional)

SERVES 4

5½oz (150g) pearl barley

4 tbsp sunflower or vegetable oil

1 large onion, chopped

1 leek, sliced into ½in (1cm) rings

1 celery stalk, cut into
¾in (2cm) pieces

2 large carrots, cut into
¾in (2cm) pieces

1 parsnip, cut into ¾in (2cm) pieces

salt and freshly ground black pepper

1 tbsp all-purpose flour

8 skinless bone-in chicken thighs

2 cups chicken stock (see p94)

1 bouquet garni

1 Put the barley in a saucepan and cover it with cold water. Place over high heat and bring to a boil. Cook for 10 minutes, skimming off foam. Drain and rinse.

2 In a large Dutch oven or heavy-bottomed saucepan with a lid, heat 2 tbsp of the sunflower oil.

Cook the onion, leek, celery, carrots, and parsnip for 10 minutes over medium heat until they color at the edges. Remove from the pan and wipe it out with paper towels.

3 Heat the remaining 2 tbsp of oil in the pan. Season the flour. Dust the chicken with the flour, shaking off excess. Cook the pieces, spaced well apart, for 3–5 minutes each side until golden. You may need to cook in batches. Set aside.

4 Pour in the stock, scraping up the residue from the pan. Return the vegetables, barley, and chicken. Add the bouquet garni.

5 Bring to a boil, then reduce the heat to a gentle simmer and cook, covered, for about 45 minutes, until the chicken is cooked through. Remove the bouquet garni before serving.

CALORIES: 513kcals/2156kJ

CARBOHYDRATE: 45g
  sugar: 10g

FAT: 17g
  saturated: 3g

SALT: 0.8g

FIBER: 6g

Spanish chicken, chorizo, and pepper stew

A quick and satisfying crowd pleaser of a recipe that adds a dash of warming spice to family meal times.

10 mins   1 hr 15 mins

SPECIAL EQUIPMENT

large Dutch oven (optional)

SERVES 4

3 tbsp olive oil

1 tbsp all-purpose flour

salt and freshly ground black pepper

8 skinless bone-in chicken pieces, thighs, drumsticks, or a mixture

1 red onion, finely sliced

1 red bell pepper, finely sliced

1 yellow bell pepper, finely sliced

2 garlic cloves, chopped

5½oz (150g) dry Spanish-style chorizo, casing removed, cut into 1in (3cm) pieces

1 heaping tsp smoked paprika

1 x 14oz (400g) can chopped tomatoes

1¾ cups chicken stock (see p94)

2 heaping tbsp chopped flat-leaf parsley leaves

a few sprigs of thyme

1 In a large Dutch oven or pot with a lid, heat 2 tbsp of the olive oil. Season the flour with salt and pepper. Dust the chicken pieces with the flour, shaking off excess. Cook them in the pan, spaced well apart, for a few minutes each side, until golden brown. Remove from the pan.

2 Heat the remaining 1 tbsp of oil and cook the onion and peppers for 5 minutes until softened, but not browned. Add the garlic and cook for another minute. Add the chorizo and cook for a few minutes until it becomes crisp at the edges and the reddish oil starts to run. Sprinkle in the smoked paprika and stir well.

3 Add the tomatoes, stock, and herbs and season to taste. Finally, return the chicken to the pan, cover, and simmer over low heat for 40–45 minutes, until the chicken is cooked (pierce a thick piece to the bone to check; there should be no trace of pink). Remove the thyme and serve.

BATCHING AND FREEZING

To get ahead, make this meal when there are only two of you for dinner. Divide the remaining 2 portions into separate freezer- and microwave-safe containers and freeze. Defrosted, and reheated in a microwave, these frozen portions make ideal lunches on busy days, with no effort. Accompany with crusty bread.

CALORIES: 485kcals/2029kJ

CARBOHYDRATE: 13g
sugar: 9g

FAT: 23g
saturated: 6.5g

SALT: 1.4g

FIBER: 3g

Mediterranean chicken

This colorful one-pot meal is stuffed full of vitamin-rich vegetables, pleasing the eye as well as the palate.

20 mins   1 hr

SERVES 4

9oz (250g) butternut squash, peeled and cut into 1in (3cm) cubes

1 red bell pepper, cut into 1in (3cm) cubes

1 yellow bell pepper, cut into 1in (3cm) cubes

2 small red onions, quartered

14oz (400g) small new potatoes, halved

2 tbsp olive oil, plus extra for greasing

1 tbsp chopped flat-leaf parsley

salt and freshly ground black pepper

8 skin-on bone-in chicken thighs

10oz (300g) cherry tomatoes

2 tbsp chopped basil leaves

4 small sprigs of rosemary

1 Preheat the oven to 350°F (180°C). In a large metal roasting pan, mix the squash, peppers, onions, and potatoes with the olive oil and parsley. Season them well and spread out in a single layer.

2 Rub the chicken thighs with a little oil, season them, and poke into the layer of vegetables.

3 Roast in the oven for 40 minutes. Remove from the oven and increase the oven temperature to 200°C (400°F).

4 Mix in the tomatoes and basil, with another splash of olive oil if necessary, and tuck in the rosemary. Spread it all out and cook for another 15–20 minutes at the top of the oven, until the chicken is crisp and the tomatoes are just starting to burst. Remove the rosemary and serve.

FEEDING A CROWD

Casseroles are ideal for large numbers, as they can be prepared ahead and need little tending. Use 2 pieces of chicken per person, and add more vegetables. Do not crowd the pan: use 2, so the ingredients can be spread out in a single layer.

CALORIES: 428kcals/1795kJ
CARBOHYDRATE: 29g
  sugar: 12.5g
FAT: 18g
  saturated: 4g
SALT: 0.4g
FIBER: 6g

Coq au vin

A classic French dish that makes a comforting winter meal. The alcohol cooks off, leaving only a rich taste.

10 mins   1 hr 10 mins

SERVES 4

4 tbsp olive oil

3½oz (100g) chopped pancetta

5½oz (150g) small button mushrooms, wiped, and halved if necessary

12 small pearl onions or shallots, peeled

4 tbsp all-purpose flour

salt and freshly ground black pepper

8 skinless bone-in chicken pieces, thighs, drumsticks, or a mixture

¼ cup brandy (optional)

1¼ cups red wine

1¼ cups chicken stock (see p94)

1 tbsp redcurrant or sour cherry jelly

1 bouquet garni

1 In a large pot with a lid, heat 2 tbsp of the oil over medium heat. Cook the pancetta, mushrooms, and small onions for 5 minutes, until golden brown. Remove from the pan.

2 Heat the remaining 2 tbsp of oil in the pan. Season 1 tbsp of the flour with salt and pepper and put on a plate. Dust the chicken with the flour, shaking off excess. Cook the chicken, well spaced (you may have to do this in batches), for 3–5 minutes each side, until golden brown. Add the brandy (if using), take it off the heat, and ignite with a match to cook off the alcohol.

3 Remove the chicken from the pan and add it to the vegetables and pancetta. Add the remaining 3 tbsp of flour to the pan and stir for a minute. Add the wine, stock, redcurrant jelly, and bouquet garni.

4 Return the chicken, pancetta, and vegetables and bring to a boil. Reduce to a simmer, cover, and cook for 40–45 minutes, until cooked through. Remove the bouquet garni to serve.

CALORIES: 564kcals/2361kJ
CARBOHYDRATE: 17g
  sugar: 5.5g
FAT: 20g
  saturated: 4g
SALT: 1.3g
FIBER: 2g

Moroccan-spiced chicken

A gently spiced stew, sweet with squash and dried apricots, this is particularly appealing to younger children.

15 mins   1 hr 10 mins

SERVES 4

1 heaping tbsp all-purpose flour

salt and freshly ground black pepper

8 skinless bone-in chicken pieces,
  thighs, drumsticks, or a mixture

4 tbsp olive oil

1 large onion, finely chopped

1 red bell pepper, sliced

1 yellow bell pepper, sliced

2 garlic cloves, roughly chopped

1 tsp ground cumin

½ tsp ground coriander

½ tsp ground cinnamon

1 tsp smoked paprika

1 tsp dried thyme

1 x 14oz (400g) can chopped tomatoes

2 cups chicken stock (see p94)

1 tbsp honey

9oz (250g) butternut squash, peeled
  and cut into ¾in (2cm) cubes

1¾oz (50g) dried apricots,
  roughly chopped

handful of cilantro leaves,
  roughly chopped

1 Place the flour in a freezer
  bag and season it well. Toss
the chicken in the bag until well
coated. Pour out into a sieve and
shake to remove excess flour.

2 Heat 2 tbsp of the oil over
  medium heat in a large,
heavy-bottomed pot with a lid.
Cook the chicken (you may need
to do this in batches), spaced
well apart, for 3–5 minutes each

side, until golden brown all over.
Set aside while you cook the
remaining pieces.

3 Heat the remaining 2 tbsp of oil
  in the pan and cook the onion,
peppers, and garlic for 3–5 minutes
until softened, but not brown. Add
all the spices and the thyme and
cook for a minute or two until they
release all their fragrances. Add
the tomatoes, stock, and honey,
and season to taste.

4 Return the chicken and bring
  to a boil. Reduce the heat to
a low simmer and cook, covered,
for 20 minutes. Add the squash
and apricots and cook, covered,
for another 20 minutes, stirring
occasionally, until the chicken
is cooked through. Stir in the
cilantro leaves to serve.

PREPARE AHEAD

Stews or slow-cooked dishes often
taste better the day after they are
made, as time allows the flavors to
develop. Cook this dish a day or two
in advance and, when it is cold, remove
the chicken from the bones and store
it in an airtight container in the fridge.
Removing the bones saves space and
allows it to reheat more easily.

CALORIES: 414kcals/1739kJ

CARBOHYDRATE: 26g
  sugar: 20g

FAT: 16g
  saturated: 3g

SALT: 0.8g

FIBER: 6g

Chicken cacciatore

Chicken breasts can be dry. Cooking them in this rich, Italian sauce will give them a succulent texture.

10 mins   50–55 mins

SPECIAL EQUIPMENT
Dutch oven

SERVES 4

1 tbsp olive oil

4 skin-on bone-in chicken breasts

1 red onion, finely chopped

2 garlic cloves, finely chopped

1 red bell pepper, sliced

2 x (14oz) 400g cans chopped tomatoes

¾ cup chicken stock (see p94)

½ tsp dried rosemary

2½oz (75g) pitted black olives

salt and freshly ground black pepper

basil leaves, to garnish

pasta or cooked rice, to serve

1 Preheat the oven to 375°F (190°C). Place half the oil in a large, heavy-bottomed Dutch oven over medium heat and brown the chicken on all sides. Remove with a slotted spoon and set aside on a plate lined with paper towels.

2 Add the remaining oil and cook the onion for 5 minutes, stirring occasionally. Add the garlic and pepper and cook for another 2 minutes. Add the tomatoes, stock, rosemary, and olives, season well, and stir.

3 Return the chicken and coat in the sauce. Bring to a boil, cover, and bake in the oven for 30–35 minutes, or until the chicken is cooked. Sprinkle with basil and serve with pasta or cooked rice.

For a different texture, use two 15oz (425g) cans of tomato sauce instead of the canned chopped tomatoes. This gives a smoother sauce for children who are not keen on "lumps."

Fussy eaters!

CALORIES: 301kcals/1267kJ
CARBOHYDRATE: 10g
    sugar: 9g
FAT: 10g
    saturated: 2g
SALT: 0.8g
FIBER: 4g

Chicken and white bean stew

Soaking dried beans is preferable to using canned. They are far cheaper and tastier.

20 mins, plus soaking   2 hrs

SERVES 4

5½oz (150g) dried white beans, such as navy or cannellini

3 tbsp olive oil

1 tbsp all-purpose flour

salt and freshly ground black pepper

8 skinless bone-in chicken pieces, thighs, drumsticks, or a mixture

1 onion, finely chopped

2 garlic cloves, finely chopped

¾ cup white wine (optional)

2 cups chicken stock (see p94), or 2½ cups if not using wine

2 heaping tbsp chopped flat-leaf parsley leaves

1 tbsp finely chopped oregano leaves

sprig of rosemary

9oz (250g) cherry tomatoes

1 Soak the beans overnight in lots of cold water. Make sure they have plenty of room to swell. Drain, rinse, and place in a large pan of water. Bring to a boil over high heat, skim off any froth, then reduce the heat and simmer for 10 minutes. Drain and rinse.

2 In a large saucepan with a lid, heat 2 tbsp of the olive oil. Season the flour with salt and pepper. Dust the chicken in the flour and cook in the pan, spaced well apart, for a few minutes on each side, until golden brown all over. Set aside.

3 Heat the remaining 1 tbsp of oil and cook the onion for 5 minutes until softened, but not browned. Add the garlic and cook for another minute. Add the wine (if using) and stock, and stir to loosen the residue from the pan.

4 Return the beans to the pan with the herbs, cover, and simmer over low heat for up to 1 hour, or until the beans are tender. Return the chicken and simmer for another 30 minutes. Remove the lid and add the tomatoes. Cook for another 15 minutes, uncovered, until the sauce reduces. Remove the rosemary before serving.

CALORIES: 489kcals/2060kJ
CARBOHYDRATE: 24g
    sugar: 4.5g
FAT: 13g
    saturated: 2.5g
SALT: 0.8g
FIBER: 10g

One-pot Spanish chicken with rice

This simple supper dish is packed full of warmly spicy flavor and is a no-fuss recipe: it practically cooks itself.

20 mins 1 hr

SERVES 4–6

4 tbsp olive oil

1 heaping tbsp all-purpose flour

salt and freshly ground black pepper

2 tsp smoked paprika, plus extra for dusting

8 boneless, skinless chicken thighs, cut into large pieces

1 onion, finely chopped

1 red and 1 orange bell pepper, cut into ¾in (2cm) cubes

1 dry, Spanish-style chorizo, approx. 7oz (200g), casing removed, cut into 1in (3cm) slices

2 garlic cloves, chopped

½ tsp cayenne pepper (optional)

2¾ cups chicken stock (see p94)

3 heaping tbsp chopped flat-leaf parsley leaves

10oz (300g) long-grain or basmati white rice

2½oz (75g) frozen peas

1 tbsp butter

1 Heat 2 tbsp of the oil in a large, heavy-bottomed saucepan with a lid. Season the flour with salt, pepper, and a little smoked paprika to taste. Dust the chicken evenly with the flour, shaking off excess. Cook the chicken, well spaced apart, for 2–3 minutes on each side over medium heat, until golden brown all over (you may need to do this in batches). Set aside and keep warm.

2 Heat the remaining oil in the pan and cook the onion and peppers for 3–5 minutes until softened and turning brown. Add the chorizo (don't worry if it breaks up) and cook for a few minutes, until beginning to turn crispy at the edges. Add the garlic, smoked paprika, and cayenne pepper (if using) and cook for 1 minute, until fragrant.

3 Add the stock, scraping up the meaty residue from the pan. Return the chicken to the pan, add 2 tbsp of the parsley, and bring to a boil. Reduce to a low simmer, cover, and cook for 10 minutes.

4 Add the rice and stir well. Cover and cook over very low heat for about 15 minutes, until the rice has cooked and absorbed most of the liquid. Stir in the peas, butter, and remaining parsley and rest, off the heat but with the lid on, for 5 minutes before serving.

CALORIES: 815kcals/3400kJ

CARBOHYDRATE: 69g
  sugar: 8g

FAT: 31g
  saturated: 10g

SALT: 1.6g

FIBER: 3.6g

Ricotta-stuffed chicken breasts

A modest effort for an impressive midweek meal, or weekend treat chic enough to serve to friends.

20 mins 20–25 mins

SERVES 4

¼ cup ricotta cheese

2 tbsp finely grated Parmesan cheese

2 tbsp finely chopped basil leaves

1 tbsp finely chopped flat-leaf parsley leaves

finely grated zest of 1 lemon

salt and freshly ground black pepper

4 boneless, skinless chicken breasts

1 tbsp olive oil

8 prosciutto slices

1 Preheat the oven to 400°F (200°C). In a bowl, mash the ricotta cheese with the Parmesan cheese, herbs, and lemon zest. Season well.

2 Take the chicken breasts and cut a pocket into the thickest side. Stuff each with one-quarter of the ricotta mixture, then rub with a little oil. Lay 2 prosciutto slices on a cutting board, overlapping slightly, and place the chicken on top. Carefully wrap the prosciutto around, making sure it meets on top. (If necessary, use a toothpick to secure.)

3 Flip the breasts over and place seam-side down on a baking sheet. Cook at the top of the oven for 20–25 minutes, until golden brown. When pressed with a finger, the meat should bounce back. Remove the toothpicks, if you used them, before serving.

CALORIES: 281kcals/1181kJ

CARBOHYDRATE: 0.3g
  sugar: 0.3g

FAT: 11g
  saturated: 4g

SALT: 1.4g

FIBER: 0g

Duck in orange sauce

Duck à l'orange is a classic, sadly fallen out of favor. This simpler recipe uses breasts for a modern twist.

20 mins 20–30 mins

SERVES 4

4 skin-on boneless duck breasts

salt and freshly ground black pepper

⅓ cup brown sugar

finely grated zest and juice of 2 large oranges

2 tbsp cider vinegar

¾ cup chicken stock (see p94)

1 tbsp cornstarch

orange slices, to garnish

CALORIES: 520kcals/2178kJ

CARBOHYDRATE: 27g
  sugar: 24.4g

FAT: 28.5g
  saturated: 8.5g

SALT: 0.7g

FIBER: 0.2g

1 With a sharp knife, score the skin of the duck in a criss-cross pattern and season well. Heat a large, non-stick frying pan over medium heat and add the duck, skin-side down. Reduce the heat to low and cook for 8–10 minutes to release the fat.

2 Increase the temperature and cook for 3–5 minutes, or until the skin is golden brown.

3 Turn the duck over and cook over medium heat for another 5 minutes. Place on a warmed plate lined with paper towels, loosely cover with foil, and set aside. Pour the fat from the frying pan and wipe it clean with paper towels.

4 Put the sugar, orange zest and juice, vinegar, and stock in the frying pan. Stir well and boil for 8–10 minutes or until reduced. Season to taste. While there is still 5 minutes cooking time left, stir the cornstarch with 3 tbsp water and add to the sauce to thicken, stirring frequently from then on.

5 Arrange the duck on serving plates, drizzle with the sauce, and garnish with the orange slices.

Crispy duck char siu

Chinese roast duck is tasty, but it is tricky to cook a whole bird. Try this easy version with duck breasts instead.

5 mins, plus marinating   25 mins

SERVES 4

4 skin-on boneless duck breasts

3 garlic cloves, crushed

3 tbsp soy sauce

3 tbsp rice wine

1 tbsp hoisin sauce

2 tbsp honey

2 tsp five-spice powder

salt and freshly ground black pepper

noodles or a green salad, to serve

1 Score the skin of the duck breasts with a knife in a criss-cross pattern, being careful not to cut down into the meat.

2 Whisk all the remaining ingredients together in a wide, shallow dish. Turn the duck breasts through the marinade to coat them on all sides, cover with plastic wrap, and leave to marinate for 2–4 hours in the fridge.

3 Preheat the oven to 400°F (200°C). Line a baking sheet with foil, to make cleaning up easier later.

4 Put the duck, skin-side down, in a frying pan and place over medium heat. Cook for 8 minutes.

5 Place the duck, skin-side up, on the baking sheet and cook at the top of the oven for 10 minutes. Rest for 5 minutes.

6 Cut the duck into slices on the diagonal and serve with stir-fried noodles or a green salad.

HOW TO FREEZE

Freeze the raw duck in the marinade. Defrost thoroughly before continuing with the recipe from step 3.

BATCHING AND FREEZING

Duck breasts can be expensive, so if you find them at a good price it is worth buying more than you need. Cook double this recipe and bag it up in portions for the freezer for a near-instant addition to a quick stir-fry anytime.

CALORIES: 576kcals/2394kJ

CARBOHYDRATE: 8g
  sugar: 8g

FAT: 44g
  saturated: 13g

SALT: 2.5g

FIBER: 0g

Zesty roasted chicken pieces

A great last-minute recipe for when all you have is some chicken and a few pantry essentials.

10 mins, plus marinating | 40-45 mins

SERVES 4

finely grated zest of 1 lemon

finely grated zest of 1 orange

2 tbsp orange juice

2 tbsp olive oil

1 tbsp honey

1 tbsp soy sauce

2 heaping tbsp chopped flat-leaf parsley leaves (optional)

8 skin-on bone-in chicken thighs, drumsticks, or a mixture

CALORIES: 321kcals/13.7kJ

CARBOHYDRATE: 4.5g
 sugar: 4.5g

FAT: 15g
 saturated: 3.5g

SALT: 1.1g

FIBER: 0g

1 Preheat the oven to 400°F (200°C). Mix all the ingredients except the chicken in a large, shallow container.

2 Add the chicken, turning to coat. Cover and leave it in the fridge for at least 2 hours, but preferably 4 if possible.

3 Put the chicken in a large baking dish, spaced well apart and in a single layer. Roast at the top of the oven for 40–45 minutes, turning occasionally, until golden brown and crispy.

VARIATION

The parsley can be omitted, or replaced with other chopped herb leaves, such as cilantro, dill, or oregano.

HOW TO FREEZE

Freeze the raw chicken in the marinade. Defrost thoroughly before cooking, and follow the recipe from the start of step 3.

Parmesan-crusted chicken

This crispy, crunchy coating is a perfect foil to the succulent and juicy chicken beneath.

15 mins | 40-45 mins

SPECIAL EQUIPMENT

food processor

SERVES 4

1 cup day-old white bread crumbs

1¾oz (50g) finely grated Parmesan cheese

2 garlic cloves, crushed

handful of basil leaves

finely grated zest of 1 lemon

salt and freshly ground black pepper

1 large egg, beaten

1 heaping tbsp all-purpose flour

8 skin-on bone-in chicken thighs

2 tbsp olive oil

1 Preheat the oven to 400°F (200°C). In a food processor, place the bread crumbs, Parmesan, garlic, basil, zest, and salt and pepper, and process until the basil turns the mixture green. Transfer into a wide, shallow bowl.

2 Place the egg in a shallow bowl and the flour in a freezer bag. Season the flour well. Put the chicken in the freezer bag and toss to coat. Pour out into a sieve and shake to remove excess flour.

3 Dip each piece of chicken in the egg, then coat well in the bread crumbs.

4 Heat the olive oil on a large baking sheet for 5 minutes, then arrange the chicken on the sheet, spaced well apart and in a single layer. Cook for 40–45 minutes, turning occasionally, until golden brown and crispy.

To make bite-sized nuggets, use diced chicken breast and reduce the cooking time to 20–25 minutes.

Fussy eaters!

CALORIES: 423kcals/1777kJ

CARBOHYDRATE: 21g
 sugar: 0.8g

FAT: 19g
 saturated: 6g

SALT: 1.1g

FIBER: 1g

Cajun-spiced chicken

This sweet, spicy marinade can be used in the oven, on the barbecue, and even under the broiler.

10 mins, plus marinating   40–45 mins

SERVES 4

2 tbsp olive oil

2 tsp light brown sugar

2 tsp paprika

½–1 tsp cayenne pepper or chili powder, to taste

1 tsp ground cumin

1 tsp dried thyme

1 tsp ground coriander

salt and freshly ground black pepper

8 skin-on bone-in chicken pieces, thighs, drumsticks, or a mixture

1 To make the marinade, mix all the ingredients together, apart from the chicken.

2 Rub the chicken in the marinade. Place in a dish, cover, and refrigerate for at least 1 hour, or preferably up to 4 hours. When ready to cook, preheat the oven to 400°F (200°C).

3 Arrange the chicken on a roasting pan, spaced well apart and in a single layer. Cook at the top of the oven for 40–45 minutes, turning occasionally, until the chicken is dark golden brown and cooked through.

HOW TO FREEZE

Freeze the raw chicken in the marinade. Defrost thoroughly before cooking, and follow the recipe from the start of step 3.

CALORIES: 321kcals/1345kJ

CARBOHYDRATE: 2.5g
sugar: 2.5g

FAT: 14g
saturated: 3g

SALT: 0.4g

FIBER: 0g

Crispy southern-baked chicken

A healthier alternative to the great tasting but fatty fried chicken that everybody loves.

10 mins, plus chilling   45 mins–1 hr

SERVES 4

⅓ cup all-purpose flour

2 tsp paprika

salt and freshly ground black pepper

1 large egg, beaten

1 cup panko bread crumbs or day-old bread crumbs

1 tsp cayenne pepper

½ tsp celery salt

8 skin-on chicken drumsticks

2 tbsp sunflower or vegetable oil

1 Put the flour, 1 tsp of the paprika, and salt and pepper in a large freezer bag. Place the egg in a shallow bowl. Put the bread crumbs, remaining 1 tsp of paprika, the cayenne, celery salt, and a good grinding of black pepper into a separate bowl and mix well.

2 Put the chicken in the freezer bag and toss to coat. Pour out into a sieve and shake to remove excess flour.

3 Dip each chicken drumstick in the egg, then coat with bread crumbs. Cover and refrigerate for at least 30 minutes (this helps the coating to stick). Preheat the oven to 350°F (180°C).

4 Heat the oil in a large, heavy pan in the oven for 10 minutes.

5 Add the chicken to the pan, spacing it well apart. It should sizzle as it hits the oil. Cook in the center of the oven for 45 minutes to 1 hour, turning once the underside is golden brown and crusty. Drain on paper towels.

VARIATION

For more crunch, try using finely crushed cornflakes instead of bread crumbs in the chicken coating.

CALORIES: 338kcals/1422kJ

CARBOHYDRATE: 27g
sugar: 1g

FAT: 13g
saturated: 3g

SALT: 1.3g

FIBER: 1g

Spicy chicken fajitas

A quick recipe and a classic crowd pleaser, with the winning "hands-on" element that is so popular with children.

15 mins, plus marinating   15 mins

SERVES 3–4

FOR THE MARINADE

2 tbsp olive oil

1 tbsp lime juice

2 tsp ground cumin

1 tsp smoked paprika, plus extra for the onions

1 tsp dried oregano

1 tsp cayenne pepper or chili powder

salt and freshly ground black pepper

FOR THE FAJITAS

2 large boneless, skinless chicken breasts, sliced

2 tbsp sunflower or vegetable oil

1 red onion, cut into ½in (1cm) slices

1 red and 1 yellow bell pepper, cut into ½in (1cm) slices

8 tortillas

TO SERVE

sour cream or plain yogurt

chili sauce

guacamole (see p290)

tomato salsa (see p288)

1 Whisk together the marinade ingredients and pour over the chicken in a bowl. Cover and refrigerate for at least 30 minutes, or up to 4 hours.

2 Preheat the broiler to its highest setting. Broil the chicken for 3–5 minutes on each side until golden and cooked. (It can also be grilled for a smoky flavor.)

3 Meanwhile, heat the sunflower oil in a large frying pan or wok over high heat and cook the onion and peppers for 5–7 minutes, or until cooked through and colored on the edges. Season with a little salt and pepper, and smoked paprika.

4 Warm the tortillas in a microwave or a low oven, following the package instructions. Serve the chicken on a platter with the vegetables, tortillas, and the sour cream and sauces, letting everyone make their own fajita.

VARIATION

Try using this marinade with beef or shrimp. The beef will need to be very thinly sliced to cook through, while the shrimp will only need to be broiled for 1–2 minutes on each side, or until pink.

These fajitas are ideal for fussy eaters because they can include only what they like in their wrap. Cooking the peppers and chicken separately makes it easy to pick these out.

Fussy eaters!

CALORIES: 565kcals/2382kJ

CARBOHYDRATE: 75g
sugar: 9g

FAT: 14g
saturated: 2g

SALT: 1g

FIBER: 7g

Spicy chicken meatballs

These are perfect alongside a vegetable and noodle stir-fry. Finely chopped chile can be added for more heat.

10 mins   10 mins

SERVES 4

14oz (400g) ground chicken

¼ cup fresh white bread crumbs

2 scallions, finely chopped

1 garlic clove, crushed

¾in (2cm) fresh ginger, finely grated

1 tbsp finely chopped cilantro leaves

1 tbsp sweet chili sauce

1 tsp lime juice

1 tsp fish sauce

2 tbsp sunflower or vegetable oil

1 Mix all the ingredients, except the oil, together in a large bowl until evenly incorporated. It's easiest to use your fingers for this; you may prefer to wear plastic food preparation gloves. Cover and refrigerate for at least 30 minutes.

2 With damp hands, shape walnut-sized balls with the chicken mixture, placing them on a plate. At this point, you may cover and chill the meatballs for up to 1 day, if that is more convenient.

3 Heat the sunflower oil in a large frying pan and cook the meatballs over medium-high heat for about 3–5 minutes, turning to color all sides, until golden and cooked through (cut one through to the center to check there is no trace of pink). You may need to do this in batches, depending on the size of the pan. Serve.

VARIATION

Try making these meatballs with ground turkey instead of chicken, for a slightly deeper and richer flavor.

BATCHING AND FREEZING

Meatballs are an ideal ingredient to prepare in bulk. Double or triple the quantities suggested and prepare the meatballs to the end of step 2. Open-freeze on a large baking sheet (make sure that it fits in your freezer first); the meatballs should not touch. Once they are frozen solid (after 2–3 hours), transfer to large freezer bags and freeze. To defrost, remove the amount needed and place them in a single layer on a plate, cover, and put in the fridge on the morning you need them. They will be ready for supper that night.

CALORIES: 211kcals/888kJ

CARBOHYDRATE: 11.5g
 sugar: 3g

FAT: 7g
 saturated: 1g

SALT: 0.8g

FIBER: 0.5g

Chicken scallops with lemon sauce

This light, bright recipe is perfect with steamed spring vegetables and potatoes.

10-15 mins   15 mins

SERVES 4

4 boneless, skinless chicken breasts

1 tbsp olive oil

salt and freshly ground black pepper

3 tbsp all-purpose flour

1 tbsp butter

1 cup chicken stock (see p94)

juice of ½ lemon

¼ cup (2oz) crème fraîche

1 tbsp finely chopped thyme leaves

½ tsp granulated sugar

1 Preheat the oven to 400°F (200°C). Flatten each chicken breast gently with a rolling pin until ¾in (2cm) thick all over.

2 Heat the oil in a large, heavy-bottomed frying pan. Season 2 tbsp of the flour. Dust the chicken with the flour, shaking off excess. Cook the chicken for 2–3 minutes on each side over medium heat, until golden. Transfer to a baking dish and cook in the hot oven for 10 minutes until cooked.

3 Meanwhile, wipe the pan clean with paper towels. Melt the butter in the pan and scatter with the remaining 1 tbsp of flour, whisking over medium heat for 1 minute. Gradually add the stock and lemon juice, whisking constantly, and bring to a boil.

4 Add the crème fraîche, thyme, and sugar, and season to taste. Cook the sauce for 5 minutes, until thick and glossy, whisking. Remove the chicken from the oven and add its juices to the sauce. Slice the chicken on the diagonal and pour the sauce over to serve.

CALORIES: 323kcals/1356kJ
CARBOHYDRATE: 9g
  sugar: 1g
FAT: 13.5g
  saturated: 7g
SALT: 0.5g
FIBER: 0.5g

Chicken in leek and mustard sauce

A super-speedy midweek supper that looks as good as it tastes, with the gentle sweetness of leeks.

10-15 mins   25 mins

SERVES 4

2 tbsp olive oil

3 tbsp all-purpose flour

salt and freshly ground black pepper

4 boneless, skinless chicken breasts

2 tbsp butter

7oz (200g) leeks, white part only, finely sliced

1¼ cups chicken stock (see p94)

¼ cup half-and-half

1 tbsp Dijon mustard

1 Preheat the oven to 400°F (200°C). Heat the oil in a large, heavy-bottomed frying pan. Season 2 tbsp of the flour with salt and pepper. Dust the chicken with the flour, shaking off excess. Cook the chicken for 2–3 minutes on each side over medium heat, until golden brown. Transfer to a baking dish and cook in the hot oven for 10 minutes until cooked, then remove from the oven, cover with foil, and rest while you make the sauce.

2 Wipe the pan with paper towels and add the butter. Cook the leeks for 10 minutes over low heat, until they soften. Stir in the remaining 1 tbsp of flour and cook for another minute.

3 Add the stock and bring to a boil. Reduce to a simmer and cook the sauce until it thickens. Add the half-and-half and mustard and cook for 2–3 minutes until thick, adding juices from the chicken. Pour the sauce over the chicken to serve.

CALORIES: 364kcals/1526kJ
CARBOHYDRATE: 10g
  sugar: 2g
FAT: 17g
  saturated: 7g
SALT: 0.8g
FIBER: 2g

Chicken with a creamy mushroom sauce

A deliciously quick dinner, perfect served with fluffy mashed potatoes to soak up the delicious juices.

20–25 mins   15 mins

SERVES 4

3 tbsp olive oil

1 tbsp butter

7oz (200g) button mushrooms, sliced

1 onion, finely chopped

2 garlic cloves, finely chopped

1 heaping tbsp all-purpose flour

salt and freshly ground black pepper

1lb 5oz (600g) boneless, skinless chicken thighs, cut into 1in (3cm) pieces

½ cup white wine (optional)

¾ cup chicken stock (see p94)

1 tbsp finely chopped sage leaves

3 tbsp heavy cream

> **CALORIES:** 377kcals/1572kJ
> **CARBOHYDRATE:** 5g
>   sugar: 1.8g
> **FAT:** 22g
>   saturated: 8g
> **SALT:** 0.6g
> **FIBER:** 1.5g

1 Heat 1 tbsp of the olive oil and the butter in a large, deep-sided frying pan. Cook the mushrooms for 5 minutes until they start to brown. Add the onion and cook for 2–3 minutes until it softens. Add the garlic, cook for 1 minute, then remove the vegetables from the pan. Wipe the pan clean with paper towels.

2 Heat the remaining 2 tbsp of oil in the pan. Season the flour with salt and pepper. Toss the chicken in the flour, shaking off excess. Cook the chicken for 8–10 minutes, turning, until golden all over. Add the wine (if using), stock, and sage and bring to a boil.

3 Add the mushroom mixture and simmer for 5 minutes, stirring occasionally, until the sauce starts to reduce. Add the cream and cook for 2–3 minutes until the chicken is cooked and the sauce is thick and creamy.

VARIATION

If cooking for young children, you can replace the wine with extra chicken stock.

Tarragon chicken

This simple oven-roasted dish is given a classic French makeover with the use of tarragon and cream.

15 mins   40–45 mins

SERVES 4

FOR THE HERB BUTTER

1 tbsp olive oil

2 tbsp butter, softened

1 heaping tbsp Dijon mustard

2 garlic cloves, crushed

2 tbsp finely chopped tarragon leaves, plus extra to serve (optional)

finely grated zest and juice of 1 lemon

salt and freshly ground black pepper

FOR THE CHICKEN

8 skin-on bone-in chicken pieces, thighs, drumsticks, or a mixture

1 tbsp all-purpose flour

2 cups chicken stock (see p94)

⅓ cup half-and-half

1 Preheat the oven to 400°F (200°C). To make the herb butter, mash the oil, butter, mustard, garlic, tarragon, lemon zest, and salt and pepper until well combined.

2 Smear the butter over the chicken and put it in a large flameproof baking dish. Squeeze the lemon over the chicken. Roast the chicken in the hot oven for 40–45 minutes until golden brown with crispy skin. Remove from the pan and keep it warm.

3 Put the baking dish over low heat and whisk in the flour, stirring for 1 minute. Gradually pour in the stock, stirring all the time to loosen the sticky residue from the pan.

4 Bring to a boil and simmer for a few minutes until the stock has thickened. Add the cream and bubble for another minute or 2 before serving.

The sauce can be poured directly over the chicken, or passed through a strainer first for children who don't like "bits".

Fussy eaters!

> **CALORIES:** 406kcals/1698kJ
> **CARBOHYDRATE:** 3.5g
>   sugar: 1g
> **FAT:** 21g
>   saturated: 8.5g
> **SALT:** 1.2g
> **FIBER:** 0.5g

Chicken pot pies

Children often love individual portions, so these gently flavored pies, filled with vegetables, are ideal.

20 mins, plus chilling   40 mins

SPECIAL EQUIPMENT
6 x 3in (7.5cm) round pie dishes

3in (7.5cm) round cutter

MAKES 6

FOR THE DOUGH
2 cups all-purpose flour, plus extra for dusting

12 tbsp butter, cut into cubes

½ tsp salt

1 egg, beaten

FOR THE FILLING
3½ cups chicken stock (see p94)

3 carrots, sliced

1lb 10oz (750g) Yukon Gold potatoes, cut into cubes

3 celery stalks, thinly sliced

6oz (175g) peas

1lb 2oz (500g) cooked boneless, skinless chicken

4 tbsp butter

1 onion, chopped

¼ cup all-purpose flour

⅔ cup heavy cream

nutmeg, to taste

sea salt and freshly ground black pepper

small bunch of flat-leaf parsley leaves, chopped

1 Preheat the oven to 400°F (200°C). To make the dough, rub the flour and butter together with your fingertips until the mixture resembles bread crumbs. Add the salt and enough cold water to form a soft dough. Wrap in plastic wrap and chill in the fridge for 30 minutes.

2 For the filling, bring the stock to a boil in a large saucepan. Add the carrots, potatoes, and celery, and simmer for 3 minutes.

Add the peas and simmer for another 5 minutes until all the vegetables are tender. Strain, reserving the stock. Cut the chicken into slivers and put in a bowl. Add the vegetables.

3 Melt the butter in a small pan over medium heat. Add the onion and cook for 3–5 minutes until softened, but not browned. Sprinkle the flour over the onions and cook for 1–2 minutes, stirring. Gradually add 2 cups of the stock, whisking all the time, and heat until the sauce comes to a boil and thickens.

4 Reduce the heat and simmer the sauce for 2 minutes, add the cream and a grating of nutmeg, then season. Now pour the sauce over the chicken and vegetables, add the parsley, and mix gently. Divide the filling evenly among six 3in (7.5cm) round pie dishes.

5 Roll the dough out on a well-floured surface to ¼in (5mm) thick. Cut out 6 circles using a 3in (7.5cm) round cutter. Brush the edge of each pie dish with water and place the dough circles on top, pressing down firmly to secure in place. Place the pies on a baking sheet and brush with the beaten egg. Cut a slit in the top of each pie and bake for 15–20 minutes.

HOW TO FREEZE
The pastry and the filling can be frozen separately for up to 1 month. Wrap the pastry in plastic wrap and then in foil to store securely in the freezer.

CALORIES: 903kcals/3771kJ	
CARBOHYDRATE: 76g sugar: 7.5g	
FAT: 52g saturated: 31g	
SALT: 1.3g	
FIBER: 9g	

Vegetable and chicken pie

A pleasant change to a pastry-topped pie. Gently flavoring with turmeric turns this into something special.

20 mins   50 mins

SERVES 2

FOR THE TOPPING

1lb (450g) large potatoes, peeled and cut into large chunks

salt and freshly ground black pepper

large pat of butter

4-5 tbsp whole milk

FOR THE FILLING

5½oz (150g) green beans, cut into ¾in (2cm) pieces

3 tbsp butter

1 red bell pepper, thinly sliced

1 leek, sliced

¼ tsp turmeric

3 tbsp all-purpose flour

1 cup milk

¾ cup (7oz) crème fraîche

8oz (225g) cooked boneless, skinless chicken, sliced

1 Preheat the oven to 400°F (200°C). Cook the potatoes in boiling salted water for 15 minutes, or until tender when pierced with a sharp knife, adding the green beans for the last 3 minutes. Drain, return the potatoes to the pan, and mash with the butter and enough milk to make a smooth mash. Season with salt and set aside. Set the green beans aside separately.

2 For the filling, melt the butter in a large pan. Add the red bell pepper and leek, and cook for 3–4 minutes until soft. Stir in the turmeric, cook for a minute, then add the flour and cook for another 2–3 minutes.

3 Pour in the milk slowly, while stirring constantly, and cook for 4–5 minutes until the sauce has thickened and looks smooth, glossy, and golden in color. Add the crème fraîche, blanched green beans, and chicken and mix well to distribute all the ingredients equally through the sauce. Do not bring to a boil at this point, or the sauce may split.

4 Season well with salt and pepper and pour the filling into an ovenproof dish. Cover with the mashed potatoes, then cook in the oven for 25 minutes until the filling is piping hot and bubbling around the edges and the potato is golden brown.

CALORIES: 1161kcals/4830kJ
CARBOHYDRATE: 67g
  sugar: 17g
FAT: 76g
  saturated: 48g
SALT: 0.9g
FIBER: 10g

Batching and freezing

Batching and freezing meals is a great standby if you have a busy schedule and little time to cook during the week. Simple sauces and stews can be made in double, or even triple, quantities and portioned up for freezing. Stale bread can be ground in a food processor to make instant bread crumbs, combined with parmesan and basil for extra flavor, then used straight from the freezer. If you have time to bake on the weekend, consider making a large batch of cookie dough (as used for Double chocolate chip cookies, p404) then open freeze the formed, unbaked cookies. Once they are frozen solid, pack the dough shapes into a freezer bag, then defrost and bake as needed for almost instant home-baked cookies even during the busiest of weeks.

"Eat the freezer" week

Eat the freezer week is a great way to save money, organize the freezer, and challenge your culinary skills all at the same time. Once every month or so, make your weekly shopping list after first going through the freezer to see what you can find. Use those overlooked items at the bottom of the freezer as the basis of your weekly menu, and add only essential items to the weekly store trip. You may be amazed at what you discover lurking in the depths of your freezer!

Labeling

A roll of freezer-proof labels will help you recognize items you may have frozen weeks ago. There are also freezer-proof pens available, and freezer bags that you can write directly onto.

Ways of freezing

By using the correct method and preparing food carefully you can freeze almost anything—from herbs to fruit cordials—saving yourself time and money in the process.

Open freezing This is one of the best ways to preserve smaller items and ensure that they do not freeze into a solid mass. Spread them out, not touching each other, on a baking sheet and freeze; once frozen solid, pack into freezer bags.

Using freezer bags Have at least two sizes of sturdy freezer bags on hand to ensure you can freeze things quickly and efficiently. Dividing up food into portion sizes helps you to make the most of the economies of scale.

Using ice-cube trays Freezing foods such as herbs, pesto, or stock in ice-cube trays gives a ready supply of portion-sized amounts. Herbs work especially well in this way, as freezing will preserve their flavors.

Freezing liquids Liquids such as soups, stocks, and even cordials can be frozen in sturdy freezer bags or well washed, plastic milk containers. Be sure to leave a small amount of space at the top, as most liquids expand on freezing.

Safe freezing

Plastics Not all plastics are suitable for freezing. Some become brittle with the low temperatures, and lids can shatter if removed while too cold. Try using freezer- and microwave-proof containers for items that can be defrosted in an emergency.

Defrosting The denser the item, the longer it will take to defrost. Ideally, long, slow overnight defrosting in the fridge is best for items such as larger pieces of meat, although smaller items can be defrosted at room temperature.

Freezer burn This occurs when food has not been adequately wrapped or stored in an airtight container. Throw away any food that has patches of discoloration on it, as the taste and quality will have been affected.

Freezing gluts Take advantage of gluts of seasonal fruit and vegetables by freezing any excess you have in pre-portioned freezer bags. Vegetables with a lower water content freeze better, but often need to be blanched first.

Freezing bread Frozen bread cuts quite easily with a sharp knife. If you use it to make sandwiches, it will defrost in time for lunch, keeping everything fresh and cool in the summer months.

Handy things to have in the freezer

★ Frozen berry mixes, such as summer fruits

★ Ice cream

★ Frozen yogurt portions for quick lunch box fillers

★ Frozen sliced bread—see top tip, above

★ Slow-cooked tomato sauce for pasta (p34)

★ Packages of ground beef, lamb, chicken, or pork

★ Homemade burgers (p278), divided by waxed paper and stacked

★ Assorted vegetables, such as peas, broccoli, and corn

Thai beef salad

The bright, vibrant flavors of this salad really sing out, making it perfect for a summer lunch.

10 mins   10 mins

SERVES 4

FOR THE SALAD

14oz (400g) thin-cut skirt
   or sirloin steak

1 tbsp sesame oil or sunflower oil

salt and freshly ground black pepper

2 Little Gem lettuces, leaves separated

large handful of watercress

8in (20cm) piece of cucumber, seeded
   and finely sliced on the diagonal

1 small red onion, finely sliced

handful of cilantro leaves,
   roughly chopped

handful of mint leaves,
   roughly chopped

1 red chile, seeded and finely
   chopped (optional)

FOR THE DRESSING

¼ cup lime juice

2 tbsp fish sauce

2 tsp light brown sugar

pinch of chile flakes (optional)

1 Heat a frying pan or grill pan. Rub the steak in the oil and season it well all over. Briefly sear over high heat on both sides so it is browned outside but still tender and juicy within. Set aside.

2 Whisk the dressing ingredients together until the sugar dissolves completely.

3 In a large bowl, mix the lettuce, watercress, cucumber, onion, herbs, and chile (if using). Slice the still-warm steak and add to the bowl with the dressing. Toss gently, then serve.

VARIATION

Large shrimp, deveined and sliced horizontally or butterflied, make a nice alternative to steak.

CALORIES: 190kcals/796kJ
CARBOHYDRATE: 5.5g
   sugar: 5g
FAT: 7.5g
   saturated: 2.5g
SALT: 1.6g
FIBER: 1g

Harissa-spiced lamb chops with chickpea mash

With spices and pantry ingredients, midweek lamb chops can be turned into something really special.

15 mins   25 mins

SERVES 4

FOR THE LAMB

½ cup fresh white bread crumbs

finely grated zest of 1 lemon

1 tbsp harissa paste

2 tbsp finely chopped cilantro leaves

2 tsp olive oil

salt and freshly ground black pepper

8 x 3½oz (100g) lamb loin chops

FOR THE CHICKPEA MASH

1 tbsp olive oil

1 red onion, finely chopped

2 garlic cloves, finely chopped

2 x 14oz (400g) cans chickpeas,
   drained and rinsed

1½ tbsp lemon juice

2 tbsp extra virgin olive oil

2 tbsp finely chopped cilantro leaves

tomato salad, to serve

1 Place the bread crumbs, zest, harissa, cilantro, and olive oil in a bowl, season, and stir well to combine evenly.

2 Preheat the broiler. Place the chops on a foil-lined baking sheet and broil on one side for 8 minutes. Turn and press the bread crumb and harissa mixture onto the uncooked side of each chop. Broil for another 8 minutes.

3 Meanwhile, make the chickpea mash. Heat the oil in a saucepan over medium heat, add the onion, and cook for 5 minutes. Add the garlic and cook for 2 minutes. Stir in the chickpeas, lemon juice, and extra virgin olive oil, and gently heat.

4 Remove from the heat and mash roughly with a potato masher; it should not be smooth. Stir in the cilantro and season generously.

5 Serve the chops with the chickpea mash and a dressed tomato salad.

PREPARE AHEAD

Make the bread crumb topping up to 3 days ahead, cover, and store in an airtight container in the fridge.

CALORIES: 594kcals/2489kJ
CARBOHYDRATE: 30g
   sugar: 2.5g
FAT: 30g
   saturated: 9g
SALT: 1.3g
FIBER: 8g

Indian lamb kebabs with cucumber and mango salad

Lamb and mint is a perennial favorite, here combined in a fresh take on a classic Indian dish, with juicy mango.

15 mins, plus marinating   10 mins

SPECIAL EQUIPMENT
8 bamboo skewers

SERVES 4

¼ cup (2oz) plain yogurt

1 tsp ground cumin

1 tsp ground coriander

½ tsp chili powder

1 tbsp honey

salt and freshly ground black pepper

1lb 5oz (500g) lamb leg or neck filet, cut into 1in (3cm) cubes

warmed naan bread, to serve

FOR THE SALAD

½ cucumber, peeled, seeded, and cut into ¼in (5mm) cubes

1 just-ripe mango, cut into ¼in (5mm) cubes

½ red onion, finely chopped

1 Little Gem lettuce, shredded

handful of mint leaves, shredded

handful of cilantro leaves, shredded

2 tbsp light olive oil

juice of 1 lime

pomegranate seeds, to garnish (optional)

1 Soak the skewers in cold water for at least 30 minutes. This will help keep them from burning.

2 Mix the yogurt, spices, and honey in a large bowl. Season the mixture generously and add the lamb, turning to coat in the spice mixture on all sides. Cover and marinate for at least 1 hour at room temperature, or up to 1 day or overnight in the fridge, if that's more convenient.

3 For the salad, combine the cucumber, mango, onion, lettuce, and herbs in a large salad bowl. Toss them in the oil and lime juice to dress all the ingredients and season generously to taste. Scatter with the pomegranate seeds (if using), and make sure all the different elements are showing.

4 Preheat the broiler to its highest setting. Thread the lamb onto the drained skewers, wiping off any excess marinade. Broil for 3–6 minutes on each side, or until the lamb is turning crispy at the edges and is cooked to your taste. Serve at once with the colorful salad and warmed naan bread.

CALORIES: 302kcals/1260kJ

CARBOHYDRATE: 12g
  sugar: 12g

FAT: 16g
  saturated: 5.5g

SALT: 0.3g

FIBER: 2g

Sticky pork skewers

These are fantastic cooked on an outdoor grill where the sugar in the marinade really caramelizes.

10 mins, plus marinating   5 mins

SPECIAL EQUIPMENT
12 bamboo skewers
hand-held blender

SERVES 4

1 pork tenderloin, approx. 14oz (400g), finely sliced

FOR THE DRY MARINADE
1 large garlic clove

1in (3cm) piece of fresh ginger

½ red chile, seeded

1 heaping tbsp chopped cilantro root or stalk

salt and freshly ground black pepper

FOR THE WET MARINADE
2 tbsp sunflower or vegetable oil

1 tbsp honey

1 tbsp soy sauce

½ tbsp fish sauce

½ tbsp light brown sugar

1. Soak the skewers in water for at least 30 minutes to keep them from burning.

2. Using a hand-held blender, roughly chop the dry marinade ingredients, add them to the wet marinade ingredients, and blend to a thick paste. Add the pork slices and turn to coat all over in the marinade.

3. Preheat the broiler to its highest setting. Thread the pork onto the skewers. Grill for 2–3 minutes on each side, until cooked and turning crispy at the edges.

VARIATION

Try this marinade with chicken, beef, or shrimp. All are equally delicious, although the cooking times will of course change according to what meat or fish you choose.

HOW TO FREEZE

The pork can be frozen in the marinade, uncooked, and kept for 3 months. Defrost it thoroughly before cooking from the start of step 3.

CALORIES: 196kcals/825kJ
CARBOHYDRATE: 6g
  sugar: 6g
FAT: 9g
  saturated: 2g
SALT: 1.2g
FIBER: 0g

Beef satay

Children love anything cooked on a skewer, so try these simple satay sticks for a tasty protein-packed treat.

10 mins, plus marinating   5 mins

SPECIAL EQUIPMENT
bamboo or metal skewers
food processor or blender

SERVES 4

2lb (900g) beef tenderloin, cut into 1in (2.5cm) chunks

3 tbsp crunchy peanut butter

FOR THE MARINADE
1 onion, quartered

2in (5cm) piece of fresh ginger, roughly chopped

3 garlic cloves, roughly chopped

2 hot red chiles, seeded

2 tbsp ketchup

2 tbsp light soy sauce

1 tbsp peanut oil

juice of 2 limes

3 tbsp brown sugar

CALORIES: 471kcals/1969kJ
CARBOHYDRATE: 16g
  sugar: 15g
FAT: 22.5g
  saturated: 8g
SALT: 2g
FIBER: 1.5g

1. If using bamboo skewers, soak them in cold water for at least 30 minutes before using. Put all the ingredients for the marinade in a blender or food processor, and blend until smooth. Put the beef chunks in a plastic freezer bag. Pour in the marinade, squish together, and seal. Leave to marinate in the fridge for at least 1 hour.

2. Thread the beef onto bamboo or metal skewers, about 5 pieces on each skewer, and reserve the marinade. Set aside while you make the peanut sauce.

3. Pour the marinade into a small non-stick pan and bring to a boil. Add the peanut butter and continue cooking over medium-high heat, stirring constantly, until the mixture thickens into a sauce. Keep warm.

4. Preheat the broiler to its highest setting. Broil the beef skewers for 5 minutes, turning frequently. Leave to rest for a few minutes, then serve with the warm peanut sauce for dipping.

Turkish-style lamb flatbreads

A quick and easy dish, try serving this with a selection of herbs and salad leaves for a deliciously different wrap.

5 mins 15 mins

SERVES 4

14oz (400g) ground lamb

bunch of scallions, white part only, finely chopped

2 garlic cloves, crushed

1 tsp ground cumin

½ tsp cayenne pepper

1 tsp smoked paprika

½ tsp ground cinnamon

1 tbsp tomato paste

salt and freshly ground black pepper

1 tbsp sunflower or vegetable oil

4 naan breads or other flatbreads

7oz (200g) crumbled feta cheese

handful of mint leaves, finely chopped

½ lemon, to serve

1 Preheat the oven to 425°F (220°C). Mix the ground lamb with the scallions, garlic, spices, and tomato paste in a bowl until well combined (it's easiest to use your hands), and season generously with salt and pepper.

2 Heat the oil in a wok or frying pan. Cook the lamb mixture over high heat for 2–3 minutes, stirring and breaking up any clumps with a wooden spoon, until browned all over.

3 Spread one-quarter of the meat mixture over each naan bread, press it down, and arrange them on 2 baking sheets. Scatter the feta and mint over the top and cook at the top of the oven for 10 minutes, until the meat is cooked through and crispy. To serve, squeeze a little lemon over each flatbread.

CLEVER WITH LEFTOVERS

If you have any leftover roast lamb, try shredding it finely and using it to replace the ground lamb in this recipe for an almost instant meal.

CALORIES: 766kcals/3199kJ

CARBOHYDRATE: 62g
  sugar: 5g

FAT: 40g
  saturated: 17g

SALT: 3g

FIBER: 0.6g

Thai-style stir-fried ground beef

Using ground meat is an easy way to introduce young children to Asian flavors—just leave out the chiles.

5 mins   10 mins

SERVES 4–6

salt

3½oz (100g) broccoli florets, cut very small

2 tbsp sunflower or vegetable oil

bunch of scallions, finely chopped

2 garlic cloves, crushed

1in (3cm) fresh ginger, finely chopped

1 tbsp finely chopped cilantro stalks, plus a handful of cilantro leaves, roughly chopped

1 red chile, seeded and finely chopped (optional)

14oz (400g) ground beef

1 tbsp fish sauce

2 tbsp soy sauce

1 tbsp lime juice

1 tsp granulated sugar

rice, to serve

1 Bring a large pan of salted water to a boil and blanch the broccoli for 1 minute, then drain and refresh it under cold water. Set aside.

2 Heat the sunflower oil in a wok or a large, deep-sided frying pan. Add the scallions, garlic, ginger, cilantro stalks, and chile (if using), and cook for a couple of minutes until colored slightly.

3 Add the ground beef and continue to cook over high heat until the meat is well browned.

4 Return the broccoli and add the fish sauce, soy sauce, lime juice, and sugar. Mix well, cooking for a minute or 2 until the broccoli is piping hot. Stir in the cilantro leaves and serve with rice.

CALORIES: 300kcals/1244kJ

CARBOHYDRATE: 4g
  sugar: 4g

FAT: 22g
  saturated: 8g

SALT: 2.3g

FIBER: 1.5g

Spicy lamb and feta meatballs

These are good with rice or couscous, or even wrapped up with salad in a tortilla for a quick lunch.

10 mins, plus chilling   10 mins

SERVES 4

14oz (400g) ground lamb

½ cup fresh white bread crumbs

1 large egg, beaten

1 tsp ground cumin

1 tsp paprika

handful of mint leaves, finely chopped

salt and freshly ground black pepper

2oz (60g) crumbled feta cheese

2 tbsp sunflower or vegetable oil

couscous, to serve

1 Mix together the ground lamb, bread crumbs, egg, spices, and mint, and season well. Gently mix in the feta cheese. Cover and chill for 30 minutes.

2 With damp hands, shape walnut-sized balls with the lamb mixture.

3 Heat the oil in a large frying pan and cook the meatballs over medium heat for 5–7 minutes, until browned all over and cooked through. Serve with couscous.

CALORIES: 350kcals/1455kJ

CARBOHYDRATE: 9g
  sugar: 0.5g

FAT: 24g
  saturated: 9g

SALT: 1g

FIBER: 0.5g

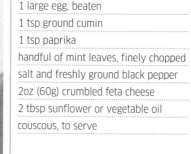

Traditional meatballs

Adding milk-soaked bread crumbs gives a light, soft texture to these family-friendly meatballs.

10 mins, plus chilling   10 mins

SERVES 4

½ cup fresh white bread crumbs

5 tbsp whole milk

9oz (250g) ground pork

9oz (250g) ground beef

1oz (30g) grated Parmesan cheese

2 tbsp finely chopped parsley leaves

1 tbsp finely chopped oregano leaves

1 tbsp finely chopped basil leaves

1 large egg, beaten

1 tsp onion powder (optional)

salt and freshly ground black pepper

olive oil, for greasing and drizzling

tomato and basil sauce (see p191), to serve

CALORIES: 353kcals/1472kJ

CARBOHYDRATE: 10g
  sugar: 1g

FAT: 21g
  saturated: 9g

SALT: 0.7g

FIBER: 0.5g

---

1 Soak the bread crumbs in the milk in a bowl for 5 minutes. In a separate large bowl, mix all the ingredients except the oil, but including the bread crumbs. Cover and chill for 30 minutes.

2 Preheat the oven to 400°F (200°C) and lightly oil a baking sheet. With damp hands, shape golf ball-sized balls with the meat and place them, spaced well apart, on the baking sheet. They should not touch, or they may cook unevenly

3 Drizzle with a little olive oil and bake at the top of the oven for 20 minutes, until browned and springy to the touch. Serve with tomato and basil sauce.

VARIATION

Make bite-sized meatballs, cooking them for 10–15 minutes, for small children as a lunchtime snack.

HOW TO FREEZE

Open-freeze the raw meatballs, in 1 layer, on a baking sheet for 2–3 hours, or until frozen solid. Transfer to a freezer bag.

Swedish meatballs with gravy

Chilling onions before grating means your eyes will water a lot less—genius!

10 mins, plus chilling   10–15 mins

SERVES 4

FOR THE MEATBALLS

1lb (450g) ground pork

¾ cup fresh white bread crumbs

½ onion, chilled and then finely grated

1 tbsp whole milk

1 egg, beaten

1 tsp granulated sugar

salt and freshly ground black pepper

2 tbsp butter

1 tbsp sunflower or vegetable oil

mashed potatoes, to serve

FOR THE GRAVY

1 heaping tbsp all-purpose flour

1 cup beef stock

1 tsp redcurrant or sour cherry jelly

1 tbsp half-and-half

CALORIES: 391kcals/1635kJ

CARBOHYDRATE: 19g
  sugar: 3g

FAT: 22g
  saturated: 9g

SALT: 0.9g

FIBER: 1g

---

1 In a large bowl, mix the pork, bread crumbs, onion, milk, egg, sugar, and seasoning until well combined. Chill for at least 1 hour.

2 Preheat the oven to 300°F (150°C). Heat the butter and oil in a large frying pan. With damp hands, shape walnut-sized balls with the mixture and cook them over low heat for 10 minutes, until browned all over and springy to the touch. You may need to do this in batches, keeping the cooked meatballs warm.

3 When the meatballs are cooked, transfer them to the oven and cover loosely with foil to keep them warm. Take the pan off the heat and sprinkle in the flour. Whisk it into the fat in the pan, then gradually whisk in the stock. Return to the heat and cook the gravy until it thickens, then reduce to a simmer, add the jelly and half-and-half, and cook for another 2–3 minutes. Taste for seasoning and serve with the meatballs and mashed potatoes.

HOW TO FREEZE

Open-freeze the raw meatballs, in 1 layer, on a baking sheet for 2–3 hours, or until frozen solid. Transfer to a freezer bag.

Pork steaks with fried apples

A super-quick, tasty meal. The fried apples make a near-instant accompaniment to the pork.

 5 mins 15 mins

SERVES 4

4 x 3½oz (100g) boneless pork chops

salt and freshly ground black pepper

2 tbsp olive oil

1 tbsp butter

4 small apples, peeled, cored, and quartered

1 tbsp lemon juice

½ tsp granulated sugar

1 Season the pork well with salt and pepper. Heat 1 tbsp of the oil in a large frying pan and cook the pork for 3–5 minutes on each side, depending on thickness, until cooked through. Set it aside, loosely covered in foil to keep it warm.

2 Add the remaining 1 tbsp of oil and the butter to the pan and allow it to bubble up. Add the apple pieces, pour in the lemon juice, sprinkle with the sugar, and season with salt and pepper.

3 Cook the apples over medium heat for 5–7 minutes, turning occasionally, until they soften and start to caramelize. Turn them gently using 2 spatulas, so the pieces don't break up. Serve each pork steak topped with one-quarter of the apples.

CALORIES: 255kcals/1073kJ

CARBOHYDRATE: 13g
   sugar: 13g

FAT: 12.5g
   saturated: 4g

SALT: 0.3g

FIBER: 3g

Steak glazed with mustard and brown sugar

If you have a kitchen blowtorch, now is the perfect time to use it! This is a special occasion dish.

 5 mins 10 mins

SERVES 4

4 x 3½–5½oz (100–150g) steaks, preferably tenderloin filet, approx. 1in (3cm) thick, at room temperature

1 tbsp olive oil

salt and freshly ground black pepper

1 tbsp Dijon mustard

1 tbsp light brown sugar

CALORIES: 184kcals/767kJ

CARBOHYDRATE: 4g
   sugar: 4g

FAT: 9g
   saturated: 3g

SALT: 0.4g

FIBER: 0g

1 Rub the steaks with the oil and season well with salt and pepper. Pan-fry or grill over high heat until cooked as you like. For rare, allow 2–3 minutes each side; for medium, 3–4 minutes each side; and for well done, 4–5 minutes each side. Allow the meat to rest for about 5 minutes, loosely covered with foil to keep warm.

2 Meanwhile, preheat the broiler to its highest setting. Brush each steak on one side with a thin layer of mustard, then sprinkle with an even layer of the sugar.

3 Broil the steaks for a minute or two only, until the sugar has melted and caramelized over the top. You don't want to cook them any further, just to create a great glazed effect.

Pork schnitzel with creamy mustard sauce

Many children like this schnitzel plain with mashed potatoes, leaving more of the delicious sauce for the adults!

10 mins, plus chilling **15 mins**

SERVES 4

FOR THE SCHNITZEL

4 x 3½oz (100g) boneless
  pork chops

salt and freshly ground black
  pepper

1 tbsp all-purpose flour

1 large egg, beaten

¾ cup day-old white bread crumbs

1 tbsp olive oil

1 tbsp butter

FOR THE SAUCE

1 tbsp olive oil

½ onion, finely chopped

1 garlic clove, crushed

½ cup white wine

¾ cup (7oz) heavy cream

1 tbsp Dijon mustard

pinch of granulated sugar

1 If the pork is a little thick, pound it gently with a rolling pin until it is about ¾in (2cm) thick all over. This also helps to tenderize it.

2 Season the flour and put it on a plate. Put the egg and bread crumbs in 2 separate shallow bowls. Dust the pork in the flour, shaking off excess, then dip it in the egg, and finally coat it in the bread crumbs. Cover and chill for at least 30 minutes (this helps the coating to stick).

3 Preheat the oven to 350°F (180°C). Heat the oil and butter in a large frying pan and cook the pork over a medium-high heat for 2–3 minutes each side, until golden brown. Transfer to a baking sheet in the oven while you make the sauce.

4 For the sauce, wipe the pan with paper towels, heat the oil, and cook the onion gently for 5 minutes. Add the garlic and cook for 1 minute. Now add the wine and allow it to reduce to almost nothing. Add the cream, mustard, and sugar and simmer until the sauce thickens. Season to taste and serve alongside the pork.

CALORIES: 577kcals/2403kJ

CARBOHYDRATE: 19g
  sugar: 3g

FAT: 42g
  saturated: 21g

SALT: 0.9g

FIBER: 1g

Pork tenderloin with apple gravy

An updated version of an old dinner party classic, this family-friendly version uses apple juice instead of wine.

5 mins   5 mins

SERVES 4

2 tbsp all-purpose flour

salt and freshly ground black pepper

1lb (450g) piece of pork tenderloin, sliced into ¾in (2cm) pieces

1 tbsp olive oil

2 tbsp butter

⅔ cup apple juice

⅔ cup chicken stock (see p94)

¼ cup half-and-half

1 tbsp finely chopped sage leaves

1 Season 1 tbsp of the flour with salt and pepper and place on a plate. Toss the meat in it, lightly coating all sides and shaking off any excess flour. Preheat the oven to 250°F (130°C).

2 Heat the olive oil and 1 tbsp of the butter in a large, deep-sided frying pan. Sear the pork pieces a few at a time for 2–3 minutes on each side until well browned. You will need to work in batches, as the pan must not be crowded or the meat will fail to form a good crust. Keep the cooked pork warm, loosely covered with foil, in the low oven.

3 Heat the remaining 1 tbsp of butter in the pan and whisk in the remaining 1 tbsp of flour. Whisk in the apple juice and stock, a little at a time, and bring to a boil. Reduce the heat to a simmer and reduce the sauce to about half its original volume, then add the half-and-half and sage, and cook until the sauce is thick and creamy. Season to taste.

4 Return the meat to the pan with any juices that have come from it, and cook for another minute or 2 until the pork is piping hot once more, and the sauce is evenly glossy.

VARIATION

For a more grown-up meal, use white wine or hard cider in place of the apple juice. The alcohol will burn off, leaving just the taste of the drink, so use a good-quality bottle.

CALORIES: 296kcals/1239kJ

CARBOHYDRATE: 9g
  sugar: 4g

FAT: 16g
  saturated: 8g

SALT: 0.4g

FIBER: 0.5g

Veal with creamy mushroom sauce

When buying veal, always try and find meat that has come from a source with a good animal welfare guarantee.

10 mins   20 mins

SERVES 4

4 veal scallops, approx.
  3½oz (100g) each

salt and freshly ground black pepper

¼ cup all-purpose flour

2 tbsp olive oil

1 tbsp butter

9oz (250g) crimini mushrooms,
  sliced

¾ cup chicken stock (see p94)

½ cup dry white wine

2 sprigs of thyme

¼ cup (2oz) heavy cream

rice, to serve

1 Place the veal between sheets of parchment paper and pound each with a meat mallet or wooden rolling pin until about ⅛in (3mm) thick. Season the scallops with salt and pepper. Place the flour on a plate, season it, and coat each scallop on both sides.

2 Heat the oil and butter in a large, non-stick frying pan that has a lid over medium heat and brown 2 of the scallops for 1 minute on each side. Set aside on a plate. Repeat to brown the remaining veal.

3 Add the mushrooms to the pan, stir well, and cook over medium heat for 5 minutes, stirring, until they have released

their juices and the juices have evaporated. Add the stock, wine, and thyme, season, and bring to a boil.

4 Return the veal to the pan and gently shake to cover the scallops in the mushroom sauce.

5 Reduce the heat, cover the pan, and simmer for 5 minutes over low heat, carefully turning once halfway through cooking. Remove the veal from the pan and place on a warmed serving plate.

6 Bring the sauce to a boil and cook for 5 minutes to reduce. Stir in the cream and heat through. Pour the sauce and mushrooms over the veal and serve with rice.

CLEVER WITH LEFTOVERS

If you have any of this delicious dish left over, you can make a quick and tasty pasta sauce. Just slice the cold meat into thin slices and reheat it. Add chicken stock (see p94) to loosen the sauce and toss it through freshly cooked tagliatelle.

CALORIES: 345kcals/1440kJ

CARBOHYDRATE: 11.5g
  sugar: 1g

FAT: 19g
  saturated: 8.5g

SALT: 0.4g

FIBER: 1.5g

Slow-cooked Moroccan lamb

For an exotic take on a family meal, try serving this aromatic lamb with couscous salad.

10 mins, plus marinating   3 hrs 30 mins

SERVES 4–6

2 tbsp olive oil

juice of 1 lemon

2 tbsp harissa paste

2 tsp smoked paprika

1 tsp ground cinnamon

salt and freshly ground black pepper

1 bone-in shoulder of lamb, approx. 3lb 3oz–4½lb (1.5–2kg)

1 Mix the oil, lemon juice, harissa, and spices in a bowl and season well. Cut slashes all over the lamb, rub in the marinade, cover, and refrigerate for at least 4 hours, preferably overnight.

2 Preheat the oven to 350°F (180°C). Place the lamb in a roasting pan where it fits snugly and pour in water to a depth of ¾in (2cm). Place a piece of parchment paper on top, then cover tightly with foil, making sure there are no gaps.

3 Cook for 3 hours. Uncover the pan and cook for 20–30 minutes. If the pan is dry, add a little water.

4 When the lamb is crisp on the outside and falling off the bone, it is ready. Strain off the liquid and separate and discard the fat. Pour the juices over the sliced lamb before serving on a platter.

CLEVER WITH LEFTOVERS

Turn leftover lamb into a wrap: serve it warmed, with Greek yogurt mixed with chopped mint leaves, and warmed Middle Eastern flatbread.

HOW TO FREEZE

Freeze the lamb, in its marinade, uncooked. Defrost thoroughly before cooking from the start of step 2.

CALORIES: 516–344kcals/2152–1435kJ
CARBOHYDRATE: 0.7–0.5g
  sugar: 0.6–0.4g
FAT: 30–20g
  saturated: 11–7.5g
SALT: 0.6–0.4g
FIBER: 0.2–0.1g

Easy Chinese roast pork

Recreate this favorite restaurant choice at home, using some clever shortcuts.

10 mins, plus marinating   40 mins

SERVES 4

2 tbsp soy sauce

1 tbsp hoisin sauce

1 tbsp honey, plus 1 tbsp for glazing

1 tbsp rice wine or dry sherry

1 tsp sunflower or vegetable oil

1 tsp light brown sugar

2 garlic cloves, crushed

1lb (450g) piece of pork tenderloin

rice, to serve

1 Mix all the ingredients—except the honey for glazing and the pork—in a bowl. Rub the marinade all over the pork, cover, and refrigerate for at least 4 hours, but preferably overnight.

2 Preheat the oven to 400°F (200°C). Put the pork on a rack over a roasting pan half filled with hot water, making sure the water does not touch the rack. Brush the meat with the remaining honey on all sides.

3 Roast at the top of the oven for 40 minutes, turning occasionally, until glossy on all sides. Serve with rice.

HOW TO FREEZE

Freeze the meat, in its marinade, uncooked. Defrost thoroughly before cooking from the start of step 2.

CALORIES: 190kcals/804kJ
CARBOHYDRATE: 9g
  sugar: 9g
FAT: 5g
  saturated: 2g
SALT: 1.6g
FIBER: 0g

Chinese-spiced pork belly

A wonderful treatment turns an inexpensive cut of meat into an Asian feast, with the best crackling ever.

10 mins, plus marinating　　1 hr 30 mins

SERVES 4

piece of boneless skin-on pork belly, approx. 1lb 10oz (750g)

2 tbsp soy sauce

1 tbsp light brown sugar

1 tbsp five-spice powder

2 tsp salt

1 tsp sunflower or vegetable oil

1 With a sharp knife, make criss-cross slits all over the skin of the pork, being careful not to cut through to the meat. (Or ask your butcher to do this.) Pat the skin dry.

2 Mix the soy sauce, sugar, five-spice powder, and 1 tsp of salt into a thick paste and rub it over the meat side of the pork, keeping all the skin dry. Refrigerate, skin-side up and uncovered, for at least 8 hours, or overnight.

3 Preheat the oven to 425°F (220°C). Place the meat, skin-side up, on a rack in a roasting pan lined with foil (making cleaning easier later). Rub the skin with the oil and remaining 1 tsp of salt. Fill the pan half full with hot water.

4 Roast the pork at the top of the oven for 30 minutes, then reduce the oven temperature to 400°F (200°C) and roast for another 45 minutes to 1 hour, until crispy. Keep an eye on the water level, and add more if it starts to get too low.

CALORIES: 507kcals/2109kJ

CARBOHYDRATE: 4g
　sugar: 4g

FAT: 39g
　saturated: 14g

SALT: 4g

FIBER: 0g

Chinese braised beef with ginger and soy sauce

For a simple supper, put some broccoli rabe in the sauce to braise for the last 5 minutes of cooking.

25 mins　　2 hrs 30 mins

SERVES 4

4 tbsp sunflower or vegetable oil

2 onions, quartered

2in (5cm) fresh ginger, finely sliced

3 garlic cloves, finely sliced

2 heaping tbsp all-purpose flour

1 tsp five-spice powder

1lb 2oz (500g) beef stew meat, cut into 1in (3cm) cubes

1¼ cups beef stock

¼ cup rice wine or dry sherry

2 tbsp soy sauce

4 dried red chiles, left whole

1 tbsp light brown sugar

salt and freshly ground black pepper

steamed rice, to serve

cilantro leaves, to serve (optional)

1 Heat 2 tbsp of the oil in a large, heavy-bottomed saucepan with a lid. Cook the onions, turning with tongs until browned all over. Add the ginger and garlic and cook for another minute. Set aside.

2 Mix the flour and ½ tsp of five-spice powder in a freezer bag and add the beef. Toss until coated on all sides, then pour out into a sieve, shaking to remove excess flour.

3 Heat the remaining 2 tbsp of oil. Cook the beef, a few pieces at a time, until browned on all sides. Return the onion mixture.

4 Add the stock, rice wine, and soy sauce and bring to a boil, stirring to dislodge any residue from the pan. Add the chiles and sugar.

5 Cover and cook over very low heat for 2 hours, then uncover and cook for 30 minutes until the meat is meltingly tender and the sauce reduced and thickened slightly. Season to taste, remove the chiles, and serve with steamed rice and a sprinkling of cilantro leaves (if using).

CALORIES: 366kcals/1528kJ

CARBOHYDRATE: 13.5g
　sugar: 7g

FAT: 18g
　saturated: 4g

SALT: 1.7g

FIBER: 1g

Pot-roast beef

Try to find a piece of well-marbled beef that will be good and juicy. Round or chuck are both good.

20 mins   2 hrs 30 mins

SERVES 4

3 tbsp olive oil

2 onions, quartered

4 large carrots, cut into
  1in (3cm) pieces

2 garlic cloves, roughly chopped

salt and freshly ground black pepper

2¼lb (1kg) round roast

2 cups red wine, or beef stock,
  or a mixture

1 tbsp redcurrant or sour cherry jelly

2 sprigs of rosemary

handful of thyme

mashed potatoes, to serve

1 Preheat the oven to 350°F (180°C). Heat 2 tbsp of the oil in a large, heavy-bottomed saucepan with a lid. Cook the onions, carrots, and garlic over medium heat until they start to color. Set aside.

2 Heat the remaining 1 tbsp of oil in the pan. Season the beef well on all sides and sear it in the oil for 2–3 minutes, turning, until browned. Set aside.

3 Add the wine and/or stock to the pan. Stir in the redcurrant or sour cherry jelly and season well. Return the meat and vegetables. Tuck in the herbs.

4 Cover and cook in the oven for 2 hours until meltingly tender. Remove the herbs before serving with mashed potatoes.

CALORIES: 511kcals/2146kJ

CARBOHYDRATE: 13.5g
  sugar: 12g

FAT: 15g
  saturated: 4g

SALT: 0.6g

FIBER: 4g

COOK'S TIP

Feeding a family can sometimes be expensive. The cheaper cuts of meat are perfectly suited to pot roasting, as the long, slow cooking time allows the meat to cook to a melting softness.

Slow pot-roast lamb shoulder

Lamb shoulder is an affordable choice for a family. Pot roasting renders it succulent and provides gravy, too.

20 mins,
plus marinating   3 hrs 40 mins

SERVES 4

4½lb (2kg) bone-in shoulder of lamb

2 tbsp olive oil

salt and freshly ground black pepper

4 sprigs of rosemary, torn into
  small pieces

4 garlic cloves, halved lengthwise

1¾ cups lamb stock

1¾ cups red wine

4 carrots, roughly chopped

1 onion, roughly chopped

4 celery stalks, roughly chopped

1 Using a sharp knife, make 8 incisions in the lamb, rub the oil all over, season well, and sprinkle with rosemary. Cover and set aside for 1 hour.

2 Preheat the oven to 325°F (160°C). Heat a roasting pan on the stove top over medium heat and sear the lamb on all sides. Place the garlic in the incisions.

3 Add the stock, wine, and vegetables. Seal tightly with foil and cook in the oven for 3–3½ hours, basting the meat and stirring the vegetables from time to time.

4 Transfer the meat and vegetables to a warmed serving plate and loosely cover with foil to keep warm and rest. Skim and discard the fat from the juices and pour into a serving bowl, along with any juices from the lamb.

5 Shred the meltingly tender lamb with 2 forks and serve with the vegetables and juices.

CALORIES: 836–557kcals/3487–2324kJ

CARBOHYDRATE: 10–6.5g
  sugar: 9–6g

FAT: 40–27g
  saturated: 16–10g

SALT: 1.1–0.7g

FIBER: 4–3g

Braised lamb with spring vegetables

Lamb neck is an inexpensive cut, and the long, slow cooking here breaks it down to a melt-in-the-mouth texture.

30 mins   2 hrs

SPECIAL EQUIPMENT
4-quart (4-liter) heavy-bottomed Dutch oven

SERVES 4

2 tbsp all-purpose flour

salt and freshly ground black pepper

1lb 5oz (600g) lamb neck filet, excess fat trimmed, cut into 1in (3cm) pieces

2 tbsp olive oil

6 baby leeks, sliced

4 shallots, halved

2 garlic cloves, finely sliced

2½ cups lamb or chicken stock (see p94)

1 bay leaf

2 sprigs of rosemary

finely grated zest of 1 lemon

5½oz (150g) Chantenay carrots, ends trimmed and halved lengthwise if large

3½oz (100g) thin green beans, topped, tailed, and halved

5½oz (150g) fresh or frozen peas

5½oz (150g) fresh or frozen baby fava beans

new potatoes, to serve

1 Place the flour in a large freezer bag, season well, and add the meat. Shake to coat the meat. Pour into a sieve to remove excess flour.

2 Heat 1 tbsp of the oil in a 4-quart (4-liter) heavy-bottomed Dutch oven over medium heat. Brown the meat in 2 batches, turning to color all sides. Remove with a slotted spoon and set aside on a plate lined with paper towels.

3 Add the remaining 1 tbsp of oil to the dish and add the leeks, shallots, and garlic. Cook over medium heat for 3 minutes, stirring occasionally.

4 Return the meat and add the stock, bay leaf, rosemary, and lemon zest. Season well and bring to a simmer, skim off any foam, then cover and simmer gently for 1½ hours.

5 Add the carrots, return to a boil, then reduce the heat and simmer gently, uncovered, for 10 minutes to reduce the sauce. Add the green beans, peas, and baby fava beans. Return to a boil, reduce the heat, and simmer for another 10 minutes, or until all the vegetables are just tender and the sauce has thickened slightly. Do not overcook the vegetables.

6 Remove the rosemary and bay leaf and serve the braised lamb with new potatoes.

BATCHING AND FREEZING

This kind of stew is ideally suited to freezing ahead. Make double or triple quantities and freeze it in family-sized portions at the end of stage 4. Defrost it thoroughly, reheat it, and add the vegetables to serve.

CALORIES: 441kcals/1839kJ
CARBOHYDRATE: 18g
  sugar: 7g
FAT: 19g
  saturated: 6.5g
SALT: 0.8g
FIBER: 11g

Greek lamb stew

This unusual stew is a meal in itself, and only needs some crusty bread to soak up the delicious juices.

20 mins · 2 hrs 5 mins

SPECIAL EQUIPMENT
large Dutch oven

SERVES 4

2 tbsp olive oil

1lb 9oz (700g) boneless shoulder or neck filet of lamb, excess fat trimmed, cut into bite-sized pieces

1 red onion, finely chopped

2 garlic cloves, finely chopped

¾ cup dry white wine

2 x 14oz (400g) cans chopped tomatoes

3½oz (100g) pitted Kalamata olives

3 sprigs of thyme

3½oz (100g) orzo pasta

3½oz (100g) feta cheese, finely chopped

small bunch of mint leaves, finely chopped

salt and freshly ground black pepper

1 Preheat the oven to 300°F (150°C). Heat 1 tbsp of the oil in a large, heavy-bottomed Dutch oven over medium heat. Brown the meat in 2 batches, remove with a slotted spoon, and set aside on a plate lined with paper towels.

2 Add the remaining 1 tbsp of oil to the casserole, stir in the onion, and cook for 5 minutes, stirring occasionally. Add the garlic and cook for 2 minutes.

3 Add the wine and tomatoes and stir. Return the lamb with the olives and thyme. Bring to a boil, season, and cover.

4 Cook in the oven for 1½ hours. Discard the thyme, add the pasta, and stir. Return to the oven for 15 minutes. Mix the feta and mint in a small dish. Season the stew to taste and serve sprinkled with the cheese mixture.

CALORIES: 576kcals/2412kJ
CARBOHYDRATE: 28g
  sugar: 8g
FAT: 29g
  saturated: 11g
SALT: 2g
FIBER: 4g

Irish stew

An economical dish that uses inexpensive cuts; with a long cooking time to ensure a rich flavor.

25 mins · 3 hrs

SPECIAL EQUIPMENT
large Dutch oven

SERVES 4

2lb (900g) stewing lamb from the neck or shoulder, excess fat trimmed, cut into 1in (3cm) pieces

4¾oz (130g) pearl barley

1 large onion, roughly chopped

3 carrots, roughly sliced

7oz (200g) rutabaga, roughly chopped

4 potatoes, roughly chopped

4 sprigs of thyme

salt and freshly ground black pepper

3½ cups hot lamb stock

crusty bread, to serve

CALORIES: 714kcals/3003kJ
CARBOHYDRATE: 68g
  sugar: 9.5g
FAT: 20g
  saturated: 8g
SALT: 1.2g
FIBER: 8g

1 Place half the meat in a large, heavy-bottomed Dutch oven. Top with half the barley, half the vegetables, and 2 of the thyme sprigs and season well. Repeat the layers to use up the remaining meat, barley, vegetables, and thyme. Season well.

2 Pour in hot stock, place over high heat, and bring to a boil. Skim off any foam that rises.

3 Cover and reduce the heat to a gentle simmer. Cook for 3 hours, stirring occasionally. Taste and adjust the seasoning. Serve in bowls with crusty bread.

PREPARE AHEAD

It can take a surprisingly long time to prepare vegetables. To get ahead, peel and chop the carrots, rutabaga, and potatoes in advance and submerge under water in a large saucepan or bowl. Left like this, they will be fine for up to 1 day in all but the very hottest kitchens.

Lamb, apricot, and chickpea tagine

If you forget to soak the dried chickpeas overnight, just replace them with a can, drained and added at the end.

25 mins, plus marinating   2 hrs 30 mins

SPECIAL EQUIPMENT
4-quart (4-liter) Dutch oven

SERVES 4

3½oz (100g) dried apricots, roughly chopped

1¾oz (50g) raisins

½ cup dry sherry (or lamb stock or orange juice)

1lb 5oz (600g) boneless shoulder of lamb, excess fat trimmed, cut into 1in (3cm) pieces

finely grated zest and juice of 1 orange

2 garlic cloves, finely chopped

salt and freshly ground black pepper

3½oz (100g) dried chickpeas, soaked overnight in water

2 tbsp olive oil

1 red onion, finely chopped

pinch of saffron strands

2 tsp ground coriander

2 tsp ground cumin

½ tsp paprika

1¾oz (50g) pine nuts

2 tbsp all-purpose flour

⅔ cup red wine

⅔ cup lamb or chicken stock (see p94)

1 x 14oz (400g) can chopped tomatoes

20 pitted black olives

juice of ½ lemon

couscous, to serve

1 Place the apricots and raisins in a small bowl and pour in the sherry (or lamb stock or orange juice). Set aside for 2 hours to plump up.

2 Place the lamb in a dish with the orange zest and juice, garlic, and seasoning. Stir well, cover, and set aside for 2 hours to marinate.

3 Drain and rinse the soaked chickpeas under running water. Place in a medium pan, cover with cold water, and bring to a boil. Reduce the heat, cover, and simmer for 1 hour. Drain. Preheat the oven to 350°F (180°C).

4 Remove the lamb from the marinade, using a slotted spoon, reserving the marinade. Heat 1 tbsp of the oil in a 4-quart (4-liter) Dutch oven and brown the meat in 2 batches, for 3 minutes each. Transfer each batch with a slotted spoon to a plate lined with paper towels.

5 Add the remaining 1 tbsp of oil to the casserole and cook the onion over medium heat. Add the spices and pine nuts and cook for 2 minutes. Stir in the flour and add the soaked fruit and sherry, reserved marinade, wine, stock, tomatoes, and chickpeas. Season.

6 Return the meat to the casserole and bring to a boil. Cover and cook in the oven for 1 hour. Remove from the oven and add the olives and lemon juice. Return to the oven for 15 minutes. Serve in warmed bowls, over couscous.

CLEVER WITH LEFTOVERS

A little leftover tagine can easily be stretched with some extra chicken stock (see p94) to make a great spicy soup.

CALORIES: 667kcals/2794kJ

CARBOHYDRATE: 42g
  sugar: 25g

FAT: 30g
  saturated: 7g

SALT: 0.8g

FIBER: 9g

Braised lamb shanks

This takes only minutes to make; hours of unattended slow cooking leave it succulent and falling off the bone.

15 mins   3 hrs 15 mins

SPECIAL EQUIPMENT
4-quart (4-liter) Dutch oven

SERVES 4

2 tbsp olive oil

4 lamb shanks

salt and freshly ground black pepper

3 celery stalks, roughly chopped

3 carrots, roughly chopped

4 shallots, roughly chopped

2 garlic cloves, finely sliced

2 sprigs of rosemary

1 bay leaf

1¼ cups red wine

2 cups lamb stock

mashed potatoes, to serve

1 Preheat the oven to 300°F (150°C). Heat the oil in a very large (4-quart/4-liter) heavy-bottomed Dutch oven over medium heat.

2 Add 2 of the shanks, season well, and brown for 5 minutes, turning occasionally. Transfer to a plate and set aside. Repeat for the remaining shanks.

3 Add the vegetables and garlic to the casserole and cook over medium heat for 5 minutes. Return the lamb and its juices and add the herbs, wine, and stock. Bring to a boil and cover. Cook in the oven for 2½–3 hours or until the meat is starting to fall off the bone.

4 Using a slotted spoon, carefully transfer the shanks and vegetables to a warmed serving dish. Remove the bay leaf and rosemary. Discard the fat from the sauce and pour it into a bowl. Serve the lamb and vegetables with mashed potatoes and the sauce.

HOW TO FREEZE

Freezing dishes that are cooked on the bone is far easier if the meat is cooled and taken off the bone first. The bones can be frozen separately to make a stock at another time, and the deboned meat will take up far less space in your freezer.

CALORIES: 468kcals/1951kJ
CARBOHYDRATE: 8g
  sugar: 7g
FAT: 22g
  saturated: 8g
SALT: 0.7g
FIBER: 3g

Blanquette de veau

This classic French dish has a rich, creamy sauce that is thickened with the careful addition of egg yolks.

15 mins   1 hr 40 mins

SPECIAL EQUIPMENT
2-quart (2-liter) Dutch oven

SERVES 4

1lb 5oz (600g) veal, cut into 1½in (4cm) pieces

1 bouquet garni

1 celery stalk, roughly chopped

1 carrot, roughly chopped

salt and freshly ground black pepper

½ cup white wine

12 pearl onions

10oz (300g) button mushrooms

2 large egg yolks

¼ cup heavy cream

chopped flat-leaf parsley leaves, to garnish

mixed basmati and wild rice, and steamed green vegetables, to serve

1 Place the veal, bouquet garni, celery, and carrot in a 2-quart (2-liter) heavy-bottomed Dutch oven. Season well and add the wine. Pour in 2 cups of water. Bring to a boil, then skim off any foam. Reduce the heat, cover, and simmer for 1 hour, stirring occasionally.

2 Add the onions and mushrooms, return to a boil, cover, and simmer for 30 minutes. Remove the bouquet garni.

3 Whisk together the egg yolks and cream in a bowl and whisk in a little of the hot cooking juices. Slowly pour the egg yolk and cream mixture into the casserole, stirring constantly. Cook gently until the sauce thickens.

4 Scatter the parsley over the veal and serve with mixed basmati and wild rice and steamed green vegetables.

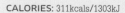

Veal is a gentle-tasting meat, and often appeals to children. If children want just the creamy sauce, leave the mushrooms and onions whole so that they can be picked out easily.

Fussy eaters!

CALORIES: 311kcals/1303kJ
CARBOHYDRATE: 5g
  sugar: 4g
FAT: 14g
  saturated: 7g
SALT: 0.3g
FIBER: 2.5g

Venison and red wine stew

Venison is an excellent source of low-fat protein, and its treatment in this recipe gives it a rich, satisfying flavor.

15 mins   **2¼–2¾ hrs**

SPECIAL EQUIPMENT
medium Dutch oven

SERVES 4

3 tbsp olive oil

4 shallots, halved

2 celery stalks, finely chopped

1 carrot, finely chopped

2 garlic cloves, finely chopped

2 tbsp all-purpose flour

½ tsp grated nutmeg

½ tsp ground allspice

salt and freshly ground black
    pepper

1½lb (675g) boneless shoulder or
    other stewing venison, cut into
    bite-sized chunks

¼ cup redcurrant or sour cherry jelly

finely grated zest and juice of
    1 orange

1¼ cups red wine

⅔ cup beef stock

1 bay leaf

potato and celeriac mash, to serve

1 Preheat the oven to 300°F
(150°C). Heat 1 tbsp of the oil
in a medium Dutch oven and gently
cook the shallots, celery, and carrot
for 3 minutes. Add the garlic and
cook for a couple more minutes.
Remove from the pot using a slotted
spoon and set aside.

2 Place the flour, nutmeg, and
allspice in a large freezer bag,
season well, and add the meat.
Shake to coat the meat in the
seasoned flour. Pour out into a sieve
and shake to remove excess flour.

3 Add the remaining 2 tbsp of
oil to the pot and brown the
meat in batches over medium heat,
removing each batch to the plate
with the vegetables.

4 Add the jelly, orange zest and
juice, wine, stock, and bay leaf
to the pot, season, and stir until the
jelly has melted.

5 Return the vegetables and
venison, stir, and bring to a
simmer. Cover and cook in the

oven for 2–2½ hours or until
the venison is tender. Remove
the bay leaf and serve the stew
with potato and celeriac mash,
made with two-thirds potato
to one-third celeriac.

CALORIES: 400kcals/1670kJ

CARBOHYDRATE: 21g
    sugar: 16g

FAT: 11g
    saturated: 2.5g

SALT: 0.4g

FIBER: 2g

Polish hunter's stew

This is considered the Polish national dish. Called *bigos* it has a bit of everything—fresh, dried, smoked, and pickled!

30 mins   3 hrs 30 mins

SPECIAL EQUIPMENT
large Dutch oven

SERVES 6–8

scant 1oz (25g) dried wild mushrooms

3 tbsp olive oil

7oz (200g) chopped pancetta

1lb 2oz (500g) pork shoulder, cut into 1in (3cm) cubes

9oz (250g) cured, smoked sausage, ideally Polish sausage such as Kiełbasa Czosnkowa, cut into chunks

1 onion, finely sliced

1 celery stalk, sliced

1 large carrot, sliced

1 leek, white part only, finely sliced

7oz (200g) green cabbage, sliced

5½oz (150g) crimini mushrooms

½ tsp caraway seeds

½ tsp juniper berries, roughly ground in a mortar and pestle

1 tsp paprika

1 bay leaf

large sprig of thyme

1 heaping tbsp all-purpose flour

salt and freshly ground black pepper

1¼ cups red wine

1¾ cups beef or chicken stock (see p94)

9oz (250g) sauerkraut, drained and rinsed

2 tbsp redcurrant jelly

1 bouquet garni

bread or boiled potatoes, to serve

1 Soak the dried mushrooms in 2 cups of boiling water. In a large Dutch oven, heat 1 tbsp of the oil over high heat. Add all the meat and sausage and brown on all sides. Remove from the casserole and set aside.

2 Heat another 1 tbsp of the oil over medium heat. Cook the onion, celery, carrot, leek, and cabbage for 10 minutes, until softened. Remove and set aside.

3 Heat the remaining 1 tbsp of oil over low heat, and cook the crimini mushrooms for 2 minutes. Return the meat and vegetables, add the caraway, juniper, paprika, bay leaf, thyme, and flour, and season well. Stir over medium heat for 2 minutes.

4 Stir in the dried mushrooms, their soaking water (leave behind any grit), wine, and stock. Add the sauerkraut, redcurrant jelly, and bouquet garni and bring to a boil. Reduce the heat to low, cover, and cook for 2 hours.

5 Remove the lid and cook for another hour, until the meat is almost falling apart. Remove the bay leaf, thyme, and bouquet garni. Serve with bread or boiled potatoes.

CALORIES: 472kcals/1967kJ
CARBOHYDRATE: 11g
  sugar: 8.5g
FAT: 27g
  saturated: 9g
SALT: 2.6g
FIBER: 5g

Brazilian pork and beans

Otherwise known as *feijoada* this, the national dish of Brazil, is made with a variety of cured and fresh pork.

15 mins, plus soaking

1 hr 45 mins

SERVES 6

1lb 2oz (500g) dried black-eyed peas

2 pig's trotters, split, or 1 ham hock

9oz (250g) pork ribs

7oz (200g) can chopped tomatoes

1 tbsp tomato paste

1 bay leaf

salt and freshly ground black pepper

2 tbsp olive oil

7oz (200g) chopped pancetta

1lb 2oz (500g) lean pork tenderloin

1 small onion, finely chopped

2 garlic cloves, finely chopped

6oz (175g) chorizo, in small chunks

1 green chile, seeded (optional)

1 Soak the beans overnight. Drain and place in a large saucepan. Cover with water, bring to a boil, and boil for 10 minutes, skimming off any foam, then lower the heat, cover, and simmer for one hour.

2 Meanwhile, place the pig's trotters or ham hock and pork ribs in a saucepan with the tomatoes, tomato paste, bay leaf, and salt and pepper. Cover with water, bring to a boil, and skim off any foam. Cover, reduce the heat, and simmer for 50 minutes.

3 Drain the beans and reserve the liquid, then return the beans to the pan. Add the meats with their cooking liquid. Add enough liquid from the beans to cover. Cook, covered, over low heat, for another 20 minutes.

4 Heat 1 tbsp of the oil in a frying pan and add the pancetta. Cook for 5 minutes, until it starts to brown. Remove it and use the same fat to brown the pork tenderloin. Add the pork and pancetta to the meat and bean mixture and cook for 10 minutes, or until everything is tender. Wipe out the frying pan, add 1 tbsp of oil, and cook the onion and garlic over medium heat for 4 minutes, stirring, until translucent. Add the chorizo and chile (if using), increase the heat, and cook for 2 minutes, stirring.

5 Add 2–3 tbsp of the cooked beans to the frying pan and mash well with the back of a spoon. Add the contents of the frying pan to the meat and beans, stir, and cook for another 10 minutes.

6 Pick the meat from the trotters or hock (discard the bones and skin). Cut the pork tenderloin into pieces. Transfer them and the rest of the meat and beans to a warmed platter, season to taste, and serve.

VARIATION

Instead of using dried beans, use two 14oz (400g) cans of beans, drained and added in step 5. Instead of black-eyed peas, try black beans, adzuki beans, red kidney beans, or pinto beans.

CALORIES: 757kcals/3178kJ

CARBOHYDRATE: 46g
sugar: 6g

FAT: 33g
saturated: 11g

SALT: 2.8g

FIBER: 10g

Boeuf bourguignon

A simplified version of a French classic, the beef here is meltingly rich and tender.

30 mins   2 hrs 45 mins

SERVES 4–6

4 tbsp olive oil

3½oz (100g) chopped pancetta

2 onions, finely chopped

4 thin carrots, cut into ¾in (2cm) slices

1 celery stalk, finely chopped

5½oz (150g) button mushrooms, halved if large

2¼lb (1kg) beef stew meat, cut into 1in (3cm) cubes

2 tbsp all-purpose flour

salt and freshly ground black pepper

1½ cups red wine

1 cup beef stock

1 bouquet garni

buttered noodles, to serve

CALORIES: 663kcals/2766kJ

CARBOHYDRATE: 15g
  sugar: 8.5g

FAT: 32g
  saturated: 10g

SALT: 1.5g

FIBER: 4.5g

1 Preheat the oven to 300°F (150°C). Heat 2 tbsp of the oil in a large casserole or Dutch oven. Cook the pancetta for a few minutes until lightly browned. Add the onions, carrots, celery, and mushrooms, and cook for 5 minutes. Set aside.

2 Pat the beef dry with paper towels. Season the flour with salt and pepper and toss the beef in it to coat. Shake off the excess.

3 Heat the remaining oil in the pan and cook the beef, in batches, until well browned. Set aside.

4 Pour the wine and stock into the pan, scraping any browned bits stuck to the bottom.. Season well, add the bouquet garni, and return the meat and vegetables.

5 Cover and cook in the oven for 2½ hours, until very tender. Remove the bouquet garni and serve with buttered noodles.

CLEVER WITH LEFTOVERS

Freeze leftover wine in ice cube trays for use in cooking. Once frozen, transfer to a freezer bag. Add a cube or two to a casserole or stew for added flavor.

Beef stroganoff

This classic Russian dish with a rich creamy sauce is a quick alternative to a stew.

10 mins   15 mins

SERVES 4

4 tbsp olive oil

14oz (400g) steak, such as sirloin, very thinly sliced

1 onion, finely chopped

5½oz (150g) button mushrooms, sliced

1 tbsp butter

2 tbsp all-purpose flour

1¼ cups beef stock

¼ cup (2oz) crème fraîche or sour cream

1 heaping tsp paprika

salt and freshly ground black pepper

½ tbsp lemon juice

1 tbsp chopped dill (optional)

buttered tagliatelle, to serve

CALORIES: 364kcals/1513kJ

CARBOHYDRATE: 8g
  sugar: 2g

FAT: 25g
  saturated: 9g

SALT: 0.4g

FIBER: 1.5g

1 Heat 2 tbsp of the oil in a large, deep-sided frying pan. Sear the steak in batches over high heat, cooking until it just colors. Set aside.

2 Heat the remaining 2 tbsp of oil in the pan and cook the onion and mushrooms over medium heat for 5 minutes until the mushrooms are golden brown, making sure not to burn the onions.

3 Add the butter and sprinkle in the flour, stirring it in. Gradually stir in the stock and cook for a few minutes until the sauce thickens. Stir in the crème fraîche and paprika and season to taste.

4 Return the beef to the pan and heat it through. Add the lemon with the dill (if using). Serve over buttered tagliatelle or pappardelle.

VARIATION

This treatment works just as well with thinly sliced chicken or pork. Add tarragon for chicken and sage for pork in the place of dill, use chicken stock (see p94) instead of beef stock, and add a spoonful of Dijon mustard to the sauce.

Beef in beer

The type of beer used here will affect the flavor, but both light and dark beers work well.

25 mins   2 hrs 45 mins

SERVES 4–6

¼ cup olive oil

1 onion, finely chopped

1 celery stalk, finely chopped

1 large carrot, finely chopped

2 garlic cloves, finely chopped

2¼lb (1kg) beef stew meat, cut into 1in (3cm) cubes

salt and freshly ground black pepper

2 tbsp all-purpose flour

12oz (330ml) bottle dark beer

1 cup beef stock

1 tsp granulated sugar

a few sprigs of thyme

3 tbsp chopped flat-leaf parsley leaves

1 Preheat the oven to 300°F (150°C). Heat half the oil in a large Dutch oven. Cook the onion, celery, and carrot for 10 minutes over medium heat, until they start to color. Add the garlic and cook for another minute. Set aside.

2 Pat the meat dry with paper towels. Season the flour and toss the beef in it, to coat. Shake off excess flour.

3 Heat the remaining oil in the pan and cook the beef, in batches, until well browned. Do not crowd the pan. Set aside.

4 Pour the beer and stock into the pan, scraping any browned bits stuck to the bottom. Season well, add the sugar, thyme, and 2 tbsp of parsley, and return the meat and vegetables.

5 Cover and cook in the oven for 2½ hours. The beef should be almost falling apart. Remove the thyme and sprinkle with the remaining parsley to serve.

CALORIES: 536kcals/2240kJ
CARBOHYDRATE: 13g
  sugar: 7g
FAT: 25.5g
  saturated: 7.5g
SALT: 0.6g
FIBER: 2g

Chili con carne

A family favorite, and a good way to introduce your children to beans such as kidney beans.

25 mins   1 hr 45 mins

SPECIAL EQUIPMENT
large Dutch oven

SERVES 4

2 tbsp olive oil

1 onion, finely chopped

1 celery stalk, finely chopped

1 green bell pepper, finely chopped

2 garlic cloves, crushed

1lb 2oz (500g) ground beef

1 tsp dried oregano

2 tsp smoked paprika

½ tsp cayenne pepper

1 tsp ground cumin

1 tsp brown sugar

salt and freshly ground black pepper

1 x 14oz (400g) can chopped tomatoes

1 cup beef stock

1 tbsp tomato paste

1 x 14oz (400g) can kidney beans, drained and rinsed

sour cream and grated Cheddar cheese, to serve (optional)

1 Heat the oil over medium heat in a large Dutch oven. Cook the onion, celery, and green bell pepper for 10 minutes, until they start to color at the edges. Add the garlic and cook for 1 minute.

2 Add the beef and cook over high heat, breaking up any clumps with a wooden spoon, until well browned. Add the oregano, spices, sugar, and seasoning and cook until the spices are fragrant.

3 Add the tomatoes, stock, and tomato paste and bring to a boil. Cover and cook over low heat for 1 hour. Uncover, add the kidney beans, and cook for another 30 minutes over very low heat, until the sauce has thickened slightly. Serve with sour cream and grated Cheddar cheese (if you like).

CALORIES: 451kcals/1881kJ
CARBOHYDRATE: 19g
  sugar: 10g
FAT: 26g
  saturated: 10g
SALT: 1.2g
FIBER: 7.5g

Cider-braised pork with fennel

Pork shoulder is an inexpensive cut, and in this recipe a long, slow braise brings out all its flavor.

25 mins   2 hrs

SERVES 4

4 tbsp olive oil

2 onions, quartered

1 fennel bulb, cut into similar-sized pieces as the onion

1lb 2oz (500g) pork shoulder, cut into 1in (3cm) cubes

salt and freshly ground black pepper

1 heaping tbsp all-purpose flour

12oz (330ml) bottle of hard cider

⅔ cup chicken stock (see p94)

1 tbsp Dijon mustard

2 tbsp finely chopped sage leaves

2 tbsp crème fraîche

1 Heat 2 tbsp of the oil in a large, heavy-bottomed saucepan with a lid. Cook the onions and fennel for 5–7 minutes, until they soften slightly. Set aside.

2 Pat the meat dry with paper towels. Season the flour and toss the pork in it, to coat. Shake off excess flour.

3 Heat the remaining 2 tbsp of oil in the pan and cook the pork, in batches, until browned. Set aside.

4 Pour the cider and stock into the pan, stirring well to dislodge any meaty residue. Season well, add the mustard and sage, and return the meat and vegetables.

5 Cover and cook over very low heat for 1½ hours until meltingly tender. Stir in the crème fraîche and heat through before serving.

COOK'S TIP

The cider in this dish can easily be replaced by apple juice, if preferred, or use half cider and half apple juice.

CALORIES: 358kcals/1496kJ
CARBOHYDRATE: 9g
  sugar: 6g
FAT: 19g
  saturated: 5g
SALT: 0.6g
FIBER: 2g

Creamy pork goulash

A delicious version of an old classic, the use of caraway adds extra depth to this rich, warming stew.

20 mins   2 hrs

SERVES 4

1 tbsp all-purpose flour

2 tsp paprika

salt and freshly ground black pepper

1lb 2oz (500g) pork shoulder, cut into 1in (3cm) cubes

4 tbsp olive oil

5½oz (150g) button mushrooms, halved if large

1 onion, finely chopped

3½oz (100g) chopped pancetta

2 garlic cloves, crushed

1 tsp caraway seeds

2 cups chicken stock (see p94)

2 tbsp cider vinegar

2 heaping tbsp sour cream

mashed potatoes and cabbage, to serve

CALORIES: 393kcals/1638kJ
CARBOHYDRATE: 5g
  sugar: 2g
FAT: 24g
  saturated: 6g
SALT: 1.4g
FIBER: 1.5g

1 Put the flour in a freezer bag with ½ tsp of the paprika and some salt and pepper. Toss the pork in it. Pour out into a sieve, shaking to remove excess flour. Heat 2 tbsp of the olive oil in a large, heavy-bottomed saucepan with a lid. Cook the pork, in batches, for a couple of minutes on each side, until well browned. Set aside.

2 Heat the remaining 2 tbsp of oil in the pan and cook the mushrooms for a few minutes until they color. Add the onion and pancetta and cook for 5 minutes until the pancetta crisps up. Add the garlic, the remaining 2 tsp of paprika, and the caraway, and cook for 1 minute.

3 Stir in the stock and vinegar, scraping up any residue, and season. Return the pork and reduce the heat to a gentle simmer.

4 Cover and cook for 45 minutes to 1 hour, then uncover and cook for another hour, stirring occasionally, until the sauce has thickened and reduced and the meat is meltingly tender. Stir in the sour cream and serve with fluffy mashed potatoes and lightly steamed cabbage.

Easy cassoulet

Try this super family-friendly version of a far more complex French classic dish for a warming winter meal.

20 mins   1 hr 50mins

SPECIAL EQUIPMENT

2-quart (2-liter) Dutch oven

SERVES 4

1 tbsp olive oil

1lb (450g) pork belly slices

4 pork and herb sausages

3½oz (100g) chopped pancetta

1 onion, roughly chopped

2 carrots, roughly chopped

2 garlic cloves, roughly chopped

1 x 14oz (400g) can cannellini beans, drained and rinsed

1 tsp dried thyme

salt and freshly ground black pepper

2 tbsp sun-dried tomato pesto

1 cup hot chicken stock (see p94)

½ cup red wine

2 tbsp chopped flat-leaf parsley leaves

1 cup fresh white bread crumbs

crusty bread, to serve

1 Preheat the oven to 350°F (180°C). Heat the oil in a 2-quart (2-liter) Dutch oven over medium heat and brown the pork belly. Transfer to a plate lined with paper towels. Add the sausages to the pot and cook, turning to brown on all sides. Transfer to the plate.

2 Add the pancetta, onion, and carrots to the pot and cook gently, stirring occasionally, for 5 minutes. Add the garlic, beans, and thyme to the pot. Season and stir well.

3 Combine the tomato pesto, stock, and wine in a bowl and stir well. Pour into the pot and stir. Arrange the pork belly and sausages in the vegetable mixture. Cover and bake in the oven for 1 hour.

4 Mix the parsley into the bread crumbs with plenty of pepper. Remove the pot from the oven and sprinkle with the bread crumbs. Return to the oven, uncovered, for 30 minutes.

5 Spoon onto warmed plates, making sure each portion gets some crispy crumb topping, and serve with crusty bread.

VARIATION

Use 5½oz (150g) of dried beans instead of canned if you have time, soaking them overnight, then simmering according to the packet instructions. Add them to the cassoulet in step 3.

CALORIES: 716kcals/2988kJ

CARBOHYDRATE: 38g
sugar: 7g

FAT: 41g
saturated: 14g

SALT: 2.7g

FIBER: 7.5g

Spicy pork and beans

This is a sort of cowboy-style barbecue pork and beans, rich with dark, smoky flavors.

20 mins, plus soaking   2 hrs 15 mins

SERVES 4

5½oz (150g) mixed dried beans, such as black-eyed, black, and cannellini beans, soaked overnight

2 tbsp olive oil

2 onions, finely chopped

2 garlic cloves, crushed

2 tsp all-purpose flour

2 tsp smoked paprika

salt and freshly ground black pepper

1lb 2oz (500g) pork shoulder, cut into 1in (3cm) cubes

½ tsp dried oregano

1 tsp dark brown sugar

2 cups beef stock

2 tbsp good-quality barbecue sauce

baked potatoes, to serve

CALORIES: 400kcals/1691kJ

CARBOHYDRATE: 32g
  sugar: 8g

FAT: 11.5g
  saturated: 3g

SALT: 0.8g

FIBER: 6.5g

1 Place the beans in a saucepan with plenty of fresh water. Bring to a boil over high heat and simmer for 10 minutes. Drain and refresh under cold water. Set aside.

2 Heat 1 tbsp of the oil in a large, heavy-bottomed pot. Cook the onions over medium heat for 5 minutes. Add the garlic and cook for another minute. Set aside.

3 Put the flour in a freezer bag with 1 tsp of the smoked paprika and salt and pepper. Toss the pork in it. Pour out into a sieve, shaking to remove excess flour.

4 Cook the pork in the remaining 1 tbsp of oil, in batches, for a couple of minutes on each side.

5 Return the onion mixture and stir in the remaining 1 tsp of smoked paprika, the oregano, and sugar. Mix in the stock and barbecue sauce and bring to a boil. Reduce to a gentle simmer and cook, covered, for 1 hour.

6 Add the beans, cover, and cook for 30 minutes. Uncover and cook for 30 minutes, adding water if needed, until the beans and pork are tender. Serve with baked potatoes.

Leftover pork chili

After a large pork roast or barbecue, you may have meat left over. Chop and freeze it ready for this easy supper.

15 mins   1 hr

SERVES 4

2 tbsp olive oil

1 onion, finely chopped

1 celery stalk, finely chopped

1 carrot, finely chopped

1 red bell pepper, cut into ½in (1cm) cubes

1 yellow bell pepper, cut into ½in (1cm) cubes

1 tsp smoked paprika

½ tsp cayenne pepper

½ tsp ground cumin

1 tsp dried oregano

1 x 14oz (400g) can chopped tomatoes

1¾ cups beef stock

salt and freshly ground black pepper

1lb 2oz (500g) cold roast pork or barbecued slow-cooked shoulder of pork (see p281), in ¾in (2cm) cubes

1 Heat the oil in a large, heavy-bottomed pot with a lid. Cook the vegetables over medium heat for 5 minutes, until they soften.

2 Add the spices and oregano and cook for another minute, until they release their fragrance. Add the tomatoes and stock and season to taste.

3 Bring to a boil, then reduce to a low simmer and cook, uncovered, for 30 minutes. Add the pork, cover, and cook for another 30 minutes until tender.

CALORIES: 356kcals/1493kJ

CARBOHYDRATE: 11g
  sugar: 10g

FAT: 13g
  saturated: 3.5g

SALT: 0.6g

FIBER: 4g

Spicy sausage casserole

Sausages are a great family standby, and this recipe is a welcome change from the standard grilled sausages.

15 mins   1 hr 15 mins

SERVES 4

4 tbsp olive oil

8 spicy sausages, such as chorizo-style or spicy Italian

2 onions, finely sliced

2 garlic cloves, crushed

1 x 14oz (400g) can chopped tomatoes

2 cups chicken stock (see p94)

1 tbsp honey

1 tbsp tomato paste

salt and freshly ground black pepper

handful of herb leaves, such as thyme, parsley, or oregano, chopped

1 Heat 2 tbsp of the oil in a large, deep-sided frying pan and cook the sausages over medium heat for 5–7 minutes, until browned all over. Remove from the pan and cool slightly before cutting into 1in (3cm) pieces.

2 Heat the remaining 2 tbsp of oil in the pan and cook the onions for 5 minutes, until softened but not browned. Add the garlic and cook for 1 minute. Add the tomatoes, stock, honey, and tomato paste, and season well. Cook, uncovered, for 45 minutes, until rich and thick. If the tomatoes have not broken up, mash briefly with a potato masher.

3 Return the sausages and cook for another 15 minutes before stirring in the chopped herbs.

CLEVER WITH LEFTOVERS

This dish is particularly good reheated and served over pasta. Chop the sausage pieces up smaller so that they reheat easily, and reheat over medium heat while the pasta cooks. If the sauce seems a little thick, let it down with some water or chicken stock (see p94).

CALORIES: 480kcals/1995kJ

CARBOHYDRATE: 14g
  sugar: 12.5g

FAT: 37g
  saturated: 12.5g

SALT: 2g

FIBER: 2g

Swedish sausage casserole

When the weather turns cold, you'll find this thick, winter stew is a simple, pleasing dish.

10 mins   35-45 mins

SERVES 4

2 tbsp light olive oil

2 tbsp unsalted butter

1 onion, roughly chopped

1 leek, white part only, trimmed and chopped

1½ tbsp all-purpose flour

3½ cups hot beef or chicken stock (see p94)

1lb 2oz (500g) waxy or semi-waxy potatoes, peeled and cut into 1in (3cm) chunks

9oz (250g) carrots, cut into ½in (1cm) rounds

8 good-quality pork sausages

1 bay leaf

1 bouquet garni

salt and freshly ground black pepper

1 In a heavy-bottomed saucepan, heat the oil and butter over medium heat. Add the onion and leek and cook gently for 5 minutes, until softened. Sprinkle over the flour and stir in. Cook for a couple of minutes, to brown the flour slightly.

2 Gradually stir in the stock and bring to a boil. It should thicken. Add the potatoes and carrots.

3 Prick the sausages with a fork and add them, making sure everything is submerged.

4 Add the bay leaf and bouquet garni, and season well. Cover and cook over low heat for 20–30 minutes, until the vegetables are soft and the sausages cooked through. The cooking time will depend on the type of potatoes. It is ready once the potatoes are cooked. Remove the bay leaf and bouquet garni, and serve.

The mild, soothing flavor of this warming dish may appeal to children. It works well, diced small, for toddlers too.

Fussy eaters!

CALORIES: 529kcals/2211kJ

CARBOHYDRATE: 37g
  sugar: 9g

FAT: 33g
  saturated: 12.5g

SALT: 2.9g

FIBER: 5.5g

Toad in the hole with onion gravy

This gravy is perfect with toad in the hole, but also with grilled chops, mashed potatoes, or your favorite sausages.

25 mins   40-45 mins

SPECIAL EQUIPMENT
10 x 12 x 2¾in (25 x 30 x 7cm)
roasting pan

SERVES 4

FOR THE TOAD IN THE HOLE
¾ cup all-purpose flour
salt and freshly ground black pepper
4 large eggs
1¼ cups whole milk
½ tsp dried sage
½ tsp spicy brown mustard
2 tbsp beef dripping or butter
8 pork and herb sausages

FOR THE ONION GRAVY
2 tbsp olive oil
3 red onions, finely sliced
2 tbsp all-purpose flour
1¼ cups vegetable stock (see p156)
splash of red wine (optional)

1 Preheat the oven to 400°F (200°C). Place the flour in a mixing bowl and season well. Break the eggs, 1 at a time, into the flour, and stir with a fork to incorporate. Gradually add the milk, whisking vigorously with a fork after each addition. Stir in the sage and mustard. Set aside.

2 Start the gravy. Heat the oil in a small, non-stick pan over medium heat. Add the onions and cook for 5 minutes. Reduce the heat, cover, and cook very gently for 30 minutes, stirring occasionally.

3 Meanwhile, put the dripping in a non-stick, heavy-bottomed roasting pan and heat for 5 minutes. Add the sausages and cook in the oven for 15 minutes. Space the sausages out evenly in the pan, then carefully pour the batter over the top. Return to the oven for 25–30 minutes, or until well-risen and golden brown.

4 Meanwhile, stir the flour into the onions and cook over medium heat for 2 minutes, stirring with a wooden spoon. Gradually pour in the stock, stirring constantly. Season to taste and add the wine (if using). Serve with slices of toad in the hole.

VARIATION

Make a vegetarian version, using vegetarian sausages, and oil instead of dripping. These sausages will not need pre-cooking, so add the sausages and batter to the hot fat at the same time.

PREPARE AHEAD

Make the batter up to 1 day in advance, cover, and refrigerate. Return to room temperature; follow the recipe from step 2.

CALORIES: 705kcals/2941kJ	
CARBOHYDRATE: 44g	
sugar: 9.5g	
FAT: 45g	
saturated: 15g	
SALT: 2.4g	
FIBER: 3g	

Sausage and butterbean goulash

This works best with German-style cooked or scalded sausages. Try cannellini beans instead of butterbeans.

10 mins · 35 mins

SERVES 4

2 tbsp olive oil

1 onion, finely chopped

1 red bell pepper, cut into ¾in (2cm) cubes

1 yellow bell pepper, cut into ¾in (2cm) cubes

2 garlic cloves, crushed

1 tbsp all-purpose flour

½ tsp cayenne pepper

½ tsp smoked paprika

1½ cups tomato sauce

1¼ cups chicken stock (see p94)

salt and freshly ground black pepper

14oz (400g) mixed German wurst, cut into ¾in (2cm) chunks

1 x 14oz (400g) can butterbeans, drained, and rinsed

2 tbsp chopped flat-leaf parsley leaves

2 tbsp sour cream

white rice or crusty bread, to serve

1 In a large, heavy-bottomed saucepan, heat the oil over low heat and gently cook the onion and peppers for 5 minutes until softened but not browned. Add the garlic and cook for another 2 minutes.

2 Add the flour, cayenne pepper, and smoked paprika and stir well. Add the tomato sauce and chicken stock to the pan and mix thoroughly. Season with salt and pepper if needed (the stock may be salty). Bring to a boil, reduce the heat, and simmer for 10 minutes.

3 Add the wurst and continue to simmer for 10 minutes. Add the butterbeans and gently simmer for a final 5 minutes. Stir in the parsley and serve with the sour cream swirled on top, or on the side, with white rice or crusty bread.

CALORIES: 464kcals/1935kJ
CARBOHYDRATE: 25g
    sugar: 7g
FAT: 29g
    saturated: 10g
SALT: 2.1g
FIBER: 7g

All-American meatloaf

A sterling family meal. Any leftovers can be pan-fried with a little oil for a quick dinner the following day.

20 mins · 1 hr

SPECIAL EQUIPMENT
food processor (optional)
9in x 5in (900g) loaf pan (optional)

SERVES 4

1 onion

1 celery stalk

1 carrot

2 tbsp olive oil, plus extra for greasing

1 garlic clove, crushed

½ cup fresh white bread crumbs

10oz (300g) ground beef

10oz (300g) ground pork

2 tbsp finely chopped parsley

½ tsp dried thyme, or 1 tbsp chopped thyme leaves

1 tsp Worcestershire sauce

2 tbsp ketchup

salt and freshly ground black pepper

1 Preheat the oven to 350°F (180°C). If you have a food processor, roughly chop the onion, celery, and carrot, then process until very finely chopped. If not, chop as finely as you can.

2 Heat the oil in a saucepan and cook the chopped vegetables over low heat for 5 minutes, until they darken slightly. Add the garlic and cook for 1 minute.

3 Next, mix the vegetables, bread crumbs, and remaining ingredients until well mixed, but not compacted.

4 Either line a shallow-sided baking sheet with waxed paper and shape the meat into an oval loaf with your hands, or lightly pack it into an oiled 9in x 5in (900g) loaf pan. Rub oil on top and bake in the middle of the oven for 45 minutes (1 hour if in a pan). Rest for 10 minutes, then slice with a sharp, serrated knife and serve with tomato sauce or creamy gravy.

CALORIES: 429kcals/1788kJ
CARBOHYDRATE: 13g
    sugar: 4g
FAT: 28g
    saturated: 9g
SALT: 0.8g
FIBER: 1g

HOW TO FREEZE

Freeze either whole, securely wrapped first in plastic wrap and then in foil, or in individually wrapped slices.

Moussaka

Good moussaka may take a while to prepare but the time taken to get the sauces right is well worth it.

1 hr   2 hrs 25mins

SPECIAL EQUIPMENT
8 x 8in (20 x 20cm) deep-sided
ovenproof dish

SERVES 4

FOR THE MEAT SAUCE
2 tbsp olive oil
1 onion, finely chopped
2 garlic cloves, finely chopped
1lb (450g) ground lamb
1 x 14oz (400g) can chopped tomatoes
1 cup beef, lamb, or chicken stock
(see p94)
¼ cup red wine (optional)
2 tbsp finely chopped parsley leaves
½ tsp dried thyme
½ tsp dried oregano
½ tsp ground cinnamon
salt and freshly ground black pepper

12oz (350g) waxy potatoes,
peeled weight
1 large eggplant, cut lengthwise
into ½in (1cm) thick slices
4 tbsp olive oil

FOR THE BÉCHAMEL SAUCE
4 tbsp butter
¼ cup all-purpose flour
1¾ cups whole milk
pinch of grated nutmeg
scant 1oz (25g) grated Parmesan
cheese
2 large eggs, beaten

1 To make the meat sauce,
heat the oil in a large, heavy-
bottomed saucepan. Cook the
onion over medium heat until it
softens, but does not color, then
add the garlic and cook for 1 minute.
Increase the heat and add the lamb.
Cook, using a wooden spoon to
break up the meat, until it browns.
Add the tomatoes, stock, wine

(if using), herbs, and cinnamon, and
season. Bring to a boil, reduce to a
simmer, and cook over low heat for
1–1¼ hours until all the liquid has
evaporated.

2 Meanwhile, boil the potatoes,
whole, in salted water, until
just cooked through. Drain, slice
lengthwise, and set aside. Preheat
the broiler to its highest setting.
Spread the eggplant on a baking
sheet, brush with 2 tbsp of the oil,
and broil until brown. Turn, brush
with the remaining 2 tbsp of oil,
and broil the other side. Set aside.

3 Preheat the oven to 350°F
(180°C). To make the béchamel
sauce, melt the butter in a small
pan over medium heat. Whisk in
the flour and cook for 2 minutes,
then take off the heat and gradually
whisk in the milk. Return to the
heat and cook, stirring, until it
thickens. Add the nutmeg, salt
and pepper, and the Parmesan

cheese, and cook over low heat for
10 minutes. Whisk in the beaten
eggs off the heat.

4 Spread half the meat into an
8 x 8in (20 x 20cm) ovenproof
dish. Cover it with half the eggplant,
then half the béchamel. Arrange
the potatoes in an overlapping
layer, then add the rest of the meat,
eggplant, and finally béchamel.
Bake for 1 hour until golden brown.
Rest for 10 minutes before serving.

CALORIES: 772kcals/3216kJ

CARBOHYDRATE: 35g
sugar: 10g

FAT: 51.5g
saturated: 20g

SALT: 1g

FIBER: 5g

Shepherd's pie

Every family should have a good recipe for this, and here is a simple, tasty version that will please everyone.

30 mins | 2 hrs

SPECIAL EQUIPMENT

8 x 8in (20 x 20cm) deep-sided ovenproof dish

SERVES 4

3 tbsp olive oil

1 onion, finely chopped

1 celery stalk, finely chopped

2 carrots, finely chopped

2 garlic cloves, crushed

1lb 2oz (500g) ground lamb

1 heaping tbsp all-purpose flour

1¾ cups chicken stock (see p94)

1 tbsp tomato paste

1 tsp Worcestershire sauce

1 bouquet garni

salt and freshly ground black pepper

1lb 9oz (700g) floury potatoes, peeled weight, cut into large chunks

2 tbsp butter

2 tbsp whole milk

1 Heat 2 tbsp of the oil in a large Dutch oven or heavy-bottomed saucepan and cook the onion, celery, and carrots for 5 minutes, until softened, but not browned. Add the garlic and cook for another minute, then set aside.

2 Heat the remaining oil in the pan and cook the lamb, using a wooden spoon to break up the meat, until it has browned all over.

Stir in the flour. Add the stock, tomato paste, Worcestershire sauce, and bouquet garni, and season to taste. Return the vegetables and bring to a boil. Reduce the heat to a simmer and cook, uncovered, for 1½ hours until the liquid has almost completely evaporated. Remove the bouquet garni.

3 Meanwhile, boil the potatoes in a saucepan of salted water for 20–25 minutes, depending on the variety, until tender when pierced with the tip of a knife. Drain well. Return to the pan, add the butter and milk, and mash well. They should be quite stiff, so start with the butter, then add the milk, a little at a time. Season to taste, cover, and keep warm until the meat is cooked.

4 Preheat the oven to 400°F (200°C). Put the lamb into an 8 x 8in (20 x 20cm) ovenproof dish, top with the potato, fork it over, and cook at the top of the oven for 30 minutes until golden.

VARIATION

Traditionally, this was made with chunks of cold roast lamb. Use the same amount of meat but only ¾ cup of chicken stock and cook for 30 minutes.

CALORIES: 577kcals/2407kJ

CARBOHYDRATE: 37g
  sugar: 7g

FAT: 32g
  saturated: 13g

SALT: 0.8g

FIBER: 5.5g

Cottage pie with sweet potato crust

Very similar in method to Shepherd's pie (see p151), this is a sweeter version really popular with children.

30 mins   2 hrs

SPECIAL EQUIPMENT
8in (20cm) square, deep-sided ovenproof dish

SERVES 4

3 tbsp olive oil

1 onion, finely chopped

1 celery stalk, finely chopped

2 carrots, finely chopped

2 garlic cloves, crushed

1lb 2oz (500g) ground beef

1 x 14oz (400g) can chopped tomatoes

1 cup beef stock

1 tbsp tomato paste

1 tsp Worcestershire sauce

1 bouquet garni

salt and freshly ground black pepper

1lb 9oz (700g) sweet potatoes, peeled weight, cut into large chunks

2 tbsp butter

CALORIES: 623kcals/2605kJ
CARBOHYDRATE: 44g
  sugar: 18g
FAT: 35.5g
  saturated: 14g
SALT: 0.9g
FIBER: 9g

1 Heat 2 tbsp of the oil in a large Dutch oven or heavy-bottomed saucepan and cook the onion, celery, and carrots for 5 minutes, until softened, but not browned. Add the garlic and cook for another minute. Set aside.

2 Heat the remaining oil in the pan and cook the beef, breaking it up with a wooden spoon, until it has browned all over. Add the tomatoes, stock, tomato paste, Worcestershire sauce, and bouquet garni, and season. Return the vegetables to the pan and bring to a boil.

3 Reduce the heat to a simmer and cook, uncovered, for 1–1¼ hours until the sauce has almost completely evaporated. Remove the bouquet garni. Preheat the oven to 400°F (200°C).

4 Meanwhile, boil the sweet potatoes for 10–15 minutes, then drain. Return to the pan, add the butter and mash. Season, cover, and keep warm.

5 Put the beef into an 8in (20cm) square, deep-sided ovenproof dish, top with the sweet potato, and cook at the top of the oven for 30 minutes, until golden brown.

Steak and wild mushroom pie

This steak pie is both comforting and extravagant. Use soaked, dried wild mushrooms if you prefer.

55 mins, plus chilling   3 hrs

SPECIAL EQUIPMENT
2-quart (2-liter) baking dish

SERVES 4–6

FOR THE FILLING

salt and freshly ground black pepper

3 tbsp all-purpose flour

2¼lb (1kg) sirloin steak, cut into 1in (2.5cm) cubes

1lb 2oz (500g) wild mushrooms, sliced

4 shallots, finely chopped

3 cups beef stock

handful of parsley leaves, chopped

FOR THE PIE DOUGH

2 cups all-purpose flour, plus extra for dusting

½ tsp fine salt

12 tbsp unsalted butter, cut into cubes

1 large egg, lightly beaten, to glaze

CALORIES: 1007kcals/4235kJ
CARBOHYDRATE: 54g
  sugar: 2.5g
FAT: 53g
  saturated: 28g
SALT: 1.5g
FIBER: 5g

1 Preheat the oven to 350°F (180°C). Season the flour and toss the steak in it to coat. Put the meat, mushrooms, and shallots in a Dutch oven. Add the stock and bring to a boil, stirring. Cover and cook in the oven for 2–2¼ hours until tender.

2 For the pie dough, sift the flour and salt into a bowl. Rub in a third of the butter. Add water to form a dough. Chill for 15 minutes. Roll out to a rectangle on a lightly floured surface. Dot the rest of the butter over two-thirds. Fold the unbuttered third over half the buttered side. Fold again so the butter is enclosed in layers of dough. Turn it over and press the edges to seal. Wrap in plastic wrap and chill for 15 minutes.

3 Roll out and fold as before, make a quarter turn, and seal. Chill for 15 minutes. Repeat 3 more times, chilling between each. Add the parsley to the meat. Spoon it into a 2-quart (2-liter) baking dish.

4 Increase the heat to 425°F (220°C). Roll out the dough and cut a strip from the edge. Dampen the rim of the dish and press on the strip. Put the rolled-out dough over the pie and seal. Brush with egg. Make a hole in the top. Chill for 15 minutes, then bake for 25–35 minutes.

Lamb, rosemary, and potato pie

This is the perfect use for leftover roast lamb, making a great Monday night dinner dish.

20 mins | 50 mins, plus resting

SPECIAL EQUIPMENT

7in (18cm) round pie dish

SERVES 4

1lb (450g) potatoes, peeled and quartered

salt and freshly ground black pepper

1 tbsp olive oil

1 onion, finely chopped

handful of rosemary sprigs, leaves picked and chopped

12oz (350g) leftover roast lamb, roughly shredded or sliced

1 tbsp all-purpose flour, plus extra for dusting

1¼ cups hot vegetable stock (see p156)

2-3 tsp mint sauce

9oz (250g) store-bought pie dough

1 large egg, lightly beaten

CALORIES: 690kcals/2885kJ
CARBOHYDRATE: 53g
  sugar: 2.5g
FAT: 39g
  saturated: 14g
SALT: 0.9g
FIBER: 4g

1 Preheat the oven to 400°F (200°C). Cook the potatoes in boiling salted water for about 15 minutes, until soft; drain and set aside. Heat the olive oil in a large pan over low heat. Add the onion and cook gently for 5 minutes until soft. Stir in the rosemary and add the lamb. Season well.

2 Stir in the flour, then pour in the stock. Stir for 10 minutes over medium heat until the liquid begins to thicken, then gently stir in the potatoes with the mint sauce. Simmer for another 10 minutes. Allow to cool slightly.

3 Divide the dough into 2 pieces, one a little larger than the other. Roll out the larger piece into a large circle on a floured work surface. Use to line a 7in (18cm) pie dish, letting the dough hang over the edges. Roll out the other piece to make the lid for the pie.

4 Spoon the lamb mixture into the bottom crust, then sit the other dough round on top. Using your finger and thumb, pinch together the edges of the dough to seal. Trim away the excess. Brush evenly with beaten egg, and bake for 40–50 minutes until the dough is cooked and golden. Let rest in the dish for at least 15 minutes before cutting into slices to serve.

Sausage and tomato tart

Sausage meat makes the basis of the filling for this delicious tart, guaranteed to please the whole family.

15 mins | 40 mins, plus cooling

SPECIAL EQUIPMENT

8in (20cm) square pie dish or fluted tart pan

ceramic baking beans

SERVES 4

8oz (225g) store-bought pie dough

all-purpose flour, for dusting

1 large egg, lightly beaten

½ tbsp olive oil

1 onion, finely chopped

14oz (400g) good-quality pork sausages, casing removed

salt and freshly ground black pepper

1 tsp dried oregano

4 tomatoes, sliced

CALORIES: 557kcals/2323kJ
CARBOHYDRATE: 35g
  sugar: 6g
FAT: 38g
  saturated: 13g
SALT: 2.5g
FIBER: 3g

1 Preheat the oven to 400°F (200°C). Roll out the dough on a floured work surface and use to line an 8in (20cm) square pie dish. Trim away excess, line the pie dough with waxed paper, and fill with baking beans. Bake in the oven for 15–20 minutes until the edges are golden. Remove the beans and paper, brush the crust with a little beaten egg, and return to the oven for 2 minutes to crisp. Set aside. Reduce the oven temperature to 350°F (180°C).

2 Meanwhile, heat the oil in a large frying pan over low heat. Add the onion and cook gently for about 5 minutes until soft. Add the sausage, breaking it up with a fork or the back of a spatula. Season well, and add the oregano. Cook, stirring, over medium-low heat for 10 minutes, until brown. Let cool, then mix in the remaining egg.

3 Spoon the sausage mixture into the crust, then layer the tomatoes over the top. Bake in the oven for about 20 minutes until lightly golden. Let for about 10 minutes, then slice in the dish or pan.

Meals for a Week

Most families these days have busy schedules, and working parents in particular benefit from a little planning ahead. It makes sense to try and cook the basis for two or three meals when you have time, maybe on the weekends, so that you have something nutritious and homemade on hand for when you don't. Some items, such as sauces and stocks can be made in batches and frozen in advance, and then defrosted as needed. A good shopping list is helpful here, as is some freezer space. Planning meals for a week will include some days when the kids need to eat separately—the family meals and dishes will need to be stretched over different mealtimes. Although it's much more efficient to try and vary one meal to suit everyone, there are times when you can take advantage of having to eat separately from your kids, so that you can cook something a little more exotic.

Family timetable

Working with your family's timetable and shopping and cooking accordingly can save you time and money, as well as reducing waste. In order to plan ahead you'll need to know what you have in the kitchen—do a weekly check of your pantry essentials before you go shopping to ensure that you aren't missing a vital ingredient when you do have the time to cook.

One meal for all

You can triple your cooking workload if cooking different meals for everyone. Make simple, healthy dishes and encourage everybody to eat the same.

Make it stretch

As part of your planning, transform one day's meal into another day's leftovers meal. For example, the roast chicken cooked for Sunday lunch can become a chicken pilaf (p229) for Tuesday's dinner.

Your plan

Keep it simple! Don't overcomplicate your weekly plan. Write down the dinners for the week and plan your weekly trip to the store, ensuring your family eats a healthy and enjoyable variety.

Sunday —
Roast chicken
(p294)

Monday —
Fish pie
(p86)

Tuesday —
Chicken pilaf
(p229)

Wednesday —
Quick paella
(p223)

Sunday

Tuesday

Thursday –
Pasta with
peas and
pancetta
(p205)

Thursday

Friday –
Chili con
carne (p143)

Saturday –
Sausage and
sweet potato
(p302)

Saturday

A healthy variety

When planning, bear in mind not just the need for meals, but different tastes as well. Try different ingredients, but remember to keep the nutrition of the meals balanced for the whole family. Ensure that you aim for everyone to achieve their five a day; sufficient protein for growth; calcium for bones; and the essential vitamins and minerals we all need.

Fish is a good source of protein, along with meat, eggs, and pulses. Aim for at least two portions of fish a week, including one portion of oily fish such as salmon or mackerel, and not too much processed meat (for example, sausages, ham, and salami).

Check out the nutritional details on the recipes in this book and see pages 10–11 for more information on a balanced diet.

Keep it simple

Don't worry if you find planning the meals for the entire week tricky at first. Aiming for the whole family to sit down together at the weekend is a good first step to creating a weekly routine.

Vegetable stock

This simple stock is the basis for hundreds of delicious soups, stews, and sauces.

5 mins   55 mins

MAKES 2 CUPS

1 tbsp olive oil

1 onion, roughly chopped

2 carrots, roughly chopped

1 celery stalk, roughly chopped (include any leaves)

1 leek, roughly chopped

¼ tsp black peppercorns

1 bay leaf

small handful of parsley

1 Heat the oil in a large, heavy-bottomed saucepan. Add the vegetables and cook them over low heat, stirring occasionally, for 10 minutes, until they soften and start to color at the edges.

2 Add 3½ cups of cold water, the peppercorns, and herbs, and bring to a boil. Reduce to a low simmer and cook for 45 minutes, or until the stock has reduced by half and tastes rich and flavorful.

Strain the stock through a sieve before using or cooling and freezing.

VARIATION

You can try adding some mushroom trimmings to give more depth to the stock.

COOK'S TIP

This stock is salt free, so is suitable for babies and young children. Salt can be added after it has reduced, if necessary. Never salt stock before cooking, as it will concentrate during the cooking process.

HOW TO FREEZE

Freezing the stock in icecube trays, then transferring them to a freezer bag, means that a few cubes at a time can be added to dishes for extra flavor.

CALORIES: 99kcals/407kJ

CARBOHYDRATE: trace
  sugar: trace

FAT: 11g
  saturated: 1.5g

SALT: trace

FIBER: 0g

Butternut squash soup

Make this rich, velvety soup more sophisticated with a garnish of sage leaves, quickly fried in light oil.

5 mins   20 mins

SPECIAL EQUIPMENT

blender or hand-held blender

SERVES 4–6

3 tbsp olive oil

1 onion, chopped

1 leek, white part only, chopped

1 celery stalk, chopped

1lb 2oz (500g) butternut squash, peeled and cut into 1in (3cm) cubes

2½ cups vegetable or chicken stock (see left or p94)

½ tbsp chopped sage leaves

salt and freshly ground black pepper

1 Heat the oil in a large, heavy-bottomed saucepan with a lid. Add the onion, leek, and celery and cook for 5 minutes until they soften, but do not brown.

2 Add the squash, stock, and sage, and season well.

3 Bring to a boil, then reduce to a gentle simmer, cover, and cook for 15 minutes until the squash is tender.

4 Blend the soup, either in a blender or using a hand-held blender, until completely smooth. Check the seasoning and serve.

VARIATION

This soup can also be made with sweet potato or pumpkin, although the cooking times for those vegetables will be slightly less; try cooking for just 10 minutes in step 3.

CALORIES: 175–117kcals/734–490kJ

CARBOHYDRATE: 12–8g
  sugar: 7–5g

FAT: 8.5–6g
  saturated: 1–0.8g

SALT: 0.6–0.4g

FIBER: 4–3g

Harvest vegetable soup

Also known as "bottom of the fridge soup," this is a great way to use up odds and ends of vegetables.

10 mins   30 mins

SPECIAL EQUIPMENT
blender or hand-held blender

SERVES 4–6

3 tbsp olive oil

1 onion, chopped

1 leek, white part only, chopped

1 celery stalk, chopped

1lb 2oz (500g) mixed root vegetables, peeled weight, such as carrots, potatoes, parsnips, and turnips, cut into even-sized cubes

2½–3½ cups vegetable or chicken stock (see left or p94)

salt and freshly ground black pepper

1 Heat the oil in a large, heavy-bottomed saucepan with a lid. Add the onion, leek, and celery and cook for 5 minutes until they soften, but do not brown.

2 Add the mixed root vegetables and 2½ cups of the stock and season well.

3 Bring to a boil, then reduce the heat to a gentle simmer. Cover and cook for 20 minutes, until the vegetables are soft.

4 Blend the soup, either in a blender or using a hand-held blender, until it is completely smooth. Add more stock if you want a thinner soup. Check the seasoning and add a swirl of cream to serve.

CALORIES: 186–124kcals/778–519kJ

CARBOHYDRATE: 14–10g
sugar: 7–4.5g

FAT: 9–6g
saturated: 1–0.8g

SALT: 0.6–0.4g

FIBER: 4.5–3g

Minted split pea and tomato soup

This soup is full of goodness, warm, and nutritious, as well as being very delicious.

10 mins   1 hr

SPECIAL EQUIPMENT
blender or hand-held blender

SERVES 6

2 tbsp olive oil

1 large onion, finely chopped

2 garlic cloves, crushed

1 x 14oz (400g) can chopped tomatoes

3½ cups vegetable stock (see left)

9oz (250g) dried split peas

2 tsp dried mint

salt and freshly ground black pepper

1 Heat the oil in a large, heavy-bottomed saucepan with a lid. Cook the onion for 5 minutes over medium heat, until it has softened, but not browned. Add the garlic and cook for another minute.

2 Add the rest of the ingredients, season well, and bring to a boil. Reduce the heat to a low simmer and cook for up to 1 hour, stirring occasionally, or until the peas have softened. Keep an eye on it: start checking after 30 minutes, as different batches of split peas cook at varying rates.

3 Blend the soup, either in a blender or using a hand-held blender. You can process until completely smooth, or leave it a little chunky if you prefer.

VARIATION

If you eat meat, try using a good-quality beef stock instead of vegetable stock for a really rich taste.

CALORIES: 229kcals/954kJ

CARBOHYDRATE: 26g
sugar: 4g

FAT: 5g
saturated: 0.7g

SALT: 0.6g

FIBER: 4.5g

French onion soup

Deep-flavored and savory, this recipe creates a soup elegant enough to serve to friends.

20 mins   50 mins

SERVES 6

4 tbsp butter

1 tbsp olive oil

2lb 4oz (1kg) white onions, finely sliced

2 garlic cloves, crushed

salt and freshly ground black pepper

2 heaping tbsp all-purpose flour

⅔ cup white wine

7 cups beef stock

a few sprigs of thyme

12 slices of baguette, each ¾in (2cm) thick

5½oz (150g) grated Gruyère cheese

CALORIES: 502kcals/2103kJ
CARBOHYDRATE: 47.5g
sugar: 11g
FAT: 18g
saturated: 10g
SALT: 2.3g
FIBER: 5g

1 Heat the butter and oil in a large, heavy-bottomed pan. Add the onions and cook over medium-low heat for about 30 minutes, until dark golden brown and well softened. Add the garlic, season well, and stir in the flour for a minute or two.

2 Gradually stir in the wine and stock, add the thyme, and cook over very low heat, uncovered, for 40 minutes, until the onions are meltingly tender and the soup reduced. Remove the thyme.

3 Preheat the broiler. Broil the baguette slices on both sides. Divide the Gruyère cheese between the slices, then melt it under the broiler. Float 2 slices of cheesy toast on each warmed bowl of soup to serve.

Potato salad with celery and capers

A straightforward potato salad can easily be livened up with these tangy, fresh flavors.

10 mins   20-25 mins

SERVES 4-6

2lb 4oz (1kg) waxy potatoes, peeled

salt and freshly ground black pepper

¼ cup good-quality mayonnaise

2 tsp Dijon mustard

1 celery stalk, finely chopped

bunch of scallions, white part only, finely chopped

1 tbsp capers, drained or rinsed, and finely chopped

1 tbsp lemon juice

1 Cook the potatoes whole in a large pan of boiling salted water for 20–25 minutes until tender. Drain and set aside to cool. When cold, cut the potatoes carefully into 1in (3cm) cubes.

2 Mix the mayonnaise, mustard, celery, scallions, capers, and lemon juice, and season well.

3 Gently toss through the diced potatoes, being careful not to break them up.

VARIATION

Chopped hard-boiled egg, or canned tuna, can also be added to this versatile salad for added protein.

CALORIES: 303–202kcals/1272–848kJ
CARBOHYDRATE: 42–28g
sugar: 3.5–2.5g
FAT: 12–8g
saturated: 2–1g
SALT: 0.7–0.5g
FIBER: 5–3.5g

Mixed leaf salad with balsamic dressing

This slightly sweet version of a standard salad dressing is popular with adults and children alike.

5 mins

SERVES 4

5½oz (150g) mixed salad leaves

FOR THE DRESSING

2 tbsp extra virgin olive oil

1 tbsp balsamic vinegar

½ tsp honey

1 tsp Dijon mustard

salt and freshly ground black pepper

1 Make the dressing by whisking all the ingredients together in a salad bowl until the mixture emulsifies.

2 Gently toss through the salad leaves to serve.

PREPARE AHEAD

Try doubling or tripling the quantities of salad dressing and seal the leftovers in a jam jar. It will store in the fridge for up to a week, and is great on steamed green vegetables and new potatoes as well as on salad.

CALORIES: 64kcals/263kJ
CARBOHYDRATE: 2.5g
  sugar: 2.5g
FAT: 6g
  saturated: 0.8g
SALT: trace
FIBER: 0.5g

Warm new potato salad with caramelized red onions

With its sweet onions and sharp dressing, this salad is perfect with barbecued beef brisket (see p282).

10 mins   15 mins

SERVES 4–6

2lb 4oz (1kg) small new potatoes, halved lengthwise

salt and freshly ground black pepper

2 tbsp olive oil

2 red onions, finely sliced

2 tbsp balsamic vinegar

1 tsp light brown sugar

FOR THE DRESSING

¼ cup extra virgin olive oil, plus extra if needed

2 tbsp red wine vinegar

2 tsp Dijon mustard

1 tsp granulated sugar

1 Cook the potatoes in plenty of boiling salted water until just tender, 10–15 minutes depending on their size. Drain well.

2 Meanwhile, heat the oil in a large, deep-sided frying pan. Cook the onions over low heat for about 10 minutes until they soften, then add the vinegar and sugar and cook for another 10 minutes until dark and glossy. Season well.

3 Whisk together the dressing ingredients in a salad bowl and season well. While the potatoes are still warm, but not too hot, toss them through the dressing. Add the red onions and serve. (If you are not serving immediately you may need a little extra oil, as the potatoes often absorb all the dressing once cool.)

CALORIES: 364–243kcals/1524–1016kJ
CARBOHYDRATE: 45–30g
  sugar: 10–7g
FAT: 17.5–12g
  saturated: 2.5–2g
SALT: 0.3–0.2g
FIBER: 4–3g

New potato, sweet potato, and tarragon salad

Delicious served with herby barbecued chicken and a green salad for a summer lunch.

10 mins   10-15 mins

SERVES 4–6

1lb 2oz (500g) small new potatoes, halved lengthwise

salt and freshly ground black pepper

1lb 2oz (500g) sweet potatoes, peeled and cut into similar-sized pieces as the new potatoes

FOR THE DRESSING

¼ cup extra virgin olive oil

3 tbsp balsamic vinegar

2 tsp Dijon mustard

2 tbsp finely chopped tarragon leaves

1 Cook the new potatoes in plenty of boiling salted water for about 12 minutes, until tender. Cook the sweet potatoes in another pan of simmering water for about 8 minutes, until tender. Do not cook them in the same pan, as the sweet potatoes are delicate and need less cooking time. Drain both well, separately.

2 In a salad bowl, whisk together all the dressing ingredients and season well. Mix through the warm new potatoes to coat. Gently mix in the sweet potatoes with your hands, making sure they do not break up. Serve warm or cold.

CALORIES: 312kcals/1314kJ

CARBOHYDRATE: 46g
  sugar: 11g

FAT: 12g
  saturated: 2g

SALT: 0.4g

FIBER: 6g

Classic coleslaw

Infinitely superior to store-bought coleslaw, this makes a great topping for baked potatoes, with grated cheese.

5 mins

SERVES 6

¼ cup good-quality mayonnaise

½ tbsp white wine vinegar

1 tsp granulated sugar

salt and freshly ground black pepper

¼ white cabbage, approx. 9oz (250g), shredded

2 large carrots, shredded

½ sweet white onion, very finely sliced

1 Mix together the mayonnaise, vinegar, and sugar until well combined. Season well.

2 Mix the shredded and sliced vegetables into the mayonnaise well, until every strand is coated in the seasoned mayonnaise.

CALORIES: 105kcals/435kJ

CARBOHYDRATE: 7g
  sugar: 7g

FAT: 8g
  saturated: 1g

SALT: 0.15g

FIBER: 3g

Spicy Asian slaw

This is fantastic served as a barbecue accompaniment, or as part of a summer buffet.

20 mins

SERVES 4

FOR THE COLESLAW

¼ red cabbage, approx. 9oz (250g), shredded

2 large carrots, shredded

½ red onion, finely sliced

1 tbsp finely chopped cilantro leaves

1 tbsp finely chopped mint leaves

FOR THE DRESSING

3 tbsp white wine vinegar or rice wine vinegar

3 tbsp light olive oil

1 tsp light brown sugar

½ tsp salt

pinch of chile flakes

1 In a large bowl, whisk together all the ingredients for the dressing until the sugar dissolves.

2 Toss through the shredded and sliced vegetables and herbs, keeping a few herbs back to scatter over the top before serving.

PREPARE AHEAD

Prepare the vegetables and store them in freezer bags in the fridge for up to 2 days. Spicy Asian slaw dressing will keep in a jar in the fridge for up to 1 week. At the last minute, simply toss the vegetables and dressing together with the just-chopped herbs.

CALORIES: 116kcals/482kJ

CARBOHYDRATE: 8g
  sugar: 7g

FAT: 8.5g
  saturated: 1g

SALT: 0.6g

FIBER: 4g

Carrot and beet salad

This richly colored salad is packed with beneficial antioxidants. Young, fresh vegetables are ideal for this.

30 mins   3–4 mins

SERVES 4–6

1lb 5oz (600g) carrots, scrubbed

bunch of beets, approx. 1lb 5oz (600g), peeled and halved

small bunch of flat-leaf parsley, leaves picked and chopped, or 1 bunch of cress, snipped

FOR THE VINAIGRETTE

6 tbsp extra virgin olive oil, plus 1 tsp for toasting the seeds

¼ cup balsamic vinegar

1 garlic clove, crushed (optional)

1¾oz (50g) sunflower or pumpkin seeds

1 tsp soy sauce (optional)

salt and freshly ground black pepper

1 Coarsely grate the raw vegetables and combine in a large bowl.

2 For the vinaigrette, whisk the oil, vinegar, and garlic (if using), together until emulsified.

3 Gently heat the remaining 1 tsp of oil in a small frying pan and toast the seeds for 3–4 minutes over medium heat, stirring frequently. Add the soy sauce at the end of cooking (if using). Most of the soy sauce will evaporate, leaving a salty taste and extra browning for the seeds.

4 Add the parsley or cress to the carrot and beets. Shake the vinaigrette again, pour over the vegetables, then season to taste. Toss the salad gently, scatter the toasted seeds over, and serve.

PREPARE AHEAD

The vegetables, vinaigrette, and seeds can be prepared and stored separately in the fridge for up to 24 hours. Return to room temperature and combine before serving.

CALORIES: 350kcals/1453kJ

CARBOHYDRATE: 27g
  sugar: 24g

FAT: 24g
  saturated: 3.5g

SALT: 0.6g

FIBER: 10g

Roasted beet, goat cheese, and walnut salad

Roasted beets have a fabulously rich, earthy flavor, and are great served warm with tangy goat cheese.

10 mins   40 mins

SERVES 4

6 small raw beets, peeled
  and quartered

2 tbsp olive oil

2½oz (75g) walnut halves

5½oz (150g) mixed salad leaves

3½oz (100g) crumbly goat cheese

FOR THE DRESSING

¼ cup extra virgin olive oil

2 tbsp cider vinegar

1 tsp Dijon mustard

1 tsp honey

salt and freshly ground black pepper

1 Preheat the oven to 400°F (200°C). Coat the beets in the oil and spread out on a large baking sheet. Bake at the top of the oven for 30–40 minutes, turning occasionally, until tender and browning slightly at the edges. Let cool.

2 Meanwhile, toast the walnuts in a dry frying pan over medium heat until they start to brown slightly at the edges, but do not burn. Take them off the heat, cool, then roughly chop.

3 In a large salad bowl, whisk together all the ingredients for the dressing until it has emulsified. Season to taste.

4 When the beets have cooled, toss the salad leaves through the dressing. Gently mix in the beets and walnuts and crumble the goat cheese over the top to serve.

CALORIES: 399kcals/1650kJ
CARBOHYDRATE: 8g
  sugar: 8g
FAT: 36g
  saturated: 8g
SALT: 0.6g
FIBER: 3g

Oven-roasted tomato bruschetta

This is a great dish to serve when tomatoes are at their peak. Use several different varieties, if possible.

10 mins   20 mins

SERVES 4

2lb 4oz (1kg) mixed ripe tomatoes,
  such as cherry, plum, yellow,
  or heirloom

6 tbsp olive oil

salt and freshly ground black pepper

8 slices ciabatta bread, each
  ¾in (2cm) thick

1 garlic clove, halved horizontally

handful of basil leaves, roughly torn

1 tbsp good-quality balsamic vinegar

1 Preheat the oven to 425°F (220°C). Cut the tomatoes in half, or quarter if large, and spread them out over 1 or 2 baking sheets in a single layer. Drizzle them with 4 tbsp of the oil, and season well. Turn carefully with your hands, to coat in the oil and seasoning, making sure that they are all lying cut-side up. Cook in the middle of the oven for 20–25 minutes until they start to soften, but still hold their shape.

2 Meanwhile, brush the ciabatta slices on both sides with the remaining 2 tbsp of oil and spread them out in a single layer on a baking sheet. Cook them at the top of the oven for 5–7 minutes on each side, until they start to brown and are crispy on both sides. Watch them carefully—they should be golden, not dark brown or scorched. Remove them from the oven and rub them on 1 side with the cut sides of the garlic.

3 Put the warm tomatoes in a bowl and gently toss in the basil and vinegar. Distribute the tomatoes evenly on the garlic-rubbed sides of the ciabatta and serve while still warm.

VARIATION

Add feta or goat cheese, crumbled on top, for a light lunch, and serve with a crisp green salad.

CALORIES: 365kcals/1530kJ
CARBOHYDRATE: 38g
  sugar: 10g
FAT: 20g
  saturated: 3g
SALT: 0.9g
FIBER: 5.5g

Zucchini fritters

To offset wateriness, salt larger zucchini as in the recipe. Smaller zucchini won't need salting.

20 mins, plus draining

10 mins

MAKES 12

7oz (200g) zucchini, coarsely grated

salt and freshly ground black pepper

3½oz (100g) ricotta cheese

1 large egg

2 tbsp all-purpose flour

3 garlic cloves, crushed

small handful of basil leaves, chopped

small handful of flat-leaf parsley leaves, chopped

light olive oil, to fry

FOR THE TZATZIKI

2 tbsp finely chopped dill fronds

7oz (200g) Greek-style yogurt

juice of ½ lemon

1 Sprinkle the zucchini with 1 tsp salt and leave to drain in a sieve over the sink for 1 hour. Water will leach out of the zucchini, leaving them firmer. Rinse and squeeze dry in a clean kitchen towel.

2 In a bowl, whisk together the ricotta cheese, egg, and flour. Add 2 of the crushed garlic cloves, the basil, and parsley, and season well. Mix in the zucchini.

3 Fill a frying pan with oil to a depth of ½in (1cm) and fry tablespoons of the zucchini batter over medium heat for 2–3 minutes on each side, until golden brown. Drain on paper towels.

4 To make the tzatziki, mix ½ of the last clove of garlic with the dill, salt and pepper, and yogurt. Add a squeeze of lemon juice, season to taste. Serve with the hot fritters.

Children may be much more willing to try some "unusual" vegetables, such as zucchini, when they are disguised in tasty fried morsels like these.

Fussy eaters!

CALORIES: 71kcals/293kJ
CARBOHYDRATE: 3g
 sugar: 1g
FAT: 5g
 saturated: 2g
SALT: trace
FIBER: 0.3g

Pea pancakes

A simple dish to prepare, the bright peas and asparagus contrast beautifully with the golden yolk of the egg.

10 mins

30 mins

SPECIAL EQUIPMENT
food processor

SERVES 4 (MAKES 8)

14oz (400g) fresh peas, shelled weight, or frozen peas, defrosted

large handful of mint leaves, finely chopped

4 tbsp melted butter, plus extra for frying

¼ cup all-purpose flour

¼ cup heavy cream

2 tbsp finely grated Parmesan cheese

6 large eggs

salt and freshly ground black pepper

large bunch of asparagus spears, woody ends removed

1 tsp extra virgin olive oill

CALORIES: 539kcals/2238kJ
CARBOHYDRATE: 23g
 sugar: 4.5g
FAT: 38g
 saturated: 19g
SALT: 0.8g
FIBER: 9g

1 Put the fresh peas in a pan and blanch in boiling water for 1–2 minutes, then drain and let cool. Frozen peas will not need this step.

2 Put the peas and mint into a food processor and pulse to a rough texture. Add the butter, flour, cream, Parmesan, and 2 of the eggs, and season. Process once more to form a stiff paste.

3 Heat a little butter in a large frying pan and add a couple of tablespoonfuls of the mixture for each pancake. Cook over medium heat and use the back of a spoon to smooth the top. After 3–4 minutes, the edges will change color and show a brownish tinge. Carefully turn them over and cook for another couple of minutes.

4 Meanwhile, bring a large pan of water to a boil and lightly poach the remaining 4 eggs until just set. Remove them with a slotted spoon.

5 As the eggs are cooking, grill the asparagus in a hot grill pan with the extra virgin olive oil, seasoning while cooking, until golden. Serve on warmed plates with the pancakes, carefully placing a poached egg on each serving.

Glazed carrots with nutmeg

A favorite accompaniment to roast chicken, the nutmeg and sugar make these carrots extra special.

5 mins   10 mins

SERVES 4

10oz (300g) thin, young carrots, peeled weight, cut into ½in (1cm) rounds

salt and freshly ground black pepper

1 tbsp butter

½ tsp granulated sugar

pinch of nutmeg

CALORIES: 56kcals/233kJ
CARBOHYDRATE: 6g
 sugar: 6g
FAT: 3.5g
 saturated: 2g
SALT: 0.1g
FIBER: 2.5g

1 Cook the carrots in plenty of boiling salted water for about 7 minutes until they are really soft. Drain well.

2 Put the butter in the pan in which you cooked the carrots and allow it to melt over a low heat. Stir in the sugar and nutmeg and cook gently until the sugar dissolves. Return the carrots, season well, and turn them in the butter until well glazed.

PREPARE AHEAD

If you have a large meal to prepare, cook the carrots to the end of step 1 ahead of time, cover, and refrigerate for up to 3 days. Reheat them in the melted butter glaze, following step 2, for 2–3 minutes until hot throughout.

Creamed spinach

This is the perfect recipe to introduce children to this healthy and nutritious green leaf.

5 mins   10 mins

SERVES 4

1 tbsp butter

1 tbsp olive oil

1 small garlic clove, crushed

14oz (400g) baby spinach leaves

½ cup heavy cream

salt and freshly ground black pepper

We all know how healthy spinach is, yet its strong taste will often put children off. Try this creamy treatment of the iron-rich vegetable alongside chicken or fish for more hard-to-please palates.

Fussy eaters!

1 Melt the butter and oil in a large, deep-sided frying pan. Cook the garlic for 1 minute, then add the baby spinach. Turn it through the oil and sauté it for 2–3 minutes, until cooked through.

2 Add the cream, season well, bring to a boil, and reduce before serving.

CALORIES: 202kcals/830kJ
CARBOHYDRATE: 2g
 sugar: 2g
FAT: 20g
 saturated: 11g
SALT: 0.4g
FIBER: 3g

Zucchini with garlic and mint

Zucchini, when eaten small, are sweet and juicy. The secret to cooking them well is in this recipe.

5 mins   5 mins

SPECIAL EQUIPMENT
large Dutch oven (optional)

SERVES 4

2 tbsp olive oil

1 tbsp butter

10oz (300g) small zucchini, sliced into ½in (1cm) rounds

1 garlic clove, crushed

1 tbsp finely chopped mint

salt and freshly ground black pepper

1 Melt the oil and butter in a large Dutch oven or heavy-bottomed saucepan with a lid, ideally one that will fit the zucchini in a single layer.

2 Add the zucchini and stir them around so that as many as possible are touching the bottom of the pan. Cover and cook over medium-high heat for 3 minutes.

3 Remove the lid, stir in the garlic and mint, and season well. Cover again and cook for another 2 minutes, shaking occasionally, until the zucchini are just cooked and golden brown in places.

CALORIES: 91kcals/373kJ

CARBOHYDRATE: 1.5g
 sugar: 1g

FAT: 9g
 saturated: 3g

SALT: trace

FIBER: 1g

Slow-cooked red cabbage

A really warming winter dish, this goes equally well with game or sausages.

10 mins   2 hrs

SPECIAL EQUIPMENT
large Dutch oven

SERVES 4–6

4 tbsp butter

2 tbsp granulated sugar

1 tsp salt

6 tbsp white wine vinegar

1 red cabbage, approx. 2lb 4oz (1kg), shredded

2 tbsp redcurrant or sour cherry jelly

2 apples, peeled and grated

salt and freshly ground black pepper

1 Preheat the oven to 325°F (160°C). Heat the butter, sugar, salt, vinegar, and 6 tbsp of water in a large Dutch oven. Bring to a boil, then reduce to a simmer and cook for just 2 minutes.

2 Add the red cabbage and stir it through. Seal the pan with a thick piece of foil, then put on the lid.

3 Cook in the center of the oven for 1½ hours. Remove the lid and stir in the jelly and apples, adding a little more water if the cabbage looks dry. Season generously, cover, and return to the oven for a final 30 minutes before serving.

CALORIES: 228–152kcals/958–639kJ

CARBOHYDRATE: 28–18g
 sugar: 28–18g

FAT: 11–7.5g
 saturated: 6.5–4.5g

SALT: 1.5–1g

FIBER: 10.5–7g

BATCHING AND FREEZING

This is one of the few vegetable dishes that freeze well. If you have a large red cabbage, just weigh it and increase the other ingredients accordingly. Cook it all and freeze leftovers for another meal.

Savoy cabbage with onions and garlic

This delicious cabbage is the perfect accompaniment to mashed potato and a warming winter stew.

5 mins   20 mins

SPECIAL EQUIPMENT
large Dutch oven (optional)

SERVES 4

2 tbsp olive oil

1 tbsp butter

1 onion, finely sliced

1 garlic clove, crushed

14oz (400g) Savoy cabbage, shredded

salt and freshly ground black pepper

CALORIES: 237kcals/998kJ
CARBOHYDRATE: 40g
  sugar: 1.5g
FAT: 6g
  saturated: 0.8g
SALT: trace
FIBER: 4.5g

---

1 Heat the oil and butter in a large Dutch oven or heavy-bottomed saucepan with a lid. Add the onion, cover, and cook over medium heat, stirring frequently, for 10 minutes, until it is well softened, but not brown. Add the garlic and cook for another minute.

2 Add the cabbage, seasoning, and ¼ cup of water. The water will practically sizzle away. Mix it all together and cover. Cook over low heat for 10 minutes, stirring occasionally, until the cabbage is cooked through.

VARIATION

For an Eastern European version, try adding ½ tsp of aromatic caraway seeds to the pan with the garlic. This version is delicious with pork, ham, or sausages.

Stir-fried green vegetables

Serve alongside many Chinese dishes, such as Chinese braised beef with ginger and soy sauce (see p133).

5 mins   5 mins

SERVES 4

salt

3½oz (100g) thin green beans

3½oz (100g) broccoli spears, or small florets

1 tbsp sesame oil or sunflower oil

3½oz (100g) sugarsnap peas, halved diagonally

bunch of scallions, cut into 1in (3cm) lengths

2 tbsp oyster sauce

1 tbsp soy sauce

1 tbsp rice wine or dry sherry

CALORIES: 66kcals/278kJ
CARBOHYDRATE: 5.5g
  sugar: 4g
FAT: 3g
  saturated: 0.5g
SALT: 1.5g
FIBER: 2.5g

---

1 In a large pan of boiling salted water, blanch the beans for 1 minute. Add the broccoli and blanch for another minute. Drain and refresh in cold water, then drain once more and set aside.

2 Heat the oil in a wok and stir-fry the sugarsnaps for 1 minute. Add the scallions and cook for another minute. With the wok off the heat, add the oyster sauce, soy sauce, and rice wine. Be careful, it will sizzle.

3 Return the wok to the heat and heat the sauce until it bubbles. Toss in the blanched vegetables and heat for another minute until they are warmed through and the sauce is reduced.

Perfect mashed potatoes

Mashed potatoes may seem easy to make but try this for a really creamy mash.

10 mins   20-30 mins

SERVES 4–6

2lb 4oz (1kg) floury potatoes, such as Russets, peeled and cut into large chunks

salt and freshly ground black pepper

¼ cup whole milk or half-and-half

2 tbsp butter

pinch of granulated sugar

1 Bring the potatoes to a boil in a large pan of cold salted water. Reduce the heat to a brisk simmer and cook, uncovered, for 20–25 minutes until soft, but not breaking up. Drain well in a colander.

2 Heat the milk and butter over low heat until the butter melts and the milk is hot, but not boiling. Add the sugar and season well. Return the potatoes to the pan and mash them well with a masher, or for a perfectly smooth result press them through a potato ricer.

3 Finally, use a wooden spoon to beat the potatoes really well. This helps make them super-smooth and fluffy.

CLEVER WITH LEFTOVERS

If you have leftover mashed potato, add any of the following in any combination for some different flavors: a handful of chopped spring onions, a handful of chopped flat-leaf parsley, 1 tbsp rinsed and chopped capers, finely grated zest of ½ lemon, and a pinch of chile flakes.

CALORIES: 255–170kcals/1074–716kJ

CARBOHYDRATE: 41–28g
  sugar: 2.5–1.7g

FAT: 7–5g
  saturated: 4–3g

SALT: 0.17–0.1g

FIBER: 4–3g

Mashed carrots and rutabaga

An accompaniment that works well with meat dishes, this is a good way to encourage kids to try rutabaga.

10 mins   20 mins

SERVES 4

10oz (300g) carrots, cut into small pieces

7oz (200g) rutabaga, cut into small pieces

salt and freshly ground black pepper

2 tbsp butter

1 tsp light brown sugar (optional)

pinch of grated nutmeg

1 Boil the vegetables together in a large pan of boiling salted water for about 20 minutes, or until soft. Drain well and return them to the pan.

2 Add the remaining ingredients and mash the vegetables well before serving.

CALORIES: 89kcals/371kJ

CARBOHYDRATE: 9g
  sugar: 9g

FAT: 5.5g
  saturated: 3.5g

SALT: 0.16g

FIBER: 4g

Rutabaga on its own has a strong taste. Yet mashed with a little butter, sugar, and some sweet carrots, it becomes a delicious, child-friendly dish.

Fussy eaters!

Green beans with toasted almonds

Liven up humble green beans with this simple twist that uses flaked almonds.

5 mins 5 mins

SERVES 4

10oz (300g) thin green beans

salt and freshly ground black pepper

2 tbsp sliced almonds

1 tbsp butter

1 Cook the green beans in plenty of boiling salted water for 3–5 minutes, or until they are tender. Drain well.

2 Meanwhile, dry-fry the almonds for a couple of minutes in a large frying pan over medium heat, turning constantly, until they begin to color, but not burn.

3 When the beans are ready, melt the butter in the pan with the almonds and toss the beans through. Season well with salt and pepper to serve.

COOK'S TIP

The same trick in this recipe can be used to liven up all types of green vegetable dishes. Simply adding a few toasted sliced almonds—or even hazelnuts—will add taste and texture.

CALORIES: 92kcals/380kJ
CARBOHYDRATE: 3g
  sugar: 2g
FAT: 7.5g
  saturated: 2.5g
SALT: trace
FIBER: 2g

Best roast potatoes

Completely indispensable with a Sunday roast; the best roast potatoes are cooked in goose fat.

10 mins 1 hr 10 mins

SERVES 4

2lb 4oz (1kg) white potatoes, such as Russet, peeled and halved

sea salt

3 heaping tbsp goose or duck fat

1 Preheat the oven to 400°F (200°C). Bring the potatoes to a boil in a large pan of salted water. Reduce the heat to a brisk simmer and cook, uncovered, for 10 minutes, until softening at the edges. Drain, return to the pan, and place over low heat for a minute to remove excess water, then remove from the heat, cover, and shake to rough up the edges.

2 Meanwhile, put the fat in a roasting pan big enough to take the potatoes in a single layer. Heat in the oven for 5 minutes.

3 Carefully remove the pan from the oven and add the potatoes. Turn to coat in fat, spread out, and sprinkle generously with salt. Roast for 45 minutes to 1 hour, turning them after they form a crust underneath.

CALORIES: 300kcals/1254kJ
CARBOHYDRATE: 40g
  sugar: 1.5g
FAT: 13g
  saturated: 8g
SALT: 0.3g
FIBER: 4.5g

Roast potatoes with rosemary and garlic

The Italians have a wonderful way of cooking potatoes in a large pan, but it is tricky. This is an easy version.

10 mins   40-45 mins

SERVES 4

2lb 4oz (1kg) waxy potatoes, peeled weight, cut into 2in (5cm) cubes

2 tbsp olive oil

2 garlic cloves, crushed

2 tbsp finely chopped rosemary

salt and freshly ground black pepper

CALORIES: 237kcals/998kJ

CARBOHYDRATE: 40g
    sugar: 1.5g

FAT: 6g
    saturated: 0.8g

SALT: trace

FIBER: 4.5g

1 Preheat the oven to 400°F (200°C). Toss all the ingredients together and spread them out in a single layer in a large roasting pan.

2 Cook for 40–50 minutes, turning occasionally, until golden brown and crispy at the edges.

FEEDING A CROWD

These simple Italian-style roast potatoes are an ideal dish for larger numbers. Just dice up as many potatoes as you need, and cook them on several baking sheets in the oven, switching the pans around during cooking so they all get to spend time at the top of the oven.

Boulangère potatoes

Try these for a healthy alternative to the more indulgent Gratin dauphinoise (see p170).

20 mins   1 hr 10 mins

SPECIAL EQUIPMENT

food processor (optional)

8 x 8in (20 x 20cm) deep-sided ovenproof dish

SERVES 4–6

2 tbsp butter, plus extra for greasing

1 tbsp olive oil

1 onion, finely sliced

1 garlic clove, crushed

2lb (900g) waxy, or yellow, potatoes, such as large Yukon Golds

salt and freshly ground black pepper

1¼ cups vegetable stock (see p156)

CALORIES: 284–190kcals/1191–794kJ

CARBOHYDRATE: 38–25.4g
    sugar: 3–1.8g

FAT: 10.5–7g
    saturated: 5–3.5g

SALT: 0.4–0.3g

FIBER: 4.5–3g

1 Preheat the oven to 350°F (180°C). Melt half the butter and the oil in a frying pan and cook the onion over medium heat for 5–7 minutes until softened, but not brown. Add the garlic and cook for another minute.

2 Finely slice the potatoes, using a food processor with a slicing attachment or a mandolin.

3 Rub an 8 x 8in (20 x 20cm) deep-sided ovenproof dish with the remaining butter. Spread in half the potatoes. Arrange the onions and garlic over the top, season well, and cover with the remaining potatoes. When you get to the top layer, arrange the potatoes nicely. Pour in the stock and dot with the remaining butter.

4 Put the ovenproof dish on a large baking sheet and cook in the center of the oven for 1 hour, or until the potatoes are soft and the top golden brown. Rest for 10 minutes before serving.

Cajun-spiced potato wedges

The spicy coating to these potato wedges works well with steak or just with a soured cream dip.

10 mins   40–50 mins

SERVES 6

4 potatoes, unpeeled and scrubbed

salt and freshly ground black pepper

1 lemon, cut into 6 wedges

12 garlic cloves

3 red onions, each cut into 8 wedges

4 bay leaves

3 tbsp lemon juice

1 tbsp tomato paste

1 tsp paprika

½ tsp cayenne pepper

1 tsp dried oregano

1 tsp dried thyme

½ tsp ground cumin

6 tbsp olive oil

1 Preheat the oven to 400°F (200°C). Cut the potatoes into thick wedges. Cook in a large pan of boiling salted water for 3 minutes, drain well, and place in a large roasting pan with the lemon, garlic, onions, and bay leaves.

2 Whisk together the remaining ingredients with 6 tbsp of water and pour evenly over the potatoes. Toss well to coat.

3 Roast for 30–40 minutes, or until the potatoes are tender and the liquid has been absorbed. Gently and frequently turn the potatoes during cooking, using a spatula. Serve hot.

CALORIES: 329kcals/1374kJ
CARBOHYDRATE: 38g
  sugar: 6g
FAT: 17g
  saturated: 2.5g
SALT: trace
FIBER: 5g

Gratin dauphinoise

Rich, creamy, and heady with garlic, this is a wonderful treat and the perfect side dish to any lamb recipe.

20 mins   1 hr

SPECIAL EQUIPMENT
food processor (optional)

8 x 8in (20 x 20cm) deep-sided ovenproof dish

SERVES 4–6

2lb 4oz (1kg) waxy, or yellow, potatoes, such as large Yukon Golds

1 tbsp butter, softened

2 garlic cloves, chopped

salt and freshly ground black pepper

1¾ cups half-and-half

1 Preheat the oven to 350°F (180°C). Finely slice the potatoes in a food processor with a slicing attachment, or a mandolin.

2 Rub an 8 x 8in (20 x 20cm) deep-sided ovenproof dish with some butter. Spread in half the potatoes. Sprinkle with the garlic, season, and arrange the remaining potatoes nicely on top.

3 Pour in the cream. You should just be able to see the cream coming up around the edges. Dot the top with the remaining butter.

4 Put the dish on a large baking sheet and cook in the center of the oven for 1 hour until the potatoes are soft, the cream has evaporated, and the top is golden. Rest for 10 minutes before serving.

PREPARE AHEAD
For an impressive side dish, make the potatoes the day before. When cold, use a ring to cut out individual servings and reheat to serve.

CALORIES: 408–272kcals/1708–1138kJ
CARBOHYDRATE: 42–28g
  sugar: 3.5–2.5g
FAT: 33–15g
  saturated: 14–9.5g
SALT: 0.2–0.1g
FIBER: 4–3g

Herby roasted roots

Most root vegetables become sweeter when roasted and can be a delicious alternative to simple roast potatoes.

10 mins · 45–55 mins

SERVES 4

2lb 4oz (1kg) mixed root vegetables, such as waxy potatoes, carrots, parsnips, or butternut squash, cut into large wedges

1 large red onion, cut into wedges

3 tbsp olive oil

handful of mixed herb leaves, such as parsley, sage, and thyme, finely chopped

salt and freshly ground black pepper

1 Preheat the oven to 400°F (200°C). Mix all the vegetables, the oil, and herbs, and season well.

2 Arrange in a single layer in a large roasting pan and roast at the top of the oven for 45–55 minutes, turning occasionally, until browned at the edges and cooked through.

CALORIES: 223kcals/936kJ
CARBOHYDRATE: 31g
    sugar: 13.5g
FAT: 9.5g
    saturated: 1.5g
SALT: trace
FIBER: 9g

Roasting vegetables brings out their natural sweetness. Children who are not fond of vegetables may enjoy them roasted.

Fussy eaters!

Potato rosti

These fabulous potato pancakes always feel like a treat. Make 4 individual-sized rosti if you prefer.

10 mins · 30 mins

SPECIAL EQUIPMENT
8–8½in (20–22cm) frying pan

SERVES 4

14oz (400g) waxy potatoes, such as Yukon Golds, peeled

salt and freshly ground black pepper

1 tbsp butter

1 tbsp olive oil

1 Bring the whole, peeled potatoes to a boil in a large pan of salted water. Reduce to a simmer and cook for 7–10 minutes, depending on size, until part-cooked but still firm. Leave to cool, then grate coarsely and toss with salt and pepper.

2 Melt the butter and oil in an 8–8½in (20–22cm) frying pan. Put the potato in the pan and squash it down with a spatula to make a large, flat pancake. Cook over medium heat for 5–7 minutes, until crispy underneath.

3 To turn, slide the potato pancake onto a large plate. Put another plate on top and flip the whole thing over, so the cooked side is on top. Slide back into the pan and cook for another 5–7 minutes until crispy underneath. Cut into wedges to serve.

VARIATION

These can be made with raw, grated potato, but the potato must be squeezed dry in a clean kitchen towel first, and the rosti will need to be cooked slowly for 35–40 minutes.

CALORIES: 128kcals/534kJ
CARBOHYDRATE: 16g
    sugar: 0.6g
FAT: 6g
    saturated: 2.5g
SALT: trace
FIBER: 2g

Baked shallots with cream and Parmesan

These are delicious served alongside a simple roast chicken, or with roast beef, ham, or pork.

10 mins   30–35 mins

SERVES 4

butter, for greasing

16 large shallots, peeled and left whole

1¼ cups heavy cream

1¾oz (50g) finely grated Parmesan cheese

freshly ground black pepper

¼ cup fresh bread crumbs

CALORIES: 390kcals/1611kJ

CARBOHYDRATE: 10g
  sugar: 5g

FAT: 35g
  saturated: 22g

SALT: 0.5g

FIBER: 2g

1 Preheat the oven to 350°C (180°C). Butter a small ovenproof dish, big enough to hold the shallots in a single, tight layer.

2 Put the shallots in a small pan of simmering water and cook them gently for 10 minutes. Drain well. Lay the shallots in the ovenproof dish.

3 In a bowl, stir together the cream and three-quarters of the Parmesan. Season with pepper and pour the cream over the shallots.

4 In a small bowl, toss together the bread crumbs, the remaining Parmesan, and plenty of pepper. Scatter it over the shallots.

5 Bake for 20–25 minutes, or until the shallots are soft and the top is golden brown and crispy.

Creamy cauliflower cheese

A classic cold weather dish, this needs nothing more than a baked potato to turn it into a main meal.

20 mins   15–20 mins

SPECIAL EQUIPMENT

10in (25cm) ovenproof dish

SERVES 4

1 cauliflower, cut into florets

4 tbsp butter

¼ cup all-purpose flour

2 cups whole milk

3½oz (100g) grated aged Cheddar cheese

salt and freshly ground black pepper

1 tbsp Dijon mustard (optional)

CALORIES: 408–272kcals/1694–1129kJ

CARBOHYDRATE: 21–14g
  sugar: 11.5–7.5g

FAT: 27–18g
  saturated: 16–11g

SALT: 1.1–0.7g

FIBER: 5–3.5g

1 Steam the cauliflower for about 7 minutes until it is tender, but still firm, then drain and arrange it in a 10in (25cm) ovenproof dish, with the stems underneath and the florets fitting together. Preheat the oven to 350°F (180°C).

2 Meanwhile, melt the butter in a small, heavy-bottomed saucepan. Whisk in the flour over low heat and cook for 2 minutes, whisking. Take off the heat and slowly whisk in the milk until smooth.

3 Return to the heat and cook, stirring constantly right into the edges of the saucepan, for 5 minutes. Add 2½oz (75g) of the cheese, the seasoning, and mustard (if using), and cook for 2 minutes until the cheese has melted and the sauce is creamy.

4 Pour the sauce over the cauliflower, scatter with the remaining cheese, and bake at the top of the oven for 15–20 minutes, or until golden brown all over.

VARIATION

Mix ¼ cup of bread crumbs with the cheese for the topping, if desired, for more crunch.

Broccoli gratin

For a change from plain-old steamed broccoli, try this warming gratin instead.

15 mins   40 mins

SERVES 4

1lb (450g) broccoli florets

4 tbsp butter

¼ cup all-purpose flour

2 cups whole milk

2¼oz (70g) grated Gruyère cheese

salt and freshly ground black pepper

⅓ cup fresh bread crumbs

1oz (30g) toasted pine nuts

finely grated zest of 1 lemon

1¾oz (50g) grated mozzarella cheese

chunks of baguette, to serve

CALORIES: 429kcals/1785kJ
CARBOHYDRATE: 22g
 sugar: 7.5g
FAT: 29.5g
 saturated: 15g
SALT: 0.9g
FIBER: 5g

1 Preheat the oven to 350°F (180°C). Put the broccoli in a steamer, largest florets at the bottom. Place over boiling water and steam for 5 minutes, or until just tender when pierced with the tip of a sharp knife. Drain well.

2 Meanwhile, melt the butter in a saucepan. Stir in the flour and cook for 2–3 minutes over medium heat, stirring. Gradually stir in the milk to make a smooth white sauce.

3 Add the Gruyère cheese and stir to melt, then season. Stir in the broccoli, then pour into a gratin dish.

4 Mix together the bread crumbs, pine nuts, lemon zest, and mozzarella, and season. Sprinkle over the broccoli. Bake for 20 minutes. Serve with baguette.

VARIATION

Try blue cheeses such as Dolcelatte or Stilton instead of Gruyère for a more piquant taste. The gratin is great with baked ham at Christmas time.

Quick creamy vegetable gratin

This is very simple to prepare if you have a food processor with a julienne attachment.

15 mins   1 hr

SPECIAL EQUIPMENT

food processor (optional)

8 x 8in (20 x 20cm) deep-sided ovenproof dish

SERVES 4–6

1lb 5oz (600g) mixed root vegetables, such as parsnips, potatoes, and carrots

1 onion, halved

salt and freshly ground black pepper

2 cups heavy cream

1¾oz (50g) grated Parmesan cheese

CALORIES: 571–380kcals/2361–1574kJ
CARBOHYDRATE: 21–14g
 sugar: 9–6g
FAT: 50–33g
 saturated: 31–21g
SALT: 0.3–0.2g
FIBER: 6–4g

1 Preheat the oven to 350°F (180°C). Julienne all the vegetables, including the onion, on your food processor. Alternatively, finely slice the onion and coarsely grate the remaining vegetables.

2 Pile the vegetables into a clean kitchen towel and wring them dry, squeezing hard, to extract as much excess moisture as you can.

3 Put them in a large bowl and toss with salt and pepper. Add the cream and Parmesan cheese and mix well, until everything is evenly amalgamated together.

4 Pack the vegetables into an 8 x 8in (20 x 20cm) ovenproof dish. Bake in the center of the oven for 1 hour, until the cream has evaporated and the top is crispy and golden brown. Rest for at least 5 minutes before serving.

PREPARE AHEAD

This crowd-pleasing side dish can be assembled in seconds if you shred the vegetables ahead of time. Keep them in sealed freezer bags in the fridge for up to 2 days until you are ready to cover them in the cream mixture and bake.

Classic ratatouille

If you have the time to make it, and summer-fresh ingredients, nothing beats this deep-flavored Provençal feast.

30 mins   50 mins, plus resting

SERVES 4

5 tbsp olive oil

1 large red bell pepper, cut into ½in (1cm) slices

2 small zucchini, cut into ½in (1cm) slices

1 white onion, halved and cut into ½in (1cm) slices

2 large ripe tomatoes, cut into wedges

1 large eggplant, cut into ½in (1cm) slices

2 large garlic cloves, finely chopped

2 tbsp finely chopped flat-leaf parsley

salt and freshly ground black pepper

1 Heat 1 tbsp of the oil in a large, heavy-bottomed frying pan. Cook the pepper for 2–3 minutes over medium heat until browned in places. Set aside.

2 Return the pan to the heat and add another 1 tbsp of the oil. Cook the zucchini for 1–2 minutes on each side until lightly browned at the edges. Set aside separately.

3 Add another 1 tbsp of the oil to the pan and cook the onion for 2–3 minutes until softened, but not browned. Add the tomatoes and cook for another 1–2 minutes until they start to break down. Set aside separately. Wipe the frying pan clean with a piece of paper towel.

4 Add the remaining 2 tbsp of the oil to the pan. When it is hot, add the eggplant slices in a single layer and cook for 3–4 minutes until browned. Turn and cook for another 1–2 minutes. Depending on the size of the frying pan, you may need to do this in batches.

5 With the pan off the heat, spread the eggplant slices out in a single layer on the bottom of the pan and top with a layer of zucchini, then a layer of peppers. Scatter with the garlic and parsley, and season well.

6 Add the tomato and onion mixture, and use a dinner plate to press down on the vegetables.

7 Cook over low heat for 30 minutes, until the vegetables are soft and have given off liquid. Turn gently with a spatula and cook, uncovered, for 10 minutes over high heat, until the liquid nearly evaporates. Let rest for at least 10 minutes before serving.

CALORIES: 186kcals/773kJ

CARBOHYDRATE: 10g
  sugar: 10g

FAT: 15g
  saturated: 2g

SALT: trace

FIBER: 5g

Oven-roasted ratatouille

A classic ratatouille (see left) is a time-consuming dish to prepare. Here's a simple baked variation for busier days.

10 mins | 1 hr

SERVES 4

1 eggplant, cut into 1in (3cm) cubes

1 red bell pepper, cut into 1in (2.5cm) cubes

1 yellow bell pepper, cut into 1in (2.5cm) cubes

1 red onion, cut into 1in (2.5cm) cubes

1 zucchini, cut into 1in (2.5cm) cubes

3 garlic cloves, roughly chopped

6 tbsp olive oil

salt and freshly ground black pepper

1 small pint of cherry tomatoes

2 tbsp roughly chopped flat-leaf parsley leaves

1 tbsp thyme leaves

1 Preheat the oven to 400°F (200°C). In a bowl, mix together the eggplant, peppers, red onion, zucchini, and garlic. Toss them in 4 tbsp of the oil and season well.

2 Spread them out into a single layer in 1 large or 2 smaller roasting pans. Drizzle with the remaining 2 tbsp of oil and bake for 40 minutes, until the vegetables are starting to turn brown at the edges. If you are using 2 oven shelves, switch the roasting pans over after 20 minutes, so that they both have a chance to cook near the top of the oven.

3 Take the vegetables out of the oven and scatter the cherry tomatoes and herbs over the top. Gently mix them in, arranging the vegetables so that most of the tomatoes are on top, and cook for another 20 minutes until the tomatoes are starting to burst and the vegetables are cooked through. Serve with crusty bread.

CLEVER WITH LEFTOVERS

Bake double or triple quantities of this and use the leftovers to make Roasted vegetable lasagna (see p207), for a near-effortless second meal.

CALORIES: 155kcals/641kJ

CARBOHYDRATE: 10g
  sugar: 9g

FAT: 12g
  saturated: 2g

SALT: trace

FIBER: 4.5g

Butternut squash tagine

Most squashes ripen as the summer draws to a close. This spicy tagine uses the best of the early-autumn produce.

20 mins · 1 hr

SERVES 4

¼ cup olive oil

2 red onions, finely chopped

1 large red bell pepper, cut into cubes

4 garlic cloves, chopped

2in (5cm) piece of fresh ginger, finely chopped

1 tsp chili powder

1 tsp ground cinnamon

2 tsp smoked paprika

2 tsp ground coriander

1 tbsp ground cumin

2 x 14oz (400g) cans chopped tomatoes

2 cups vegetable stock (see p156)

2 tbsp honey

salt and freshly ground black pepper

14oz (400g) butternut squash, cut into cubes

1 x 7oz (200g) can chickpeas

3½oz (100g) dried apricots, chopped

bunch of cilantro leaves, chopped

herby couscous, to serve

1 Pour the oil into a large pan. Add the onions, red bell pepper, garlic, and ginger, and cook over low heat, stirring, for 2 minutes until they are just beginning to soften, but not brown.

2 Add the chili powder, cinnamon, smoked paprika, ground coriander, and ground cumin, and continue to cook for another 2 minutes over low heat to release all the flavors of the spices. Add the tomatoes, stock, and honey, stir to combine, and season well. Increase the heat to bring the sauce to a boil, then stir and reduce the heat once more. Simmer slowly, uncovered, for 30 minutes.

3 Add the butternut squash, chickpeas, and dried apricots and continue to cook for 10–15 minutes until the squash is just soft but the pieces are not falling apart. Add a little more water if it is beginning to look a little dry. Season to taste and stir in the cilantro leaves before serving. Serve the tagine with some herby couscous.

VARIATION

Canned chickpeas are used here for convenience, although dried chickpeas that have been soaked overnight, then simmered until soft according to the package instructions, give a more robust texture to the tagine.

CALORIES: 339kcals/1428kJ

CARBOHYDRATE: 44g
  sugar: 32g

FAT: 13.5g
  saturated: 2g

SALT: 0.6g

FIBER: 11g

Braised lentils

A healthy dish that works particularly well with sausages or pork, or as an alternative to many potato side dishes.

10 mins   50 mins

SERVES 4

10oz (300g) brown lentils, washed and drained

salt and freshly ground black pepper

2 tbsp olive oil

1 onion, finely chopped

1 large carrot, finely chopped

1 celery stalk, finely chopped

1 garlic clove, finely chopped

1 heaping tbsp all-purpose flour

2 cups vegetable stock (see p156)

1 Cook the lentils in a large pan of boiling salted water for 20–30 minutes (depending on the type of lentils), until cooked, but still firm. Drain and set aside.

2 Heat the oil in a large, heavy-bottomed saucepan. Cook the onion, carrot, and celery for 7–10 minutes until softened, but not browned. Add the garlic and cook for another minute.

3 Sprinkle in the flour, stir, and cook for another minute or two, before stirring in the stock.

4 Add the lentils and season well. Bring them to a boil, then reduce the heat to a gentle simmer and cook for 7–10 minutes until the lentils are soft and the braise has thickened slightly.

CALORIES: 171kcals/718kJ
CARBOHYDRATE: 19g
  sugar: 4.5g
FAT: 6.5g
  saturated: 1g
SALT: trace
FIBER: 6g

BATCHING AND FREEZING

This is not only tasty, it is also good for you. Prepare double or triple quantities and freeze it in family-sized portions.

Spring vegetable stew

Serve this with simple grilled chicken or fish. The stew brings a lovely garlic flavor of its own.

10 mins   5 mins

SERVES 4

salt and freshly ground black pepper

8–10 asparagus stalks, woody ends broken off, chopped into ¾in (2cm) lengths, tips and stalks kept separate

3½oz (100g) frozen petits pois

1 tbsp butter

1 tbsp olive oil

2 small zucchini, quartered lengthwise, cut into ½in (1cm) cubes

4 large scallions, white part only, cut into ½in (1cm) pieces

1 garlic clove, finely chopped

3-4 tbsp white wine

½ cup half-and-half

1 tbsp finely chopped mint leaves

1 In a large pan of boiling salted water, blanch the asparagus stalks together with the petits pois for 1 minute. Add the asparagus tips and cook for another 1 minute. Drain the vegetables and refresh immediately in a large bowl of cold water, then drain again.

2 In the same pan, melt the butter with the oil. Add the zucchini and scallions and cook for 2–3 minutes until they start to brown at the edges. Add the garlic and cook for another minute. Add the wine (it will bubble up and almost evaporate), then the cream, and season well.

3 Add the blanched vegetables to the pan and cook for another minute or two over high heat until the sauce has reduced and thickened. Stir in the mint to serve.

CALORIES: 163kcals/672kJ
CARBOHYDRATE: 6g
  sugar: 4g
FAT: 11.5g
  saturated: 5.5g
SALT: trace
FIBER: 4g

Sweet potato, red onion, and thyme galettes with chile

A store-bought butter-based puff pastry is a great time saver, all but indistinguishable from homemade pastry.

20 mins   50 mins

MAKES 6

FOR THE FILLING

2 sweet potatoes, approx. 10oz (300g) peeled weight, cut into ½in (1cm) cubes.

2 red onions, cut into ½in (1cm) cubes

1 tbsp olive oil

salt and freshly ground black pepper

½ red chile, seeded and finely chopped

1 tsp finely chopped thyme leaves

FOR THE PASTRY

12oz (375g) store-bought puff pastry

all-purpose flour, for dusting

1 egg yolk, beaten

1 Preheat the oven to 400°F (200°C). Toss the sweet potatoes and red onions in the oil in a large bowl and season well with salt and pepper. Turn the vegetables out onto a baking sheet and bake for 30 minutes until softened and golden at the edges.

2 Roll out the puff pastry on a lightly floured surface into a square about 12 x 16in (30 x 40cm)

and cut it into quarters. Lay the pastry rectangles on baking sheets. Brush them with the egg yolk.

3 Toss the cooked vegetables with the chile and thyme and divide equally between the pastries. Spread the vegetables out, leaving a ½in (1cm) clear border to each pastry.

4 Bake for 20 minutes, or until the pastry is puffed up and golden brown at the edges, and the bases are firm to the touch. The pastries are best eaten hot, but set aside to cool the most ferocious heat of the oven for 5 minutes before serving with a leafy green salad.

PREPARE AHEAD

The cooked galettes can be covered and stored in the fridge for up to 2 days. Warm through again just before serving.

CALORIES: 317kcals/1329kJ

CARBOHYDRATE: 34g
    sugar: 5g

FAT: 18g
    saturated: 8g

SALT: 0.6g

FIBER: 3.5g

Whole wheat spinach and potato pasties

Chill these pasties in the fridge before baking; this helps firm up the pastry and hold them together during cooking.

45 mins   30-35 mins

MAKES 4

FOR THE PASTRY

1 cup whole wheat flour

1 cup all-purpose flour, plus extra for dusting

11 tbsp butter, chilled and diced

½ tsp salt

1 egg, beaten, to glaze

FOR THE FILLING

10oz (300g) unpeeled waxy potatoes, such as Yukon Golds, cut into small chunks

8oz (225g) spinach

1 garlic clove, finely chopped

9oz (250g) ricotta cheese

2½oz (75g) finely grated Grana Padano cheese

grated nutmeg

salt and freshly ground black pepper

1 To make the pastry, rub the flours and butter together with your fingertips until the mixture resembles bread crumbs. Add the salt and about ¼ cup of cold water to form a soft dough. Wrap in plastic wrap and chill for 30 minutes.

2 For the filling, cook the potato in a small saucepan of boiling water for 10 minutes. Drain and set aside to cool. Place the spinach in a colander and pour boiling water over it from a teapot to wilt. Squeeze out the liquid and chop finely. Place in a large bowl with the garlic, cheeses, nutmeg, salt and pepper, and stir well. Set aside.

3 Preheat the oven to 375°F (190°C). Line 2 baking sheets with parchment paper. Mix the potato and spinach mixture.

4 On a well-floured surface, cut the dough into 4 equal pieces. Roll each piece into a circle 8in

(20cm) across and ¼in (5mm) thick. Using a plate about 8in (20cm) in diameter, cut out a circle from each rolled circle of dough.

5 Arrange one-quarter of the filling on half of each circle, leaving a ½in (1cm) border around the edge. Brush the edges with the beaten egg, then bring them together to seal, and crimp. Chill for 10 minutes.

6 Place the pasties on the prepared baking sheets and brush with the remaining beaten egg. Cut a slit in the top of each pasty and bake for 20–25 minutes. Serve the pasties either hot or cold.

For children, try using butternut squash or sweet potatoes in place of the potatoes for a sweeter taste to this healthy filling.

Fussy eaters!

CALORIES: 795kcals/3321kJ

CARBOHYDRATE: 69g
  sugar: 4g

FAT: 47g
  saturated: 28g

SALT: 1.8g

FIBER: 6.5g

Auvergne torte

This warming pie from France is an ideal lunch when it's cold outside; it's very comforting in the depths of winter.

30 mins,
plus chilling

1 hr 15 mins

SPECIAL EQUIPMENT
9in (23cm) deep-dish metal pie plate with sloping sides

SERVES 8

FOR THE FILLING
2 tbsp butter

1 large onion, finely sliced

1 garlic clove, finely chopped

3½oz (100g) chopped bacon

1lb 6oz (650g) waxy new potatoes, peeled and finely sliced

3½oz (100g) Cantal cheese, or Wensleydale or mild Cheddar, grated

1 tbsp finely chopped flat-leaf parsley

salt and freshly ground black pepper

¾ cup half-and-half

1 large egg yolk

FOR THE PASTRY
1lb 2oz (500g) store-bought puff pastry

all-purpose flour, for dusting

1 large egg yolk, beaten with 1 tbsp cold water, to glaze

1 Melt the butter in a large saucepan. Add the onion and cook over medium heat for 10 minutes. Add the garlic and bacon and cook for another 5 minutes until the onion is soft, but not brown.

2 Preheat the oven to 350°F (180°C). Roll out the puff pastry on a floured surface and, using a 9in (23cm) deep-dish metal pie plate as a template, cut from one end a circle large enough to top the pie. Use the rest of the pastry to line the plate, leaving a ½in (1cm) overhang around the edges. Wrap and chill the base and the top for 20 minutes.

3 Brush the inside of the pastry crust, including the edges, with some of the egg yolk mixture. Reserve the remainder.

4 Layer the pastry crust with one-third of the potatoes. Cover them with half the onion and bacon mixture and half the cheese. Scatter in half the parsley and season with salt and pepper.

5 Repeat the procedure and finish with a final layer of potatoes. Whisk together the half-and-half and the egg yolk, and pour it over the pie filling. Top the pie with the pre-cut circle of pastry, pressing it down around the edges to seal. Crimp the edges.

6 Brush the top of the pie with the remaining egg yolk mixture and cut 2 small slits in the top to allow steam to escape. Place the pie on a baking sheet and bake for

1 hour until well cooked, puffed up, and golden brown. Set aside to rest for 15–20 minutes before serving.

CLEVER WITH LEFTOVERS
This filling torte tastes great even when it's left to cool of, and is a wonderful addition to a picnic, or perfect for lunch on the go.

CALORIES: 476kcals/1990kJ

CARBOHYDRATE: 37g
  sugar: 3g

FAT: 31g
  saturated: 16g

SALT: 1.3g

FIBER: 3g

Eggplant Parmigiana

This dish needs nothing more than crusty bread and a crisp green salad to make a simple but delicious supper.

30 mins | 1 hr 45 mins, plus resting

SPECIAL EQUIPMENT
10in (25cm) ovenproof dish

SERVES 4–6

FOR THE TOMATO SAUCE
3 tbsp olive oil

1 onion, finely chopped

2 garlic cloves, crushed

1 x 14oz (400g) can chopped tomatoes

1 tbsp tomato paste

1 tsp granulated sugar

2 tbsp roughly chopped flat-leaf parsley leaves

salt and freshly ground black pepper

FOR THE REST
6–8 tbsp olive oil, plus extra for drizzling

2 eggplants, cut into ½in (1cm) thick slices

1 ball mozzarella, approx. 4½oz (125g), cut into ½in (1cm) slices

2 tbsp roughly chopped basil leaves

¾ cup fresh white bread crumbs

scant 1oz (25g) finely grated Parmesan cheese

crusty bread, to serve

1 Heat the oil for the tomato sauce in a heavy-bottomed saucepan and cook the onion over medium heat for 5 minutes. Add the garlic and cook for another minute.

2 Add the tomatoes, fill the empty can with water, and pour that in too. Stir in the tomato paste, sugar, and parsley, and season well. Bring to a boil, reduce the heat to a low simmer, and cook for 1 hour, until thickened.

3 Meanwhile, heat 2 tbsp of the oil for the rest in a frying pan and cook the eggplant for 2–3 minutes each side, in batches, until golden. You will need more oil as you go. Drain on paper towels. (You can cook these on a grill, brushing with oil. This uses less oil and gives a smoky flavor.) Preheat the oven to 350°F (180°C).

4 Spread half the eggplant in a 10in (25cm) ovenproof dish. Top with half the sauce, then all the mozzarella. Scatter with the basil, then top with the rest of the eggplant. Cover with the rest of the sauce.

5 Mix the bread crumbs and Parmesan and scatter over the top. Drizzle with oil and bake for 40–45 minutes until golden and crisp. Rest for 5 minutes, then serve with crusty bread.

BATCHING AND FREEZING
Make double or triple quantities of this sauce. It can be frozen (in meal-sized portions), used as a pasta sauce, or mixed with Traditional meatballs (see p127) for an easy spaghetti and meatballs supper.

CALORIES: 442–295kcals/1838–1226kJ

CARBOHYDRATE: 22–14.5g
sugar: 8–5g

FAT: 34–22.5g
saturated: 9–6g

SALT: 0.9–0.6g

FIBER: 5–3g

Zucchini stuffed with herby rice

This dish turns some leftover rice and a few zucchini into a tasty side dish with added crunch.

20 mins   15–20 mins

SERVES 4

4 zucchini, approx. 5½oz (150g) each

2 tbsp olive oil, plus extra for drizzling

1 onion, finely chopped

2 garlic cloves, crushed

2 tbsp butter

9oz (250g) cooked, cold white rice, preferably basmati

large handful of mixed soft herb leaves, such as flat-leaf parsley, dill, and chives, finely chopped

salt and freshly ground black pepper

½ cup fresh bread crumbs

2 tbsp finely grated Parmesan cheese

1 Preheat the oven to 400°F (200°C). Slice each zucchini in half horizontally and use a teaspoon to scoop out most of the flesh, being sure to leave a shell of about ½in (1cm). Finely chop and reserve the scooped-out flesh. Place the zucchini shells on a baking sheet and bake for 10 minutes until softened slightly.

2 Meanwhile, make the stuffing. Heat the oil in a large, heavy-bottomed frying pan and cook the onion for 5 minutes until softened, but not browned. Add the reserved zucchini flesh and cook for another 2–3 minutes until it softens. Add the garlic and butter and cook for a final minute.

3 Take the pan off the heat and stir in the rice and herbs until well combined, then season well. In a separate bowl, mix the bread crumbs and Parmesan and season well. Stir once more until well combined.

4 When the zucchini has cooked for 10 minutes, stuff them with the rice mixture, mounding it up in the zucchini shells, and evenly sprinkle the Parmesan bread crumbs overtop. Drizzle the tops with a little oil and return to the oven to bake for 15–20 minutes, or until the zucchini shells are soft but still holding their shape and the topping has become golden brown and crunchy. Serve.

A crunchy, cheesy bread crumb topping can make vegetables much more enticing to children. Try the same crunchy topping on thickly sliced and baked juicy tomatoes or on cauliflower cheese.

Fussy eaters!

CALORIES: 294kcals/1228kJ

CARBOHYDRATE: 31g
  sugar: 4g

FAT: 15g
  saturated: 6g

SALT: 0.5g

FIBER: 3g

Baked tomatoes stuffed with couscous, black olives, and feta

These summery baked tomatoes are an ideal accompaniment to a simple grilled or baked fish dish.

20 mins | 15 mins, plus resting

SERVES 4

4–8 beefsteak or other large tomatoes, depending on size

⅔ cup couscous

2 tbsp olive oil, plus extra for drizzling

⅔ cup boiling vegetable stock (see p156)

2 large scallions, finely chopped

8 pitted black olives, finely chopped

finely grated zest of ½ lemon

1¾oz (50g) feta cheese, crumbled

2 tbsp finely chopped mint leaves

1 tbsp finely chopped chives

freshly ground black pepper

1 Preheat the oven to 400°F (200°C). Slice the tops off the tomatoes and carefully scoop out and discard the interior flesh, reserving the tops for later.

2 Put the couscous in a wide, shallow dish and rub in 1 tbsp of the oil with your fingers (to keep the grains from sticking together). Pour in the stock, stir briefly, and immediately cover tightly with plastic wrap. Leave for 10 minutes, then uncover. The couscous should be soft and the liquid absorbed. Fluff the couscous with a fork and let cool slightly.

3 When the couscous has cooled, add the remaining ingredients, except the tomatoes, with the remaining 1 tbsp of oil. Season well with pepper (the feta and olives are salty enough), and carefully stuff the tomatoes with the mixture.

4 Place the tomatoes in a small ovenproof dish that fits them tightly, put the reserved tops on, and drizzle with oil. Bake in the hot oven for 15 minutes, until the tomatoes are soft but still hold their shape and the tops are golden. Rest for 5 minutes, then serve.

VARIATION

Drizzle salmon fillets with olive oil, season well, and cook surrounded by the tomatoes for a one-dish meal.

CALORIES: 224kcals/941kJ

CARBOHYDRATE: 25g
    sugar: 14g

FAT: 10g
    saturated: 3g

SALT: 0.7g

FIBER: 5g

Eggplant stuffed with goat cheese, pine nuts, and apricots

Take inspiration from the Middle East to transform eggplant into a delicious vegetarian main course.

20 mins | 50 mins

SERVES 2–4

2 large eggplants

2 tbsp olive oil, plus extra for rubbing

1oz (30g) pine nuts

1 red onion, finely sliced

1 garlic clove, crushed

1¾oz (50g) dried apricots, finely chopped

¾ cup fresh white bread crumbs

3½oz (100g) firm goat cheese, finely chopped or crumbled

2 tbsp finely chopped dill fronds

2 tbsp finely chopped mint leaves

1 tsp smoked paprika

salt and freshly ground black pepper

1 Preheat the oven to 375°F (190°C). Halve the eggplants lengthwise and cut a criss-cross into the cut side, without piercing the skin. Rub with oil and bake, cut-sides up, for 30 minutes. Scoop out the interior, leaving a shell of ¼in (5mm). Chop the flesh.

2 Heat a large frying pan and dry-fry the pine nuts for 3–4 minutes. Put them in a bowl and wipe the pan with paper towels.

3 Heat the 2 tbsp of oil in the pan. Cook the onion for 5 minutes, until soft. Add the eggplant flesh. Cook for 3–4 minutes, then add the garlic for 1 minute.

4 Add the onion mixture to the pine nuts with the apricots, bread crumbs, goat cheese, herbs, and smoked paprika, and season.

5 Divide the stuffing between the eggplant halves and bake for 20 minutes until golden brown.

VARIATION

Sprinkle the tops of the eggplant with 1¾oz (50g) of grated mozzarella cheese before cooking.

CALORIES: 328kcals/1369kJ

CARBOHYDRATE: 24g
    sugar: 10.5g

FAT: 21g
    saturated: 6g

SALT: 0.8g

FIBER: 6g

Sweet potato and eggplant curry

Keep jars of good curry pastes in your pantry and you'll always have the basis of a quick, tasty meal.

 15 mins   30 mins

SERVES 4

salt and freshly ground black pepper

14oz (400g) potatoes, peeled and cut into ¾in (2cm) cubes

14oz (400g) sweet potatoes, peeled and cut into ¾in (2cm) cubes

1 tbsp vegetable oil

1 onion, finely chopped

2 garlic cloves, finely chopped

1 eggplant, cut into ¾in (2cm) cubes

¼ cup mild curry paste (such as korma)

1 x 14oz (400g) can chopped tomatoes

1 cup vegetable stock (see p156)

3 tbsp chopped cilantro leaves

basmati rice and plain yogurt, to serve

1 Bring a saucepan of salted water to a boil, add the potato and sweet potato, and cook for 10 minutes. Drain and set aside.

2 Meanwhile, heat the oil in a large pan over medium heat and cook the onion for 5 minutes. Add the garlic and eggplant and cook for another 2 minutes.

3 Add the curry paste to the pan and stir well. Add the tomatoes, stock, and cooked potatoes, and stir to combine. Season, cover, and simmer for 20 minutes.

4 Stir in the cilantro. Serve the curry with rice and topped with a spoonful of yogurt.

Try cooking this mild, tasty, low-fat vegetarian curry for teenagers who have a craving for a take-out.

 Fussy eaters!

CALORIES: 258kcals/1089kJ
CARBOHYDRATE: 43g
  sugar: 11g
FAT: 7g
  saturated: 0.5g
SALT: 0.8g
FIBER: 8g

Mushroom and spinach curry

Try this as a side dish with Mild creamy chicken curry (see p98), or as a main course dish for a vegetarian.

  15 mins   30 mins

SERVES 4

1 tbsp vegetable oil

2 onions, sliced

4 garlic cloves, finely chopped

1½in (4cm) piece of fresh ginger, finely chopped

4 cardamom pods

1 red chile, seeded and finely chopped (optional)

1 cinnamon stick

1 tsp ground coriander

1 tsp ground cumin

1 tsp turmeric

½ tsp ground nutmeg

9oz (250g) crimini or portabello mushrooms, roughly chopped

9oz (250g) button mushrooms

1¼ cups vegetable stock (see p156)

salt and freshly ground black pepper

7oz (200g) spinach

¼ cup (2oz) plain yogurt

toasted cashew nuts and naan bread or chapatis, to serve

1 Heat the oil in a large saucepan over medium heat and cook the onions for 5 minutes. Add the garlic and ginger and cook for 2 minutes, stirring occasionally.

2 Add the spices to the pan and stir well. Add the mushrooms and stir to coat in the spices.

3 Pour in the stock, season, and bring to a boil, then cover and reduce the heat to a simmer. Cook for 15 minutes.

4 Stir in the spinach and cook for another 2 minutes. Remove the cinnamon stick and cardamom pods (if possible), then stir in the yogurt, sprinkle in the cashew nuts, and serve with naan bread or chapatis.

CALORIES: 87kcals/363kJ
CARBOHYDRATE: 6g
  sugar: 5g
FAT: 4.5g
  saturated: 0.8g
SALT: 0.3g
FIBER: 4g

Pumpkin and coconut curry

The sweet flesh of pumpkin complements creamy coconut milk perfectly. Add chopped red chile for more heat.

15 mins   30 mins

SERVES 4

1 tbsp vegetable oil

1 red onion, finely chopped

2 garlic cloves, finely chopped

1½lb (700g) pumpkin or butternut squash flesh, cut into 1in (3cm) cubes

¼ cup medium curry paste

1 cup vegetable stock (see p156)

1¼ cups reduced-fat coconut milk

salt and freshly ground black pepper

rice, to serve

1 Heat the vegetable oil in a large saucepan placed over medium heat. Add the onion and cook for 5 minutes until it has softened, but not browned. Add the garlic and cook for another 2 minutes, until it smells fragrant, but has not burned or turned dark brown.

2 Increase the heat to high, add the pumpkin cubes, and cook for 2 minutes, stirring constantly, so it does not stick to the bottom of the pan.

3 Reduce the heat to medium and stir in the curry paste to coat, then cook for 2 minutes, stirring occasionally.

3 Add the stock and coconut milk, season, and stir well to combine. Increase the heat and bring the curry to a boil, then reduce the heat to a gentle simmer.

4 Cover and simmer very gently for 20 minutes, or until the flavors and textures are harmonious. Stop cooking when the pumpkin is tender, but not falling apart. Serve with rice.

VARIATION

Use 12oz (350g) butternut squash and 12oz (350g) sweet potato, both cut into cubes, as an alternative to the pumpkin.

COOK'S TIP

Feeding one vegetarian in a family can often be difficult. But this mild tasting, substantial vegetarian curry should please everyone, carnivores included.

CALORIES: 212kcals/890kJ

CARBOHYDRATE: 18g
  sugar: 10g

FAT: 13.5g
  saturated: 7g

SALT: 0.6g

FIBER: 4g

Vegetarian kids

With some careful planning, it's possible to ensure that a vegetarian child receives all the nutrients necessary to grow and thrive. You will need to ensure that their diet contains adequate amounts of protein and iron—this can be achieved by providing two to three portions of vegetable proteins (see opposite) or nuts each day (don't give whole nuts to children under five). For family meals, it's easier to cook just once. If other members of the family are meat eaters, try serving a roast chicken or cooking a pork chop alongside a vegetarian meal, or adapt to eating less meat overall as a family, a healthy option for all.

Types of vegetarianism

Some vegetarians avoid meat but eat fish; some avoid meat and fish; and vegans choose to avoid all animal products, including dairy. If you are a vegan household, or your child becomes a vegan, you will need to provide high-calorie foods to meet the energy needs of a growing child, such as bananas and peanut butter. Use vegetable oils in cooking, such as canola and avocado oils, which are a good source of healthy monounsaturated fats. Parents of vegetarian or vegan children are well advised also to seek specialist advice from their doctor or nutritionist.

The importance of a balanced diet

If your child wishes to follow a vegetarian diet, it's vital that they are aware of the importance of eating a balanced diet that includes all the essential nutrients.

Vitamins and minerals Iron is found in dark green vegetables, beans, fortified cereals, and dried fruit. Vitamin C, which aids iron absorption, is found in citrus and kiwis, broccoli, tomatoes and bell peppers. Dairy products contain vitamin A, and vitamin D can be found in fortified cereals, eggs, and oily fish such as salmon.

Vitamins and minerals

Protein

Meat-free days

It is increasingly acknowledged that a little less meat is a good thing. So if a child becomes a vegetarian, take your cue from them and have at least two meat-free family meals a week.

Get kids cooking

The teenage years are often when people choose to cut meat from their diet. Use this interest in food as an opportunity to teach them how to cook in preparation for adulthood.

Protein Beans and legumes, such as lentils, chickpeas, and kidney beans, are good sources of proteins for vegetarians. Nut and seed butters also provide protein.

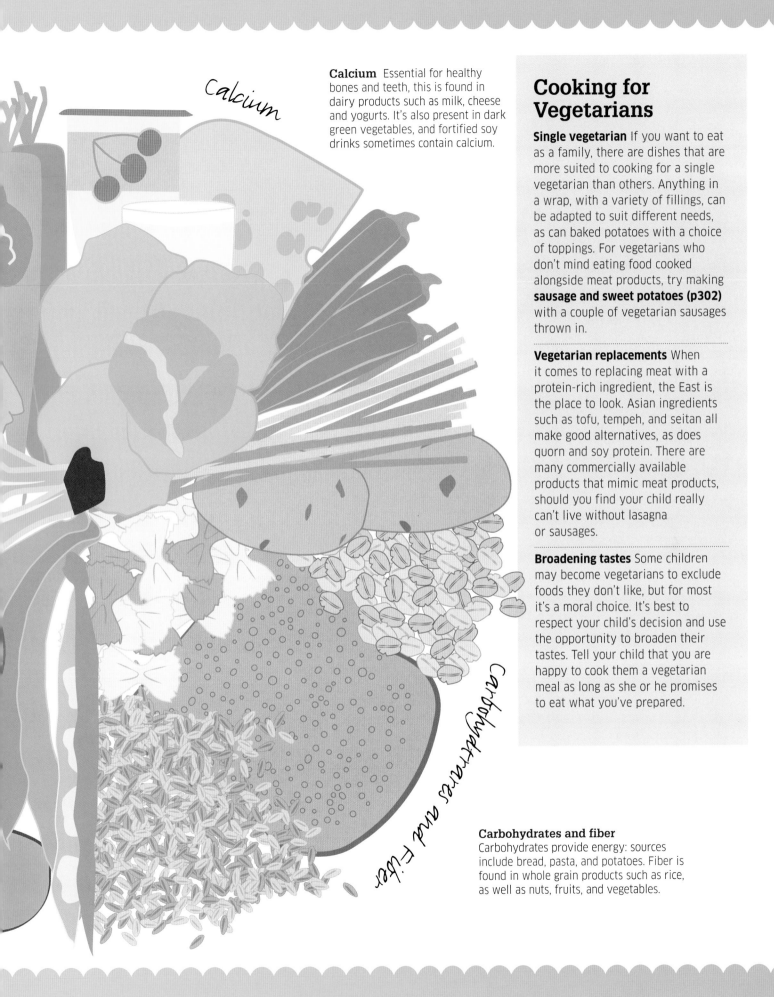

Calcium Essential for healthy bones and teeth, this is found in dairy products such as milk, cheese and yogurts. It's also present in dark green vegetables, and fortified soy drinks sometimes contain calcium.

Calcium

Carbohydrates and Fiber

Cooking for Vegetarians

Single vegetarian If you want to eat as a family, there are dishes that are more suited to cooking for a single vegetarian than others. Anything in a wrap, with a variety of fillings, can be adapted to suit different needs, as can baked potatoes with a choice of toppings. For vegetarians who don't mind eating food cooked alongside meat products, try making **sausage and sweet potatoes (p302)** with a couple of vegetarian sausages thrown in.

Vegetarian replacements When it comes to replacing meat with a protein-rich ingredient, the East is the place to look. Asian ingredients such as tofu, tempeh, and seitan all make good alternatives, as does quorn and soy protein. There are many commercially available products that mimic meat products, should you find your child really can't live without lasagna or sausages.

Broadening tastes Some children may become vegetarians to exclude foods they don't like, but for most it's a moral choice. It's best to respect your child's decision and use the opportunity to broaden their tastes. Tell your child that you are happy to cook them a vegetarian meal as long as she or he promises to eat what you've prepared.

Carbohydrates and fiber
Carbohydrates provide energy: sources include bread, pasta, and potatoes. Fiber is found in whole grain products such as rice, as well as nuts, fruits, and vegetables.

Pasta salad with shrimp and pesto

Homemade pesto takes just minutes to prepare and the flavor is far superior to store-bought varieties.

20 mins   10-12 mins

SPECIAL EQUIPMENT
food processor

SERVES 4

salt and freshly ground black pepper

7oz (200g) dried pasta, such as fusilli

2oz (60g) basil leaves

scant 1oz (25g) toasted pine nuts

scant 1oz (25g) grated Parmesan

2 garlic cloves, roughly chopped

⅓ cup extra virgin olive oil

finely grated zest of 1 lemon, plus 1 tbsp lemon juice

9oz (250g) cooked, peeled large shrimp

CALORIES: 420kcals/1759kJ

CARBOHYDRATE: 36g
  sugar: 1.5g

FAT: 22g
  saturated: 4g

SALT: 1g

FIBER: 2.5g

---

1 Bring a large pan of salted water to a boil and cook the pasta according to the package instructions. Drain and rinse under cold running water until the pasta is cold. Drain well and set aside.

2 Place the basil, pine nuts, Parmesan cheese, garlic, oil, and lemon zest and juice in a food processor and pulse until well blended.

3 Place the pasta in a large serving bowl and stir in the pesto. Season well with pepper and stir to combine. Carefully stir in the shrimp. Serve with hunks of whole grain bread.

BATCHING AND FREEZING

Try making double quantities of this pesto and freezing it in small portions. It can be used over pasta, to liven up a pizza crust, or can even be kneaded into some simple homemade ciabatta bread.

Summer pasta salad

Kids love pasta, so try to expand their horizons with this tasty Italian-style pasta salad.

20 mins   10-12 mins

SERVES 4

salt and freshly ground black pepper

9oz (250g) dried pasta, such as farfalle

5½oz (150g) cherry tomatoes

5½oz (150g) bocconcini (mini mozzarella cheese balls), drained

2 avocados, cut into large chunks

2oz (60g) pitted black olives

large handful of basil leaves

juice of 1 lemon

¼ cup extra virgin olive oil

1 tsp Dijon mustard

2 tbsp chopped chives

1 garlic clove, finely chopped

CALORIES: 611kcals/2554kJ

CARBOHYDRATE: 47g
  sugar: 3g

FAT: 40g
  saturated: 10g

SALT: 0.6g

FIBER: 7g

---

1 Bring a large pan of salted water to a boil and cook the pasta according to the package instructions. Drain and rinse under cold running water until the pasta is cold. Drain well and set aside.

2 Place the tomatoes, bocconcini, avocados, and olives in a large serving bowl. Tear the basil leaves and add to the bowl. Season well and toss carefully to combine.

3 In a bowl, combine the lemon juice, oil, mustard, chives, and garlic. Season and stir well.

4 Add the cold pasta to the bowl and pour in the dressing. Stir gently but well and serve with warm ciabatta.

COOK'S TIP

If you find it hard to get hold of bocconcini, buy a ball of fresh mozzarella and dice it into pieces the same size as the cherry tomatoes.

Bean thread noodle salad

This light yet vibrant summer salad is refreshing and perfect as part of an Asian-inspired meal or buffet lunch.

20 mins

SERVES 4

7oz (200g) dried Chinese bean thread noodles or thin rice noodles

1 large carrot, shaved using a vegetable peeler

4in (10cm) cucumber, halved lengthwise, seeded, and finely sliced on the diagonal

4 scallions, white parts only, finely sliced on the diagonal

1 mango, not too ripe, finely julienned

handful of mint leaves, roughly chopped

handful of cilantro leaves, roughly chopped

FOR THE DRESSING

juice of 2 limes

2 tbsp white wine vinegar or rice wine vinegar

1 tsp granulated sugar

pinch of salt

1 Put the noodles in a large bowl and cover with boiling water. Leave for 4 minutes, or according to the package instructions, until they are soft but still have a bite to them. Stir and separate the strands with chopsticks when you first pour the water over them, and once or twice afterwards. Drain and refresh under cold water, then drain thoroughly.

2 Meanwhile, assemble the rest of the salad ingredients in a bowl, keeping back a few herbs to serve. Preparing the salad vegetables over the bowl means you will capture all the juices. Pat the noodles completely dry with paper towels and add the cold, drained noodles to the bowl.

3 Whisk together the dressing ingredients and toss it through the salad. Serve, scattered with the reserved herbs.

VARIATION

Adding cooked large shrimp, shelled, deveined, and halved horizontally, makes this a lovely light summer lunch.

COOK'S TIP

If you can locate only the fatter ⅛in- (3mm-) wide variety of dried rice noodles, soak them for about 10 minutes, or according to the package instructions, being sure to separate them well with chopsticks, as in step 1.

CALORIES: 228kcals/957kJ

CARBOHYDRATE: 48g
   sugar: 10g

FAT: 0.5g
   saturated: 0.1g

SALT: 0.5g

FIBER: 3g

Tomato, bean, and pasta soup

If you make this ahead of time, you may need to add more water when reheating, as it thickens on standing.

15 mins   45–50 mins

SERVES 4–6

1 tbsp olive oil

1 onion, finely chopped

1 carrot, finely chopped

2 garlic cloves, finely chopped

2 x 14oz (400g) cans chopped tomatoes

1 x 14oz (400g) can butterbeans, drained and rinsed

1 x 14oz (400g) can cannellini beans, drained and rinsed

2 cups vegetable stock (see p156)

salt and freshly ground black pepper

2½oz (75g) mini dried pasta shapes

1 tsp finely chopped basil leaves

grated Cheddar cheese, to serve

1 Heat the oil in a large saucepan over medium-low heat. Add the onion and carrot and cook for about 5 minutes, stirring occasionally, until softened, but not browned. Add the garlic and cook for another minute, or until it is fragrant, but not browned.

2 Add the tomatoes, beans, and stock. Season, cover, and simmer gently for 25 minutes, stirring occasionally.

3 Add the pasta and cook the soup for another 15 minutes, stirring occasionally so it does not stick to the pan. Add a little more water if the soup seems to be becoming too thick.

4 Add the basil and stir it through, then ladle the soup into warmed bowls and sprinkle with grated cheese to serve.

COOK'S TIP

Cooking your own beans is cheaper and tastier. For every 14oz (400g) can, soak ½ cup of dried beans overnight. Cook according to the package instructions (without salt) before adding them to the soup.

CALORIES: 242kcals/1024kJ

CARBOHYDRATE: 38g
  sugar: 10g

FAT: 4.5g
  saturated: 0.5g

SALT: 1.6g

FIBER: 11.5g

Raw tomato and basil sauce

This super-quick sauce is perfect for using up flavorful, ripe tomatoes, if you are lucky enough to have a glut.

10 mins

SPECIAL EQUIPMENT
food processor

SERVES 4

1lb 2oz (500g) very ripe tomatoes

¼ cup olive oil

1 tbsp tomato paste

1 garlic clove, crushed

handful of basil leaves

salt and freshly ground black pepper

finely grated Parmesan cheese,
 to serve

CALORIES: 123kcals/510kJ

CARBOHYDRATE: 4g
 sugar: 4g

FAT: 11.5g
 saturated: 2g

SALT: trace

FIBER: 2g

1 Cut a small slit in the bottom of each tomato and place in a large bowl. Cover with boiling water. Set aside for 1 minute, until the skins start to peel back.

2 Transfer with a slotted spoon to a bowl of cold water. Peel the tomatoes. (At this point you can quarter each and remove the seeds with a teaspoon, if you want a dryer sauce.) Cut the flesh into cubes.

3 Put the tomatoes and other ingredients in a food processor, season generously, and process to a rough sauce.

4 Toss the sauce through cooked pasta and serve with finely grated Parmesan cheese.

VARIATION

For a special dish, sauté small bay scallops in butter for a couple of minutes, and toss them through cooked pasta with this sauce (this version is better without Parmesan).

Slow-cooked tomato sauce

A classic tomato sauce is the basis of so many good family meals. The secret is in the long cooking time.

10 mins   45 mins-1hr

SERVES 4

3 tbsp olive oil

1 onion, finely chopped

2 garlic cloves, crushed

1 x 14oz (400g) can chopped tomatoes

1 tbsp tomato paste

1 tsp granulated sugar

2 tbsp roughly chopped
 flat-leaf parsley leaves

salt and freshly ground black pepper

2 tbsp roughly chopped basil leaves

1 Heat the oil in a heavy-bottomed saucepan and cook the onion over medium heat for about 5 minutes until softened, but not browned. Add the garlic and cook for 1 minute.

2 Add the tomatoes, then fill the empty can with water and pour it in. Stir in the tomato paste, sugar, and parsley, and season well.

3 Bring the sauce to a boil, reduce the heat to a low simmer, and cook, uncovered, for 45 minutes to 1 hour, until thickened. If the tomatoes are taking a while to break down, mash with a potato masher to help them along. Stir in the basil to serve.

For young children who don't like "chunks," it can be a good idea to blend the sauce until smooth with a hand-held blender.

Fussy eaters!

CALORIES: 106kcals/440kJ

CARBOHYDRATE: 6g
 sugar: 5.5g

FAT: 8.5g
 saturated: 1g

SALT: 0.1g

FIBER: 1.5g

Arrabbiata sauce

This is traditionally served with penne. Alter the amount of chile flakes depending on how spicy you like it.

10 mins | 1 hr

SERVES 4–6

3 tbsp olive oil

1 onion, finely chopped

2 garlic cloves, crushed

1 tsp dried chile flakes

1 x 14oz (400g) can chopped tomatoes

½ cup red wine (optional)

1 tbsp tomato paste

1 tsp granulated sugar

2 tbsp roughly chopped flat-leaf parsley leaves

salt and freshly ground black pepper

2 tbsp chopped basil leaves (optional)

1 Heat the oil in a heavy-bottomed saucepan and cook the onion over medium heat for about 5 minutes, until softened, but not browned. Add the garlic and chile flakes and cook for 1 minute.

2 Add the tomatoes, then fill the empty can three-quarters full with water and pour it in with the wine (if using). If not using wine, add a whole canful of water. Stir in the tomato paste, sugar, and parsley, and season well.

3 Bring to a boil, reduce the heat to a low simmer, and cook, uncovered, for 45 minutes to 1 hour, stirring occasionally, until thickened. If the tomatoes are taking a while to break down, mash with a potato masher to help them along. Stir through the basil (if using) and serve.

HOW TO FREEZE

It is best to freeze this sauce without the basil, adding it after defrosting, or the green herb will oxidize and turn black in the freezer.

CALORIES: 127kcals/529kJ

CARBOHYDRATE: 6g
  sugar: 5.5g

FAT: 8.5g
  saturated: 1g

SALT: 0.1g

FIBER: 1.5g

Tomato and mascarpone pasta

This is a perfect way to use up overripe tomatoes, and is made beautifully creamy by the mascarpone.

10 mins | 10–15 mins

SERVES 4

salt and freshly ground black pepper

10oz (300g) dried pasta

4 large, overripe tomatoes, approx. 1lb 5oz (600g) in total

2 tbsp olive oil

2 garlic cloves, crushed

¼ cup mascarpone

¼ cup finely grated Parmesan cheese

2 tbsp roughly chopped basil leaves

1 Bring a large pan of salted water to a boil to cook the pasta. Before adding the pasta, use the boiling water to help peel the tomatoes (see p191). Cut them into fairly small cubes.

2 Use the boiling water to cook the pasta according to the package instructions.

3 Heat the oil in a large frying pan. Add the tomatoes and garlic and cook for 2 minutes until they start to break down.

4 Add ¾ cup of water and cook over high heat for about 5 minutes, or until the tomatoes have completely broken down and the sauce is very thick. (You can use a potato masher to help this process along.) Drain the pasta and return it to the pan.

5 Season the sauce well and stir in the mascarpone. Cook for another minute or two until the mascarpone has dispersed and the sauce is thick and creamy. Toss through the pasta and cook over low heat for 2 minutes until the pasta has absorbed some of the sauce. Take it off the heat, toss through the Parmesan cheese and basil, and serve.

CALORIES: 460kcals/1942kJ

CARBOHYDRATE: 58g
  sugar: 7g

FAT: 18g
  saturated: 8g

SALT: 0.4g

FIBER: 5g

Pasta primavera

This delicate, tasty sauce is an easy and delicious way to get plenty of green vegetables into your family's diet.

10 mins   20 mins

SERVES 4

salt and freshly ground black pepper

3½oz (100g) sugarsnap peas

4½oz (125g) thin asparagus spears, halved

3½oz (100g) baby zucchini, quartered lengthwise

14oz (400g) dried linguine or fettuccine

1 tbsp olive oil

2 garlic cloves, finely sliced

1 shallot, finely chopped

2 tbsp extra virgin olive oil

⅔ cup (5oz) low-fat crème fraîche

½ tsp grated nutmeg

finely grated zest of 1 lemon, plus juice of ½ lemon

2 tbsp torn basil leaves

2 tbsp chopped flat-leaf parsley leaves

3½oz (100g) baby spinach

Parmesan cheese shavings and ciabatta, to serve

1 Bring a large pot of salted water to a boil and add the sugarsnap peas, asparagus, and zucchini. Return to a boil and cook for 3 minutes, or until the vegetables are just tender, but still brightly colored and al dente. Drain well, then run under cold water to set the color. Drain once more, and set aside in a colander over the kitchen sink.

2 Refill the pot used for cooking the vegetables with more salted water and bring it to a boil. Cook the pasta according to the package instructions. Meanwhile, heat the olive oil in a small pan over medium heat and sauté the garlic and shallot for 2 minutes.

3 In a medium bowl, combine the extra virgin olive oil, crème fraîche, nutmeg, lemon zest and juice, basil, and parsley. Add the cooked garlic and shallot. Stir well and season generously with pepper.

4 Drain the pasta well in the same colander as the vegetables to reheat them slightly, then return the pasta and vegetables to the pot. Add the spinach and stir until it wilts. Add the herby sauce to the pasta and stir to coat.

5 Transfer to warmed serving bowls, top with Parmesan shavings, and serve with ciabatta.

PREPARE AHEAD

The herby sauce can be prepared up to 1 day in advance, covered, and kept in the fridge until needed. Whisk it once more to emulsify before use.

CALORIES: 505kcals/2135kJ

CARBOHYDRATE: 73g
sugar: 4.5g

FAT: 15g
saturated: 5g

SALT: 0.1g

FIBER: 6.5g

Angel hair pasta with arugula pesto

Homemade pesto is great, but can be expensive to make using just basil. Try this arugula-basil version instead.

10 mins, plus resting   10 mins

SPECIAL EQUIPMENT
food processor

SERVES 4

3½oz (100g) pine nuts

1¾oz (50g) arugula leaves

large handful of basil leaves, approx. ½oz (15g)

1¾oz (50g) finely grated Parmesan cheese, plus extra for serving

1 garlic clove, crushed

¾ cup extra virgin olive oil

salt and freshly ground black pepper

10oz (300g) dried angel hair or other long, thin pasta

CALORIES: 820kcals/3416kJ
CARBOHYDRATE: 54g
  sugar: 3g
FAT: 59g
  saturated: 9g
SALT: 0.3g
FIBER: 4g

1 Dry-fry the pine nuts in a frying pan over medium heat for 2 minutes, stirring constantly, or until golden brown, but not burnt. Pour out of the pan and set aside to cool.

2 Once the nuts are cold, put them in a food processor with the arugula, basil, Parmesan, and garlic, and grind to a medium-coarse paste. With the motor running, pour in the oil in a slow, steady stream until you have a loose, vivid green paste. Check the seasoning and adjust if necessary. The pesto tastes better if you can rest it, covered, for 30 minutes to allow the flavors to develop.

3 Boil the pasta according to the package instructions, drain it (reserving a ladleful of the cooking water), and return it to the pan with the reserved water. Stir the pesto through the pasta and serve, sprinkled with extra Parmesan cheese.

VARIATION

After step 1, set aside ¾oz (20g) of the pine nuts, sprinkling them over just before serving, for more texture.

Pantry spaghetti

A great recipe to cook when you have nothing—you'll probably have at least these essentials.

10 mins   15 mins

SPECIAL EQUIPMENT
food processor

SERVES 4

10oz (300g) dried spaghetti

salt and freshly ground black pepper

7oz (200g) good-quality day-old white bread or baguette

3 tbsp olive oil, plus extra if needed

2 tbsp butter

2 garlic cloves, crushed

1¾oz (50g) finely grated Parmesan cheese

CALORIES: 572kcals/2413kJ
CARBOHYDRATE: 79g
  sugar: 3g
FAT: 20g
  saturated: 7g
SALT: 1.1g
FIBER: 5g

1 Cook the spaghetti in a large pan of boiling salted water according to the package instructions.

2 Cut the bread into large chunks and pulse it in a food processor to coarse bread crumbs. (Leaving the crusts on gives larger crumbs and so a better texture to the finished dish.)

3 Heat the oil and butter in a large frying pan. Cook the garlic for a minute over medium heat until fragrant. Add the bread crumbs and continue to cook until golden brown and crispy, adding a little extra oil if the bread crumbs appear dry.

4 Drain the pasta and return to the pan, with a little oil tossed through to keep it from sticking together. Toss through the bread crumbs and Parmesan cheese and season well to serve.

VARIATION

Try adding a pinch of chile flakes with the garlic, or 4 chopped anchovies, or a handful of black olives.

Pasta with butternut squash

This dish is perfect for those slightly cooler days, as it has the comfort of cream and the warmth of red chiles.

20 mins   30 mins

SPECIAL EQUIPMENT
blender or food processor

SERVES 4

7oz (200g) butternut squash, peeled and diced

1–2 tbsp olive oil

salt and freshly ground black pepper

1 garlic clove, crushed

½ red chile, seeded and finely chopped

8 sage leaves

⅔ cup half-and-half

scant 1oz (25g) Parmesan cheese, grated, plus extra to serve

12oz (350g) dried conchiglie pasta

CALORIES: 451kcals/1906kJ
CARBOHYDRATE: 66g
  sugar: 5g
FAT: 14g
  saturated: 7g
SALT: 0.2g
FIBER: 5g

1 Preheat the oven to 400°F (200°C). Toss the squash in a little oil, season it well with salt and pepper, and roast for about 30 minutes, or until soft. Remove it from the oven and leave to cool for a few minutes.

2 Meanwhile, gently cook the garlic, chile, and sage in a little oil for 2–3 minutes.

3 Once the butternut squash has cooled slightly, put it into a blender or food processor. Add the half-and-half, Parmesan, garlic, chile, sage leaves, plenty of pepper, and a little salt. Blend it all to a coarse purée, adding 1–2 tbsp water if it looks too thick.

4 Cook the pasta until al dente and drain it. Quickly reheat the sauce in the pasta pan, adding more water if it seems a little stiff. Put the pasta back into the pan and mix it well, allowing the sauce to coat the pasta. Serve with plenty of Parmesan.

Pasta with creamy zucchini

If your children are wary of eating zucchini, try grating it into the sauce instead.

15 mins   15 mins

SERVES 4

2 tbsp butter

1 tbsp olive oil

1 garlic clove, crushed

14oz (400g) baby zucchini, quartered lengthwise

10oz (300g) long dried pasta, such as spaghetti, linguine, fettuccine, or pappardelle

salt and freshly ground black pepper

1¼ cups half-and-half

finely grated zest and juice of 1 lemon

¾oz (20g) finely grated Grana Padano cheese, plus extra to serve

pinch of grated nutmeg

CALORIES: 530kcals/2224kJ
CARBOHYDRATE: 56g
  sugar: 5g
FAT: 27g
  saturated: 15g
SALT: 0.3g
FIBER: 4g

1 Heat the butter and oil in a large, non-stick frying pan over medium heat. Add the garlic and zucchini and cook gently for 10 minutes, stirring occasionally.

2 Meanwhile, cook the pasta in boiling salted water according to the package instructions.

3 Return to the zucchini mixture and add the half-and-half, lemon zest and juice, Grana Padano cheese, nutmeg, salt, and plenty of pepper. Heat through gently.

4 Drain the pasta and serve immediately, with the sauce tossed through and extra grated Grana Padano cheese.

VARIATION

For a crispy garnish, broil 8 slices of prosciutto under a hot broil until crisp. Break into small pieces and sprinkle over the pasta just before serving.

Blue cheese and broccoli pasta sauce

This is a delicious sauce to stir through pasta shapes. Cook 14oz (400g) of dried pasta to serve four people.

10 mins   15 mins

SPECIAL EQUIPMENT
food processor

SERVES 4

9oz (250g) broccoli, in bite-sized florets

¾ cup (7oz) low-fat crème fraîche

7oz (200g) Dolcelatte or gorgonzola cheese, rind removed and roughly chopped

finely grated zest of 1 lemon, plus 1 tbsp lemon juice

freshly ground black pepper

¼ tsp ground nutmeg

3 tbsp chopped walnuts, to serve

1 Place the broccoli in a steamer and cook until just tender (up to 5 minutes). Drain well. Transfer to a food processor and blend to a bright green purée.

2 Place the crème fraîche and cheese in a medium saucepan over low heat and stir until the cheese has melted to form a smooth sauce. Stir in the lemon zest and juice, plenty of pepper, and the nutmeg.

3 Scrape the broccoli purée into the pan and stir well. Pour the sauce over cooked pasta and sprinkle with the walnuts to serve.

Blue cheese has a strong flavor. For very young children, try replacing it with cream cheese and a handful of grated Parmesan, for a milder sauce.

Fussy eaters!

CALORIES: 707kcals/2971kJ
CARBOHYDRATE: 72g
  sugar: 3.5g
FAT: 33g
  saturated: 16g
SALT: 2.1g
FIBER: 7g

Classic carbonara

Even when you think you have nothing in the fridge, you may have the ingredients for this creamy sauce.

15 mins   25 mins

SERVES 4

7oz (200g) thick-cut bacon

salt and freshly ground black pepper

14oz (400g) dried long pasta, such as spaghetti, linguine, fettuccine, or pappardelle

¾ cup half-and-half

4 large eggs, lightly beaten

1¼oz (40g) finely grated Parmesan cheese, plus extra to serve

2 tbsp chopped flat-leaf parsley leaves, to garnish

tomato and basil salad, to serve

1 Heat a large, non-stick frying pan over medium heat. Add the bacon and cook, turning, until crisp. Transfer to a plate lined with paper towels.

2 Bring a large pan of salted water to a boil and cook the pasta according to package instructions.

3 Meanwhile, measure the half-and-half into a large liquid measuring cup and stir in the eggs, Parmesan cheese, and pepper. Snip the bacon into pieces with kitchen scissors, and stir into the egg.

4 Drain the pasta and return to the pan, pour in the egg mixture, and place over low heat. Stir for 2 minutes, or until the sauce has thickened and clings to the strands of pasta. Divide between warmed bowls, season with pepper, and sprinkle with parsley. Serve with extra Parmesan and a tomato and basil salad.

CALORIES: 716kcals/3011kJ
CARBOHYDRATE: 72g
  sugar: 3g
FAT: 33g
  saturated: 14g
SALT: 2g
FIBER: 4g

Three cheese pasta

This rich, cheesy sauce is a heartening recipe to make on a cold day. The pine nuts add crunch and texture.

10 mins   15 mins

SERVES 4

salt and freshly ground black pepper

14oz (400g) dried long pasta, such as spaghetti, linguine, fettuccine, or pappardelle

1lb 2oz (500g) fat-free ricotta

9oz (250g) cream cheese with garlic and herbs

1oz (30g) finely chopped flat-leaf parsley leaves

scant 1oz (25g) finely grated Pecorino Romano cheese

1¾oz (50g) toasted pine nuts, very finely chopped

pinch of grated nutmeg

1 Bring a large pan of salted water to a boil and cook the pasta according to the package instructions.

2 Meanwhile, place the ricotta and cream cheese in a saucepan over very low heat, stirring occasionally, until a smooth sauce is formed.

3 Stir in the parsley, Pecorino Romano, and pine nuts, and heat through, stirring constantly, until piping hot.

4 Drain the pasta (reserving a ladleful of the cooking water) and return it to the pan with the reserved water.

5 Season the cheese sauce well with pepper and nutmeg, pour over the cooked pasta, stir, and serve immediately.

VARIATION

This tasty sauce can be varied to suit whatever odds and ends of cheese you have available. Just grate small pieces and add to the heating ricotta.

CALORIES: 796kcals/3335kJ
CARBOHYDRATE: 76g
    sugar: 8g
FAT: 42g
    saturated: 21g
SALT: 0.7g
FIBER: 4.5g

Easy carbonara

This simple, delicious sauce can be tossed together in less time than the pasta takes to cook.

10 mins   10 mins

SERVES 4

3½oz (100g) prosciutto slices

salt and freshly ground black pepper

14oz (400g) quick-cook dried long pasta, such as spaghetti, linguine, fettuccine, or pappardelle

⅔ cup (5oz) low-fat crème fraîche

⅔ cup half-and-half

1¼oz (40g) finely grated Parmesan cheese, plus extra to serve

arugula salad, to serve

1 Preheat the broiler to its highest setting. Line a baking sheet with foil. Place the slices of prosciutto on the foil-lined pan and broil for 3–4 minutes on one side until crispy. Set aside.

2 Bring a large pan of salted water to a boil and cook the pasta according to package instructions.

3 Drain the pasta and return it to the pan. Crumble in the crispy broiled ham and stir in the crème fraîche, half-and-half, and cheese. Season well with pepper. Serve with extra Parmesan and an arugula salad.

PREPARE AHEAD

This simple yet luxurious dish is ideal for midweek entertaining. To get ahead, the prosciutto can be broiled, crumbled up, and stored in the fridge in an airtight container for up to 2 days.

CALORIES: 578kcals/2439kJ
CARBOHYDRATE: 71g
    sugar: 3g
FAT: 20g
    saturated: 11g
SALT: 1.5g
FIBER: 4g

Smoked salmon and crème fraîche pasta

A simple yet stylish way to pull together a fabulous supper with just a few ingredients from the fridge.

5 mins   10 mins

SERVES 4

10oz (300g) dried pasta

salt and freshly ground black pepper

¾ cup (7oz) low-fat crème fraîche

4oz (120g) smoked salmon, finely chopped

1 tbsp finely chopped capers, rinsed, or more to taste

finely grated zest of ½ lemon

2 tbsp finely chopped dill

finely grated Parmesan cheese, to serve

1 Cook the pasta in a large pan of boiling salted water according to the package instructions.

2 Meanwhile, beat the crème fraîche in a bowl until smooth. Add the smoked salmon, capers, lemon zest, and dill, and season.

3 Drain the pasta (reserving a ladleful of the cooking water) and return it to the pan with the reserved water. Toss the sauce through the pasta and return it to the heat, stirring just long enough both for the pasta to soak up some of the sauce and for the sauce to heat through. Serve with the Parmesan cheese.

Sometimes children will surprise you with a liking for stronger, piquant flavors but for those who don't, you can exclude the dill and capers.

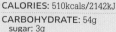
Fussy eaters!

CALORIES: 510kcals/2142kJ
CARBOHYDRATE: 54g
  sugar: 3g
FAT: 25g
  saturated: 15g
SALT: 1.2g
FIBER: 2.2g

Spaghetti alle vongole

The classic Italian dish is made with fresh clams, but this version uses a can for a pantry supper.

15 mins   1 hr 5 mins

SERVES 4

3 tbsp olive oil

1 onion, finely chopped

2 garlic cloves, crushed

1 x 7oz (280g) can clams

1 x 14oz (400g) can chopped tomatoes

1 tbsp tomato paste

1 tsp granulated sugar

2 tbsp roughly chopped flat-leaf parsley leaves

salt and freshly ground black pepper

10oz (300g) dried spaghetti

1 Heat 2 tbsp of the oil in a heavy-bottomed saucepan and cook the onion over medium heat for about 5 minutes, until softened, but not browned. Add the garlic and cook for a minute. Drain the clams, reserving the liquid. Cover and refrigerate the clams.

2 Add the tomatoes and clam liquid to the onions. Stir in the tomato paste, sugar, and parsley, and season well. Bring to a boil, reduce the heat to a low simmer, and cook for about 1 hour until thickened and reduced. If the tomatoes are taking a while to break down, mash with a potato masher to help them along.

3 When the sauce is nearly ready, cook the spaghetti in a large pan of boiling salted water according to the package instructions. Drain the spaghetti (reserving a ladleful of the cooking water), and return it to the pan with the reserved water.

4 Add the clams and remaining oil to the sauce and allow to heat through, before tossing in the cooked spaghetti.

CALORIES: 387kcals/1634kJ
CARBOHYDRATE: 59g
  sugar: 8.5g
FAT: 10g
  saturated: 1.5g
SALT: 0.3g
FIBER: 5g

Tuna, tomato, and black olive pasta sauce

Another pantry recipe, the addition of tuna and black olives to a basic tomato sauce gives added flavor.

15 mins **1 hr 10 mins**

SERVES 4

2 tbsp olive oil

1 onion, finely chopped

2 garlic cloves, crushed

1 x 14oz (400g) can chopped tomatoes

1 tbsp tomato paste

1 tsp granulated sugar

2 tbsp roughly chopped flat-leaf parsley leaves

salt and freshly ground black pepper

1 x 7oz (185g) can tuna, drained, and flaked with a fork

1¾oz (50g) pitted black olives, roughly chopped

2 tbsp roughly chopped basil leaves

finely grated Parmesan cheese, to serve

1 Heat the oil in a heavy-bottomed saucepan and cook the onion over medium heat for about 5 minutes, until softened but not browned. Add the garlic and cook for 1 minute.

2 Add the tomatoes, then fill the empty can with water and pour it in. Stir in the tomato paste, sugar, and parsley, and season well. Bring the sauce to a boil, reduce it to a low simmer, and cook for about 1 hour, until thickened and reduced, stirring occasionally. If the tomatoes are taking a while to break down, mash with a potato masher to help them along.

3 When the sauce has reduced and is rich and thick, add the tuna and olives and heat through.

4 Remove from the heat and stir in the basil before serving over your favorite pasta, with the Parmesan cheese.

CALORIES: 178kcals/742kJ

CARBOHYDRATE: 6g
  sugar: 6g

FAT: 11g
  saturated: 1.5g

SALT: 0.4g

FIBER: 2g

Linguine with spicy shrimp and tomato sauce

Adding Parmesan cheese is not traditional with shellfish pasta recipes, but feel free to have some if you want!

20 mins | 1 hr

SERVES 4

14oz (400g) shell-on, cooked shrimp

2 tbsp olive oil

1 onion, finely chopped

2 garlic cloves, crushed

1 tsp chile flakes

1 x 14oz (400g) can chopped tomatoes

1 tbsp tomato paste

1 tsp granulated sugar

2 tbsp roughly chopped flat-leaf parsley leaves

salt and freshly ground black pepper

10oz (300g) dried linguine

1 First, shell the shrimp and devein them. Cover and refrigerate. Put the shells in a saucepan and pour in a 2in (5cm) depth of water. Bring to a boil, reduce to a low simmer, and cook for 25–30 minutes until the liquid has reduced by about half. Strain.

2 Heat the oil in a heavy-bottomed saucepan and cook the onion over medium heat for about 5 minutes, until softened but not browned. Add the garlic and chile flakes and cook for 1 minute.

3 Add the tomatoes and shrimp stock. Stir in the tomato paste, sugar, and parsley, and season well. Bring the sauce to a boil, reduce the heat to a low simmer, and cook for about 45 minutes until thickened and reduced. If the tomatoes are taking a while to break down, mash gently with a potato masher to help them along.

4 When the sauce is nearly ready, cook the linguine in boiling salted water according to the package instructions. Drain (reserving a ladleful of the cooking water) and return it to the pan with the reserved water.

5 Add the shrimp to the sauce and cook for 2 minutes, or until heated through, being careful not to overcook. Toss the sauce through the linguine to serve.

CLEVER WITH LEFTOVERS

Whenever you are peeling shrimp, don't throw the shells away; they have an amazing flavor. Bag them up and freeze them until you have enough to prepare the stock for this dish, or for the basis of hundreds of shellfish soups and sauces.

CALORIES: 467kcals/1971kJ

CARBOHYDRATE: 59g
sugar: 7g

FAT: 11g
saturated: 1.5g

SALT: 0.2g

FIBER: 4.5g

Spaghetti Bolognese

A household standard, but the long, slow cooking time here turns the everyday into something special.

20 mins   1 hr

SERVES 4

2 tbsp olive oil

1 onion, finely chopped

1 celery stalk, finely chopped

1 carrot, finely chopped

2 garlic cloves, crushed

1lb 2oz (500g) ground beef

1 x 14oz (400g) can chopped tomatoes

1 cup beef stock

1 tbsp tomato paste

1 tsp granulated sugar

2 tbsp roughly chopped flat-leaf
   parsley leaves

1 tsp dried oregano

salt and freshly ground black pepper

10oz (300g) dried spaghetti

finely grated Parmesan cheese, to serve

1 Heat the oil in a large, heavy-bottomed saucepan and cook the onion, celery, and carrot over medium heat for 5 minutes, until softened, but not browned. Add the garlic and cook for 1 minute. Add the ground beef and cook it over high heat, breaking any clumps up with a wooden spoon and turning to brown all over.

2 Add the tomatoes and stock. Stir in the tomato paste, sugar, parsley, and oregano, and season generously. Slowly bring to a boil, then reduce the heat to a low simmer, and cook for about 1 hour, or more if needed, until the sauce has thickened and reduced, and smells rich.

3 When the sauce is nearly ready, cook the spaghetti until just al dente in boiling salted water according to the package instructions. Drain the pasta (reserving about a ladleful of the cooking water) and return it to the pan along with the reserved water.

4 Toss the sauce through the spaghetti and serve with plenty of Parmesan cheese.

VARIATION

Substitute some of the stock with a small glass of red wine for a richer flavor, if you are cooking for adults.

CALORIES: 641kcals/2692kJ

CARBOHYDRATE: 60g
   sugar: 10g

FAT: 27g
   saturated: 10g

SALT: 0.6g

FIBER: 6g

Conchigliette with sausage and tomato sauce

Sausages are an easy standby, but can get boring. Remove the casing and mix into this child-friendly pasta sauce.

10 mins   30-40 mins

SERVES 4

1 tbsp olive oil

1 red onion, finely chopped

2 garlic cloves, finely chopped

8 pork and herb sausages

1 tsp dried oregano

1 tsp dried marjoram

½ tsp fennel seeds

salt and freshly ground black pepper

2 x 15oz (500g) cans tomato sauce

5½oz (150g) dried conchigliette or other small pasta shapes

finely grated Parmesan cheese, garlic bread, and salad, to serve

1 Heat the oil in a large pan over medium heat and cook the onion for 5 minutes, until translucent and softened, but not browned.

2 Add the garlic, sausages, oregano, marjoram, and fennel seeds. Season and stir well, breaking the sausages up with a wooden spoon so the meat browns all over. Cook over medium heat for 5 minutes, stirring constantly so it does not stick. Add the tomato sauce, cover, and simmer for 10 minutes.

3 Add the conchigliette and cook over low heat for 10 minutes, or until cooked, stirring regularly. If the mixture threatens to become too dry, add a splash of water.

4 Spoon into bowls, sprinkle generously with Parmesan cheese, and serve with garlic bread and a green salad.

BATCHING AND FREEZING

A frozen portion of Slow-cooked tomato sauce (see p191) works well here. For a quick version, defrost the sauce in the morning. Add it to cooked pasta and sausages for an instant family supper.

CALORIES: 510kcals/2136kJ

CARBOHYDRATE: 48g
  sugar: 4g

FAT: 25g
  saturated: 8.5g

SALT: 2.1g

FIBER: 5g

Spaghetti and meatballs

It's best to make the meatballs fairly small for this dish, as it makes it easier to pick them up with the spaghetti.

30 mins, plus chilling   1 hr 10 mins

SERVES 4

FOR THE MEATBALLS

½ cup fresh bread crumbs

5½oz (150g) ground pork

5½oz (150g) ground beef

¾oz (20g) finely grated Parmesan cheese, plus extra for serving

1 tbsp finely chopped parsley leaves

1 large egg yolk

salt and freshly ground black pepper

FOR THE SAUCE AND PASTA

4 tbsp olive oil

1 onion, finely chopped

2 garlic cloves, crushed

1 x 14oz (400g) can chopped tomatoes

1 tbsp tomato paste

1 tsp granulated sugar

2 tbsp roughly chopped flat-leaf parsley leaves

10oz (300g) dried spaghetti

2 tbsp roughly chopped basil leaves (optional)

1 In a large bowl, mix all the meatball ingredients until well combined, seasoning generously. Cover and chill for at least 30 minutes.

2 For the sauce, heat 2 tbsp of the oil in a heavy-bottomed saucepan and cook the onion over medium heat for about 5 minutes, until softened, but not browned. Add the garlic and cook, stirring, for another minute.

3 Add the tomatoes, then fill the empty can with water and pour it in. Stir in the tomato paste, sugar, and parsley, and season well. Bring to a boil, reduce it to a low simmer, and cook for about 1 hour, until thickened. If the tomatoes are taking a while to break down, mash with a potato masher.

4 When the sauce is nearly ready, cook the spaghetti in boiling salted water according to the package instructions. Drain the pasta (reserving a ladleful of the cooking water) and return it to the pan with the reserved water.

5 Meanwhile, heat the remaining 2 tbsp of oil in a large, heavy-bottomed frying pan. Roll the meat mixture into 1in (3cm) balls and cook for 5 minutes over medium heat, shaking frequently, until browned all over and cooked through. They should be springy to the touch. Drain on paper towels.

6 Mix the sauce through the spaghetti with the basil (if using) and turn it into a large, wide, warmed serving bowl. Scatter in the meatballs (this helps to portion out the meatballs when serving), and serve with plenty of grated Parmesan cheese.

VARIATION

Use all ground pork, or all ground beef, or even substitute ground turkey for the ground pork, to suit your family's diet and budget.

HOW TO FREEZE

Open-freeze the raw meatballs on a baking sheet, then transfer to a freezer bag and keep for up to 3 months. You can then remove only as many as you want. The cooked sauce can be frozen separately and kept for up to 6 months.

CALORIES: 606kcals/2548kJ

CARBOHYDRATE: 64g
  sugar: 7g

FAT: 26g
  saturated: 7.5g

SALT: 0.6g

FIBER: 5g

Penne with creamy butternut squash and bacon

This creamy, savory sauce is simply one of the nicest things you can eat with pasta, sweet and comforting.

15 mins   30 mins

SERVES 4

14oz (400g) butternut squash, chopped into ½in (1cm) cubes

3 tbsp olive oil

salt and freshly ground black pepper

10oz (300g) dried penne

1 onion, finely chopped

5½oz (150g) thick-cut bacon, cut into ½in (1cm) strips

1 large garlic clove, crushed

1¼ cups half-and-half

1 tbsp finely chopped sage leaves

1¼oz (40g) finely grated Parmesan cheese

1 Preheat the oven to 400°F (200°C). Toss the butternut squash in 2 tbsp of the oil, season it well, and spread it out over a large baking sheet. Bake at the top of the oven for 20 minutes, turning once, until golden brown and cooked through.

2 Cook the penne in boiling salted water according to the package instructions. Drain the pasta (reserving a ladleful of the cooking water) and return it to the pan with the reserved water.

3 Meanwhile, heat the remaining 1 tbsp of oil in a large frying pan. Cook the onion over medium heat for 5 minutes, until it is softened, but not browned. Add the bacon and cook for 3–4 minutes, stirring, until it is browned and crispy. Add the garlic and cook for 1 minute.

4 Add the half-and-half and sage and allow it to bubble up. Add the squash and cook until the half-and-half reduces and begins to be absorbed into the other ingredients, about 3 minutes.

5 Use a potato masher or the back of a wooden spoon to lightly crush some of the squash pieces, and stir these in to further thicken the sauce. Take the pan off the heat and stir in the Parmesan cheese. Taste for seasoning and stir through the penne to serve.

VARIATION

Add a little chile (try 1 red chile, seeded and finely chopped, or ½ tsp chile flakes) with the garlic for a spicier dish. Omit the chile if you are serving small children.

CALORIES: 670kcals/2809kJ

CARBOHYDRATE: 64g
sugar: 9g

FAT: 36g
saturated: 15.5g

SALT: 1.5g

FIBER: 6g

Pasta with peas and pancetta

Another quick, tasty pasta that relies just on a few pantry essentials to make a great supper.

10 mins   15 mins

SERVES 4

10oz (300g) dried shell pasta, such as conchigliette

salt and freshly ground black pepper

5½oz (150g) frozen peas or petits pois

2 tbsp olive oil

7oz (200g) chopped pancetta

2 tbsp butter

2 garlic cloves, crushed

1¾oz (50g) finely grated Parmesan cheese, plus extra for serving

1 Cook the pasta in boiling salted water according to the package instructions. A minute or two before the end of cooking, throw the peas in with the pasta to cook through. Drain (reserving a ladleful of the cooking water) and return it to the pan with the reserved water.

2 Meanwhile, heat the oil in a large frying pan. Cook the pancetta for 3–5 minutes over medium heat until crispy. Add the butter and garlic and cook for another minute, then remove from the heat.

3 Toss the garlicky pancetta through the pasta and peas, and follow with the Parmesan cheese. Season well to taste and serve with extra Parmesan cheese.

VARIATION

If you have no pancetta, use chopped up smoked bacon, as this is like pancetta in flavor.

CALORIES: 587kcals/2461kJ
CARBOHYDRATE: 57g
    sugar: 2.5g
FAT: 29g
    saturated: 11.5g
SALT: 1.9g
FIBER: 5.5g

Quick tomato, bacon, and garlic pasta

Using ripe, peeled tomatoes is a great standby when you don't have time to cook a canned tomato sauce.

10 mins   15 mins

SERVES 4

salt and freshly ground black pepper

10oz (300g) dried pasta

4 large, ripe tomatoes, approx. 1lb 5oz (600g) in total

1 tbsp olive oil

5½oz (150g) thick-cut bacon, cut into ½in (1cm) strips

1 tbsp butter

2 garlic cloves, crushed

handful of basil leaves, finely chopped

finely grated Parmesan cheese, to serve

1 Bring a large pan of salted water to a boil for the pasta. Before cooking the pasta, use the water to peel the tomatoes (see p191), then cut the flesh into small cubes. Then cook the pasta according to the package instructions.

2 Meanwhile, heat the oil in a large frying pan. Cook the bacon for 3 minutes over medium heat until brown and crispy. Add the butter and garlic and cook for 1 minute.

3 Add the tomatoes and three ladles of the pasta water to the pan and bring to a boil. Reduce the heat to a simmer and cook until the tomatoes have broken down and the sauce is thick, about 5 minutes. Use a potato masher to help break the tomatoes down, if necessary. Season to taste and stir in the basil.

4 Drain the pasta (reserving a ladleful of the cooking water) and return it to the pan with the reserved water. Toss through the tomato sauce and serve with the Parmesan cheese.

CALORIES: 443kcals/1866kJ
CARBOHYDRATE: 57g
    sugar: 6g
FAT: 16g
    saturated: 6g
SALT: 1.3g
FIBER: 5g

Lasagna Bolognese

No one ever gets tired of lasagna. If you have time to assemble the different parts, it will always be appreciated.

30 mins   2 hrs, plus resting

SPECIAL EQUIPMENT

10in (25cm) ovenproof dish

SERVES 4–6

3½oz (100g) dried lasagna sheets

green salad and crusty bread, to serve

FOR THE BOLOGNESE SAUCE

2 tbsp olive oil

1 onion, finely chopped

1 celery stalk, finely chopped

1 carrot, finely chopped

2 garlic cloves, crushed

1lb 5oz (600g) ground beef

1 x 14oz (400g) can chopped tomatoes

1 cup beef stock

1 tbsp tomato paste

1 tsp granulated sugar

2 tbsp chopped flat-leaf parsley leaves

1 tsp dried oregano

salt and freshly ground black pepper

FOR THE CHEESE SAUCE

5 tbsp butter

⅓ cup all-purpose flour

2 cups whole milk

2½oz (75g) grated aged Cheddar cheese

1 Cook the meat sauce as for Spaghetti Bolognese (see p201).When the sauce is nearly ready, preheat the oven to 350°F (180°C).

2 For the cheese sauce, melt the butter in a small, heavy-bottomed saucepan. Whisk in the flour over low heat and cook for 2 minutes, whisking constantly, until the mixture bubbles and separates. Take the pan off the heat and whisk in the milk, a little at a time, whisking well between each addition, until it has all been added and the sauce is smooth. Return to the heat and cook, stirring constantly, until it thickens.

3 Reduce the heat to low and cook, stirring occasionally, for 5 minutes. Be sure to whisk right into the edges of the saucepan, as this is where the sauce can burn if left undisturbed. Add 1¾oz (50g) of the cheese, season well, and cook for another 2 minutes until the cheese has melted and the sauce is smooth, thick, and creamy.

4 Spread one-third of the meat sauce over a 10in (25cm) ovenproof dish. Top with a layer of lasagna sheets and one-third of the cheese sauce. Repeat twice more, finishing with the cheese sauce. Sprinkle the scant 1oz (25g) of reserved cheese on top and cook in the middle of the oven for 45 minutes to 1 hour until golden brown and a knife goes easily through the center. Rest for 10 minutes, then serve with green salad and plenty of crusty bread.

BATCHING AND FREEZING

Getting ahead with supper can be easy if you have made a double or triple batch of Bolognese sauce (see p201) and frozen it in family-sized portions. Defrost a portion and you can make this lasagna in half the time.

CALORIES: 892kcals/3716kJ

CARBOHYDRATE: 44.5g
  sugar: 13.5g

FAT: 57g
  saturated: 28g

SALT: 1.4g

FIBER: 4g

Roasted vegetable lasagna

Meat-free days are a good thing, but sometimes difficult to manage for the whole family. This makes them easy.

25 mins   30 mins

SPECIAL EQUIPMENT
11 x 8 x 2in (28 x 20 x 5cm) ovenproof dish

SERVES 4

3 tbsp olive oil

2 red onions, roughly chopped

1 eggplant, cut into 1in (3cm) cubes

1 red and 1 yellow bell pepper, cut into 1in (3cm) pieces

1 zucchini, cut into 1in (3cm) cubes

1 bulb fennel, finely sliced

3 garlic cloves, roughly chopped

1 tsp dried rosemary

1 tsp dried basil

salt and freshly ground black pepper

2 cups tomato sauce

1¾ cups (14oz) low-fat crème fraîche

2 large eggs, beaten

2oz (60g) finely grated Parmesan cheese

8oz (225g) fresh lasagna sheets

3½oz (100g) grated mozzarella cheese

garlic bread, to serve

1 Preheat the oven to 400°F (200°C). Pour the oil into a large roasting pan and heat in the oven for 5 minutes.

2 Add all the vegetables to the pan with the garlic, herbs, and plenty of seasoning. Stir well and return the pan to the oven for 30 minutes, stirring occasionally. Remove, then stir the tomato sauce into the roasted vegetables.

3 Meanwhile, place the crème fraîche, eggs, and Parmesan in a bowl, season with pepper, and whisk together with a fork. Place half the vegetables in the bottom of a 11 x 8 x 2in (28 x 29 x 5cm) ovenproof dish and top with half the lasagna. Repeat the layers.

4 Pour the egg mixture over the lasagna and top with the mozzarella cheese. Place the dish on a baking sheet and bake for 30 minutes. Serve with garlic bread.

CALORIES: 635kcals/2660kJ
CARBOHYDRATE: 46g
  sugar: 9g
FAT: 36g
  saturated: 17g
SALT: 0.7g
FIBER: 6g

Spinach and ricotta cannelloni

This soothing vegetarian dish makes a welcome change to the more usual meat-filled lasagna. Great on cold days.

25 mins   50 mins

SERVES 4

4 tbsp butter, plus extra for greasing

10oz (300g) spinach

2 garlic cloves, finely chopped

salt and freshly ground black pepper

15oz (425g) ricotta cheese, drained

½ tsp grated nutmeg

16 dried cannelloni tubes

¼ cup all-purpose flour

2 cups whole milk

1¼oz (40g) finely grated Grana Padano cheese

1 Preheat the oven to 350°F (180°C). Butter a medium, shallow ovenproof dish.

2 Bring a large pan, containing a ½in (1cm) depth of water, to a boil, add the spinach, and stir until wilted. Drain and press out excess water. Chop the spinach.

3 Melt 1 tbsp of the butter in a medium pan and sauté the garlic for 2 minutes. Add the spinach, season, and stir well. Remove from the heat and stir in the ricotta cheese and nutmeg. Carefully fill the cannelloni with the spinach mixture and place the tubes in the buttered dish.

4 Meanwhile, melt the remaining 3 tbsp of the butter in a large pan. Whisk in the flour over low heat and cook for 2 minutes, whisking constantly. Take the pan off the heat and whisk in the milk, a little at a time, whisking well between each addition, until it has all been added. Return to the heat and cook, stirring constantly, until it thickens.

5 Reduce the heat to low and cook, stirring occasionally, for 5 minutes. Be sure to whisk right into the edges of the saucepan, as this is where the sauce can burn if left undisturbed. Season well and pour over the filled cannelloni. Sprinkle the cheese over the top in an even layer. Place on a baking sheet and bake for 30 minutes.

VARIATION

Reduce the amount of ricotta to 13oz (375g), and add 1¾oz (50g) finely chopped sun-dried tomatoes to the filling mixture.

CALORIES: 761kcals/3191kJ
CARBOHYDRATE: 78g
  sugar: 10g
FAT: 36g
  saturated: 22g
SALT: 1.1g
FIBER: 6g

Cheesy tuna and corn pasta bake

Tuna is a great pantry essential, being relatively inexpensive, yet packed full of low-fat protein.

10 mins   35 mins

SPECIAL EQUIPMENT
2-quart (2-liter) flameproof casserole

SERVES 4

salt and freshly ground black pepper

12oz (350g) dried fusilli

4 tbsp butter

¼ cup all-purpose flour

2 cups whole milk

5¾oz (160g) grated white Cheddar cheese

2 x 14oz (400g) cans tuna in spring water, drained and flaked

1 x 7oz (195g) can corn (no added salt or sugar), drained

1 tbsp tomato paste

1 tsp dried thyme

1¼oz (40g) cheese tortilla chips, roughly crushed

steamed green beans, to serve

CALORIES: 984kcals/4132kJ
CARBOHYDRATE: 92g
  sugar: 11g
FAT: 34g
  saturated: 18g
SALT: 1.9g
FIBER: 6g

1 Preheat the oven to 350°F (180°C). Bring a large pan of salted water to a boil, add the pasta, and cook according to the package instructions. Drain.

2 Meanwhile, melt the butter in a 2-quart (2-liter) flameproof casserole dish. Whisk in the flour over low heat. Cook for 2 minutes, whisking constantly until the mixture bubbles and separates.

3 Take the pan off the heat and whisk in the milk, a little at a time, whisking well between each addition, until it has all been added and the sauce is smooth. Return to the heat and cook, stirring, until it thickens. Reduce the heat to low and cook, stirring occasionally, for 5 minutes. Be sure to whisk right into the edges of the saucepan, as this is where the sauce can burn.

4 Add 3oz (90g) of the cheese and stir until melted. Add the tuna, corn, tomato paste, and thyme. Season and stir well.

5 Add the cooked pasta to the sauce and stir well to coat. Sprinkle the crushed tortilla chips over the pasta and top with the remaining cheese. Bake in the oven for 15 minutes. Serve with steamed green beans.

Chicken and broccoli pasta bake

A fantastic idea for leftovers, and perfect for making Sunday's roast chicken stretch to Monday night's supper.

20 mins | 30 mins, plus resting

SPECIAL EQUIPMENT
10in (25cm) ovenproof dish

SERVES 4

10oz (300g) small dried pasta shapes, such as mini conchigliette or macaroni

7oz (200g) small broccoli florets

5 tbsp butter

⅓ cup all-purpose flour

2 cups whole milk

1¾oz (50g) grated aged Cheddar cheese

salt and freshly ground black pepper

leftover roast chicken (ideally 10oz/300g), chopped small

1 cup day-old bread crumbs

scant 1oz (25g) finely grated Parmesan cheese

1 Preheat the oven to 400°F (200°C). Boil the pasta according to the package instructions. A couple of minutes before it is ready, throw in the broccoli and cook until al dente. Drain the pasta and broccoli and return them to the pan.

2 Meanwhile, melt the butter in a small, heavy-bottomed saucepan. Whisk in the flour over low heat. Continue to cook for 2 minutes, whisking constantly, until the mixture bubbles and separates. Take the pan off the heat and whisk in the milk, a little at a time, whisking well between each addition, until it has all been added and the sauce is smooth.

3 Return to the heat and cook, stirring constantly, until it thickens. Reduce the heat to low and continue to cook, stirring occasionally for 5 minutes.

Be sure to whisk into the edges of the saucepan, as this is where the sauce can burn if left undisturbed.

4 Add the Cheddar cheese, season well, and cook for 2 minutes until the cheese has melted and the sauce is smooth, thick, and creamy.

5 Pour the sauce over the pasta and broccoli, add the chicken, and stir until well combined. Be gentle, so as not to break up the broccoli florets. Check the seasoning and pour the mixture into a 10in (25cm) ovenproof dish. Mix the bread crumbs and Parmesan and sprinkle an even layer on top.

6 Cook the pasta at the top of the oven for 20–25 minutes, until golden brown on top with crisp bread crumbs, and bubbling around the edges. Rest for at least 5 minutes before serving.

VARIATION

If you do not have leftover chicken, or your family does not eat meat, try adding a large can of drained, flaked salmon or tuna to the pasta in step 5 before baking.

CALORIES: 800kcals/3365kJ
CARBOHYDRATE: 82g
  sugar: 8g
FAT: 31.5g
  saturated: 18g
SALT: 1.2g
FIBER: 6g

"Mac and cheese"

A thick, creamy mac and cheese is everybody's idea of a tasty supper. This is the ultimate family favorite.

10 mins   15 mins

SERVES 4

10oz (300g) dried macaroni

salt and freshly ground black pepper

4 tbsp butter

¼ cup all-purpose flour

2 cups whole milk

5½oz (150g) grated aged
Cheddar cheese

1¾oz (50g) finely grated
Parmesan cheese

steamed broccoli, to serve

1 Cook the macaroni in boiling salted water according to the package instructions. Drain and transfer to a shallow ovenproof dish.

2 Meanwhile, melt the butter in a saucepan. Whisk in the flour over low heat and cook for 2 minutes, whisking constantly, until the mixture bubbles and separates.

3 Take the pan off the heat and whisk in the milk, a little at a time, whisking well between each addition, until it has all been added and the sauce is smooth. Return to the heat and cook, stirring until it thickens. Reduce the heat to low and cook, stirring occasionally, for 5 minutes. Be sure to whisk right into the edges of the saucepan, as this is where the sauce can burn if left undisturbed. Add 3½oz (100g) of the Cheddar cheese and stir until it has melted. Preheat the broiler to its highest setting.

4 Pour the sauce over the macaroni, season with pepper, and stir well to coat. Sprinkle in the remaining 1¾oz (50g) of Cheddar cheese and the Parmesan. Place on a baking sheet and broil for 5 minutes, or until bubbling. Serve with steamed broccoli.

Mac and cheese is an easy, ever-popular way to ensure children are getting enough calcium and protein.

Fussy eaters!

CALORIES: 679kcals/2847kJ
CARBOHYDRATE: 67g
  sugar: 7g
FAT: 33g
  saturated: 20g
SALT: 1.2g
FIBER: 3.5g

Pastitsio

This delicious Greek pasta bake is rich, filling, and gently spiced; a hit with children and adults alike.

20 mins   1 hr 40 mins

SERVES 4

1 tbsp olive oil

1 onion, finely chopped

2 garlic cloves, finely chopped

14oz (400g) lean ground lamb

½ tsp ground nutmeg, plus extra for the cheese sauce

1 tsp ground cumin

1 tsp ground coriander

1 tsp dried thyme

1 tsp dried oregano

1 bay leaf

¾ cup red wine

1 x 14oz (400g) can chopped tomatoes

salt and freshly ground black pepper

10oz (300g) dried macaroni

¼ cup chopped cilantro leaves

2 tomatoes, sliced

steamed green beans and crusty white bread, to serve

FOR THE CHEESE SAUCE

2 tbsp butter

2 tbsp all-purpose flour

1¼ cups whole milk

1¾oz (50g) finely grated Parmesan cheese

3½oz (100g) feta cheese, crumbled

2 large eggs, lightly beaten

1 Heat the oil in a large pan over medium heat. Cook the onion for 5 minutes. Add the garlic and cook for another minute. Add the lamb and cook for 5 minutes, breaking it up to brown all over.

2 Stir in the spices, dried herbs, and bay leaf, and cook for 2 minutes, stirring. Add the wine and tomatoes, season, cover, and simmer for 45 minutes. Preheat the oven to 350°F (180°C).

3 Meanwhile, bring a large pan of salted water to a boil and cook the macaroni for 2 minutes less than instructed on the package. Drain and run under cold water.

4 Add the pasta and cilantro to the lamb, stir, and remove the bay leaf. Spoon the lamb sauce into a shallow ovenproof dish.

5 Meanwhile, make the cheese sauce. Melt the butter in a pan. Whisk in the flour over low heat for 2 minutes. Take the pan off the heat and whisk in the milk gradually. Return to the heat and cook, stirring, until it thickens. Stir in both cheeses. Remove from the heat, stir in the eggs, and season well with nutmeg and pepper.

6 Pour the cheese sauce over the lamb mixture and top with the sliced tomatoes. Bake for 40 minutes. Serve with steamed green beans and crusty white bread.

PREPARE AHEAD

Like other layered recipes, such as Lasagna Bolognese (see p206), all the elements of this dish can be made up to 2 days ahead. It is safest to add the eggs to the cheese sauce only when ready to assemble and bake.

CALORIES: 789kcals/3316kJ

CARBOHYDRATE: 67g
  sugar: 11g

FAT: 35g
  saturated: 17g

SALT: 1.8g

FIBER: 5.5g

Baked gnocchi with cheese sauce

Gnocchi is an excellent standby for any busy family's fridge. A few additions turn it into something special.

10 mins   25 mins

SERVES 4

3 tbsp butter

3 tbsp all-purpose flour

2 cups whole milk

1 tsp English mustard

2¼oz (70g) grated Gruyère cheese

salt and freshly ground black pepper

1lb 2oz (500g) store-bought gnocchi

5½oz (150g) bocconcini (small mozzarella cheese balls)

3½oz (100g) cherry tomatoes, halved

green salad, to serve

1 Preheat the oven to 400°F (200°C). Melt the butter in a pan. Whisk in the flour over low heat. Cook for 2 minutes, whisking constantly, until the mixture bubbles and separates.

2 Take the pan off the heat and whisk in the milk, a little at a time, whisking well between each addition, until it has all been added and the sauce is smooth. Return to the heat and cook, stirring constantly, until it thickens. Reduce the heat to low and cook, stirring occasionally, for 5 minutes. Be sure to whisk right into the edges of the saucepan, as this is where the sauce can burn if left undisturbed.

3 Add the mustard and Gruyère cheese and stir until the cheese has melted and the sauce is smooth, thick, and creamy. Season well.

4 Place the gnocchi in a shallow ovenproof dish, pour in the sauce, and arrange the mozzarella balls and cherry tomatoes, cut-side up, on top. Bake for 15 minutes. Spoon onto warmed plates and serve with a green salad.

CALORIES: 555kcals/2314kJ
CARBOHYDRATE: 53g
   sugar: 7g
FAT: 27g
   saturated: 17g
SALT: 2.4g
FIBER: 3g

Crispy gnocchi with Bolognese sauce

If you have some Bolognese sauce in the freezer, this tasty, family-friendly meal can be ready in minutes.

20 mins   1 hr 30 mins

SERVES 4

1 tbsp olive oil

1 onion, finely chopped

2 garlic cloves, finely chopped

1lb 2oz (500g) lean ground beef

1 tsp dried oregano

1 tsp dried marjoram

1 x 15oz (500g) can tomato sauce

⅔ cup red wine

1 bay leaf

salt and freshly ground black pepper

1lb 2oz (500g) store-bought gnocchi

¾ cup fresh white bread crumbs

¼oz (40g) finely grated Parmesan cheese

arugula salad, to serve

CALORIES: 590kcals/2464kJ
CARBOHYDRATE: 57g
   sugar: 2g
FAT: 18.5g
   saturated: 8g
SALT: 2g
FIBER: 4.5g

1 Heat the oil in a large pan over medium heat and cook the onion for 5 minutes. Add the garlic and cook for 2 minutes.

2 Stir the meat into the pan and cook for 5 minutes, breaking it up with a wooden spoon, or until browned. Stir in the dried herbs, tomato sauce, wine, and bay leaf. Season well and bring to a boil, then reduce the heat, partially cover, and simmer gently for 1 hour, stirring occasionally. Preheat the oven to 375°F (190°C).

3 Put the gnocchi in a shallow ovenproof dish. Mix the bread crumbs, Parmesan cheese, and plenty of pepper in a bowl.

4 Pour the Bolognese sauce over the gnocchi and sprinkle with the cheesy bread crumbs. Place the dish on a baking sheet and bake for 15 minutes, or until the crumbs are crispy. Spoon onto plates and serve with arugula salad.

PREPARE AHEAD

Assemble this recipe up to 2 days in advance, cover, and refrigerate. Simply bake as in step 4 to finish.

Fiery pepper noodles

A wonderfully spicy vegetarian dish, where the contrasting lime and chile work well with the crunchy peanuts.

30 mins   **4 mins**

SERVES 4

1 red bell pepper

1 green bell pepper

1 tbsp sunflower or vegetable oil

4 scallions, chopped

1 garlic clove, finely chopped

1 zucchini, finely chopped

1 or 2 green jalapeño or poblano chiles, seeded and chopped

1 tsp grated fresh ginger

1 tbsp chopped flat-leaf parsley leaves

1 tbsp chopped cilantro, plus a few torn leaves, to serve

finely grated zest and juice of 1 lime

¼ cup crunchy peanut butter

3 tbsp soy sauce

1 tbsp dry sherry

1lb 2oz (500g) fresh egg noodles

2oz (60g) chopped roasted peanuts, to serve

1 Preheat the oven to 400°F (200°C). Put the peppers on a baking sheet and cook for 25–30 minutes until they begin to char. Remove from the oven, put in a plastic bag, and let cool before removing the stalks and skin, seeding, and roughly chopping. (Watch out, as the juices inside will be hot.)

2 Heat the oil in a wok or large frying pan over high heat. Add the scallions, garlic, and zucchini, and stir-fry for 1 minute, constantly moving the ingredients so they do not stick and burn to the pan. Add the peppers, chiles, ginger, herbs, lime zest and juice, peanut butter, soy sauce, sherry, and ½ cup of water. Stir until the peanut butter melts into the rest of the sauce.

3 Add the noodles and toss for 2 minutes until piping hot throughout. Pile into warmed bowls and sprinkle with the peanuts and a few torn cilantro leaves to serve.

Teenagers often dislike vegetables, yet love take-out. Cook this tasty Asian stir-fry and see if you can convert them!

Fussy eaters!

CALORIES: 450kcals/1873kJ	
CARBOHYDRATE: 44g	
sugar: 8g	
FAT: 23g	
saturated: 4g	
SALT: 2.4g	
FIBER: 5.5	

Dan dan noodles

An easy version of the spicy Sichuan classic, simplified to include easily available ingredients.

10 mins   10 mins

SERVES 4

10oz (300g) dried Chinese egg noodles

salt

7oz (200g) small broccoli florets

¼ cup soy sauce

1 tbsp tahini paste

1 tbsp cornstarch

2 tsp sesame oil

2 tsp chili oil

1 tbsp balsamic vinegar

1 tsp granulated sugar

⅔ cup chicken stock (see p94)

2 tbsp sunflower or vegetable oil

2 garlic cloves, finely chopped

1in (3cm) piece of fresh ginger, finely chopped

12oz (350g) ground pork

bunch of scallions, finely chopped, to serve

1¾oz (50g) salted peanuts, roughly chopped, to serve (optional)

CALORIES: 673kcals/2822kJ
CARBOHYDRATE: 60g
   sugar: 7.5g
FAT: 32g
   saturated: 8g
SALT: 3.5g
FIBER: 7g

1 Cook the noodles in a large pan of boiling salted water according to the package instructions. Drain well. Keep them in a bowl of cold water until needed (to keep them from sticking together). Meanwhile, cook the broccoli for 2 minutes in a pan of boiling salted water, then drain and refresh under cold water.

2 To make the sauce, whisk the soy sauce, tahini, and cornstarch to a thick paste, then whisk in the sesame oil, chili oil, vinegar, sugar, and stock.

3 Heat the sunflower oil in a large wok and stir-fry the garlic and ginger for 1 minute, until it starts to color. Add the pork and stir-fry over high heat, breaking it up with a wooden spoon, until it browns. Add the sauce and allow to boil until it thickens, for about 2 minutes.

4 Add the drained noodles and broccoli, stirring them in well to make sure they are well coated with the sauce and heated through. Serve scattered with the scallions and peanuts (if using).

VARIATION

Omit or decrease the amount of chili oil if you are making this recipe for young children. Leave the chili oil bottle on the side for adults who want to pep up their noodles.

Pad thai

Take-out is often not a healthy choice. Homemade versions mean you know exactly what's in the food.

15 mins   15 mins

SERVES 8

1¼lb (550g) medium or thick dried rice noodles

3 tbsp sunflower or vegetable oil

4 large eggs, lightly beaten

1 tsp shrimp paste (optional)

4 hot red chiles, seeded and finely chopped

6 boneless, skinless chicken breasts, cut into ¼in (5mm) slices

2 bunches of scallions, finely chopped

splash of Thai fish sauce, such as nam pla

juice of 2 limes

2 tbsp brown sugar

salt and freshly ground black pepper

10oz (300g) unsalted peanuts

handful of cilantro leaves, finely chopped

lime wedges, to serve

CALORIES: 681kcals/2847kJ
CARBOHYDRATE: 61g
   sugar: 7g
FAT: 26g
   saturated: 5g
SALT: 0.6g
FIBER: 0.5g

1 Put the noodles in a large bowl, cover with boiling water, and leave for 8 minutes, or until soft. Drain and set aside. Meanwhile, put 1 tbsp of the oil in a large wok over high heat and swirl around the pan. Add the beaten egg and swirl it around the wok for about a minute, or until it begins to set—don't let it set completely—then remove, chop, and set aside.

2 Add the remaining 2 tbsp of oil to the pan, then add the shrimp paste (if using) and chiles, and stir. With the heat still high, add the chicken and stir vigorously for 5 minutes, or until it is no longer pink. Stir in the scallions, fish sauce, lime juice, and sugar, and toss together well. Cook for a few minutes until the sugar has dissolved, then season well with salt and pepper. Return the egg to the pan.

3 Add the noodles to the pan and toss together to coat with the sauce, then add half the peanuts and half the cilantro and toss again. Transfer to a large, shallow warmed serving bowl and scatter with the rest of the peanuts and cilantro. Garnish with lime wedges to serve.

Singapore noodles

This vegetable-packed dish is mildly spiced with curry powder, which you can reduce or omit as preferred.

25-30 mins   25 mins

SERVES 4

2 tbsp vegetable oil

5½oz (150g) boneless, skinless chicken breast, cut into strips

16 raw tiger shrimp, shelled and deveined

1 onion, finely sliced

2 garlic cloves, finely chopped

1in (3cm) piece of fresh ginger, finely chopped

1 red chile, seeded and finely chopped

1 red bell pepper, finely sliced

3½oz (100g) baby corn

3½oz (100g) sugarsnap peas

3½oz (100g) beansprouts

1 tsp turmeric

2 tsp mild curry powder

2 tbsp soy sauce

10oz (300g) fresh vermicelli rice noodles

3 large eggs, lightly beaten

salt and freshly ground black pepper

sliced scallions, to garnish

1 Heat half the oil in a wok or very large, non-stick frying pan over medium heat. Add the chicken and cook for 5 minutes or until cooked through, stirring. Remove from the wok and place on a plate lined with paper towels.

2 Add the shrimp to the pan and cook for 2–3 minutes until the shrimp turn pink and are cooked through, stirring occasionally. Transfer to the plate with the chicken.

3 Pour in the remaining 1 tbsp of oil and, over medium heat, cook the onion for 2 minutes. Add the garlic, ginger, and chile, and cook for 1 minute.

4 Add the remaining vegetables, turmeric, and curry powder and stir-fry for 5 minutes.

5 Stir in the soy sauce and noodles and cook for 3 minutes. Push the mixture in the wok to one side and pour the egg into the other

side of the pan. Stir constantly and, once cooked, stir the egg into the noodles. Season.

6 Return the chicken and shrimp to the pan and stir until heated through. Serve the noodles garnished with scallions.

CALORIES: 549kcals/2299kJ

CARBOHYDRATE: 68g
sugar: 6g

FAT: 12g
saturated: 2g

SALT: 1.9g

FIBER: 3g

After school

Preschool children usually need to eat between 5 and 6pm, and school aged children often return home ravenous. In addition, long working days for many parents have the unfortunate consequence that, for many families, sitting down together to eat rarely happens midweek. It would be lovely if families could sit down and eat together every night, but if that's not a realistic idea, then a bit of planning and a few simple recipes can help you.

Children's dinners

Cooking for children and adults separately can be tiresome and time-consuming, so if you can't sit down to a family meal, try to cook things that you will all enjoy, even at different times. Mild curries or chilis can be spiced up after the children have eaten, and easily reheated. Leftovers from an adult meal can often be used to make the children's dinner the following day, with chicken folded into a pasta sauce or fish used as a basis for fishcakes. When time is short, quick cook pasta with butter and cheese, cheese on toast, or ham and cheese quesadillas all make a tasty and nutritious meal. Alternatively, for an almost instant snack, arrange a platter with pick-and-mix food, such as hummus, pita bread, hard-boiled eggs, and chopped raw vegetables.

Drinks

Children often drink a lot of fruit juices. Try sticking to water as the drink of choice between mealtimes, and water down fresh juices to help prevent tooth decay.

Meals for kids

To help you keep your sanity and avoid spending hours in the kitchen, plan ahead and keep weekday meals fairly simple.

Spicy chicken and tomato curry (p98) This colorful dish makes a tasty adult supper and can be served to children the next day with garlic bread, rice, and some yogurt to temper the spices, if necessary.

Mac and cheese (p210) Easy to prepare and universally loved by children, this comforting dish is a weekday winner. You can add variety with extra ingredients such as bacon, tomatoes, or broccoli.

A balanced snack

Breakfast may be rushed and it's hard to be certain what children have eaten for their lunch at school, so snack time is the best way of making sure your children have a balanced meal and include some vegetables and fruit in their diet.

Variety

It's easy to get stuck in a rut when preparing children's meals, especially when time is short. Planning ahead helps to ensure that you give them a good spread of meat, fish, and vegetarian dishes throughout the week.

Banana and date mini muffins (p58) A substantial and healthy after-school snack, such as these delicious muffins, should keep your children going until you've had a chance to prepare the evening meal at a time to suit you.

After-school snacks

Healthy snacks are an important part of a child's diet, but make sure that they don't overload on sugary, processed foods that keep them from eating well-balanced, home-cooked meals. Try the following quick bites:

Granola breakfast bars (p474)

Homemade hummus (p388) andvegetable sticks

Grissini (p444)

Mixed nuts, dried fruit, and seeds

A full fruit bowl

Banana, mango, and yogurt smoothie (p32)

Toasted muffins and crumpets

Rice cakes

Frittata

Fruity ice pops (p59)

No-cook desserts

Chopped up fruit with added juice make a colorful fruit salad, or serve favorite fruits with thick yogurt and honey. Keep a bag of frozen banana chunks on hand to whip up banana ice cream (see p328) in a minute.

Assemble fruit such as grapes, pineapple, apple, and strawberries onto skewers.

Jeweled rice salad

This pretty salad is a fantastic centerpiece at a buffet, along with some grilled meats and leafy green salads.

20 mins, plus cooling   20 mins

SERVES 4

9oz (250g) mixed basmati and wild rice

2 cups vegetable stock (see p156)

seeds from 2 pomegranates

finely chopped flesh of 1 orange

2oz (60g) dried apricots, chopped

1¼oz (40g) sliced almonds

6 scallions, finely chopped

3 tbsp chopped cilantro leaves

2 tbsp chopped flat-leaf parsley leaves

FOR THE DRESSING

finely grated zest and juice of 1 orange

juice of 1 lemon

2 tbsp extra virgin olive oil

1 tsp Dijon mustard

1 garlic clove, finely chopped

salt and freshly ground black pepper

1 Cook the rice in the stock according to the package instructions (about 20 minutes). Set aside to cool.

2 For the dressing, in a small bowl combine the orange zest and juice, lemon juice, oil, mustard, garlic, and seasoning. Whisk together with a fork to combine.

3 Transfer the cooled rice to a serving dish and stir in the dressing. Add the remaining ingredients and stir well. Cover and keep in the fridge until ready to serve.

COOK'S TIP

To free the seeds from the pomegranates quickly and easily, first cut them in half. Then hold each pomegranate-half cut-side down over a bowl and, using a wooden spoon, bash the skin until the shell is empty. Pick out and discard any white pith.

CALORIES: 429kcals/1795kJ
CARBOHYDRATE: 66g
  sugar: 19g
FAT: 12g
  saturated: 1g
SALT: 0.1g
FIBER: 6g

Curried rice salad

Serve this with Easy chicken tikka skewers and raita (see p100) for an Indian-inspired summertime meal.

15 mins, plus cooling   25 mins

SERVES 4

9oz (250g) brown basmati rice

2 cups vegetable stock (see p156)

1 tbsp medium curry powder

1¾oz (50g) raisins

1 red onion, very finely sliced

2¾oz (80g) dried cranberries

1¾oz (50g) shelled pistachio nuts

1oz (30g) flaked coconut

1 green bell pepper, finely chopped

FOR THE DRESSING

3 tbsp mango chutney

1 tbsp olive oil

juice of ½ lemon

salt and freshly ground black pepper

1 Place the rice, stock, curry powder, and raisins in a saucepan and cook the rice according to the package instructions (about 25 minutes). Set aside.

2 In a small bowl, combine the dressing ingredients. Whisk together with a fork to combine. Transfer the cooled rice to a serving dish and pour in the dressing.

3 Add the onion, cranberries, nuts, coconut, and green bell pepper to the rice and stir well. Cover and keep in the fridge until ready to serve.

CLEVER WITH LEFTOVERS

A near-instant version of this salad can be made using leftover cooked and chilled rice (see the guidelines for cooked rice, p9). Simply mix the curry powder with the dressing ingredients and toss it through the cold rice with the nuts, fruits, and vegetables.

CALORIES: 524kcals/2208kJ
CARBOHYDRATE: 67g
  sugar: 19g
FAT: 16g
  saturated: 6g
SALT: 0.4g
FIBER: 7g

Simple Parmesan risotto

This basic but fabulous risotto relies as much on the cooking method as the ingredients.

15 mins   30-35 mins

SERVES 4

2 tbsp olive oil

1 onion, finely chopped

1 garlic clove, finely chopped

2½ cups hot vegetable or chicken stock (see p156; p94)

10oz (300g) risotto rice, such as Arborio or Carnaroli

¼ cup white wine (optional)

2oz (60g) finely grated Parmesan cheese, plus extra to serve

1 tbsp butter

salt and freshly ground black pepper

1 Heat the oil in a large, heavy-bottomed, deep-sided frying pan. Cook the onion over medium heat for five minutes. Add the garlic and cook for another minute.

2 Keep the stock gently simmering on the stove near the risotto pan.

3 Add the rice to the onion pan and stir it in the oil and onions to coat. When it begins to sizzle, pour in the wine (if using) and allow it to evaporate.

4 Now pour in the stock a ladleful at a time, stirring the rice constantly, for about 20 minutes, allowing all the liquid to evaporate from the pan between ladlefuls.

5 When the rice is cooked but still al dente, stop adding the liquid and continue to cook it, stirring, until it is quite dry (the cheese and butter will loosen it up again).

6 Take off the heat and stir in the Parmesan and butter, season, then serve with extra Parmesan.

VARIATION

Once you have mastered a basic risotto, try adding leftover chicken, handfuls of herbs, or different cheeses as you like.

CALORIES: 484kcals/2017kJ
CARBOHYDRATE: 58g
  sugar: 2g
FAT: 13g
  saturated: 6g
SALT: 0.9g
FIBER: 0.5g

Butternut squash risotto

It's well worth roasting the squash before adding it to the risotto; it gives a lovely deep, rich, sweet flavor.

10 mins   1 hr 25 mins

SPECIAL EQUIPMENT
food processor (optional)

SERVES 4-6

1 butternut squash, approx. 1¾lb (800g) prepared weight

2 tbsp olive oil, plus extra for drizzling

1 onion, finely chopped

1 garlic clove, finely chopped

2½ cups hot vegetable or chicken stock (see p156; p94)

10oz (300g) risotto rice, such as Arborio or Carnaroli

¼ cup white wine (optional)

2 tbsp chopped sage leaves

2oz (60g) finely grated Parmesan cheese, plus extra to serve

1 tbsp butter (optional)

salt and freshly ground black pepper

1 Preheat the oven to 400°F (200°C). Slice the squash in half lengthwise and scoop out the seeds. Place on a baking sheet, drizzle with oil, and cover with foil. Bake for 1 hour, until soft.

2 When the squash is nearly cooked, start the risotto. Heat the oil in a large, heavy-bottomed, deep-sided frying pan. Cook the onion over medium heat for 5 minutes. Add the garlic and cook for another minute.

3 Keep the stock simmering on the stove near the risotto pan. Add the rice to the onion pan, and stir. When it sizzles, pour in the wine (if using) and allow to evaporate. Continue to add stock a ladleful at a time, stirring, for 20 minutes, allowing the liquid to evaporate between ladlefuls.

4 Scoop out the squash flesh and mash it, or purée in a food processor with 2 tbsp of stock.

5 Add the squash and sage to the risotto and cook for five minutes, until most of the liquid has evaporated. The rice should be cooked, but still al dente. Add the Parmesan and butter (if using), and season. Serve with extra Parmesan.

CALORIES: 553kcals/2316kJ
CARBOHYDRATE: 73g
  sugar: 10g
FAT: 14g
  saturated: 6g
SALT: 0.8g
FIBER: 5g

Minted pea and shrimp risotto

Sweet peas and shrimp contrast well with the sharp Parmesan and creamy rice.

10 mins   25 mins

SPECIAL EQUIPMENT
food processor or hand-held blender

SERVES 4

14oz (400g) frozen peas

salt and freshly ground black pepper

2½ cups fish or vegetable stock (see p156)

1 tbsp olive oil

1 onion, finely chopped

1 garlic clove, finely chopped

10oz (300g) risotto rice, such as Arborio or Carnaroli

½ cup white wine (optional)

10oz (300g) cooked, shelled, and deveined large shrimp

1oz (30g) finely grated Parmesan cheese, plus extra to serve

2 tbsp chopped mint leaves

1 tbsp butter (optional)

CALORIES: 542kcals/2262kJ
CARBOHYDRATE: 68g
   sugar: 4g
FAT: 11g
   saturated: 4.5g
SALT: 1.9g
FIBER: 7g

1 Cook the peas in boiling salted water for 2 minutes, until just cooked. Drain, refresh under cold water, then purée with about ¾ cup of the stock in a food processor, or with a hand-held blender, until smooth. Put the remaining stock in a saucepan over low heat, and keep it simmering on the stove with a ladle nearby.

2 Heat the oil in a large, heavy-bottomed, deep-sided frying pan. Cook the onion over medium heat for 5 minutes until it softens, but does not brown. Add the garlic and cook for another minute.

3 Add in the rice and stir to coat. When it sizzles, stir in the wine (if using) and allow it to evaporate.

4 Add the stock a ladleful at a time, stirring constantly, for 20 minutes, allowing the liquid to evaporate between ladlefuls.

5 Add the puréed peas and cook for 2 minutes, or until most of the liquid evaporates. The rice should be al dente. Add the shrimp and another ladle of stock and heat through for 2 minutes.

6 Take the pan off the heat, add the Parmesan, mint, and butter (if using), and season well to taste. Sprinkle with extra Parmesan to serve.

Oven-baked risotto

If you don't have time to stir a risotto for 20 minutes, try this trouble-free baked version instead.

10 mins   25-30 mins

SPECIAL EQUIPMENT
large, heavy-bottomed Dutch oven

SERVES 4

2 tbsp butter

1 tbsp olive oil

1 onion, finely chopped

2 garlic cloves, finely chopped

10oz (300g) mixed mushrooms, such as crimini, shiitake, and oyster, roughly chopped

14oz (400g) risotto rice

2½ cups vegetable or chicken stock (see 156; p94)

⅔ cup dry white wine

salt and freshly ground black pepper

10oz (300g) cooked chicken, chopped into bite-sized pieces

1¼oz (40g) grated Grana Padano cheese, plus extra to serve

¼ cup chopped parsley leaves

CALORIES: 670kcals/2801kJ
CARBOHYDRATE: 78g
   sugar: 2g
FAT: 16g
   saturated: 7g
SALT: 1.4g
FIBER: 2g

1 Preheat the oven to 400°F (200°C). Heat the butter and oil in a large, heavy-bottomed Dutch oven over low heat. Once the butter has melted, add the onion and garlic and cook gently for 5 minutes.

2 Add the mushrooms and rice and stir well to coat in the butter and oil. Pour in the stock and wine, bring to a boil, season, and stir well.

3 Cover and cook in the oven for 20 minutes or until the rice is tender, stirring a couple of times.

4 Remove from the oven and stir in the chicken, Grana Padano cheese, and parsley. Return to the oven for 5 minutes, or until the chicken is heated through. Serve with pepper and extra Grana Padano, for sprinkling.

VARIATION

For a spinach and hot-smoked salmon risotto, omit the mushrooms and chicken, and stir in 10oz (300g) flaked, hot-smoked salmon fillets, and 3½oz (100g) spinach 5 minutes before the end of the cooking time.

Mozzarella-stuffed risotto balls

A fantastic way to use up leftover risotto, these Italian *arancini* make a great snack that children love.

20 mins, plus resting • 10 mins

MAKES 12

14oz (400g) cooked, cold Simple Parmesan risotto (see p219)

2oz (60g) mozzarella cheese, cut into 12 x ½in (1cm) cubes

¼ cup all-purpose flour

1 large egg, beaten

1 cup day-old bread crumbs or panko bread crumbs

3½ cups sunflower or vegetable oil, for deep-frying

1 Keep your hands damp to mold the risotto balls. Take a walnut-sized spoonful of risotto and mold it in your palm so it creates a flattened circle. Place a piece of the mozzarella in the middle of the rice and mold the rice around it, rolling it to make a ball. Make sure the mozzarella is well covered, and be sure to pack the risotto down well. Continue until you have 12 balls.

2 Put the flour, egg, and bread crumbs in 3 wide, shallow bowls. Roll each risotto ball first in the flour, then in the egg, and finally coat it well in the bread crumbs. Place on a plate, cover with plastic wrap, and rest in the fridge for at least 30 minutes (this will help the coating to stick).

3 When you are ready to cook the risotto balls, preheat the oven to 300°F (150°C). Heat the oil in a large, heavy-bottomed saucepan to a depth of 4in (10cm). It will be ready to use when a small piece of bread dropped in sizzles and turns golden brown.

4 Cook the risotto balls a few at a time for two minutes until golden brown all over. Remove with a slotted spoon and drain on paper towels. Keep warm in the oven while you cook the rest.

VARIATION

Try this with other risottos, but make sure they are fairly smooth in texture, as these will adhere more easily to the bread crumb coating. Adding a spicy tomato sauce for dipping cuts through the richness of the risotto balls.

CALORIES: 188kcals/789kJ
CARBOHYDRATE: 18g
  sugar: 0.5g
FAT: 10g
  saturated: 3g
SALT: 0.9g
FIBER: 0.5g

Crispy risotto cakes

These are stylish leftovers. Serve with grilled fish and a poached egg on top for a simple, sophisticated meal.

5 mins • 30 mins

SPECIAL EQUIPMENT

4in (10cm) cookie cutter or ring mold

SERVES 4

1¾lb (800g) cooked, cold risotto, such as Simple Parmesan risotto (see p219)

1¾oz (50g) finely grated Parmesan cheese

handful of flat-leaf parsley or basil leaves, finely chopped (optional)

salt and freshly ground black pepper

olive oil, for brushing

1 Preheat the oven to 450°F (230°C). In a bowl, mix together the risotto, Parmesan, and herbs (if using), and season well.

2 Use a 4in (10cm) round cutter or mold to make cakes of the mixture: place the cutter or mold on a work surface and spoon in one-quarter of the risotto mixture, squashing it in and flattening it off nicely. Remove the cutter or mold. Repeat to make four cakes.

3 Brush each risotto cake with a little oil on one side and place oil-side down on a non-stick baking sheet. Brush the upper side with oil and bake at the top of the oven for 25 minutes, turning carefully after 15 minutes, or until golden and crispy on the outside but soft and yielding within.

VARIATION

Make bite-sized Crispy risotto cakes for an instant canapé, serving them with arugula pesto (see p194).

CALORIES: 646kcals/2710kJ
CARBOHYDRATE: 66g
  sugar: 2g
FAT: 33g
  saturated: 12g
SALT: 4.9g
FIBER: 1g

Paella

As with any recipe involving fresh clams or mussels, discard any that do not close when firmly tapped on a sink.

35 mins   35 mins

SERVES 4

2 tbsp olive oil

4 boneless, skinless chicken thighs, halved

1¾oz (50g) chorizo, thinly sliced

1¾oz (50g) chopped pancetta

2 garlic cloves, finely chopped

1 Spanish onion, finely chopped

1 green bell pepper, sliced

1 red bell pepper, sliced

9oz (250g) Spanish short-grain rice, such as paella rice

generous pinch of saffron strands

1 tsp smoked paprika

2 tbsp dry sherry

¾ cup dry white wine

2 cups chicken stock (see p94)

4 tomatoes, peeled, seeded, and roughly chopped (see p191)

salt and freshly ground black pepper

3½oz (100g) fresh or frozen peas

12–16 fresh mussels or clams, scrubbed, rinsed, and beards removed

7oz (200g) raw, shelled, and deveined large shrimp

5½oz (150g) scallops

¼ cup chopped flat-leaf parsley leaves

juice of ½–1 lemon

1 Heat half the oil in a very large non-stick frying pan with a lid over medium heat. Cook the chicken for 5 minutes. Set aside.

2 Add the chorizo, pancetta, garlic, and onion and cook for 3 minutes, stirring occasionally. Add the peppers and cook for 1 minute.

3 Stir in the rice and spices for 1 minute. Add the sherry, wine, stock, tomatoes, and seasoning, and bring to a boil. Reduce the heat to a simmer, return the chicken, cover, and cook for 15 minutes. Add the peas and mussels, cover, and cook for 5 minutes. Discard any mussels that don't open.

4 Meanwhile, in a small pan, heat the remaining 1 tbsp of oil over medium heat and cook the shrimp and scallops for only 2 or 3 minutes, until just cooked through and opaque. Add to the paella and stir well. Stir the parsley and lemon juice into the paella and serve immediately.

CALORIES: 663kcals/2774kJ

CARBOHYDRATE: 61g
  sugar: 10g

FAT: 16g
  saturated: 4g

SALT: 1.7g

FIBER: 5g

Quick paella

Frozen foods can often help you out when time is short, and frozen seafood adds flavor and body to this dish.

10 mins   35–40 mins

SERVES 4

1 tbsp olive oil

7oz (200g) boneless, skinless chicken breast, cut into strips

14oz (400g) frozen seafood mix, defrosted and drained

1 Spanish onion, sliced

2 garlic cloves, finely chopped

1 tsp turmeric

1 tsp smoked paprika

salt and freshly ground black pepper

10oz (300g) long-grain white rice

3½ cups hot chicken stock (see p94)

3½oz (100g) frozen thin green beans

3½oz (100g) frozen peas

juice of ½ lemon

1 Heat half the oil in a very large, non-stick frying pan with a lid over medium heat. Add the chicken and cook for 5 minutes, stirring occasionally. Remove from the pan and set aside.

2 Add the seafood mix to the pan and cook for 2 minutes, stirring occasionally. Remove from the pan using a slotted spoon and set aside with the chicken.

3 Wipe the pan dry with paper towels and add the remaining ½ tbsp of oil. Add the onion and cook for 5 minutes. Add the garlic and cook for 1 minute.

4 Add the spices, seasoning, and rice to the pan and stir to coat for 1 minute. Add the stock, bring to a boil, cover, and simmer for 10–15 minutes.

5 Add the beans to the pan, stir well, and cook for another 3 minutes, then add the peas and cook for 2 minutes.

6 Return the cooked chicken and seafood to the pan and heat through over high heat for a final 2 minutes, stirring constantly. Squeeze in the lemon and serve immediately.

CALORIES: 522kcals/2188kJ

CARBOHYDRATE: 62g
   sugar: 2.5g
FAT: 6g
   saturated: 1g
SALT: 1.3g
FIBER: 3g

Cashew and zucchini rice

You can serve this nutty, gingery pilaf on its own or as an accompaniment to grilled lamb or fish.

15 mins   40 mins

SERVES 4

1–2 tbsp olive oil

1 onion, finely chopped

salt and freshly ground black pepper

4in (10cm) piece of fresh ginger, finely grated

4 zucchini, quartered lengthwise and chopped into bite-sized pieces

3 garlic cloves, finely chopped

1 tbsp cider vinegar

pinch of cayenne pepper

7oz (200g) long-grain white rice

approx. 3 cups hot vegetable stock (see p156)

2½oz (75g) cashew nuts, roughly chopped

bunch of scallions, green part only, thinly sliced

bunch of cilantro, leaves only, chopped

CALORIES: 356kcals/1484kJ

CARBOHYDRATE: 44g
   sugar: 4.5g
FAT: 13g
   saturated: 2.5g
SALT: 0.2g
FIBER: 3g

1 Heat 1 tbsp of oil in a large, heavy-bottomed pan with a lid over medium heat, add the onion, and cook for 3 minutes until soft. Season with salt and pepper, increase the heat, and stir in the ginger and zucchini.

2 Cook for 5 minutes until the zucchini are lightly golden (adding more oil, if necessary), then add the garlic and cook for another 3 minutes.

3 Increase the heat, add the vinegar, let it cook for 1 minute, then stir in the cayenne pepper and rice. Add a little stock and turn it so all the grains are coated.

4 Bring to a boil, add enough stock to cover, cover with a lid, and simmer gently for about 20 minutes, or until the rice is tender. Add more stock when needed.

5 Stir in the cashew nuts, scallions, and half the cilantro, taste, and season as needed. Sprinkle with the remaining cilantro to serve.

HOW TO FREEZE

Grated fresh ginger freezes well, so wrap small quantities in plastic wrap, freeze, and you'll always have some on hand.

Jamaican rice and peas

The kidney beans in this tasty dish are known as "gungo peas" in Jamaica and "pigeon peas" in Trinidad.

10 mins   45 mins

SERVES 4

1 x 14oz (400g) can kidney beans, drained and rinsed

1 x 14oz (400ml) can coconut milk

1 large onion, finely chopped

1 green bell pepper, finely chopped or sliced

salt and freshly ground black pepper

4½oz (125g) long-grain white rice

chile powder, to garnish

1 Put the beans, coconut milk, onion, and green bell pepper in a saucepan. Season to taste with salt and pepper and simmer over low heat for 5 minutes.

2 Stir in the rice, cover, and cook gently for 35 minutes, or until the rice is tender, stirring. Serve sprinkled with chile powder.

PREPARE AHEAD

The dish can be prepared in advance (but cool it quickly and store it carefully, following the guidelines on the Clever with Leftovers feature on pp322–323). To reheat, place in a shallow dish and tightly cover with foil. Reheat in a preheated oven at 350°F (180°C) for 15 minutes, or until piping hot.

CALORIES: 379kcals/1590kJ

CARBOHYDRATE: 42g
  sugar: 6g

FAT: 18g
  saturated: 15g

SALT: 0.6g

FIBER: 7g

Chinese fried rice with shrimp and chicken

If your family has favorite crunchy vegetables, vary the ingredients here according to what they like.

15 mins   40 mins

SERVES 8

2lb (900g) white basmati rice

salt and freshly ground black pepper

5 tbsp sunflower or vegetable oil

1lb (450g) raw, shelled, and deveined shrimp, chopped

4 large boneless, skinless chicken breasts, cut into 1in (2.5cm) strips

15oz (425g) chopped pancetta

8oz (225g) mushrooms, chopped

3in (7.5cm) piece of fresh ginger, finely sliced

8oz (225g) frozen peas, defrosted

4 large eggs, lightly beaten

2 tbsp dark soy sauce

2 tbsp mirin

bunch of scallions, finely sliced

small handful of flat-leaf parsley leaves, finely chopped

1 Rinse the rice, then place in a large pan, cover with boiling water, and add salt. Cover with a lid, bring to a boil, and cook for 15–20 minutes, or until done. Drain well and set aside to cool completely.

2 Meanwhile, heat 1 tbsp of the oil in a wok over high heat, add the shrimp, season, and cook until pink. Set aside. Heat another 1 tbsp of the oil, add the chicken, season, and stir-fry for 5 minutes, or until no longer pink. Set aside.

3 Heat another 1 tbsp of the oil, add the pancetta, and cook over medium-high heat until crispy and golden. Set aside. Wipe the wok with paper towels, then heat another 1 tbsp of the oil. Add the mushrooms and ginger and stir-fry for 5 minutes. Add the peas for the last minute. Set aside.

4 Heat the final 1 tbsp of oil in the wok, then pour in the eggs and cook gently, stirring, for 1 minute. Add the rice and stir well, then stir in the shrimp, chicken, pancetta, mushrooms, and peas. Add the soy sauce and mirin and stir for 5 minutes. Transfer to a serving dish, top with the scallions and parsley, and serve.

CALORIES: 733kcals/3057kJ

CARBOHYDRATE: 88g
  sugar: 2g

FAT: 24g
  saturated: 6g

SALT: 2.7g

FIBER: 2g

Mexican red rice

Try this as a side dish for dishes that have a little heat, such as Spicy pork and beans (see p146).

5 mins | 30 mins, plus resting

SERVES 4

2 tbsp olive oil

1 onion, finely chopped

1 garlic clove, finely chopped

1 red chile, seeded and finely chopped

7oz (200g) long-grain white rice

1 cup tomato paste

2 cups vegetable stock (see p156)

2 tsp smoked paprika

salt and freshly ground black pepper

1 tbsp butter

1 heaping tbsp chopped cilantro leaves (optional)

1 Heat the oil in a heavy-bottomed saucepan with a lid. Cook the onion over medium heat for 5 minutes, until it softens, but does not brown. Add the garlic and chile and cook for another minute.

2 Add the rice and cook it over low heat, stirring constantly, for 2–3 minutes, until it starts to turn translucent. Add the tomato paste, stock, and smoked paprika and season well.

3 Bring the rice to a boil, reduce the heat to low, cover, and simmer for 25 minutes until the rice is tender and all the liquid has been absorbed.

4 Take the rice off the heat, stir in the butter, cover, and rest for 5 minutes. Serve, scattered with cilantro (if using).

CALORIES: 286kcals/1190kJ

CARBOHYDRATE: 41g
  sugar: 3g

FAT: 9g
  saturated: 3g

SALT: 0.4g

FIBER: 1g

CLEVER WITH LEFTOVERS

If you have leftover cooked rice, use this recipe as the inspiration for a Mexican-style refried rice, using a combination of just enough paste and chicken stock (see p94) to color and flavor the dish, without making it too moist.

Moroccan spiced rice

This exotic rice dish is full of flavor, and would be delicious with Slow-cooked Moroccan lamb (see p132).

15 mins | 20-25 mins

SERVES 4

1 tbsp olive oil

1 onion, very finely sliced

2 garlic cloves, finely chopped

2 tsp ras el hanout spice mix

9oz (250g) long-grain white rice

2 cups vegetable stock (see p156)

1 x 14oz (400g) can chickpeas, drained

2¼oz (70g) dried apricots, chopped

2¼oz (70g) dried figs, finely chopped

1 preserved lemon, finely chopped

salt and freshly ground black pepper

1oz (30g) toasted sliced almonds

2 tbsp chopped cilantro leaves

2 tbsp chopped mint leaves

1 Heat the oil in a large pan over medium heat. Add the onion and cook for 5 minutes, until it has softened. Add the garlic and cook for 1 minute.

2 Stir in the spice mix and cook for 1 minute. Add the rice and stir to coat in the spices.

3 Add the stock, chickpeas, apricots, figs, and preserved lemon. Season, bring to a boil, stir well, cover, and cook according to the package instructions (about 10–15 minutes).

4 Remove from the heat and stir in the almonds, cilantro, and mint. Serve hot, or cool and chill and serve cold. (If serving cold, add the herbs only once the rice has cooled, and follow the guidelines for cooked rice, see p9.)

CALORIES: 374kcals/1568kJ

CARBOHYDRATE: 63g
  sugar: 16g

FAT: 8g
  saturated: 0.7g

SALT: 0.6g

FIBER: 3.5g

Dirty rice

A classic recipe from the Deep South, this dish gets its name from the color given by the meat.

15 mins   1 hr, plus resting

SPECIAL EQUIPMENT
large Dutch oven, ideally cast-iron

SERVES 6

4 tbsp olive oil

1 onion, finely chopped

½ celery stalk, finely chopped

1 green bell pepper, finely chopped

9oz (250g) ground pork

7oz (200g) chicken livers, trimmed and finely chopped

1 green chile, seeded and finely chopped

2 garlic cloves, finely chopped

1 tsp smoked paprika

1 tsp coriander seeds, crushed

10oz (300g) long-grain white rice

salt and freshly ground black pepper

2½ cups hot chicken stock (see p94)

large sprig of thyme

handful of flat-leaf parsley leaves, finely chopped

1 tbsp finely chopped oregano leaves

1 Preheat the oven to 325°F (160°C). Heat 3 tbsp of the oil in a large Dutch oven and add the onion, celery, and green bell pepper. Cook gently for 5 minutes, until soft. Set aside.

2 Add the remaining oil, then the pork and chicken livers. Increase the heat to high and cook, turning, until the meat is well browned, about 5 minutes.

3 Add the chile, garlic, smoked paprika, and coriander seeds and cook for 2 minutes. Return the vegetables, then stir in the rice. Season well and add the hot stock and thyme. Bring to a boil, stir, cover, and cook in the oven for 30–40 minutes, stirring once or twice, until the rice is cooked and the stock absorbed.

4 Remove and rest for 5 minutes. Remove the thyme, stir in the chopped herbs, taste for seasoning, and serve.

CALORIES: 326kcals/1360kJ

CARBOHYDRATE: 27g
  sugar: 2.5g

FAT: 12.5g
  saturated: 3g

SALT: 0.5g

FIBER: 1g

Thai coconut rice

Traditional flavorings of coconut and kaffir lime leaves are mixed with plain rice to make this popular Asian dish.

25 mins   40 mins

SERVES 4–6

¼oz (10g) bunch of cilantro

2 tbsp olive oil

2 tbsp butter

1 red chile, finely chopped (seed it if you want a milder dish)

2 shallots, finely chopped

2½oz (75g) Thai red curry paste

finely grated zest of 1 lime

14oz (400g) Thai jasmine rice

1 tsp salt

1 14oz (400ml) can coconut milk

large pinch of shredded kaffir lime leaves

2 scallions, thinly sliced

1 Pick the cilantro leaves from the stalks, finely chop the stalks, and reserve the leaves.

2 Heat the oil and butter in a large frying pan with a lid over low heat. Add the chile and shallots and cook, stirring, for 5 minutes, or until they start to turn golden. Stir in the curry paste and cook for 30 seconds.

3 Add the lime zest, cilantro stalks, rice, and salt and mix together until the grains of rice are coated in the curry paste. Pour in the coconut milk, then fill the empty can with water and add that too. Stir well. Bring to a simmer over medium heat, stirring occasionally so the rice doesn't stick. Scatter in the lime leaves and simmer, uncovered, for 5 minutes.

4 Stir the rice thoroughly, then cover the pan and leave over very low heat for 15 minutes, or until the rice is tender. If all the liquid has been absorbed but the rice is still not quite ready, add a little extra water until it is tender. When ready to serve, stir in the scallions and sprinkle with the reserved cilantro leaves.

CALORIES: 684kcals/2855kJ

CARBOHYDRATE: 80g
  sugar: 1.5g

FAT: 32g
  saturated: 19g

SALT: 1.8g

FIBER: 0.3g

Quick rice with tomatoes, shrimp, and peas

This is a great standby lunch or dinner dish, which has a sweetness that is particularly popular with children.

5 mins   10 mins

SERVES 4-6

1 tbsp olive oil

2 tbsp butter

2 large ripe tomatoes, peeled, seeded, and chopped (see p191)

2 garlic cloves, crushed

7oz (200g) frozen peas

2¼lb (1kg) cooked, cold white basmati rice

7oz (200g) cooked, shelled, and deveined small shrimp

salt and freshly ground black pepper

handful of finely chopped basil leaves

CALORIES: 517kcals/2180kJ

CARBOHYDRATE: 77g
  sugar: 1g

FAT: 13g
  saturated: 5.5g

SALT: 0.2g

FIBER: 3.5g

1 Heat the oil and 1 tbsp of the butter in a wok. Cook the tomatoes and garlic for 1 minute, then add the peas and cook for another 2 minutes until they defrost and start to heat through.

2 Add the rice and shrimp and continue to cook over high heat, stirring constantly, until the rice is heated through.

3 Season well and stir in the remaining 1 tbsp of butter and the basil, to serve.

CLEVER WITH LEFTOVERS

It is common to have a small amount of rice left over after a meal. Make sure you follow the storage guidelines on the Clever with Leftovers feature on pp322-323 to avoid potential risks.

COOK'S TIP

The quantities in this quick stir-fry can be an instant lunch for one, or a meal for a toddler, or for older children—just vary them accordingly.

Lemon rice

This is a wonderfully tangy side dish from South India that can be easily rustled up when you are in a hurry.

10 mins   5 mins

SERVES 4

3 tbsp vegetable oil

1 tsp yellow mustard seeds

6 green cardamom pods, split

10 fresh or dried curry leaves

2 red chiles, split lengthwise

½ tsp turmeric

½in (1cm) piece of fresh ginger, finely chopped

1 garlic clove, crushed

3 tbsp lemon juice, or to taste

10oz (300g) cooked, cold white basmati rice

2oz (60g) cashews, lightly toasted

2 tbsp chopped cilantro leaves

1 Heat the oil in a large frying pan, add the spices, ginger, and garlic, and cook over medium heat for 2 minutes, or until aromatic, stirring all the time.

2 Add the lemon juice and cook for 1 minute, then add the rice. Stir until the rice is heated through and coated in the spices.

3 Transfer to a serving dish, scatter with the cashews and cilantro, and serve at once.

CALORIES: 264kcals/1101kJ

CARBOHYDRATE: 24g
  sugar: 1g

FAT: 16g
  saturated: 3g

SALT: trace

FIBER: 0.7g

Oven-baked dal

This wonderful pilaf takes a little time to prepare, but once it is in the oven it takes care of itself.

30 mins   30 mins

SPECIAL EQUIPMENT
large Dutch oven

SERVES 4–6

3½oz (100g) yellow split peas

salt and freshly ground black pepper

7oz (200g) white basmati rice

2 tbsp sunflower or vegetable oil

2 tbsp butter

1 onion, finely chopped

2 garlic cloves, finely chopped

1in (3cm) piece of fresh ginger, finely chopped

1 red chile, seeded and chopped

1 tsp chile powder

1 tsp ground coriander

1 tsp ground cumin

1 tsp turmeric

¼ cup (2oz) plain yogurt

1½ cups vegetable stock (see p156)

1 Put the split peas in a large pan of boiling salted water and cook, uncovered, for about 20 minutes, or until they are just cooked through. Drain, rinse under cold water, and set aside.

2 Meanwhile, put the rice in a sieve and run it under a cold tap for a couple of minutes, rubbing it together with your fingers, to get rid of excess starch. Drain and set aside.

3 Preheat the oven to 325°F (160°C). Heat the oil and butter in a large Dutch oven. Cook the onion over medium heat for 5 minutes, until softened, but not browned. Add the garlic, ginger, and chile and cook for another minute. Add the ground spices and cook over low heat for a minute until they start to smell fragrant. Add the yogurt and cook over a low heat until it reduces and thickens.

4 Add the rice, split peas, and stock and stir well. Cook in the center of the hot oven for 30 minutes, stirring halfway, until the rice is cooked and the liquid evaporated. Season to taste and serve.

CALORIES: 392kcals/1638kJ
CARBOHYDRATE: 54g
  sugar: 3g
FAT: 13g
  saturated: 5g
SALT: 0.2g
FIBER: 3g

Turkey, almond, and cranberry pilaf

A perfect post-Thanksgiving meal, soothing and nutritious. Pep it up with a little hot sauce, if you like.

15 mins   40 mins

SPECIAL EQUIPMENT
Dutch oven

SERVES 4

1 tbsp olive oil

1 onion, finely chopped

3 garlic cloves, finely chopped

9oz (250g) white basmati rice

2½ cups vegetable stock (see p156)

12oz (350g) cooked turkey, sliced

salt and freshly ground black pepper

6oz (175g) dried cranberries

3oz (90g) sliced almonds, toasted

handful of thyme sprigs, leaves picked

1 Heat the oil in a Dutch oven over low heat. Add the onion and cook gently for about 5 minutes until soft. Add the garlic and cook, stirring, for a minute. Stir in the rice to coat well.

2 Pour in the stock and bring to a boil. Reduce the heat slightly and stir in the turkey. Simmer gently, covered, adding more hot stock or water if needed, for 20–25 minutes, or until the stock has been absorbed and the rice is tender. Season generously.

3 Just before serving, add the cranberries, almonds, and thyme and gently stir through. Serve hot.

CLEVER WITH LEFTOVERS

A large roast turkey always provides plenty of leftovers. Crack a few leftover almonds, if you have them, and chop them up to replace the sliced almonds in this festive pilaf.

CALORIES: 615kcals/2574kJ
CARBOHYDRATE: 82g
  sugar: 34g
FAT: 12g
  saturated: 1.5g
SALT: 0.2g
FIBER: 3g

Chicken pilaf

Adding yogurt and coconut to this dish gives it both a depth of flavor and also a rich, creamy texture.

15 mins   25 mins

SERVES 3–4

1 tbsp vegetable oil

2 tbsp butter

1 onion, finely sliced

2 chicken breasts, chopped into chunks

1 tsp turmeric

1 tsp ground cinnamon

1 tsp ground coriander

1 tsp ground cumin

8oz (225g) long-grain white rice

2 cups chicken stock (see p94)

2½oz (75g) golden raisins

salt and freshly ground black pepper

2 tbsp chopped cilantro leaves

¼ cup (2oz) low-fat plain yogurt

2 tbsp flaked coconut

1 Heat the oil and butter in a heavy-bottomed saucepan over medium heat. Add the onion and cook for 2 minutes. Add the chicken chunks and cook for 5 minutes, stirring occasionally.

2 Add the spices to the pan and cook for 1 minute. Add the rice and stir for another minute to coat in the spices.

3 Add the stock and golden raisins to the pan, season, and bring to a boil. Cover, reduce the heat, and simmer for 15 minutes.

4 Stir the cilantro and yogurt into the rice. Divide between four warmed plates and sprinkle with the coconut, to serve.

CLEVER WITH LEFTOVERS

The rice can be served cold as a substantial salad, or make rissoles: remove and shred the chicken, then mix it back into the rice. Form balls or rissoles and follow the recipe for coating and frying Mozzarella-stuffed risotto balls (see p221) for a light lunch or tasty supper dish.

CALORIES: 501kcals/2096kJ

CARBOHYDRATE: 57g
  sugar: 15g

FAT: 15g
  saturated: 9g

SALT: 0.6g

FIBER: 2g

Nasi goreng

If your family like spicy dishes, try this Indonesian rice recipe. Add extra vegetables if you like.

15 mins   20 mins

SERVES 4

2 tbsp olive oil

2 large eggs

salt and freshly ground black pepper

1 red bell pepper, finely sliced

1 orange bell pepper, finely sliced

1 garlic clove, finely chopped

1½in (4cm) piece of fresh ginger, finely chopped

1 red chile, seeded and finely chopped

8 scallions, finely chopped

5½oz (150g) raw large shrimp, shelled and deveined

1lb 5oz (600g) cooked white rice

7oz (200g) cooked chicken, finely chopped

2 tbsp soy sauce, plus extra to serve

1 Heat 1 tbsp of the oil in a large, non-stick frying pan over medium heat. Crack the eggs into a small bowl, season well, and whisk with a fork.

2 Pour the beaten egg into the pan and swirl it to make a thin omelet. Cook for 3 minutes or until set. Transfer to a plate, cut into ribbons, and set aside.

3 Heat the remaining oil in the pan and add the peppers, garlic, ginger, chile, and scallions. Cook over medium heat for 5 minutes, stirring occasionally.

4 Add the shrimp to the pan and stir-fry for 2 minutes. Add the rice, chicken, and soy sauce and heat for 5 minutes, stirring occasionally, then stir in the omelet ribbons.

5 Serve the nasi goreng in warmed bowls, with extra soy sauce to season.

CALORIES: 458kcals/1929kJ

CARBOHYDRATE: 49g
  sugar: 5g

FAT: 17g
  saturated: 4g

SALT: 1.8g

FIBER: 2.2g

FEEDING A CROWD

This is just the kind of dish to take center stage at a buffet or large gathering. Surround it with vegetable curries, bowls of minted yogurt, and store-bought naan bread and poppadoms, and it will be a real feast!

Brown rice stir-fry

Brown rice really comes into its own in this super-healthy stir-fry. It's nutty and deliciously savory.

10 mins   10 mins

SERVES 4

5½oz (150g) sugarsnap peas, cut into ½in (1cm) pieces

2 asparagus spears, cut into ½in (1cm) pieces

salt

2 tbsp sunflower or vegetable oil

5½oz (150g) zucchini, cut into ½in (1cm) cubes

4 scallions, finely sliced

2 garlic cloves, finely chopped

1½in (4cm) piece of fresh ginger, finely chopped

1 green chile pepper, seeded and finely chopped

1¾lb (800g) cooked, cold brown rice

2 tbsp oyster sauce

2 tbsp soy sauce

2 tbsp rice wine or dry sherry

2 tbsp pumpkin seeds

2 tbsp sunflower seeds

1 Blanch the sugarsnap peas and asparagus in a large pan of boiling salted water for 1 minute, then drain and refresh them under cold water.

2 Heat the oil in a large wok and stir-fry the zucchini over high heat for 2 minutes until they start to color. Add the scallions, garlic, ginger, and chile and cook for another minute.

3 Add the blanched vegetables and cook for a minute, then add the rice with the remaining ingredients. Stir-fry for a minute or two until everything is well combined and the rice is hot.

VARIATION

Dried seaweed, reconstituted and finely chopped, makes a lovely umami-packed addition to this dish.

> **CALORIES:** 441kcals/1856kJ
> **CARBOHYDRATE:** 67g
>   sugar: 4g
> **FAT:** 14g
>   saturated: 2g
> **SALT:** 2.5g
> **FIBER:** 5g

One-pot Indian rice

One-pot meals are a real lifesaver when time is short but you want to produce an enjoyable family meal.

15 mins   25 mins

SERVES 4

1 tbsp vegetable oil

1 onion, finely chopped

2 garlic cloves, finely chopped

1 red bell pepper, finely chopped

1 green bell pepper, finely chopped

¼ cup medium curry powder

9oz (250g) white basmati rice

2 cups vegetable stock (see p156)

salt and freshly ground black pepper

1oz (30g) toasted sliced almonds

9oz (250g) cooked shrimp, shelled and deveined

¾ cup (7oz) plain low-fat yogurt

2 tbsp finely chopped mint leaves

2 tbsp finely chopped cilantro leaves

1 Heat the oil in a heavy-bottomed saucepan over medium heat and cook the onion for 5 minutes.

2 Add the garlic and peppers and cook for 1 minute. Stir in the curry powder and rice and cook for 1 minute, stirring constantly.

3 Stir in the stock, season well, and bring to a boil. Cover and simmer over low heat for 12–15 minutes. When the rice is nearly cooked, stir in the almonds and shrimp to heat through.

4 Meanwhile, place the yogurt in a small serving bowl and stir in the herbs. Set aside.

5 Serve the rice on warmed plates with a dollop of the mint and cilantro yogurt on top.

VARIATION

Add 9oz (250g) chopped, cooked chicken to the rice at the end of cooking, instead of the shrimp, and heat through thoroughly.

> **CALORIES:** 442kcals/1847kJ
> **CARBOHYDRATE:** 56g
>   sugar: 9g
> **FAT:** 11.5g
>   saturated: 1.5g
> **SALT:** 0.2g
> **FIBER:** 2g

Chinese chicken and rice

Simply serve with some steamed bok choy for an aromatic and deliciously different one-pot meal.

10 mins | 30 mins, plus resting

SERVES 4

1 tsp sesame oil

1 tbsp soy sauce

2 tbsp rice wine or dry sherry

14oz (400g) boneless, skinless chicken thighs, cut into 1in (3cm) chunks

2 tbsp sunflower or vegetable oil

1 bunch of scallions, finely sliced

2 garlic cloves, finely chopped

1in (3cm) piece of fresh ginger, finely chopped

1 red chile, seeded and finely chopped

1 tsp five-spice powder

2½ cups chicken stock (see p94)

10oz (300g) long-grain white rice, or jasmine rice

steamed bok choy, to serve

1 Mix together the sesame oil, soy sauce, and half the rice wine in a shallow dish. Add the chicken, stir to coat, cover, and refrigerate in the marinade for up to 1 hour.

2 Heat the sunflower oil in a heavy-bottomed saucepan with a lid. Drain the chicken from its marinade (reserve any of the remaining marinade) and cook it for 2–3 minutes, until colored all over. Add the scallions, garlic, ginger, and chile and cook for another 2 minutes. Now add the five-spice powder and cook for 1 minute.

3 Add the stock, remaining rice wine, and any marinade and stir in the rice. Bring the rice to a boil, then reduce the heat to a low simmer and then cook, covered, for 20–25 minutes, until the rice is cooked and all the liquid has evaporated.

4 Take it off the heat and rest it, covered, for 5 minutes before serving with steamed bok choy.

VARIATION

If you can find Chinese sausages, add a couple of these, casings peeled and sliced, with the chicken.

CALORIES: 464kcals/1945kJ
CARBOHYDRATE: 57g
  sugar: 1g
FAT: 5g
  saturated: 1g
SALT: 1.4g
FIBER: 0.5g

Chicken and chickpea pilaf

This one-pot rice dish is full of flavor and easy to make. It just needs a crisp green salad on the side.

20 mins | 35 mins

SERVES 4

pinch of saffron threads

2 tsp vegetable oil

6 boneless, skinless chicken thighs, cut into small pieces

2 tsp ground coriander

1 tsp ground cumin

1 onion, sliced

1 red bell pepper, chopped

2 garlic cloves, crushed

8oz (225g) long-grain white rice

2½ cups hot chicken stock (see p94)

2 bay leaves

1 x 14oz (400g) can chickpeas, drained and rinsed

2oz (60g) golden raisins

2oz (60g) sliced almonds or pine nuts, toasted

3 tbsp chopped flat-leaf parsley leaves

1 Crumble the saffron threads into a small bowl, add 2 tbsp of boiling water, and set aside for at least 10 minutes.

2 Meanwhile, heat half the oil in a large saucepan, then add the chicken, coriander, and cumin and cook over medium heat for 3 minutes, stirring frequently.

3 Remove from the pan and set aside. Lower the heat, add the rest of the oil, the onion, red bell pepper, and garlic, and cook for 5 minutes, or until softened.

4 Stir in the rice, return the chicken to the pan, and pour in about three-quarters of the stock. Add the bay leaves and saffron with its soaking water and bring to a boil. Simmer for 15 minutes, or until the rice is almost cooked, adding more stock as needed.

5 Stir in the chickpeas and golden raisins and continue cooking until the rice is tender. Transfer to a warmed serving platter and serve hot, sprinkled with the toasted nuts and chopped parsley.

CALORIES: 566kcals/2371kJ
CARBOHYDRATE: 66g
  sugar: 14g
FAT: 14g
  saturated: 2g
SALT: 1g
FIBER: 5g

Vegetable biryani

This tasty Indian dish is packed full of vegetables, and the cashew nuts add protein for vegetarians, too.

20-30 mins 40-45 mins

SERVES 4–6

14oz (400g) white basmati rice

salt and freshly ground black pepper

2 tbsp vegetable oil

1 large onion, finely chopped

1in (2.5cm) piece of fresh ginger, finely chopped

2 garlic cloves, finely chopped

1 tsp ground coriander

2 tsp ground cumin

1 tsp turmeric

½–1 tsp chile powder

3 cups vegetable stock (see p156)

2 sweet potatoes, finely chopped

7oz (200g) thin green beans, halved

7oz (200g) small cauliflower florets

1 tsp garam masala

juice of 1 lemon

handful of cilantro leaves, chopped

1¾oz (50g) unsalted cashew nuts

raita and poppadoms, to serve

1 Rinse the rice, then pour into a large pan of salted water, and cook according to the package instructions. Drain and set aside.

2 Meanwhile, heat the oil in a large pan over medium heat and cook the onion for 5 minutes. Add the ginger and garlic and cook for 2 minutes. Add the spices and cook for 1 minute, stirring.

3 Stir in the stock, season, and bring to a boil. Add the sweet potatoes, cover, and simmer for 10 minutes. Stir in the beans and cauliflower and cook for another 10 minutes.

4 Return the rice to heat through. Stir in the garam masala and lemon juice. Season to taste and stir in the cilantro and nuts. Serve with raita and poppadoms.

VARIATION

Instead of the sweet potatoes use 3 sliced carrots or ½ chopped butternut squash.

CALORIES: 621kcals/2598kJ

CARBOHYDRATE: 102g
 sugar: 10g

FAT: 13g
 saturated: 2g

SALT: 0.2g

FIBER: 7g

Vietnamese stir-fried ground pork and rice

Fresh mint leaves, sour lime, salty fish sauce, and a touch of sweetness make this stir-fry extremely tasty.

10 mins 15 mins

SERVES 4

3½oz (100g) thin green beans, chopped into ¾in (2cm) pieces

salt

3½oz (100g) small broccoli florets

3½oz (100g) sugarsnap peas, chopped into ¾in (2cm) pieces

4 tbsp sunflower or vegetable oil

1 tsp sesame oil

4 scallions, finely sliced

2 garlic cloves, finely chopped

1in (3cm) piece of fresh ginger, finely chopped

14oz (400g) ground pork

1¾lb (800g) cooked, cold white rice, such as basmati or jasmine

1 tbsp Thai fish sauce

juice of 1 lime, plus 1 extra lime, to serve

2 tbsp soy sauce

2 tbsp oyster sauce

1 tsp granulated sugar

2 tbsp finely chopped mint leaves

2 tbsp finely chopped cilantro leaves

1 Blanch the beans in boiling salted water for 1 minute, then add the broccoli and sugarsnap peas and blanch for another minute. Drain, refresh under cold water, then drain again.

2 In a wok, heat 2 tbsp of the sunflower oil and the sesame oil and cook the scallions, garlic, and ginger over high heat for 2 minutes. Add the pork and cook for 5 minutes, until brown, then remove from the wok. Wipe the wok with paper towels.

3 Heat the remaining sunflower oil and cook the green vegetables for 2 minutes. Return the pork.

4 Add the rice, fish sauce, lime juice, soy sauce, oyster sauce, and sugar, and cook for another 2 minutes until heated through. Stir in the herbs and serve with extra lime wedges to squeeze over.

CALORIES: 565kcals/2373kJ

CARBOHYDRATE: 59g
 sugar: 1.5g

FAT: 24g
 saturated: 6g

SALT: 0.9g

FIBER: 2g

Jambalaya

This one-pot meal captures the authentic Creole and Cajun flavors of Louisiana in the Deep South.

30 mins   45 mins

SPECIAL EQUIPMENT
large Dutch oven

SERVES 4–6

4 tbsp sunflower or vegetable oil

4 boneless, skinless chicken thighs, cut into bite-sized pieces

8oz (225g) mix of garlic and spicy sausages, (and smoked, if liked), cut into thick slices

1 onion, finely chopped

2 garlic cloves, finely chopped

1 red bell pepper, finely chopped

1 green bell pepper, finely chopped

1 celery stalk, thinly sliced

1 Scotch bonnet chile, seeded and chopped, or to taste

12oz (350g) long-grain white rice

1 tsp chile powder

1 tsp Worcestershire sauce

2 tbsp tomato paste

2 bay leaves

2 tsp dried thyme

1 tsp salt

½ tsp smoked paprika

pinch of sugar

freshly ground black pepper

1 x 14oz (400g) can chopped tomatoes

2 cups vegetable stock (see p156)

12 large raw shrimp, shelled and deveined

hot pepper sauce, to serve

1 Heat half the oil in a large Dutch oven over high heat. Cook the chicken for 10 minutes, or until the juices run clear. Set aside on paper towels.

2 Add the remaining oil to the pan and heat. Add the sausages, except the smoked sausages (if using), and cook, stirring, for 5 minutes, or until browned. Remove with a slotted spoon and set aside with the chicken.

3 Add the onion, garlic, peppers, celery, and chile to the pan and cook for 5 minutes, or until softened, stirring frequently. Add the rice and chile powder and cook, stirring, for 2 minutes. Add the Worcestershire sauce and tomato paste and cook, stirring, for another minute.

4 Return the chicken to the Dutch oven with all the sausages, including smoked (if using), the bay leaves, thyme, salt, paprika, and sugar, and season to taste with pepper. Pour in the tomatoes and the stock and bring to a boil, stirring. Reduce the heat to its lowest setting, cover, and simmer for 12–15 minutes, or until the peppers are tender.

5 Add the shrimp, cover, and simmer for 3 to 5 minutes, or until the shrimp are pink. The rice should be tender and the mixture a little soupy. Transfer to a warmed serving bowl and serve with hot pepper sauce.

CALORIES: 734kcals/3068kJ

CARBOHYDRATE: 78g
sugar: 11g

FAT: 25g
saturated: 6g

SALT: 2.6g

FIBER: 3.5g

The hard-working fridge

A hard-working, well-organized fridge can save you time as well as being more energy efficient, allowing cool air to circulate to keep food at the right temperature. It can be helpful to go through the fridge just before a supermarket trip, and throw out anything that is past its use-by-date, or make a mental note to use up anything that has been hanging around a little too long (these items can form the basis of your next few meals).To prevent germs multiplying, your fridge should be kept clean, and all food should be wrapped or stored in covered containers. When refrigerating leftovers, allow hot food to cool first.

What goes where

Storing things in designated spaces in your fridge means that you can see at a glance when you are running low of a staple item. Most modern fridges have special storage areas for cheese, eggs, and vegetables—using these frees up space for bulkier items. Fridges often have movable shelves, too. Try positioning these at different heights to optimize the space that you have. A small top shelf is ideal for shorter things like jars, for example.

Best chilled

Many items say "refrigerate after opening". Storing items such as ketchup, mustard, and jelly will prolong their shelf life and keep them tasting fresher for longer.

How to store

Ensure that items are accessible, visble, and not too crammed. The back of the fridge will be colder than the door, so plan carefully to make your food last longer.

Leftovers Most leftovers will keep for 2–3 days in the fridge, providing they are well wrapped or stored in an airtight container. Delicate items such as shellfish and fish should be kept overnight only.

Meat Meat must always be carefully stored. For hygiene reasons you should try and store it separately from other foodstuffs, if not on its own shelf then at least in a designated area, well wrapped.

Vegetables Most vegetables are best stored in the large drawers at the bottom of the fridge. Keeping one side for the tougher root vegetables means that more delicate items such as lettuce can be protected from damage.

Essential fridge stock

⭐ Cheeses – a hard cheese (such as cheddar), a soft cheese (such as brie), feta, and parmesan

⭐ Butter – salted and unsalted for baking

⭐ Eggs – try using free range or organic, if possible

⭐ Yogurts – flavored, plain, and Greek yogurt

⭐ Creams – heavy cream and sour cream

⭐ Curry pastes

⭐ Good quality sauces – such as tartar, horseradish, and hollandaise

⭐ Mustards – English, Djon, and grain mustards

⭐ Good-quality mayonnaise

⭐ Prepared ginger, chile paste, and garlic in tubes or jars

Temperature check

The wrong temperature not only wastes energy, it can result in spoiled food. Use a fridge thermometer to make sure that the fridge stays between 37–41°F.

Inviting layout

Make the inside of the fridge look appealing to kids. Ensure that there's fresh, colorful fruit for snacking, so that when they're hungry, they head to the fridge rather than the cookie jar.

Zucchini, mint, and feta frittata

This light, summery frittata is perfect for a summer picnic, cut into wedges and served cold.

10 mins   15 mins, plus resting

SPECIAL EQUIPMENT
10in (25cm) heavy-bottomed, ovenproof frying pan

SERVES 4–6

2 tbsp olive oil

9oz (250g) zucchini, cut into ½in (1cm) cubes

1 garlic clove, crushed

6 large eggs

1 tbsp heavy cream

scant 1oz (25g) finely grated Parmesan cheese

2 tbsp chopped mint leaves

salt and freshly ground black pepper

3½oz (100g) feta cheese, cut into ½in (1cm) cubes

1 tbsp butter

1 Heat the oil in a 10in (25cm) heavy-bottomed, ovenproof frying pan and cook the zucchini over medium heat for 3–5 minutes until they start to brown. Add the garlic and cook for 1 minute. Transfer to a plate and wipe the pan with paper towels. Preheat the broiler to its highest setting.

2 Whisk together the eggs, cream, Parmesan, and mint, then season well. Add the garlicky zucchini and the feta cheese and mix well.

3 Melt the butter in the frying pan over medium heat and pour the egg mixture into the pan. Cook for 5 minutes, without moving it at all, until the edges start to set.

4 Transfer the pan to the broiler and cook for another 5 minutes, until the frittata is set and the top golden brown. Rest for 5 minutes before cutting into wedges to serve.

CALORIES: 326kcals/1353kJ
CARBOHYDRATE: 1.5g
  sugar: 1.5g
FAT: 28g
  saturated: 11g
SALT: 1.4g
FIBER: 0.8g

Red bell pepper and chorizo frittata

This hearty frittata can be served for brunch, or even cut into small squares and served as a canapé.

10 mins   35–40 mins, plus resting

SPECIAL EQUIPMENT
10in (25cm) heavy-bottomed, ovenproof frying pan

SERVES 4–6

1 tbsp olive oil

2 red bell peppers, cut into ½in (1cm) cubes

5½oz (150g) dry Spanish-style chorizo, casing removed and cut into small cubes (don't worry if it crumbles)

1 garlic clove, crushed

6 large eggs

1 tbsp heavy cream

scant 1oz (25g) finely grated Parmesan cheese

2 tbsp chopped basil leaves

salt and freshly ground black pepper

1 tbsp butter

1 Heat the oil in a 10in (25cm) heavy-bottomed, ovenproof frying pan and cook the peppers over low heat for 15–20 minutes until they are tender. Add the chorizo and cook for 3–4 minutes until browned in places, throwing in the garlic 1 minute before the end of cooking. Transfer to a plate and wipe the pan with paper towels. Preheat the broiler to its highest setting.

2 Whisk together the eggs, cream, Parmesan cheese, and basil, and season well. Add the pepper and chorizo mixture and stir well.

3 Melt the butter in the frying pan over medium heat and pour in the egg mixture. Cook for 5 minutes, without moving it at all, until the edges start to set.

4 Transfer the pan to the broiler and cook for another 5 minutes until the frittata is set and the top golden brown. Rest for 5 minutes before cutting into wedges to serve.

CALORIES: 361kcals/1500kJ
CARBOHYDRATE: 6g
  sugar: 5.5g
FAT: 29g
  saturated: 11g
SALT: 1g
FIBER: 2g

Egg salad

A step up from traditional egg mayonnaise, try this spread on whole wheat toast for a quick, delicious lunch.

10 mins, plus cooling   10 mins

SERVES 4

6 large eggs

6 tbsp good-quality mayonnaise

1 tbsp lemon juice

1 celery stalk, finely chopped

1 heaping tbsp finely chopped dill

1 heaping tbsp Dijon mustard

1 large scallion, finely chopped

salt and freshly ground black pepper

paprika (optional)

1 Bring a saucepan of water to a boil, lower in the eggs on a large spoon, and boil for 8 minutes. Remove with a slotted spoon, run under cold water, and let cool. Peel the eggs.

2 In a large bowl, beat together all the remaining ingredients, except the optional paprika, until well combined.

3 Finely chop the eggs and gently mix them into the mayonnaise mixture, being careful not to break up the eggs too much. Serve sprinkled with paprika (if using).

COOK'S TIP

Try using this as a filling for a tasty packed lunch, especially for a vegetarian child. It is tasty but not overpowering. It is also a good source of protein.

CALORIES: 288kcals/1191kJ

CARBOHYDRATE: 0.5g
 sugar: 0.4g

FAT: 27g
 saturated: 5g

SALT: 0.6g

FIBER: 0.2g

Piperade

This recipe is from the Basque region of France, where the peppers are sweetened by long hours of sunshine.

5 mins   20 mins

SERVES 4

2 tbsp olive oil

1 large onion, finely sliced

2 garlic cloves, crushed

1 red bell pepper, chopped

1 green bell pepper, chopped

3oz (85g) Serrano ham or Bayonne ham, chopped

4 tomatoes, chopped

8 large eggs, beaten

salt and freshly ground black pepper

2 tbsp chopped flat-leaf parsley leaves

1 Heat the oil in a large frying pan and cook the onion over low heat until softened. Add the garlic and peppers and cook for 5 minutes, stirring occasionally.

2 Add the ham and cook for 2 minutes, then add the tomatoes and cook for 2–3 minutes, or until any liquid has evaporated.

3 Pour the eggs into the pan and scramble, stirring frequently. Season to taste with salt and pepper, sprinkle with parsley, and serve.

COOK'S TIP

For a simple shortcut, use roasted peppers from a jar. They come preserved in either brine or olive oil. Drain and chop before use.

CALORIES: 300kcals/1257kJ

CARBOHYDRATE: 10g
 sugar: 9g

FAT: 19g
 saturated: 5g

SALT: 1.5g

FIBER: 4g

Baked eggs with ham and cheese

This simple, nursery-style dish makes a fantastic breakfast for children, and is popular with adults, too.

5 mins   15 mins

SPECIAL EQUIPMENT
4 x 5fl oz (150ml) ramekins

SERVES 4

butter, for greasing

3oz (85g) ham, finely chopped

4 large eggs

salt and freshly ground black pepper

1¾oz (50g) grated mild Cheddar cheese

buttered toast sticks, to serve

1 Preheat the oven to 350°F (180°C). Butter four 5fl oz (150ml) ramekins and place them on a baking sheet.

2 Divide the ham evenly between the ramekins. Press it down in the center to make a dip for the egg to sit in.

3 Carefully break an egg into the hollow in each ramekin and season well. Top each egg with one-quarter of the cheese.

4 Bake for 15 minutes, or until the eggs are just cooked. The yolks will still be a little runny, so continue to cook for another 5 minutes if you like your yolks well cooked. Serve immediately along with buttered toast sticks for dipping.

CLEVER WITH LEFTOVERS

Try adapting this recipe, replacing the ham with some cold roast meat, or poached salmon, or even leftover gravy. These will all make an easy, comforting supper dish.

CALORIES: 170kcals/708kJ

CARBOHYDRATE: 0.2g
  sugar: 0.2g

FAT: 13g
  saturated: 5.5g

SALT: 1g

FIBER: 0g

Mexican eggs

This family favorite is a great way to turn eggs into a main meal. Add chile if you want more heat.

5 mins   25 mins

SPECIAL EQUIPMENT
10in (25cm) heavy-bottomed, ovenproof frying pan

SERVES 4

1 tbsp olive oil

2 garlic cloves, crushed

1 x 14oz (400ml) tomato sauce

1 tsp smoked paprika

salt and freshly ground black pepper

1 tbsp chopped cilantro leaves

4 large eggs

4 thick slices of country-style bread

CALORIES: 228kcals/958kJ

CARBOHYDRATE: 22g
  sugar: 4g

FAT: 10g
  saturated: 2.5g

SALT: 1.2g

FIBER: 2g

1 Heat the oil in a 10in (25cm) heavy-bottomed, ovenproof frying pan over medium heat and cook the garlic for 1 minute until it begins to color. Add the tomato sauce and smoked paprika and season well. Bring to a boil, reduce to a gentle simmer, and cook for 20 minutes until thickened and reduced.

2 Five minutes before it is ready, Preheat the broiler to its highest setting. Stir most of the cilantro into the tomato mixture.

3 When the sauce is ready, take it off the heat. Make 4 holes in the sauce with the back of a spoon. Crack an egg into each hole and put the pan under the hot broiler for 2–3 minutes, until the eggs have just set. Meanwhile, broil or toast the slices of bread.

4 Scoop a little of the tomato sauce over the top of each piece of toast, then top it with an egg and sprinkle over the reserved cilantro to serve.

Roasted portobello mushrooms with scrambled eggs on toast

A lovely way to serve eggs, this makes an unusual and luxurious breakfast or supper dish.

10 mins   20 mins

SERVES 4

¼ cup olive oil

2 tbsp chopped parsley leaves

salt and freshly ground black pepper

4 large flat mushrooms, such as Portobello, stems discarded

6 large eggs

¼ cup heavy cream

1 heaping tbsp finely chopped chives

2 tbsp butter

4 thick slices of country-style bread

1 Preheat the oven to 400°F (200°C). In a bowl, mix the oil and parsley and season. Brush the mixture all over the mushrooms, place on a baking sheet, and roast for 20 minutes until tender.

2 Just before the mushrooms are ready, whisk together the eggs, cream, and chives and season well.

3 Heat a large, heavy-bottomed frying pan and melt the butter. Scramble the eggs in the pan over low heat for 3–4 minutes, using a wooden spoon and a slow, scraping motion to move them around so all the egg comes in contact with the heat. Be sure to get into every area of the bottom and the corners of the pan so the egg cooks evenly.

4 Meanwhile, broil or toast the bread. When the toast is ready, spoon over the juices from the mushrooms and top each piece with a mushroom, gill-side up.

5 While the egg is still a little soft or liquid (it will continue to cook off the heat), place one-quarter of it into each mushroom to serve.

VARIATION

For a special treat, drizzle the tops of the eggs sparingly with good-quality truffle oil just before serving.

CALORIES: 464kcals/1930kJ

CARBOHYDRATE: 19g
  sugar: 1.5g

FAT: 36g
  saturated: 13g

SALT: 1g

FIBER: 2g

Poached eggs with grilled asparagus

A fabulous appetizer or light lunch. Dip the asparagus in the egg yolk as if it were a toast stick.

5 mins   10 mins

SERVES 4

1 bunch of asparagus, woody ends removed

1 tbsp olive oil

salt and freshly ground black pepper

4 large eggs

1 Heat a grill pan and rub the asparagus spears with the oil. Cook on the grill pan over medium heat for 5–7 minutes (depending on thickness), turning occasionally, until they are tender and charred in places. Sprinkle them with salt and pepper.

2 When the asparagus is nearly ready, bring a large pan of salted water to a boil. Crack an egg into a teacup and gently slide into the bubbling water. Repeat for all the eggs (using a teacup helps them maintain their shape). Poach the eggs in very gently simmering water for about 3 minutes until the white is set but the yolk is still runny. (The trick to perfect poached eggs is that they must be very fresh; this helps the white to stay together in a neat shape.)

3 Transfer the asparagus to warmed plates, place an egg on top of each pile, and sprinkle with black pepper.

COOK'S TIP

If you don't have a grill pan, try cooking the asparagus under a hot broiler instead.

CALORIES: 128kcals/530kJ

CARBOHYDRATE: 1g
  sugar: 1g

FAT: 10g
  saturated: 2g

SALT: 0.2g

FIBER: 1.5g

Zucchini and goat cheese omelet

The vibrant green of zucchini combines with the creamy white of goat cheese in this tasty omelet.

10 mins   5 mins

SERVES 1

3 large eggs, lightly beaten

1 small zucchini, grated

salt and freshly ground black pepper

pat of butter

1¾oz (50g) soft goat cheese, crumbled

small handful of thyme, leaves picked (optional)

1 Put the eggs and zucchini in a bowl. Season with salt and pepper. Melt the butter in a small, non-stick frying pan over medium-high heat until foaming, then pour in the egg mixture, swirling it around the pan to cover the bottom. Gently slide a rubber spatula under the edges.

2 When the omelet is beginning to cook around the edges, scatter in the goat cheese so that it is evenly covered. Continue cooking until the center is still just a little wet. Remove from the heat and leave for 2 minutes to set;

the heat of the pan will continue to cook the omelet. (Do not overcook it; you do not want it to be rubbery in texture.)

3 Evenly sprinkle in a little black pepper and scatter with the thyme leaves (if using). Carefully slide the omelet out of the pan (a rubber spatula will help with this) and serve immediately.

Try serving vegetables grated, well cooked, and disguised in a dish such as this. Omit the fresh thyme for fussy eaters, as it has a rather "grown-up" taste.

Fussy eaters!

CALORIES: 514kcals/2135kJ

CARBOHYDRATE: 2g
  sugar: 2g

FAT: 41g
  saturated: 20g

SALT: 1.6g

FIBER: 1g

Herby feta and spinach filo pie

Spinach works well with strong, sharp cheeses. In this Greek pie it is encased in crispy filo pastry with herbs.

30 mins   1 hr, plus cooling

SPECIAL EQUIPMENT

8in (20cm) round springform pan

SERVES 6

FOR THE FILLING

2lb (900g) spinach

7 tbsp butter, plus extra for greasing

2 onions, finely chopped

2 garlic cloves, finely chopped

4oz (120g) roasted peppers in oil, drained and chopped

handful of basil leaves, torn

3 tbsp chopped mint leaves

3 tbsp chopped parsley leaves

salt and freshly ground black pepper

10oz (300g) feta cheese, crumbled

FOR THE PASTRY

6 sheets store-bought filo pastry, 16 x 12in (40 x 30cm)

1 Pack the spinach into a large saucepan, cover, and cook, stirring occasionally, until just wilted. Drain well in a colander. Set aside, still draining, to cool.

2 Melt scant 1oz (25g) of the butter and cook the onions for 3 minutes. Add the garlic and cook for one minute. Stir in the peppers and herbs and set aside. Preheat the oven to 400°F (200°C). Grease and line an 8in (20cm) round springform pan.

3 Chop the spinach. Stir into the onion mixture and season. Melt the remaining butter. Brush the pan with butter. Cover with a sheet of pastry, leaving it overhanging, and brush with butter. Repeat to use all the pastry, arranging each sheet at an angle to the one beneath. Add half the onion mixture, the feta, then the remaining onion. Pull the overhanging pastry over the top, brushing with the last of the butter.

4 Place on a baking sheet. Bake for 35–40 minutes, until crisp. Leave for 10 minutes, then release from the pan. Serve hot or warm.

CALORIES: 438kcals/1814kJ

CARBOHYDRATE: 28g
  sugar: 8g

FAT: 28g
  saturated: 16g

SALT: 3.2g

FIBER: 5g

Broiled halloumi salad

Halloumi, a Cypriot sheep cheese, is delicious served warm. Work quickly, as it hardens on cooling.

10 mins, plus marinating   5–10 mins

SERVES 4 (as an appetizer)

9oz (250g) halloumi cheese with mint, cut into 8 slices

finely grated zest and juice of 1 lime

2 tbsp extra virgin olive oil

1 red chile, seeded and finely chopped (optional)

freshly ground black pepper

1¾oz (50g) pitted Kalamata olives

5½oz (150g) cherry tomatoes, halved

2 tbsp chopped cilantro leaves

2 tbsp chopped flat-leaf parsley leaves

¾oz (20g) toasted pine nuts

2¼oz (70g) arugula

4 pita breads, warmed, to serve

CALORIES: 305kcals/1270kJ

CARBOHYDRATE: 8g
  sugar: 1.5g

FAT: 27g
  saturated: 12g

SALT: 1.9g

FIBER: 1g

1 Place the sliced cheese in a single layer in a shallow dish. Evenly sprinkle over the lime zest and juice, oil, chile, and a good grinding of pepper and turn the cheese slices to coat them. Cover and set aside to marinate for 30 minutes at room temperature.

2 Meanwhile, place the remaining ingredients (except the pita bread) in a large bowl and toss to combine. Divide the salad between 4 plates. Preheat the broiler to its highest setting.

3 Line a baking sheet with foil. Using a slotted spoon, remove the cheese from the marinade (reserve the marinade) and place on the sheet. Broil for 3–5 minutes on each side, turning carefully, until golden brown. The cheese will not melt, but should soften slightly.

4 Place 2 slices of halloumi on top of each plate of salad. Drizzle the reserved marinade evenly over each portion, to act as a dressing, and serve with warmed pita bread.

Herby goat cheese spread

A simple spread to serve as an appetizer or dip, or even to make an interesting sandwich filling.

5 mins

SERVES 4–6

9oz (250g) soft goat cheese, at room temperature

9oz (250g) cream cheese, at room temperature

3 heaping tbsp finely chopped basil leaves

3 heaping tbsp finely chopped chives

finely grated zest of 1 lemon

salt and freshly ground black pepper

toasted baguette, to serve (optional)

1 Put the 2 cheeses in a large bowl and beat with a wooden spoon until any lumps have been removed and the mixture is completely smooth and evenly blended together.

2 Add the herbs and lemon zest and mix them in. Season well with pepper and a little salt (the goat cheese can be quite salty). Serve with toasted baguette (if using), or in a sandwich with roasted vegetables.

CLEVER WITH LEFTOVERS

Use this recipe as a guide to use up any soft cheese and herbs you may have, varying the taste with the addition of smoked paprika, pesto (see p194), or a handful of finely grated Parmesan cheese.

CALORIES: 474kcals/1960kJ

CARBOHYDRATE: 0.6g
  sugar: 0.6g

FAT: 46g
  saturated: 30g

SALT: 1.4g

FIBER: 0g

Herby baked feta with pita chips

A wonderfully simple appetizer or snack. Leave out the chile if you are feeding young children.

5 mins | 20 mins

SERVES 4 (as an appetizer)

7oz (200g) package of feta cheese

1 tsp finely grated orange zest

1 tsp finely chopped red or green chile

1 tbsp finely chopped mint leaves

½ tbsp honey

3-4 tbsp olive oil

freshly ground black pepper

3 pita breads

1 Preheat the oven to 400°F (200°C). Put the cheese in a small ovenproof dish and sprinkle evenly with the zest, chile, and mint. Drizzle in the honey and 1 tbsp of the oil and season well with pepper (feta cheese is quite salty, so you shouldn't need any salt). Bake for 20 minutes until softened and golden brown.

2 Meanwhile, with a sharp knife, carefully pry and cut apart the 2 layers of each pita bread. Brush each side of the bread with a little of the oil, then pile them on top of each other. Use a large knife to cut them into irregular triangle-shaped pieces, each about 2in (5cm) large. Spread them out in 1 layer across 2 baking sheets and bake at the top of the oven for 5–7 minutes, turning once, until golden brown and crisp. Swap the positions of the baking sheets halfway, so each spends time at the top of the oven.

3 Use the pita chips to scoop up the baked feta while it is still hot (it will harden as it cools).

VARIATION

Serve the baked feta as a light lunch with a green salad and some fresh, crusty bread, instead of the pita chips.

CALORIES: 340kcals/1423kJ
CARBOHYDRATE: 29g
  sugar: 4g
FAT: 19g
  saturated: 8g
SALT: 2.5g
FIBER: 1g

Baked ricotta

Try this easy vegetarian dish as a light lunch, scooping it up with plenty of warm, crusty bread.

10 mins | 30 mins

SPECIAL EQUIPMENT
4 x 5fl oz (150ml) ramekins

SERVES 4

vegetable oil, for greasing

1lb 2oz (500g) ricotta cheese, drained

1 large egg, beaten

1¾oz (50g) finely grated Parmesan cheese

3 tbsp thyme leaves

1 tbsp chopped rosemary leaves

salt and freshly ground black pepper

⅓ cup fresh white bread crumbs

breadsticks or crackers, to serve

1 Preheat the oven to 350°F (180°C). Brush four 5fl oz (150ml) ramekins with oil and place on a baking sheet.

2 Put the ricotta, egg, Parmesan, thyme, rosemary, and plenty of seasoning in a mixing bowl and beat well. Divide among the prepared ramekins.

3 Season the bread crumbs and sprinkle over the ricotta mixture. Bake in the oven for 30 minutes. Serve hot with breadsticks or crackers for dipping.

PREPARE AHEAD
These make a fantastic vegetarian lunch choice. They can be prepared ahead and stored in the fridge for up to 1 day. For best results, bring to room temperature before baking.

CALORIES: 271kcals/1131kJ
CARBOHYDRATE: 6g
  sugar: 2.5g
FAT: 19g
  saturated: 11g
SALT: 0.7g
FIBER: 0g

Mozzarella en carrozza

These Italian-style fried sandwiches are rich, crispy, and oozing with melted mozzarella.

15 mins 10-15 mins

SERVES 4

2 balls of mozzarella cheese, approx. 4½oz (125g) each, sliced

8 thick slices of white bread, crusts removed

¼ cup all-purpose flour

salt and freshly ground black pepper

2 large eggs

2 tbsp milk

2 tbsp olive oil

1 Carefully pat each of the mozzarella slices dry with paper towels; be gentle and try not to tear them. Arrange them evenly over 4 slices of the bread, leaving a ½in (1cm) gap all round the edges to act as a border.

2 Place the remaining slices of bread on top of the cheese and press the bread together all around the edges.

3 Put the flour on a plate and season well. Beat the eggs and milk in a shallow dish, large enough for a sandwich to fit in, and whisk together with a fork until well combined.

4 Heat half the oil in a large, non-stick frying pan over medium heat. Coat one of the sandwiches in the flour and then in the egg mixture. Add to the pan. Repeat with the second sandwich. Cook for 2–3 minutes on each side, turning once, until golden brown. Do not let them burn; reduce the heat slightly if they threaten to do so. Remove and keep warm.

5 Add the remaining oil to the pan and cook the last 2 sandwiches. Serve immediately.

VARIATION

Thinly spread each slice of bread with sundried tomato pesto and add a slice of prosciutto to 4 of the slices before topping with the mozzarella and remaining bread.

CALORIES: 500kcals/2092kJ

CARBOHYDRATE: 48g
  sugar: 2.5g

FAT: 23g
  saturated: 11g

SALT: 1.8g

FIBER: 2.2g

Brie and cranberry walnut toasts

This combination of nutty bread, tart cranberries, and oozing melted cheese is simply delicious.

5 mins 5 mins

SERVES 4 (as a snack)

8 slices of walnut bread

½ cup cranberry sauce

9oz (250g) soft, ripe Brie cheese, cut into thin slices

leafy green salad, to serve (optional)

1 Preheat the broiler to a medium-hot setting. Lay the slices of bread on a baking sheet or in the broiler pan and toast them under the broiler on each side until golden brown, making sure they don't burn. (Or toast the bread in a toaster.)

2 Spread each slice of toast evenly with 1 tbsp of cranberry sauce and cover evenly with the slices of Brie.

3 Put the toasts back under the broiler and cook for 2–3 minutes, or until the Brie is melted and bubbling. (You may have to do this in batches.) Serve as a snack or with a leafy green salad.

CLEVER WITH LEFTOVERS

This is a really great way to use up leftover cranberry sauce and cheeses after Christmas, when small, easy-to-prepare snacks come into their own.

CALORIES: 444kcals/1861kJ

CARBOHYDRATE: 39g
  sugar: 13g

FAT: 24g
  saturated: 12g

SALT: 1.7g

FIBER: 1.5g

Cheese croquettes

Inspired by a Spanish tapa, these croquettes are loved by children and adults alike. Try adding ham, if you like.

25 mins, plus chilling — 20 mins

SERVES 4

3 tbsp butter

1½ cups all-purpose flour

1¼ cups whole milk

9oz (250g) coarsely grated manchego cheese

pinch of nutmeg

salt and freshly ground black pepper

2 large eggs, beaten

1 cup day-old white bread crumbs or panko crumbs

vegetable oil, for deep-frying

Tomato salsa (see p288), or ketchup, to serve

1 Line a baking sheet with parchment paper. Melt the butter in a small, non-stick pan over low heat. Whisk in ½ cup of the flour and cook for 2 minutes.

2 Take the pan off the heat and whisk in the milk a little at a time, whisking well between each addition, until the sauce is smooth.

3 Return to the heat and cook, stirring constantly, until it thickens. Reduce the heat to low and cook, stirring occasionally, for 5 minutes.

4 Add the cheese, nutmeg, and seasoning, remove from the heat, and stir until the cheese has melted. Cover and cool, then chill in the fridge for at least 1 hour.

5 Stir ½ cup more of the flour into the chilled mixture and divide it into 8 equal portions. Place the remaining ½ cup of flour, the eggs, and the bread crumbs in 3 shallow dishes, seasoning the flour well.

6 Using a spooon and your fingers, shape one portion of the mixture into a sausage shape. Coat in the flour, dip in the egg, then in the bread crumbs. Place on the baking sheet. Repeat to make 8. Cover and chill for 1 hour.

7 Heat the oil to 350°F (180°C) in a medium, heavy-bottomed pan. To check the temperature of the oil without a thermometer, add a cube of bread. It should turn golden after 1 minute. Cook the croquettes in 2 batches for 3 minutes or until

golden. Transfer to a plate lined with paper towels. Serve with Tomato salsa (see p288) or ketchup.

VARIATION

To make the perfect classic cheese sauce, follow the method for making the croquettes base, but use ¼ cup of flour, 2 cups of milk, and 2½oz (75g) grated sharp Cheddar cheese. Omit the nutmeg, but season well.

CALORIES: 815kcals/3398kJ
CARBOHYDRATE: 49g
  sugar: 5g
FAT: 56g
  saturated: 25g
SALT: 1.7g
FIBER: 2.5g

Twice-baked cheese soufflés

A true soufflé can be nerve-wracking to serve at a dinner party, but twice-baked soufflés are a fail-safe alternative.

10 mins, plus chilling

40 mins

SPECIAL EQUIPMENT

4 x 5fl oz (150ml) ramekins
or soufflé dishes

electric hand-held mixer

SERVES 4

2 tbsp butter, plus extra
for greasing

2 tbsp all-purpose flour

¾ cup whole milk

½ tsp ground mustard

pinch of grated nutmeg

salt and freshly ground black pepper

2 large eggs, separated

1¾oz (50g) grated Gruyère cheese

2 tbsp finely grated Parmesan cheese

1 Preheat the oven to 350°F (180°C). Butter four 5fl oz (150ml) ramekins or soufflé dishes and place in a small baking dish.

2 Melt the butter in a small, non-stick pan over low heat. Whisk in the flour and cook for 2 minutes, whisking constantly, until the mixture bubbles.

3 Take the pan off the heat and whisk in the milk a little at a time, whisking well between each addition, until it has all been added and the sauce is smooth.

4 Return the pan to the heat and bring to a boil, then reduce the heat and simmer for 2 minutes to thicken, stirring constantly. Be sure to whisk right into the edges of the saucepan as this is where the sauce can burn.

5 Remove from the heat and add the ground mustard, nutmeg, seasoning, egg yolks, and Gruyère cheese. Stir well. Whisk the egg whites with an electric hand-held mixer until stiff, then carefully fold into the cheese mixture.

6 Divide between the ramekins. Pour a ¾in (2cm) depth of just-boiled water into the baking dish. Carefully transfer to the oven and bake for 20 minutes.

7 Remove from the oven and cool completely. Use a knife to loosen the soufflés from the ramekins, then invert onto a buttered heatproof dish. Chill.

8 Preheat the oven to 400°F (200°C). Sprinkle each soufflé with Parmesan and bake for 10 minutes. Serve immediately.

HOW TO FREEZE

After the first cooking at the end of step 6, cool, unmold, and open-freeze the soufflés, then transfer to a large freezer bag. When ready to serve, remove as many as you need, stand them separately on a plate or tray, cover, and defrost thoroughly in the fridge (not at room temperature). Cook the soufflés within 1 day.

CALORIES: 288kcals/1199kJ

CARBOHYDRATE: 10g
sugar: 2.5g

FAT: 21g
saturated: 12g

SALT: 0.8g

FIBER: 0.5g

Cheesy potato bake

The ultimate in comfort food and a great recipe for cold days. It is equally good on its own, or as a rich side dish.

20 mins   35 mins, plus resting

SPECIAL EQUIPMENT

8in (20cm) deep-sided, ovenproof dish

SERVES 4–6

1¾lb (800g) waxy or yellow potatoes, such as large Yukon Golds

salt and freshly ground black pepper

2 tbsp butter, plus extra for greasing

2 tbsp all-purpose flour

2 cups whole milk

4½oz (125g) grated sharp cheese, such as Cheddar

green salad, to serve

1 Preheat the oven to 375°F (190°C). Peel and slice the potatoes into ⅛–¼in (3–5mm) slices. Put them in a large pan of boiling salted water and return to a boil. Reduce to a gentle simmer and cook for 5 minutes until the slices are tender, but not breaking up. Drain well.

2 Meanwhile, make the cheese sauce. Melt the butter in a small, heavy-bottomed saucepan. Whisk in the flour over low heat. Continue to cook for 2 minutes, whisking constantly, until the mixture bubbles and separates.

3 Take the pan off the heat and slowly whisk in the milk, a little at a time, whisking well between each addition, until it has all been added and the sauce is smooth. Return to the heat and cook, stirring constantly, until it thickens. Continue to cook, stirring now and then, for 5 minutes. Be sure to whisk right into the edges of the saucepan as this is where the sauce can burn if left undisturbed.

4 Add 1¾oz (50g) of the cheese, season well, and cook for another 2 minutes until the cheese has melted and the sauce is smooth, thick, and creamy.

5 Rub the inside of an 8in (20cm) deep-sided, ovenproof dish with the butter. Layer one-third of the potato slices in the dish, then top with one-third of the sauce and one-third (scant 1oz/25g) of the remaining grated cheese. Repeat twice more, seasoning as you go. When you get to the last layer of potatoes, arrange the slices so that the dish will look attractive after it has been baked.

6 Put the dish on a large baking sheet and cook in the oven for 30 minutes, until the potatoes are soft when pierced with the tip of a knife and the top is golden brown and bubbling. Rest for 5 minutes before serving with a green salad.

CALORIES: 437kcals/1826kJ

CARBOHYDRATE: 38g
sugar: 7g

FAT: 24g
saturated: 15g

SALT: 0.9g

FIBER: 3.5g

Cheese and onion pie

Soft and sweet slow-cooked onions make the perfect foil for the buttery pastry and rich cheeses in this pie.

20 mins

1 hr, plus resting

SERVES 4–6

1 tbsp olive oil

2 tbsp butter

2 garlic cloves, finely chopped

2 red onions, finely sliced

salt and freshly ground black pepper

2lb (900g) floury potatoes, such as Russets, peeled and cut into bite-sized chunks

5½oz (150g) grated mozzarella cheese

3½oz (100g) grated Emmental cheese

¼oz (40g) finely grated Parmesan cheese

2 x 7½oz (215g) sheets (8½ x 11in/ 22 x 28cm) store-bought puff pastry

1 large egg, beaten

mixed salad, to serve

1 Preheat the oven to 400°F (200°C). Line a baking sheet with parchment paper.

2 Heat the oil and butter in a large, non-stick frying pan over medium heat and gently cook the garlic and onions for 25 minutes, stirring occasionally, until softened and just beginning to be tinged with gold. They should be sweet and not too brown. If they seem to be browning too fast, reduce the heat to its lowest setting and cover the pan, so the onions sweat.

3 Meanwhile, bring a large pan of salted water to a boil, add the potatoes, and cook for 10 minutes, or until just tender to the point of a knife. Drain.

4 Add the cooked potatoes to the frying pan and cook over medium heat for 5 minutes, turning carefully halfway through. Remove the pan from the heat, season well, and stir in the cheeses.

5 Place one of the rectangles of pastry on the lined baking sheet. Spoon the filling into the center, leaving a ¾in (2cm) border around the edges. Brush the edges with water. Place the second pastry sheet over the filling and gently stretch it to cover the first sheet. Press the pastry sheets firmly together to seal. Brush with the egg and, using a sharp knife, make three 1½in (4cm) slashes in the top crust to allow the steam to escape.

6 Place on a baking sheet and bake for 20–25 minutes, or until browned. Remove from the oven and place the sheet on a wire rack to rest for 5 minutes. Serve hot, with a mixed salad.

VARIATION

For alternative fillings, you can try half Russets and half sweet potatoes, or half potato and half butternut squash.

HOW TO FREEZE

If you intend to freeze the pie, use chilled pastry, not pre-frozen, for the crust (you should not freeze pastry that has already been frozen). Assemble the pie and freeze at the end of step 5, omitting the egg glaze. Defrost, glaze, and follow step 6.

CLEVER WITH LEFTOVERS

If you have some odds and ends of different cheeses to use up, they can easily be part of this dish.

CALORIES: 622kcals/2596kJ

CARBOHYDRATE: 53g
sugar: 4.5g

FAT: 36g
saturated: 19g

SALT: 1.2g

FIBER: 3.5g

Cheesy soufflé omelet

This is an easy but impressive standby for a light supper or lunch dish. Serve with a green salad.

5 mins | 5–10 mins, plus resting

SPECIAL EQUIPMENT

10in (25cm) non-stick frying pan

SERVES 2

4 large eggs, separated

1 tbsp heavy cream

scant 1oz (25g) finely grated Parmesan cheese

salt and freshly ground black pepper

1 tbsp butter

1¾oz (50g) grated aged cheese, such as Cheddar (any sharp cheese will be good)

CALORIES: 449kcals/1864kJ

CARBOHYDRATE: 0.3g
 sugar: 0.3g

FAT: 38g
 saturated: 18g

SALT: 1.3g

FIBER: 0g

1 Whisk the egg whites to soft peaks. In a separate bowl, whisk the cream and Parmesan into the egg yolks and season well. Fold in the egg whites gently until they are well combined.

2 Heat the butter in a 10in (25cm) non-stick frying pan. Add the egg mixture and cook over low heat for 5 minutes, until the sides have set, without moving it. Scatter the cheese over the omelet and carefully fold it in half.

3 Continue to cook for another couple of minutes, then turn it out onto a plate and rest it for a minute or two. The middle will continue to cook as it rests. Cut in half to serve.

COOK'S TIP

Any simple omelet can be made to look far more substantial simply by separating the eggs and whisking the whites. Fold them in gently, without knocking out the air, for a fluffy, voluminous omelet.

Spanish tortilla

Slices of these thick omelets are served in bars all over Spain. They are best eaten at room temperature.

10 mins | 40 mins, plus cooling

SPECIAL EQUIPMENT

8in (20cm) non-stick frying pan

SERVES 4

3 tbsp olive oil

1 large Spanish onion, finely chopped

4 large eggs

9oz (250g) cooked, cooled new potatoes, cut into ½in (1cm) cubes

salt and freshly ground black pepper

CALORIES: 222kcals/925kJ

CARBOHYDRATE: 13g
 sugar: 3g

FAT: 15g
 saturated: 3g

SALT: 0.2g

FIBER: 2g

1 Heat 2 tbsp of the oil in an 8in (20cm) non-stick frying pan. Cook the onion over low heat for 10 minutes, until softened. Set aside. Wipe the pan with paper towels.

2 Beat the eggs in a large bowl. Add the onions and potatoes and season well, stirring gently.

3 Heat the remaining oil in the pan. Pour in the egg mixture and cook over low heat for 20 minutes, covered, until the edges start to pull away from the pan. The middle will not be cooked.

4 Loosen the tortilla with a spatula and put a plate on top. Turn the tortilla onto the plate. Slide it back into the pan, uncooked-side down, and cook for 10 minutes over low heat, or until cooked through. Serve at room temperature.

VARIATION

Although not strictly authentic, it is fun to add other ingredients to a tortilla. Try roasted peppers from a jar, drained, olives, or whole roasted garlic cloves.

Ham and cheese family omelet

When you need a quick meal and don't want to cook individual omelets, try this easy family recipe.

 5 mins 5–10 mins

SPECIAL EQUIPMENT
10in (25cm) heavy-bottomed, ovenproof frying pan

SERVES 4

6 large eggs

1 tbsp heavy cream

salt and freshly ground black pepper

1 tbsp butter

1¾oz (50g) ham, chopped

2½oz (75g) grated cheese, such as Cheddar or Monterey Jack

CALORIES: 272kcals/1129kJ
CARBOHYDRATE: 0.2g
  sugar: 0.2g
FAT: 22g
  saturated: 10g
SALT: 1g
FIBER: 0g

1 Preheat the broiler to its highest setting. Beat the eggs and cream in a bowl and season well.

2 Heat the butter in a 10in (25cm) heavy-bottomed, ovenproof frying pan over medium heat. When it is bubbling, pour in the egg mixture. Cook the omelet over medium heat for 2–3 minutes, moving it gently with a spatula.

3 When the edges of the omelet start to set, take it off the heat. Scatter in the ham and cheese.

4 Transfer the pan to the broiler and cook for 2–3 minutes until the top has set and is golden brown. Cut into wedges to serve.

CLEVER WITH LEFTOVERS

Some odds and ends of cheese and a few slices of ham can be turned into a quick family lunch using this easy recipe. Add leftover boiled potatoes, fried until crispy, to make it more substantial.

Pancetta and pea frittata

A frittata is basically a broiled omelet, and a mainstay of Italian family cooking. This one makes a great lunch.

 10 mins 15 mins, plus resting

SPECIAL EQUIPMENT
10in (25cm) heavy-bottomed, ovenproof frying pan

SERVES 4–6

1 tbsp olive oil

3½oz (100g) chopped pancetta

6 large eggs

1 tbsp heavy cream

scant 1oz (25g) finely grated Parmesan cheese

salt and freshly ground black pepper

3½oz (100g) frozen peas

1 tbsp butter

CALORIES: 318kcals/1318kJ
CARBOHYDRATE: 3g
  sugar: 0.7g
FAT: 26g
  saturated: 10g
SALT: 1.3g
FIBER: 2g

1 Heat the oil in a 10in (25cm) heavy-bottomed, ovenproof frying pan. Cook the pancetta for 3–5 minutes until it starts to brown at the edges. Transfer to a plate. Wipe the pan with paper towels. Preheat the broiler to its highest setting.

2 Whisk together the eggs, cream, and Parmesan and season well (go easy on the salt, as the Parmesan and pancetta are salty). Add the peas (they will cook in the frittata) and pancetta, and mix well.

3 Melt the butter in the frying pan over medium heat and pour in the egg mixture. Cook for 5 minutes, without moving it, until the edges start to set.

4 Transfer the pan to the broiler and cook for 5 minutes until the frittata is set and golden brown. Rest for at least 5 minutes. Cut into wedges and serve warm or at room temperature.

Easy entertaining

Easy entertaining

Whether it's a Sunday lunch with extended family, dinner with friends, or a children's birthday party, there are times when you want to do something a little special. What you cook will depend on the occasion but also on the season, the number of guests, and the time you have available. If you're hosting a large gathering, for example, try to serve dishes that can be prepared ahead, so you have more time to spend with your guests.

Rally the troops

A large part of entertaining is the serving and clearing of the meal, as well as the preparation. If you are planning a big gathering, try to ensure that some of your nearest and dearest (family, friends, or children) are happy to help in some way so that everything doesn't fall to you. Give each person a specific job beforehand, and make sure the work is distributed evenly and appropriately, so no one feels over-burdened and everyone is able to fulfill their role. Even small children can pass around appetizers or snacks—if you don't mind a few of them disappearing along the way!

Something for everyone

Family gatherings will often include everyone from toddlers to grandparents, so you'll need to serve a selection of dishes that will cater to all tastes. A platter of child-friendly bites such as Chicken patties (p56), carrot and cucumber sticks, and some

Texas-style barbecue spare ribs (p280) are ideal for entertaining friends in the summer. Serve with Barbecued corn-on-the cob (p287) on the side, some tasty salsas, and plenty of green salad.

Pumpkin and cinnamon waffles (p265) make a mouthwatering weekend brunch. Served warm with maple syrup and apple slices they are an appealing and indulgent treat for guests.

cut-up grapes and strawberries, should keep the under-fives happy at a get-together. Find out, too, if any of your guests have food allergies or specific dietary requirements so that you can provide something they can eat. Avoid serving any dishes that contain raw eggs, for example, to pregnant women.

Planning the menu

Choose light but tasty starters to whet the appetite, perhaps some Home-cured gravlax (p309) or, if you're having a barbecue Lemongrass-marinated shrimp skewers (p274), followed by a main course that makes a good centerpiece. For special occasions Boeuf en croute (p318) or a Roast turkey with all the trimmings (p314 and pp316-7) will make a splash. For a Sunday supper there are favorites such as Crispy pork belly with applesauce (p299), or spice things up with Chinese roast duck pancakes (p321) that people can assemble themselves. If you want a vegetarian main course, try an impressive Mediterranean vegetable and goat cheese timbale (p305) or make a casserole without the meat.

Cooking for a crowd

If the weather is good and you choose to barbecue, you can prepare a variety of meat, vegetarian, and side dishes to suit all palates, and which your guests can mix and match for themselves. In winter, casseroles, one-pots, or a large roast might fit the bill. When you are feeding a crowd, select more economical cuts of meat, such as a whole pork shoulder, and cook it long and slow to bring out its full flavor. Try Slow-cooked shoulder of pork with cider gravy, p301. If you opt to provide a buffet for your guests, be sure to include vegetarian options such as Individual mushroom and leek pies (p304) and hold these back especially to serve to your vegetarian guests.

Knock-out desserts

Some easy-to-prepare desserts are real crowd pleasers. A pavlova (Strawberry pavlova, p345) can be made as large as you need it to be. Prepare the fruit and whip the cream then the whole thing can be assembled at the last minute. Homemade ice creams, such as Quick banana ice cream (p328), served in cones will please most guests on a hot summer's day. A fruity crumble such as Berry and banana crumble (p350) is perfect on a cold winter's day, or you could pile up Raspberry cream meringues (p484) for an impressive display on a buffet table.

Strawberry pavlova (p345) is a perennial favorite that can be topped with seasonal fruits at any time of the year. It makes a fine centerpiece and can be quickly put together on the day.

Entertaining with children

While meeting up with friends and family is great fun for adults, grown-up conversation over a lingering lunch isn't always the way children want to spend their day. To make sure that everyone enjoys the event, spend a little time thinking about what might keep the little ones out of trouble while you catch up with friends.

Get them involved

Getting children to design and draw table place cards and write people's names on them before the party is a good way to get them excited and help them feel involved.

Give them their own table

A children's table can be a good idea—but set it up like the adults' one so they don't feel left out. They can eat at their own pace, although you will need to keep checking on them. Make the table fun by covering it with white paper and distributing crayons to the younger guests, so they can draw and color their own tablecloth.

Timing

Be aware that younger children need to eat earlier than adults, they may like different things, and will often finish their meal much sooner too. Catering to their tastes and timing will give your adult guests a more enjoyable time.

Stay spill free

It may not be elegant, but serving juice boxes to small children instead of drinks in glasses makes sense, especially as they often end up walking around with them.

Keep them busy

Have a plan for what to do with the kids once they have finished eating. Provide a selection of games and toys for younger children, or ask an older child to lead some games or perhaps do a bit of babysitting so that the children are happily occupied for a little longer.

Get the kids to help make this colorful Rainbow popcorn (p367) to serve when the guests arrive.

Eggs Benedict with smoked salmon

Follow the advice on partially-cooked eggs (see p11) when feeding pregnant women.

10 mins   5 mins

SPECIAL EQUIPMENT
blender

SERVES 2

FOR THE HOLLANDAISE SAUCE
7 tbsp unsalted butter
1 large egg yolk
½ tbsp lemon juice
salt and freshly ground black pepper

FOR THE REST
4 large eggs
2-4 English muffins
5½oz (150g) smoked salmon

CALORIES: 913kcals/3826kJ
CARBOHYDRATE: 29g
  sugar: 2.5g
FAT: 70g
  saturated: 34g
SALT: 3.6g
FIBER: 2g

1 To make the sauce, melt the butter over low heat, making sure it does not split. Put the egg yolk, lemon juice, and seasoning into a blender and blend briefly. With the motor running, pour in the melted butter drop by drop, accelerating to a thin stream, until it has emulsified to a thick sauce. Serve it as soon as possible.

2 Meanwhile, boil a large pan of salted water, then reduce the heat to a low simmer. Crack an egg into a teacup and gently slide into the bubbling water. Repeat for all the eggs. Poach for 3 minutes, until the white is set but the yolk is still runny. Remove with a slotted spoon.

3 At the same time, toast the muffins. If you like thick muffins use 4, cutting a thin slice off each one to add the egg, otherwise split 2 muffins horizontally to make 4 halves. When they are toasted, divide the salmon between them and top each with a poached egg and a little hollandaise sauce.

Eggs Benedict with crispy bacon

Try this version of Eggs Benedict with salty, crisp bacon and crunchy walnut bread.

10 mins   5 mins

SPECIAL EQUIPMENT
blender

SERVES 2

FOR THE HOLLANDAISE SAUCE
7 tbsp unsalted butter
1 large egg yolk
½ tbsp lemon juice
salt and freshly ground black pepper

FOR THE REST
6 slices thick-cut bacon
4 large eggs
4 thick slices of walnut bread, or multigrain bread, crusts removed

CALORIES: 934kcals/3913kJ
CARBOHYDRATE: 37g
  sugar: 2g
FAT: 73g
  saturated: 36g
SALT: 3.1g
FIBER: 1.5g

1 Make the hollandaise sauce as for Eggs Benedict with smoked salmon (see left).

2 Meanwhile, preheat the broiler to its highest setting. Cut each bacon slice in half horizontally, to make 12 short slices, and broil until crisp. Keep warm.

3 Next, poach the eggs. Boil a large pan of salted water and reduce the heat to a low simmer. Crack an egg into a teacup and gently slide into the bubbling water. Repeat for all the eggs. Poach for 3 minutes, until the white is set but the yolk is still runny. Remove with a slotted spoon.

4 Meanwhile, toast the bread. Top each piece with 3 half slices of crispy bacon, a poached egg, and a little hollandaise sauce.

PREPARE AHEAD
You could broil the bacon 1 day in advance and reheat it in a microwave until it sizzles.

Eggs Florentine

A great vegetarian option; make sure you drain the spinach before serving to keep the toast dry.

15 mins | 5 mins

SPECIAL EQUIPMENT
blender

SERVES 2

FOR THE HOLLANDAISE SAUCE

14 tbsp unsalted butter, plus
  1 tbsp extra for the spinach

2 large egg yolks

¾–1 tbsp lemon juice, to taste

salt and freshly ground black pepper

FOR THE REST

9oz (250g) baby spinach leaves

4 large eggs

4 thick slices of whole wheat bread,
  crusts removed

CALORIES: 1169kcals/4894kJ
CARBOHYDRATE: 31g
  sugar: 4g
FAT: 104g
  saturated: 59g
SALT: 1.6g
FIBER: 5.3g

1 Make the sauce as for Eggs Benedict with smoked salmon (see far left), adding lemon to taste.

2 Next, cook the spinach. Heat the extra 1 tbsp of butter in a large saucepan and add the spinach. Season it well and cook for a minute or two, stirring frequently, until it wilts completely. Drain well, squeezing out excess water, then return to the pan, mix in 2 tbsp of the hollandaise sauce, and put the lid on to keep it warm.

3 Next, poach the eggs. Boil a large pan of salted water and reduce the heat to a low simmer. Crack an egg into a teacup and gently slide into the bubbling water. Repeat for all the eggs. Poach gently for 3 minutes, until the white is set but the yolk still runny. Remove with a slotted spoon.

4 Meanwhile, toast the slices of bread. When they are toasted, top each piece with a spoonful of creamy spinach, a poached egg, and a little hollandaise sauce.

Huevos rancheros

A classic Mexican dish of "ranch-style eggs" makes a substantial breakfast with a fabulous chile kick.

20 mins | 50 mins

SERVES 4

6 tbsp olive oil

1 onion, finely chopped

2 garlic cloves, crushed

2 dried chiles, finely chopped

1 scant tsp smoked paprika

1 x 14oz (400g) can chopped tomatoes

½ tsp granulated sugar

1 tbsp chopped flat-leaf parsley leaves

salt and freshly ground black pepper

10oz (300g) cooked new potatoes,
  cut into ¾in (2cm) cubes

7oz (200g) spicy chorizo, casing
  removed, cut into ¾in (2cm) cubes

4 large eggs

2 tbsp chopped cilantro leaves

CALORIES: 452kcals/1881kJ
CARBOHYDRATE: 21g
  sugar: 6g
FAT: 32g
  saturated: 8g
SALT: 1g
FIBER: 3g

1 Heat 4 tbsp of the oil in a small saucepan. Add the onion and cook over medium heat for 5 minutes until softened. Add the garlic, chiles, and paprika and cook for one minute. Add the tomatoes, sugar, and parsley and bring to a boil. Season, reduce the heat, and simmer for 30 minutes. Set aside.

2 In a large, heavy-bottomed frying pan, heat the remaining 2 tbsp of oil over medium heat. Cook the potatoes for 5 minutes, add the chorizo, and cook for 5 minutes.

3 Remove the pan from the heat and stir in the tomato salsa. Make 4 large holes in the mixture and crack the eggs into the holes. Return to the heat and cook for 5 minutes. Sprinkle with the cilantro and serve from the pan.

PREPARE AHEAD

This recipe can be made in advance up to the point you put the eggs into the mixture. Cover and chill the cooked chorizo and tomato base overnight in the fridge, then add the eggs in the morning and cook for a quick, tasty breakfast treat.

Croque-madame

A once-in-a-while treat, this is the ultimate ham and cheese sandwich—try it and see.

10 mins   10 mins

SERVES 4

2 tbsp butter, plus extra for the bread

8 slices of good-quality white bread

7oz (200g) grated Gruyère cheese

1 tbsp Dijon mustard (optional)

salt and freshly ground black pepper

4 thick slices of good-quality ham, or 5½oz (150g) thinly sliced ham

1 tbsp sunflower or vegetable oil

4 small eggs

1 Butter each slice of bread on both sides. Set aside 1¾oz (50g) of the cheese. Make sandwiches by spreading 4 slices of bread with a little mustard, (if using), then a layer of grated cheese, firmly pressed down. Season well, then add a piece of ham, another layer of cheese, and a second piece of bread.

2 Melt the 2 tbsp of butter in a large, non-stick frying pan and cook 2 sandwiches carefully over medium heat for 2–3 minutes each side, pressing them gently with a spatula, until golden brown. Keep warm while you cook the remaining 2 sandwiches. Wipe the pan with paper towels.

3 Preheat the broiler to its highest setting. Place the cooked sandwiches on a baking sheet and top each with one-quarter of the reserved grated cheese. Broil until the cheese has melted and is bubbling.

4 Meanwhile, heat the sunflower oil in the frying pan and cook the eggs how you like them. Top each sandwich with a fried egg and serve with a pile of shoestring fries.

VARIATION

A classic croque-madame uses béchamel sauce in place of the melted cheese on top of the sandwich. Make a little classic cheese sauce (see p244), and try grilling 1–2 tbsp on top of each sandwich instead of the grated cheese.

CALORIES: 555kcals/2319kJ

CARBOHYDRATE: 31g
  sugar: 2.9g

FAT: 34g
  saturated: 17g

SALT: 3.3g

FIBER: 1.8g

Cheesy scrambled eggs on English muffins

Turn simple scrambled eggs into an attractive brunch dish with melting cheese, herbs, and toasted muffins.

5 mins   5 mins

SERVES 4

8 large eggs

¼ cup heavy cream

salt and freshly ground black pepper

4 English muffins

4 tbsp butter

3½oz (100g) finely grated Gruyére cheese

2 tbsp finely chopped chives, plus extra to serve (optional)

1 Whisk the eggs and cream together, then season well. Slice the muffins in half and toast. Melt the butter in a non-stick frying pan.

2 When the butter has melted, pour the egg mixture into the pan. Cook gently for a minute or two, moving it around slowly with a wooden spoon. Scatter the cheese and chives on top and continue to cook until the eggs are soft and just set and the cheese has melted.

3 Pile the cheesy scrambled eggs on the toasted muffins and serve with chives sprinkled over (if using).

VARIATION

If your family eats meat, cook chopped bacon in the pan before adding the egg mixture for a new twist on eggs and bacon.

CALORIES: 599kcals/2499kJ

CARBOHYDRATE: 29g
  sugar: 2.6g

FAT: 41g
  saturated: 21g

SALT: 1.8g

FIBER: 2g

Turkish eggs

This dish, known as *menemen* in Turkey, is spicy and utterly addictive. Add more chile if you like it hot.

15 mins   40-45 mins

SERVES 4

1 tbsp olive oil

1 onion, sliced

1 green bell pepper, sliced

1 red bell pepper, sliced

1 orange bell pepper, sliced

⅔ cup (6oz) Greek yogurt

3 tbsp chopped mint leaves

2 garlic cloves, crushed

1 red chile, seeded and finely chopped

1 x 14oz (400g) can of chopped tomatoes

pinch of granulated sugar

salt and freshly ground black pepper

4 large eggs

3 tbsp roughly chopped cilantro leaves

1 Heat the oil in a large, non-stick frying pan over medium heat and cook the onion for 5 minutes. Add the peppers to the pan and cook for 20 minutes, stirring occasionally.

2 Meanwhile, place the yogurt, mint, and garlic in a small serving bowl and stir together. Cover and set aside.

3 Add the chile, tomatoes, and sugar to the frying pan, season well, and cook for 10 minutes.

4 Make 4 hollows in the tomato mixture and crack an egg into each. Cover the pan and cook for 5–10 minutes, or until the eggs are cooked to your liking.

5 Sprinkle the dish with the cilantro and serve with the herb and garlic yogurt.

CALORIES: 208kcals/871kJ

CARBOHYDRATE: 13g
  sugar: 13g

FAT: 12g
  saturated: 4g

SALT: 0.5g

FIBER: 4g

Baked eggs with spinach

Easy to put together and very healthy, this manages to taste far more indulgent than it really is.

15 mins   20 mins

SPECIAL EQUIPMENT
4 x 5fl oz (150ml) ramekins

SERVES 4

2 tbsp butter, plus extra for greasing

12oz (350g) frozen spinach

salt and freshly ground black pepper

¼ tsp grated nutmeg

½ cup (4oz) Greek-style yogurt

4 large eggs

1 Preheat the oven to 350°F (180°C). Butter four 5fl oz (150ml) ramekins and place on a baking sheet.

2 Cook the spinach in a pan according to the package instructions. Drain well and set aside to cool. Once cooled, squeeze out any water and chop it finely.

3 Heat the butter in the pan the spinach was cooked in. Add the spinach and stir in the seasoning and nutmeg. Remove from the heat and stir in the yogurt.

4 Divide the creamy spinach between the ramekins and press down in the centers to make dips for the eggs to sit in.

5 Carefully break an egg into each ramekin and season well. Bake for 15 minutes, or until the eggs are just cooked.

VARIATION

For a more luxurious dish, replace the yogurt with the same amount of heavy cream, pouring a little over each egg before baking.

PREPARE AHEAD

Make the spinach mixture the night before, cover, and chill. Return the ramekins to room temperature before adding the eggs and baking as in step 5.

CALORIES: 198kcals/821kJ

CARBOHYDRATE: 2.5g
  sugar: 2.5g

FAT: 16g
  saturated: 7.5g

SALT: 0.7g

FIBER: 2.5g

British breakfast frittata

An all-in-one breakfast treat, which is easier to make and serve than cooking a buffet for the whole family.

20 mins   30–35 mins, plus resting

SPECIAL EQUIPMENT
8in (20cm) non-stick cake pan

SERVES 4

1 tbsp olive oil

5½oz (150g) thick-cut bacon, chopped

2½oz (75g) button mushrooms, quartered

5½oz (150g) cooked, cold potatoes, cut into ½in (1cm) cubes

4 large eggs

1 tbsp heavy cream

salt and freshly ground black pepper

2½oz (75g) cherry tomatoes, halved

butter, for greasing

1oz (30g) grated cheese, such as Cheddar

CALORIES: 299kcals/1234kJ
CARBOHYDRATE: 7g
  sugar: 1g
FAT: 23g
  saturated: 8g
SALT: 1.5g
FIBER: 1.2g

1 Preheat the oven to 375°F (190°C). Heat the oil in a heavy-bottomed frying pan and cook the bacon gently for 3 minutes until it starts to brown. Add the mushrooms and cook over high heat for another 5 minutes until browned all over. Add the potatoes and cook for a final 2 minutes.

2 Whisk together the eggs and cream in a large bowl and season well. Add the cooked mushroom mixture and the cherry tomatoes and mix well.

3 Grease an 8in (20cm) non-stick cake pan with the butter and pour in the egg mixture. Make sure all the bits are distributed evenly and the egg just covers the filling. Sprinkle with the cheese and bake for 20–25 minutes, until just set, golden brown on top, and puffed up at the sides.

4 Remove from the oven and rest for at least 5 minutes. Cut into wedges and serve warm or at room temperature.

VARIATION
You can use slices of cooked sausage instead of the bacon. Cook them in the same way so they crisp up a little.

Sweet potato, spinach, and feta tortilla

This vegetarian feast can be served for breakfast, lunch, or even cold as a picnic dish as it's so easy to transport.

20 mins   40 mins, plus resting

SPECIAL EQUIPMENT
10in (25cm) non-stick, ovenproof frying pan

SERVES 4

7oz (200g) sweet potatoes, cut into ½in (1cm) cubes

2 tbsp olive oil

2 tbsp butter

3½oz (100g) baby spinach

6 large eggs

1 tbsp heavy cream

salt and freshly ground black pepper

3½oz (100g) feta cheese, crumbled

CALORIES: 367kcals/1526kJ
CARBOHYDRATE: 11g
  sugar: 3.5g
FAT: 29g
  saturated: 12g
SALT: 1.5g
FIBER: 2.5g

1 Preheat the oven to 375°F (190°C). Toss the sweet potatoes in 1 tbsp of the oil, space out on a baking sheet, and roast for 15–20 minutes, until cooked through and browning at the edges.

2 Heat the remaining 1 tbsp of the oil and 1 tbsp of the butter in a 10in (25cm) non-stick, ovenproof frying pan. Add the spinach and cook over high heat for 2 minutes, until it wilts. When the spinach is cool enough to handle, squeeze it well to drain off excess moisture, then chop it up.

3 Whisk together the eggs and cream in a large bowl and season well. Add the sweet potato, spinach, and feta and mix well.

4 Melt the remaining butter in the pan over medium heat and pour in the egg mixture. Cook for 5 minutes, without moving it, until the edges start to set.

5 Transfer the pan to the oven and cook for another 10 minutes, until the tortilla is set and browned on top. Rest for at least 5 minutes before cutting into wedges to serve warm or at room temperature.

Breakfast burrito

A sort of total-breakfast-in-a-wrap, these burritos are particularly popular with teenagers.

20 mins   10 mins

SERVES 4

12 slices bacon

2 tbsp sunflower or vegetable oil

9oz (250g) cooked, cold potatoes, cut into ½in (1cm) cubes

4 large eggs

1 tbsp heavy cream

salt and freshly ground black pepper

6 tbsp ketchup, plus extra to serve (optional)

1 tsp smoked paprika

1 tbsp butter

4 x 8in (20cm) flour tortilla

3½oz (100g) grated cheese, such as Cheddar

1 Preheat the broiler to its highest setting and broil the bacon until it is crispy. Meanwhile, heat half the oil in a large, non-stick frying pan, add the potatoes, and cook until crispy all over, then set aside. Wipe the pan with paper towels.

2 Whisk the eggs with the cream and season well. Mix the ketchup with the smoked paprika.

3 Once the bacon and potatoes are ready, make the scrambled eggs. Heat the butter in the frying pan and cook the egg mixture over low heat until they are barely cooked and still quite loose. At the same time, lay out the tortillas and put 3 slices of bacon in a line across the middle of each. Top each with one-quarter of the potatoes, still keeping in a line across the center, and add a smear of the spicy ketchup. Finish each by topping with one-quarter of the scrambled eggs and one-quarter of the cheese, again remembering to keep the filling in a compact rectangle down the middle of each tortilla.

4 To make the burritos, tuck the sides in over the filling, then roll the longer top and bottom edges up and over the filling, to make a parcel. Press down gently.

5 Heat the remaining 1 tbsp of oil in a clean frying pan. Put the burritos seam-side down into the pan and cook for 2–3 minutes over a medium heat, until golden brown and crispy. Press down with a spatula to seal. Turn carefully and cook for 2–3 minutes. Depending on the size of your pan you may need to do this in 2 batches.

6 Serve the burritos sliced in half on a diagonal, with extra spicy ketchup (if desired).

VARIATION

Cooked sausage pieces, mushrooms, tomatoes, or even chiles are all good options for the filling here.

CALORIES: 724kcals/3023kJ

CARBOHYDRATE: 49g
  sugar: 7g

FAT: 44g
  saturated: 17g

SALT: 4.5g

FIBER: 3.3g

Spicy chorizo and cherry tomato bruschetta

This quick and easy bruschetta makes a tasty, instant brunch, or a simple snack at any time of the day.

5 mins   5 mins

SERVES 4

1 tbsp olive oil

1 tbsp butter

9oz (250g) cherry tomatoes, halved

9oz (250g) dry Spanish-style chorizo, casing removed, cut into ½in (1cm) cubes

salt and freshly ground black pepper

1 tbsp balsamic vinegar

8 slices of ciabatta bread, cut ¾in (2cm) thick

2 tbsp finely chopped basil leaves

1 Heat the oil and butter in a large, non-stick frying pan. Add the tomatoes and cook for 2 minutes, until they begin to cook.

2 Add the chorizo and continue to cook for 2–3 minutes, until the tomatoes begin to break down and the chorizo colors. Season well and add the balsamic vinegar.

3 Toast or broil the ciabatta bread. When the chorizo mixture is ready, take it off the heat, mix in the basil, and serve it piled on top of the bruschetta.

CLEVER WITH LEFTOVERS

You can use up tomatoes that are almost overripe in this recipe; briefly cooking them in olive oil with plenty of seasoning really brings out their flavor.

CALORIES: 408kcals/1709kJ

CARBOHYDRATE: 32g
  sugar: 5g

FAT: 23g
  saturated: 8g

SALT: 1.8g

FIBER: 3g

Potato pancakes with smoked salmon

Cook extra mashed potatoes in the week and you'll have the basis of this fabulous weekend brunch dish.

10 mins   10-15 mins

SERVES 4

1lb (450g) cooked, cold mashed potatoes

1 large egg, beaten

1 tbsp all-purpose flour, plus extra for dusting

salt and freshly ground black pepper

2 tbsp olive oil

3½oz (100g) smoked salmon, thinly sliced

¼ cup sour cream

2 tbsp chopped dill

lemon wedges, to serve

1 Place the potato, egg, and flour in a mixing bowl. Season well and stir to combine. Divide into 8 equal portions and, with flour-dusted hands, shape into rounds about 2¾in (7cm) in diameter.

2 Heat the oil in a large, non-stick frying pan over medium heat. Carefully add the pancakes to the pan. Cook for 10–15 minutes, occasionally turning the pancakes carefully with a metal spatula, until they are browned and hot right through.

3 Transfer the pancakes to warmed plates. Top each with smoked salmon, sour cream, and dill. Season well with black pepper and serve with lemon wedges.

CALORIES: 288kcals/1199kJ

CARBOHYDRATE: 21g
  sugar: 2g

FAT: 18g
  saturated: 7g

SALT: 0.9g

FIBER: 2g

Sausage and tomato breakfast casserole

A classic American breakfast dish, this is quick to assemble and delicious.

15 mins, plus resting | 40 mins

SPECIAL EQUIPMENT
10in (25cm) ovenproof dish

SERVES 4–6

1 tbsp olive oil

7oz (200g) thick pork sausages, casings removed, cut into chunks

butter, for greasing

3½oz (100g) stale baguette or other coarse white bread, crusts removed, and cut into ½in (1cm) cubes

4 scallions, finely sliced

1 large ripe tomato, peeled, seeded, and chopped (see p191)

2½oz (75g) grated sharp cheese, such as Cheddar

6 large eggs

½ cup half-and-half

½ cup whole milk

salt and freshly ground black pepper

1 Heat the oil in a non-stick frying pan. Add the sausage to the pan and brown it off, chopping it up with a spatula, turning it over, and moving it around until it is broken into large lumps and is well browned on all sides. Remove the pan from the heat.

2 Grease a 10in (25cm) ovenproof dish with the butter. Spread out the bread in a single layer in the bottom of the dish, then evenly scatter over the sausage. Sprinkle in the scallions and tomato, then top with the cheese.

3 Lightly beat together the eggs, half-and-half, and milk and season well. Pour the egg mixture evenly into the dish, then set aside to rest for about 15 minutes. Preheat the oven to 350°F (180°C).

4 Bake the casserole in the hot oven for 30–40 minutes until puffed up and golden brown and a skewer comes out clean.

VARIATION
Cooked bacon, chorizo, chopped ham, or sautéed mushrooms would all be welcome additions to this versatile dish.

PREPARE AHEAD
Assemble the casserole the night before, increasing the milk to ⅔ cup. Cover and chill. Cook the next morning.

CALORIES: 512kcals/2134kJ

CARBOHYDRATE: 19g
  sugar: 5g

FAT: 37g
  saturated: 15g

SALT: 2g

FIBER: 1.5g

Potato, pancetta, and red onion hash

Cold, leftover boiled potatoes can be chopped up to turn this hash into a quick brunch or lunch dish.

 10 mins 25 mins

SERVES 4

salt and freshly ground black pepper

2¼lb (1kg) floury potatoes, such as Russet, peeled and cut into bite-sized chunks

1 tbsp olive oil

2 red onions, finely chopped

3½oz (100g) chopped pancetta

2 tbsp finely chopped chives

baked beans and ketchup, to serve

1 Bring a saucepan of salted water to a boil, add the potatoes, and cook for 10 minutes. Drain.

2 Meanwhile, heat the oil in a large, non-stick frying pan over medium heat and cook the onions for 5 minutes. Add the pancetta, season well, and cook for another 5 minutes, stirring occasionally.

3 Add the cooked potatoes to the frying pan and cook over high heat for about 15 minutes, stirring frequently.

4 Divide the hash between warmed plates and sprinkle with the chives. Serve with baked beans and a dollop of ketchup.

VARIATION

For a more substantial meal, serve each portion of hash topped with a fried egg (keep the yolks runny, if you like them that way, as they will form a "sauce" for the hash).

CALORIES: 300kcals/1263kJ
CARBOHYDRATE: 44g
  sugar: 4g
FAT: 9g
  saturated: 2.5g
SALT: 0.8g
FIBER: 5g

Corn fritters with tomato salsa

These sweet fried morsels are popular with children, although omit the chile and Tabasco sauce.

20 mins   10 mins

SPECIAL EQUIPMENT
food processor or blender

MAKES 14–16

FOR THE FRITTERS

2 corn cobs, approx. 9oz (250g)

1 cup self-rising flour

1 tsp baking powder

2 large eggs, lightly beaten

¼ cup milk

1 tsp smoked paprika

2 scallions, green and white part separated, finely chopped

2 tbsp chopped cilantro leaves

1 red chile, seeded and finely chopped (optional)

salt and freshly ground black pepper

2 tbsp sunflower or vegetable oil

FOR THE SALSA

2 ripe tomatoes, peeled and roughly chopped (see p191)

2 tbsp chopped cilantro leaves

2 tbsp extra virgin olive oil

dash of Tabasco or chili sauce

1 Hold the corn upright on a board and with a sharp knife cut downward to shear off the kernels.

2 Sift the flour and baking powder into a bowl. Gradually whisk in the eggs and milk to make a batter. Mix in the corn, paprika, the whites of the onions, cilantro, and chile (if using). Season.

3 Heat the oil in a frying pan and add the batter in tablespoons. Use the back of the spoon to spread the fritters out and cook them for 2–3 minutes on each side until golden. Repeat to cook all the mixture, adding more oil if needed.

4 Put the tomatoes, cilantro, scallion greens, olive oil, and Tabasco into a food processor or blender, and process until chunky. Taste for seasoning and serve with the hot fritters.

CALORIES: 90kcals/373kJ
CARBOHYDRATE: 9g
  sugar: 1g
FAT: 5g
  saturated: 0.8g
SALT: 0.2g
FIBER: 1g

Salmon kedgeree

This Anglo-Indian dish is traditionally made with smoked haddock, but here salmon adds a touch of class.

20 mins · 20 mins

SERVES 4

10oz (300g) undyed smoked haddock fillets

10oz (300g) salmon fillets

7oz (200g) basmati rice

salt and freshly ground black pepper

pinch of saffron threads

4 tbsp butter

4 hard-boiled eggs

2 tbsp chopped parsley leaves, plus extra to serve

lemon wedges and buttered whole wheat toast, to serve

1 Place the fish in a single layer in a large frying pan. Pour in enough water to cover and heat gently to simmering point. Simmer for 5 minutes, then drain.

2 Meanwhile, cook the rice in boiling salted water with the saffron for 10–12 minutes, or according to the package instructions. When it is cooked, drain, and stir in the butter.

3 Flake the fish into large chunks and add them to the rice, removing any tiny pin bones you find as you do so. Discard the skin.

4 Remove the yolks from the hard-boiled eggs and reserve. Chop the egg whites and stir into the rice. Add the parsley and season to taste with salt and pepper.

5 Divide the mixture between warmed plates and crumble the reserved egg yolks across the top with more chopped parsley. Serve with lemon wedges and triangles of buttered whole wheat toast.

CALORIES: 574kcals/2395kJ

CARBOHYDRATE: 37g
  sugar: 1g

FAT: 28g
  saturated: 11g

SALT: 1.9g

FIBER: trace

Classic buttermilk pancakes

You can make these pancakes with whole milk instead, but using tangy buttermilk makes them lighter.

15 mins · 10–12 mins

MAKES 20

2 cups self-rising flour, sifted

1 tsp baking powder

2 tbsp granulated sugar

⅔ cup buttermilk

½ cup whole milk

2 large eggs, lightly beaten

1 tsp vanilla extract

scant 1oz (25g) butter, melted and cooled, plus extra for cooking, plus extra to serve

maple syrup, to serve

1 Use a large balloon whisk to mix together the flour, baking powder, and sugar in a large bowl.

2 Measure the buttermilk and milk into a bowl, then add the eggs and vanilla extract and whisk it well. Whisk in the cooled, melted butter.

3 Make a well in the center of the flour mixture and slowly whisk in the milk mixture, using the whisk to bring in the flour gradually from the edges of the well, until it has formed a thick batter.

4 Pour the batter back into the bowl. Heat a pat of butter in a large, non-stick frying pan and pour out as many 3¼–4in (8–10cm) pancakes as will fit comfortably in the pan. Cook them for 2 minutes on each side, turning when the edges are set and bubbles appear and pop on the surface. When they are cooked, keep them warm on a plate under a clean kitchen towel while you cook the rest. Serve with butter and maple syrup.

VARIATION

Try adding 1 heaping tsp ground cinnamon to the pancake batter for a sweet-spicy, aromatic flavor.

CALORIES: 75kcals/317kJ

CARBOHYDRATE: 10g
  sugar: 2g

FAT: 3g
  saturated: 1.5g

SALT: 0.3g

FIBER: 0.5g

Banana, yogurt, and honey pancake stack

Try stacking pancakes for a luxurious breakfast treat. Younger children especially love their sweet fluffiness.

10 mins   15-20 mins

SERVES 6

1½ cups self-rising flour, sifted

1 tsp baking powder

2 tbsp granulated sugar

1 cup whole milk

2 large eggs, lightly beaten

½ tsp vanilla extract

2 tbsp unsalted butter, melted and cooled, plus extra for cooking

2-3 bananas

¾ cup (7oz) Greek yogurt

honey, to serve

1 Sift the flour and baking powder into a large bowl and add the sugar. In a bowl, whisk together the milk, eggs, and vanilla extract. Make a well in the center of the flour mixture and whisk in the milk mixture, a little at a time, bringing in the flour as you go. Finally, whisk in the cooled, melted butter until the mixture is smooth.

2 Melt a pat of butter in a large, non-stick frying pan. Pour tablespoons of the batter into the pan, leaving space between them for the batter to spread. Each pancake should become about 3¼–4in (8–10cm) in diameter, but don't worry too much.

3 Cook over medium heat, reducing the heat if they seem to be cooking too fast. Turn the pancakes when small bubbles appear on the surface and pop. Cook for another 1–2 minutes until golden brown and cooked through.

4 Slice the bananas diagonally to produce 2in- (5cm-) long strips. Place a warm pancake on a plate and top with a spoonful of yogurt and slices of banana. Top with another pancake, more yogurt, banana, and honey. Finish the stack with a third pancake, topped with a spoonful of yogurt and drizzled generously with honey.

VARIATION

These pancakes are great with honey, but you can also eat them with maple syrup too.

Even the most fervent fruit-avoider can be persuaded to eat bananas if you mash them into the yogurt in this dish.

Fussy eaters!

CALORIES: 317kcals/1336kJ

CARBOHYDRATE: 40g
  sugar: 17g

FAT: 13g
  saturated: 7g

SALT: 0.8g

FIBER: 2g

Blueberry pancakes

Blueberries are a great source of vitamins, and this is a delicious way of introducing them into the family diet.

10 mins   10 mins

MAKES 20

2 cups self-rising flour, sifted

1 tsp baking powder

2 tbsp granulated sugar

⅔ cup buttermilk

½ cup whole milk

2 large eggs

1 tsp vanilla extract

2 tbsp butter, melted and cooled, plus extra for cooking and to serve

5½oz (150g) blueberries

maple syrup, to serve

1 Make the pancake batter as for Classic Buttermilk Pancakes (see p263).

2 Heat a pat of butter in the frying pan and pour out 3¼–4in (8–10cm) pancakes. Once you have poured them into the pan, sprinkle some of the blueberries on top; the batter will rise up around the berries as they cook.

3 Cook the pancakes for 2 minutes on each side, turning when the edges are set and bubbles appear and pop on the surface. When cooked, keep them warm on a plate under a clean kitchen towel while you cook the rest. Serve with butter and maple syrup.

COOK'S TIP

Frozen blueberries will do just as well as fresh fruit, so you can cook these out of season. Add the berries straight from the freezer; they will defrost and cook at the same time as the pancakes and will not break down too much either.

CALORIES: 80kcals/335kJ
CARBOHYDRATE: 10g
  sugar: 3g
FAT: 3g
  saturated: 1.5g
SALT: 0.2g
FIBER: 0.6g

Pumpkin and cinnamon waffles

Adding canned pumpkin and spices to these waffles gives them a wonderfully autumnal taste.

20 mins   5 mins

SPECIAL EQUIPMENT

waffle maker or waffle iron

SERVES 6

1½ cups self-rising flour, sifted

¼ cup light brown sugar

1 tsp baking powder

2 tsp ground cinnamon

2 large eggs, separated

1¼ cups whole milk

1 tsp vanilla extract

4 tbsp butter, melted and cooled

⅔ cup (5oz) canned pumpkin purée

vegetable oil, for greasing (optional)

maple syrup, sliced bananas, or cooked apple wedges, to serve

1 In a bowl, use a balloon whisk to mix the flour, brown sugar, baking powder, and cinnamon.

2 Whisk together the egg yolks, milk, vanilla extract, melted butter, and pumpkin purée. Using a clean whisk, whisk the egg whites to firm peaks. Stir the pumpkin mixture into the flour mixture until evenly combined.

3 Preheat the waffle maker or iron, and oil it if that is suitable for the model you own. Gently fold the egg whites into the batter until they are well combined. Spoon a ladleful of the batter onto the hot waffle iron (or the amount that is recommended by the manufacturer) and spread it almost to the edge. Close the lid and bake until golden.

4 Serve immediately with maple syrup, sliced bananas, or buttery fried apple wedges.

COOK'S TIP

If you cannot find canned pumpkin purée, make your own by roasting and puréeing pumpkin, but increase the amount of sugar and cinnamon in the mix, to taste.

CALORIES: 270kcals/1131kJ
CARBOHYDRATE: 34g
  sugar: 11g
FAT: 11.5g
  saturated: 6g
SALT: 0.7g
FIBER: 2g

Apple pancake

Making one large pancake instead of individual ones means you'll be able to sit down to eat with the family.

10 mins, plus resting

15–20 mins

SPECIAL EQUIPMENT

10in (25cm) non-stick, ovenproof frying pan

SERVES 4–6

½ cup all-purpose flour, sifted

pinch of salt

1 tsp ground cinnamon

½ cup whole milk

3 large eggs, lightly beaten

½ tsp vanilla extract

2 tbsp butter

2 apples, peeled, cored, and sliced into thin wedges

1 tsp lemon juice

2 heaping tbsp light brown sugar

confectioners' sugar, to serve

CALORIES: 280kcals/1166kJ

CARBOHYDRATE: 30g
  sugar: 17g

FAT: 13g
  saturated: 6g

SALT: 0.6g

FIBER: 3g

1 In a bowl, whisk together the flour, salt, and ½ tsp of the cinnamon. Gradually whisk in the milk, then add the eggs and vanilla extract. Cover the bowl with a clean kitchen towel and set aside to rest for 30 minutes.

2 Preheat the oven to 450°F (230°C). About 10 minutes before the batter has finished resting, melt the butter in a 10in (25cm) non-stick, ovenproof frying pan. Cook the apples and the lemon juice over medium-high heat for 5 minutes, stirring occasionally, until the wedges are golden brown. Add the sugar and remaining ½ tsp of cinnamon and gently stir it, off the heat, until it dissolves.

3 Pour the batter over the apples and transfer to the hot oven. Bake for 15–20 minutes until the pancake is well puffed up and golden brown. It will deflate as it cools (this is normal).

4 Turn the pancake onto a warmed plate, so the apples are on top, replacing any apples that stick to the pan. Dust evenly with confectioners' sugar and serve while piping hot.

Brioche French toast with yogurt and maple syrup

This quick and easy brunch dish is a favorite with younger children because it is soft and sweet.

5 mins

10-15 mins

SERVES 4

3 large eggs

½ cup half-and-half

⅔ cup whole milk

2 tbsp granulated sugar

pinch of nutmeg

1 tsp vanilla extract

2 tbsp butter

8 large or 12 small slices of brioche

Greek yogurt and maple syrup, to serve

CALORIES: 500kcals/2086kJ

CARBOHYDRATE: 52g
  sugar: 19g

FAT: 26g
  saturated: 14.5g

SALT: 0.9g

FIBER: 2g

1 In a large, wide bowl, whisk together the eggs, half-and-half, milk, sugar, nutmeg, and vanilla extract until well combined. Heat the butter in a large, non-stick frying pan over medium heat.

2 Dip each slice of brioche in the egg mixture, turning it once to make sure it is well soaked, then hold it over the bowl for a few seconds so any excess liquid drips off.

3 Cook the brioche over medium heat for 2–3 minutes each side until it is golden brown, crispy on the outside, and soft within. Serve each portion with a spoonful of Greek yogurt and a drizzle of maple syrup.

VARIATION

If you cannot find brioche, any sweet yeasted bread, such as challah, will do just as well. At Christmastime, try pannettone, or even Stollen (see p420), for an indulgent, festive treat.

Summer fruit salad

Dressing this fruit salad in a refreshing lemon and mint syrup helps the fruits stay fresh and colorful.

10 mins

SERVES 4–6

2 tbsp granulated sugar

juice of ½ lemon

2 tbsp finely chopped mint leaves

½ small cantaloupe melon, peeled, seeded, and cut into ½in (1cm) cubes

3½oz (100g) strawberries, halved or quartered, depending on size

1¾oz (50g) blueberries

1¾oz (50g) green, seedless grapes, halved

2 kiwi fruit, peeled and cut into ½in (1cm) cubes

1 Put the sugar, lemon juice, and 2 tbsp of water in a small, heavy-bottomed saucepan, place over low heat, and heat gently until the sugar melts. Cool, then stir in the mint.

2 Mix all the fruit together in a decorative bowl and toss it with the syrup. Chill until required.

COOK'S TIP

Use any combination of fruits, but try to avoid bananas or really ripe raspberries, which will disintegrate when mixed with the other fruit.

PREPARE AHEAD

Cut fruit can discolor quickly, but dressing it in this simple sugar syrup means it will stay fresh and vibrant even when prepared 1 day in advance.

CALORIES: 84kcals/355kJ

CARBOHYDRATE: 17g
  sugar: 17g

FAT: trace
  saturated: trace

SALT: trace

FIBER: 2g

Autumn fruit compote

When the temperature is cooler, try this seasonal fruit salad for breakfast or dessert, served hot or cold.

10 mins, plus soaking   15 mins

SERVES 4

3½oz (100g) dried apples

3½oz (100g) dried figs

3½oz (100g) dried prunes

1 cinnamon stick

½ vanilla bean, halved lengthwise

finely grated zest and juice of 1 orange

1 tbsp brown sugar

Greek-style yogurt, to serve

1 Place all the dried fruits in a mixing bowl. Add the cinnamon, vanilla bean, and orange zest and juice. Pour in ¾ cup of boiling water. Cover the bowl and set aside overnight.

2 In the morning, transfer the contents of the bowl to a saucepan. Add the sugar and ⅔ cup of cold water and bring to a boil.

3 Reduce the heat and simmer very gently, uncovered, for 15 minutes. Remove the vanilla bean and cinnamon stick. Serve with a dollop of Greek-style yogurt.

VARIATION

Any combination of dried fruits works well—try using apricots, peaches, or dates, or a mixture of dried berries. For a warming winter compote, add 2 finely chopped balls of stem ginger in syrup, plus 2 tbsp of the syrup.

CALORIES: 165kcals/703kJ

CARBOHYDRATE: 38g
  sugar: 38g

FAT: trace
  saturated: trace

SALT: trace

FIBER: 8g

Granola

Making your own is a cost-effective way of ensuring you have exactly what you like in a tasty brunch cereal.

10-15 mins   30 mins, plus cooling

SERVES 4–6

1½ cups old-fashioned oats

1¾oz (50g) mixed seeds, such as sunflower, sesame, pumpkin, and flaxseed

1¾oz (50g) unsalted nuts, such as cashews, almonds, hazelnuts, and walnuts, chopped

1 tbsp light olive oil, plus extra for greasing

2 tbsp honey

3½ tbsp maple syrup

scant 1oz (25g) dried blueberries

scant 1oz (25g) dried cranberries

scant 1oz (25g) dried cherries

½oz (15g) unsweetened coconut

Greek yogurt or milk, to serve

CALORIES: 439kcals/1838kJ
CARBOHYDRATE: 54g
  sugar: 29g
FAT: 20g
  saturated: 4g
SALT: trace
FIBER: 6

1 Preheat the oven to 300°F (150°C). Place the oats, seeds, and nuts in a large mixing bowl. Add the oil, honey, and syrup and stir well to combine.

2 Pour the mixture onto a large, lightly oiled baking sheet and spread out into an even layer. Cook for 15 minutes.

3 Mix together the berries, cherries, and coconut, add to the pan, and bake for another 15 minutes.

4 Leave in the pan to cool completely. When cold, break the granola into small pieces and transfer to an airtight container. To serve, layer Greek yogurt and granola into four glass dishes. Alternatively, serve with milk.

COOK'S TIP

This keeps for up to a month in an airtight container. As it gets older, it may benefit from a brief reheating in the oven to crisp up once more.

Tropical breakfast smoothies

Using frozen fruit is an easy way to make this instant healthy smoothie, with no fruit preparation required.

5 mins

SPECIAL EQUIPMENT
blender

MAKES 4 GLASSES

2 bananas

7oz (200g) frozen mango cubes

½ cup Greek yogurt

3 tbsp honey

2 cups apple juice

ice cubes, to serve (optional)

CALORIES: 207kcals/879kJ
CARBOHYDRATE: 41g
  sugar: 41g
FAT: 3.5g
  saturated: 2g
SALT: trace
FIBER: 2.5g

1 Place all the ingredients in a blender and process until you have a thick, smooth drink. Make sure you only half-fill the blender to prevent splashes. (You may have to blend your smoothies in batches.)

2 Pour into glasses to serve. Add ice cubes if you like, or if it is a particularly hot day.

VARIATION

Try adding ¼ cup of oats to the smoothie mix before blending to make a breakfast in a glass. You can use whole milk instead of apple juice, if you prefer; the drink will be creamier and less sweet.

HOW TO FREEZE

Any leftover smoothie can be frozen in an ice cream machine, according to the manufacturer's instructions, to make instant tropical fruit ice cream.

Banana and oatbran muffins

These muffins are a tasty and healthy choice for a late leisurely brunch; delicious eaten when they're still warm.

20 mins   20 mins

SPECIAL EQUIPMENT

12 paper muffin liners and/or
12-hole muffin pan

electric hand-held mixer

MAKES 12

8 tbsp butter, softened, plus extra
for greasing (if using a pan)

1¼ cups all-purpose flour

1 tsp baking soda

1 tsp baking powder

1 tsp ground cinnamon

¾ cup oatbran

1¾oz (50g) chopped walnuts (optional)

½ cup brown sugar

2 large eggs, lightly beaten

3 ripe bananas, mashed

½ cup whole milk

1 Preheat the oven to 375°F (190°C). Place 12 paper muffin liners in a 12-hole muffin pan, or simply place the liners on a baking sheet, or grease a 12-hole muffin pan with butter.

2 Sift the flour, baking soda, baking powder, cinnamon, and oatbran into a large bowl. Pour in any bran left in the sieve. Add the walnuts (if using). Stir well.

3 Place the butter and brown sugar in a separate mixing bowl and cream together, using an electric hand-held mixer, until very light and fluffy. (This could take as much as 5 minutes, so be patient!) Add the eggs and mix well. Stir in the bananas and milk.

4 Pour the wet mixture into the dry and stir to combine. Do not over-mix or the muffins will be heavy. Divide the mixture between the paper liners or muffin pan holes.

5 Bake for 20 minutes (start checking after 15), or until a toothpick inserted into a muffin comes out clean. Transfer to a wire rack to cool.

HOW TO FREEZE

As soon as the muffins have cooled, open-freeze them on a baking sheet. When they are frozen solid (after about 3 hours), transfer them to a large freezer bag and seal. This way you can remove and defrost only as many as you need, and they won't turn stale.

CALORIES: 192kcals/811kJ
CARBOHYDRATE: 29g
 sugar: 14g
FAT: 6g
 saturated: 1.5g
SALT: 0.4g
FIBER: 2g

Cinnamon rolls

Let these rolls proof overnight in the fridge so they are ready to bake in time for a brunch treat.

40 mins, plus proving   **25–30 mins**

SPECIAL EQUIPMENT

12in (30cm) springform cake pan

MAKES 10–12

½ cup whole milk

7 tbsp unsalted butter, plus extra for greasing

2 tsp dried yeast

¼ cup granulated sugar

3¾ cups all-purpose flour, sifted, plus extra for dusting

1 tsp salt

1 large egg, plus 2 large egg yolks

vegetable oil, for greasing

FOR THE FILLING AND GLAZE

2 tbsp ground cinnamon

½ cup light brown sugar

2 tbsp unsalted butter, melted

1 large egg, lightly beaten

¼ cup granulated sugar

1 In a pan, heat ½ cup of water, the milk, and butter until melted. Let it cool to just warm, then whisk in the yeast and 1 tbsp of the sugar. Cover for 10 minutes.

2 Place the flour, salt, and remaining sugar in a large bowl. Make a well in the center of the dry ingredients and pour in the warm milk mixture. Whisk the egg and egg yolks and add to the mixture. Combine to form a rough dough. Place on a floured surface and knead for 10 minutes. Add extra flour if it's too sticky.

3 Put in an oiled bowl, cover with plastic wrap, and keep in a warm place for 2 hours until well risen. Meanwhile, prepare the filling by mixing the cinnamon with the brown sugar.

4 When the dough has risen, turn it out onto a floured work surface and gently knock it back. Roll it out into a rectangle, measuring about 16 x 12in (40 x 30cm). Brush with

the melted butter. Scatter with the filling, leaving a ½in (1cm) border on one long side. Brush this with the egg.

5 Press the filling with the palm of your hand to ensure it sticks to the dough. Roll the dough up, working toward the egg-brushed border. Do not roll too tightly.

6 Cut into 10–12 equal pieces with a serrated knife, being careful not to squash the rolls. Grease and line a 12in (30cm) springform cake pan. Pack in the rolls, cut-sides up. Cover and proof for 1–2 hours until well risen.

7 Preheat the oven to 350°F (180°C). Brush with egg and bake for 25–30 minutes. Heat 3 tbsp of water with the sugar for the glaze until sugar has dissolved. Brush on the rolls and let cool for at least 15 minutes before serving.

HOW TO FREEZE

You can open-freeze the rolls when just baked, then transfer to a large freezer bag. This way you can defrost only as many as you need each time. You can also freeze the uncooked rolled dough at the end of step 5.

CALORIES: 400kcals/1685kJ

CARBOHYDRATE: 60g
  sugar: 22g

FAT: 14g
  saturated: 8g

SALT: 0.5g

FIBER: 2.5g

Buttermilk biscuits

These biscuits are a staple served at breakfast with bacon, sausage, or scrambled eggs.

10 mins   10–12 mins

SPECIAL EQUIPMENT

food processor (optional)

2¾in (7cm) round biscuit cutter

MAKES 6

1⅔ cups self-rising flour, sifted, plus extra for dusting

2 tsp baking powder

½ tsp fine salt

8 tbsp butter, chilled and cut into cubes

¾ cup buttermilk

1 large egg, lightly beaten

1 Preheat the oven to 450°F (230°C). In a large bowl, or the bowl of a food processor, mix together the flour, baking powder, and salt. Add the butter and rub it in, or pulse-blend, until the mixture resembles fine bread crumbs.

2 Make a well in the center of the flour mixture and stir in the buttermilk. You will need to use your hands to bring the dough together. Gently knead the mixture on a floured work surface to form a soft dough.

3 Gently roll the dough out to a thickness of 1in (3cm). Cut rounds out of the dough with a 2¾in (7cm) biscuit cutter. Gently bring the dough back together and re-roll it to cut out as many as possible.

4 Brush each biscuit with a little of the egg. Bake in the top of the oven for 10–12 minutes, until they have risen and are golden brown.

COOK'S TIP

The secret to light, fluffy biscuits is to handle the dough as little as possible, so cut them out close together to minimize the need to re-roll. Also, cut straight down with the biscuit cutter when you cut the biscuits out. If you twist the cutter as you work the dough, the edges of the biscuits will become compressed, stick together, and rise unevenly.

HOW TO FREEZE

Open-freeze the biscuits on a baking sheet the moment they are cool. When frozen solid, transfer to a freezer bag. This way you can defrost only as many as you need each time, and they won't turn stale.

CALORIES: 318kcals/1336kJ

CARBOHYDRATE: 37g
  sugar: 2g

FAT: 16g
  saturated: 9g

SALT: 1.5g

FIBER: 2g

Cooking for allergies

If your child has an allergy, follow to the letter the specific advice given by your doctor, who will have detailed guidance about what to avoid and how to cater for your child safely. Whether or not your own child has an allergy, sooner or later your child will have a playdate or throw a party with a friend who has some kind of food allergy. The most common childhood allergies are often to wheat, dairy, eggs, or nuts. Ideally, the parent of a child with an allergy should inform you in advance of what they cannot eat, along with some easy advice as to how to cook for them. Also, if the child has allergy medication, don't forget to get this from their parent, with instructions on how to use it.

What to cook

This will very much depend on the severity of the child's allergy. Sometimes excluding a certain food from your guest's plate will be enough. At other times it will be easier, and safer, if you avoid serving anyone any foods containing the allergen during the visit. However, some small children who have an allergy to uncooked or undercooked egg whites can easily consume items such as cakes, which contain eggs that have been well cooked. In this case, double check with their parent first.

Allergen-free kitchens

Depending on the severity of your guest's allergy, kitchen hygiene can play a part in ensuring a healthy and happy playdate. Be sure to use knives and boards fresh from the dishwasher, and avoid preparing any foods with the allergen in it using the same equipment. Try not to serve packaged or processed foods, if possible, and if you do serve them do so only after you have carefully read through the list of ingredients on the label.

Common allergens

Once you know what your guest is allergic to, take time to find out which food products contain that ingredient. Always read the label carefully because sometimes these allergens can be found in the most surprising things.

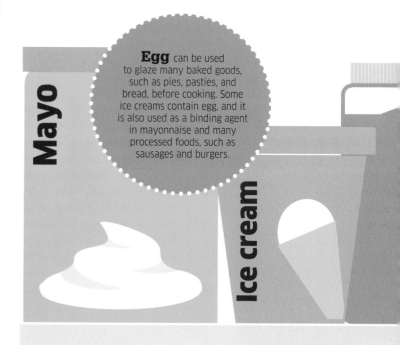

Egg can be used to glaze many baked goods, such as pies, pasties, and bread, before cooking. Some ice creams contain egg, and it is also used as a binding agent in mayonnaise and many processed foods, such as sausages and burgers.

Peanuts are classified as a legume and do not come under the same grouping as tree nuts. Peanuts can produce some of the most severe reactions in an allergic child, so it is wise to be especially cautious when buying pre-packaged food. Always check the label carefully and if in doubt, leave it out.

Milk may well be in cheese, butter, margarine, cream, yogurt, and ice cream, but it can also appear in some more surprising products. Check foodstuffs made using milk or milk powder, such as chocolate, cakes, cookies, soups, and even sausages.

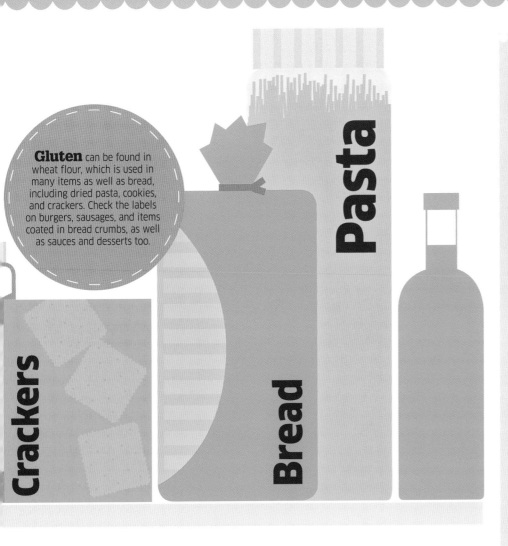

Gluten can be found in wheat flour, which is used in many items as well as bread, including dried pasta, cookies, and crackers. Check the labels on burgers, sausages, and items coated in bread crumbs, as well as sauces and desserts too.

Pasta

Bread

Crackers

Common substitutes

⭐ **Gluten** These days there are many specially produced wheat-free items to buy, from cookies and cakes to bread and pasta. However, don't forget to consider simple things such as oats and rice as a natural substitute if you can't get ahold of these products.

⭐ **Milk** Many children who are allergic to dairy products, or cows' milk, can happily consume goats' milk, soy milk, or even almond milk. Remember, too, that many delicious cheeses are made from sheeps' milk.

⭐ **Eggs** These can be easily avoided when served just as plain eggs, but they are present in cakes, cookies, and pastries. Eggs are used in baking to add air and moisture, so for best results look for egg-free recipes that use ingredients that produce equivalent effects, such as baking powder and milk or yogurt.

⭐ **Peanuts** These are also fairly easy to avoid in their simple state, and there are some good substitutes available. Health food stores sell many nut butters, such as almond, cashew, or macadamia. If the child is allergic to tree nuts, it's probably best to avoid peanuts, too.

Cereal

Tree nuts is a common food allergy in both children and adults and can cause severe allergic reactions. Many cakes and cookies may contain nuts, and some products produced in the same factory may have trace elements that can trigger a reaction.

Pesto includes pine nuts so avoid this if your guest is allergic to tree nuts.

Pesto

Read food labels

Read the labels on foodstuffs very carefully and check with a reputable website so that you know exactly which ingredients you are looking for, for each allergy. Some labels also specify allergens in the "contains" line.

Chicken satay with peanut sauce

This traditional Malaysian street food is incredibly addictive. Leave out the chile if making it for children.

15 mins, plus marinating   10 mins

SPECIAL EQUIPMENT
blender

8 bamboo skewers

SERVES 4

12oz (350g) boneless, skinless chicken breast, finely sliced

lime wedges, to serve

FOR THE MARINADE

1 stalk lemongrass, peeled of hard layers and finely chopped

2 scallions, white part only, roughly chopped

¾in (2cm) fresh ginger, roughly chopped

1 garlic clove, roughly chopped

½ tsp turmeric

1 tbsp light brown sugar

2 tbsp soy sauce

½ tbsp fish sauce

1 tbsp sunflower or vegetable oil

FOR THE PEANUT SAUCE

⅔ cup crunchy peanut butter

½ cup coconut milk

1 tbsp sweet chili sauce

1 tbsp soy sauce

1 tbsp fish sauce

1 tsp chile flakes (optional)

juice of ½ lime

1 Puree the marinade ingredients in a blender to a paste. Pour over the chicken and toss. Leave for 1 hour. Soak 8 bamboo skewers. Prepare the grill for cooking.

2 Meanwhile, put the ingredients for the sauce in a pan and stir over low heat until it loosens.

3 Thread the chicken onto the skewers, folding each piece of meat if necessary. Grill on a hot barbecue for 2–3 minutes on each side, until crispy. Serve with the sauce and lime wedges.

COOK IN THE OVEN
Preheat the broiler to its highest setting and line a broiler pan with foil. Broil the chicken for 2-3 minutes on each side.

HOW TO FREEZE
The uncooked, marinated chicken can be frozen for up to 3 months. Defrost thoroughly before cooking the recipe from the start of step 2.

CALORIES: 422kcals/1759kJ

CARBOHYDRATE: 12g
 sugar: 9g

FAT: 27g
 saturated: 9g

SALT: 3.7g

FIBER: 0g

Lemongrass-marinated shrimp skewers

Serve these alongside Chicken satay skewers (see left) for an Asian-inspired family feast.

15 mins, plus marinating   10 mins

SPECIAL EQUIPMENT
blender or food processor

8 bamboo skewers

SERVES 4

2 garlic cloves, roughly chopped

½ red chile, seeded and roughly chopped

2 lemongrass stalks, bottom (thickest) one-third only, peeled of hard layers and roughly chopped

1in (3cm) fresh ginger, finely chopped

1 tbsp chopped cilantro roots or stalks

2 tbsp fish sauce

2 tsp light brown sugar

1 tbsp lime juice, plus lime wedges, to serve

40 raw, shelled, and deveined large shrimp

1 Prepare the grill for cooking. To make the marinade, simply put all the ingredients, except the shrimp, in a blender or food processor and pulse to a fine paste.

2 Toss the shrimp in the marinade, cover, and leave in the fridge to marinate for 1 hour. Meanwhile, soak 8 bamboo skewers in water, as this will help to keep them from burning on the grill.

3 Thread 5 shrimp onto each skewer, threading through the top and bottom of the shrimp to make a curved "C"-shape. Grill the shrimp on the barbecue for 2–3 minutes on each side, until pink and charred in places. Serve with a squeeze of lime.

COOK IN THE OVEN
Preheat the broiler to its highest setting and line the broiler pan with foil. Lay the shrimp skewers on the pan and broil for 2-3 minutes on each side.

HOW TO FREEZE
Wrap well and freeze the marinated, uncooked shrimp. Defrost thoroughly, covered, in the fridge before use.

CALORIES: 128kcals/541kJ

CARBOHYDRATE: 3g
 sugar: 3g

FAT: 1g
 saturated: 0.1g

SALT: 2g

FIBER: 0g

Beef teriyaki

Try this delicious, all-purpose Japanese-style marinade with chicken, fish, and shrimp, as well as with beef.

15 mins, plus marinating | 15 mins

SPECIAL EQUIPMENT
4 bamboo skewers

SERVES 4

1 garlic clove, finely chopped

¾in (2cm) fresh ginger, finely chopped

3 tbsp mirin

3 tbsp soy sauce

3 tbsp sake

1lb (450g) sirloin steak, trimmed of any fat and cut into 1in (2.5cm) cubes

1 red bell pepper, cut into 1in (2.5cm) pieces

1 yellow bell pepper, cut into 1in (2.5cm) pieces

vegetable oil, for brushing

1 tbsp olive oil

Jeweled rice salad (see p218), to serve

1 Soak 4 bamboo skewers in water, to keep them from burning on the grill. Prepare the grill for cooking.

2 Combine the garlic, ginger, mirin, soy sauce, and sake in a small bowl and whisk together. Place the beef in a shallow dish, pour in the marinade, and stir well.

Cover and set aside to marinate, at room temperature, for about 30 minutes.

3 Using a slotted spoon, remove the beef from the marinade and place on a plate. Pour the remaining marinade into a small pan. Place the pan over high heat, bring to a boil, and simmer for 10 minutes.

4 Meanwhile, thread the beef onto the skewers, alternating with pieces of pepper.

5 Brush a little vegetable oil on the grill rack. Brush the skewers with olive oil and cook for 2–3 minutes on each side until slightly charred.

6 Serve the skewers with Jeweled rice salad (see p218), with the sauce drizzled over the top.

COOK IN THE OVEN

Preheat the broiler to its highest setting and line a broiler pan with foil. Place the kebabs on the and broil them for 2–3 minutes on each side.

CALORIES:	217kcals/909kJ
CARBOHYDRATE:	6g
sugar:	6g
FAT:	8g
saturated:	2.5g
SALT:	2.2g
FIBER:	2g

Barbecued mackerel with fennel, tomato, and herb salad

The strong flavors of mackerel are complemented well by this robust marinade and the bright, zingy salad.

20 mins, plus marinating   6 mins

SERVES 4 (as a light meal)

1 hot red chile, seeded and finely chopped

1 tbsp small capers, rinsed, dried, and chopped

2 tbsp olive oil, plus extra for brushing

juice of 1 lemon, plus extra lemon wedges to serve

4 large skin-on mackerel fillets

salt and freshly ground black pepper

FOR THE SALAD

1 bulb fennel, thinly sliced

9oz (250g) cherry tomatoes, halved

2 red chiles, seeded and thinly sliced lengthwise

½ bunch chives, snipped into 1in (2.5cm) lengths

large handful of flat-leaf parsley, chopped

4 sprigs of dill, chopped

2 tbsp olive oil

juice of ½ lemon

1 garlic clove, crushed

1 Mix together the chile, capers, olive oil, and lemon juice in a wide, shallow bowl. Add the mackerel fillets and season well on both sides. Rub the mixture over the fish, cover, and marinate in the fridge for 1 hour.

2 Prepare the grill for cooking, and brush the rack lightly with oil. Cook the fish, skin-side down, for 2–3 minutes, or until the skin is golden brown and crispy. Turn it gently, brush the cooked sides with the excess marinade, and cook for another 2–3 minutes. Remove from the heat and divide between 4 warmed serving plates.

3 Put the salad ingredients in a serving bowl, toss gently, and serve with the fish, with lemon wedges for squeezing.

CALORIES: 504kcals/2089kJ
CARBOHYDRATE: 3g
  sugar: 2.5g
FAT: 40g
  saturated: 7g
SALT: 0.6g
FIBER: 2.1g

Blackened salmon

A spice rub, rather than a marinade, is useful to have in your grilling repertoire, and works for meat and fish.

5 mins, plus resting   10 mins

SERVES 4

1 tsp cayenne pepper

1 tsp celery salt

2 tsp dried oregano

1½ tbsp light brown sugar

freshly ground black pepper

4 skinless salmon fillets, approx. 5½oz (150g) each

1 tbsp olive oil

lemon or lime wedges, to serve

1 Prepare the grill for cooking. Grind all the dry ingredients together in a mortar and pestle to a fine consistency.

2 Rub all sides of the salmon fillets with the spice rub, cover, and rest in the fridge for 1 hour to let the flavors soak into the fish. Drizzle each piece of fish with a little oil and rub it gently all over.

3 Grill the salmon on the barbecue for 2–3 minutes on each side, until brown and crispy, but still moist. Serve with lemon or lime wedges to squeeze over.

COOK IN THE OVEN

Preheat the broiler to its highest setting. Broil the salmon fillets for 3-4 minutes on each side, or less if you like them rare in the middle (although for this the fish must be very fresh).

HOW TO FREEZE

The spice-rubbed, uncooked salmon fillets can be well wrapped and frozen for up to 3 months. Defrost thoroughly in the fridge before cooking.

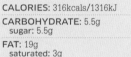

CALORIES: 316kcals/1316kJ
CARBOHYDRATE: 5.5g
  sugar: 5.5g
FAT: 19g
  saturated: 3g
SALT: 1.2g
FIBER: 0g

Grill 277

Barbecued tuna steaks with cucumber and red onion relish

Tuna is a fabulous fish to cook on the grill; its robust, meaty texture means the steaks hold together well.

10 mins, plus marinating   10 mins

SERVES 4

6in (15cm) piece of cucumber

2 tbsp rice wine or white wine vinegar

1 tsp granulated sugar

pinch of chile flakes

pinch of salt

¼ red onion, finely sliced

4 tuna steaks, approx.
 3½oz (100g) each

1 tbsp olive oil

1 tsp smoked paprika

salt and freshly ground black pepper

lemon or lime wedges, to serve

1 Prepare the grill for cooking. Slice the cucumber in half lengthwise and scoop out the seeds with a spoon. Slice each half again lengthwise to make 4 long, thin pieces. Slice thinly on a diagonal.

2 In a bowl, whisk together the vinegar, sugar, chile flakes, and salt. Mix in the sliced cucumber and red onion, cover, and leave in the fridge to rest for 30 minutes (this helps soften the taste of the raw onion).

3 Rub each tuna steak on both sides with a little oil and smoked paprika and season them well. Cook the tuna on the hot grill for 2–3 minutes on each side for medium, or 3–4 minutes for well

done (and less for rare tuna, but only serve it this way if it is very fresh). It is easy to see if the tuna has cooked on one side, as the fish will turn opaque from the bottom upward when looked at from the side. Remember that the fish will continue to cook when removed from the grill.

4 Serve with the cucumber relish and a wedge of lemon or lime to squeeze over.

COOK IN THE OVEN

Preheat the broiler to its highest setting. Broil the tuna for 3-4 minutes on each side for medium-rare, or 2-3 minutes each side, if you prefer them rare.

PREPARE AHEAD

Preparing this cucumber relish a few hours ahead of time will not only save time when you are finishing the dish, but also help the flavors to develop.

CALORIES: 174kcals/729kJ

CARBOHYDRATE: 2g
 sugar: 1.5g

FAT: 7.5g
 saturated: 1.5g

SALT: 4g

FIBER: 0.8g

Lamb koftes

These fragrantly spiced Middle Eastern kebabs are made of ground lamb, and take only minutes to cook.

15 mins   10-15 mins

SPECIAL EQUIPMENT

8 bamboo skewers

SERVES 4

vegetable oil, for greasing

1lb 2oz (500g) ground lamb

1 onion, finely chopped

1 garlic clove, finely chopped

½ tsp cayenne pepper

2 tsp ground cumin

2 tsp ground coriander

salt and freshly ground black pepper

warmed pita breads and coleslaw (see p160), to serve

1 Before you start, soak 8 bamboo skewers in water for 30 minutes. This will help keep them from burning on the grill. Prepare the grill for cooking. Brush a little oil on the grill rack.

2 Place the lamb, onion, garlic, cayenne, cumin, and coriander in a medium bowl, season well, and mix together with a fork.

3 Divide the mixture into 8 equal portions and shape them into chubby sausages, each 4–5in (10–12cm) long. Then thread the sausages onto the pre-soaked bamboo skewers.

4 Cook the lamb koftes on the grill for 10–15 minutes, turning frequently to ensure even cooking. Serve the koftes in warmed pita breads with coleslaw.

COOK IN THE OVEN

Preheat the broiler to its highest setting and line a baking sheet with foil. Place the koftes on the lined baking sheet and broil them for 10-15 minutes, turning frequently to ensure even cooking.

HOW TO FREEZE

Open-freeze the koftes raw at the end of step 3. Transfer to a freezer bag for up to 3 months. Defrost before cooking.

CALORIES: 254kcals/1059kJ
CARBOHYDRATE: 2g
  sugar: 1g
FAT: 17g
  saturated: 8g
SALT: 0.2g
FIBER: 0.5g

Beef burgers

Do not use very lean meat for a burger, or it will be dry. A little fat keeps the burger juicy, basting it from within.

15 mins,   10 mins
plus chilling

SERVES 4

14oz (400g) good-quality ground beef

¼ cup fresh white bread crumbs

1 large egg yolk

½ red onion, very finely chopped

½ tsp ground mustard

½ tsp celery salt

1 tsp Worcestershire sauce

freshly ground black pepper

TO SERVE

4 burger buns

lettuce

tomato

finely sliced red onions

mayonnaise

mustard

relish

CALORIES: 290kcals/1208kJ
CARBOHYDRATE: 10g
  sugar: 1g
FAT: 18g
  saturated: 7g
SALT: 1g
FIBER: 0.6g

1 Prepare the grill for cooking. In a large bowl, mix together all the ingredients for the burgers until well combined.

2 With damp hands (to help keep the mixture from sticking to your fingers), divide the mixture into 4 balls and roll each between your palms until smooth. Flatten each ball out into a large, fat disk, 1in (3cm) high, and pat the edges in to tidy them up.

3 Place the burgers on a plate, cover with plastic wrap, and chill for 30 minutes (this helps them keep their shape while cooking).

4 Cook over a hot grill for 6–8 minutes, turning as needed, until the meat is springy to the touch and the edges charred.

5 Serve with a selection of buns and accompaniments and let everyone assemble their own burgers as they prefer.

COOK IN THE OVEN

These can be cooked under a hot, preheated broiler, or in a large, non-stick frying pan, for 3-4 minutes on each side, until they are springy to the touch and well browned.

Minted lamb burgers

A real favorite, these burgers are exceptionally tasty and always juicy, as ground lamb has extra fat.

10 mins, plus chilling

10 mins

SERVES 4

14oz (400g) ground lamb

¼ cup fresh white bread crumbs

1 large egg yolk

½ red onion, very finely chopped

1 tbsp dried mint, or 2 tbsp finely chopped mint leaves

½ tsp ground cinnamon

½ tsp ground cumin

salt and freshly ground black pepper

TO SERVE

4 burger buns, or 2 large pita breads, halved

lettuce

tomato

finely sliced red onions

Tzatziki (see p290)

mustard

relish

1 Prepare the grill for cooking. In a large bowl, mix together all the ingredients for the burgers until well combined.

2 With damp hands (to help keep the mixture from sticking to your fingers), divide the mixture into 4 balls and roll each one between your palms until smooth. Flatten each ball out to a large, fat disk, 1in (3cm) high, and pat the edges in to tidy them up.

3 Place the burgers on a plate, cover with plastic wrap, and chill for 30 minutes (this helps them keep their shape on cooking).

4 Cook over a hot grill for 6–8 minutes, turning as needed, until the meat is springy to the touch and the edges charred.

5 Serve with a selection of buns or pita breads and the suggested accompaniments, and let everyone assemble their own burgers as they prefer.

COOK IN THE OVEN

These can be cooked under a hot, preheated broiler, or in a large, non-stick frying pan, for 3-4 minutes on each side, until they are springy to the touch and well browned.

CALORIES: 260kcals/1087kJ

CARBOHYDRATE: 10g
  sugar: 1g

FAT: 15g
  saturated: 7g

SALT: 0.4g

FIBER: 1g

Spicy turkey burgers

Try making small versions of these Asian-inspired burgers, serving with sweet chili sauce, as a canapé.

15 mins, plus chilling

10 mins

SERVES 4

14oz (400g) ground turkey

⅓ cup fresh white bread crumbs

1 tbsp sweet chili sauce

4 scallions, white part only, finely sliced

¼ cup finely chopped cilantro leaves

¾in (2cm) fresh ginger, finely grated

1 red chile, seeded and finely chopped

salt and freshly ground black pepper

TO SERVE

4 burger buns

lettuce

tomato

finely sliced red onions

mayonnaise

Greek yogurt

sweet chili sauce

1 Prepare the grill for cooking. In a large bowl, mix together all the ingredients until well combined.

2 With damp hands (to help keep the mixture from sticking to your fingers), divide the mixture into 4 balls and roll each one between your palms until smooth. Flatten each ball out to a large, fat disk, 1in (3cm) high, and pat the edges in to tidy them up. Place the burgers on a plate, cover with plastic wrap, and chill for 30 minutes (this helps them keep their shape while cooking).

3 Cook over a hot grill for 6–7 minutes, turning as needed, until the meat is springy to the touch and the edges charred.

4 Serve with a selection of buns and accompaniments, and let everyone build their own burgers.

COOK IN THE OVEN

These can be cooked under a hot broiler, or in a large, non-stick frying pan, for 3 minutes on each side, until they are springy to the touch and well browned.

HOW TO FREEZE

The burgers can be open-frozen, uncooked, then transferred to a freezer bag for up to 3 months. You can defrost just as many as you need.

CALORIES: 244kcals/1027kJ

CARBOHYDRATE: 16g
  sugar: 2.5g

FAT: 7g
  saturated: 3g

SALT: 0.5g

FIBER: 0.8g

Butterflied leg of lamb

A whole, grilled leg of lamb is an easy yet impressive way to feed a crowd. Ask the butcher to butterfly the leg.

10 mins, plus marinating   35-45 mins

SPECIAL EQUIPMENT
2 large metal skewers

SERVES 6

½ cup red wine

2 tbsp olive oil

4 garlic cloves, roughly chopped

zest of 1 orange, peeled off with a potato peeler, plus its juice

4 sprigs of rosemary, scrunched up (this will let the essential oils out)

freshly ground black pepper

boned leg of lamb, butterflied, approx. 2¾lb–3lb 3oz (1.2–1.5kg)

sea salt

1 Make the marinade by mixing together all the ingredients except the lamb and sea salt in a large, shallow dish big enough to hold the lamb in a single layer.

2 Rub the marinade over the meat. Leave it skin-side down and cover with plastic wrap. Leave in the fridge to marinate for at least 8 hours, or overnight.

3 Prepare the grill for cooking. Remove the meat from the marinade and wipe off any garlic, orange, or herb pieces. Use 2 large metal skewers to skewer it from corner to corner.

4 Sprinkle liberally with sea salt and grill it over a medium barbecue for 35–45 minutes, turning occasionally using the skewers. Place the lamb on a warmed platter, lightly cover with foil, and rest for 10 minutes before serving.

COOK IN THE OVEN
The lamb can be cooked in a roasting pan in a preheated oven at 400°F (200°C) for 35–45 minutes, depending on how you like your meat. You will not need to skewer it if cooked in an oven.

CALORIES: 591kcals/2450kJ
CARBOHYDRATE: 0.4g
  sugar: 0.2g
FAT: 47g
  saturated: 11g
SALT: 1.2g
FIBER: 0g

Texas-style barbecued spare ribs

This Southern-style sauce has a dark, sweet, smoky flavor that is universally popular.

30 mins, plus marinating   40-50 mins

SERVES 4

2 tbsp sunflower or vegetable oil

1 red onion, finely chopped

2 garlic cloves, crushed

½ cup ketchup

2 tbsp red wine vinegar

2 tbsp molasses

1 tsp Worcestershire sauce

2 tsp smoked paprika

½ tsp cayenne pepper

¼ tsp celery salt

freshly ground black pepper

8-12 meaty pork spare ribs

1 Heat the oil in a small pan and cook the onion over medium heat for 5 minutes until softened. Add the garlic for one minute. Add the remaining ingredients, apart from the ribs, with ½ cup of water and whisk. Bring the mixture to a boil, reduce the heat to a low simmer, and cook, uncovered, for 20 minutes until it has reduced to a thick sauce. Let it cool.

2 Reserve half of the sauce for serving. Rub the rest into the ribs, cover, and leave to marinate in the fridge for at least 2 hours. Prepare the grill for cooking.

3 Grill the ribs over a medium barbecue for 20–30 minutes, turning frequently, and basting with any remaining sauce from the marinade bowl, until tender and charred in places. Warm up the remaining sauce to serve alongside.

COOK IN THE OVEN
Cook in a preheated oven at 400°F (200°C) for 20–25 minutes, turning once, until tender and charred in places.

BATCHING AND FREEZING
The cooked, cooled sauce can be frozen for up to 6 months, or make double the recipe and freeze half for another time.

CALORIES: 541kcals/2251kJ
CARBOHYDRATE: 15g
  sugar: 14g
FAT: 36g
  saturated: 11g
SALT: 1.8g
FIBER: 0.8g

Slow-cooked shoulder of pork

Also known as pulled pork, this is cooked until it falls apart juicily, shredded, then smothered in delicious sauce.

30 mins, plus marinating

3 hrs, plus resting

SPECIAL EQUIPMENT
hand-held blender or food processor

SERVES 6–8

2 tbsp sunflower or vegetable oil, plus extra for rubbing

1 onion, finely chopped

2 garlic cloves, crushed

½ cup ketchup

¼ cup cider vinegar

1 tsp Tabasco or other hot sauce

1 tsp Worcestershire sauce

1 tsp ground mustard

2 tbsp honey

4½lb (2kg) bone-in pork shoulder

salt, for rubbing

selection of flour tortillas, sour cream, Tomato salsa (see p288), Guacamole (see p290), lettuce, and finely sliced red onions, to serve

1 Heat the oil in a small, heavy-bottomed pan. Cook the onion over medium heat for 5 minutes until softened. Add the garlic gand cook for 1 minute. Add the remaining ingredients, apart from the pork and salt, with ½ cup of water, and whisk well.

2 Bring to a boil, reduce the heat to a simmer, and cook, uncovered, for 20 minutes until reduced to a thick sauce. Use a hand-held blender or food processor to blend it until smooth. Cool.

3 Rub the pork in the sauce, cover, and marinate in the fridge for at least 4 hours, but preferably overnight. Preheat the oven to 350°F (180°C). Put the pork and marinade in an oven pan just big enough to fit it. Put a piece of waxed paper over the top (to keep the skin from sticking to the foil) and seal with a double layer of foil. Cook the pork for 2½ hours.

4 Prepare the grill for cooking. Remove the meat from the oven. Pat the skin dry with paper towels and rub in a little oil, then some salt. Grill it over a hot barbecue for 10–15 minutes on each side, skin-side down first; carefully turn with tongs, but do not turn it until the crackling is crispy and charred in places.

5 Meanwhile, pour the juices from the oven pan into a saucepan and first pour, then skim off all the fat. Reduce the sauce over medium heat to a thick pouring consistency.

6 Cut the crackling off the meat and leave it uncovered (or it will go soft) while you rest the meat wrapped in foil for 10 minutes. When ready to serve, cut the crackling into shards. Shred the pork into a juicy pile, pour the sauce over the top, and serve, with the tortillas and accompaniments.

COOK IN THE OVEN

After step 3, remove the meat from the oven, strain off the juices into a saucepan, and skim off the fat. Rub the meat with a little oil and scatter it with sea salt. Increase the oven temperature to 450°F (230°C) and cook the pork, uncovered, for 30 minutes, until the crackling is crisp. Reduce the juices as in step 5 to serve with the shredded meat.

CALORIES: 335kcals/1411kJ

CARBOHYDRATE: 7g
  sugar: 7g

FAT: 12g
  saturated: 3.5g

SALT: 1.1g

FIBER: 0.4g

Barbecued beef brisket

This "two-heat" method of cooking brisket ensures that it is crispy on the outside but remains tender within.

30 mins, plus marinating　　3 hrs 15 mins

SERVES 4–6

1 tbsp sunflower or vegetable oil

½ onion, finely chopped

1 garlic clove, crushed

3–4 tbsp ketchup

2 tbsp balsamic vinegar

2 tbsp dark brown sugar

1 tsp Worcestershire sauce

1 tsp ground cumin

½ tsp cayenne pepper

freshly ground black pepper

piece of beef brisket, approx. 2¼lb (1kg)

1 Heat the oil in a small pan. Cook the onion over low heat for 10 minutes, until softened. Add the garlic and cook for 1 minute.

2 Add the remaining ingredients, apart from the brisket, with 3–4 tbsp of water. Bring to a boil, reduce the heat, and simmer for 10 minutes to give a thick sauce.

3 Place the brisket in a bowl, rub it all over with the sauce, cover,

and marinate in the fridge for at least 4 hours, or overnight.

4 Preheat the oven to 325°F (160°C). Put the brisket in a roasting pan, cover it with the marinade, and seal with a double layer of foil. Cook for 3 hours.

5 Prepare the grill for cooking. Unwrap the meat, baste with the cooking juices, then grill it over a hot barbecue for 5–7 minutes each side until a crust develops. Serve sliced thinly with pickles, mustard, coleslaw (see p160), and Potato salad (see p158).

COOK IN THE OVEN

Cook the brisket as described in step 4, then unwrap it, increase the oven temperature to 450°F (230°C), and cook for another 30 minutes.

CALORIES: 284kcals/1195kJ

CARBOHYDRATE: 9g
　sugar: 8.5g

FAT: 12g
　saturated: 4.5g

SALT: 0.6g

FIBER: 0.2g

Dry-rubbed barbecued steak

Rubbing the steak with this spicy mix and allowing it to rest lets the flavors really permeate the meat.

5–10 mins, plus resting　　5–10 mins, plus resting

SPECIAL EQUIPMENT

spice grinder (optional)

SERVES 4

2 tsp smoked paprika

2 tsp ground mustard

1 tsp garlic salt

1 tsp dried thyme

1 tbsp light brown sugar

freshly ground black pepper

4 steaks, such as flank or sirloin, approx. 5½oz (150g) each

1 tbsp olive oil

1 In a mortar and pestle or a spice grinder, mix the dry ingredients together to form a fine powder.

2 Rub each steak all over with the spice mix and wrap each one with plastic wrap. Let rest in the fridge for 4–6 hours. Prepare the grill for cooking.

3 Unwrap the steaks and allow them to come to room temperature. Drizzle with a little oil and grill on a hot barbecue for 2–3 minutes on each side if you want medium-rare (3–4 minutes for medium, or 4–5 for well done), turning only after the underside has crusted up.

4 Remove from the heat and allow to rest for 5 minutes, covered with foil, before serving.

COOK IN THE OVEN

These can be rubbed in a little olive oil and pan-fried for 4–8 minutes, turning occasionally, depending on thickness and how you like steak cooked.

HOW TO FREEZE

The rubbed, uncooked steaks can be well wrapped individually, as in step 2, then frozen for up to 3 months. Defrost thoroughly before cooking.

CALORIES: 226kcals/949kJ

CARBOHYDRATE: 4g
　sugar: 4g

FAT: 9g
　saturated: 3g

SALT: 1.2g

FIBER: 0g

Classic barbecued chicken

This barbecue sauce is really easy to adapt to your particular taste, by adding more chili sauce, honey, or mustard.

40 mins, plus marinating   30–40 mins

SPECIAL EQUIPMENT
hand-held blender (optional)

SERVES 4

2 tbsp sunflower or vegetable oil

1 onion, finely chopped

2 garlic cloves, crushed

⅔ cup ketchup

3-4 tbsp cider vinegar

1 tsp Tabasco or other hot chili sauce

1 tsp Worcestershire sauce

2 tbsp honey

1 tbsp Dijon mustard

1 tsp smoked paprika

8 skin-on bone-in chicken drumsticks or thighs

1 Heat the oil in a small, heavy-bottomed saucepan. Cook the onion gently over medium heat for 5 minutes, until it is softened, but not browned. Add the garlic and cook for another minute.

2 Add the remaining ingredients, apart from the chicken, with ⅔ cup of water, and whisk, being sure to get into all the corners of the pan where honey can stick and burn.

3 Bring the mixture to a boil, reduce the heat to a low simmer, and cook, uncovered, for 25–30 minutes until it has reduced to a thick sauce. You can at this stage use a hand-held blender to purée the sauce completely smooth, if you prefer (some children don't like "chunks"). Allow to cool.

4 Cut 2–3 slashes on each side of the chicken pieces, where the meat is thickest. Toss the chicken in the cooled barbecue sauce, cover, and marinate, if you have time, for at least a few hours, or overnight, in the fridge. Prepare the grill for cooking.

5 Grill the chicken over a medium barbecue for about 30 minutes for drumsticks and 40 minutes for thighs, turning frequently, and basting with leftover sauce as it cooks. The meat will separate slightly where it has been slashed, which enables it to cook right through and gives a bigger surface area for the sauce. Check to see if the meat is cooked by gently piercing it with a sharp knife up to the bone. The juices should run clear.

COOK IN THE OVEN
These can be cooked in a preheated oven at 375°F (190°C) for 40–45 minutes, turning halfway through.

BATCHING AND FREEZING
Make double or triple quantities of this simple sauce and freeze what you don't need for another day, using it up within 6 months. The sauce can also be used to make a quick dish of oven-roasted chicken wings.

CALORIES: 404kcals/1696kJ
CARBOHYDRATE: 19.5g
  sugar: 19g
FAT: 16g
  saturated: 3.5g
SALT: 2.3g
FIBER: 1g

Lemon, garlic, and herb grilled chicken

This flavorful Mediterranean-inspired marinade is also great for rubbing on rabbit before grilling.

10 mins, plus marinating 30-40 mins

SERVES 4

juice of 1 lemon

2 tbsp olive oil

2 garlic cloves, crushed

1 tbsp Dijon mustard

2 heaping tbsp thyme leaves

2 heaping tbsp finely chopped flat-leaf parsley leaves

1 heaping tbsp finely chopped rosemary leaves

salt and freshly ground black pepper

8 skin-on bone-in chicken drumsticks or thighs

1 Mix together all the ingredients except the chicken and season the marinade well.

2 Cut 2–3 slashes on each side of the chicken pieces, where the meat is thickest. Toss the chicken in the herby sauce, cover, and marinate for at least 2 hours in the fridge. Prepare the grill for cooking.

3 Grill the chicken over a medium barbecue for about 30 minutes for drumsticks and 40 minutes for thighs, turning frequently, and basting with leftover sauce as it cooks. The meat will separate slightly where it has been slashed, which enables it to cook right through and gives a bigger surface area for the sauce. Check if the meat is cooked by gently piercing it with a sharp knife up to the bone. The juices should run clear.

COOK IN THE OVEN

The chicken can be cooked in a preheated oven at 375°F (190°C) for 40–45 minutes, turning halfway through.

HOW TO FREEZE

The marinated, uncooked chicken can be frozen for up to 3 months. Defrost in the fridge before cooking as in step 3.

CALORIES: 338kcals/1411kJ

CARBOHYDRATE: 0.5g
  sugar: 0.2g

FAT: 18g
  saturated: 4g

SALT: 0.5g

FIBER: 0g

Chinese barbecued chicken wings

Chicken wings are inexpensive, and are an easy and ever-popular way to feed a hungry family.

10 mins, plus marinating 25 mins

SERVES 4

2 tbsp soy sauce

1 tbsp rice wine or dry sherry

1 tbsp brown sugar

1 tbsp sunflower or vegetable oil

2 tbsp honey

1 garlic clove, crushed

¾in (2cm) fresh ginger, finely grated

1 tsp five-spice powder

16 large chicken wings

CALORIES: 240kcals/1007kJ

CARBOHYDRATE: 11g
  sugar: 11g

FAT: 10g
  saturated: 2g

SALT: 1.5g

FIBER: 0g

1 Mix together all the ingredients, except the chicken, in a large bowl.

2 Toss the chicken wings through the marinade, cover, and marinate in the fridge for at least 1 hour. Prepare the grill for cooking.

3 Cook the wings over a hot grill, turning frequently, and basting with the leftover marinade for 10–15 minutes, until they are well cooked and charring slightly at the edges.

COOK IN THE OVEN

These can be cooked on a baking sheet in a preheated oven at 450°F (230°C) for 20-25 mins, turning halfway through.

HOW TO FREEZE

The marinated, uncooked wings can be frozen for up to 3 months. Defrost thoroughly in the fridge before cooking from the start of step 3.

Jamaican jerk chicken

Serve this spicy chicken with Mango salsa (see p288) and Jamaican rice and peas (see p224) for a Caribbean feast.

10 mins, plus marinating   30-40 mins

SPECIAL EQUIPMENT
blender or food processor

SERVES 4

4 scallions, roughly chopped

1 garlic clove, chopped

¾in (2cm) fresh ginger, finely chopped

1 red chile, seeded and finely chopped, or more to taste

¼ cup sunflower or vegetable oil

2 tbsp soy sauce

1 tbsp cider vinegar

juice and finely grated zest of ½ lime

½ tsp dried thyme

½ tsp ground allspice

¼ tsp ground nutmeg

¼ tsp ground cinnamon

1 tbsp dark brown sugar

salt and freshly ground black pepper

8 skin-on bone-in chicken drumsticks or thighs

1 To make the marinade, put all the ingredients except the chicken in a blender or food processor, season well, and process to a thick, smooth sauce. You may have to scrape down the sides with a spatula during the process.

2 Cut 2 or 3 slashes on each side of the chicken pieces, where the meat is thickest. Toss the chicken in the jerk sauce to coat all over, cover, and marinate for at least 2 hours in the fridge, if you have time, for the flavors to permeate throughout the meat, turning once halfway through if possible. When you are ready to cook, prepare the grill for cooking.

3 Grill the chicken over a medium barbecue for about 30 minutes for drumsticks, and 40 minutes for thighs, turning frequently, and basting often with leftover jerk sauce as it cooks.

4 The meat will separate slightly where it has been slashed, which enables it to cook right through and gives a bigger surface area for the sauce. Check if the meat is cooked by gently piercing it with a sharp knife up to the bone. The juices should run clear.

COOK IN THE OVEN

These can be cooked in a preheated oven at 375°F (190°C) for 40-45 minutes, turning halfway.

HOW TO FREEZE

Freeze the marinated, uncooked chicken for up to 3 months. Defrost thoroughly before cooking from step 3.

CALORIES: 384kcals/1605kJ

CARBOHYDRATE: 4.5g
sugar: 4.5g

FAT: 21.5g
saturated: 4.5g

SALT: 1.8g

FIBER: 0.2g

Whole spatchcocked grilled chicken

Spatchcocking is removing the backbone from a chicken, allowing it to flatten out and therefore cook more easily.

10 mins,
plus marinating

30–40 mins

SPECIAL EQUIPMENT
2 large metal skewers

SERVES 4–6

½ cup white wine

juice and finely grated zest of
1 lemon

2 tbsp olive oil

large handful of herbs, such as
rosemary, parsley, thyme, or
tarragon, finely chopped

1 tsp garlic salt

freshly ground black pepper

1 medium chicken

1 To make the marinade, whisk together all the ingredients, except the chicken, and pour it into a large, shallow dish, big enough to fit the flattened chicken.

2 To spatchcock the chicken, lay it upside down on a cutting board, breast-side down. Take a pair of kitchen scissors and cut either side of the backbone. Turn the chicken over, press it out flat, tuck the wings in, and press down hard along the breast bone with your palm until you feel it snap. Slash the skin a few times where the meat is thickest, rub all over with the marinade, then cover and place in the fridge, skin-side down, for at least 2 hours. Prepare the grill for cooking.

3 Take 2 large metal skewers and skewer the chicken from corner to corner diagonally, and again the other way. This will help keep the chicken together on the grill and make turning it easier.

4 Grill the chicken, mainly skin-side down, for 30–40 minutes over a medium barbecue, turning it occasionally. Use the skewers to turn the chicken, but pick them up while wearing oven mitts as they will be very hot.

5 The meat will separate slightly where it has been slashed, which enables it to cook right through and gives a bigger surface area for the sauce. Check if the meat is cooked by gently piercing it with a sharp knife up to the bone.

The juices should run clear. Remove the skewers and serve the chicken whole, carving it at the table.

COOK IN THE OVEN
The chicken can be cooked in a roasting pan in a preheated oven at 350°F (180°C) for 1 hour. Preheat the broiler to its highest setting and finish off the bird under the broiler, turning it once. It should be starting to char in places.

CALORIES: 291kcals/1226kJ

CARBOHYDRATE: 0.5g
sugar: 0.5g

FAT: 8g
saturated: 1.5g

SALT: 1g

FIBER: 0g

Grilled corn on the cob with lime and chile butter

This butter is an easy way to flavor grilled meat, fish, or vegetables. It freezes well for up to 6 months.

10 mins   10 mins

SERVES 4

8 tbsp unsalted butter, softened

finely grated zest of 1 lime

½ tsp chile powder or cayenne pepper

½ tsp sea salt

freshly ground black pepper

4 corn cobs

a little olive oil

1 Prepare the grill for cooking. In a small bowl, mash the butter with the lime zest, chile powder, sea salt, and black pepper.

2 Cut a square of waxed paper, about 6in (15cm) square. Put the butter in the middle of one edge of the paper and shape it like a sausage. Roll the butter sausage up in the paper, then twist the ends so the butter forms a tight shape. Leave in the freezer for at least 30 minutes before use (or freeze until needed).

3 Cook the corn cobs in a large pan of boiling water for up to 5 minutes until the corn is tender (this will depend on the size and age of the cobs). Drain well, rub them in a little oil, and grill for 6 minutes over a hot barbecue, turning them frequently, until they are lightly charred on all sides.

4 Serve the corn with a ½in- (1cm-) thick disk of the chilled butter on top to melt.

COOK IN THE OVEN

The corn on the cob can be boiled as usual, then broiled for a few minutes until lightly charred.

CALORIES: 287kcals/1195kJ

CARBOHYDRATE: 16g
  sugar: 2g

FAT: 23g
  saturated: 13g

SALT: 0.6g

FIBER: 2g

Grilled eggplant with garlicky minted yogurt

These Middle Eastern-inspired eggplant slices are a good vegetarian option at a barbecue.

10 mins   15 mins

SERVES 3–4

¼ cup olive oil

1 tbsp chopped cilantro

½ tsp ground cumin

2 garlic cloves, crushed

3 tbsp chopped mint leaves

salt and freshly ground black pepper

2 large eggplants, cut into ¾in (2cm) slices

¾ cup Greek yogurt

CALORIES: 164kcals/677kJ

CARBOHYDRATE: 4g
  sugar: 3.5g

FAT: 15g
  saturated: 4g

SALT: 0.1g

FIBER: 3g

1 Prepare the grill for cooking. In a small bowl, mix together the oil, cilantro, cumin, one of the crushed garlic cloves, and 1 tbsp of the mint, and season well.

2 Brush the slices of eggplant with the herby oil and grill them over a hot barbecue for 3–5 minutes on each side until soft and charred in places.

3 Meanwhile, make the sauce by mixing together the Greek yogurt, remaining crushed garlic clove, and remaining 2 tbsp of mint. Season well and serve in a bowl alongside the eggplant slices.

COOK IN THE OVEN

The eggplant slices can be cooked under a preheated broiler, or on a grill pan for 2–3 minutes each side until they are soft and charred in places.

Mango salsa

This is the perfect accompaniment to Jamaican jerk chicken (see p285) or Blackened salmon (see p276).

10 mins

SERVES 4

2 ripe-but-firm mangoes

2 tbsp finely chopped mint leaves

1 red chile, seeded and finely chopped

juice of 1 lime

salt

1 First, pit the mangoes. Hold a mango firmly on its side on a cutting board. With a sharp knife, cut just to one side of the central line; you should feel the edge of the mango pit. When you hit the pit, carefully curve your knife around it. Repeat with the other side, to give you 2 "cheeks" of mango and the central piece, with the pit in it.

2 Cut off as much flesh as possible from the central piece and discard the pit. Cut a ½in (1cm) criss-cross design in the flesh of the mango cheeks, with a small sharp knife, being careful not to pierce the skin, but going right up to it. Push up the skin of each cheek so that it flips inside out: you should get a "hedgehog" effect of mango cubes. Cut these off at the bottom into a bowl.

3 Add any pieces of mango you removed from the pit, making sure all the skin has been removed. Repeat for the other mango. Add the rest of the ingredients to the bowl, toss them together, and season to taste with salt.

CALORIES: 43kcals/184kJ

CARBOHYDRATE: 10g
  sugar: 10g

FAT: 0g
  saturated: 0g

SALT: 0.5g

FIBER: 2.5g

Tomato salsa

This classic salsa is also known as *pico de gallo* in Mexican cuisine. It makes a great salsa for tortilla chips.

5 mins, plus resting

SERVES 4

4 large ripe tomatoes, seeded and finely chopped (see p191)

6 scallions, finely sliced

handful of cilantro leaves, finely chopped

1 mild green chile, seeded and finely chopped

juice of 1 lime

1 tbsp olive oil

pinch of granulated sugar

salt and freshly ground black pepper

1 Simply mix all the ingredients together in a bowl, being sure that every component is evenly spread throughout the salsa.

2 Let at room temperature for 15 minutes before serving, for the flavors to amalgamate. Don't leave it much longer than that, or the juice will leach out of the tomatoes, giving a more liquid result.

COOK'S TIP

If your knife skills are not great, roughly chop the ingredients, then pulse them in a food processor to the desired consistency. The salsa will be more liquid this way.

CALORIES: 56kcals/234kJ

CARBOHYDRATE: 5g
  sugar: 5g

FAT: 3g
  saturated: 0.5g

SALT: trace

FIBER: 2g

Lemongrass and chile salsa

This salsa transforms grilled fish or skewers of barbecued white meat into an Asian delicacy.

20 mins,
plus chilling

SERVES 6

2 lemongrass stalks, outer leaves discarded

2 heaping tbsp chopped Thai basil leaves, plus 6 extra whole leaves

1 tsp finely grated fresh ginger

1 whole red chile, seeded and finely chopped

1 tbsp honey or granulated sugar

3 tbsp soy sauce

2 tsp fish sauce

6 tbsp lime juice

1 Slice off the tops of the lemongrass stalks and discard them. Smash down on the bulb ends with the side of a large knife, or pound using a kitchen mallet. Chop very finely and place in a bowl.

2 Add the basil, ginger, and chile. Pour in the honey or sugar, soy sauce, fish sauce, and lime juice and stir well.

3 Cover and chill for at least 1 hour to give the flavors time to amalgamate and develop.

4 Just before serving, stir in the reserved whole basil leaves, pressing them slightly to release their fragrance.

CALORIES: 15kcals/65kJ

CARBOHYDRATE: 3.5g
  sugar: 3.5g

FAT: 0g
  saturated: 0g

SALT: 1.7g

FIBER: 0g

Roasted red bell pepper and corn salsa

This chunky salsa is ideal alongside a thick piece of barbecued fish, or a plainly grilled steak.

15 mins   30 mins

SERVES 4

2 large or 3 medium red bell peppers

½ tbsp olive oil, plus extra for rubbing

1 corn cob

1 tbsp chopped flat-leaf parsley leaves

1 tbsp chopped basil leaves

2 tbsp freshly squeezed orange juice

salt and freshly ground black pepper

1 Prepare the grill for cooking. Rub the peppers with a little oil and roast them over a hot barbecue, turning occasionally, until they are just cooked and the skin is charred in places. Cool.

2 Meanwhile, cook the corn in boiling water for 5 minutes until just tender. Drain, transfer it to the hot barbecue, and grill it for another 5 minutes until the kernels are charred in places. Cool.

3 In a bowl, whisk together the herbs, orange juice, and oil and season well. Peel and seed the red bell peppers, being careful of any liquid that will be inside them, as it will be hot. Cut the flesh into ½in (1cm) cubes and add it to the bowl.

4 Hold the cooled corn upright and rest it on a cutting board with one hand. Carefully slice the cooked kernels off with a sharp knife. Add these to the bowl and toss together before serving.

COOK IN THE OVEN

If you do not want to light the grill, roast the peppers and finish the corn under the broiler or in a grill pan.

CALORIES: 83kcals/346kJ

CARBOHYDRATE: 10.5g
  sugar: 7g

FAT: 3.5g
  saturated: 0.5g

SALT: trace

FIBER: 2.5g

Guacamole

This classic is great with tortilla chips, as a cooling side dish with spicy food, or on a grilled burger.

5 mins

SERVES 4

4 ripe avocados, halved, pitted, and peeled

1 large tomato, peeled, seeded, and finely chopped (see p191)

¼ red onion, very finely chopped

1 red chile, seeded and very finely chopped

1 garlic clove, crushed

handful of cilantro, finely chopped

juice of 1 lime

salt and freshly ground black pepper

1 Place each halved avocado cut-side down on a cutting board. Cut them into small cubes and place in a large, shallow bowl.

2 Take a large fork and gently mash the avocado, leaving it rough and with a few of the cubes still showing. (Cutting the avocado first helps maintain some texture to the finished dish.)

3 Add the remaining ingredients and gently fold them in with the fork. Season to taste and serve immediately, or cover with plastic wrap and chill until needed.

CLEVER WITH LEFTOVERS

Overripe avocados can be turned into this delicious guacamole. Just cut out any discolored parts and use the rest.

CALORIES: 298kcals/1229kJ

CARBOHYDRATE: 5g
   sugar: 2.5g

FAT: 30g
   saturated: 7g

SALT: trace

FIBER: 7.5g

Tzatziki

Traditionally served in Greece as an appetizer with pita bread, this dip can also be served with lamb dishes.

10 mins

SERVES 4

4in (10cm) piece of cucumber, quartered lengthwise and seeded

¾ cup (7oz) Greek yogurt or thick plain yogurt

1 tbsp finely chopped mint leaves

1 tbsp finely chopped dill

1 small garlic clove, crushed

1 tbsp lemon juice

salt and freshly ground black pepper

1 Grate the lengths of cucumber into a sieve, pressing them down to remove most of the excess water.

2 Put the grated cucumber in a clean kitchen towel and squeeze it well to remove the last of the water. Place the squeezed ball of cucumber on a cutting board and chop it up to make it even finer.

3 Mix it together with the remaining ingredients and season to taste. Cover and chill until needed.

Serve this delicious dip with a big pile of crudités including carrots, cucumber, and celery, to encourage fussy eaters to eat more vegetables.

Fussy eaters!

CALORIES: 49kcals/203kJ

CARBOHYDRATE: 3g
   sugar: 3g

FAT: 3g
   saturated: 2g

SALT: 0.2g

FIBER: 0.2g

Baked bananas with chocolate

The simplest of grilled desserts, yet one of the most delicious. Sadly, it's hard to replicate in the oven.

5 mins   10 mins

SERVES 4

4 ripe bananas

3½oz (100g) dark, light, or white chocolate chips, or a combination

vanilla ice cream, to serve

1 Prepare the grill for cooking. Take each banana and cut down, lengthwise, through the skin into the middle of the banana to make a deep slit.

2 Stuff the slit with one-quarter of the chocolate. Push the banana back together and wrap tightly in foil. Repeat to stuff and wrap all the bananas.

3 Cook the bananas over a hot grill for 10 minutes, turning them once. Take off the foil and serve them from their skins, with a spoonful of vanilla ice cream on top.

PREPARE AHEAD

Get the bananas ready for cooking by stuffing them and wrapping them in foil earlier in the day, then toss them on the grill as you serve the main course for a stress-free outdoor dessert.

CALORIES: 225kcals/947kJ

CARBOHYDRATE: 35g
  sugar: 33.5g

FAT: 8g
  saturated: 5g

SALT: trace

FIBER: 1.5g

Grilled pineapple with vanilla ice cream and butterscotch sauce

Another easy grilled dessert, this pineapple looks dramatic and tastes fabulous with cold ice cream.

10 mins   10 mins

SERVES 4

8 slices of pineapple, trimmed well and cut ½–¾in (1–2cm) thick

2 tbsp melted butter

FOR THE SAUCE

5 tbsp unsalted butter

½ cup dark brown sugar

⅔ cup heavy cream

pinch of salt

½ tsp vanilla extract

vanilla ice cream, to serve

1 Prepare the grill for cooking. To make the sauce, melt the butter in a small, heavy-bottomed saucepan. Take it off the heat and whisk in the sugar until it has completely amalgamated. Whisk in the cream, salt, and vanilla extract.

2 Return the sauce to the heat, bring it to a boil, then reduce the heat to a low simmer. Allow it to simmer gently for 10 minutes. Serve warm or cooled—it will thicken as it cools.

3 Meanwhile, grill the pineapple. Brush it on both sides with a little melted butter, then grill it over a hot barbecue for 2–3 minutes on each side, until charred in places and starting to soften.

4 Serve the pineapple with vanilla ice cream and the warm butterscotch sauce to pour overtop.

COOK ON THE STOVE

You can cook the buttered pineapple on a preheated grill pan until it displays black char marks on each side.

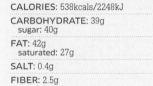

CALORIES: 538kcals/2248kJ

CARBOHYDRATE: 39g
  sugar: 40g

FAT: 42g
  saturated: 27g

SALT: 0.4g

FIBER: 2.5g

Unexpected guests

It's usually a pleasure when family or friends turn up unexpectedly, but when it comes around to mealtimes this can be problematic. As a good host you may feel duty bound to invite them to eat, yet worried that you have nothing special to serve. The arrival of another family may double the amount of people to feed, and mass catering can be quite an undertaking. However, with a little ingenuity, a few willing volunteers to set the table or keep guests occupied, and the contents of a well-stocked pantry and fridge, a tasty meal can be conjured up in a matter of minutes.

How to cheat

If you have just one or two extra people at the table, then adding to the carbohydrates you are serving will make the dish go further—potatoes, pasta, or rice are usually on hand. A basket of bread will help fill up your guests too. There are several "cheat" ingredients that are life savers when you have to rustle up a whole meal. Good quality frozen pastry and staples like sausages, individually packed chicken breasts, and fish fillets defrost relatively quickly, or you can make a meal from canned and dried ingredients (see pp14–15).

Snack time treats if you have frozen cookie dough, you can quickly bake some cookies. With frozen puff pastry, you can defrost a sheet in about 30 minutes on the counter and add savory toppings such as olives, anchovies, or slices of eggplant and tomato, or fruit such as apples or canned apricots to make tarts. Bake for 15 minutes.

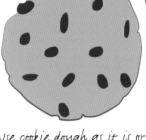

Use cookie dough as it is or add chopped nuts, chocolate chips, or dried fruit.

Make it Special

Even if you are serving the simplest of meals, good presentation is the key to good entertaining. A few fresh flowers, attractive tableware, and even a hastily ironed tablecloth will give the meal a celebratory appearance. Then add a few interesting toppings to give even simple meals a sophisticated spin.

Stale bread cut into big chunks and fried makes the best croutons. Add a swirl of cream or crème fraîche too.

1 Soup with croutons

For a lunchtime treat, start off with an onion sautéed in a little olive oil, then add any combination of root vegetables you have available to make a version of the Harvest vegetable soup (p157). Use a carton of stock from the pantry. For a special treat fry up some croutons and sprinkle them on top.

sprinkle some chopped up toasted walnut halves on dishes for added flavor.

Tasty morsels

While your guests are enjoying a pre-dinner glass of wine, rustle up some quick nibbles to stop them getting too peckish. Pitta bread crisps (see p242) can be prepared in minutes and make a delicious light bite.

Use whatever berries you have available. Strawberries, raspberries, or blueberries are ideal.

Simple baked goods

If you find you have afternoon guests, then a few speedy baked items will almost certainly go down well.

Scones (p440) are one of the easiest things to prepare, and the quickest things to bake. Bear in mind that they need no further decoration and can be served warm from the oven–they make the perfect last-minute treat.

If you are out of bread but want to serve some homemade soup, then **Soda bread** (p450) is the thing for you. Its rustic appearance and wholesome taste make a perfect match for some warming, wintery soup, and the lack of yeast in the recipe means that you don't have to wait for it to rise.

Using a few simple ingredients you can whip up these delicious **Quick cheese pastries** (p442) in a matter of minutes. Use whatever cheese you have available.

For a brunch treat, try making these tasty **Savory breakfast muffins** (p442) and serving them warm from the oven, with some scrambled eggs. If you don't have ham and cheese, substitute canned sweet corn, seeded and finely diced tomatoes, or briefly sautéed mushrooms.

2 Pasta with nuts

Pasta dishes are easy to put together using whichever dried pasta you have with a sauce you have batch cooked and saved in the freezer. To give it a twist, add some nuts, such as walnuts or pine nuts, and sprinkle on top or mix in.

3 Ice cream with fruit

It's rare for someone to refuse some good quality, homemade ice cream (p329). Jazz up your dessert with some chocolate sauce and some chopped fresh fruit, or a selection of cake sprinkles for younger visitors.

Roast chicken

A simple roast chicken can be a marvelous thing, and should be the backbone of any home cook's repertoire.

5 mins   1¼–1½ hrs, plus resting

SERVES 4–6

1 good-quality chicken, 3lb 3oz–4½lb (1.5–2kg)

1 tbsp butter, softened

salt and freshly ground black pepper

½ lemon

1 Preheat the oven to 450°F (230°C). Wipe the chicken skin dry with paper towels. Undo the string that holds the legs together and work the legs away from the body slightly. This will help the legs to cook more quickly and prevent the breast from drying out.

2 Rub the butter all over the bird, then season it well inside and out. Place it in a roasting pan

and squeeze the lemon over the chicken, putting the squeezed-out lemon shell inside the cavity. Pour water to a depth of ⅛in (3mm) around the chicken; this will help to make the gravy later.

3 Roast the chicken for about 15 minutes, then reduce the oven temperature to 350°F (180°C) and roast it for another 20 minutes per 1lb 2oz (500g), or until the juices run clear when you insert a skewer into the thickest part of the thigh.

4 When the chicken is cooked, remove it from the pan and rest it for 10 minutes, lightly covered with foil, while you make the gravy (see p307).

BATCHING AND FREEZING

The leftover carcass can be frozen in a large freezer bag. Collect 3 or 4 chicken carcasses, then use them to make a triple quantity of chicken stock (see p94). Reduce the stock to intensify the flavors, then freeze in small amounts to add great-tasting richness to sauces, stews, and gravies.

CALORIES: 219kcals/922kJ

CARBOHYDRATE: 0g
  sugar: 0g

FAT: 6g
  saturated: 2.5g

SALT: 0.3g

FIBER: 0g

Herby roast chicken

An herby butter spread under the skin of the chicken keeps the bird moist and succulent during cooking.

10 mins   1¼–1½ hrs, plus resting

SERVES 4–6

1 good-quality chicken, 3lb 3oz–4½lb (1.5–2kg)

3 tbsp butter, softened

1 tbsp finely chopped tarragon leaves

1 tbsp finely chopped flat-leaf parsley leaves

1 tbsp thyme leaves

1 garlic clove, crushed

grated zest and juice of ½ lemon

salt and freshly ground black pepper

1 tbsp olive oil

1 Preheat the oven to 450°F (230°C). Wipe the chicken skin dry with paper towels. Undo the string and work the legs away from the body (see recipe, left).

2 Make an herb butter by mashing together the butter, herbs, garlic, and lemon zest. Season well.

3 Loosen the skin where the breasts begin and slide your fingers gently between skin and breast as far as you can on either side without tearing the skin.

4 Push the herb butter under the skin, patting down to spread the butter out. Put the chicken in a roasting pan.

5 Rub the skin with the oil and season. Squeeze the half lemon over the top, then put the lemon shell in the cavity. Roast for 15 minutes, then reduce the oven temperature to 350°F (180°C) and roast for 20 minutes per 1lb 2oz (500g), or until the juices run clear. Rest for 10 minutes, covered with foil.

PREPARE AHEAD

A perfect picnic dish, cook this up to 2 days ahead, then serve cold with Potato salad (see p158), green salad, and bread.

HOW TO FREEZE

Remove the chicken from the bones in big chunks before freezing for up to 3 months. Smaller pieces may dry out.

CALORIES: 273kcals/1143kJ

CARBOHYDRATE: 0g
  sugar: 0g

FAT: 12g
  saturated: 5g

SALT: 0.4g

FIBER: 0g

Roast chicken and root vegetables

Cooking a whole chicken in a pan of colorful root vegetables will give you a convenient and healthy meal in one.

20 mins | 1 hr 15 mins, plus resting

SERVES 4–6

1 good-quality chicken, 3lb 3oz–4½lb (1.5–2kg)

4 large potatoes, peeled and quartered

3 large carrots, cut into 1in (3cm) chunks

2 parsnips, cut into 1in (3cm) chunks

2 leeks, white part only, cut into 1in (3cm) chunks

2 tbsp olive oil

salt and freshly ground black pepper

1 tbsp butter, softened

½ lemon

½ cup white wine or chicken stock (see p94)

1 Preheat the oven to 400°F (200°C). Wipe the skin of the chicken dry with paper towels. Undo the string and work the legs away from the body slightly (see recipe, far left).

2 Put the vegetables in a large roasting pan, toss them with the oil, and season well. Push them to the sides of the pan to make room for the chicken.

3 Rub the chicken all over with the butter and season it well. Put the chicken into the space you made in the roasting pan, surrounded by the vegetables. (Do not put it on top, or the vegetables may cook unevenly.) Squeeze the half lemon over the breast, then put the squeezed-out lemon shell inside the cavity.

4 Pour the wine or stock around the vegetables and roast in the oven for about 1¼ hours, turning the vegetables occasionally, or until the chicken juices run clear when you insert a skewer into the thickest part of the thigh.

5 Rest the chicken for 10 minutes, lightly covered with foil. Pour any juices that come from the chicken back into the vegetables, then carve the chicken and serve with the vegetables and juices.

COOK'S TIP

Roasting the vegetables with the chicken will soak up a lot of the chicken juices, and not leave much for a gravy. Try serving it with a "wet" vegetable such as slow-cooked Savoy cabbage (see p166), or even with Bread sauce (see p317).

CLEVER WITH LEFTOVERS

Make extra root vegetables when you roast this dish. Then take the cold leftover roasted roots, mix them with leftover gravy and chicken stock (see p94), and purée with an electric hand-held blender for an instant roast chicken and root vegetable soup.

CALORIES: 444kcals/1868kJ
CARBOHYDRATE: 37g
 sugar: 9g
FAT: 11g
 saturated: 3g
SALT: 0.4g
FIBER: 8.5g

Rosemary and garlic leg of lamb on a bed of potatoes

Lamb and rosemary are a classic combination, and garlic gives even more flavor to this delicious Sunday roast.

25 mins   1 hr 30 mins, plus resting

SERVES 4-6

3lb 3oz (1.5kg) floury potatoes, such as Russets, peeled and thinly sliced

salt and freshly ground black pepper

2 cups lamb or vegetable stock (see p156)

4 sprigs of rosemary

4½lb (2kg) bone-in leg of lamb

4 garlic cloves, halved

steamed cabbage, to serve

1 Preheat the oven to 450°F (230°C). Arrange the potato slices in a large roasting pan. Season well and pour in the stock. Place 2 of the rosemary sprigs on top of the potatoes.

2 Using a small, sharp knife, make lots of deep cuts in the meaty side of the lamb roast. Tear the remaining rosemary sprigs into several smaller pieces and carefully insert the pieces into the cuts, along with the halved garlic cloves. Season the lamb well all over and place the meat, with its rosemary- and garlic-side up, centrally on top of the bed of potatoes.

3 Roast the lamb for 15 minutes. Reduce the oven temperature to 350°F (180°C) and cook the lamb for 1¼ hours.

4 Take the pan out of the oven and place the lamb on a warmed platter. Cover it with foil and set aside to rest for 20 minutes to allow the meat to relax, making it moist and easy to carve.

5 Meanwhile, return the pan with the potatoes to the turned-off oven to keep them hot.

6 Carve the meat and spoon over any cooking juices. Serve with the potatoes and steamed cabbage.

COOK'S TIP

For crunchier potatoes, arrange them in a shallow layer in a larger roasting pan. For softer, more yielding potatoes, use a smaller roasting pan and arrange the potatoes in a deeper layer. Check to see if they are tender in the center (using a knife) before serving.

CALORIES: 638kcals/2675kJ

CARBOHYDRATE: 40g
  sugar: 1.5g

FAT: 23g
  saturated: 10g

SALT: 0.7g

FIBER: 4g

Butterflied leg of lamb with salsa verde

A boneless roast takes less time to cook than a bone-in leg of lamb, and is easier to cook exactly as you want it.

20 mins | 45 mins, plus resting

SPECIAL EQUIPMENT
mini food processor

SERVES 4–6

medium-sized leg of lamb, butterflied, approx. 1¾–2¼lb (800g–1kg)

1 tbsp olive oil

salt and freshly ground black pepper

FOR THE SALSA VERDE

½oz (15g) basil leaves

½oz (15g) flat-leaf parsley leaves

½oz (15g) mint leaves

3 tbsp lemon juice

6 anchovy fillets

1 tbsp capers, drained and rinsed

2 tsp Dijon mustard

1 garlic clove, crushed

⅔ cup extra virgin olive oil

1 Preheat the oven to 400°F (200°C). Unroll the lamb into a roasting pan, skin-side up. Push the meat together slightly, as some parts are thicker than others, and this will give a piece of even thickness as far as possible. Rub it with the olive oil and season evenly and generously all over.

2 Cook the lamb in the oven for 40–45 minutes for medium rare, 50–55 minutes for medium, and 1 hour for well done. Remove from the oven and rest, lightly covered in foil, for 10 minutes.

3 Meanwhile, make the salsa verde. Put all the ingredients except the extra virgin olive oil, into a mini food processor. Purée them with a little of the oil until they make a rough paste, then pour in the remaining oil, with the food processor on, in a thin stream, until you have a thick, vibrant, and emulsified green sauce. Season to taste, going easy on the salt.

4 Serve the lamb in thin slices with any pan juices drizzled over the top and a bowl of the salsa verde on the side.

COOK'S TIP
Carve the lamb in sections to give a range of thicknesses and doneness. This allows everyone to choose how thick and how well done they like their meat.

CALORIES: 591kcals/2450kJ
CARBOHYDRATE: 0.4g
sugar: 0.2g
FAT: 47g
saturated: 11g
SALT: 1.2g
FIBER: 0g

Slow-cooked shoulder of lamb with minty gravy

This method gives tender, deliciously moist lamb. Be sure to drain off the excess fat before making the gravy.

15 mins,
plus marinating

4 hrs 30 mins,
plus resting

SERVES 6

3 sprigs of rosemary, leaves
    finely chopped

6 sage leaves, finely chopped

2 tbsp olive oil

salt and freshly ground black pepper

3lb 3oz (1.5kg) bone-in shoulder
    of lamb

2 cups vegetable stock (see p156)

1 tbsp all-purpose flour

3 tbsp red wine

2 tbsp finely chopped mint leaves

mashed potatoes, to serve

1 In a small bowl, combine the rosemary, sage, oil, and seasoning. Using a small, sharp knife, score the lamb in a criss-cross pattern and rub the herb mixture all over. Set aside to marinate for 1 hour at room temperature. Preheat the oven to 425°F (220°C).

2 Place the lamb in a medium roasting pan and cook for 20 minutes. Remove the pan from the oven and reduce the oven temperature to 300°F (150°C). Baste the lamb with the cooking juices and skim off any excess fat.

3 Add the stock to the pan and stir well. Cover the pan tightly with foil. Return the lamb to the oven and cook for 4 hours, basting it thoroughly every 30 minutes with the cooking juices.

4 Remove the lamb from the pan and place on a warmed plate, covered loosely with foil. Set aside for at least 20 minutes to allow the meat to relax. Strain the juices from the pan into a bowl. Set aside for 2 minutes to allow the fat to rise to the surface. Carefully pour and spoon the fat out and discard.

5 Return 2–3 tbsp of the cooking juices to the roasting pan and place over medium heat on the stove. Stir in the flour and cook for 2 minutes. Gradually stir in the remaining cooking juices and the wine, stirring constantly with a wooden spoon. Season to taste and stir in the mint. Remove any fatty outer layer of the lamb that was not rendered during cooking and, using a spoon and fork, take the lamb off the bone.

6 Serve the succulent chunks of lamb with the minty gravy, mashed potatoes, and green vegetables of your choice.

CALORIES: 382kcals/1595kJ

CARBOHYDRATE: 2g
    sugar: 0.1g

FAT: 21g
    saturated: 8g

SALT: 0.4g

FIBER: 0g

Crispy pork belly with applesauce

Nothing beats good crackling on roast pork. Simply follow these easy instructions to get it perfect every time.

10 mins, plus resting | 1 hr 30 mins, plus resting

SERVES 4

piece of boneless, skin-on pork belly, approx. 2¼lb (1kg)

1 tbsp olive oil

salt and freshly ground black pepper

2 cups apple juice

2 cups chicken stock (see p94)

4 sweet apples, peeled, cored, and roughly chopped

2 tbsp heavy cream (optional)

CALORIES: 852kcals/3553kJ
CARBOHYDRATE: 28g
  sugar: 28g
FAT: 57g
  saturated: 21g
SALT: 0.8g
FIBER: 4g

1 With a sharp knife, make criss-cross slits all over the skin of the pork, being careful not to cut through to the meat underneath. (You can ask your butcher to do this for you.) Rub the skin dry with paper towels and leave the meat to rest, uncovered, in the fridge for at least 4 hours, but preferably overnight. This will help the skin crisp while cooking.

2 Preheat the oven to 450°F (230°C). Place the meat, skin-side up, on a rack inside a roasting pan. Rub it with the oil and salt all over the top, being sure to get inside the slits in the skin. Pour the apple juice and stock into the roasting pan, being careful not to splash the meat.

3 Roast the pork at the top of the oven for 30 minutes, then reduce the oven temperature to 400°F (200°C) and roast it for another 1 hour until the skin is crispy. Keep an eye on the level

of the liquid and add more water if it starts to get too low. You should be left with about ½in (1cm) of liquid in the pan.

4 Meanwhile, make the applesauce. Put the apples and 6 tbsp of water into a small saucepan with a tight-fitting lid. Cook over low heat for 10–15 minutes (depending on the type of apple used), checking them from time to time and adding 1 tbsp of extra water if the pan seems dry, until they are completely broken down. Break the apples up with a potato masher, if necessary. If the mixture seems too wet, cook it uncovered to evaporate any excess water, stirring from time to time to make sure it does not scorch, until you have a smooth, thick purée.

5 Remove the pork from the oven and wrap it in foil to keep it warm while you make the gravy. (It is a good idea to separate the crackling from the pork at this

stage as wrapping it in foil will soften it, so leave the crackling uncovered in the turned-off oven.) Skim off and discard as much of the fat as possible from the cooking liquid.

6 Put the roasting pan with the meat juices directly on the stove top and bring to a boil. Reduce the heat to a simmer and cook for 5 minutes, whisking occasionally, until they have thickened and reduced. Taste for seasoning and add the cream (if using).

VARIATION

If your family includes any chile lovers, you can pep up this applesauce with a pinch of dried chile flakes, or to taste.

BATCHING AND FREEZING

The applesauce can be made ahead, in double or triple quantities, and frozen in family portion-sized amounts for up to 6 months until needed.

Fennel-rubbed pork

Many Italian recipes pair pork and fennel, and for a very good reason. Try this Italian-style dish to find out why.

15 mins | 1 hr 35 mins, plus resting

SERVES 4

3 tbsp olive oil

3 tbsp fennel seeds

1 tbsp dried rosemary

2 garlic cloves, finely chopped

salt and freshly ground black pepper

2¾lb (1.25kg) boned and rolled pork loin

1¼ cups vegetable or chicken stock (see p156; p94)

½ cup dry white wine or apple juice

2 tsp cornstarch

1 Preheat the oven to 475°F (240°C). Add 1 tbsp of the oil to a medium roasting pan and heat it in the oven for 5 minutes.

2 Meanwhile, crush the fennel seeds and rosemary in a mortar and pestle. Transfer to a big bowl. Add the garlic, remaining 2 tbsp of oil, and seasoning and stir well.

3 Roll the pork in the fennel mixture until coated. Place in the hot pan and roast for 20 minutes.

4 Reduce the oven temperature to 375°F (190°C) and roast for 30 minutes per 1lb 2oz (500g). When there are 30 minutes to go, pour in the stock and wine.

5 When there are 10 minutes to go, remove from the oven. Return the temperature to 475°F (240°C). Place the pork in a clean pan and cook for the final 10 minutes. Place on a warmed plate, cover with foil, and set aside.

6 Skim the fat from the juices. Place the pan with the juices on the stove top. Stir to pick up residue. Mix the cornstarch with 2 tbsp of cold water and stir in until the juices thicken. Season and strain into a serving bowl. Serve with the pork.

CALORIES: 500kcals/2102kJ
CARBOHYDRATE: 2.5g
  sugar: 0.1g
FAT: 22.5g
  saturated: 5.5g
SALT: 0.7g
FIBER: 0g

Roast beef

Roast beef, Yorkshire puddings (see p303), and gravy make a tasty British-style Sunday dinner.

10 mins | 1½–1¾ hrs, plus resting

SERVES 4–6

3lb 3oz (1.5kg) beef rump roast

salt and freshly ground black pepper

1 tbsp olive oil

2 tbsp beef dripping (optional)

2 tbsp all-purpose flour

1¼ cups beef or vegetable stock (see p156)

Yorkshire puddings (see p303), to serve

1 Preheat the oven to 400°F (200°C). Season the beef with salt and pepper.

2 Heat the oil in heavy-bottomed roasting pan on the stove top and sear the roast on all sides.

3 Place in the oven and roast the beef for 20 minutes. Reduce the oven temperature to 325°F (160°C) and cook the beef for 15 minutes per 1lb (450g) for rare, or 20 minutes per 1lb (450g) for medium-rare.

4 Remove the roast from the pan, place on a warmed plate, and cover with foil. Set aside for at least 20 minutes to allow the meat to relax, making it moist and easy to carve.

5 Meanwhile, place the roasting pan on the stove top and warm the cooking juices through (if you don't have any juices, add the dripping). Stir in the flour and cook for 2–3 minutes, stirring to form a smooth paste. Gradually add the stock, stirring, to make a rich gravy. Pour in any juices from the rested beef and stir well. Carve the meat and serve with Yorkshire puddings (see p303) and the gravy.

CALORIES: 568kcals/2392kJ
CARBOHYDRATE: 6g
  sugar: 1g
FAT: 20g
  saturated: 8g
SALT: 0.9g
FIBER: 0g

CLEVER WITH LEFTOVERS

Leftover roast beef and roast potatoes can make the basis of a delicious hash. Try serving it with a beet, orange, and watercress salad and some Horseradish crème fraîche (see p303).

Slow-cooked shoulder of pork with cider gravy

Shoulder of pork is an inexpensive and large cut, and roasts far better than a more traditional (but drier) unsmoked ham.

10 mins, plus resting   **3 hrs,** plus resting

SERVES 6–8

1 bone-in shoulder of pork, preferably with the skin on, approx. 4½lb (2kg)

1 tbsp olive oil

salt and freshly ground black pepper

1¼ cups cider

¾ cup chicken stock (see p94)

1 tbsp all-purpose flour

CALORIES: 460kcals/1941kJ

CARBOHYDRATE: 3g
  sugar: 1.5g

FAT: 15g
  saturated: 5g

SALT: 0.6g

FIBER: 0g

---

1 With a sharp knife, make criss-cross slits all over the skin of the pork, being careful not to cut through to the meat underneath. (You can ask your butcher to do this for you.) Rub the skin dry with paper towels and let the meat rest, uncovered, in the fridge for at least 4 hours, but preferably overnight. This will help the skin crisp while cooking.

2 Preheat the oven to 350°F (180°C). Place the meat skin-side up in a roasting pan, rub it with the oil, and rub salt all over the top, being sure to get inside the slits in the skin.

3 Pour the cider and stock into the roasting pan, being careful not to splash the top of the meat. Cover the skin with a piece of waxed paper (this will help to keep the skin from sticking to the foil), then cover the whole roasting pan with foil, sealing it tightly so that no steam escapes.

3 Roast the pork for 2½ hours, then remove the foil and waxed paper, increase the oven temperature to 450°F (230°C), and roast for 30–40 minutes until the skin is crisp. Remove the pork from the oven and wrap it in foil to keep it warm while you make the gravy. (It is a good idea to separate the crackling from the pork at this stage, as wrapping it in foil will soften it, so leave the crackling uncovered in the turned-off oven.)

4 To make the gravy, skim about ¼ cup of the pork fat from the top of the cooking juices into a saucepan and set it over low heat. Whisk in the flour and cook it for 2–3 minutes, whisking constantly, until it bubbles and starts to change color. Meanwhile, skim off and discard as much of the remaining fat as possible from the cooking liquid, then pour the juices into the pan a little at a time, whisking as you go, until you have a thick, rich gravy. Taste for seasoning. Bring it to a boil, reduce to a simmer, and cook for 5 minutes before serving with the pork and crackling.

COOK'S TIP

One of the best kitchen devices ever invented is a fat-separating measuring cup. The fat floats to the top of any liquid poured in, and you pour from a spout at the bottom of the cup. This allows you to use as much as possible of the natural juices from a roast, while leaving the fat behind.

Roast chicken and vegetables

When time is short, this is the ideal all-in-one and near-effortless tasty family meal.

10 mins   40 mins

SERVES 4

8 Yukon Golds, quartered lengthwise

3 large carrots, cut into 1in (3cm) chunks

2 large parsnips, cut into 1in (3cm) chunks

2 leeks, cut into 1in (3cm) chunks

8 skin-on bone-in chicken drumsticks, thighs, or a mixture

2 tbsp olive oil

1 tbsp thyme leaves

1 tbsp finely chopped flat-leaf parsley leaves

salt and freshly ground black pepper

CALORIES: 684kcals/2880kJ

CARBOHYDRATE: 77g
  sugar: 11g

FAT: 18g
  saturated: 4g

SALT: 0.6g

FIBER: 14g

1 Preheat the oven to 400°F (200°C). Put the vegetables and chicken pieces in a large roasting pan; it should be big enough to fit them in a single layer. Drizzle them with the oil, sprinkle in the herbs, and season well.

2 Toss everything together so that it is well coated with the herby oil and spread it out in a single layer, with the chicken skin-side up and evenly spaced between the vegetables.

3 Bake for 40 minutes until the chicken is cooked, the skin crispy, and the vegetables coloring at the edges.

PREPARE AHEAD

For a Sunday dinner that is ready in an hour, prepare this dish ahead. Store the chicken and vegetables, tossed in oil and seasoned, in the fridge until needed. While the oven is preheating, turn the ingredients into a large oven pan until they come to room temperature, then cook as in step 3.

Sausage and sweet potatoes

This quick and delicious recipe makes a great midweek supper for all the family. Young children will love it.

10 mins   45 mins

SERVES 4

4 Yukon Golds, halved lengthwise

2 sweet potatoes, peeled and cut into chunks

1 red onion, cut into 6 or 8 wedges through the root

1 red bell pepper, cut into 1in (3cm) chunks

8 fresh sausages, not smoked

2 tbsp olive oil

1 tbsp thyme leaves

2 tsp smoked paprika

salt and freshly ground black pepper

2½oz (75g) cherry tomatoes

1 Preheat the oven to 400°F (200°C). Put the vegetables and sausages in a roasting pan large enough to fit them in a single layer. Drizzle with the oil, sprinkle with the thyme and paprika, and season.

2 Toss everything together so it is well coated with the oil, and spread it out in a single layer with the sausages evenly spaced between the vegetables.

3 Bake for 30 minutes, then add the cherry tomatoes, toss everything, and spread it out again. Cook for another 15 minutes until the sausages are crispy, the vegetables coloring at the edges, and the tomatoes have softened.

CALORIES: 587kcals/2461kJ

CARBOHYDRATE: 63g
  sugar: 12g

FAT: 28g
  saturated: 9g

SALT: 2.3g

FIBER: 8g

These roasted dinners are a great way to accommodate the likes and dislikes of the whole family. Cook a variety of vegetables and everyone can pick the ones they like.

Fussy eaters!

Prime rib with horseradish crème fraîche

You will be amazed at how quick it is to roast a proper Sunday dinner, and this rib roast makes a treat.

15 mins, plus resting   1¼–1½ hrs

SERVES 4

1 tbsp olive oil

salt and freshly ground black pepper

3lb 3oz (1.5kg) prime rib roast (2 ribs), on the bone

4 carrots, chopped into large chunks

4 parsnips, chopped into large chunks

2 red onions, quartered

¾ cup (7oz) half-fat crème fraîche

3 tbsp creamed horseradish sauce

mashed potatoes, to serve

1 Preheat the oven to 425°F (220°C). Place the oil in a sturdy roasting pan and put it in the oven to preheat for 5 minutes.

2 Generously season the beef. Remove the roasting pan from the oven and place on the stove top over medium heat. Add the beef and turn to brown it all over.

3 Remove the beef to a plate. Put the chopped vegetables into the pan and stir to coat in the oil and juices. Arrange in an even layer and place the beef on top.

4 Roast for 20 minutes. Reduce the oven temperature to 325°F (160°C). Cook for 15 minutes per 1lb (450g) for rare, or 20 minutes for medium-rare.

5 Meanwhile, place the crème fraîche and horseradish sauce in a small serving dish and stir well.

6 Remove the roast from the pan, place on a warmed plate, and cover with foil. Set aside for at least 20 minutes to rest. Cover the roasted vegetables with foil and leave in the oven to keep hot.

7 Pour any juices from the rested meat into the pan and stir well to coat the vegetables. Carve the beef and serve with the vegetables, juices, mashed potatoes, and the horseradish crème fraîche.

CALORIES: 659kcals/2763kJ
CARBOHYDRATE: 27g
  sugar: 18g
FAT: 27g
  saturated: 12g
SALT: 0.9g
FIBER: 11g

Yorkshire puddings

Substitute vegetable shortening for dripping, for a vegetarian dish. The recipe will work just as well.

10 mins   20–25 mins

SPECIAL EQUIPMENT
2 x 4-hole Yorkshire pudding pans

SERVES 4

2 tbsp beef dripping

1 cup all-purpose flour

½ tsp salt

1 large egg, lightly beaten

¾ cup whole milk

1 Preheat the oven to 425°F (220°C). Divide the beef dripping between two 4-hole Yorkshire pudding pans and place the pans in the oven to heat for at least 5 minutes.

2 Sift the all-purpose flour into a medium mixing bowl. Add the salt and egg and stir well to combine. Gradually add the milk, whisking with a fork to combine. Slowly add ½ cup of cold water and whisk to form a smooth, thin batter.

3 Pour or spoon the batter evenly between the heated pans. Cook for 20–25 minutes, or until risen and golden.

PREPARE AHEAD
The batter can be made up to 1 hour in advance and kept, covered, at room temperature. If you're planning to keep it for more than 1 hour, cover and refrigerate for up to 3 hours.

CALORIES: 228kcals/957kJ
CARBOHYDRATE: 25g
  sugar: 3g
FAT: 11g
  saturated: 5.5g
SALT: 0.6g
FIBER: 1g

Individual mushroom and leek potato pies

This comforting wintry vegetable dish is perfect to serve vegetarian guests alongside a traditional Sunday lunch.

15 mins   20 mins, plus resting

SPECIAL EQUIPMENT

4 x 3in- (8cm-) wide, 1½in- (4cm-) high metal rings

SERVES 4

4 large Portobello mushrooms

4 tbsp olive oil

2 tbsp butter

2 leeks, cut into ¾in (2cm) chunks

2 tbsp all-purpose flour

⅔ cup whole milk

2½oz (75g) blue cheese, such as Stilton, crumbled

salt and freshly ground black pepper

2 cups mashed potatoes

1 heaping tbsp whole grain mustard

1 Preheat the oven to 400°F (200°C). Brush the mushrooms with half the oil and cook them on a grill pan or under a hot broiler for 3 minutes on each side until they soften.

2 Heat the remaining 2 tbsp of oil and the butter in a small saucepan. Cook the leeks, covered, over low heat for 5–7 minutes, stirring occasionally until they soften. Add the flour to the pan and mix it into the leeks, then gradually stir in the milk.

3 Bring the sauce to a boil, then reduce the heat to a simmer and cook until it thickens. Add the cheese and continue to stir until the cheese has melted. Season with pepper (the cheese is quite salty).

4 Place four 3in- (8cm-) wide, 1½in- (4cm-) high metal rings on a baking sheet. Put a mushroom in the bottom of each ring, gill-side up. It should fit neatly. Cover the mushrooms with the cheesy leek mixture and season well.

5 Reheat the mashed potatoes slightly in a microwave to soften them, then beat in the mustard and taste for seasoning. Divide the potatoes between the metal rings and finish the top nicely.

6 Bake for 15–20 minutes until the top is golden brown and the vegetables cooked through. Let rest for 5 minutes before carefully running a small, sharp knife around the inside of the ring and easing the pies out onto warmed plates to serve.

VARIATION

Try mixing the grilled mushrooms and cheesy leek mixture, omitting the potato, and dividing the mixture between 4 ramekins. Cover each with a disk of store-bought all-butter puff pastry, and bake as in step 6.

PREPARE AHEAD

These pies can be prepared up to 1 day ahead, covered, and chilled. Simply return them to room temperature before cooking as in step 6.

CALORIES: 410kcals/1703kJ

CARBOHYDRATE: 23g
  sugar: 4g

FAT: 30g
  saturated: 13g

SALT: 0.8g

FIBER: 4.5g

Mediterranean vegetable and goat cheese timbale

This individual tower of summery flavors can be served to vegetarian guests, or used as an appetizer.

15 mins

20 mins,
plus resting

SPECIAL EQUIPMENT

4 x 3in- (8cm-) wide, 1½in- (4cm-)
high metal rings

SERVES 4

2 large sweet potatoes, cut into
8 x ¾in (2cm) slices

1 large eggplant, cut into
8 x ¾in (2cm) slices

olive oil, for brushing

2 large tomatoes, thinly sliced

¼ cup finely chopped basil leaves

salt and freshly ground black pepper

4½oz (125g) goat cheese,
finely sliced

1 Preheat the oven to 400°F
(200°C). Brush the sweet
potatoes and eggplant with the
oil and cook them on a grill pan
or under a hot broiler for 3–4
minutes on each side, until they are
softened and charred in places.

2 Place a slice of the sweet
potatoes in each of four 3in-
(8cm-) wide, 1½in- (4cm-) high
metal rings on a baking sheet. If the
potato does not fit in neatly, break
off bits of a bigger slice to fill any
gaps. Top each with a slice of
tomato, divide over half the basil,
and season well. Cover each with
a slice of eggplant and divide over
half the cheese. Press down well,
then repeat the layers, finishing
with the goat cheese.

3 Bake for 15–20 minutes, until
the top is golden brown and
the vegetables are cooked through.
Let rest for 5 minutes before
carefully running a small, sharp
knife around the inside of the ring
and easing the vegetable towers
out onto warmed plates to serve.

VARIATION

If you have a single guest, you will
need ½ sweet potato, 2 slices of
eggplant, ½ tomato, and 1oz (30g)
goat cheese to make one portion.

PREPARE AHEAD

This timbale can be assembled up to
1 day ahead, covered, and chilled.
Return it to room temperature before
cooking as in step 3.

COOK'S TIP

If one of your guests is vegetarian, it
can be difficult to cook for them and
everyone else at the same time. This
individual vegetarian dish can be made
in advance, then served alongside a
summery herby roast chicken to make
a great warm-weather meal.

CALORIES: 254kcals/1069kJ

CARBOHYDRATE: 28g
sugar: 10g

FAT: 12g
saturated: 6g

SALT: 0.6g

FIBER: 6g

Sage and onion stuffing balls

Cooking the stuffing separately from the meat gives it a deliciously crispy exterior.

15 mins, plus cooling   35 mins

SERVES 4

butter, for greasing

1 tbsp olive oil

1 large onion, very finely chopped

1½ cups fresh white bread crumbs

2 tbsp finely chopped sage leaves

salt and freshly ground black pepper

1 large egg, lightly beaten

1 Preheat the oven to 350°F (180°C). Butter a medium, shallow, ovenproof dish.

2 Heat the oil in a saucepan over medium heat, cover, and gently cook the onion for 10 minutes. Let cool.

3 Stir in the bread crumbs, sage, and a generous amount of seasoning. Add the egg and stir.

4 Using your hands, form the stuffing into 8 equal-sized balls. Place in the buttered dish and bake for 20–25 minutes.

VARIATION

Alternatively, cook the stuffing balls in the roasting pan around a chicken or turkey for the last 30 minutes of roasting time. To cook the stuffing inside a chicken or turkey, make as above up to the end of step 3 and then loosely stuff the neck end of the bird just before roasting.

PREPARE AHEAD

These simple stuffing balls can be prepared ahead. Open-freeze on a baking sheet, then bag up and store in a freezer bag for up to 6 months. Defrost in a single layer on a plate and bake as usual.

CALORIES: 142kcals/597kJ

CARBOHYDRATE: 21g
  sugar: 2.5g

FAT: 5g
  saturated: 1g

SALT: 0.5g

FIBER: 1.5g

Chestnut-cranberry stuffing

Chestnuts, apples, and cranberries turn ground sausage into a suitable accompaniment to a holiday feast.

15 mins   30 mins

SERVES 6

butter, for greasing

4½oz (125g) pork sausage

2 cups fresh brown bread crumbs

1 tsp dried thyme

finely grated zest of 1 lemon

1 red eating apple, unpeeled, cored, and finely chopped

1oz (30g) dried cranberries

7oz (200g) cooked, peeled chestnuts, roughly chopped

1 large egg, lightly beaten

salt and freshly ground black pepper

1 Preheat the oven to 350°F (180°C). Butter a medium ovenproof dish.

2 Place all the ingredients in a medium mixing bowl, season generously, and stir well to combine.

3 Using your hands, form the stuffing into 18 equal-sized balls. Place into the prepared dish and bake for 20 minutes.

VARIATION

To cook the stuffing inside a chicken or turkey, loosely stuff the neck end of the bird just before roasting. Never stuff with a stuffing containing raw egg or meat ahead of time, as that poses a risk of food poisoning.

PREPARE AHEAD

This stuffing can be cooked a day or two ahead, covered and chilled, then covered with foil and reheated when the turkey is out of the oven and resting.

CALORIES: 229kcals/965kJ

CARBOHYDRATE: 34g
  sugar: 9.5g

FAT: 7g
  saturated: 2g

SALT: 0.9g

FIBER: 3g

Herby apricot stuffing

Meat eaters and vegetarians alike will enjoy digging into this fruity apricot stuffing.

15 mins 30 mins

SERVES 4–6

butter, for greasing

3½oz (100g) dried apricots, finely chopped

juice of 1 orange

1 piece crystallized ginger, finely chopped

1 cup fresh white bread crumbs

¾oz (20g) toasted pine nuts

3 tbsp chopped flat-leaf parsley leaves

4 sprigs of rosemary, leaves chopped

¼ cup vegetable shortening vegetable suet

1 large egg, lightly beaten

salt and freshly ground black pepper

1 Preheat the oven to 350°F (180°C). Butter a medium ovenproof dish.

2 Place all the ingredients in a medium mixing bowl, season generously, and stir well to combine.

3 Spoon the stuffing into the prepared dish and bake for 30 minutes.

VARIATION

If you do not have pine nuts, chopped hazelnuts, pecans, or almonds can be substituted instead.

COOK'S TIP

To cook the stuffing in a chicken or turkey, loosely stuff the neck end of the bird just before roasting. This stuffing would also be great inside a boned pork loin.

CALORIES: 323kcals/1354kJ

CARBOHYDRATE: 35g
  sugar: 17g

FAT: 17g
  saturated: 6g

SALT: 0.6g

FIBER: 3.5g

Classic pan gravy

This is a proper old-fashioned, rich and thick gravy, just like our grandmothers used to make.

5 mins 10 mins

SERVES 4

pan juices from a roast

1 heaping tbsp all-purpose flour

up to 1¼ cups chicken stock (see p94), if needed

2 tbsp sherry or marsala (optional)

1 tbsp redcurrant jelly

salt and freshly ground black pepper

1 When the roast has cooked and is resting, pour off all the cooking juices into a bowl.

2 Add 3 tbsp of the fat, which floats to the top, back into the roasting pan. Place the roasting pan over low heat and add the flour. Cook the flour, whisking constantly, for 2–3 minutes until it bubbles and starts to color.

3 Meanwhile, skim off as much of the remaining fat as possible from the cooking liquid and discard it, then pour the juices into the flour mixture a little at a time, whisking as you go, until you have a thick, rich gravy. Use the chicken stock if you need more liquid. Add the sherry (if using) and the redcurrant jelly and taste for seasoning. Bring it to a boil, making sure the jelly has melted, reduce to a simmer, and cook for 5 minutes before serving.

VARIATION

For a lighter gravy, just add a little white wine to the cooking juices (omit the flour, sherry, and jelly), and whisk over low heat until they reduce to a thinner gravy, then season to taste.

CALORIES: 72kcals/300kJ

CARBOHYDRATE: 5g
  sugar: 2.5g

FAT: 3g
  saturated: 0.5g

SALT: 0.2g

FIBER: 0g

Sausage and mustard mash canapés

These simple canapés will please young and old alike, and preparing them ahead saves time on the day.

20 mins 45 mins

SPECIAL EQUIPMENT
piping bag fitted with ½in (1cm) star-shaped nozzle

MAKES 40

4 large white potatoes, approx. 1lb 2oz (500g) in total

salt and freshly ground black pepper

2 tbsp butter

1 tbsp Dijon mustard

1 tbsp wholegrain mustard

40 cooked cocktail sausages

handful of chopped flat-leaf parsley leaves, to serve

1 Preheat the oven to 400°F (200°C). Simmer the potatoes in salted water for 20–25 minutes, or until tender. Drain well, then mash to a smooth purée with the butter and mustards, using a potato ricer if possible, for a really smooth result. Season well.

2 Meanwhile, slit each sausage down the middle. They should almost open flat.

3 When the mash has cooled a little, put it into a piping bag fitted with a ½in (1cm) star-shaped nozzle. Pipe into each sausage and lay on a baking sheet.

4 Cook at the top of the hot oven for 15–20 minutes, until the potato is crispy. Allow to cool a little and sprinkle with parsley before serving.

PREPARE AHEAD
These sausages can be prepared to the end of step 3 a day ahead of a party and kept, covered, in the fridge. For a large party, double or triple the quantities and bake in batches, so you can serve hot sausages to guests in 2 or 3 waves.

CALORIES: 62kcals/257kJ
CARBOHYDRATE: 3g
    sugar: 0.5g
FAT: 4g
    saturated: 1.5g
SALT: 0.4g
FIBER: 0g

Roasted asparagus and prosciutto bundles

This easy but elegant dish makes a great appetizer, and each bundle is one perfect serving.

10 mins 15 mins

SERVES 4 (as an appetizer)

24 thin asparagus spears

2 tbsp olive oil

salt and freshly ground black pepper

4 prosciutto slices

1 Preheat the oven to 450°F (230°C). Trim the asparagus spears of their woody ends, put them on a plate, and rub with 1 tbsp of olive oil. Season well.

2 Lay a slice of the prosciutto on a board and put one-quarter of the asparagus spears in the middle. Carefully wrap the prosciutto around the asparagus to make a neat parcel, leaving the tips exposed. Lay it on a baking sheet with the seam of the meat facing down. Repeat to make 4 parcels. Brush the prosciutto with the remaining olive oil.

3 Bake at the top of the hot oven for 15 minutes, until the prosciutto is crispy and the asparagus cooked through. Serve as it is, or with a Hollandaise sauce (see p254), or a poached egg.

COOK'S TIP

As well as an appetizer, this makes a lovely vegetable side dish to serve with salmon fillets or chicken breasts.

CALORIES: 119kcals/492kJ
CARBOHYDRATE: 2g
    sugar: 2g
FAT: 9g
    saturated: 3g
SALT: 0.2g
FIBER: 2.5g

Home-cured gravlax and dill mayonnaise

Gravlax, which means "buried salmon" in Swedish, is delicious, and relatively inexpensive to make at home.

20 mins,
plus 3 days
marinating

SPECIAL EQUIPMENT
food processor or blender

SERVES 6–10

2 tbsp coarse sea salt

3 tbsp granulated sugar

1 tsp freshly ground black pepper

1¾oz (50g) dill, finely chopped, stalks included

1¾lb (800g) piece of very fresh salmon from the center of the fillet (most of a side of salmon)

rye or pumpernickel bread, to serve

FOR THE DILL MAYONNAISE

2 large very fresh egg yolks (see food safety note on raw eggs, p11)

1 tbsp rice wine vinegar, or to taste

2 tbsp Dijon mustard

¼ cup roughly chopped dill stalks

½ tbsp granulated sugar

salt and freshly ground black pepper

2 cups sunflower or vegetable oil

1 In a small bowl, mix the salt, sugar, black pepper, and dill. Cut the salmon across the middle to form 2 equal-sized pieces. Lay 1 piece, skin-side down, on the edge of a roll of plastic wrap. Cover the flesh of the fish with the dill mixture, then put the second piece of salmon on top of the first, skin-side up.

2 Wrap the salmon a few times in the plastic wrap, being careful to wrap both lengthwise and widthwise so it is entirely enclosed in a tight parcel. Place on a trivet in a deep roasting pan. Refrigerate the salmon for 3 days, turning it morning and evening so that each side of the fish gets soaked in the marinade.

3 After 3 days, carefully unwrap the fish—there will be a lot of juice from the marinade. Put the fish, skin-side down, on a cutting board and gently scrape away most of the dill that remains on top of the flesh with a sharp knife.

4 To make the mayonnaise, put the egg yolks, vinegar, mustard, dill, and sugar into the bowl of a food processor or blender, and season well. Add a little of the oil and process to a smooth paste. With the motor running, slowly add the remaining oil in a thin stream, until the mixture thickens and emulsifies. Taste and adjust the acidity with more vinegar, if needed. Refrigerate until needed, and for up to 1 day.

5 The salmon can now be carved from the skin in thin slices at a sharp angle, as you would carve a side of smoked salmon. Serve with the dill mayonnaise and some rye or pumpernickel bread.

VARIATION

Gravlax is very adaptable. Flavor the salt and sugar cure with alcohol, such as vodka, or add grated raw beets for a stunning pink cure.

CALORIES: 206kcals/856kJ

CARBOHYDRATE: 3g
  sugar: 3g

FAT: 14g
  saturated: 2g

SALT: 1.3g

FIBER: 0g

Summery shrimp towers

Most of these impressive appetizers can be prepared ahead, then it's just a simple assembly job before serving.

30 mins   15 mins

SPECIAL EQUIPMENT

4 x 3in- (8cm-) wide and 1½in- (4cm-) high metal rings

SERVES 4

2 large beefsteak tomatoes

5 tbsp olive oil

salt and freshly ground black pepper

1 large eggplant, cut into 8 x ¾in (2cm) slices

2 avocados, halved and pitted

1 lemon

2 tbsp finely chopped basil leaves

1 tbsp balsamic vinegar

20 raw tiger shrimp, shelled, heads removed, and deveined

1 Trim the tops and bases off the tomatoes (save them for stock) and slice each in half horizontally. Heat 1 tbsp of the oil in a large, non-stick grll pan or frying pan and cook the halves for 4–5 minutes each side, seasoning after turning, until cooked but not collapsing. Set aside. Wipe the pan with paper towels.

2 Add 2 tbsp of the olive oil to the pan and cook the eggplant slices for 8–10 minutes each side, seasoning them after turning, until golden brown and cooked through. Drain them on paper towels.

3 Dice the flesh of the avocados into small cubes and mix with the juice of ½ lemon, the basil, balsamic vinegar, and 1 tbsp of the olive oil.

4 To assemble the towers, put a 3in- (8cm-) wide and 1½in- (4cm-) high metal ring in the middle of a plate and add a tomato half, squishing it in slightly. Add a spoonful of the avocado mix, then 2 slices of the eggplant, and finally another spoonful of avocado. Season every layer lightly as you build the tower.

5 When you are ready to serve, quickly pan-fry the shrimp in the remaining 1 tbsp of olive oil for 2–3 minutes, until they change color to a vivid pink. Season them well and squeeze over the remaining ½ lemon. Top each tower with 5 shrimp, nicely arranged, then carefully remove the ring to serve.

CALORIES: 333kcals/1380kJ

CARBOHYDRATE: 6g
  sugar: 5g

FAT: 29g
  saturated: 6g

SALT: 0.26g

FIBER: 6g

Smoked oyster soup

This sophisticated soup is a great dinner party appetizer. No one will realize it's actually quite simple to make.

10 mins   30 mins

SPECIAL EQUIPMENT

blender

SERVES 4 (as an appetizer)

2 tbsp olive oil

1 onion, finely chopped

2 large white potatoes, approx. 12oz (350g) in total, peeled and roughly chopped

1 x 3oz (85g) can of smoked oysters in sunflower oil, drained and rinsed

3½ cups fish stock

¼ cup whipping cream, plus extra to serve

salt and freshly ground black pepper

1 tbsp dry sherry (optional)

1 Heat the olive oil in a large, heavy-bottomed saucepan. Cook the onion over low heat, covered, for 5–7 minutes until it softens, but is not brown.

2 Add the potatoes, smoked oysters, fish stock, and cream, and season with a little salt and pepper. Bring the soup to a boil, then reduce to a simmer, partially cover, and cook for 20–25 minutes, until the potatoes are soft.

3 Purée the soup until smooth (if you are using a blender, you may have to do this in batches; it is important not to fill the blender more than one-third full with hot liquid). Now pass it through a sieve so that it is completely smooth.

4 Return the soup to the pan and heat it gently. Add the sherry (if using) and serve with a swirl of cream in the center of the bowls and a sprinkling of pepper.

CALORIES: 209kcals/869kJ

CARBOHYDRATE: 17g
  sugar: 2g

FAT: 13g
  saturated: 5g

SALT: 2.5g

FIBER: 2g

Mini naan toasts with roasted vegetables and goat cheese

These pretty little appetizers taste as delicious as they look, and can be prepared well in advance.

30 mins   35 mins

SPECIAL EQUIPMENT

1½in (4cm) round cutter

MAKES 40

½ eggplant, approx. 5½oz (150g), cut into ½in (1cm) cubes

½ red bell pepper, approx. 3½oz (100g), cut into ½in (1cm) cubes

1 zucchini, approx. 4¼oz (120g), cut into ½in (1cm) cubes

½ red onion, approx. 3½oz (100g), finely chopped

2 tbsp olive oil, plus extra if needed

salt and freshly ground black pepper

2 plain naan breads

3½oz (100g) soft goat cheese

3½oz (100g) cream cheese, softened

2 tbsp finely chopped basil leaves

1 Preheat the oven to 400°F (200°C). Put the eggplant, red bell pepper, zucchini, and onion in a large roasting pan in a single layer. Toss with the olive oil and season.

2 Cook for 20 minutes, turning after 15 minutes, until soft and charred at the edges. Set aside to cool, adding ½ tbsp of oil if they look dry. Taste for seasoning.

3 Meanwhile, cut the naan breads into small circles using a 1½in (4cm) round cutter and put on a baking sheet. Cook for 10–15 minutes until golden brown and crispy. Set aside to cool.

4 In a bowl, beat the goat cheese, cream cheese, and basil and season well. When ready to serve, spread each piece of bread with a little herby goat cheese and top with 1 tsp of vegetables, pressing down slightly so the vegetables stick to the cheese.

PREPARE AHEAD

The separate parts of this canapé can be made up to 2 days ahead and stored in airtight containers (the vegetables and the cheese should be stored in the fridge).

CALORIES: 45kcals/189kJ

CARBOHYDRATE: 3.5g
sugar: 0.5g

FAT: 3g
saturated: 1g

SALT: 0.15g

FIBER: 0.5g

Roast side of salmon with cucumber and dill salad

A whole side of salmon makes a stunning, popular centerpiece at a party or buffet, and is really simple to prepare.

20 mins, plus draining   25 mins

SPECIAL EQUIPMENT
food processor

SERVES 6-8

1 skinless and boneless side of salmon

1 tbsp olive oil

salt and freshly ground black pepper

2 lemons, cut into wedges, to serve

plain yogurt, to serve

FOR THE SALAD

2 cucumbers, very finely sliced with a food processor

2 tbsp coarse sea salt

2 tbsp granulated sugar

¼ cup rice wine vinegar

handful of dill, finely chopped

1 For the salad, toss the cucumber in the salt, put in a colander, and weigh down with a plate. Leave in the sink for 1 hour to remove the excess water. Rinse briefly, put it into a clean kitchen towel, and squeeze to remove excess water.

2 Preheat the oven to 425°F (220°C). Whisk the sugar and vinegar with 2 tbsp of boiling water to dissolve in a bowl. Toss in the cucumber and dill, cover, and chill for at least 30 minutes.

3 Put the salmon on a very large baking sheet and rub with the oil. Season well and roast at the top of the oven for 20–25 minutes, until cooked, but moist in the middle.

4 Serve the salmon with lemon wedges, the cucumber and dill salad, and a bowl of plain yogurt.

CLEVER WITH LEFTOVERS

Cold roast salmon is perfect to mix into fishcakes (see p85), or with mayonnaise and leftover Cucumber and dill salad (drained well first) to serve with crackers and salad leaves for a light lunch.

CALORIES: 374kcals/1557kJ

CARBOHYDRATE: 5g
  sugar: 5g

FAT: 22g
  saturated: 4g

SALT: 1.4g

FIBER: 0.5g

Catalan seafood zarzuela

This traditional Catalan stew makes an opulent appetizer or summer lunch. Add more mussels if you can't find clams.

15 mins   25 mins

SERVES 4

1 tbsp olive oil

1 onion, finely chopped

2 garlic cloves, finely chopped

1¼ cups dry white wine

1¼ cups fish stock

2 tbsp tomato paste

generous pinch of saffron threads

salt and freshly ground black pepper

12 fresh mussels, scrubbed, and beards removed (discard any that stay open when sharply tapped)

12 fresh clams, scrubbed (discard any that stay open when sharply tapped)

10oz (300g) firm white fish fillets, such as haddock or cod, pin-boned, skinned, and cut into bite-sized pieces

2 squid pouches (approx. 6oz/175g in total), sliced into ¼in- (5mm-) thick rings

8 raw large shrimp, shells on, deveined

3 tbsp chopped flat-leaf parsley leaves

crusty bread, to serve

1 Heat the oil in a deep-sided frying pan over medium heat and cook the onion for 10 minutes, covered. Add the garlic and cook for 1 minute. Add the wine and simmer for 5 minutes. Add the stock, tomato paste, and saffron and season. Return to a simmer, add the clams and mussels, and cook for 3 minutes.

2 Add the white fish, squid, and shrimp and cook for 2 minutes. Cover and cook for 5 minutes more. Discard any mussels or clams that do not open on cooking. Stir in the parsley. Serve with crusty bread.

VARIATION

Saffron is a very expensive spice, and not to everyone's taste. For a less authentic, but still delicious stew with a smoky edge, add 1 tsp of smoked paprika instead.

CALORIES: 314kcals/1319kJ

CARBOHYDRATE: 7g
  sugar: 3g

FAT: 6g
  saturated: 1g

SALT: 2.3g

FIBER: 0.5g

Roast turkey

Cooked this way, the turkey will be juicy and delicious. Look for a smaller turkey as they are easier to cook correctly.

10 mins | 2½–3 hrs, plus resting

SERVES 8–10

8–10lb (4–5kg) turkey

2 tbsp butter

salt and freshly ground black pepper

handful of thyme sprigs

1 Preheat the oven to 325°F (160°C). Remove any giblets from inside the turkey and use them to make a stock.

2 Weigh the turkey so you can calculate its cooking time, then place it in a large roasting pan. Smear the breast with the butter, and season the bird well inside and out. Pop the thyme into the cavity.

3 Place greaseproof paper over the breast of the turkey, then cover it with a large sheet of foil, sealing it to the roasting pan so no steam will escape.

4 Roast the turkey for 15 minutes per 1lb (450g) of weight. Remove the foil for the last 30 minutes and

increase the oven temperature to 400°F (200°C), so the skin can brown nicely. Remove the turkey from the oven and rest it, covered in foil, for at least 30 minutes before serving.

VARIATION

Try spreading the butter underneath the skin of the bird, easing the skin gently from the breast, before roasting.

COOK'S TIP

To ensure a turkey is cooked through, use a meat thermometer to test the thickest part of the thigh. It should have a temperature of 160°F (71°C).

CLEVER WITH LEFTOVERS

A turkey yields a lot of meat. The cold leftover meat can be used in place of cooked cold chicken in any of the recipes in this book.

CALORIES: 248kcals/1048kJ

CARBOHYDRATE: 0g
  sugar: 0g

FAT: 5g
  saturated: 2.5g

SALT: 0.3g

FIBER: 0g

Stuffed roast goose

Try roasting a rich goose instead of a turkey at your next holiday gathering.

20 mins   3¼ hrs, plus resting

SERVES 6–8

9lb (4.5kg) goose with giblets

4 onions, finely chopped

10 sage leaves, chopped

4 tbsp butter, melted and cooled

1 cup fresh bread crumbs

1 large egg yolk

salt and freshly ground black pepper

2 tbsp all-purpose flour

tart applesauce, to serve

1 Preheat the oven to 450°F (230°C). Remove excess fat from inside the goose. Prick the skin all over with a fork. Make a stock with the giblets, reserving the liver.

2 Boil the onions and chopped goose liver in a little water for 5 minutes, then drain. Mix with the sage, butter, bread crumbs, egg, and seasoning. Stuff loosely into the cavity and sew up with a trussing needle and kitchen string, or secure with a skewer. Cover the wings and drumsticks with foil.

3 Place the goose upside down on a rack in a deep roasting pan. Roast for 30 minutes, then turn the goose over and roast for another 30 minutes. Drain off the fat in the roasting pan (reserve it). Cover with foil, reduce the oven temperature to 375°F (190°C), and roast for 1½ hours. Drain off the fat again. Remove the foil and roast for a final 30 minutes. Put on a warm serving dish and rest for 30 minutes.

4 To make the gravy, heat 3 tbsp of goose fat in a pan, stir in the flour, and cook for 5 minutes over low heat. Gradually whisk in enough hot giblet stock to make a gravy. Pour off all the fat from the roasting pan and pour in the gravy, stirring up the brown juices. Strain.

5 Carve the goose and serve with the gravy, stuffing, and a tart applesauce.

COOK'S TIP

The clear fat rendered early in cooking is great saved in the fridge and used to roast potatoes. Discard the cloudy or brown fat rendered in the later stages.

CALORIES: 559kcals/2328kJ

CARBOHYDRATE: 12g
  sugar: 8g

FAT: 38g
  saturated: 13g

SALT: 0.4g

FIBER: 2g

Brussels sprouts with pancetta and chestnuts

Many die-hard sprout haters will love this sweet and meaty treatment of the vegetables.

10 mins   15 mins

SERVES 4–6

salt and freshly ground black pepper

1lb 2oz (500g) baby Brussels sprouts

1 tbsp butter, plus extra if needed

1 tbsp olive oil

3½oz (100g) chopped pancetta

3½oz (100g) cooked and peeled chestnuts, roughly chopped

1 Bring a large pan of salted water to a boil. Cook the Brussels sprouts for 4–5 minutes, until they are just cooked, then drain well and refresh them under cold water. Drain again and set aside.

2 In a wok, heat the butter and olive oil. When the butter has melted, add the pancetta and cook over medium heat for 3–4 minutes, until it is crispy. Add the chestnuts and cook for another minute.

3 Add the Brussels sprouts and cook for another 2–3 minutes, until heated through, adding a little more butter if necessary and seasoning well with pepper (not salt as the pancetta is quite salty).

CALORIES: 237kcals/990kJ

CARBOHYDRATE: 13g
  sugar: 5.5g

FAT: 16g
  saturated: 6g

SALT: 1g

FIBER: 8g

VARIATION

For an Asian take on sprouts, shred the blanched sprouts. Stir-fry in 2 tbsp of oil over high heat, adding 1 finely chopped chile, 1 finely grated garlic clove, and 1in (2.5cm) finely grated fresh ginger. Finish with a splash each of soy sauce and rice wine.

Bacon-wrapped sausages

Serve these with pancakes and scrambled eggs for a child-friendly Easter brunch.

10 mins   30 mins

SERVES 4

10 slices thick-cut bacon

20 cocktail sausages

1 Preheat the oven to 400°F (200°C). Take a slice of bacon, place it on a cutting board, and scrape the blade of a knife along it, while pulling on its end, so the bacon stretches out. Cut each piece in half to make 20 short, thin slices.

2 Wrap each cocktail sausage in a half-piece of bacon, then put them on a baking sheet with the ends of the bacon facing down.

3 Cook in the hot oven for 20–30 minutes, turning occasionally, until the bacon is crispy and the sausages cooked through.

PREPARE AHEAD

These can be prepared up to 2 days in advance and stored on their baking sheet, well wrapped in plastic wrap, in the fridge. Return to room temperature for 30 minutes before cooking as directed.

HOW TO FREEZE

The cocktail sausages can be wrapped and frozen, uncooked, for up to 8 weeks. Defrost thoroughly before cooking.

CALORIES: 416kcals/1725kJ

CARBOHYDRATE: 5g
  sugar: 1.5g

FAT: 33g
  saturated: 12g

SALT: 3.8g

FIBER: 0g

Cranberry sauce

Fresh cranberries are easy to buy in winter, so try using them to make this delicious, fresh cranberry sauce.

5 mins   10 mins

SERVES 8

12oz (350g) pack of cranberries

¾ cup orange juice

¼ cup tbsp port

⅔ cup granulated sugar

1 Put the cranberries in a small, heavy-bottomed pan and cover them with the orange juice and port. Add the sugar.

2 Bring the liquid to a boil, then reduce to a simmer and cook over low heat for 10 minutes, until the cranberries have softened and burst and the mixture has thickened and reduced.

VARIATION

Adapt the sauce recipe to your family's tastes. For a more tart sauce, reduce the amount of sugar to taste. Cranberry sauce also works well with many winter spices: try adding ½ tsp of allspice, or ground ginger, or freshly ground black pepper to the recipe.

PREPARE AHEAD

You can make this up to 3 days ahead and store, in an airtight container, in the fridge. Either reheat gently to serve, or serve it cold.

COOK'S TIP

For a smoother finish, use a hand-held blender to briefly purée the finished sauce to your desired consistency.

CALORIES: 85kcals/362kJ

CARBOHYDRATE: 19g
  sugar: 19g

FAT: 0g
  saturated: 0g

SALT: trace

FIBER: 1.5g

Bread sauce

A classic British accompaniment to roast turkey, chicken, or pheasant, this subtly spiced sauce is deeply comforting.

5 mins   10 mins
plus resting

SERVES 6–8

2 cups whole milk

1 onion, peeled and halved
  horizontally (across its equator)

6 cloves

2 cups fresh white bread crumbs

salt and freshly ground black pepper

grated nutmeg, to serve (optional)

pat of butter, to serve (optional)

CALORIES: 130kcals/550kJ

CARBOHYDRATE: 21g
  sugar: 3.5g

FAT: 3g
  saturated: 1.5g

SALT: 0.6g

FIBER: 0.5g

1 Put the milk, onion, and cloves in a small saucepan and bring them to a boil. Turn the heat off and cover the pan, leaving the onion and cloves to infuse for at least 1 hour.

2 When you are ready to cook the bread sauce, remove the onion and cloves from the milk, add the bread crumbs, and season well. Heat the sauce over medium heat until it is warmed through and thickened. Stir in a grating of fresh nutmeg and a pat of butter to serve (if using).

PREPARE AHEAD

To get ahead at Christmas time, infuse and strain the milk a couple of days ahead, cover, and store in the fridge. The bread crumbs can also be made in advance and frozen until needed.

Boeuf en croûte

Also known as Beef Wellington, this rich and luxurious dish is simple to finish off and serve; perfect for entertaining.

45 mins **45–60 mins, plus standing**

SERVES 6

2¼lb (1kg) filet of beef, cut from the thick end and trimmed of fat

salt and freshly ground black pepper

2 tbsp sunflower or vegetable oil

3 tbsp unsalted butter

2 shallots, finely chopped

1 garlic clove, crushed

9oz (250g) mixed wild mushrooms, finely chopped

1 tbsp brandy or Madeira

1lb 2oz (500g) store-bought all-butter puff pastry

1 large egg, lightly beaten

1 Preheat the oven to 425°F (220°C). Season the meat all over with salt and pepper. Heat the oil in a large frying pan and cook the beef until browned all over. Place in a roasting pan and roast for 10 minutes. Remove and leave it to cool.

2 Melt the butter in a pan. Cook the shallots and garlic for 2–3 minutes, stirring, until softened. Add the mushrooms and cook, stirring, for 4–5 minutes until the juices evaporate. Add the brandy and let it bubble for 30 seconds. Let cool.

3 Roll out one-third of the dough to a rectangle about 2in (5cm) larger than the beef. Place on a baking sheet and prick with a fork.

4 Bake for 12–15 minutes until crisp. Cool, then spread one-third of the mushroom mixture in the center. Place the beef on top and spread over the remaining mushroom mixture. Roll out the remaining dough and place over the beef. Brush the egg around the edges of the raw dough, and press them down on the cooked dough base to seal.

5 Brush the egg all over the dough. Slit the top for steam to escape. Bake for 30 minutes for rare, 35 for medium-rare, or 45 for well done. If the dough starts to become too brown, cover it loosely with foil. Remove from the oven and let it stand for 10 minutes before serving. Slice with a very sharp knife.

VARIATION

This is undoubtedly an expensive dish for a special occasion, but to save a few pennies, substitute ordinary field mushrooms for button mushrooms. For extra flavor, add a handful of dried wild mushrooms, soaked in boiling water for 30 minutes, then drained and chopped, to the fresh mushrooms.

CALORIES: 662kcals/2764kJ

CARBOHYDRATE: 29g
  sugar: 1.5g

FAT: 41g
  saturated: 19g

SALT: 0.9g

FIBER: 8g

Herb-crusted rack of lamb with red wine sauce

Simple but impressive, and a great centerpiece for a special meal. Double the ingredients to serve more people.

15 mins, plus resting   12–22 mins

SPECIAL EQUIPMENT
food processor

SERVES 4

1½ tbsp olive oil

2 x 6-bone racks of lamb, Frenched

¾ cup fresh bread crumbs

1 tbsp chopped rosemary leaves

2 tbsp chopped flat-leaf parsley leaves

1 tbsp thyme leaves

salt and freshly ground black pepper

2 tbsp Dijon mustard

FOR THE SAUCE

⅔ cup red wine

⅔ cup lamb or beef stock

2 tbsp redcurrant jelly

mashed potatoes and thin green beans, to serve

1 Preheat the oven to 400°F (200°C). Heat the oil in a roasting pan over medium heat and cook the lamb racks for 1 minute on each side, until browned all over. Discard any excess oil and set the meat aside.

2 Put the bread crumbs, herbs, and seasoning in the small bowl of a food processor and process them for a minute, until the herbs turn the bread crumbs bright green. Brush the meaty side of each rack with 1 tbsp of the mustard. Firmly pat half the herb mixture onto the mustard-covered side of each rack. Shake off any excess.

3 Roast the lamb for 10 minutes for rare meat, 15 minutes for medium, and 20 minutes for well done. Let rest, loosely covered with foil, for 5 minutes.

4 To make the sauce, put the wine and stock into a heavy-bottomed saucepan and bring to a boil. Stir in the redcurrant jelly until it has melted, reduce to a low simmer, and cook for 10 minutes until reduced. Season with pepper, to taste.

5 Carve the lamb into chops and serve 3 per person with a little of the sauce, mashed potatoes, and thin green beans.

COOK'S TIP

For the best presentation, cover the Frenched bones with foil before roasting and they will maintain their whiteness and not scorch.

CALORIES: 387kcals/1619kJ

CARBOHYDRATE: 14g
  sugar: 5.5g

FAT: 19g
  saturated: 6g

SALT: 1.2g

FIBER: 0.5g

Whole glazed ham

Buying a pre-cooked ham means that it simply needs to be brought up to a safe temperature to eat.

20 mins   **2½ hrs**

SERVES 8–10

4½lb (2kg) piece of smoked ham

FOR THE GLAZE

3 heaping tbsp smooth marmalade

2 tbsp pineapple juice

1 tbsp honey

1 heaping tbsp light brown sugar

2 tbsp whole grain mustard

salt and freshly ground black pepper

1 Preheat the oven to 325°F (160°C). Put the ham, skin-side up, on a rack inside a large roasting pan, and pour water to a depth of 1in (3cm) into the pan. Cover tightly with foil, making sure it is well sealed so that no steam escapes. Cook for 2 hours.

2 Meanwhile, in a pan, mix the glaze ingredients and bring to a boil. Reduce to a simmer and cook for 5–7 minutes, until thick.

3 Remove the ham from the oven and increase the temperature to 400°F (200°C).

Cut a criss-cross in the fat. Brush some glaze over the top.

4 Return the ham to the oven for 30 minutes, brushing with glaze every 10 minutes until browned and crispy. Serve hot with mashed potatoes and Slow-cooked red cabbage (see p165).

CLEVER WITH LEFTOVERS

This will give you plenty of leftovers. It is a great standby in the holidays when you can serve it cold for days afterward, with baked potatoes, or in sandwiches and omelets.

COOK'S TIP

To cook a larger ham, simply calculate cooking time as 30 minutes per 1lb 2oz (500g) of meat, increasing the temperature for the final 30 minutes.

CALORIES: 362kcals/1527kJ

CARBOHYDRATE: 6g
  sugar: 6g

FAT: 11g
  saturated: 4g

SALT: 5.7g

FIBER: 0g

Chinese roast duck and pancakes

This recipe is likely to become a favorite with all the family; children love to assemble their own pancake rolls.

20 mins   1 hr 10 mins

SERVES 4

4 duck legs

1 heaping tsp five-spice powder

1 tsp coarse sea salt

freshly ground black pepper

1 cucumber

2 bunches of scallions

2 x 4oz packages of Chinese pancakes

12oz jar of hoisin sauce or plum sauce

1 Preheat the oven to 325°F (160°C). Prick the skin of the duck legs all over with a fork. Mix the five-spice powder, salt, and plenty of pepper and rub it all over the legs.

2 Put the duck legs, skin-side up, on a rack inside a roasting pan and cook them for 45 minutes. Then increase the oven temperature to 425°F (220°C) and cook them for another 25 minutes until the skin is crispy and the duck is cooked through.

3 Meanwhile, prepare the vegetables. Cut the cucumber in quarters, lengthwise, then use a teaspoon to scoop the seeds from each piece. Cut each long piece into 4 chunks, then cut each chunk lengthwise into thin strips, so that you are left with a pile of thin cucumber batons. Cut the scallions into thin strips.

4 When the duck is ready, place it on a cutting board and pull both meat and crispy skin from the bones with 2 forks. Keep it warm.

5 Heat the Chinese pancakes according to the package instructions. Serve the duck with the shredded vegetables, pancakes, and the hoisin or plum sauce.

CALORIES: 497kcals/2082kJ

CARBOHYDRATE: 31g
sugar: 17.5g

FAT: 16g
saturated: 3.5g

SALT: 2.3g

FIBER: 3g

Smart with leftovers

In the past, cooking with leftovers would have been a cornerstone of the repertoire of every family cook. For most families, meat products were expensive, and fruits and vegetables available only seasonally, so it made sense to make the most of what you had, when you had it. These days food is much more easily available, and it's easy to feel that we don't have the time or experience to turn the odds and ends in the fridge into another meal. Often we can end up discarding what we cannot easily cook. However, with a few helpful hints you can save time as well as money, and cut back on food waste.

Good things to keep

There are times when it makes sense to deliberately cook more than needed, just for the leftovers. Cold roast meat, a roast chicken carcass with meat left on it, and extra pasta are all worth keeping in the fridge. If cooking extra rice, be sure to cool the leftovers as quickly as possible (ideally within an hour). Only store the leftover rice in the fridge for one day, and make sure it is steaming throughout when reheating. Use leftover meat for salads or sandwiches, and cook up the chicken carcass to make a rich stock (p84). Even leftover vegetables can be added to a soup or stir-fry, and staples like eggs, cheese, and store-bought pastry can help to turn leftovers into delicious dishes in minutes.

Good things to save (and what to turn them into)

⭐ Mashed potatoes (fishcakes, potato pancakes)

⭐ Basmati rice (salads, stir-fries)

⭐ Simple risotto (risotto cakes, involtini)

⭐ Sausages (hearty soups, pasta sauces)

⭐ Cooked bacon (sandwiches, salads)

⭐ Slow-cooked barbecued pork (wraps)

⭐ Croissants, especially the chocolate ones (bread and butter pudding p349)

New dishes from leftovers

Transforming your leftovers into brand new family meals takes only a little effort. Roasts can provide a lot of extra meat to use, and excess rice or potatoes just need the addition of something tasty to produce the next day's supper.

roast pork

Roast pork If you made a hearty Sunday roast you will probably have lots of leftover meat. With the addition of some pantry essentials, you can produce a very tasty Monday night supper, such as Leftover pork chili (p146).

Risotto

Adult meals to toddler dishes

Turn any roast chicken left over from Sunday dinner into a simple supper for the children. Make a pasta casserole using small pasta shapes, the leftover chicken, some Easy cheesy sauce (p34), and a handful of frozen peas.

Mashed potatoes

Risotto The remaining rice from a simple risotto dish can be turned into crispy involtini, such as Mozzarella-stuffed risotto balls (p221), in a matter of minutes. Spread out the leftover rice in a large container so that it dries out well to make it easier to handle the next day.

Leftovers into lunches

Leftover rice, pasta, or even boiled new potatoes can all form the basis of some wonderful portable food, suitable for a lunch box, such as Jeweled rice salad (p218), Potato salad with celery and capers (p158), or Pasta salad with shrimp and pesto (p188).

Mashed potatoes If you know you will need extra mashed potatoes for a recipe such as Smoked haddock fishcakes (p84), make sure you mash the potatoes with almost no added liquid before removing what you will need for the next day.

Soft fruit bruschetta with mascarpone

A quick and impressive dessert that makes the most of seasonal summer fruits.

10 mins, plus macerating　　5 mins

SERVES 4

2 tbsp confectioners' sugar

½ tbsp balsamic vinegar

7oz (200g) strawberries, cut into raspberry-sized chunks

2 ripe peaches, peeled and cut into raspberry-sized chunks

5½oz (150g) raspberries

4 large or 8 small thick slices of brioche or challah bread

2 tbsp butter, softened

7oz (250g) tub of mascarpone

CALORIES: 562kcals/2354kJ

CARBOHYDRATE: 48g
sugar: 27g

FAT: 37g
saturated: 24g

SALT: 0.6g

FIBER: 4.5g

1 In a bowl, mix 1 tbsp of the confectioners' sugar with the vinegar until the sugar has dissolved.

2 Add the strawberries and mix through. Leave to macerate at room temperature for about 30 minutes. Stir in the peaches and raspberries.

3 Meanwhile, spread the slices of brioche with a little butter on both sides and toast them on a preheated grill pan, or under a broiler. Spread thickly with the mascarpone (you may not need the whole tub) and top each evenly with the berry mixture. Dust with the remaining confectioners' sugar and serve immediately.

VARIATION

Omit the berries and use 3–4 peaches instead. Once the brioche is toasted and topped, sprinkle with 1 tbsp dark brown sugar and broil under a hot broiler, or blast with a blowtorch, until glazed.

Summer pudding

Make this classic, elegant dessert when summer fruits are at their best, and serve with cream.

15 mins, plus chilling　　5 mins

SPECIAL EQUIPMENT

1-quart (900ml) pudding mold or bowl

SERVES 4

1¼lb (550g) prepared mixed berries, such as raspberries, redcurrants, strawberries, blackcurrants, or blueberries, plus extra for serving

½ cup granulated sugar

8 thin slices of white bread, crusts cut off

heavy cream, softly whipped, to serve

CALORIES: 266kcals/1131kJ

CARBOHYDRATE: 57g
sugar: 34g

FAT: 1g
saturated: 0.2g

SALT: 0.7g

FIBER: 5g

1 Place the fruit and sugar in a saucepan and add 3 tbsp of water. Heat until simmering and cook for 5 minutes.

2 Line a 1-quart (900ml) pudding mold with 6 slices of the bread. Carefully spoon the fruit and all the juices into the lined bowl and cover with the remaining bread, cutting to fit if necessary. Place a saucer on top and then a 14oz (400g) can to weigh it down. Place in the fridge overnight.

3 Just before serving, remove the saucer and can and place a serving plate over the bowl. Invert the pudding onto the plate and top with a few fresh berries to decorate. Cut into wedges and serve with the heavy cream.

VARIATION

Later in the year, try autumn pudding. Simmer sliced apples for 20 minutes, adding blackberries and the sugar for the last 5 minutes (the total weight of fruit should be 1¼lb/550g).

Raspberry towers

This easy yet impressive dessert is perfect for entertaining and can be assembled at the last minute.

30 mins, plus chilling   35 mins

SPECIAL EQUIPMENT

2¾in (7cm) round cookie cutter

SERVES 4

5 tbsp butter

½ cup granulated sugar

1 large egg yolk

½ tsp vanilla extract

pinch of salt

1 cup all-purpose flour, sifted, plus extra for dusting

¾ cup heavy cream

1 tbsp confectioners' sugar, plus extra for dusting

10oz (300g) raspberries

1 Beat the butter and granulated sugar together until fluffy. Beat in the yolk, vanilla, and salt. Stir in the flour to make a dough. Wrap in plastic wrap and chill for 30 minutes. Preheat the oven to 350°F (180°C).

2 Roll out the dough as thinly as possible on a floured surface and cut out 12 rounds with a 2¾in (7cm) cookie cutter. Any leftover dough can be frozen.

3 Bake for 10 minutes on a baking sheet lined with parchment paper until golden at the edges. Leave on the pan for a couple of minutes, then transfer to a wire rack to cool completely.

4 Whip the cream with the confectioners' sugar until stiff. Spread a spoonful of cream on a cookie and cover with raspberries. Take a second cookie and spread a thin layer of cream underneath. Stick it on top. Repeat, finishing the tower with the nicest-looking cookie. Dust with confectioners' sugar to serve.

CLEVER WITH LEFTOVERS

Purée extra fruit with 1 tbsp confectioners' sugar and pass through a nylon sieve to make a sauce to serve with the Raspberry towers.

HOW TO FREEZE

Any uncooked dough can be wrapped in plastic wrap and frozen for up to 12 weeks. Defrost thoroughly before baking.

CALORIES: 687kcals/2871kJ

CARBOHYDRATE: 65g
  sugar: 40g

FAT: 44g
  saturated: 27g

SALT: 0.6g

FIBER: 4g

Warm winter fruit salad

There's no need to miss out on fresh fruits in fall or winter; try them warm with a sweet syrup.

20 mins   35 mins

⅓ cup granulated sugar

⅔ cup red wine

finely grated zest and juice of 1 orange, plus 2 oranges, peeled and sliced into rounds

1 cinnamon stick

2 ripe pears, quartered, cored, and peeled

4 plums, halved and pitted

1 Place the sugar in a medium, heavy-bottomed pan and add 1¼ cups of water. Place over medium-low heat to dissolve the sugar. When it has all completely dissolved, increase the heat and bring it to a boil, then reduce the heat once more and simmer for 10 minutes.

2 Add the wine, orange zest and juice, and cinnamon stick to the pan and bring to a boil.

3 Reduce the heat and add the pears and plums. Cover and simmer over medium heat for

10 minutes, or until the fruit is tender (test by piercing a big piece with a knife; it should meet no resistance). Stir in the orange slices.

4 Carefully remove the fruit from the pan using a slotted spoon, taking as little liquid as possible with the pieces, and set aside in a serving dish.

5 Boil the syrup over high heat for 10 minutes to reduce it; it should thicken slightly. Remove the cinnamon stick from the syrup and pour it over the fruit. Serve warm or at room temperature.

CALORIES: 193kcals/819kJ

CARBOHYDRATE: 39g
  sugar: 40g

FAT: 0g
  saturated: 0g

SALT: trace

FIBER: 4.5g

Cherry and almond clafoutis

This French classic is easy to rustle up from a few pantry and fridge essentials.

15 mins   30-35 mins

SPECIAL EQUIPMENT

11 x 8 x 2in (28 x 20 x 5cm) ovenproof dish

electric hand-held mixer

SERVES 4

2 tbsp butter, melted, plus extra for greasing

2 large eggs

¼ cup vanilla or granulated sugar

2 tbsp all-purpose flour, sifted

½ cup whole milk

1 x 14oz (440g) can pitted black cherries in syrup, drained

1oz (30g) sliced almonds

sifted confectioners' sugar and whipped cream, to serve

CALORIES: 267kcals/1122kJ

CARBOHYDRATE: 29g
  sugar: 26g

FAT: 14g
  saturated: 5g

SALT: 0.3g

FIBER: 0.8g

---

1 Preheat the oven to 350°F (180°C). Butter a 11 x 8 x 2in (28 x 20 x 5cm) ovenproof dish.

2 Place the eggs and vanilla sugar or granulated sugar in a large bowl and whisk with an electric hand-held mixer until light and fluffy, then fold in the flour. Pour in the melted butter and whisk until well combined. Add the milk and stir well.

3 Arrange the cherries in the ovenproof dish and pour the batter over. Sprinkle the almonds on top and place the dish on a baking sheet.

4 Bake for 30–35 minutes, until risen and golden brown. Dust with confectioners' sugar and serve with whipped cream.

VARIATION

In the summer, when fresh berries are cheap and plentiful, use these instead. Try raspberries, blackcurrants, blueberries, or blackberries instead of the canned cherries.

Apricot clafoutis

Canned apricots taste just fine in this French favorite, when fresh are out of season.

10 mins   35 mins, plus cooling

SERVES 4

unsalted butter, for greasing

9oz (250g) ripe apricots, halved and pitted, or 1 x 14oz (400g) can apricot halves, drained

1 large egg, plus 1 large egg yolk

2 tbsp all-purpose flour, sifted

¼ cup granulated sugar

⅔ cup heavy cream

¼ tsp vanilla extract

thick cream or crème fraîche, to serve (optional)

CALORIES: 322kcals/1342kJ

CARBOHYDRATE: 21g
  sugar: 17.5g

FAT: 24g
  saturated: 14g

SALT: 0.1g

FIBER: 2g

---

1 Preheat the oven to 400°F (200°C). Lightly grease a baking dish that is big enough to fit the apricots in a single layer. Place the apricots in a single layer in the dish; there should be space between them.

2 In a bowl, whisk together the egg, egg yolk, and the flour. Whisk in the granulated sugar. Finally add the cream and vanilla extract and whisk thoroughly to form a smooth custard.

3 Pour the custard around the apricots, so the tops are just visible. Bake on the top rack of the oven for 35 minutes, until puffed up and lightly golden brown in places. Remove and let cool for at least 15 minutes before eating. It is best served warm with thick cream or crème fraîche.

PREPARE AHEAD

The clafoutis is best when it's freshly baked and served warm, but it can be cooked up to 6 hours ahead and served at room temperature.

Summer fruits with easy "brûlée" topping

This simple little trick can turn a luscious fruit salad into something far more special.

10 mins, plus resting and chilling

SERVES 4–6

14oz (400g) mixed soft summer fruits, such as strawberries, raspberries, peaches, or blueberries

2½ tbsp granulated sugar

¾ cup (7oz) heavy cream

¾ cup (7oz) Greek yogurt

1 tsp vanilla extract

4 heaping tbsp brown sugar, plus extra if needed

1 Make a fruit salad by cutting the fruit into similar-sized chunks, about ½in (1cm), or the same size as your smallest fruit, discarding the peach pits, if using. Mix in 1 tbsp of the granulated sugar and leave to macerate, at room temperature, for 1 hour.

2 Whisk together the cream and remaining granulated sugar until it is thick. Gently fold in the Greek yogurt and vanilla extract until well combined and chill until needed.

3 When the fruit is ready, spread it out in a large shallow bowl and cover it with a thick layer of the whipped cream mixture. Sprinkle in the brown sugar as evenly as possibly, until there is a thin, even layer all over the cream, and you cannot see it underneath. You may need a little more sugar, depending on the diamater of your serving bowl.

4 Chill the fruit salad in the fridge for 30 minutes, until the sugar has dissolved and there are no granules left.

COOK'S TIP

It is often hard to measure thick liquids. As a guide, ¾ cup of Greek yogurt will weigh about 7oz (200g), so weigh the yogurt if you find it easier.

CALORIES: 274kcals/1141kJ
CARBOHYDRATE: 21g
 sugar: 21g
FAT: 20g
 saturated: 13g
SALT: 0.2g
FIBER: 1.5g

Mango kulfi

This Indian-inspired iced dessert can also be made into child-sized popsicles, using a popsicle mold and sticks.

15–20 mins, plus freezing   5 mins

SPECIAL EQUIPMENT

blender or food processor

4 x 5fl oz (150ml) ramekins or popsicle molds

SERVES 4

⅔ cup whipping cream

6 cardamom pods, crushed

pinch of saffron strands

¾ cup sweetened condensed milk

2 ripe mangoes, flesh only, roughly chopped

1¾oz (50g) pistachio nuts, roughly chopped (optional)

CALORIES: 420kcals/1762kJ
CARBOHYDRATE: 37g
 sugar: 37g
FAT: 26g
 saturated: 13g
SALT: 0.2g
FIBER: 2.5g

1 Put the cream, cardamom, and saffron in a small saucepan and gently heat for 5 minutes. Remove from the heat and let cool.

2 Put the condensed milk and mango into a blender or food processor and strain the cream into it through a sieve or tea strainer. Blend until completely smooth. Press through a sieve if you want to make sure there are no stray lumps, but this is not essential.

3 Scatter the bottom of four 5fl oz (150ml) cup ramekins or popsicle molds with a few chopped pistachios (if using), then pour in the kulfi mixture and freeze at least overnight, or until needed.

4 To serve, fill a bowl with hot water and carefully dip the bottom of each ramekin or popsicle briefly into the water to loosen the kulfi. Be careful not to allow the water to drip onto the kulfi. Run a small knife around the edge of each ramekin, and turn the kulfi onto individual serving plates, or simply remove from the popsicle molds and serve.

Strawberry semifreddo

This frozen dessert is a delicious alternative to simply eating strawberries with cream and sugar.

20 mins, plus freezing

SPECIAL EQUIPMENT

20cm (8in) springform tin

blender or food processor

SERVES 6–8

vegetable oil, for greasing

8oz (225g) strawberries, hulled, plus extra whole strawberries, to decorate

1 cup heavy cream

½ cup confectioners' sugar

4oz (115g) meringues, coarsely crushed

3 tbsp raspberry liqueur

redcurrants, to serve

FOR THE COULIS

8oz (225g) strawberries, hulled

¼–½ cup confectioners' sugar

1–2 tsp lemon juice, brandy, grappa, or balsamic vinegar, to taste

CALORIES: 282kcals/1177kJ

CARBOHYDRATE: 28g
  of which sugar: 28g

FAT: 17g
  of which saturates: 10g

SALT: 0.1g

FIBER: 0.8g

1 Lightly brush a 8in (20cm) springform pan with vegetable oil, then line the bottom with waxed paper and set aside.

2 Purée the strawberries in a blender or food processor. Whip the cream and confectioners' sugar until it holds its shape. Fold the strawberry purée and cream together, then fold in the crushed meringues and liqueur. Turn the mixture into the pan, smooth the surface, cover with plastic wrap, and freeze for at least 6 hours.

3 To make the coulis, purée the strawberries in a blender or food processor, then press through a fine nylon sieve to remove the seeds. Stir in ¼ cup confectioners' sugar and taste for sweetness, adding more sugar if necessary. Flavor with the lemon juice to taste.

4 Just before serving, remove the semifreddo from the pan, peel away the paper, and slice with a warmed knife. Serve with the coulis, and decorate with whole strawberries and redcurrants.

HOW TO FREEZE

This can be stored in the freezer for up to 3 months. It's best to seal it securely with foil if keeping for longer than 1 week.

Quick banana ice cream

This is the quickest and easiest ice cream you will ever make and it's super healthy, too!

5 mins, plus freezing

SPECIAL EQUIPMENT

food processor

SERVES 4

4 ripe bananas

1 tsp vanilla extract

1 Simply peel the bananas, chop them into ¾in (2cm) chunks, and put them in a freezer container. Seal, and put in the freezer until frozen.

2 When the bananas are frozen solid, process them in a food processor with the vanilla extract, until you have a smooth, thick ice cream. You may need to scrape down the sides a couple of times during the process.

3 Either eat the softened banana ice cream immediately, or freeze for a few minutes for it to firm up once more before serving.

VARIATION

A few spoonfuls of chocolate and hazelnut spread, or smooth peanut butter, added to the food processor works well here, too.

CLEVER WITH LEFTOVERS

If you have ripening bananas that you can't use up quickly enough, peel them, cut into chunks, and freeze on a plate. When they are frozen solid, transfer to a freezer bag and add more bananas until you have enough to make this ice cream.

CALORIES: 119kcals/504kJ

CARBOHYDRATE: 27g
  of which sugar: 25g

FAT: 0g
  of which saturates: 0g

SALT: trace

FIBER: 2g

Quick chocolate and hazelnut ice cream

This is another quick ice cream that does not rely on the traditional custard base of other recipes.

5 mins, plus churning and freezing

SPECIAL EQUIPMENT

blender or food processor

ice-cream maker

SERVES 4

1 cup whole milk

1 cup heavy whipping cream

10oz (300g) chocolate and hazelnut spread

1 tsp vanilla extract

1 Simply puree all the ingredients in a blender or food processor to a smooth, thick liquid.

2 Pour the ice-cream base slowly into an ice-cream maker and churn it until it is a thick, scoopable ice cream.

3 Transfer it to a plastic container and freeze until needed.

CLEVER WITH LEFTOVERS

If you have a jar of chocolate and hazelnut spread that you cannot use up quickly enough, try it in this delicious ice cream recipe.

CARLORIES: 701kcals/2916kJ

CARBOHYDRATE: 45g
of which sugar: 45g

FAT: 55g
of which saturates: 17g

SALT: 0.1g

FIBER: 0g

Classic vanilla ice cream

It's hard to beat a classic vanilla ice cream! This is the perfect accompaniment to so many pies and tarts.

10 mins, plus chilling and churning   5-10 mins

SPECIAL EQUIPMENT

ice-cream maker

SERVES 4

1 cup heavy whipping cream

2 cups whole milk

6 large egg yolks

½ cup granulated sugar

1 tsp vanilla extract

1 Heat the cream and milk in a heavy-bottomed saucepan over a medium heat, until hot, but not boiling.

2 Whisk together the egg yolks, sugar, and vanilla extract. Very gradually whisk the hot cream and milk into the egg mixture in a thin stream, whisking constantly.

3 Return the custard to the rinsed-out pan and heat over a medium heat, whisking constantly, until it thickens and just coats the back of a spoon. Do not heat it too fast or for too long, or the eggs will "scramble" in the custard. Take it off the heat and transfer it to a cold bowl immediately, continuing to whisk for a couple of minutes in order to cool it down.

4 Cool the custard completely, then cover the surface with a layer of plastic wrap (placing it directly on the custard) to prevent a skin from forming. Transfer it to the fridge and chill it for a minimum of 4 hours, or overnight.

5 Pour the chilled custard into an ice-cream maker and churn it until it is a thick, scoopable ice cream. Transfer it to a plastic container and freeze until needed.

PREPARE AHEAD

The custard needs to be thoroughly chilled before churning, so you can make it up to a day ahead and keep it in the fridge until you make the ice cream.

CALORIES: 522kcals/2176kJ

CARBOHYDRATE: 38g
of which sugar: 38g

FAT: 37g
of which saturates: 20g

SALT: 0.2g

FIBER: 0g

Blueberry ripple ice cream

Vitamin-rich blueberries make a lovely sweet, colorful ripple to swirl through homemade vanilla ice cream.

20 mins, plus chilling and churning   5–10 mins

SPECIAL EQUIPMENT
blender or food processor
ice-cream maker

SERVES 4

1 cup whipping cream

2 cups whole milk

6 large egg yolks

½ cup granulated sugar

1 tsp vanilla extract

FOR THE RIPPLE

3½oz (100g) blueberries

2 tbsp granulated sugar

1 Heat the cream and milk in a heavy-bottomed saucepan until hot, but not boiling.

2 Whisk together the egg yolks, sugar, and vanilla. Gradually whisk the hot cream and milk into the egg mixture in a thin stream.

3 Return the custard to the rinsed-out pan and heat over medium heat, whisking constantly, until it just coats the back of a spoon. Do not heat it too fast or the eggs will "scramble." Transfer to a cold bowl, whisking to cool it.

4 Cool the custard completely, then cover the surface with a layer of plastic wrap (placing it directly on the custard). Chill it for at least 4 hours, or overnight.

5 Meanwhile, make the blueberry ripple by putting the blueberries and sugar in a small saucepan and cooking over low heat for 3–4 minutes until the fruit softens, stirring once or twice. Put the mixture in a blender or food processor, blend until completely smooth, then pass it through a nylon sieve into a bowl to get rid of the tiny blueberry seeds. Let cool.

6 Pour the chilled custard into an ice-cream maker and churn until it is a thick, scoopable ice cream. Transfer the ice cream to a wide, shallow plastic container and pour the ripple over the surface in thick, irregular lines. Use a chopstick to swirl it through the ice cream. Freeze until needed.

VARIATION

To make butterscotch ripple, melt 2 tbsp unsalted butter in a small, heavy-bottomed saucepan. Take it off the heat and whisk in ¼ cup dark brown sugar until combined. Whisk in ⅓ heavy cream, a pinch of salt, and ¼ tsp vanilla extract. Bring it to a boil, then reduce to a low simmer. Simmer gently for 5 minutes. Let cool. Add to the ice cream as in the main recipe at step 6 (see left).

CALORIES: 566kcals/2362kJ

CARBOHYDRATE: 48g
sugar: 48g

FAT: 37g
saturated: 20g

SALT: 0.2g

FIBER: 0.5g

Raspberry meringue ice cream

This light yet rich ice cream truly tastes like summer in a bowl. Make it when the berries are cheap and plentiful.

20 mins, plus chilling and churning

5-10 mins

SPECIAL EQUIPMENT
blender or food processor
ice-cream maker

SERVES 4

1 cup whipping cream

2 cups whole milk

6 large egg yolks

½ cup granulated sugar

1 tsp vanilla extract

FOR THE RIPPLE

3½oz (100g) raspberries

2 tbsp granulated sugar

¾oz (20g) meringues (approx. 2 pre-made meringue nests)

1 Heat the cream and milk in a heavy-bottomed saucepan over medium heat until hot, but not boiling.

2 Whisk together the egg yolks, sugar, and vanilla extract. Very gradually whisk the hot cream and milk into the egg mixture in a thin stream, whisking constantly.

3 Return the custard to the rinsed-out pan and heat over medium heat, whisking constantly, until it thickens and just coats the back of a spoon. Do not heat it too fast or for too long, or the eggs will "scramble" in the custard. Take it off the heat and transfer it to a cold bowl immediately, continuing to whisk for a couple of minutes to cool it down a little.

4 Cool the custard completely, then cover the surface with a layer of plastic wrap (placing it directly on the surface) to prevent a skin from forming. Transfer it to the fridge and chill it for a minimum of 4 hours, or overnight.

5 Meanwhile, make the raspberry ripple by putting the raspberries, sugar, and 1 tbsp of water in a blender or food processor. Blend until completely smooth, then pass it through a nylon sieve to get rid of any seeds. Put the meringues into a plastic bag and smash them with a rolling pin to make small "pebbles" of meringue.

6 Pour the chilled custard into an ice-cream maker and churn it until it is a thick, scoopable ice cream.

7 Transfer the ice cream to a wide, shallow plastic container and stir in the meringue pieces, being sure to distribute them fairly evenly. Pour the ripple over the surface in thick irregular lines. Use a chopstick to swirl it through the ice cream. Freeze until needed.

VARIATION

Substitute the raspberries with strawberries for the British Eton mess combination in an ice cream.

CALORIES: 577kcals/2410kJ
CARBOHYDRATE: 50g
  sugar: 50g
FAT: 37g
  saturated: 20g
SALT: 0.2g
FIBER: 0.8g

Rocky road ice-cream pie

A great dessert to serve in hot weather with chocolate ice cream and nuts, making it the ultimate sweet treat.

20 mins, plus cooling, chilling, and freezing

10 mins

SPECIAL EQUIPMENT
food processor

9in (22cm) loose-bottomed, fluted tart pan

SERVES 8

FOR THE COOKIE CRUST
9oz (250g) vanilla wafers

¼ cup granulated sugar

8 tbsp butter, melted and cooled

FOR THE FILLING
1 liter (1¾ pints) good-quality chocolate ice cream

1oz (30g) mini marshmallows

1¾oz (50g) pecans, roughly chopped

1¾oz (50g) blanched almonds, roughly chopped

CALORIES: 654kcals/2731kJ

CARBOHYDRATE: 50g
    sugar: 34g

FAT: 46g
    saturated: 23g

SALT: 0.7g

FIBER: 0.4g

1 Preheat the oven to 350°F (180°C). To make the cookie crust, crush the wafers by hand or in a food processor. Mix with the sugar and melted butter until it resembles wet sand.

2 Pour the wafer mixture into a 9in (22cm) loose-bottomed, fluted tart pan and press it firmly into the bottom and sides. Make sure the mixture is as packed as possible and that it climbs at least 1¼in (3cm) up the sides of the pan. Bake for 10 minutes, then set aside to cool. Once cold, cover and store in the fridge until needed.

3 For the filling, transfer the ice cream to the fridge 15 minutes before needed, to allow it to soften. Spoon it into a food processor (don't put the whole block in as it will be too hard to break down). Process until creamy and smooth. Scrape it into a bowl and fold in most of the marshmallows and nuts. Pour into the prepared crust and freeze for 1 hour, or until firm.

4 To serve the ice-cream pie, remove it from the freezer and leave it in the fridge for 20–30 minutes to soften before serving, scattered with the remaining marshmallows and nuts.

Blackberry and apple pie

A sweet apple would work well here, but tart Granny Smiths give a good flavor to this pie.

35-40 mins, plus chilling

50-60 mins

SPECIAL EQUIPMENT
1-quart (1-liter) pie dish

pie funnel

SERVES 4-6

1½ cups all-purpose flour, plus extra for dusting

1½ tbsp granulated sugar

¼ tsp salt

3 tbsp lard or white vegetable shortening, chilled and cut into cubes

4 tbsp unsalted butter, chilled and cut into cubes

FOR THE FILLING
1lb 15oz (875g) Granny Smith apples, peeled, cored, and cut into cubes

juice of 1 lemon

¾ cup granulated sugar, or to taste

1lb 2oz (500g) blackberries

CALORIES: 462kcals/1953kJ

CARBOHYDRATE: 73g
    sugar: 49g

FAT: 16g
    saturated: 8.5g

SALT: 0.2g

FIBER: 8g

1 Sift the flour, sugar, and salt into a bowl. Add the lard and butter and rub together until crumbs form. Sprinkle in water, 1 tbsp at a time, stopping as soon as clumps form. Press lightly into a ball, wrap in plastic wrap, and chill for 30 minutes.

2 Put the apples in a bowl, add the lemon juice and all but 2 tbsp of the sugar, and toss. Add the blackberries and toss again.

3 Roll out the dough on a floured surface. Cut off a ¾in (2cm) strip that will reach around the rim of a 1-quart (1-liter) pie dish. Roll the rest out to 3in (7.5cm) larger in diameter than the dish. Place a pie funnel or upturned ovenproof cup in the dish. Spoon the fruit around.

4 Moisten the rim of the dish with water and press on the strip of dough. Brush it with water and press on the pie top. Cut a hole over the funnel and trim the edges. Chill for 15 minutes. Preheat the oven to 375°F (190°C). Bake for 50–60 minutes. Sprinkle with the remaining sugar to serve.

PREPARE AHEAD
The dough can be made up to 2 days ahead, wrapped in plastic wrap, and kept in the fridge until needed.

Pumpkin pie

This is a delicate version of the classic dessert, with warm tones of cinnamon and pumpkin pie spice.

30 mins, plus chilling

1–1¼ hrs

SPECIAL EQUIPMENT
food processor (optional)

9in (22cm) loose-bottomed tart pan

baking beans

SERVES 6–8

1 cup all-purpose flour, plus extra for dusting

7 tbsp unsalted butter, chilled and cut into cubes

¼ cup granulated sugar

1 large egg yolk

½ tsp vanilla extract

FOR THE FILLING

3 large eggs

½ cup light brown sugar

1 tsp ground cinnamon

1 tsp pumpkin pie spice

¾ cup heavy cream

1 x 14oz (425g) can processed pumpkin, or 14oz (400g) roasted and puréed pumpkin

thick cream or vanilla ice cream, to serve (optional)

1 To make the dough, rub together the flour and butter, or pulse-blend in a food processor, to form fine crumbs. Stir in the sugar. Beat together the egg yolk and vanilla. Mix into the dry ingredients to form a soft dough, adding a little water if needed. Wrap in plastic wrap and chill for 1 hour.

2 Preheat the oven to 350°F (180°C). Roll out the dough on a floured surface to a thickness of ⅛in (3mm). It will be fragile, so if it starts to crumble, bring it together with your hands and knead it gently to get rid of any cracks. Use it to line a 9in (22cm) loose-bottomed tart pan, leaving an overlapping edge of at least ¾in (2cm). Prick the bottom all over with a fork. Line the crust with parchment paper and weigh it down with baking beans.

3 Place the crust on a baking sheet and blind-bake it for 20 minutes. Remove the beans and paper; if the center looks damp, or raw, which means it is uncooked, return it to the oven for 5 minutes.

4 For the filling, in a large bowl, whisk together the eggs, sugar, spices, and cream. When they are well blended, beat in the canned or puréed pumpkin to make a smooth filling. Partially pull out an oven rack from the center of the oven and place the crust on it. Pour the filling into the crust and slide the rack back into the oven.

5 Bake for 45–50 minutes until the filling is quite set, but before it begins to bubble up at the edges. Trim the dough edge with a small, sharp knife while still warm, then leave the pie to cool in its pan for at least 15 minutes before turning out. Serve warm with thick cream or vanilla ice cream.

PREPARE AHEAD

The blind-baked, unfilled crust can be stored in an airtight container for up to 3 days, or frozen for up to 12 weeks.

CALORIES: 320kcals/1337kJ

CARBOHYDRATE: 21g
  sugar: 8g

FAT: 25g
  saturated: 15g

SALT: 0.1g

FIBER: 1.5g

Banoffee pie

This version of the modern classic is incredibly rich and sweet, just as it should be, and is great for a party.

20 mins, plus chilling | 5 mins

SPECIAL EQUIPMENT
9in (22cm) round springform cake pan or loose-bottomed tart pan

SERVES 6–8

9oz (250g) vanilla wafers

7 tbsp unsalted butter, melted and cooled

FOR THE CARAMEL

4 tbsp unsalted butter

¼ cup light brown sugar

1 x 14oz (400g) can condensed milk

FOR THE TOPPING

2 large, ripe bananas

1 cup heavy cream

a little dark chocolate, for grating

CALORIES: 665kcals/2785kJ

CARBOHYDRATE: 60g
   sugar: 44g

FAT: 44g
   saturated: 27g

SALT: 0.7g

FIBER: 0.6g

---

1 Line a 9in (22cm) round springform cake pan or loose-bottomed tart pan with parchment paper. Put the wafers in a plastic bag and crush with a rolling pin. Mix the wafers with the butter, pour into the pan, and press down. Cover and refrigerate.

2 To make the caramel, melt the butter and sugar in a small, heavy-bottomed saucepan over medium heat. Add the condensed milk and bring to a boil. Reduce the heat and simmer for 2–3 minutes, stirring. It will thicken and take on a light caramel color. Pour over the bottom and leave to set.

3 Once set, remove from the pan and transfer to a serving plate. Slice the bananas diagonally into ¼in (5mm) disks and use them to cover the caramel.

4 Whip the cream and smooth it over the pie. Decorate with grated chocolate and chocolate curls, made by peeling chocolate with a vegetable peeler.

PREPARE AHEAD

The pie will keep in an airtight container in the refrigerator for 2 days, and can be frozen for up to 8 weeks.

Cherry lattice pie

Here, the classic cherry pie is topped with a decorative latticed crust.

40–45 mins, plus chilling | 20–25 mins

SPECIAL EQUIPMENT
9in (23cm) loose-bottomed flan pan

SERVES 8

FOR THE DOUGH

2 cups all-purpose flour, plus extra for dusting

1 tsp salt

1 cup lard or white vegetable shortening, chilled and cut into cubes

5 tbsp unsalted butter, chilled and cut into cubes

1 large egg, to glaze

FOR THE FILLING

1lb 2oz (500g) cherries, pitted

¾ cup granulated sugar

3 tbsp all-purpose flour

¼ tsp almond extract (optional)

CALORIES: 474kcals/1992kJ

CARBOHYDRATE: 58g
   sugar: 33g

FAT: 25g
   saturated: 12g

SALT: 0.6g

FIBER: 2.5g

---

1 To make the dough, sift the flour and ½ tsp salt into a bowl. Rub the lard and butter into the flour with your fingertips, until the mixture resembles bread crumbs. Sprinkle with 3 tbsp water and mix until the dough forms a ball. Wrap in plastic wrap and chill for 30 minutes.

2 Preheat the oven to 400°F (200°C) and put in a baking sheet. Roll out two-thirds of the dough on a floured surface and use to line a 9in (23cm) loose-bottomed flan pan with some dough hanging over the edge. Press the dough into the dish and chill for 15 minutes.

3 For the filling, place the cherries in a bowl and add the sugar, flour, and almond extract (if using). Stir until well mixed, then spoon into the pan.

4 Roll out the remaining dough into a rectangle. Cut out 11 strips, each ½in (1cm) wide, and arrange them in a lattice pattern on top of the pie. Trim the edges of the dough. Beat the egg and use this to glaze the lattice and to secure the strips to the edge of the pie. Bake for 20–25 minutes until the dough is golden brown. Serve at room temperature or chilled.

Apple pie

Perhaps the ultimate in home-baked comfort food, this fall pie is best served warm with vanilla ice cream.

30–35 mins, plus chilling   50–55 mins

SPECIAL EQUIPMENT

9in (23cm) shallow pie dish

SERVES 6–8

2½ cups all-purpose flour, plus extra for dusting

½ tsp salt

1¼ cups chilled lard or white vegetable shortening, plus extra for greasing

2 tbsp granulated sugar, plus extra for sprinkling

1 tbsp milk, for glazing

FOR THE FILLING

2¼lb (1kg) tart apples

juice of 1 lemon

2 tbsp all-purpose flour

½ tsp ground cinnamon, or to taste

¼ tsp grated nutmeg, or to taste

½ cup granulated sugar, or to taste

1 Sift the flour and salt into a bowl. Add the lard, cutting it in with 2 butter knives. With your fingertips, rub the fat into the flour until crumbs form, lifting the mixture to aerate it. Add the sugar. Sprinkle with 6–7 tbsp of cold water and mix it in with a fork.

2 Press the crumbs into a ball, wrap, and chill for 30 minutes. Meanwhile, grease a 9in (23cm) shallow pie dish. Flour a work surface. Roll two-thirds of the dough out to a round, 2in (5cm) larger than the diameter of the dish. Using the rolling pin, drape the dough over the dish, then gently push it into the contours. Trim any excess dough, then chill for 15 minutes until firm.

3 For the filling, peel the apples, quarter, and cut out the cores. Set each quarter, cut-side down, on a cutting board and cut into evenly sized thin slices.

4 Put the apple slices in a bowl and pour in the lemon juice. Toss to coat. Sprinkle the flour, cinnamon, nutmeg, and sugar over the apples and toss again to coat. Put the apple in the pie dish and arrange so that they are slightly mounded in the center.

5 Brush the rim of the dough with water. Roll the rest of the dough to an 11in (28cm) round. Wrap it around the rolling pin and drape it over the filling. Trim the top crust and press the edges together to seal, crimping them with the back of a knife as you go.

6 Cut an "x" in the top crust and gently pull back the point of each triangle to reveal the filling. Roll out the trimmings, then cut into strips and moisten. Lay over the pie crust in a criss-cross pattern. Brush the pie with the milk so that it bakes to a golden color. Sprinkle with sugar and chill for 30 minutes.

7 Meanwhile, preheat the oven to 425°F (220°C). Bake for 20 minutes. Reduce to 350°F (180°C) and bake for 30–35 minutes. Insert a skewer through the steam vent to make sure the apples are tender (it should meet no resistance). Serve warm.

HOW TO FREEZE

The pie can be assembled, wrapped in plastic wrap, then sealed well with foil. This way, it can be frozen for up to 12 weeks and is the perfect way to preserve a glut of apples at harvest time. Defrost the pie thoroughly and bake as in step 7.

CALORIES: 492kcals/2072kJ
CARBOHYDRATE: 73g
  sugar: 40g
FAT: 19g
  saturated: 8g
SALT: 0.5g
FIBER: 5g

Lemon meringue pie

The sharpness of lemon combined with a vanilla meringue topping makes this pie a legendary family favorite.

30 mins   40–50 mins

SPECIAL EQUIPMENT

9in (23cm) loose-bottomed tart pan

baking beans

SERVES 8

3 tbsp butter, cut into cubes, plus extra for greasing

14oz (400g) store-bought pie dough

3 tbsp all-purpose flour, plus extra for dusting

6 large eggs, at room temperature, separated

3 tbsp cornstarch

1½ cups granulated sugar

juice of 3 lemons

1 tbsp finely grated lemon zest

½ tsp cream of tartar

½ tsp vanilla extract

1 Preheat the oven to 400°F (200°C). Lightly grease a 9in (23cm) loose-bottomed tart pan. Roll out the dough on a floured surface and use it to line the pan.

2 Line the dough with parchment paper, then fill with baking beans. Place on a baking sheet and bake for 10–15 minutes or until pale golden. Remove the paper and beans and bake for 5 minutes until golden all over. Reduce the oven temperature to 350°F (180°C). Let the crust cool slightly.

3 Place the egg yolks in a bowl and lightly beat. Combine the cornstarch, flour, and 1 cup of the sugar in a saucepan. Slowly add 1½ cups of water and heat gently, stirring, until the sugar dissolves and there are no lumps. Increase the heat slightly and stir for 3–5 minutes, or until the mixture starts to thicken.

4 Beat several spoonfuls of the hot mixture into the egg yolks. Pour this back into the pan and slowly bring to a boil, stirring. Boil for 3 minutes, then stir in the lemon juice, zest, and butter. Boil for another 2 minutes or until thick and glossy, stirring constantly. Remove the pan from the heat; cover to keep warm.

5 Whisk the egg whites in a large bowl until foamy. Sprinkle in the cream of tartar and whisk, adding the remaining sugar 1 tbsp at a time. Add the vanilla with the last of the sugar, whisking until thick and glossy.

6 Place the crust on a baking sheet, pour in the lemon filling, then top with the meringue, spreading it to cover the filling up to the crust edge. Be careful not to spill it over the dough, or the tart will be hard to remove from the pan.

7 Bake for 12–15 minutes, or until lightly golden. Transfer to a wire rack and cool completely. Turn out of the pan to serve.

COOK'S TIP

If you are not careful, the meringue topping can slide around on top of the lemon filling. Make sure it is touching the crust around the entire pie before baking, to stop it from dislodging.

CALORIES: 578kcals/2431kJ

CARBOHYDRATE: 81g
  sugar: 53g

FAT: 24g
  saturated: 9g

SALT: 0.7g

FIBER: 1.5g

Tarte aux pommes

This French classic uses both cooking apples that stew down to a purée and dessert apples that keep their shape.

20 mins, plus chilling

50-55 mins

SPECIAL EQUIPMENT

9in (22cm) loose-bottomed tart pan
baking beans

MAKES 8 SLICES

14oz (375g) store-bought pie dough

all-purpose flour, for dusting

4 tbsp unsalted butter

1lb 10oz (750g) Gala apples, peeled, cored, and chopped

½ cup granulated sugar

finely grated zest and juice of ½ lemon

2 tbsp Calvados or brandy

2 Granny Smith apples

2 tbsp apricot jam, sieved, for glazing

1 Roll the dough out on a floured surface to ⅛in (3mm) thick and use it to line a 9in (22cm) loose-bottomed tart pan, leaving an overlap of at least ¾in (2cm). Prick with a fork. Chill for 30 minutes.

2 Preheat the oven to 400°F (200°C). Line the dough with parchment paper and baking beans. Bake for 15 minutes. Remove the paper and beans, then bake for 5 minutes until golden.

3 Meanwhile, melt the butter in a saucepan and add the Gala apples. Cover and cook over low heat, stirring occasionally, for 15 minutes, or until soft and mushy.

4 Push the cooked apple through a nylon sieve to make a smooth purée, then return it to the saucepan.

Reserve 1 tbsp of granulated sugar and add the rest to the apple purée. Stir in the lemon zest and Calvados or brandy. Return it to the heat and simmer, stirring, until it thickens.

5 Spoon the purée into the crust. Peel, core, and thinly slice the Granny Smith apples and arrange in concentric circles on top of the purée. Brush with the lemon juice and sprinkle with the reserved granulated sugar.

6 Bake for 30–35 minutes, or until the apple slices have softened and are turning golden. Use a small, sharp knife to trim the excess dough for a neat edge.

7 Warm the apricot jam and brush it over the top. Cut into slices and serve.

COOK'S TIP

A glaze will make any homemade fruit tart look as appetizing as those in a bake shop. Apricot jam works well for apples and pears, but for a red fruit tart brush with warmed redcurrant jelly. Press jam through a sieve before using as a glaze, to remove any lumps of fruit.

PREPARE AHEAD

The tart will keep in an airtight container for up to 2 days. Reheat at 350°F (180°C) for 15 minutes before serving.

CALORIES: 365kcals/1534kJ

CARBOHYDRATE: 45g
    sugar: 25g

FAT: 18g
    saturated: 7.5g

SALT: 0.5g

FIBER: 2.5g

Tarte Tatin

This tart is named after two French sisters, who earned a living by baking their father's favorite apple tart.

45-50 mins, plus chilling   35-50 mins

SPECIAL EQUIPMENT
food processor with dough hook
9-10in (23-25cm) ovenproof pan

SERVES 8

1¾ cups all-purpose flour, plus extra for dusting

2 large egg yolks

1½ tbsp granulated sugar

pinch of salt

5 tbsp unsalted butter, softened

FOR THE FILLING

8 tbsp butter

1¼ cups granulated sugar

14-16 apples, approx 5½lb (2.4kg) in total

1 lemon

crème fraîche, to serve (optional)

CALORIES: 523kcals/2208kJ
CARBOHYDRATE: 75g
  sugar: 60g
FAT: 27g
  saturated: 14g
SALT: 0.2g
FIBER: 9g

1 For the dough, sift the flour into a food processor fitted with a dough hook and add all the other ingredients with 1 tbsp of water. Work the ingredients together until they form a ball. Wrap in plastic wrap and chill for 30 minutes until firm.

2 For the filling, melt the butter in a 9–10in (23–25cm) ovenproof pan. Stir in the sugar. Cook over medium heat, stirring occasionally, until caramelized to deep golden. Let it cool to tepid.

3 Meanwhile, peel, halve, and core the apples. Cut the lemon in half and rub the apples all over with it, to prevent discoloration. Add the apples, cut-sides down, to the caramel pan. Cook over high heat for 15–25 minutes. Turn once.

4 Remove from the heat. Cool for 15 minutes. Preheat the oven to 375°F (190°C). Roll out the dough on a floured surface to a round, 1in (2.5cm) larger than the pan. Tuck the edges of the dough around the apples. Bake for 20–25 minutes until golden. Cool to tepid, then set a plate on top, hold firmly together, and invert. Spoon some caramel over the apples. Serve with crème fraîche (if using).

Apricot tart

This classic French tart is filled with a delicate custard and juicy apricots and makes a delicious dessert.

30 mins, plus chilling   50 mins-1 hr

SPECIAL EQUIPMENT
food processor (optional)
9in (22cm) loose-bottomed tart pan
baking beans

SERVES 6-8

FOR THE DOUGH

1¼ cups all-purpose flour, plus extra for dusting

1 tbsp granulated sugar

7 tbsp unsalted butter, softened, cut into pieces

1 large egg, separated

FOR THE FILLING

¾ cup heavy cream

¼ cup granulated sugar

2 large eggs, plus 1 large egg yolk

½ tsp vanilla extract

1 x 14oz can apricot halves, drained

confectioners' sugar, for dusting

CALORIES: 382kcals/1598kJ
CARBOHYDRATE: 28g
  sugar: 13g
FAT: 27g
  saturated: 16g
SALT: 0.1g
FIBER: 1.5g

1 To make the dough, rub the flour, sugar, and butter together with your fingertips, or pulse-blend in a food processor, until the mixture resembles fine crumbs. Add the egg yolk and enough water to form a soft dough. Wrap and chill for 30 minutes. Preheat the oven to 350°F (180°C).

2 Roll out the dough on a floured surface to ⅛in (3mm) thick and use to line a 9in (22cm) loose-bottomed tart pan, leaving an overhang of at least ½in (1cm). Prick with a fork, brush with the egg white to seal, line with parchment paper, and fill with baking beans. Bake for 20 minutes. Remove the beans and paper, and bake for another 5 minutes. Trim off the ragged edges while warm.

3 For the filling, whisk the cream, sugar, eggs, yolk, and vanilla in a bowl. Lay the apricots, cut-sides down, over the tart crust. Place on a baking sheet and pour the cream mixture over the fruit. Bake for 30–35 minutes until just set. Allow to cool to room temperature before dusting with confectioners' sugar to serve.

HOW TO FREEZE

This crust can be wrapped well in plastic wrap, then sealed with foil and frozen for up to 12 weeks.

Treacle tart

A classic English tart that remains a favorite. Treacle can be hard to find in the US, but molasses can be used instead.

30 mins, plus chilling

50–55 mins

SPECIAL EQUIPMENT

food processor (optional)

9in (22cm) loose-bottomed tart pan

baking beans

hand-held blender

SERVES 6–8

1 cup all-purpose flour, plus extra for dusting

7 tbsp unsalted butter, chilled and cut into cubes

¼ cup granulated sugar

1 large egg yolk

½ tsp vanilla extract

FOR THE FILLING

¾ cup corn syrup

¾ cup heavy cream

2 large eggs

finely grated zest of 1 orange

1 cup brioche or croissant crumbs

thick cream or ice cream, to serve

1 Using your fingertips, rub together the flour and butter, or pulse-blend in a food processor, to form fine crumbs. Stir in the sugar. Beat together the egg yolk and vanilla extract and mix them into the dry ingredients. Bring the mixture together to form a soft dough, adding a little water if it seems dry. Wrap in plastic wrap and chill for 30 minutes. Preheat the oven to 350°F (180°C).

2 Roll out the dough on a floured surface to 1/8in (3mm) thick. It will be quite fragile, so if it starts to crumble, just bring it together with your hands and gently knead it to get rid of any cracks. Line a 9in (22cm) loose-bottomed tart pan with the rolled-out dough, leaving an overlapping edge of at least ¾in (2cm) all around the rim. Prick the bottom all over with a fork.

3 Line the dough with parchment paper and baking beans. Place it on a baking sheet, and blind-bake for 20 minutes. Remove the beans and paper, and return it to the oven for 5 minutes. Reduce the oven temperature to 340°F (170°C).

4 For the filling, measure out the corn syrup into a large measuring cup. Measure the cream on top of it (the density of the syrup will keep the two separate, making measuring easy). Add the eggs and orange zest, and process together with a hand-held blender until well combined. Alternatively, transfer to a bowl and whisk. Gently fold in the brioche crumbs.

5 Place the tart crust on a baking sheet, pull out an oven rack from the center of the oven, and put the baking sheet on it. Pour the filling into the crust and carefully slide the rack back into the oven.

6 Bake the tart for 30 minutes until just set, but before the filling starts to bubble up. Trim the crust edge with a small, sharp knife while still warm, then leave to cool in its pan for at least 15 minutes before turning out. Serve warm with thick cream or ice cream.

COOK'S TIP

Try using eggs and cream to lighten the more traditional filling of bread crumbs and syrup. This process incorporates more air and creates a mousse-like effect.

PREPARE AHEAD

The unfilled crust can be stored in an airtight container for up to 3 days, or wrapped well in plastic wrap, sealed with foil, and frozen for up to 12 weeks.

CALORIES: 452kcals/1895kJ

CARBOHYDRATE: 45g
  sugar: 27g

FAT: 28g
  saturated: 16g

SALT: 0.4g

FIBER: 1g

Strawberry tart

Master the basics of this fresh fruit tart and you can adapt it by replacing the strawberries with other soft fruit.

40 mins, plus chilling   25 mins

SERVES 6-8

SPECIAL EQUIPMENT

9in (22cm) loose-bottomed tart pan

baking beans

INGREDIENTS

1 cup all-purpose flour, plus extra for dusting

7 tbsp unsalted butter, chilled and cut into cubes

¼ cup granulated sugar

1 large egg yolk

½ tsp vanilla extract

6 tbsp redcurrant jelly, for glazing

10oz (300g) strawberries, thickly sliced

FOR THE CRÈME PÂTISSIÈRE

½ cup granulated sugar

5 tbsp cornstarch

2 large eggs

1 tsp vanilla extract

1¾ cups whole milk

1 In a bowl, rub the flour and butter together to form fine crumbs. Stir in the sugar. Beat together the egg yolk and vanilla extract, and add them to the flour mixture. Bring together to a dough, adding a little water if needed. Wrap in plastic wrap and chill for 30 minutes.

2 Preheat the oven to 350°F (180°C). Roll out the dough on a floured surface to ⅛in (3mm) thick. Use the rolled-out dough to line a 9in (22cm) loose-bottomed tart pan, leaving an overlapping edge of about ¾in (2cm). Use a pair of scissors to trim any excess dough that hangs down further than this.

3 Prick the dough bottom all over with a fork to prevent air bubbles from forming as it bakes. Carefully line the dough with a piece of parchment paper.

4 Scatter baking beans over the paper. Place on a baking sheet and bake for 20 minutes. Remove the beans and paper and bake for 5 minutes more. Trim the excess dough while it is still warm. Melt

the redcurrant jelly with 1 tbsp of water and brush a little over the crust. Let cool.

5 For the crème pâtissière, beat the sugar, cornstarch, eggs, and vanilla extract in a bowl. In a heavy-bottomed saucepan, bring the milk to a boil and take it off the heat just as it bubbles. Pour the hot milk onto the egg mixture in the bowl, whisking all the time.

6 Return the mixture to a pan and bring to a boil over medium heat, whisking constantly. When it thickens, reduce the heat to low and continue to cook gently, stirring constantly, for 2–3 minutes. Transfer to a bowl, cover with plastic wrap directly on its surface, and let cool completely.

7 Beat the crème pâtissière until smooth and spread it over the crust with a spatula. Top with the strawberries. Heat the jelly glaze again and brush over the strawberries, then leave to set. Remove from the pan to serve.

PREPARE AHEAD

This tart is best eaten on the day it is made, but the components will keep well overnight if properly stored. Wrap the crust well and keep it in an airtight container. Pour the crème pâtissière into a bowl, place plastic wrap directly onto its surface, and also cover the bowl with plastic wrap before storing in the fridge. The next day, scrape the crème pâtissière into the crust, slice the strawberries, and arrange over the top, as in step 7.

CALORIES: 353kcals/1490kJ

CARBOHYDRATE: 48g
   sugar: 30g

FAT: 15g
   saturated: 9g

SALT: 0.1g

FIBER: 1g

Raspberry tart with chocolate cream

A fruit tart with a twist, here the crème pâtissière is enriched with chocolate—a perfect partner for fresh raspberries.

40 mins, plus chilling   **20-25 mins**

SERVES 6-8

SPECIAL EQUIPMENT
9in (22cm) loose-bottomed tart pan

baking beans

INGREDIENTS
1 cup all-purpose flour, plus extra for dusting

3 tbsp cocoa powder

7 tbsp unsalted butter, chilled and cut into cubes

¾ cup granulated sugar

1 large egg yolk, plus 2 large eggs

1½ tsp vanilla extract

5 tbsp cornstarch, sifted

2 cups whole milk

6oz (175g) good-quality dark chocolate, broken into pieces

14oz (400g) raspberries

confectioners' sugar, for dusting

1 Rub together the flour, cocoa, and butter, until they resemble fine crumbs. Stir in ¼ cup of the sugar. Beat the egg yolk with ½ tsp of vanilla extract and add to the flour mixture to form a soft dough. Add a little cold water if it seems too stiff. Wrap in plastic wrap and chill for 30 minutes.

2 Preheat the oven to 350°F (180°C). Roll the dough out on a floured surface to ⅛in (3mm) thick. Use it to line a 9in (22cm) loose-bottomed tart pan, leaving an overlapping edge of ¾in (2cm), trimming the excess with scissors. Prick the bottom with a fork.

3 Line the dough with parchment paper and weigh down with baking beans. Place on a baking sheet and bake for 20 minutes. Remove the beans and paper and return it to the oven for another 5 minutes. Trim off the excess dough with a sharp knife while still warm.

4 For the crème pâtissière, beat together the remaining ¼ cup of sugar, the cornstarch, whole eggs, and the remaining 1 tsp of vanilla extract. In a pan, bring the milk and 3½oz (100g) of the chocolate to a boil, whisking all the time. Take it off the heat just as it starts to bubble up. Pour the milk onto the egg mixture, whisking all the time as you do.

5 Return the chocolate mixture to the cleaned-out pan and bring to a boil over medium heat, whisking constantly. When it bubbles and begins to thicken, reduce the heat to its lowest setting and cook for 2–3 minutes, again whisking all the time. Pour into a bowl, cover the surface with plastic wrap to prevent a skin from forming, and let cool.

6 Melt the remaining chocolate in a bowl set over a pan of simmering water (make sure the bowl does not touch the water), and brush around the inside of the tart crust to seal and add a new layer of texture. Let set. Beat the cold chocolate crème pâtissière with a wooden spoon and pour into the crust, smoothing it down evenly with a spatula or palette knife.

7 Arrange the raspberries over the chocolate crème pâtissière, remove the tart from the pan, and serve dusted with the confectioners' sugar.

PREPARE AHEAD
This tart is best eaten on the day it is made, but can be stored, without the berries, in the fridge overnight. Add the raspberries and confectioners' sugar to serve.

CALORIES: 443kcals/1867kJ

CARBOHYDRATE: 53g
sugar: 37g

FAT: 22g
saturated: 13g

SALT: 0.2g

FIBER: 3.5g

Tarte au citron

This French classic is both rich and refreshing, with melt-in-the-mouth dough and a tangy, smooth, creamy filling.

35 mins, plus chilling 45 mins

SPECIAL EQUIPMENT
food processor (optional)
9½in (24cm) loose-bottomed tart pan
baking beans

SERVES 6–8

1¼ cups all-purpose flour, plus extra
for dusting

6 tbsp butter, chilled

3 tbsp granulated sugar

1 large egg, lightly beaten

FOR THE FILLING

5 large eggs

¾ cup granulated sugar

finely grated zest and juice of
4 lemons, plus extra zest to serve

1 cup heavy cream

confectioners' sugar, to serve

1 To make the dough, rub together the flour and butter with your fingertips, or pulse them in a food processor until the mixture looks like fine crumbs. Stir in the sugar until well combined. Add the egg and draw the mixture together, first with a fork and then with your hands, to form a ball of dough. If it is too dry and crumbly to come together, carefully add water, 1 tbsp at a time, until it does.

2 On a lightly floured surface, roll out the dough into a large circle of even thickness, and use it carefully to line a 9½in (24cm) loose-bottomed tart pan, pushing it well into the contours. Cover and chill for at least 30 minutes.

3 For the filling, beat the eggs and sugar. Whisk in the lemon zest and juice and then the cream until evenly blended. Transfer to a bowl, cover, and chill for 1 hour.

4 Preheat the oven to 375°F (190°C) and put in a baking sheet. Line the crust with parchment paper, fill with baking beans, and bake blind on the hot sheet for 10 minutes. Remove the paper and beans and bake for another 5 minutes on the pan, or until the dough bottom is crisp with no sign of damp or raw dough.

5 Reduce the oven temperature to 275°F (140°C). With the tart pan still on the baking sheet, pull out the oven rack, pour in the lemon filling, being careful not to allow it to spill over the edges, and slide the rack back in. Bake for 30 minutes, or until the filling has just set but retains a slight wobble.

6 Remove the tart from the oven and let cool on a wire rack. Turn out of the pan and serve, dusted with confectioners' sugar and sprinkled with lemon zest.

PREPARE AHEAD

The unfilled crust can be prepared ahead and stored in an airtight container for up to 3 days, or well wrapped in plastic wrap, sealed with foil, and frozen for up to 12 weeks.

COOK'S TIP

Try to choose unwaxed lemons, especially if a recipe calls for lemon zest. If these are unavailable, scrub the fruits to remove the wax coating. Pick lemons that are heavy for their size, indicating that they have lots of juice.

CALORIES: 496kcals/2075kJ

CARBOHYDRATE: 47g
sugar: 32g

FAT: 31g
saturated: 17g

SALT: 0.4g

FIBER: 1g

Plum tart

The perfect use for plums that are a little tart to eat on their own; baking brings out their sweetness.

40 mins, plus chilling and resting

25-30 mins

SPECIAL EQUIPMENT
electric hand-held mixer

8in (20cm) loose-bottomed tart pan

SERVES 4

FOR THE DOUGH
1 cup all-purpose flour, plus extra for dusting

6 tbsp unsalted butter, chilled and cut into cubes

¼ cup granulated sugar

1 large egg yolk

FOR THE FILLING
6 tbsp unsalted butter, softened

⅓ cup granulated sugar

2 large eggs, lightly beaten

2 tbsp all-purpose flour

1 cup ground almonds

3 plums, quartered and pitted

¼oz (10g) sliced almonds

confectioners' sugar, to serve

crème fraîche, to serve

1 To make the dough, rub the flour and butter together to form fine crumbs. Stir in the sugar. Add the egg yolk to the flour mixture and bring together to form a smooth dough, adding 1–2 tbsp of cold water if necessary. Wrap in plastic wrap and chill for 1 hour. Preheat the oven to 350°F (180°C).

2 For the filling, place the butter and sugar in a bowl and whisk with an electric hand-held mixer until pale and fluffy. Whisk in the eggs, flour, and ground almonds to form a smooth paste.

3 On a floured work surface, roll the dough out into a circle large enough to line an 8in (20cm) loose-bottomed tart pan. Place the dough in the pan, pressing down well into the bottom and around the edges. Trim any excess dough and prick the bottom of the tart with a fork. Place the pan on a baking sheet.

4 Spoon the almond paste into the crust and, using the back of a spoon, spread it out to form an even layer. Arrange the plum quarters, skin-side up, in the almond paste and sprinkle in the sliced almonds.

5 Bake the tart for 25–30 minutes, or until golden and set. Let the tart cool slightly in the pan for 5 minutes, then carefully remove it. Sift confectioners' sugar overtop and serve warm with crème fraîche.

VARIATION
Peeled, halved, quartered, and cored pears, or quartered and pitted apricots, can be used as an alternative to the plums. Slightly underripe or tart fruits will work well.

PREPARE AHEAD
Make the dough up to 24 hours in advance, wrap in plastic wrap, and keep in the fridge until ready to use.

CALORIES: 841kcals/3533kJ

CARBOHYDRATE: 69g
sugar: 40g

FAT: 57g
saturated: 27g

SALT: 0.2g

FIBER: 2.5g

Lemon meringue roulade

The traditional filling for a Lemon meringue pie (see p336) is given a new twist in this incredibly light dessert.

30 mins   15 mins

SPECIAL EQUIPMENT

10 x 14in (25 x 35cm) Swiss roll pan
electric hand-held mixer

SERVES 8

5 large egg whites, at room temperature

1 cup granulated sugar

½ tsp white wine vinegar

1 tsp cornstarch

½ tsp vanilla extract

1 cup heavy cream

4 tbsp good-quality lemon curd

confectioners' sugar, for dusting

1 Preheat the oven to 350°F (180°C) and line a 10 x 14in (25 x 35cm) Swiss roll pan with parchment paper. Whisk the egg whites with an electric hand-held mixer on high speed, until stiff peaks form. Reduce the speed and whisk in the sugar, a little at a time, until thick and glossy.

2 Mix the vinegar, cornstarch, and vanilla extract and fold them in, trying to keep the mixture as well aerated as possible. Spread the mixture into the pan and bake in the center of the oven for 15 minutes. Remove from the oven and set it aside. Allow it to cool to room temperature.

3 Meanwhile, whisk the cream until thick but not stiff; it should remain unctuous. Fold in the lemon curd roughly until just mixed; a few ripples will enhance the roulade. Sprinkle confectioners' sugar over a fresh sheet of parchment paper.

4 Carefully turn the cooled roulade out of the pan onto the sugared parchment. Spread the lemon cream over the unbaked side of the roulade with a palette knife. Use the parchment to roll up the meringue firmly, but without squeezing out the cream. Place seam-side down on a serving plate, cover, and chill until needed. Sift over confectioners' sugar to serve.

PREPARE AHEAD

The meringue can be made up to 3 days in advance and stored, unfilled, in an airtight container. If you want to store it this way, it helps to roll it up loosely, using a clean sheet of parchment paper, and store it in the roll. If you store it flat, it may crack when you try to roll it.

CALORIES: 275kcals/1149kJ

CARBOHYDRATE: 28g
    sugar: 28g

FAT: 17g
    saturated: 10g

SALT: 0.1g

FIBER: 0g

Strawberry pavlova

Freeze your leftover egg whites, one at a time if necessary, until you have enough to make this well-loved dessert.

15 mins   1 hr 15 mins

SPECIAL EQUIPMENT
electric hand-held mixer

SERVES 8

6 large egg whites, at room temperature

pinch of salt

approx. 1½ cups granulated sugar

2 tsp cornstarch

1 tsp vinegar

1¼ cups heavy cream

strawberries, to decorate

1 Preheat the oven to 350°F (180°C). Line a baking sheet with parchment paper. Draw an 8in (20cm) diameter circle on the parchment paper with a pencil. Reverse the parchment, so the pencil mark is underneath and won't transfer to the meringue.

2 Put the egg whites in a large, clean, grease-free bowl with the salt. Using an electric hand-held mixer, whip the egg whites until stiff peaks form. Start whisking in the sugar 1 tbsp at a time, whisking well after each addition. Continue whisking until the whites are stiff and glossy. Mix the cornstarch and vinegar and whisk them in. Spoon into a mound inside the circle on the parchment, spreading it to the edges of the circle. Form neat swirls, using a palette knife, as you spread out the meringue.

3 Bake for 5 minutes, then reduce the oven temperature to 250°F (120°C) and cook for 1¼ hours. Let cool completely in the oven. Whip the cream until it holds its shape. Spoon onto the meringue base and decorate with the strawberries, hulled, and halved or sliced. Serve in wedges.

PREPARE AHEAD
The meringue base will keep in a dry, airtight container for up to 3 days; keep it away from extremes of heat or cold. Whip and add the cream, and add the berries, just before serving.

CALORIES: 377kcals/1578kJ

CARBOHYDRATE: 46g
  sugar: 46g

FAT: 20g
  saturated: 12.5g

SALT: 0.3g

FIBER: 0g

Eton mess

This is a crowd-pleasing dessert that's quick to make, and even quicker if you use store-bought meringues.

10 mins,
plus chilling

SERVES 6

2 cups heavy cream

1 tsp vanilla extract

2 tbsp granulated sugar

5½oz (150g) meringues

10oz (300g) strawberries, chopped quite small

5½oz (150g) raspberries

CALORIES: 548kcals/2275kJ
CARBOHYDRATE: 33g
    sugar: 33g
FAT: 45g
    saturated: 28g
SALT: 0.1g
FIBER: 1.5g

1 Whip the cream until it is very stiff, then whisk in the vanilla extract and fold in the sugar.

2 Place the meringues in a freezer bag and smash with a rolling pin to break into uneven pebble-sized pieces. It's nice to have a mixture of large pieces and smaller crumbs for the best texture.

3 Fold together the cream mixture, the meringues, and the fruit. Cover and chill for at least 1 hour before serving.

VARIATION

Try replacing half the heavy cream with Greek yogurt for a lighter taste.

CLEVER WITH LEFTOVERS

This is a dish that is easy to adapt to include any berries that need to be used up quickly. Their ripe juices will enhance the dessert.

Chocolate amaretti roulade

An irresistible combination of crunchy cookie, soft cream, and yielding chocolate cake.

30 mins   20 mins

SPECIAL EQUIPMENT

9 x 13in (23 x 33cm) Swiss roll pan
electric hand-held mixer

SERVES 4

6 large eggs, separated

¾ cup granulated sugar

½ cup cocoa powder

confectioners' sugar, for dusting

1¼ cups heavy cream or whipping cream

2–3 tbsp Amaretto or brandy

20 amaretti cookies, crushed, plus 2 extra, to serve

1¾oz (50g) dark chocolate, grated

CALORIES: 863kcals/3594kJ
CARBOHYDRATE: 55g
    sugar: 55g
FAT: 61g
    saturated: 32g
SALT: 0.7g
FIBER: 2.5g

1 Preheat the oven to 350°F (180°C). Line a 9 x 13in (23 x 33cm) Swiss roll pan with parchment paper. Put the egg yolks and granulated sugar in a heatproof bowl set over simmering water and whisk for 10 minutes until pale, thick, and creamy. Remove from the heat. Whisk the egg whites to soft peaks.

2 Sift the cocoa into the egg yolk mixture and gently fold in with the egg whites. Pour into the pan. Bake for 20 minutes, until just firm.

3 Turn onto a sheet of parchment paper dusted with confectioners' sugar. Remove the pan, leave the top paper, and cool for 30 minutes.

4 Whip the cream until soft peaks form. Peel the paper from the cake, trim the edges, then drizzle with Amaretto. Spread with the cream and scatter with most of the amaretti and chocolate.

5 Starting from a short side, roll it up. Sprinkle over the remaining amaretti and chocolate and dust with confectioners' sugar.

Sticky toffee pudding

A modern classic that never fails to please. A fabulous dessert to serve to guests on a cold day.

20 mins | 35–40 mins, plus resting

SPECIAL EQUIPMENT

1-quart (1-liter) deep, ovenproof dish

electric hand-held mixer

SERVES 4–6

8 tbsp butter, plus extra for greasing

3½oz (100g) chopped dates

½ tsp baking soda

1 cup light brown sugar

1¼ cups heavy cream

1 large egg, lightly beaten

1 cup self-rising flour, sifted

whipped cream or custard, to serve

1 Preheat the oven to 350°F (180°C). Butter a 1-quart (1-liter) deep, ovenproof dish.

2 Place the dates and baking soda in a heatproof bowl. Pour in ½ cup of boiling water, stir well, and set aside for 10 minutes.

3 Place 5 tbsp of the butter, ½ cup of the sugar, and the cream in a non-stick pan. Heat gently until the sugar dissolves, then bring to a boil for 3 minutes. Pour half the sauce into the dish.

4 Put the remaining sugar and butter in a bowl and beat with an electric hand-held mixer. Whisk in the egg and the date mixture. Fold in the flour and pour into the dish, on top of the sauce. Bake for 35–40 minutes, or until a skewer comes out clean. Leave for 5 minutes, then invert onto a dish. Serve with whipped cream or custard and the reserved sauce.

VARIATION

For a sticky toffee and walnut pudding, fold in 2½oz (75g) chopped walnuts at the same time as the flour.

CALORIES: 637kcals/2654kJ

CARBOHYDRATE: 54g
  sugar: 40g

FAT: 45g
  saturated: 28g

SALT: 0.8g

FIBER: 2g

Chocolate brownie pudding

This decadent dessert is delicious, but very rich, and a little goes a long way.

15 mins | 45–50 mins

SPECIAL EQUIPMENT

electric hand-held mixer

12 x 8in (30 x 20cm) ovenproof dish

SERVES 6–8

½ cup all-purpose flour

½ cup cocoa powder

4 large eggs

1 cup light brown sugar

¾ cup granulated sugar

1 tsp vanilla extract

14 tbsp butter, melted and cooled, plus extra for greasing

vanilla ice cream, to serve

1 Preheat the oven to 325°F (160°C). Sift the flour and cocoa powder together.

2 Put the eggs, sugars, and vanilla extract into a large bowl and whisk with an electric hand-held mixer for 3–4 minutes until the mixture is light and fluffy.

3 Fold in the flour mixture until it is well-combined. Finally, mix in the melted butter.

4 Pour the batter into a greased 12 x 8in (30 x 20cm) ovenproof dish and place it inside a large roasting pan. Carefully pour hot water into the pan until it is halfway up the sides of the ovenproof dish.

5 Transfer the pan carefully to the oven and bake for 45–50 minutes until it is cooked at the edges, but still a little wobbly in the center. Serve warm with vanilla ice cream.

CALORIES: 447kcals/1872kJ

CARBOHYDRATE: 50g
  sugar: 46g

FAT: 25g
  saturated: 15g

SALT: 0.7g

FIBER: 1.5g

PREPARE AHEAD

Make this to the end of step 3 up to 1 day ahead, cover, and keep in the fridge until needed. Return to room temperature before cooking as in steps 4 and 5.

Classic bread and butter pudding

A favorite for generations, this is also an economical dish for the whole family.

15 mins, plus soaking

25–35 mins, plus resting

SERVES 4

2 tbsp butter, softened, plus extra for greasing

6 slices of day-old white bread, crusts cut off

1¾oz (50g) golden raisins

2 cups whole milk

2 large eggs, lightly beaten

½ tsp ground cinnamon

finely grated zest of 1 lemon

3 tbsp granulated sugar

custard, to serve

1 Grease a medium ovenproof dish. Butter the bread and cut each slice into 4 triangles.

2 Arrange half the bread in the bottom of the dish. Sprinkle in half the golden raisins. Top with the remaining bread, in neat rows, and the remaining golden raisins.

3 Place the milk, eggs, cinnamon, lemon zest, and 2 tbsp of the sugar in a bowl and whisk together with a fork until well combined. Pour the mixture over the bread. Set aside for at least 15 minutes, for the custard to soak into the bread, then push the golden raisins under the custard so they don't burn in the oven. When ready to bake, preheat the oven to 350°F (180°C).

4 Sprinkle the remaining sugar over the top of the pudding and bake for 25–35 minutes, or until golden brown. Remove from the oven and set aside for 10–15 minutes. Serve warm, with custard.

CALORIES: 376kcals/1596kJ
CARBOHYDRATE: 47g
    sugar: 26g
FAT: 16g
    saturated: 8g
SALT: 1g
FIBER: 1.5g

PREPARE AHEAD

Make up to the end of step 3 (but don't preheat the oven), cover, and chill for up to 1 day, before baking as in step 4.

Panettone and marmalade bread and butter pudding

The sophisticated and subtle flavor of panettone and the tang of marmalade add interest to this dessert.

20 mins, plus soaking

30 mins, plus resting

SERVES 4

butter, for greasing

9oz (250g) panettone, sliced

½ cup marmalade

¾ cup whole milk

3 large eggs, lightly beaten

finely grated zest and juice of 1 orange

3 tbsp heavy cream

¼ cup light brown sugar

½ tsp pumpkin pie spice

whipped cream, to serve

1 Butter a medium ovenproof dish. Spread each slice of panettone with marmalade. Arrange the slices neatly in the buttered dish.

2 In a bowl, combine the milk, eggs, orange zest and juice, cream, sugar, and pumpkin pie spice. Whisk together with a fork until well combined.

3 Pour the mixture over the panettone, gently re-submerge the bread under the mixture with the back of a fork, and set aside for 15 minutes. Preheat the oven to 325°F (160°C).

4 Place the dish on a baking sheet and bake for 30 minutes. Serve warm or at room temperature, with whipped cream.

CALORIES: 537kcals/2255kJ
CARBOHYDRATE: 75g
    sugar: 50g
FAT: 21g
    saturated: 11g
SALT: 0.8g
FIBER: 1.5g

VARIATION

For a festive version, add 2–3 tbsp of crystallized and candied fruits and ginger to this recipe, chopping them finely and adding them under the top layer of panettone.

Chocolate croissant bread and butter pudding

An unapologetically indulgent dessert, this is one to save for a special occasion.

15 mins, plus soaking

30 mins, plus resting

SPECIAL EQUIPMENT
electric hand-held mixer

SERVES 4

butter, for greasing

4 pains au chocolat, thinly sliced

¾ cup heavy cream

¾ cup whole milk

1 vanilla bean, split, seeds scraped out and reserved

2 tbsp granulated sugar

3 large egg yolks

1¾oz (50g) white chocolate chips or buttons

confectioners' sugar, to serve

half-and-half, to serve

> CALORIES: 716kcals/2978kJ
> CARBOHYDRATE: 47g
>   sugar: 26g
> FAT: 55g
>   saturated: 30g
> SALT: 0.8g
> FIBER: 2g

1 Preheat the oven to 400°F (200°C). Butter a medium ovenproof dish and arrange the sliced pastries in the dish.

2 Place the cream, milk, vanilla bean, and scraped-out seeds in a small, non-stick pan over medium heat. Gently heat to a simmer.

3 Meanwhile, put the sugar and yolks in a heatproof bowl and whisk with an electric hand-held mixer until pale and creamy.

4 Stir the white chocolate into the milk mixture and stir constantly until melted. Remove the vanilla bean from the milk mixture. Pour the milk mixture over the egg mixture, whisking constantly.

5 Pour the mixture back into the rinsed-out pan, and heat gently until thickened, stirring constantly with a wooden spoon. Pour the thickened custard over the pastry slices and set aside for 15 minutes. Bake in the oven for 20 minutes, then leave to rest for at least 10 minutes. Sift over confectioners' sugar and serve with half-and-half.

Creamy rice pudding

The comforting taste of childhood. Serve with a spoonful of fruity strawberry jam for added nostalgia.

5 mins

2 hrs 10 mins, plus resting

SPECIAL EQUIPMENT
medium Dutch oven

SERVES 4

2 tbsp butter

3½oz (100g) short-grain pudding rice

¼ cup vanilla or golden granulated sugar

3½ cups whole milk

⅔ cup heavy cream

grated nutmeg, to taste

> CALORIES: 585kcals/2439kJ
> CARBOHYDRATE: 49g
>   sugar: 30g
> FAT: 38g
>   saturated: 24g
> SALT: 0.5g
> FIBER: 0.2g

1 Preheat the oven to 275°F (140°C). Melt the butter in a medium Dutch oven over low heat.

2 Add the rice to the dish and stir well to coat in the butter. Stir the sugar into the rice and pour in the milk and cream. Stir well to combine.

3 Over medium heat, stirring constantly, gradually bring to a simmer. Sprinkle in the nutmeg, cover, and bake in the oven for 2 hours. Set aside to rest for 20 minutes before serving.

VARIATIONS

For an extra treat, stir in a handful of dark, white, or milk chocolate chips. For added flavor and texture, stir in 1¾oz (50g) dried fruit, such as golden raisins, chopped apricots, figs, or prunes, and ½ tsp ground cinnamon, just before resting in step 3.

Chocolate lava cakes

Usually thought of as a restaurant dessert, chocolate lava cakes are surprisingly easy to prepare at home.

20 mins, plus chilling   12–15 mins

SPECIAL EQUIPMENT
4 x 4in (10cm) ramekins

SERVES 4

11 tbsp unsalted butter, cut into cubes, plus extra for greasing

1 heaping tbsp all-purpose flour, sifted, plus extra for dusting

5½oz (150g) good-quality dark chocolate, broken into pieces

3 large eggs

¼ cups granulated sugar

cocoa powder or confectioners' sugar, for dusting (optional)

ice cream, to serve (optional)

CALORIES: 633kcals/2655kJ

CARBOHYDRATE: 43g
    sugar: 41g

FAT: 47g
    saturated: 28g

SALT: 0.2g

FIBER: 1.5g

1 Preheat the oven to 400°F (200°C). Grease the sides and bottoms of four 4in (10cm) ramekins. Sprinkle with a little flour, pouring out any excess. Line the bottoms with parchment paper.

2 Gently melt the chocolate and butter in a heatproof bowl over simmering water (the bowl must not touch the water). Cool slightly.

3 In a separate bowl, whisk the eggs and sugar. Beat in the chocolate mixture. Fold in the flour. Divide between the ramekins.

4 Cook in the middle of the oven for 12–15 minutes. The middles should still be soft to the touch. Run a knife around the edges. Turn the fondants onto serving plates and peel off the parchment.

5 Dust with cocoa powder or confectioners' sugar, if desired, and serve with ice cream.

PREPARE AHEAD
The raw mixture in the ramekins can be covered and refrigerated overnight, or frozen for up to 1 week. Return to room temperature before cooking.

Berry and banana crumble

An unusual mixture, this sweet dish with its soft, unctuous texture makes a great family dessert.

10–15 mins   30–40 mins

SERVES 4–6

14oz (400g) frozen mixed berries, such as blackberries, blackcurrants, redcurrants, strawberries, and raspberries

2 bananas, thickly sliced

⅔ cup all-purpose flour, sifted

7 tbsp butter, chilled and cut into cubes

½ cup oats

¼ cup vanilla or granulated sugar

1¼oz (40g) toasted sliced almonds

custard, to serve

CALORIES: 328kcals/1370kJ

CARBOHYDRATE: 36g
    sugar: 19g

FAT: 18g
    saturated: 9g

SALT: 0.3g

FIBER: 4.5g

1 Preheat the oven to 350°F (180°C). Place all the fruit in a medium baking dish.

2 Put the flour in a large mixing bowl and rub in the butter with your fingertips until the mixture resembles coarse bread crumbs. Stir in the oats, sugar, and almonds.

3 Sprinkle the crumble mixture over the fruit and use the back of a metal spoon to smooth it into an even layer.

4 Place the dish on a baking sheet and bake for 30–40 minutes, or until golden brown. Serve hot with custard.

VARIATION
Try adding 3 tbsp of chopped pecans or walnuts to this topping, or stir in ½ tsp of ground cinnamon.

Plum crumble

Orange and ginger add flavor to the plums, and walnuts add crunch to the topping, in this twist on a classic.

15 mins   35 mins

SERVES 4–6

14oz (400g) plums, halved and pitted

finely grated zest and juice of 1 orange

2 tbsp granulated sugar

½ tsp ground ginger

¾ cup whole wheat flour, sifted

¾ cup all-purpose flour, sifted

14 tbsp butter, chilled and cut into cubes

¾ cup light brown sugar

1¾oz (50g) walnuts, roughly chopped

heavy cream, to serve

CALORIES: 553kcals/2311kJ

CARBOHYDRATE: 56g
  sugar: 36g

FAT: 34g
  saturated: 18g

SALT: 0.5g

FIBER: 4.5g

1 Preheat the oven to 400°F (200°C). Place the halved plums, orange zest and juice, granulated sugar, and ginger in a medium ovenproof dish. Stir well to coat the plums.

2 Place the flours into a mixing bowl. Rub in the butter until the mixture resembles coarse bread crumbs. Stir in the brown sugar and walnuts.

3 Spoon the crumble mixture over the plums, pressing it down with the back of a metal spoon to form an even layer.

4 Place the dish on a baking sheet and bake for 35 minutes. Serve hot or warm with heavy cream.

PREPARE AHEAD

The topping can be prepared up to 2 days in advance and kept in an airtight container in the fridge until needed.

Apple and cinnamon crumble

The spice makes all the difference to this dessert, making the crumble even more appetizing.

20 mins   35 mins

SERVES 4–6

1lb 10oz (750g) apples, peeled, cored, and thinly sliced

½ cup granulated sugar

2 tsp ground cinnamon

1¼ cups all-purpose flour

6 tpsp butter, cut into cubes

vanilla ice cream, to serve

CALORIES: 314kcals/1325kJ

CARBOHYDRATE: 48g
  sugar: 28g

FAT: 12g
  saturated: 7.5g

SALT: 0.3g

FIBER: 4g

1 Preheat the oven to 400°F (200°C). Place the apple slices, scant 2 tbsp of the granulated sugar, and 1 tsp of the cinnamon in a medium ovenproof dish. Stir well to coat the apple slices.

2 Sift the all-purpose flour and remaining ground cinnamon into a mixing bowl. Rub in the butter until the mixture resembles coarse bread crumbs. Stir in ¼ cup of the granulated sugar.

3 Spoon the mixture over the fruit, pressing it down with the back of a metal spoon to form an even layer. Sprinkle the remaining 2 tbsp of sugar over the top. Place the dish on a baking sheet and bake for 35 minutes. Serve hot with vanilla ice cream.

VARIATION

Use 13oz (375g) blackberries and 13oz (375g) apples to make a blackberry and apple crumble. In this case, omit the ground cinnamon.

Cinnamon apple cake

This recipe is delicious either warm as a dessert with cream or cold with a cup of coffee.

30 mins   25-30 mins

SPECIAL EQUIPMENT
9½in (24cm) square baking pan

SERVES 8–12

8 tbsp butter, cut into cubes, plus extra for greasing

1⅔ cups all-purpose flour, sifted, plus extra for dusting

3-4 apples (depending on size)

1 tbsp lemon juice

3 large eggs

1 cup, plus 1 tbsp granulated sugar

6 tbsp milk

¼ cup half-and-half

1 tbsp baking powder

2 tsp ground cinnamon

CALORIES: 523kcals/2207kJ
CARBOHYDRATE: 52g
    sugar: 28g
FAT: 32g
    saturated: 19g
SALT: 0.3g
FIBER: 2g

1 Preheat the oven to 400°F (200°C). Grease a 9½in (24cm) square baking pan with butter and dust with flour.

2 Peel, core, quarter, and slice the apples, and put in a bowl of water with the lemon juice to prevent browning.

3 Whisk the eggs and 1 cup of the sugar until thick and pale, and the whisk leaves a trail when lifted out of the mixture.

4 Put the butter, milk, and half-and-half in a pan and melt gently, then bring to a boil. Let cool briefly, then stir into the egg mixture. Fold in the flour and baking powder. Pour into the pan.

5 Drain the apples and arrange over the batter. Mix the remaining sugar with the cinnamon and sprinkle over. Bake for 25–30 minutes until golden. Let cool in the pan, then cut into squares.

VARIATION

This cake can be adapted for many other autumn fruits. Try it with pitted plums or apricots, or even pears.

Rhubarb crumble cake

This cake has a rich, almond-scented crumble topping covering sharp, sweet rhubarb.

20 mins   50 mins-1 hr, plus resting

SPECIAL EQUIPMENT
8in (20cm) springform cake pan
electric hand-held mixer

SERVES 6–8

FOR THE CAKE

14 tbsp unsalted butter, softened, plus extra for greasing

¾ cup granulated sugar

2 large eggs, lightly beaten

1⅔ cups self-rising flour, sifted

½ tsp ground ginger

2 tbsp milk

5½oz (150g) rhubarb, trimmed and chopped into bite-sized pieces

FOR THE TOPPING

⅓ cup all-purpose flour

5 tbsp unsalted butter, chilled and cut into cubes

½ tsp ground cinnamon

2 tbsp demerara sugar

2 tbsp ground almonds

custard or whipped cream, to serve

1 Preheat the oven to 325°F (160°C). Grease an 8in (20cm) springform cake pan and line with parchment paper.

2 Place the butter and sugar in a bowl. Beat with an electric hand-held mixer until light.

3 Add the eggs and beat until well combined. Fold in the flour and ginger, then the milk.

4 Spoon the mixture into the pan. Push the rhubarb pieces into the batter, spreading them evenly.

5 In a bowl, rub the flour and butter to coarse crumbs. Stir in the cinnamon, sugar, and almonds. Sprinkle over the cake and press down lightly. Bake for 50 minutes to 1 hour until a skewer emerges clean. Leaving it in the pan, cool for 20 minutes.

6 Remove from the pan. Serve warm with custard, or at room temperature with whipped cream.

CALORIES: 523kcals/2207kJ
CARBOHYDRATE: 52g
    sugar: 28g
FAT: 32g
    saturated: 19g
SALT: 0.3g
FIBER: 2g

Easy treacle spongecake

A great last-minute family dessert with ingredients all from the pantry and fridge.

10-15 mins   7-10 mins

SPECIAL EQUIPMENT

1-quart (1-liter) microwaveable pudding bowl

electric hand-held mixer

SERVES 4-6

5 tbsp butter, softened, plus extra for greasing

¼ cup corn syrup

⅓ cup granulated sugar

2 large eggs, lightly beaten

1¼ cups self-rising flour, sifted

3-4 tbsp milk

custard, heavy cream, or vanilla ice cream, to serve

1 Grease a 1-quart (1-liter) microwaveable pudding bowl and spoon the corn syrup into it.

2 Place the butter and sugar into a mixing bowl and cream them together using an electric hand-held mixer. Add the eggs, a little at a time, beating well between each addition.

3 Add the flour to the mixture and beat until a smooth mixture is formed. Add enough milk to give a soft dropping consistency. Spoon the mixture over the syrup in the bowl and level the surface.

4 Microwave the pudding on low (at about 600 watts, if possible) for 7 minutes, or until the cake is just slightly moist and a skewer comes out clean. If the pudding is not cooked, continue to cook it for 1 minute intervals on low, testing after each minute, for up to a total of 10 minutes.

5 Let stand for 5 minutes, before carefully inverting onto a serving dish. Serve immediately with custard, heavy cream, or vanilla ice cream.

CALORIES: 290kcals/1213kJ

CARBOHYDRATE: 37g
  sugar: 21g

FAT: 13g
  saturated: 7g

SALT: 0.6g

FIBER: 1g

Blueberry cobbler

A classic American summer fruit dessert, easy to make, and great for a hungry family.

15 mins   30 mins

SERVES 6-8

FOR THE FILLING

1lb (450g) blueberries

2 apples, or 2 large peaches, sliced

2 tbsp granulated sugar

finely grated zest of ½ lemon

FOR THE COBBLER

2 cups self-rising flour

2 tsp baking powder

⅓ cup granulated sugar, plus 1 tbsp for sprinkling

pinch of salt

5 tbsp unsalted butter, chilled and cut into cubes

½ cup buttermilk

1 large egg, lightly beaten

handful of sliced almonds

custard, or heavy cream, to serve (optional)

CALORIES: 225kcals/946kJ

CARBOHYDRATE: 30g
  sugar: 25g

FAT: 10g
  saturated: 5.5g

SALT: 0.5g

FIBER: 2g

1 Preheat the oven to 375°F (190°C). Put the fruit in a shallow ovenproof dish and stir in the sugar and zest. For the cobbler, sift the flour, baking powder, granulated sugar, and salt into a bowl. Add the butter and rub with your fingers, until the mixture resembles crumbs.

2 Beat together the buttermilk and egg, add to the flour mixture, and mix to form a dough. Place walnut-sized spoonfuls over the fruit, leaving space for the mix to spread. Lightly press down to help them combine with the fruit.

3 Evenly sprinkle in the almonds and remaining sugar. Bake for 30 minutes until bubbling. If it browns quickly, cover with foil. Insert a skewer into the middle of the center "cobble": it should emerge clean. If not, return to the oven for 5 minutes, then test again. Let cool briefly before serving straight from the dish, with plenty of custard or heavy cream. This is best eaten on the same day.

PREPARE AHEAD

If you have time earlier in the day to prepare the fruit filling and the dry ingredients for the cobbler, this dessert can be assembled in 5 minutes.

Blueberry ripple cheesecake

The marbled effect on this cheesecake is really simple to achieve, but always looks impressively professional.

20 mins   50 mins

SPECIAL EQUIPMENT

8in (20cm) deep springform cake pan
food processor

SERVES 8

4 tbsp unsalted butter, plus extra for greasing

4½oz (125g) vanilla wafers

5½oz (150g) blueberries

⅔ cup granulated sugar, plus 3 tbsp extra

14oz (400g) cream cheese, softened

9oz (250g) mascarpone

2 large eggs, plus 1 large egg yolk

½ tsp vanilla extract

2 tbsp all-purpose flour, sifted

FOR THE COMPOTE

3½oz (100g) blueberries

1 tbsp granulated sugar

squeeze of lemon juice

1 Preheat the oven to 350°F (180°C). Grease the bottom and sides of an 8in (20cm) deep springform cake pan. Put the wafers in a plastic bag and crush with a rolling pin until they form fine crumbs. Melt the butter in a saucepan set over low heat; it should not begin to turn brown.

2 Add the crumbs to the pan and stir until they are coated in butter. Remove from the heat. Press the crumbs into the bottom of the pan, pushing them down with the back of a spoon.

3 Put the blueberries and 3 tbsp of the sugar in a food processor and purée until smooth. Push the mixture through a nylon sieve (metal will taint it) into a small pan. Boil, and then simmer for 3–5 minutes, or until thickened and jam-like. Set aside.

4 Place the remaining sugar and last 5 cheesecake ingredients in the rinsed-out food processor.

Purée the mixture until smooth and very well combined. Pour the mixture onto the wafer bottom, and smooth the top with a palette knife. Drizzle over the berry "jam" and make swirls in it, by drawing a metal skewer back, forth, and around through the mix.

5 Wrap the sides of the cake pan with foil and put it into a deep roasting pan. Boil a pot of water and pour in enough to come halfway up the cake pan; this prevents cracking. Bake for 40 minutes, until set but still a bit wobbly. Turn off the oven and wedge open the door.

6 After 1 hour, remove the cake and place on a wire rack. Remove the sides of the pan. Slide 1 or 2 metal spatulas or palette knives between the wafer base and the bottom of the pan. Carefully transfer the cheesecake to a serving plate, platter, or cake stand, and let cool completely.

7 Meanwhile, put all the ingredients for the compote in a small pan. Heat the compote gently, stirring occasionally, until all the sugar dissolves. Transfer to a bowl to serve.

VARIATION

Change the fruits for the ripple according to the season, though remember that the colors will be dulled after baking.

CALORIES: 645kcals/2694kJ
CARBOHYDRATE: 45g
  sugar: 33g
FAT: 48g
  saturated: 29g
SALT: 0.7g
FIBER: 0.5g

Vanilla cheesecake with summer fruit coulis

This is an indulgent dessert but the rich creaminess is cut by the sharp, fruity flavors of the sauce.

20 mins, plus chilling   50 mins

SPECIAL EQUIPMENT
9in (23cm) springform cake pan
hand-held blender

SERVES 8–10

FOR THE CHEESECAKE
4 tbsp unsalted butter, plus extra for greasing

8oz (225g) vanilla wafers, finely crushed

1 tbsp demerara sugar

1½lb (675g) cream cheese, at room temperature

4 large eggs, separated

¾ cup granulated sugar

1 tsp vanilla extract

2 cups (16oz) sour cream

FOR THE FRUIT COULIS
10oz (300g) frozen summer fruits

¼ cup granulated sugar

1 Preheat the oven to 350°F (180°C). Grease a 9in (23cm) springform cake pan and line it with parchment paper. Melt the butter in a pan over medium heat. Add the wafer crumbs and demerara sugar, and stir until blended. Press the crumbs into the bottom of the pan with the back of a spoon.

2 Beat the cream cheese, egg yolks, ½ cup of the granulated sugar, and the vanilla in a bowl until blended. In a separate bowl, beat the egg whites until stiff. Fold the egg whites into the cream cheese mixture. Pour into the pan and smooth the top.

3 Place the pan in the oven and bake for 45 minutes until set. Remove the pan from the oven and let stand for 10 minutes.

4 Meanwhile, increase the oven temperature to 475°F (240°C). Combine the sour cream and remaining ¼ cup of granulated sugar in a bowl and beat well. Pour over the cheesecake and smooth the top. Bake the cheesecake for 5 minutes. Transfer it to a wire rack to cool completely, then cover and chill for at least 6 hours.

5 To make the summer fruit coulis, put the frozen fruit, sugar, and 3 tbsp of water into a small saucepan with a lid. Cover, place over medium heat, and bring to a boil, then remove the lid, stir, and simmer the fruit for about 5 minutes, or until it is soft.

6 Blend the fruit with a hand-held blender until smooth, then press it through a nylon sieve to remove all the seeds. It can be served warm or cold, and will thicken as it cools.

VARIATION
Instead of a mixture of fruits, try making the coulis just with blackcurrants, for a tart sauce that makes a dramatic color contrast with the cheesecake.

PREPARE AHEAD
The cheesecake and the coulis can both be made up to 3 days ahead, covered, and stored in the fridge until needed. Both should be served slightly chilled, but not fridge-cold, or the flavors will be dulled.

CALORIES: 738kcals/3070kJ
CARBOHYDRATE: 46g
　sugar: 34g
FAT: 58g
　saturated: 34g
SALT: 1g
FIBER: 0.4g

Lemon cheesecake

This cold-set cheesecake needs no baking, and thus produces a lighter, more delicate result.

30 mins, plus chilling   5 mins

SPECIAL EQUIPMENT

9in (22cm) round springform cake pan

SERVES 8

9oz (250g) vanilla wafers

7 tbsp unsalted butter, in cubes

juice and finely grated zest of 2 lemons

1 tbsp (10g) powdered gelatin

12oz (350g) cream cheese, at room temperature

¾ cup granulated sugar

1¼ cups heavy cream

1 Line a 9in (22cm) round springform cake pan with parchment paper. Put the wafers in a bag and crush to crumbs with a rolling pin. Melt the butter and pour over the crushed wafers, mixing well to combine. Press the wafer mixture firmly into the bottom of the pan using a wooden spoon.

2 Place the lemon juice in a small heatproof bowl. Sprinkle the gelatin over the surface of the lemon juice and let stand for 5 minutes to soften. Place the bowl over a pan of hot water and stir until all the granules are dissolved. Set aside to cool. Beat together the cream cheese, granulated sugar, and lemon zest until smooth.

3 In a separate bowl, whisk the heavy cream to soft peaks. Make sure it is not stiff. Beat the gelatin mixture into the cream cheese mixture, stirring well to combine. Gently fold the whisked cream into the cheese mixture. Be careful not to lose volume.

4 Pour the cheese mixture onto the chilled wafer base and spread evenly. Smooth the top with a damp palette knife or the back of a damp spoon. Chill for at least 4 hours or overnight. Run a sharp, thin knife around the inside of the pan. Gently turn the cheesecake onto a plate, making sure you remove the parchment paper before cutting into slices.

CALORIES: 655kcals/2732kJ
CARBOHYDRATE: 45g
  sugar: 30g
FAT: 51g
  saturated: 31g
SALT: 0.8g
FIBER: 0.5g

Amaretti and apricot trifle

A sophisticated new twist on an old classic that takes minutes to prepare with items from the pantry.

15 mins, plus chilling

SERVES 4–6

5¾oz (160g) amaretti cookies

2 tbsp sherry (optional)

1 x 14oz (410g) can apricot halves, drained (juice reserved) and roughly chopped

1lb 2oz (500g) fresh custard

1¼ cups heavy cream, whipped

1 Place all but 3 of the amaretti cookies in a glass serving dish. Sprinkle the sherry (if using) or 2 tbsp of the reserved apricot juice over the cookies.

2 Evenly spread all but 2 tbsp of the apricots over the cookies. Pour the custard over the fruit. Top with the cream and spread out in an even layer.

3 Crumble the reserved cookies. Decorate the trifle with them, and the reserved apricots. Cover and chill for 2 hours before serving, but serve on the day of making.

VARIATION

This trifle is also delicious (and looks dramatic) made with canned, drained morello cherries, and sprinkled with sliced almonds as well as amaretti.

CLEVER WITH LEFTOVERS

Slightly stale amaretti cookies will give a welcome crunch to this trifle.

CALORIES: 515kcals/2140kJ
CARBOHYDRATE: 35g
  sugar: 30g
FAT: 37g
  saturated: 19g
SALT: 0.2g
FIBER: 0.7g

Tiramisu

Irresistible to everyone, this version omits the usual alcohol for a more family-friendly dessert.

20 mins,
plus chilling

SERVES 4-6

1lb 2oz (500g) mascarpone cheese

½ cup confectioners' sugar, sifted

3 tbsp fromage frais or crème fraîche

1¼ cups strong cold coffee

6oz (175g) ladyfingers

1 tbsp cocoa powder

1 Place the mascarpone, confectioners' sugar, and fromage frais in a bowl and beat until soft and well combined.

2 Pour the coffee into a shallow bowl and dip the ladyfingers into it, one at a time, to moisten.

3 Arrange one-third of the fingers in a glass serving bowl. Top with one-third of the mascarpone mixture, spreading it out in an even layer to cover the ladyfingers. Repeat this layering twice more, finishing with a layer of mascarpone.

4 Sift over the cocoa powder. Cover with plastic wrap and chill for at least 1 hour, or overnight, before serving.

VARIATION

Top the tiramisu with finely grated chocolate instead of the cocoa powder. White, dark, or milk chocolate, or a combination of the three, will all work well. For an even more chocolatey tiramisu, melt 5½oz (150g) of chocolate and layer it in, along with the mascarpone and ladyfingers.

CALORIES: 486kcals/2035kJ

CARBOHYDRATE: 32g
sugar: 25g

FAT: 36g
saturated: 24g

SALT: 0.3g

FIBER: 0.8g

Profiteroles

These cream-filled choux pastry buns, drizzled with chocolate sauce, make a deliciously decadent dessert.

30 mins   22 mins

SPECIAL EQUIPMENT

2 piping bags with a ½in (1cm) plain nozzle and ¼in (5mm) star nozzle

SERVES 4

4 tbsp unsalted butter

½ cup all-purpose flour, sifted

2 large eggs, lightly beaten

FOR THE FILLING AND TOPPING

1½ cups heavy cream

7oz (200g) good-quality dark chocolate, broken into pieces

2 tbsp butter

2 tbsp corn syrup

1 Preheat the oven to 425°F (220°C). Line 2 large baking sheets with parchment paper.

2 Put the butter and ⅔ cup of water into a pan and melt. Bring to a boil, remove from the heat, and pour in the flour. Beat until it forms a ball. Cool for 10 minutes.

3 Gradually beat in the eggs to form a stiff, smooth, shiny paste. Spoon into a piping bag with a ½in (1cm) plain nozzle. Pipe walnut-sized rounds and bake for 20 minutes, until golden. Slit the side of each and bake for 2 minutes to crisp, then transfer to a wire rack to cool.

4 For the filling and topping, pour ½ cup cream into a pan and whip the rest to soft peaks. Add the chocolate, butter, and syrup to the cream in the pan and heat gently. Pile the whipped cream into a piping bag fitted with a ¼in (5mm) star nozzle and pipe into the buns. Serve with the sauce.

HOW TO FREEZE

The unfilled buns can be open-frozen, then transferred to a freezer bag and frozen for up to 12 weeks.

CALORIES: 1008kcals/4185kJ

CARBOHYDRATE: 47g
sugar: 37g

FAT: 87g
saturated: 53g

SALT: 0.3g

FIBER: 2.5g

Pannacotta

This simple Italian dessert makes a refreshing end to a meal, served with a fruit compote or fresh fruit salad.

10 mins, plus setting   5 mins

SPECIAL EQUIPMENT

4 x 5fl oz (150ml) ramekins

SERVES 4

1½ cups half-and-half

1 cup whole milk

½ cup granulated sugar

1 tbsp (10g) powdered gelatin

1 tbsp sunflower or vegetable oil

fruit compote, fruit coulis, or fruit salad, to serve

1 Heat 1¼ cups half-and-half and milk in a saucepan. When it is hot, but not boiling, pour it into a bowl and whisk in the sugar until dissolved.

2 Meanwhile, pour the remaining half-and-half into a bowl and sprinkle the gelatin over the top. Let soak for 5 minutes then add it to the hot cream. Heat very gently, stirring, until the gelatin dissolves.

3 Rub the insides of four 5fl oz (150ml) cup ramekins with a piece of paper towel dipped in the oil. Divide the cream mixture between the ramekins, cover, and cool. Transfer to the fridge for at least 2 hours, or until the cream has set.

4 To serve, fill a bowl with hot water and carefully dip the bottom of each ramekin into the water. Run a small knife around the edge of each ramekin, and turn the pannacottas onto plates. Garnish with fruit compote, fruit coulis (see p355), or a fruit salad.

VARIATION

For a Middle Eastern flavor add ½ tsp ground cardamom and 1 tbsp rose water to the cream at the end of step 2.

CALORIES: 359kcals/1499kJ

CARBOHYDRATE: 29g
    sugar: 29g

FAT: 24g
    saturated: 14g

SALT: 0.2g

FIBER: 0g

Crème brûlée

This custard is richer than a crème caramel, and has a sweet, bitter, burnt sugar topping.

10 mins   30-40 mins

SPECIAL EQUIPMENT

4 x 7fl oz (200ml) ramekins

kitchen blowtorch (optional)

SERVES 4

5 large egg yolks

¼ cup granulated sugar, plus 4 tbsp extra for the topping

1 tsp vanilla extract

2 cups whipping cream

1 Preheat the oven to 325°F (160°C). Whisk together the egg yolks, granulated sugar, and vanilla extract. Heat the cream gently over low heat until hot, but not starting to boil. Pour the cream into the egg yolk mixture, whisking constantly.

2 Place four 7fl oz (700ml) ramekins in a roasting pan. Pour the custard mixture into the ramekins. Carefully fill the roasting pan halfway up the sides of the ramekins with hot water, being careful not to splash any into the custards. Transfer to the oven and cook for 30–40 minutes until they are just set, but still wobbling slightly in the middle.

3 Refrigerate the custards for at least 2 hours. When you are ready to serve, sprinkle 1 tbsp of granulated sugar over each custard and gently spread it out with the back of a teaspoon. Preheat the broiler to its highest setting, or take out your blowtorch (if using).

4 If using a broiler, place the custards on a baking sheet, put them very close to a very hot broiler, and watch them carefully. Remove them when the sugar has melted to a dark brown caramel. Alternatively, use a kitchen blowtorch to melt the sugar, sweeping the flame evenly over the sugar until it melts.

CLEVER WITH LEFTOVERS

The egg whites left over from this dish can be frozen for a Pavlova (see p345), or for meringues. Don't worry if you can't remember how many egg whites you have frozen, just weigh them and double the weight to calculate how much sugar to use in the meringue recipe.

CALORIES: 686kcals/2842kJ

CARBOHYDRATE: 36g
    sugar: 36g

FAT: 57g
    saturated: 33g

SALT: 0.1g

FIBER: 0g

Crème caramel

These desserts are not as difficult as they seem, gentle cooking in a water bath will help them come out perfectly.

10 mins, plus chilling

30 mins

SPECIAL EQUIPMENT

4 x 7fl oz (200ml), or 6 x 5fl oz (150ml) ramekins

SERVES 4–6

1 cup granulated sugar

2 cups whole milk

2 large eggs, plus 2 large egg yolks

1 tsp vanilla extract

1 Preheat the oven to 350°F (180°C). Put ⅔ cup of the sugar into a small, heavy-bottomed saucepan and mix in 2 tbsp of water. Now heat the sugar over medium heat until it dissolves; do not stir the mixture at all, or it will spoil. Once the sugar has melted, gently swirl the pan occasionally to ensure it cooks evenly. Watch the sugar carefully as it will start to change color suddenly. Once it is a golden brown caramel color, take it off the heat and carefully distribute it evenly between four 7fl oz (200ml) or six 5fl oz (150ml) ramekins. Pick up each ramekin and swirl it around to make sure the bottom and a bit of the sides are coated in the caramel.

2 Heat the milk over low heat. Whisk together the eggs, egg yolks, vanilla, and remaining ⅓ cup of granulated sugar until well combined. When the milk is hot but not boiling, pour it over the egg mixture and whisk it well. To prevent bubbles in the finished caramel, rest the mixture for 30 minutes in the fridge at this point.

3 Place the ramekins in a roasting pan. Pour the custard mixture into the ramekins. Carefully fill the roasting pan halfway up the sides of the ramekins with hot water, being careful not to splash any into the custards. Transfer to the oven and cook for 25–30 minutes until they are just set, but still wobbling slightly in the middle.

4 Refrigerate for at least 2 hours. To serve, run a small, sharp knife around the insides of the ramekins and turn them onto small serving plates, being sure to scrape all the caramel over the top.

VARIATION

Try adding 1 tbsp cocoa powder to the heating milk for a chocolate caramel. Or, for a touch of crunch, scatter the desserts with chopped roasted pecan nuts.

CALORIES:	252kcals/1065kJ
CARBOHYDRATE:	40g
sugar:	40g
FAT:	7g
saturated:	3g
SALT:	0.2g
FIBER:	0g

Quick chocolate mousse

Truly the easiest mousse in the world. It is made with raw egg whites, so the usual advice applies (see p11).

20 mins, plus chilling

SERVES 4

7oz (200g) good-quality dark chocolate, about 70 percent cocoa solids, broken into pieces

4 large eggs, separated

1 tbsp liqueur, such as blackcurrant or orange (optional)

1 Put the chocolate in a heatproof bowl over a pot of simmering water. The bowl should not touch the water. Melt the chocolate gently over the heat, stirring occasionally. Remove from the heat and allow it to cool completely, but not to solidify again. Whisk the egg whites to stiff peaks.

2 When the chocolate is cool enough, beat in the egg yolks, and then the liqueur (if using). The mixture will stiffen slightly. Take one-third of the egg whites and beat them into the melted chocolate mixture. This will loosen the chocolate up enough to be able to fold in the remaining egg whites.

3 Gently fold the remaining egg whites into the chocolate, making sure they are completely combined, but trying to keep in as much air as possible.

4 Pour the mousse into 1 large or 4 small serving bowls. Chill until firm before serving.

CALORIES: 354kcals/1481kJ

CARBOHYDRATE: 31g
    sugar: 31g

FAT: 21g
    saturated: 10g

SALT: 0.2g

FIBER: 1.5g

This is very rich, and if you have younger children, they might like it made with a milk chocolate with lower cocoa solids.

Fussy eaters!

Creamy custard

The secret to any custard is to heat it gently, so that the eggs do not scramble.

5 mins   10 mins

SERVES 4

1¼ cups whole milk

2 large egg yolks

1 tbsp granulated sugar

¼ tsp vanilla extract

1 tsp cornstarch

1 Heat the milk until it is hot, but not boiling. In a bowl, whisk together the egg yolks, sugar, vanilla extract, and cornstarch.

2 Gradually pour the hot milk into the eggs in a thin stream, whisking it continuously. Return the mixture to the rinsed-out saucepan and place over medium heat, whisking constantly, until it starts to bubble.

3 Reduce the heat to a low simmer and cook for another 5 minutes, until the mixture thickens and coats the back of a wooden spoon.

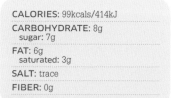

CALORIES: 99kcals/414kJ

CARBOHYDRATE: 8g
    sugar: 7g

FAT: 6g
    saturated: 3g

SALT: trace

FIBER: 0g

VARIATION

To make a chocolate custard, which is especially appealing to children, add 1 tbsp cocoa powder with the cornstarch. For a more grown-up custard, stir in 1–2 tbsp of Irish cream liqueur when the custard is ready to be served.

French crêpes

Even if you only make crêpes once a year, a good, stress-free recipe will help you cook them with style!

10 mins, plus resting 15–20 mins

SPECIAL EQUIPMENT

electric hand-held mixer

7in (18cm) non-stick frying pan

MAKES 8

¾ cup all-purpose flour

2 large eggs, lightly beaten

¾ cup whole milk

2 tbsp butter, melted

sunflower or vegetable oil, for cooking

FOR THE FILLING

sliced bananas and chocolate spread

stewed apple and ground cinnamon

maple syrup and walnuts

1 Sift the flour into a large bowl. Add the eggs and ¼ cup of the milk and, using an electric hand-held mixer, whisk well to combine.

2 Gradually add the remaining milk, whisking constantly. Stir in both the melted butter and ¼ cup of cold water. Whisk well to give a thin, smooth batter. Set aside to rest for 30 minutes, covered with a clean kitchen towel.

3 Brush the bottom of a 7in (18cm) non-stick frying pan with a little oil. Heat over high temperature on the stovetop.

4 Carefully pour in just enough batter to coat the bottom of the pan and swirl the pan to give an even layer of batter. Cook for 40–60 seconds or until the crêpe is set.

Flip over using a palette knife and cook the other side; reducing the burner temperature if the crêpe is browning too quickly.

5 Remove from the pan and place on a warmed plate. Repeat to cook 7 more crêpes, occasionally brushing the pan with more oil. Stack the crêpes up with a sheet of waxed paper between each, and cover the stack with foil to keep them all warm. Serve the crêpes with bowls containing the banana, apple, and walnut fillings.

PREPARE AHEAD

The crêpe batter can be made up to 2 hours in advance. It is best to cover and chill it after 30 minutes to avoid any risk of taint or fermentation, especially in hot weather.

Slice bananas, oranges, or strawberries, mix with chocolate spread, and use this as a filling to introduce fruit into the diet of children who say they don't like fruit.

Fussy eaters!

CALORIES: 124kcals/519kJ

CARBOHYDRATE: 10g
sugar: 1.5g

FAT: 7g
saturated: 3g

SALT: 0.1g

FIBER: 0.5g

Honey and mustard roasted sausages

These are a favorite at both children's and adults' parties. Make more than you think you'll need...

5 mins | 25 mins, plus resting

MAKES 20

20 good-quality cocktail sausages

1 tbsp sunflower or vegetable oil

2 tbsp honey

2 tbsp grain mustard

1 Preheat the oven to 400°F (200°C). Prick the sausages all over with a small fork and put them in a roasting pan. Toss them in the oil so that they are all well covered, then roast at the top of the oven for 20 minutes, turning occasionally, until they are browned and cooked through.

2 In a small bowl, whisk together the honey and mustard. Remove the cooked sausages from the oven, toss them in the honey mixture, and return them to the oven for 5 minutes, turning once, until they are glazed with the honey mixture and sticky.

3 Remove from the oven and let rest for 5 minutes before serving.

PREPARE AHEAD

The sausages can be precooked up to the end of step 1, up to 2 days ahead, covered, and refrigerated. Finish them in the oven with the honey glaze just before serving.

CALORIES: 61kcals/256kJ

CARBOHYDRATE: 2.5g
  sugar: 2g

FAT: 4.5g
  saturated: 1.5g

SALT: 0.4g

FIBER: 0g

Oven-baked potato skins with sour cream dip

These crispy potato skins are a real hit at a party and are a reasonably healthy option, as well as fun to eat.

10 mins | 10 mins

SERVES 4

4 large baking potatoes

2 tbsp sunflower or vegetable oil

salt and freshly ground black pepper

⅔ cup sour cream

4 scallions, finely sliced

1 Preheat the oven to 400°F (200°C). Bake the potatoes in the oven for up to 1 hour, until they are cooked through. Set aside to cool; this will make cutting them more manageable.

2 Cut each potato in half and scoop out all but ¼ in (5mm) of the potato from the skins. Set this aside for another time, perhaps to make mashed potato or fishcakes. Cut each halved potato skin into 4 long, thin slices. Brush on all sides with oil and place, skin-side down, on a baking sheet. Sprinkle them with salt and return to the oven for 20 minutes, until crispy and golden brown on top.

3 Mix together the sour cream and scallions and season well. Serve the potato skins with the sour cream dip.

PREPARE AHEAD

The potatoes can be baked up to 2 days in advance, so try to cook them when you are using the oven for something else anyway. The potato flesh can be used to make the Sausage and mustard mash canapés (see p308), if you are serving them at the party as well.

CALORIES: 317kcals/1330kJ

CARBOHYDRATE: 42g
  sugar: 4g

FAT: 13g
  saturated: 5g

SALT: trace

FIBER: 4.5g

Mini-pizzas

These individual pizzas are perfect party-sized children's snacks, and can be topped and cooked at the last minute.

20 mins, plus rising   10 mins

SPECIAL EQUIPMENT
food processor with dough hook (optional)

MAKES 10

FOR THE CRUSTS
2 cups bread flour, plus extra for dusting

¼ tsp salt

1½ tsp dried yeast

1 tbsp olive oil, plus extra for greasing

FOR THE TOPPING
1 x 14oz (400g) can crushed tomatoes, or 1½ cups tomato sauce

2 garlic cloves, crushed

1 tbsp olive oil

freshly ground black pepper

selection of prepared pizza toppings

5½oz (150g) finely sliced mozzarella

1 Put the flour and salt into a large bowl, or the bowl of a food processor fitted with a dough hook. Dissolve the yeast in ⅔ cup of warm water, then add the oil.

2 If making by hand, make a well in the center of the flour. Gradually pour in the liquid, stirring to form a rough dough. Use your hands to bring it together. Turn the dough out onto a floured work surface. Knead for up to 10 minutes, until smooth, glossy, and elastic.

3 If making in a food processor, turn the machine on to a low speed. Pour in the liquid a little at a time, until the mixture begins to come together. You may need to turn off the machine and scrape down the sides once or twice to ensure that all the flour is incorporated. Increase the speed to medium and continue to knead for 5–7 minutes, until smooth, glossy, and elastic.

4 Put the dough in an oiled bowl and cover loosely with plastic wrap. Let rise in a warm place for 2 hours, or until doubled in size.

5 Meanwhile, make the tomato sauce. Put the tomatoes, garlic, and olive oil into a small saucepan and season well with pepper. Bring to a boil, reduce the heat to a low simmer, and cook for 45 minutes to 1 hour, until you have a rich, thick sauce. Taste for seasoning.

6 When ready to cook, preheat the oven to 450°F (230°C). When the dough has risen, turn it onto a lightly floured work surface and knead it briefly. Divide it into 10 equal-sized pieces and roll each one out to a diameter of 5–6in (12–15cm). Lay them on several baking sheets.

7 Top the mini-pizzas with 1 tbsp of the tomato sauce, spread thinly, and any toppings you would like. Finish with a thin layer of mozzarella cheese, and cook at the top of the hot oven for 10 minutes, until golden brown and crispy.

PREPARE AHEAD
The dough can be made the day before up to step 4 and left to rise slowly in the fridge overnight. Just before the party, roll the crusts out and have them ready to top and cook at the last minute.

Put out bowls of toppings and encourage children to build their own pizzas. This way they are more likely to eat them. Try ham, black olives, mushrooms, peppers, or pineapple.

Fussy eaters!

CALORIES: 151kcals/673kJ

CARBOHYDRATE: 19g
sugar: 1.5g

FAT: 5.5g
saturated: 2.5g

SALT: 0.4g

FIBER: 1.5g

Triple decker sandwiches

Getting children to eat anything healthy at a party is not easy; making the savory choices attractive helps.

10 mins

MAKES 36 (bite-sized sandwiches)

8 slices of thin-cut whole wheat bread

4 slices of thin-cut white bread

softened butter or margarine, for spreading

4 slices of ham

16 thin slices of cucumber

¼ cup cream cheese, softened

1 Spread all the slices of bread on one side only with softened butter or margarine.

2 Place 4 of the whole wheat bread slices, buttered-side up, on a cutting board, and lay a piece of ham on each.

3 Top the ham with a white slice of bread, buttered-side down. Butter the top of the bread, then put 4 pieces of cucumber on top of each.

4 Finally, spread the buttered side of the remaining whole wheat bread with 1 tbsp of cream cheese spread per slice and put it, cheese-side down, on the cucumber to make a three-tiered sandwich. Press down well.

5 Trim the sandwiches of their crusts, then cut each sandwich into 9 small squares to serve.

PREPARE AHEAD

These sandwiches can be made with frozen bread slices and left to defrost for 1 day in the fridge, packed in an airtight container or wrapped in foil. Trim them of their crusts, but do not cut them until the last minute to keep them from drying out.

CALORIES: 37kcals/157kJ
CARBOHYDRATE: 4g
  sugar: 0.3g
FAT: 2g
  saturated: 1g
SALT: 0.2g
FIBER: 0.6g

Sushi sandwiches

Turn party sandwiches into something special with these easy-to-make sushi versions.

20 mins

MAKES 24 (bite-sized sandwiches)

6 large slices of white or whole wheat bread, crusts removed

1 x 7oz (185g) can of tuna, drained

¼ cup good-quality mayonnaise, plus 1 tbsp

2 scallions, finely chopped

salt and freshly ground black pepper

½ large red bell pepper, finely sliced

½ cucumber, seeded and finely sliced

1 Roll each slice of bread out as thinly as you can with a rolling pin. Mash together the tuna, ¼ cup of mayonnaise, and scallions and season well. Make sure the resulting paste is smooth.

2 Lay a slice of bread out widthwise. Spread a little extra mayonnaise in a ½in (1cm) line at one long edge of the piece of bread farthest from you (to help the sandwich stick together).

Spread a thin layer of tuna over the bread, stopping where the line of mayonnaise starts. Lay a line of red bell pepper at the long edge of the bread nearest to you, and top it with a thin line of cucumber.

3 Pick up the edge nearest you, fold it over the vegetables, then roll until it sticks itself together with the mayonnaise. Trim the edges and cut into 4 pieces, using a sawing action so the shape does not get spoiled. Serve upright.

VARIATION

A vegetarian version can be made with cream cheese, carrot sticks, and a layer of arugula or watercress.

CALORIES: 56kcals/235kJ
CARBOHYDRATE: 4.5g
  sugar: 0.5g
FAT: 3g
  saturated: 0.5g
SALT: 0.2g
FIBER: 0.5g

Cheesy chicken meatballs

These chicken meatballs are easy-to-handle finger food and an ideal choice for a children's party.

10 mins, plus chilling   10 mins

MAKES 20

10oz (300g) ground chicken

½ cup fresh white bread crumbs

¾oz (20g) finely grated Parmesan cheese

2 tbsp finely chopped flat-leaf parsley

salt and freshly ground black pepper

1 tbsp olive oil

1 tbsp butter

1 In a bowl, mix all the ingredients together, apart from the oil and butter, and season well. You may need to use your hands to really get them well combined.

2 Form the mixture into walnut-sized balls and roll them between damp hands to firm them up. Place on a plate, cover, and refrigerate for at least 30 minutes before use.

3 Heat the oil and butter in a large, non-stick frying pan and cook the chicken balls over medium heat for 5–7 minutes, turning occasionally, until they are golden brown and springy to the touch.

VARIATION

Add mushrooms or red bell peppers to the meatballs, ground in a mini food processor, for extra goodness.

HOW TO FREEZE

The cooked meatballs can be cooled and open-frozen on a baking sheet, then transferred into freezer bags for easy storage. Defrost and reheat thoroughly before serving. Use up within 8 weeks.

CALORIES: 39kcals/166kJ

CARBOHYDRATE: 2g
  sugar: 0.1g

FAT: 2g
  saturated: 1g

SALT: 0.1g

FIBER: 0.1g

Tuna and corn melts

A few hot snacks are welcome at a children's party, and these melts are always popular.

5 mins   10–15 mins

MAKES 8

8 x ½in- (1.5cm-) thick slices of baguette

2 tbsp olive oil

7oz (185g) can of tuna, drained

¼ cup canned corn, drained

2 scallions, finely chopped (optional)

2 tbsp mayonnaise

2½oz (75g) grated cheese, such as Cheddar

salt and freshly ground black pepper

1 Preheat the oven to 425°F (220°C). Place the slices of baguette on a baking sheet and brush both sides with a little oil. Bake at the top of the oven for 5–7 minutes, turning once, until lightly browned on both sides. Set aside.

2 In a bowl, mash together the tuna, corn, scallions (if using), mayonnaise, and half the cheese and season well.

3 Divide the topping equally between the baguette slices, and top each piece with some of the remaining cheese. Bake the slices in the hot oven for another 5–7 minutes, until they are hot and the cheese has melted to a nice golden brown. Remove from the oven and allow to cool for at least 5 minutes before serving.

PREPARE AHEAD

These can be prepared up to the point of baking, covered, then stored in the fridge for up to 1 day. Remove from the fridge and bake in the hot oven as in step 3.

CALORIES: 243kcals/1022kJ

CARBOHYDRATE: 23g
  sugar: 2g

FAT: 11.5g
  saturated: 3.5g

SALT: 1g

FIBER: 1.5g

Mini-burgers

These are hard to beat. Make them for your family and friends. They'll soon ask you to make them again!

30 mins   15 mins

MAKES 12–16

FOR THE BURGERS

9oz (250g) ground beef

1¾oz (50g) finely grated Parmesan

¼ cup fresh bread crumbs

1½ tbsp olive oil

½ garlic clove, crushed

1 tbsp finely chopped onion

1 large egg, lightly beaten

1 tsp dried oregano

olive oil, for frying

TO SERVE

16 mini-bread rolls

2 tomatoes, thinly sliced

lettuce leaves

jar of tomato sauce or tomato salsa

CALORIES: 159kcals/669kJ

CARBOHYDRATE: 16.5g
   sugar: 1g

FAT: 7g
   saturated: 2g

SALT: 0.6g

FIBER: 1g

1 Mix all the ingredients for the burgers in a bowl. Use your hands to mix everything well.

2 Form the mixture into balls about the size of walnuts and then flatten them. Chill the mini-burgers in the fridge. Wash your hands well.

3 Place a large frying pan over medium heat and add a little oil. Cook the burgers for about 5 minutes, turning once halfway. Make sure the meat is cooked through by sticking a fork in and making sure the juices that run out are clear. If they are not, continue to cook for another minute, then check again.

4 Carefully cut the rolls in half. Fill each roll with a cooked burger, a tomato slice, a lettuce leaf, and some tomato sauce.

CLEVER WITH LEFTOVERS

Bread crumbs are also useful to coat fish sticks, fishcakes, chicken nuggets, and a multitude of other great dishes. Make bread crumbs every time you have bread turning stale by blending it in a food processor to fine crumbs. Freeze in a bag.

Fish and potato wedges

Fish and chips is a favorite meal around the world. Try these sweet potato wedges with the fish instead.

15 mins   25 mins

SPECIAL EQUIPMENT
oil thermometer

SERVES 4

FOR THE WEDGES

2 large sweet potatoes

2 tbsp olive oil

FOR THE BATTERED FISH

1 cup all-purpose flour

1 tsp baking soda

1 tsp paprika

⅔ cup cold sparkling water

pinch of black pepper

1 cup sunflower or vegetable oil

10oz (300g) white fish, such as pollock or haddock, cut into ½in (1cm) strips

CALORIES: 446kcals/1880kJ

CARBOHYDRATE: 52g
   sugar: 9g

FAT: 18g
   saturated: 2.5g

SALT: 1g

FIBER: 6g

1 Preheat the oven to 400°F (200°C). Scrub the sweet potatoes and slice into wedges.

2 Place the wedges on a large baking sheet and pour the olive oil over them. Roast for 25 minutes, or until lightly browned.

3 Meanwhile, to make the batter, put the flour, baking soda, paprika, and sparkling water in a mixing bowl, season with black pepper, then whisk until smooth.

4 Heat the sunflower oil in a deep-sided frying pan to 375°F (190°C). Coat the fish in the batter.

5 Carefully lower a few strips of the fish into the oil, being careful not to crowd the pan. After about 2 minutes, when it's golden brown, it's ready. Remove with a slotted spoon, drain on paper towels, and serve with the wedges.

COOK'S TIP

This batter puffs up because of the air trapped by the baking soda and sparkling water, which expands when heated. Add these to any batter for deep-frying.

Rainbow popcorn

Try making this vividly colored popcorn for a (slightly) healthier alternative to the usual store-bought treats.

10 mins, plus drying   10 mins

MAKES 1 LARGE BOWL

½ tbsp sunflower or vegetable oil

¼ cup popcorn kernels

¾ cup granulated sugar

2 tbsp butter

3 different food colorings

1 Heat the oil in a large, heavy-bottomed saucepan with a lid. Add the popcorn and shake the pan so it spreads out into a single layer. Cover and place over high heat until the popcorn starts to pop. Reduce the heat to low and continue to cook, covered, until the popping noises have stopped. Shake the pan occasionally, but don't lift the lid too early, or the popcorn will shoot out of the pan.

2 Transfer the popcorn carefully to a large bowl to cool, being careful to leave behind any unpopped kernels at the bottom of the saucepan.

3 Make a sugar syrup by gently melting together the sugar, butter, and 3 tbsp of water. Bring to a boil and reduce the heat to a simmer, stirring constantly, until the sugar has melted. Divide the mixture between 3 small bowls and add a few drops of different food coloring to each bowl until you have the desired shade.

4 Divide the cooled popcorn into 3 separate large bowls and pour the colored syrup over each bowl, one at a time. You can use a large spoon or your hands to mix the color into the popcorn (hands are more effective, but it is a messy job so you might want to wear plastic food preparation gloves).

5 Once the popcorn is colored, spread a large sheet of waxed paper over a table and lay it out to dry, in a single layer, with the colors separated. When it is dry, toss it a little to break it up, then serve it in a large glass bowl, mixed together.

CALORIES: 1250kcals/5258kJ
CARBOHYDRATE: 224g
sugar: 151g
FAT: 33g
saturated: 16g
SALT: 0.4g
FIBER: 5g

Mini-sausage rolls

These are lovely, easy versions of sausage rolls, and use just a few store-bought ingredients.

15 mins   15 mins

MAKES 36 (bite-sized sausage rolls)

12 good-quality cocktail sausages

1 x 14oz pack ready-rolled puff pastry

all-purpose flour, for dusting

1 large egg, lightly beaten

1 Preheat the oven to 425°F (220°C). Line 2 baking sheets with parchment paper.

2 Use a pair of scissors to cut through a sausage casing and gently ease it away, leaving a casingless sausage. Re-roll it with your hands, and repeat, to get 12 even-sized rolls of sausage.

3 Lay the sheet of puff pastry out onto a lightly floured work surface and roll it out just a little, if necessary, to form a 9½ x 14in (24 x 36cm) rectangle. Cut this into twelve 2½ x 5in (6 x 12cm) pieces.

4 Brush a pastry square lightly with egg. Place a sausage at the end nearest you, then roll it up so that the pastry overlaps slightly, sealing in the sausage. Place each seam-side down and cut it with a sharp knife into 3. Repeat to make 36 bite-sized rolls. Brush with egg and bake for 15 minutes.

5 Remove the sausage rolls from the oven and transfer them to a wire rack to cool until you are ready to serve them, either warm or cold.

HOW TO FREEZE

The sausage rolls can be open-frozen, uncooked, then transferred to a freezer bag until needed. Defrost as many as you need on a plate, then bake as in step 4. Use up within 8 weeks.

CALORIES: 56kcals/233kJ
CARBOHYDRATE: 3.5g
sugar: 0.2g
FAT: 4g
saturated: 1.5g
SALT: 0.2g
FIBER: 0g

Kids' parties

The first birthday party you throw for your child can be a nerve-wracking experience, but do take comfort in the fact that when children are very young they may not remember much of it! Even so, the pressure from your child and other parents to produce a marvelous party can be intense. A house full of children, high on sugar and each others' company, needs to be managed well, so plan to spend most of your time with the children, not in the kitchen. Prepare as much as you can ahead of time including checking for any food allergies or vegetarian guests. Finally, don't feel everything must be picture-perfect.

The perfectly balanced party

When you're planning a party meal for young children, remember that they probably will not eat a great deal. Inevitably they will be over-excited and less interested in the food than the party itself, so it makes sense to produce a number of small, bite-sized choices that will cover a variety of tastes. Try to balance hot with cold; sweet with savory, so that there is a bit of everything.

savory first

A good trick is to lay the table with a variety of savory items first and hold back the sweet treats until these healthier foods have been eaten.

Chips later

Try keeping back the chips for a while, and then "remembering" to get them from the kitchen. By this time, hopefully, your guests will have eaten at least one sandwich!

What to serve

It's a party, so the children will want a few classic treats sugar-coated with frosting and sprinkles, but tempt them with healthy options too by making them look appealing with flags, colorful accompaniments, and fun serving dishes.

Hot options You may want to include some hot food items, such as these Mini burgers (p366), especially if the weather is cold. Keep the portions bite-sized and easy to handle and get everyone to dive into them while they're still warm.

For a bit of extra indulgence, decorate these jellies with sprinkles or a dollop of whipped cream.

Sweet treats Colorful food always gets the tastebuds tingling, such as these vibrantly colored Traffic-light jellies (p371). Add these to a well-decorated table, maybe one with a theme, alongside bright and cheery plates and party hats.

Give your frosting texture by making gentle grooves with a small palette knife.

Serving the cake This Butterfly cake (p375) is easy to make and can be decorated with pretty pastel-colored frosting shapes and sparkles. Both this and the Caterpillar cake (p377) can be baked and then frozen uniced for up to three months.

Bite-sized sushi-roll sandwiches look unusual and very appealing.

Savory eats Serve up sandwiches that are the right size for little fingers and make them as attractive as possible. This is a particularly good idea for any "healthy" savory options, such as these pinwheel Sushi sandwiches (p364).

Drinks If you want to reduce the sugar rush, try serving some fresh fruit-based cordials or chilled flavored milkshakes instead of sugary soft drinks and juices. Make them look grown-up adding straws or cocktail umbrellas.

Healthy party choices

Here are some healthy or less sugary choices for party food.

★ Small sandwiches with plain fillings and the crusts removed

★ Cocktail sausages, hot or cold (p362)

★ Cherry tomatoes and cucumber slices

★ Grapes and strawberries

★ Fruit kebabs (snip off the sharp end of the wooden skewer before serving)

★ Rainbow popcorn (p367)

★ Mini muffins, such as Banana and date mini muffins (p58)

★ Small squares of Oatmeal bars or homemade Granola breakfast bars (p474)

★ Mini pizzas (p460)

★ Fruit juice "cocktails"

★ Fruity ice pops (p59)

Party bags

Children probably won't be hungry enough to eat the birthday cake at the party, so wrap slices in a napkin and put them in the party bags to take home. Depending on the age of the children (and the views of their parents) sweets may not always be appropriate in the party bags. Try giving little toys instead.

Easy cheesy straws

This is the simplest way to make a quick puff pastry, but if time is short use store-bought instead.

20 mins, plus chilling   15 mins

MAKES 15

7 tbsp butter

1 cup all-purpose flour, sifted, plus extra for dusting

¼ tsp salt

1 large egg yolk

1 tsp smoked paprika

3½oz (100g) finely grated cheese, such as aged Cheddar

1 Freeze the butter for 30 minutes, until semi-frozen. Dust a large grater with flour (to keep the butter from sticking). Grate the butter into a large bowl. Rub in the flour and salt with your fingers. Add 4–5 tbsp of cold water and bring it together to form a dough. Wrap it in plastic wrap and chill for 30 minutes. Preheat the oven to 400°F (200°C).

2 Roll the dough out on a floured work surface into a rectangle about 8 x 12in (20 x 30cm).

3 Brush the surface of the dough with the egg yolk and sprinkle over the smoked paprika. Sprinkle the cheese over in a thin layer, and press it in well with the flat of your hands. Fold the dough in half and press down well to enclose the cheese totally.

4 Cut the dough into 15 strips, each about ½in (1cm) wide. Hold the top of each strip and twist the bottom a few times to make a dough spiral.

5 Place the cheese straws onto a baking sheet and bake for 15 minutes at the top of the oven. Cool on the pan for 5 minutes, then transfer to a wire rack to cool completely.

HOW TO FREEZE

The cheese straws can be open-frozen at the end of step 4, then transferred to a freezer bag for up to 12 weeks. Defrost thoroughly in the fridge and bake as in step 5.

CALORIES: 82kcals/342kJ
CARBOHYDRATE: 4.5g
  sugar: 0.1g
FAT: 6g
  saturated: 4g
SALT: 0.2g
FIBER: 0.3g

Pretzeldogs

These are simple to prepare and guaranteed to be a hit at any child's party.

30 mins, plus proofing   15-20 mins, plus resting

MAKES 8

1¼ cups white bread flour, plus extra for dusting

¾ cup all-purpose flour

½ tsp salt

1 tbsp granulated sugar

1 tsp dried yeast

½ tbsp sunflower or vegetable oil, plus extra for greasing

8 hot dogs

mustard (optional)

FOR THE GLAZE

1 tbsp baking soda

coarse sea salt

1 Put the flours, salt, and sugar in a bowl. Sprinkle the yeast over ⅔ cup of warm water in a separate bowl. Stir, leave for 5 minutes to dissolve, and add the oil.

2 Pour the liquid into the flour mixture, stirring to a dough. Knead for 10 minutes until pliable. Put into an oiled bowl, cover, and leave in a warm place for 1–2 hours until doubled in size.

3 Turn onto a floured work surface and knock back. Divide it into 8 pieces. Take each piece and roll it to 18in (45cm) long.

4 Take each hot dog and brush with mustard (if using). Wrap the pretzel dough around it in a spiral to seal completely, with only the top and bottom showing.

5 Place on baking sheets lined with parchment paper, cover with oiled plastic wrap and a kitchen towel, and leave in a warm place for about 30 minutes until well puffed up. Preheat the oven to 400°F (200°C).

6 Dissolve the baking soda in 3½ cups of boiling water in a pan. Poach the hotdogs in the water, in batches of 3, for 1 minute. Remove with a slotted spatula, dry on a kitchen towel, and return to the baking sheets.

7 Scatter with sea salt and bake for 15 minutes until golden brown and shiny. Remove from the oven and cool on a wire rack for 5 minutes before serving. These are best eaten while still warm, but can be stored in an airtight container in the refrigerator overnight.

CALORIES: 171kcals/722kJ
CARBOHYDRATE: 28g
  sugar: 3g
FAT: 4.5g
  saturated: 1.5g
SALT: 2.3g
FIBER: 1.5g

Sparkly chocolate-dipped breadsticks

Make these chocolate-dipped breadsticks as a pretty, sweet snack that isn't all about sugar.

20 mins, plus setting   5 mins

MAKES 12

2½oz (75g) good-quality chocolate

granulated sugar, to rest the breadsticks in

12 breadsticks

jar of small sprinkles

1 Put the chocolate in a small heatproof bowl over a saucepan of simmering water, making sure the bowl does not touch the water. Remove as soon as the chocolate melts. Transfer to a small, high glass, so it is 2in (5cm) deep.

2 Pour sugar 1in (2.5cm) deep into 3 glasses. These will help the dipped breadsticks dry without touching (see photo, below).

3 Dip a breadstick into the melted chocolate, tilting the glass to get a greater depth of chocolate. Carefully drip off any excess back into the glass (they should be sparingly coated), and push the undipped end into the sugar in 1 of the glasses. Continue to dip all the breadsticks. (If you work quickly you could dip all 12 breadsticks in one go, but otherwise do half at a time.) Set aside until slightly tacky but not entirely set, about 20 minutes.

4 Hold a chocolate-dipped breadstick over a bowl and pour the sprinkles generously over so they stick, and the extras fall into the bowl below. Repeat for all the chocolate-dipped breadsticks.

5 Wait until the chocolate has set, then serve. These are best served on the day they are made.

> CALORIES: 115kcals/488kJ
> CARBOHYDRATE: 20g
>   sugar: 11g
> FAT: 3g
>   saturated: 2g
> SALT: 0.3g
> FIBER: 0.8g

Traffic-light jellies

Fresh, sugar-free fruit juices make a healthier jelly. These take most of the day to set, but only minutes to make.

15 mins, plus setting   5 mins

SPECIAL EQUIPMENT

10 small plastic glasses, to hold ⅔ cup each

MAKES 10

3 x (10g) packages unflavored powdered gelatin

2 cups of 3 different fresh fruit juice, such as pineapple, cranberry, kiwi, and apple (try to get different colors)

1 Place ¼ cup of one of the fruit juices in a small bowl. Sprinkle one package of gelatin over the top and allow it to soften for 5-10 minutes.

2 Heat the remaining 1¾ cups of the juice gently over low heat in a small saucepan. Take the pan off the heat. Add the gelatin and juice mixture, whisking to dissolve. Cool, then divide equally between 10 small plastic glasses. Chill to set.

3 Repeat the process with the second jelly, making sure you choose a contrasting color to the first. Make sure the second fruit juice mixture is cold before pouring it carefully on top of the set jelly.

4 Repeat the process with the final fruit juice and return to the fridge to set before serving.

PREPARE AHEAD

These jellies can be made up to 3 days ahead and kept, covered in plastic wrap, in the fridge until needed. As the process of setting is a long one, they can also be made over 2 or 3 days.

> CALORIES: 61kcals/260kJ
> CARBOHYDRATE: 12g
>   sugar: 12g
> FAT: 0g
>   saturated: 0g
> SALT: trace
> FIBER: 0.2g

Chocolate-dipped strawberries

A simple fruity snack is all the better after being dipped in rich, dark chocolate.

15 mins   5 mins

SERVES 8

14oz (400g) strawberries, not too ripe

3½oz (100g) good-quality dark chocolate, more than 60 percent cocoa solids, broken into pieces

1 Wash and dry the strawberries well. Try to leave the hulls in, as this makes the finished fruit easier to pick up.

2 Put the chocolate in a small heatproof bowl and place over a saucepan of simmering water, making sure the bowl does not touch the water. Stir frequently and remove it as soon as it melts.

3 Line a large baking sheet with waxed paper. Hold each strawberry by its leaves and dip the end in the chocolate, so half of the fruit is covered in chocolate.

Allow any excess chocolate to drip off back into the bowl, then place the strawberries on the baking sheet, making sure they do not touch each other.

4 Put in a cool place to set. These should be served the same day, as the chocolate will soften if the strawberries are overripe, or if they are kept in the fridge for too long.

VARIATION

Dip orange segments, pineapple pieces, or even large grapes, for a chocolatey fruit platter.

CALORIES: 77kcals/324kJ

CARBOHYDRATE: 10g
  sugar: 10g

FAT: 3.5g
  saturated: 2g

SALT: 0g

FIBER: 1g

Frozen fruity yogurt popsicles

These summery treats are packed full of vitamin-rich blueberries and have a lovely vivid color.

5 mins,
plus freezing

SPECIAL EQUIPMENT

blender or hand-held blender

popsicle molds

MAKES 6–8

16oz (2 cups) plain yogurt

7oz (200g) blueberries

⅔ cup confectioners' sugar

1 Simply blend all the ingredients together in a blender, or using a hand-held blender, until they are smooth, then freeze in popsicle molds for up to 8 weeks.

2 Put the molds carefully under running hot water for a minute to help release the popsicles when you are ready to serve them.

VARIATION

Try making these with other soft fruits, such as strawberries, peaches, or raspberries, and serve all at once for a range of flavors and colors. Just keep the weight of fruit for each batch to 7oz (200g).

CLEVER WITH LEFTOVERS

If you have a few leftover berries or other summer soft fruit that need to be used up quickly, scale this recipe down to make just 1 or 2 popsicles at a time. That way, you will soon build up a rainbow of different colors.

CALORIES: 100kcals/425kJ

CARBOHYDRATE: 16g
  sugar: 16g

FAT: 2g
  saturated: 1g

SALT: 0.1g

FIBER: 0.3g

Chocolate cake pops

These create a fabulous centerpiece, and you can customize the chocolate color and sprinkles to suit your party.

45 mins | **20–25 mins, plus chilling**

SPECIAL EQUIPMENT

electric hand-held mixer

7in (18cm) round cake pan

food processor

25 popsicle sticks or wooden skewers (sharp ends removed)

MAKES 25

7 tbsp unsalted butter, softened

½ cup granulated sugar

2 large eggs

¾ cup self-rising flour

3 tbsp cocoa powder

1 tsp baking powder

½ cup store-bought chocolate fudge frosting

9oz (250g) white chocolate

assorted bright cake sprinkles

1 Preheat the oven to 350°F (180°C). Place the butter and sugar in a large bowl and cream it with an electric hand-held mixer until light and fluffy. Whisk in the eggs one at a time. Sift together the flour, cocoa, and baking powder and fold into the batter.

2 Pour the batter into a greased and lined 7in (18cm) round cake pan, then level the surface and bake for 20–25 minutes until a skewer comes out clean. Turn onto a wire rack. When the cake is cool, process it in a food processor until it resembles fine crumbs.

3 Weigh out 10oz (300g) of cake crumbs and put them into a mixing bowl. Mix in the chocolate fudge frosting. Using dry hands, roll into balls, each the size of a walnut. You should get about 25 balls. Put them on a plate, cover, and refrigerate for several hours or freeze for up to 30 minutes until they are quite firm, but not frozen.

4 Line 2 baking sheets with waxed paper. Melt the cake covering according to the package instructions. Dip the ends of 25 popsicle sticks in it, one at a time, then push into the cake balls.

5 Dip the cake pops, one at a time, into the molten chocolate mixture, tilting the bowl to help, and lift them out without moving them around. Make sure the chocolate covers the balls up to the stick, as this helps them stay stuck. Allow excess chocolate to drip back into the bowl.

6 Over a bowl, to catch the stray pieces, sprinkle each cake pop with brightly colored sprinkles and transfer them to the lined baking sheets to dry. (To ensure a smooth, round finish, you can stick the lollipop sticks into an apple that has first been cut in half and placed cut-side down. This will help the cake pops dry without any marks to the surface, but can be a rather

delicate business.) Continue until all the balls are coated. You will have to work fast at this stage, as the chocolate can harden quickly. These should be eaten the same day they are made, and kept fairly cool, but not cold, for storage purposes.

HOW TO FREEZE

Open-freeze the chilled, undipped cake balls on a baking sheet, then transfer to freezer bags for up to 1 month. Defrost almost completely, but keep them cold and firm before coating and finishing with sprinkles.

CALORIES: 147kcals/615kJ

CARBOHYDRATE: 15g
  sugar: 13g

FAT: 8.5g
  saturated: 5g

SALT: 0.2g

FIBER: 0.3g

Flowery cupcakes

Make these pretty spring-like cupcakes for a girl's birthday party treat.

25 mins   16–18 mins

SPECIAL EQUIPMENT

electric hand-held mixer

12 cupcake liners

deep 12-hole muffin pan

MAKES 12

7 tbsp butter, softened

⅔ cup granulated sugar

3 large eggs, lightly beaten

1 tsp vanilla extract

1½ cups self-rising flour

1 tsp baking powder

3½ tbsp milk

FOR THE BUTTERCREAM

7 tbsp butter, softened

1⅔ cups confectioners' sugar

½–1 tsp green food coloring

store-bought sugar flowers, or store-bought colored icing, to decorate

CALORIES: 319kcals/1340kJ
CARBOHYDRATE: 41g
  sugar: 29g
FAT: 16g
  saturated: 9g
SALT: 0.6g
FIBER: 0.7g

1 Preheat the oven to 350°F (180°C). Place the butter and sugar in a bowl and use an electric hand-held mixer to beat them until light and fluffy. Whisk in the eggs and vanilla extract.

2 Sift together the flour and baking powder. Whisk the flour mixture and the milk into the batter alternately. Place 12 cupcake liners in a deep 12-hole muffin pan (this will help them keep their shape).

3 Spoon the cake batter into the liners, filling each two-thirds full. Bake for 16–18 minutes until springy to the touch. Transfer to a wire rack to cool.

4 To make the buttercream, beat the butter, confectioners' sugar, and food coloring until smooth and creamy.

5 When the cakes are cold, cover them in buttercream, using the back of a spoon dipped in warm water to smooth the surface. Decorate with store-bought sugar flowers, or cut your own using store-bought colored icing.

PREPARE AHEAD
The cakes can be made 1 day ahead and stored, un-iced, in an airtight container. Ice them on the day they are to be eaten.

Rocky road squares

These chocolatey treats are very rich, so be sure to cut them into small party-sized pieces.

15–20 mins, plus chilling

SPECIAL EQUIPMENT

7in (18cm) square baking pan

MAKES 36

9oz (250g) dark chocolate, broken into squares

11 tbsp unsalted butter, plus extra for the pan

2 tbsp corn syrup

7oz (200g) shortbread cookies

1¾oz (50g) raisins

1¾oz (50g) dried cranberries

3½oz (100g) mini-marshmallows

CALORIES: 110kcals/460kJ
CARBOHYDRATE: 13g
  sugar: 10g
FAT: 6g
  saturated: 4g
SALT: 0.1g
FIBER: 0.3g

1 Put the chocolate, butter, and syrup in a large, heatproof bowl and melt it over a saucepan of simmering water, making sure the bowl does not touch the water. When it has melted, cool slightly.

2 Put the cookies into a plastic bag and smash with a rolling pin until you have small, broken pieces.

3 Mix the cookies into the chocolate mixture. Next mix in the dried fruit and marshmallows.

4 Grease a 7in (18cm) square baking pan with butter and line with parchment paper. Pour in the mixture and press it down firmly with the back of a spoon.

5 Cover and refrigerate for 2 hours, before removing from the pan and cutting into 36 squares with a sharp knife. In warm weather, store these in the fridge.

VARIATION

You can use milk chocolate if you prefer, which will be less rich for young children. Also try varying the type of dried fruit or cookies used.

Butterfly cake

You can decorate this pretty cake any way you like, with bright colored sprinkles, flowers, or even small sweets.

40 mins | 35–40 mins, plus cooling

SPECIAL EQUIPMENT

9½in (24cm) round cake pan
electric hand-held mixer
ruler
cake board (optional)

SERVES 15

14 tbsp unsalted butter, softened, plus extra for greasing
¾ cup granulated sugar
1 tsp vanilla extract
4 large eggs
1½ cups all-purpose flour, sifted
1 tsp baking powder
2 tbsp milk, if needed

FOR THE ICING

2 cups confectioners' sugar
8 tbsp butter, softened
red food coloring
cake decorations, such as sprinkles and sweets, to decorate

1 Preheat the oven to 325°F (160°C). Grease a 9½in (24cm) cake pan and line the bottom with parchment paper.

2 In a large bowl, whisk the butter and sugar with an electric hand-held mixer for at least 5 minutes, until light and fluffy. Whisk in the vanilla.

3 Whisk in the eggs one at a time, making sure to incorporate as much air as possible. Fold in the flour and baking powder until just blended. If it seems stiff, add the milk. Pour the batter into the pan.

4 Bake in the center of the hot oven for 35–40 minutes, until a skewer comes out clean. Cool in the pan for 5 minutes, then turn it out to cool completely on a wire rack.

5 For the icing, beat together the confectioners' sugar and butter until smooth and creamy. Add drops of food coloring until you reach your desired shade of pink. Add a splash of boiling water if it is too stiff.

6 To make the butterfly shape, place the cake on a cutting board and use a bread knife to cut off any rise on the top, so it is completely flat. Turn it over, so the cut side is underneath. Now take a ruler and use it to measure a ¾in- (2cm-) wide strip in the center of the cake. Cut this out and you will be left with 1 long, thin strip of cake and 2 semi-circular pieces. Set the thin strip aside. Now reverse the semi-circles so they are back to back. Cut each semi-circle into 2, roughly two-thirds and one-third each, using the finished picture as a guide. When the pieces are cut and you separate them, they should look like butterfly wings.

7 Ice and decorate the thin cake strip (the body of the butterfly) and place it in the middle of a serving plate or cake board (if using). Ice each wing piece individually, put it in place using a long palette knife or spatula, and use a small palette knife to touch up any areas that have been smeared.

Decorate each before you go on to the next, so the icing does not harden before you begin to press your chosen decorations into it.

COOK'S TIP

Use a paper template to work out the shape. The best cake to use is one with a slightly firmer texture such as this pound cake, as it will be easier to ice, but use an electric hand-held mixer to lighten the texture.

HOW TO FREEZE

The cooked cake, un-iced, can be wrapped well in plastic wrap, sealed with foil, then frozen for up to 12 weeks. Defrost the cake thoroughly before cutting it to shape and icing.

CALORIES: 350kcals/1478kJ
CARBOHYDRATE: 39g
  sugar: 30g
FAT: 20g
  saturated: 12g
SALT: 0.2g
FIBER: 0.5g

Chocolate cake

This is a light, chocolate layer cake and sometimes only chocolate cake will do—especially at party time.

30-40 mins   25-30 mins

SPECIAL EQUIPMENT

2 x 8in (20cm) round, non-stick cake pans

electric hand-held mixer

SERVES 4

12 tbsp unsalted butter, softened, plus extra for greasing

⅔ cup granulated sugar

3 large eggs, lightly beaten

1¼ cups self-rising flour

3 tbsp cocoa powder

½ tsp of baking powder

FOR THE TOPPING

3½oz (100g) plain chocolate

3½oz (100g) milk chocolate

¾ cup heavy cream, at room temperature

1 Grease two 8in (20cm) round, non-stick cake pans and line the bottoms with parchment paper. Cream the butter and sugar together in a bowl until they are light and fluffy. Gradually beat in the egg.

2 Preheat the oven to 350°F (180°C). Sift the flour, cocoa powder, and baking powder into the bowl and fold them into the creamed mixture. Divide this between the pans, smoothing the tops with a palette knife. Bake for 20–25 minutes, or until firm, then turn onto a wire rack.

3 Break both the chocolate bars into a bowl and gently melt them over a pan of simmering water. Remove the bowl from the pan. Let cool for 5 minutes, then stir in the cream and let thicken for a few minutes.

4 Make sure the cakes are cool before putting on the topping. Put one cake on a serving plate and spread one-quarter of the topping over it. Put the other cake on top and spread the rest of the topping over the top and sides until the cake is evenly coated. Let set.

VARIATION

Melt 3½ oz (100g) white chocolate and pour it into a parchment paper-lined sheet. Let it set. Break it into small pieces and use it to decorate the cake.

COOK'S TIP

The eggs should be at room temperature and added slowly, or the mixture may curdle. If it does, mix in a little flour.

CALORIES: 410kcals/1717kJ

CARBOHYDRATE: 33g
sugar: 24g

FAT: 29g
saturated: 17g

SALT: 0.3g

FIBER: 1.5g

Caterpillar cake

This classic caterpillar is fun, but the basic body shape could be adapted to make a snake cake, if you prefer.

40 mins   30-35 mins

SPECIAL EQUIPMENT

10in (25cm) bundt cake pan (optional)

electric hand-held mixer

rectangular cake board, or similar, at least 12 x 8in (30 x 20cm)

SERVES 15

14 tbsp unsalted butter, softened, plus extra for greasing

¾ cup granulated sugar

1 tsp vanilla extract

4 large eggs

1¼ cups all-purpose flour

½ cup cocoa powder

1 tsp baking powder

2 tbsp whole milk, if needed

FOR THE ICING

1⅔ cups confectioners' sugar

7 tbsp unsalted butter, softened

green food coloring

TO DECORATE

1oz (30g) dark chocolate chips

2 white chocolate chips

2 chocolate buttons

dark green and brown icing pens

sprinkles (optional)

2 green drinking straws (optional)

1 Preheat the oven to 325°F (160°C). Grease a 10in (25cm) bundt pan. Sprinkle a little flour into the pan, then shake to form a fine layer all over. Pour out excess flour and set aside. (If you do not have a bundt pan, see the Cook's Tip.)

2 Beat the butter and sugar with an electric hand-held mixer for 5 minutes, until fluffy. Add the vanilla, then the eggs, beating in as much air as possible.

3 Sift the flour, cocoa powder, and baking powder together, then fold it in. If it seems too stiff, add the milk. Pour into the pan.

4 Bake for 30–35 minutes, until the cake has risen. Cool in the pan for 5 minutes, then turn onto a rack.

5 To make the icing, beat the confectioners' sugar and butter until light and creamy. Add the green food coloring a little at a time until you reach a light green for the face. Set aside ¼ cup, then continue to add food coloring until you reach a dark green for the body.

6 Place the cake on a board and use a bread knife to cut off any rise, so it is flat. Cut in half, to give 2 "C"-shaped pieces. Now cut one-quarter off one of the pieces—this will become the head. Use the picture (below) as a guide to put the body together. Trim the head and tail into a rounded shape.

7 Ice each piece, place it on the cake board, and use a small palette knife to touch up any areas that have been smeared. Use the lighter colored icing for the head.

8 Smooth over any cracks in the icing and place dark chocolate chips along the body, on both sides, for legs. Use icing to stick the white chocolate chips to the chocolate buttons, then fix them on as "eyes." Leave for 1 hour. Use the icing pens to draw on body sections and a smiley mouth. Add sprinkles and drinking straw antennae, if you like.

COOK'S TIP

If you do not have a bundt pan you can use a 9½in (24cm) round cake pan. Prepare as above both the pan and a small (2½in/6.5cm) ovenproof ramekin. Place the ramekin upside down in the pan before pouring the batter around.

CALORIES: 334kcals/1408kJ

CARBOHYDRATE: 35g
  sugar: 28g

FAT: 20g
  saturated: 12g

SALT: 0.3g

FIBER: 1g

Food to go

Food to go

Whether you're planning a picnic, packing children's lunch boxes, or trying to save a little money by taking your lunch to work, here are a range of ideas to eat healthily on the go. Beyond the ordinary sandwich, there is a wealth of possibilities from wraps to hearty salads, protein-packed frittatas to mini pies and pastries. Homemade healthy snacks help you and your family avoid eating processed packaged foods when you're hungry out and about.

Pantry essentials

Keeping a few basics in the fridge as well as some pantry essentials means a sudden sunny day can be the excuse for an impromptu picnic. Cans of tuna, salmon, and beans can be the basis of an array of salads and sandwiches. Refrigerator staples such as a good-quality mayonnaise, mustard, pickles, and cheeses make it easy to put together a tasty, portable lunch.

Be creative with bread

Don't get stuck in the habit of using sliced bread for everything. Experiment by making wraps using tortillas, stuffing pita pockets, or even making savory muffins. For a family picnic try cooking mini frittatas with different fillings or put together a Whole stuffed ciabatta (p387)—it's one of the easiest things to transport, as it's meant to be squashed, and can be cut into chunks when you need to eat.

Homemade hummus and crudités (p388), is easy to make and always popular. Crudités could be carrots, celery, or broccoli; or take breadsticks.

Stuffed ciabatta (p387) makes an ideal picnic food. Tasty and easy to carry, it can be sliced when you arrive and served with salad.

Lunch boxes for all

It's very easy to pack the same few items in a child's lunch box day after day, once you know what they like—sandwiches, fruit, something sweet—but no wonder they get bored! On a cold winter's day send them off with warming Harvest Vegetable soup and crusty bread (p157), or when it's warm outside pack some crunchy vegetables and homemade Hummus (p388). Bake a batch of Tuna empanadas (p397), which are robust enough to transport and perfect for small appetites. Packed lunches aren't just for children—you can save time and money taking your lunch to work, too. Try a slice of Red bell pepper and tomato frittata (p236) and salad or why not roast a pan of vegetables (see Oven-roasted ratatouille p175) on a Sunday, and use them over the following two or three days. Eat in a salad, a wrap, or as the filling of a sandwich in a crusty roll spread with a little Herby goat cheese spread (p241). You can add a little stock or water and purée them into a hearty soup, if the weather is cold.

Picnic ideas

The prospect of a picnic on a warm day means you need to think of some tasty portable foods. Lightly grilled vegetables, chunky salads, and overstuffed wraps all seem to taste better eaten outside. Think beyond the usual sandwiches, and try planning ahead by baking Individual pork pies (p399) for a special occasion. Take salads that won't wilt or get squashed such as Cannellini bean, tuna, and red onion (p390), or assemble items such as Chicken Caesar wraps (p386) when you get there.

Proper packaging

The proper packaging can make carrying and eating a meal on the go fuss free. Make sure you choose sturdy containers with tight-fitting lids, or bento boxes with compartments, to separate different courses. Wide-mouthed thermal containers with spoons that fit into the lid can be used to carry hot soups or stews for a warm midday meal.

Snacks on the run

Reuse small plastic containers, well washed, to transport snacks on the go. A handful of dried fruit, nuts, and seeds makes a healthy snack to keep on your desk. Young children will happily snack on a few fistfuls of their favorite cereal or raisins, stashed in a small container. Even teenagers are more likely to grab a healthy snack when presented with some

homemade Granola breakfast bars (p474) or Savory breakfast muffins (p442) as they rush out of the door. To avoid the temptation of unnecessary junk food or snacks, why not bake a batch of the Banana and date mini muffins (p58), which are as good for adults as they are for children? Freeze them the day they are made, then take one or two straight from the freezer to have as a healthy mid-morning snack, along with some freshly chopped fruit packed in an airtight container.

Granola breakfast bars (p474), are a nutritious snack for hungry teens on the run, adults' packed lunches, or after-school snacks for kids.

Sweet potato and goat cheese mini frittatas (p396) make an ideal lunch box item for adults or children, just add some green salad.

Keep it fresh

To keep things fresh and cool in the warmer months, try freezing children's juice boxes or even water bottles before packing their lunch. The frozen liquid will keep everything in the lunchbox cool, and defrost perfectly in time for lunch, ensuring that they'll have a cool drink on a hot day.

Roll wraps up tightly in foil or plastic wrap to keep them fresh or pack the wraps and filling separately for older children to compile themselves.

Double-decker turkey and avocado sandwiches

Serving layered sandwiches is an easy way to make a simple sandwich more attractive.

10 mins

SERVES 4

3 heaping tbsp good-quality mayonnaise

1 heaping tsp Dijon mustard

salt and freshly ground black pepper

butter, softened, for spreading

12 large slices of multigrain bread

2 handfuls of salad leaves

5½oz (150g) thinly sliced turkey breast

2 avocados, thinly sliced

½ lemon

CALORIES: 614kcals/2572kJ

CARBOHYDRATE: 55g
  sugar: 4g

FAT: 32g
  saturated: 9g

SALT: 2g

FIBER: 10g

---

1 Mix the mayonnaise and mustard together and season well. Butter 8 slices of bread on one side only, and 4 slices carefully on both sides.

2 Lay 4 of the single side-buttered slices on a cutting board, buttered-sides up. Top each slice with one-quarter of the salad leaves, pressing them into the bread gently. Lay one-quarter of the turkey on top of each and spread with a thin layer of the mayonnaise.

3 Put a double-side-buttered slice of bread on each sandwich, then layer one-quarter of the avocado over each, drizzle with a little lemon juice, and season well.

4 Top each with a final slice of bread, buttered-side down, and press down well to hold everything together. Carefully trim the crusts off the bread and cut into halves on a diagonal to serve, or pack into a container for transportation.

Herby goat cheese pinwheel sandwiches

These little sandwich bites make a very appealing addition to a picnic spread.

15 mins

MAKES 16

3½oz (100g) soft goat cheese, softened

3½oz (100g) cream cheese, softened

1 heaping tbsp finely chopped basil leaves

1 heaping tbsp finely chopped chives

finely grated zest of ½ lemon

salt and freshly ground black pepper

4 large slices of soft whole wheat bread

butter, softened, for spreading

1 Put the 2 cheeses in a large bowl with the herbs and lemon zest and beat with a wooden spoon until combined. Season well with pepper and a little salt (be careful as goat cheese can be quite salty).

2 Trim the crusts off the bread and roll each slice out with a rolling pin until it is as flat as possible. Spread each slice with butter on one side only.

3 Spread each slice of bread with one-quarter of the cheese mixture and roll it up, starting from a short edge. Trim the edges neatly with a serrated knife and cut each roll in half, then in half again, to make 4 pieces per sandwich. Serve cut-sides up to show the swirled effect, or pack into a container for transportation.

Pinwheels are fun for children to help make and eat. Try using slices of ham as well as the cheese, or use plain or flavored cream cheese.

Fussy eaters!

CALORIES: 78kcals/326kJ

CARBOHYDRATE: 4g
  sugar: 0.2g

FAT: 6g
  saturated: 3.5g

SALT: 0.3g

FIBER: 0.8g

Roast beef, watercress, and horseradish mayo sandwiches

Sandwiches can be easily enlivened by flavoring some good, store-bought mayonnaise.

10 mins

SERVES 4

3 heaping tbsp good-quality mayonnaise

1 heaping tsp horseradish sauce

salt and freshly ground black pepper

butter, softened, for spreading

8 large slices of sourdough or rye bread

2 handfuls of watercress

7oz (200g) rare roast beef, thinly sliced

CALORIES: 408kcals/1717kJ
CARBOHYDRATE: 37g
sugar: 2.5g
FAT: 18g
saturated: 4g
SALT: 1.4g
FIBER: 2.5g

1 Mix the mayonnaise and horseradish together and season well. Butter each slice of bread on one side only.

2 Lay 4 of the buttered slices on a cutting board, buttered-sides up. Top each slice with a layer of the watercress, pressing it into the bread gently. Then layer one-quarter of the beef on each slice, and spread with a thin layer of the mayonnaise.

3 Top with the final slice of bread, buttered-side down, and press down well to hold everything together. Cut into halves to serve, or pack into a container for transportation.

CLEVER WITH LEFTOVERS

These sandwiches are a cunning and delicious way to use up leftovers from a Sunday roast. Just make sure the slices of beef are rare and carved very thinly.

Roast beet, goat cheese, and arugula sandwiches

These are fabulous for a picnic or packed lunch, or try them at home with toasted bread instead.

10 mins   45 mins

SERVES 4

4 small beets, approx. 2½oz (75g) each, peeled and sliced ¼in (5mm) thick

1 tbsp olive oil

salt and freshly ground black pepper

8 large slices sourdough or other rustic bread

butter, softened, for spreading

7oz (200g) soft goat cheese

2 handfuls of arugula leaves

CALORIES: 436kcals/1832kJ
CARBOHYDRATE: 41g
sugar: 8g
FAT: 22g
saturated: 12g
SALT: 2g
FIBER: 4.5g

1 Preheat the oven to 400°F (200°C). Place the beet slices on a baking sheet, brush them with the olive oil, and season them well. Bake them at the top of the oven for 20 minutes, turning once, until they are lightly browned and cooked through. Remove them from the oven and set aside to cool.

2 Spread the slices of bread with butter on one side only. Spread 4 slices with one-quarter each of the goat cheese, season with a little pepper, then add a layer of the cooled beet slices.

3 Top the beets with a layer of the arugula and finish the sandwich with a final slice of bread, buttered-side down. Cut in half to serve, or pack into a container for transportation.

White bean purée, alfalfa, and carrot pita pockets

A delicious mix of moist softness and crunch makes these portable pockets ideal to pack for lunch or a picnic.

15 mins

SPECIAL EQUIPMENT
food processer

SERVES 4

1 x 14oz (400g) can of cannellini
   beans, drained and rinsed (reserve
   2 tbsp of the liquid)

2 large garlic cloves, crushed

2 heaping tbsp finely chopped
   flat-leaf parsley leaves

1 tbsp olive oil

¼ tsp salt

freshly ground black pepper

2 tbsp lemon juice

4 whole wheat pita breads

1 large carrot, coarsely grated

1¾oz (50g) alfalfa shoots or
   other shoots

1 To make the bean purée, put the beans, garlic, parsley, olive oil, salt, pepper, lemon juice, and 1 tbsp of the bean liquid into a food processer and process to a rough paste. If it is too thick add another 1 tbsp of the liquid (but remember this needs to be a thick paste to hold up well in the pita bread).

2 Cut each pita in half and open to make 8 small pockets. Spread a layer of bean purée on both inside faces of the pockets.

3 Sprinkle a little carrot and alfalfa into each. Serve layered on top of each other with the stuffing showing, or pack into a container for transportation.

VARIATION

It is easy to adapt this bean purée to your taste. Add roasted red bell peppers for a sweet, red-tinged purée, or roasted garlic for a mellow version (omit the crushed garlic in the latter case).

CALORIES: 287kcals/1203kJ

CARBOHYDRATE: 45g
   sugar: 6.5g

FAT: 5g
   saturated: 0.7g

SALT: 1.8g

FIBER: 12g

Pulled pork wraps

This is a great way to use up any leftover Slow-cooked shoulder of pork (see p281), in an instantly portable meal.

10 mins

SERVES 4

12oz (350g) cooked pulled pork, such as leftover Slow-cooked shoulder of pork (see p281)

2 heaping tbsp good-quality barbecue sauce

4 large wraps

4 large Romaine lettuce leaves

½ cucumber, halved, seeded, and finely sliced

3 tbsp sour cream

1 Shred the pork finely and mix it with the barbecue sauce. Lay the wraps on a work surface. Flatten the lettuce leaves by pressing down on the central rib, and put a large lettuce leaf onto each wrap, with the leaf starting at the edge nearest you. Layer a line of the sliced cucumber along the lettuce leaf, about 1in (3cm) thick, and top each line of cucumber with ½ tbsp of the sour cream.

2 Lay one-quarter of the pork along each line of sour cream. Now take the remaining sour cream and smear a little, with the back of a spoon, all over the piece of wrap furthest from you (it should cover one-third of the wrap). This helps it stick together.

3 Carefully roll up the wrap by picking up the side nearest to you and folding it over the filling. Continue to roll it away from you until the wrap meets itself and sticks together with the sour cream. Slice each end off carefully and cut the wraps in half on a diagonal to serve, or wrap and pack into a container for transportation.

CALORIES: 380kcals/1599kJ

CARBOHYDRATE: 42g
  sugar: 4g

FAT: 9g
  saturated: 3.6g

SALT: 0.9g

FIBER: 3g

Shrimp, sweet chili, and Greek yogurt wraps

Sweet, fresh-tasting pea shoots, juicy shrimp, and sharp yogurt make a wonderful combination.

10 mins

SERVES 4

4 large wraps

1¾oz (50g) pea shoots, mixed baby salad leaves, or arugula

½ cucumber, halved, seeded, and finely sliced

6oz (175g) package of cooked, shelled large shrimp, sliced in half horizontally and deveined

3 heaping tbsp Greek yogurt

4 tsp Thai sweet chili sauce

salt and freshly ground black pepper

1 Lay the wraps on a work surface and divide the pea shoots between them, starting at the edge nearest you and covering about one-third of the wrap. Layer one-quarter of the cucumber, then the shrimp, along the pea shoots, and top each with ½ tbsp of yogurt and 1 tsp of chili sauce. Season.

2 Take the remaining yogurt and smear a little, with the back of a spoon, all over the piece of each wrap furthest from you (it should cover one-third of the wrap). This helps it stick together.

3 Fold the side nearest to you over the filling. Roll it away from you until it sticks together with the yogurt. Slice each end off and halve on a diagonal to serve, or pack for transportation.

CLEVER WITH LEFTOVERS

These wraps can easily be adapted to contain any leftover cooked fish (but avoid smoked fish for this recipe).

CALORIES: 249kcals/1054kJ

CARBOHYDRATE: 43g
  sugar: 5g

FAT: 2g
  saturated: 1g

SALT: 1.2g

FIBER: 3g

Chicken Caesar wraps

This delicious wrap, with its piquant dressing, has all the flavors of a chicken Caesar salad in a portable form.

10 mins, plus cooking   15–20 mins

SERVES 4

1 tbsp olive oil

salt and freshly ground black pepper

2 boneless, skinless chicken breasts

FOR THE SAUCE

4 anchovy fillets

2 tsp lemon juice

2 tsp Dijon mustard

½ cup good-quality mayonnaise

¼ cup finely grated Parmesan cheese

½ tsp Worcestershire sauce

4 large wraps

4 large Romaine lettuce leaves

1 Preheat a grill pan. Brush it with olive oil and season the chicken breasts on both sides. Grill the chicken over medium heat for 5–10 minutes on each side (depending on size), until charred in places on the outside and cooked through. Let cool. If you are in a hurry, slice it now into thin strips, as it will cool more quickly.

2 While the chicken is cooling, make the Caesar sauce. Put the anchovies and lemon juice in a bowl and mash them with the back of a spoon until the anchovy has turned to paste. (Alternatively, use a mortar and pestle.) Add the mustard, mayonnaise, Parmesan cheese, and Worcestershire sauce, and mix well. Check the seasoning and add some pepper.

3 To assemble the wraps, lay them out on a work surface. Flatten the lettuce leaves by pressing down on the central rib, and put a leaf onto each wrap, with the leaf starting at the edge nearest you. Layer one-quarter of the sliced chicken along the lettuce leaf, and top each line with a good smear of the Caesar sauce, reserving a little to seal the wraps.

4 Take the remaining Caesar sauce and smear a little, with the back of a spoon, all over each piece of wrap farthest away from you (it should cover about one-third of the wrap). This will help the wrap stick together. Then carefully roll up the wrap by picking up the side nearest to you and folding it over the filling. Continue to roll it

away from you until the wrap bread meets itself and sticks together with the Caesar sauce.

5 Slice each end off carefully and cut the wraps in half on a diagonal to serve.

CLEVER WITH LEFTOVERS

If you have cold, leftover roast chicken or turkey, use it here instead of grilling fresh chicken breast. You'll need about 10oz (300g) of meat in total.

CALORIES: 575kcals/2406kJ

CARBOHYDRATE: 40g
    sugar: 1.5g

FAT: 33g
    saturated: 7g

SALT: 1.7g

FIBER: 2g

Whole stuffed ciabatta with mozzarella and grilled vegetables

This is incredibly tasty and simple to transport, and will easily feed a family of four.

10 mins, plus chilling | 15 mins, plus cooling

SERVES 4

½ eggplant, cut into ½in (1cm) slices

2 zucchini, cut into ½in (1cm) slices

4–6 tbsp olive oil

salt and freshly ground black pepper

1 large beefsteak tomato

1 ciabatta loaf

2 roasted red bell peppers from a jar, drained, and sliced

ball of mozzarella, approx. 4½oz (125g), thinly sliced

handful of basil leaves

1 Preheat a large grill pan or a broiler to its highest setting. Brush the slices of eggplant and zucchini on both sides with olive oil and season them well. Either grill or broil them for 2–4 minutes each side, until they are charred in places and cooked through. Put them on a large plate in a single layer to cool.

2 Slice about ½in (1cm) off each end of the tomato, reserving these pieces. Slice the remaining tomato as thinly as possible.

3 Cut the ciabatta in half, leaving a hinge so you can open it out flat. Drizzle both sides with a little olive oil. Take the ends of the tomato and rub both sides of the bread with the cut side, to soften and flavor the bread, then discard the ends.

4 Cover one side of the loaf with the eggplant, zucchini, and red bell peppers, then top with mozzarella. Sprinkle with the basil, season, then add the tomato.

5 Close the loaf and press down on it hard. Wrap it very tightly in plastic wrap, going around it a few times until it is completely covered and compressed. Leave in the fridge with a weight (such as a cutting board and some cans) on top for at least 4 hours, turning once. Unwrap and slice to serve, or transport in the wrapping and slice at a picnic.

CALORIES: 435kcals/1812kJ
CARBOHYDRATE: 36g
    sugar: 4g
FAT: 25g
    saturated: 6.5g
SALT: 1.2g
FIBER: 8g

Baked Parmesan and rosemary crisps

These easy home-baked crisps transform a simple wrap into a gourmet snack.

5 mins | 5-7 mins

SERVES 4

4 large wraps

2 tbsp olive oil

2 tsp rosemary leaves, finely chopped

¼ cup finely grated Parmesan cheese

freshly ground black pepper

Hummus or Baba ghanoush, to serve (see p388)

1 Preheat the oven to 400°F (200°C). Lay the wraps on a work surface and brush all over on both sides with the olive oil.

2 Scatter them with the rosemary and Parmesan and season well with pepper. Place on a baking sheet.

3 Bake them at the top of the oven for 5–7 minutes until golden brown, puffed up, and crispy. Watch them carefully for the last minute, as they burn quickly.

4 Remove them from the oven, then transfer to a wire rack to cool. When they are cool, break them into jagged, irregular pieces and serve with Hummus or Baba ghanoush (see p388).

VARIATION

While it is best to stick with Parmesan cheese for these crisps, you can vary the woody herbs to suit your personal preference. Try the same amount of thyme leaves, or chopped oregano leaves. Soft herbs, such as basil, should not be used here, because they will burn in the oven.

CALORIES: 295kcals/1242kJ
CARBOHYDRATE: 39g
    sugar: 1g
FAT: 10.5g
    saturated: 4g
SALT: 0.8g
FIBER: 2.2g

Hummus

This simple hummus can be adjusted with more garlic or lemon juice, or additional spices, if desired.

5 mins

SPECIAL EQUIPMENT
blender or food processor

SERVES 4 (as part of a mezze)

1 x 14oz (400g) can of chickpeas, drained and rinsed (reserve ¼ cup of liquid)

2 tbsp tahini

2 tbsp olive oil, plus extra to serve

2 tbsp lemon juice, or to taste

1 large garlic clove, crushed, or to taste

¼ tsp ground cumin

¼ tsp salt

freshly ground black pepper

spinkling of paprika

crudités, to serve

1 Put all the ingredients, except the paprika, into a blender or food processor, and process until completely smooth.

2 Taste and adjust the seasoning, or the amount of garlic or lemon juice, as desired.

3 Serve the hummus in a bowl with a swirl of olive oil and a sprinkling of paprika, and some crudités on the side.

VARIATION

Hummus can be flavored to suit your family. Add a handful of pitted black olives, or roasted red bell pepper strips, to the mix before blending, or sprinkle with smoked paprika instead of plain for a more subtle twist.

CLEVER WITH LEFTOVERS

Because it is so adaptable, hummus is an excellent way to use up all kinds of odds and ends. Add any leftover plain beans or lentils (as long as the total weight remains the same), or try a small handful of leftover soft herb leaves.

CALORIES: 167kcals/698kJ
CARBOHYDRATE: 9.5g
  sugar: 0.5g
FAT: 12g
  saturated: 1.5g
SALT: 0.6g
FIBER: 4g

Baba ghanoush

Try this delicious smoky Middle Eastern dip with Pita chips (see p242), or just scooped up with fresh bread.

10 mins   30 mins, plus cooling

SPECIAL EQUIPMENT
food processor or blender

SERVES 4 (as part of a mezze)

1 large eggplant

2 tbsp olive oil

1 tbsp lemon juice

3 tbsp tahini

1 garlic clove, crushed

1 tsp smoked paprika

salt and freshly ground black pepper

crudités, or Pita chips (see p242), to serve

1 Preheat the oven to 450°F (230°C). Prick the eggplant all over with a fork, then rub it with 1 tbsp of the olive oil. Place on a baking sheet and bake at the top of the hot oven for 25–30 minutes, turning once, until the skin has completely blackened and the interior is very soft.

2 Remove the eggplant from the oven and let cool. When it is cold, cut it in half and scoop out the flesh into the bowl of a food processor or blender. Add the remaining ingredients and purée the mixture to a rough paste. Taste and adjust the seasoning. Serve with some crudités or Pita chips (see p242).

CALORIES: 129kcals/535kJ
CARBOHYDRATE: 2g
  sugar: 1.5g
FAT: 12.5g
  saturated: 2g
SALT: trace
FIBER: 3g

Baba ghanoush tends to be a favorite with everyone who tastes it, so it's worth trying out with children who claim to dislike eggplant.

Fussy eaters!

Artichoke and scallion dip

A pantry recipe that has sophisticated and subtle flavors, but takes just minutes to make.

5 mins

SPECIAL EQUIPMENT
food processor or blender

SERVES 6 (as part of a mezze)

1 x 14oz (390g) can of artichoke hearts, drained

1 garlic clove, halved

3 scallions, coarsely chopped

2 tbsp good-quality mayonnaise

salt and freshly ground black pepper

1 Place the artichokes, garlic, scallions, and mayonnaise in a food processor or blender and process to form a smooth purée.

2 Season to taste with salt and pepper, then spoon into a serving bowl, cover, and refrigerate until ready to use.

VARIATION

If you can find jarred, grilled artichokes, use the same amount to add an agreeably smoky edge to this dip, and sprinkle the finished dip with smoked paprika, too.

PREPARE AHEAD

The dip can be made up to 24 hours in advance, covered with plastic wrap, and chilled until ready to serve.

COOK'S TIP

Good with pita bread, vegetable crudités, or breadsticks. Alternatively, spread on to chunks of French bread.

CALORIES: 48kcals/199kJ
CARBOHYDRATE: 2.5g
  sugar: 2.5g
FAT: 4g
  saturated: 0.5g
SALT: 0.2g
FIBER: 1g

Red bell pepper salad

In Spanish, this dish is called *ensaladilla de pimientos*. Sweet red bell peppers are stewed, then served cold.

10 mins   25 mins

SERVES 4
(as part of a mezze)

3 tbsp olive oil

6 red bell peppers, cut into broad strips

2 garlic cloves, finely chopped

9oz (250g) ripe tomatoes, peeled, seeded, and chopped (see p191)

2 tbsp chopped flat-leaf parsley leaves

salt and freshly ground black pepper

1 tbsp sherry vinegar

1 Heat the oil in a large frying pan, add the peppers and garlic, and cook over low heat for 5 minutes, stirring. Add the tomatoes, increase the heat, and bring to simmering point, then reduce the heat to low, cover, and cook for 12–15 minutes.

2 Stir in the parsley, season well with salt and pepper, and cook for another 2 minutes.

3 Using a slotted spoon, remove the peppers and arrange them in a serving dish.

4 Add the vinegar to the juices in the pan, increase the heat, and simmer the sauce for 5–7 minutes, or until reduced and thickened. Pour the sauce over the peppers and allow the salad to cool.

CLEVER WITH LEFTOVERS

Process any leftover salad in a food processor until smooth. Whisk in enough olive oil to make the mixture into the consistency of a salad dressing and use to coat the salad leaves or roasted vegetables.

CALORIES: 158kcals/655kJ
CARBOHYDRATE: 15g
  sugar: 15g
FAT: 9g
  saturated: 1.5g
SALT: trace
FIBER: 5.5g

Cannellini bean, tuna, and red onion salad

This classic Italian salad is a great dish to take on a picnic because it is quite robust and easy to transport.

10 mins

SERVES 4

3 tbsp olive oil

1 tbsp red wine vinegar

salt and freshly ground black pepper

1 x 7oz can of tuna in olive oil, drained

1 red onion, quartered and very finely sliced

2 tbsp capers, drained or rinsed, and roughly chopped

1 x 14oz (410g) can of cannellini beans, drained and rinsed

handful of flat-leaf parsley leaves, finely chopped

1 In a bowl, whisk together the olive oil and vinegar and season well. Pour the tuna into the bowl and mash it gently with a fork to break it up a little, leaving some chunks.

2 Add the remaining ingredients and toss the salad well until everything has a good coating of dressing. Serve, or pack into a container for transportation.

VARIATION

If serving at home, simply add a bag of salad leaves and some halved cherry tomatoes to make a complete meal.

CLEVER WITH LEFTOVERS

This salad is also great served with leftover cold mackerel instead of tuna, or with any canned beans instead of the cannellini used here.

CALORIES: 231kcals/965kJ
CARBOHYDRATE: 13g
    sugar: 3.5g
FAT: 13g
    saturated: 2g
SALT: 1.5g
FIBER: 6g

Watermelon salad

Seedless watermelons save a lot of work, and are more manageable in size than the seeded varieties.

15 mins

SERVES 4–6

1¾oz (50g) pumpkin seeds

1lb 2oz (500g) watermelon (prepared weight), cut into ¾in (2cm) chunks

1 red onion, quartered and very finely sliced

handful of mint leaves, roughly chopped

salt and freshly ground black pepper

1 tbsp extra virgin olive oil

1 tsp balsamic vinegar

3½oz (100g) feta cheese, crumbled

CALORIES: 208kcals/866kJ
CARBOHYDRATE: 12.5g
    sugar: 10.5g
FAT: 14g
    saturated: 5g
SALT: 0.9g
FIBER: 1.5g

1 In a non-stick frying pan, dry-fry the pumpkin seeds over medium heat until they start to color and pop. Set aside to cool.

2 In a large bowl, toss together the watermelon, red onion, and mint leaves and season well. Drizzle in the olive oil and balsamic vinegar and mix it into the salad.

3 Put the salad in a bowl or container and scatter in the cooled pumpkin seeds and feta cheese to serve.

VARIATION

This salad is easy to adapt to your family's tastes. Leave out the red onion, if you prefer, or use a hard goat cheese, or mozzarella, instead of feta.

Tuna and artichoke pasta salad

This hearty meal-in-one salad is enhanced by a few pantry ingredients and some fresh green beans.

15 mins   10 mins

SERVES 4

7¾oz (220g) quick-cook pasta shapes

3½oz (100g) thin green beans, trimmed and halved

1 x 7oz (200g) can of tuna in spring water, drained and flaked

1 x 14oz (400g) can of cannellini beans, drained and rinsed

10 sundried tomatoes in oil, drained and roughly chopped (oil reserved)

1 x 9oz (250g) jar artichoke hearts in oil, drained (oil reserved)

finely grated zest and juice of 1 lemon

1 tsp whole grain mustard

salt and freshly ground black pepper

3 tbsp chopped flat-leaf parsley leaves

leaves from 3 sprigs of basil, torn

1 Bring a large pan of water to a boil and cook the pasta according to the package instructions, adding the green beans 4–5 minutes before the end of cooking time. Drain and rinse under cold running water until the pasta is cold. Drain well and place in a serving dish. Add the tuna, cannellini beans, tomatoes, and artichokes and stir well.

2 Place 3 tbsp of the oil from the sundried tomatoes and 3 tbsp of the oil from the drained artichokes in a small bowl. Stir in the lemon zest and juice, mustard, and seasoning.

3 Pour the lemon-mustard dressing over the pasta. Add the herbs and toss well to coat. Cover and chill until ready to serve.

VARIATION

For a vegetarian version, omit the tuna and add a 9oz (250g) jar of roasted pepper strips instead, and a handful of rinsed capers or green olives.

CALORIES: 411kcals/1740kJ

CARBOHYDRATE: 51g
  sugar: 5g

FAT: 11g
  saturated: 1g

SALT: 1.9g

FIBER: 13g

Orzo salad with tomato vinaigrette

Orzo is a tiny pasta that resembles rice and is quite versatile, adapting to many different flavors.

10 mins   10 mins

SPECIAL EQUIPMENT
mini food processor

SERVES 4–6

7oz (200g) orzo pasta

salt and freshly ground black pepper

2 large ripe tomatoes, peeled, seeded, and roughly chopped (see p191)

2 tbsp olive oil

2 tsp balsamic vinegar

handful of basil leaves, roughly torn

10 black olives, pitted, and chopped

1 Cook the orzo in plenty of boiling salted water according to the package instructions. Drain it, then rinse under cold water and let cool.

2 Put the tomatoes, olive oil, vinegar, and basil in a mini food processer and season generously. Process the mixture to make a thick tomato dressing.

3 When the orzo is cold, mix the tomato dressing through and add the olives. Serve.

VARIATION

For an alternative sauce, try using Arugula pesto (see p194), or a jar of good-quality, store-bought pesto loosened with olive oil, instead of the tomato vinaigrette.

CLEVER WITH LEFTOVERS

This salad can be made with a variety of vegetables that need to be used up. Chopped celery, sweet peppers, or green beans would all be successful additions.

CALORIES: 251kcals/1061kJ

CARBOHYDRATE: 38g
  sugar: 4g

FAT: 8g
  saturated: 1g

SALT: 0.15g

FIBER: 3.5g

Mediterranean vegetable couscous

This lovely summer salad can be adapted to include any vegetables you have available and that are in season.

20 mins, plus cooling   30–40 mins

SERVES 4–6

1 small or ½ large eggplant, cut into ½in (1cm) cubes

1 red bell pepper, cut into ½in (1cm) cubes

1 zucchini, cut into ½in (1cm) cubes

1 red onion, cut into ½in (1cm) cubes

¼ cup olive oil

salt and freshly ground black pepper

2 cups couscous

1 tbsp powdered vegetable stock

2½ tbsp extra virgin olive oil

juice of 1 large lemon

handful of basil leaves, roughly chopped

handful of flat-leaf parsley leaves, roughly chopped

1 Preheat the oven to 400°F (200°C). Put the eggplant, red bell pepper, zucchini, and red onion in a roasting pan and toss them with 2 tbsp of the olive oil. Season them well, spread them out in a single layer, and cook them at the top of the oven for 30–40 minutes, turning them once, until they are well cooked and browned at the edges. Remove them from the oven and allow to cool.

2 Put the couscous into a large, shallow bowl and drizzle in the remaining 1½ tbsp of the olive oil. Rub the olive oil into the couscous with your hands to ensure that all the grains have a covering of oil (this will help to keep them from sticking together). Scatter in the powdered vegetable stock and mix it in with a fork.

3 Pour 2 cups of boiling water over the couscous and stir it in briefly with a fork. The water should just cover the couscous (if it does not, add a little more). Immediately cover the bowl with a tight layer of plastic wrap, sealing it well to ensure that no steam escapes. Let steam for 5 minutes, then remove the plastic wrap and test the grains, which should be nearly soft, and all the water soaked in. Fluff the couscous with a fork and let cool, fluffing it again occasionally to make sure it does not stick together.

4 When the vegetables and the couscous have cooled, assemble the salad by tossing them together in a large bowl along with the extra virgin olive oil, the lemon juice, and herbs. Season to taste and serve.

VARIATION

Try this recipe with green summer vegetables and arugula dressing. Make the dressing by processing together ¼ cup extra virgin olive oil, scant 1 cup roughly chopped arugula leaves, ¼ cup lemon juice, and salt and pepper until it is a thick, dark green liquid. Add the dressing to the cooked couscous, then toss in ¾ cup each of frozen fava beans and petit pois, cooked, drained, and cooled, with a handful of roughly chopped mint leaves. Crumble 3½oz (100g) feta cheese over the top to serve.

CALORIES: 361kcals/1500kJ

CARBOHYDRATE: 42g
  sugar: 5g

FAT: 18g
  saturated: 2.5g

SALT: 1.6g

FIBER: 3g

Apricot, pine nut, and cilantro couscous

This Middle Eastern-inspired salad is equally good with dishes such as Slow-cooked Moroccan lamb (see p132).

12 mins, plus cooling

SERVES 4–6

2 cups couscous

1½ tbsp olive oil

1 tbsp powdered vegetable stock

1¾oz (50g) pine nuts

3½oz (100g) dried apricots, finely chopped

large handful of cilantro leaves, finely chopped

4½ tbsp extra virgin olive oil

juice of 1 large lemon

salt and freshly ground black pepper

CALORIES: 461kcals/1917kJ

CARBOHYDRATE: 47g
  sugar: 11g

FAT: 27g
  saturated: 3g

SALT: 1.6g

FIBER: 3g

1 Put the couscous in a bowl and drizzle in the 1½ tbsp of olive oil. Rub it into the couscous, scatter in the powdered vegetable stock, and mix it in.

2 Measure 2 cups of boiling water into a liquid measuring cup. Pour it over the couscous and stir briefly. The water should just cover the couscous. Immediately seal with plastic wrap.

3 Leave for 5 minutes, then test the grains, which should be nearly soft, and all the water soaked in. Fluff the couscous and let cool, fluffing it occasionally to separate the grains.

4 Meanwhile, dry-fry the pine nuts in a non-stick frying pan over medium heat, stirring, until they color. Be careful, as they can burn quickly. Set aside to cool.

5 Toss together the cooled couscous, pine nuts, apricots, and cilantro. Mix in the extra virgin olive oil and lemon juice and season to taste.

Panzanella

Good-quality bread is a joy, and even when it is past its best it can be used in this delectable Italian salad.

15 mins, plus standing

SERVES 4–6

12oz (350g) unsliced stale dense-textured white bread, such as ciabatta or sourdough, roughly torn into bite-sized pieces

1lb 5oz (600g) mixed tomatoes, at room temperature, such as red, yellow, green, purple baby plum, cherry, or beefsteak, all roughly chopped into bite-sized chunks

1 red onion, finely chopped

2 garlic cloves, finely chopped

2 tbsp capers in brine, drained

salt and freshly ground black pepper

leaves from 1 bunch of basil, roughly torn

FOR THE DRESSING

6 tbsp extra virgin olive oil

3 tbsp red wine vinegar

½ tsp ground mustard

½ tsp granulated sugar

1 Place the bread, tomatoes, onion, garlic, and capers in a large serving bowl. Season well and stir to combine.

2 Place the dressing ingredients in a small bowl, season, and stir well. Pour over the bread and tomato mixture and stir to coat.

3 Set aside for at least 10 minutes and up to 2 hours, at room temperature, to allow the flavors to mingle. Stir the basil leaves into the salad just before serving.

VARIATION

Add pitted black olives and drained anchovies for a salad with more robust and piquant flavors.

CALORIES: 396kcals/1664kJ

CARBOHYDRATE: 47g
  sugar: 8.5g

FAT: 19g
  saturated: 3g

SALT: 1.7g

FIBER: 4.5g

Quick pink pickled onions

These quick pickles make a great addition to a picnic to serve with cold meats or Individual pork pies (see p399).

5 mins,
plus chilling

SERVES 4–8

2 tbsp granulated sugar

2 tsp salt

¾ cup cider vinegar

2 red onions, halved and very finely sliced

1 Put the sugar and salt in a bowl and add a little of the vinegar. Whisk until the salt and sugar crystals have dissolved, then add the rest of the vinegar.

2 Toss through the onions and cover. Leave at room temperature for 1 hour before serving, or packing into a sterilized jam jar (see Cucumber and dill pickles, right) for transportation.

VARIATION

For even pinker onions, add a small chunk of raw beet to the vinegar mixture before adding the onion. Stir it once or twice, to distribute the vibrant color, before serving or storing.

PREPARE AHEAD

These pickled onions will keep in the fridge for up to 1 week, packed in a sterilized, sealed jar. Make sure they are always covered with vinegar.

CALORIES: 34kcals/142kJ
CARBOHYDRATE: 7g
   sugar: 6g
FAT: 0g
   saturated: 0g
SALT: 1g
FIBER: 0.7g

Cucumber and dill pickles

These "refrigerator pickles" are almost instant, so try out making your own portable pickles.

10 mins, plus
sterilizing,
and chilling

SPECIAL EQUIPMENT

2 x 7fl oz (200ml) jam jars with lids

MAKES 2 JARS

¼ cup granulated sugar

2 tsp salt

¾ cup white wine vinegar or rice wine vinegar

freshly ground black pepper

4–5 pickling (small) cucumbers, thinly sliced

1 tbsp finely chopped dill fronds

½ tsp dill seeds, lightly crushed

1 Preheat the oven to 275°F (140°C). Wash two 7fl oz (200ml) jam jars, place upside-down on a baking sheet, and put in the oven for at least 15 minutes. This will sterilize them. Put the lids in a metal bowl and pour a kettleful of boiling water over. Leave for 5 minutes, then remove and let drain. Dry well with paper towels.

2 Put the sugar and salt in a bowl and add a little vinegar. Whisk until the salt and sugar dissolve, then add the rest of the vinegar and a good grinding of pepper.

3 Once the jars are cold, layer the cucumbers into the jars, adding a sprinkling of chopped dill and a few dill seeds between each layer.

4 When the jars are full, pour in the vinegar mixture and seal. Shake them to disperse the liquid evenly and refrigerate overnight for them to get really crispy.

PREPARE AHEAD

These pickles will keep in the fridge for up to 1 month, packed in a sterilized, sealed jar (see above). Make sure they are always covered with vinegar.

CALORIES: 156kcals/649kJ
CARBOHYDRATE: 30g
   sugar: 30g
FAT: 0g
   saturated: 0g
SALT: 4g
FIBER: 3g

Homemade mayonnaise

There is nothing difficult about making mayonnaise, and a food processer makes it even easier.

10 mins

SPECIAL EQUIPMENT
food processor

MAKES 1 CUP

2 large egg yolks

¼ tsp salt

2 tsp lemon juice

1 cup sunflower or vegetable oil

1 tsp Dijon mustard, or more, to taste

1 tsp white wine vinegar, or more, to taste

1 Put the egg yolks, salt, lemon juice, and 2 tsp of water in a food processor. Blend for a minute.

2 Add the oil in a very slow, thin stream, really little more than a few drops at a time to begin with, with the motor running all the time.

3 As the mixture starts to thicken, continue to add the oil in a thin, steady stream. Once it emulsifies to a thick mayonnaise, add the mustard and vinegar, taste, and add more of either if desired. Refrigerate until needed.

VARIATION

After the mayonnaise is made, chopped herbs, crushed garlic, or spices can be added as you like.

PREPARE AHEAD

The mayonnaise will keep, covered, in the fridge for up to 3 days. Be aware that it contains raw eggs, so the usual food safety rules apply (see p11).

CALORIES: 89kcals/368kJ
CARBOHYDRATE: 0g
  sugar: 0g
FAT: 10g
  saturated: 1g
SALT: 0.1g
FIBER: 0g

Potted shrimp

These individual servings make a lovely picnic treat, served simply spread on crusty whole wheat bread.

15 mins, plus chilling   10 mins

SPECIAL EQUIPMENT
4 x 4½fl oz (125ml) ramekins

SERVES 4

20 tbsp unsalted butter

2 tsp lemon juice

pinch of grated nutmeg

salt and freshly ground black pepper

12oz (350g) cooked and peeled small shrimp, or brown shrimp

1 First, clarify the butter. Put it into a small saucepan over low heat. As it melts, foam will come to the surface; pour the pan and skim it off. Gently pour the butter into a bowl, through a strainer. Stop pouring before the whitish milk solids in the pan come out; discard the solids. You should have a bowl of golden, clear butter.

2 Clean the saucepan and return to the heat with three-quarters of the butter and the remaining ingredients. Simmer for 5 minutes.

3 Remove the shrimp with a slotted spoon and pack them into four 4½fl oz (125ml) ramekins, pressing down with a spoon. Now strain the butter from the pan over the shrimp, stopping when you see the residue is about to come out.

4 Cover and chill until set (at least 2 hours). Melt the remaining butter and pour over the shrimp to create a thin seal. Cover and chill once more until set. Remove from the fridge 15–20 minutes before serving, for the butter to soften.

VARIATION

Try using the same amount of white crab, or diced salmon, instead of shrimp, adding 1 tbsp of chopped dill to the salmon at the point of potting.

CALORIES: 625kcals/2612kJ
CARBOHYDRATE: 0g
  sugar: 0g
FAT: 62g
  saturated: 41g
SALT: 1.2g
FIBER: 0g

Salmon rillettes

This piquant pâté from France should be prepared with a fairly rough texture.

15 mins

SERVES 4

4 tbsp butter, softened

9oz (250g) hot-smoked salmon, skinned

¼ cup (2oz) Greek yogurt

finely grated zest and juice of ½ lemon

2 tbsp snipped chives

1 x 2½oz (50g) jar of salmon caviar

handful of watercress and lemon wedges, to serve

1 Put the butter in a bowl and beat with a wooden spoon until smooth. Break up the salmon into small pieces, add to the bowl, and mash with a fork.

2 Add the yogurt, lemon zest and juice, and chives, and stir until evenly combined.

3 Spoon on to serving plates and top with caviar. Serve with watercress sprigs and lemon wedges to squeeze over.

VARIATION

Use the same quantity of poached fresh salmon fillet to make poached salmon rillettes, removing the skin after the fish has been cooked.

PREPARE AHEAD

The rillettes can be made up to 24 hours in advance, covered, and stored in the fridge, or frozen for up to 8 weeks.

COOK'S TIP

For attractive canapés, spread the rillettes, 1 tsp of caviar, and a sprig of watercress onto small rounds of pumpernickel, cut with a round cutter.

CALORIES: 252kcals/1047kJ

CARBOHYDRATE: 1g
  sugar: 1g

FAT: 20g
  saturated: 10g

SALT: 3.1g

FIBER: 0.3g

Sweet potato and goat cheese mini frittatas

These pocket-sized frittatas with their sweet, rich flavors make great portable snacks.

10 mins   35-40 mins

SPECIAL EQUIPMENT

6-hole muffin pan

6 paper liners (optional)

MAKES 6

9oz (250g) sweet potato, cut into ½in (1cm) cubes

1 tbsp olive oil, plus extra for greasing (optional)

salt and freshly ground black pepper

1 tbsp thyme leaves

1¾oz (50g) goat cheese, cut into small cubes

4 large eggs

2 tbsp heavy cream

CALORIES: 162kcals/678kJ

CARBOHYDRATE: 8.5g
  sugar: 2.5g

FAT: 11g
  saturated: 4.5g

SALT: 0.3g

FIBER: 1.3g

1 Preheat the oven to 400°F (200°C). Toss the sweet potato in the oil and spread in a single layer on a baking sheet. Season well and roast at the top of the oven for 20 minutes, turning halfway, until browned in places and cooked. Let cool. Reduce the oven temperature to 350°F (180°C).

2 In a bowl, toss the cooled sweet potatoes, thyme, and goat cheese, and season. Grease a 6-hole muffin pan well with a little oil, or line it with paper liners, and divide the mixture between them.

3 Whisk the eggs and cream, season, and divide equally over the sweet potato. Use a teaspoon to mix the egg into the filling.

4 Bake in the top of the hot oven for 15–20 minutes, until puffed up and golden brown. If you have just greased the pan, allow to cool in the pan until barely warm before removing to a wire rack. If you are using liners, allow to cool in the pan for 5 minutes before removing and cooling completely on a wire rack.

Tuna empanadas

Originally from Spain and Portugal, these savory pastries called empanadas translate as "wrapped in bread."

45 mins, plus chilling | 40–50 mins

SPECIAL EQUIPMENT
3½in (9cm) round cutter

MAKES 24

2½ cups all-purpose flour, plus extra for dusting

sea salt

6 tbsp unsalted butter, cut in cubes

2 large eggs, lightly beaten, plus extra for glazing

FOR THE FILLING

1 tbsp olive oil, plus extra for greasing

1 onion, finely chopped

½ cup canned tomatoes, drained weight

2 tsp tomato paste

1 x 5oz (140g) can of tuna, drained

2 tbsp finely chopped parsley

freshly ground black pepper

1 To make the dough, sift the flour into a bowl with ½ tsp salt. Add the butter and rub it in. Mix in the eggs with 4–6 tbsp of water. Wrap in plastic wrap and chill for 30 minutes.

2 Heat the oil in a frying pan, add the onion, and cook over medium heat for 5 minutes. Add the tomatoes, tomato paste, tuna, and parsley, and season with pepper. Reduce the heat and simmer for 10–12 minutes, stirring occasionally. Allow to cool.

3 Preheat the oven to 375°F (190°C). Roll out the pastry to ⅛in (3mm) thick. Cut out 24 rounds with a 3½in (9cm) round cutter. Put 1 tsp of the filling on each. Brush the edges with water, fold over, and pinch together.

4 Place on an oiled baking sheet and brush with egg. Bake for 25–30 minutes. Serve warm.

PREPARE AHEAD

These keep in the fridge for 2 days. Reheat in an oven at 325°F (160°C) for 10 minutes before serving.

CALORIES: 115kcals/484kJ

CARBOHYDRATE: 14g
  sugar: 0.7g

FAT: 4.5g
  saturated: 2g

SALT: 0.15g

FIBER: 1g

Sausage rolls

Classic finger food for picnics and parties, these are so easy to make you may never go back to store-bought.

30 mins, plus chilling   10–12 mins, plus cooling

MAKES 24

9oz (250g) store-bought puff pastry

all-purpose flour, for dusting

1½lb (675g) ground sausage

1 small onion, finely chopped

1 tbsp thyme leaves

1 tbsp finely grated lemon zest

1 tsp Dijon mustard

1 large egg yolk

sea salt and freshly ground black pepper

1 large egg, lightly beaten, for glazing

CALORIES: 114kcals/477kJ

CARBOHYDRATE: 5g
  sugar: 0.7g

FAT: 8g
  saturated: 3g

SALT: 0.6g

FIBER: 0g

---

1 Preheat the oven to 400°F (200°C). Line a baking sheet with parchment paper and chill. Cut the pastry in half. Roll each piece out on a floured surface to a 12 x 6in (30 x 15cm) rectangle, then cover and chill for 30 minutes. Mix the sausage with the onion, thyme, lemon zest, mustard, and egg yolk. Season.

2 Lay the pastry on a flat surface. Form the sausage mixture into 2 logs and place a log in the center of each piece of pastry. Brush the pastry with the egg, roll it over, and press to seal. Cut each roll into 12.

3 Place on the chilled pan, make 2 snips at the top of each roll with scissors, then brush with egg. Bake for 10–12 minutes or until golden and flaky. Serve warm, or transfer to a wire rack to cool.

PREPARE AHEAD

These can be stored in an airtight container in the fridge for 2 days, or frozen, uncooked, for up to 8 weeks.

Cornish pasties

Although not traditional, a splash of Worcestershire sauce adds a depth of flavor to the pasty filling.

20 mins, plus chilling   40–45 mins, plus cooling

MAKES 4

7 tbsp lard, chilled and cut into cubes

4 tbsp unsalted butter, chilled and cut into cubes

1½ cups all-purpose flour, plus extra for dusting

½ tsp salt

1 large egg, lightly beaten, for glazing

FOR THE FILLING

9oz (250g) beef skirt steak, trimmed and cut into ½in (1cm) cubes

2¾oz (80g) rutabaga , peeled and cut into ¼in (5mm) cubes

3½oz (100g) waxy potatoes, peeled and cut into ¼in (5mm) cubes

1 large onion, finely chopped

splash of Worcestershire sauce

1 tsp all-purpose flour

salt and freshly ground black pepper

CALORIES: 700kcals/3091kJ

CARBOHYDRATE: 62g
  sugar: 4g

FAT: 44g
  saturated: 20g

SALT: 0.8g

FIBER: 5g

---

1 Rub the lard and butter into the flour until it resembles fine crumbs. Add the salt and enough water to form a soft dough. Knead briefly on a floured surface. Wrap in plastic wrap and chill for 1 hour.

2 Preheat the oven to 375°F (190°C). Mix all the filling ingredients and season well. On a well-floured work surface, roll the dough out to ¼in (5mm) thick. Using a saucer, cut 4 circles from the dough. Re-roll the scraps.

3 Fold the circles in half, then flatten them out again, leaving a slight mark down the center. Pile one-quarter of the filling into each circle, leaving a ¾in (2cm) border all around. Brush the border of the dough with a little beaten egg.

4 Pull both edges up over the filling and press to seal. Crimp the seal with your fingers. Brush a little beaten egg all over the pasties. Bake in the center of the oven for 40–45 minutes until golden brown. Allow to cool for at least 15 minutes before eating warm or cold.

PREPARE AHEAD

These will keep, covered, in the fridge for 2 days–reheat at 350°F (180°C) for 20 minutes; or freeze the assembled pasties, uncooked, for up to 8 weeks.

Individual pork pies

Try making these bite-sized pork pies for a special picnic treat. Remember to pack a jar of mustard, too.

40 mins, plus chilling   **1 hr**

SPECIAL EQUIPMENT

food processor (optional)

12-hole muffin pan

small funnel (optional)

MAKES 12

FOR THE FILLING

7oz (200g) pork belly, trimmed of fat and skin and cut into cubes

7oz (200g) pork shoulder, trimmed and cut into cubes

1¾oz (50g) bacon, trimmed and cut into cubes

10 sage leaves, finely chopped

sea salt and freshly ground black pepper

¼ tsp nutmeg

¼ tsp allspice

FOR THE HOT WATER PASTRY

3 cups all-purpose flour, plus extra for dusting

½ tsp fine salt

⅔ cup lard or beef dripping, cut into cubes

1 large egg, lightly beaten, for glazing

FOR THE JELLY (OPTIONAL)

½ tbsp unflavored powdered gelatin

1 cup chicken stock (see p94)

1 Preheat the oven to 400°F (200°C). Put all the ingredients for the filling into a food processor and pulse until the meat is chopped, but not mushy.

2 To make the hot water pastry, place the flour and salt in a bowl and make a well in the middle. Combine lard or dripping with ⅔ cup boiling water in a bowl and stir until the fat melts.

3 Pour the liquid into the flour and mix. You will need to use your hands to bring it into a soft dough. Be careful, as it will be hot. Cut off one-quarter of the dough, wrap it in a clean kitchen towel, and set it aside somewhere warm.

4 You need to work quickly as the dough hardens as it cools. Turn the dough onto a well-floured work surface and roll it out to ¼in (5mm) thick. Cut out 12 circles big enough to line a 12-hole muffin pan, allowing them to overlap the edges. Pack the filling into each and brush egg around the edges.

5 Roll out the set-aside dough. Cut out 12 lids to fit the crusts. Top the filling with the lids and press down the sides to seal. Brush with egg. Use a chopstick to make a hole in each pie if you wish to fill it with jelly later, or cut 2 slits to allow the steam to escape if you don't.

6 Bake for 30 minutes, then reduce the oven temperature to 325°F (160°C) and cook for 30 minutes. Let cool for 10 minutes before turning out.

7 To make the jelly, pour ¼ cup of chicken stock into a bowl. Sprinkle in the gelatin and let sit 5 minutes. Heat the remaining stock and add the gelatin, stirring until it dissolves. Cool. Once the liquid starts to thicken, use a small funnel to pour it into each pie. Refrigerate to set overnight. These will keep, covered and chilled, for up to 3 days.

CALORIES: 312kcals/1303kJ

CARBOHYDRATE: 24g
 sugar: 0.5g

FAT: 18g
 saturated: 7g

SALT: 0.4g

FIBER: 1.4g

Baking

Baking

If you follow a few basic rules, baking can be quite straightforward, and even novice bakers can achieve great results. Follow the recipe carefully, measure out ingredients accurately, be patient, and with the clever tips on this page you should do well. Baking is a great way to get kids interested in cooking—cookies, scones, and cakes are always popular treats to start with. Some store-bought baked goods are made with unhealthy amounts of sugar, salt, and fat, so by making your own you will know exactly what your family is eating. Baked goods are perfect for snacks, picnics, and parties, as well as everyday treats, and nothing beats the smell of bread or cookies baking in the oven.

Get organized

The most important thing to do before you start is to read all the way through the recipe before attempting it for the first time. You may be overwhelmed with the desire to get started, but you need to be sure that you have enough time to see all the stages of a recipe through, especially if it involves pauses for rising or proofing. It's important to make sure ingredients are at the temperature stated in the recipe, too. Using cake pans of the correct size is also vital to the success of a recipe, so make sure they are the size stipulated. Finally, adjust your oven shelves to the desired height before you heat the oven, and make sure the oven reaches the correct temperature well before you are due to start baking.

Master the basics first, such as a classic sponge cake with an easy filling, like this Victoria sponge cake (p423). As your confidence grows you can get more ambitious with the recipes you tackle.

Useful baking equipment

Essentials	Good to have
Digital scales	Spatula
Wooden spoons	Silicone paper
Balloon whisk	Baking spray
Mixing bowls	Electric hand-held mixer
Fine metal sieve	Food processor or standing mixer
Good-quality, heavy baking pans and sheets in various sizes	Cookie cutters
	Piping set
Waxed paper	Oven thermometer
Measuring spoons	

Know your chemistry

Cooking may be an art, but baking is a science. The artistry can come after the science, by all means, but there is a basic chemistry involved in turning simple ingredients into light baked goods. The essential component of many recipes is air—this is introduced through the fermentation of yeast, the leavening of rising agents such as baking powder, or the simple addition of stiffly whisked egg whites. A light touch when folding in dry ingredients, egg whites, or bringing together pastry or scones, is essential, so try not to be heavy handed or overmix ingredients. When transferring cake mix to a pan, smooth the top gently, but try to avoid pressing down and expelling all the air. When baking bread, make sure you allow time for the yeast to become active and aerate the dough, which will help it rise and give it a light texture.

Savory bakes, such as this moist Zucchini and feta loaf (p453) are well worth the effort. Home-baked loaves and bakes are versatile and ideal for packed lunches, picnics, and afternoon snacks.

Rise to the occasion

There are so many mouthwatering treats here that it's going to be hard to know where to start. Cookies are easy to tackle, and the supremely useful Slice and bake butter cookies (p407) use a cookie dough you can make and store in the fridge or freezer until you need it. If you have guests and want to impress, choose a Lemon drizzle cake (p421) or Coffee and Walnut cake (p429), or wow your dinner guests with an irresistible Genoise cake with raspberries and cream (p422). For a party, choose from Red velvet cupcakes with cream cheese icing (p415) or an Angel food cake (p418), or frost the delicious Rich fruit cake (p419) for a special celebration.

Try something different

Don't forget the savory bakes! For some easy savory treats, start with some store-bought puff pastry for Quick cheese pastries (p442) or mix up some Savory breakfast muffins (p442) for a weekend treat. Home-baked bread is also wonderful. If you don't have time to allow for rising and proofing, start by trying some quick breads such as Brown soda bread (p450) or Sweet potato and rosemary rolls (p452), and build up your confidence before tackling a Rosemary foccacia (p447) or some delicious home-baked Pretzels (p445).

Tips for success

There's no mystery to making your own delicious and nutritious baked goods. These few tricks of the trade will show you how easy it can be.

Look after your ingredients

Store flours and sugars in airtight containers to keep them fresh, dry, and moisture free.

Weigh

Invest in some digital scales to ensure that you are accurate with your measurements.

Spray

Baking sprays help to distribute a thin, even layer of fat around the pan, which helps to stop cakes from sticking.

Line

Cut reusable silicone baking sheets to the size of your cake pans for a perfect, non-stick result every time.

Test

Many ovens, especially older ones, do not always heat up accurately to the temperature the recipe requires; they may run hotter, or colder. A simple in-oven thermometer that hangs from the shelves will help you get to and maintain the correct temperature for a successful bake.

Rest

If a recipe says to rest something, there is usually a reason. Most cookies, for example, will need a few minutes resting on their baking sheets to firm up before you move them, or they will break. It may be tempting to cut into warm bread, but if you do it straight from the oven, the result will be stodgy, rather than light, moist bread.

Store

Home-baked goods keep fresher for longer if you store them correctly. Have plenty of different-sized airtight containers for cookies and cakes, and wrap fruit cakes in foil to stop the moisture from escaping, before putting them in a pan. Covering the top of a delicately iced cake in waxed paper helps preserve the decorations.

Fats

For sweet pastry, use a good quality, unsalted butter to give a perfectly crisp texture. Savory pastry can be made with half butter, half lard for an old-fashioned, crumbly pastry. Cooking margarine gives an airy texture to cakes.

Oat and raisin cookies

These crisp, crumbly cookies are packed full of fiber-filled oats and sweet raisins for a healthier treat.

10 mins   15 mins

MAKES 15

11 tbsp butter

½ cup granulated sugar

1 cup self-rising flour, sifted

1 cup oats

1¾oz (50g) raisins

1 tsp baking soda

1 Preheat the oven to 350°F (180°C). Melt the butter in a large saucepan over low heat. Allow it to cool while you measure out the other ingredients.

2 Mix the sugar, flour, oats, and raisins into the cooled, melted butter and stir well.

3 In a cup, mix the baking soda with 1 tbsp boiling water until it dissolves, then mix it well into the cookie mixture.

4 Take 1 tbsp of the mixture and roll it into a ball between your hands. Flatten it slightly and put it on a baking sheet. Repeat to use up all the dough, spacing them well apart on the pan, as they will spread.

5 Bake in the center of the oven for 12–15 minutes until they turn golden brown. Remove the cookies from the oven and let cool on their baking sheets for 5 minutes (they will break if you do not), then transfer them to a wire rack to cool completely.

CALORIES: 164kcals/687kJ

CARBOHYDRATE: 19g
sugar: 9g

FAT: 9g
saturated: 5g

SALT: 0.4g

FIBER: 1g

Double chocolate chip cookies

The ultimate chocolate treat—try these freshly baked and still warm with a cold glass of milk.

10 mins   15 mins

SPECIAL EQUIPMENT
electric hand-held mixer

MAKES 15

7 tbsp butter, softened

½ cup granulated sugar

½ cup light brown sugar

1 large egg, lightly beaten

1 tsp vanilla extract

1¼ cups all-purpose flour

¼ cup cocoa powder

½ tsp baking powder

¼ tsp salt

1 tbsp whole milk

3½oz (100g) chocolate chips

1 Preheat the oven to 180°C (350°F). In a large bowl, cream together the butter and sugars until light and fluffy, then beat in the egg and vanilla extract.

2 Sift the flour, cocoa powder, baking powder, and salt together, and mix it in to the cookie mixture, until it is well combined. Mix in the milk.

3 Fold in the chocolate chips. Place tablespoons of the cookie mixture onto several baking sheets, spaced well apart as they will spread on cooking.

4 Bake the cookies in the center of the oven for 15 minutes, until just cooked. Let cool on the baking sheets for 5 minutes before transferring them to a wire rack to cool completely.

HOW TO FREEZE
The baked cookies can be frozen in an airtight container for up to 6 months. Defrost thoroughly before eating.

CALORIES: 180kcals/758kJ

CARBOHYDRATE: 25g
sugar: 17g

FAT: 8g
saturated: 5g

SALT: 0.2g

FIBER: 0.6g

Pistachio and cranberry oat cookies

Using pistachios and cranberries brings a healthy, chewy bite to these easy-to-make cookies.

20 mins   10–15 mins

SPECIAL EQUIPMENT
electric hand-held mixer

MAKES 24

7 tbsp unsalted butter, softened

1 cup light brown sugar

1 large egg, lightly beaten

1 tsp vanilla extract

1 tbsp honey

1 cup self-rising flour, sifted

1 cup oats

pinch of salt

3½oz (100g) pistachios, lightly toasted and roughly chopped

3½oz (100g) dried cranberries, roughly chopped

a little milk, if needed

1 Preheat the oven to 375°F (190°C). Put the butter and sugar in a bowl and cream with an electric hand-held mixer until smooth. Add the egg, vanilla extract, and honey and beat well.

2 Add the flour, oats, and salt, stirring with a wooden spoon to combine. Add the chopped nuts and cranberries, and mix until thoroughly combined. If the mixture is too stiff, add a little milk until it becomes pliable.

3 Take walnut-sized pieces and roll them into balls between your palms. Place on 2 or 3 baking sheets lined with parchment and flatten slightly, spacing them well apart on the pan.

4 Bake for 10–15 minutes until golden brown (you may need to do this in batches). Leave on the pan to cool, then transfer to a wire rack. These will keep in an airtight container for up to 5 days.

VARIATION

Once you have mastered this recipe for oat cookies, try experimenting with different combinations of fresh or dried fruit and nuts, or adding seeds such as sunflower seeds and pumpkin seeds into the cookie dough mixture.

CALORIES: 145kcals/611kJ

CARBOHYDRATE: 19g
  sugar: 12g

FAT: 6g
  saturated: 2.5g

SALT: 0.1g

FIBER: 1g

Pistachio, cranberry, and orange biscotti

Try baking these colorful Italian cookies as a festive treat or gift, packaging them in a colorful jar or tin.

15 mins   45–50 mins

MAKES 25–30

2 cups self-rising flour, plus extra for dusting

½ cup granulated sugar

3½oz (100g) shelled unsalted pistachios, toasted and chopped

1¾oz (50g) dried cranberries, roughly chopped

finely grated zest of 1 orange

2 large eggs

1 tsp vanilla extract

4 tbsp unsalted butter, melted and cooled

1 Preheat the oven to 350°F (180°C). Line 1 or 2 baking sheets with parchment paper. Sift the flour into a large bowl. Stir in the sugar, pistachios, and cranberries. Whisk together the orange zest, eggs, vanilla extract, and butter. Gradually stir into the flour.

2 Turn the dough onto a floured work surface. With your hands, form it into two 8in (20cm) logs. Place on a lined baking sheet and bake for 25 minutes in the middle of the oven. Cool slightly.

3 With a serrated knife, cut the logs on a slant into 1½–2in- (3–5cm-) thick slices. Put the biscotti on 1 or 2 baking sheets, as needed, and return to the oven for 20 minutes to dry even more, turning halfway through with a palette knife. Cool the biscotti on a wire rack to harden them and allow any moisture to escape. These will keep in an airtight container for up to 1 week.

CALORIES: 80kcals/338kJ

CARBOHYDRATE: 10g
  sugar: 5g

FAT: 3.5g
  saturated: 1g

SALT: 0.1g

FIBER: 0.5g

Pecan sandies

These addictive cookies are so-called because they have the texture (though not the taste!) of fine sand.

15 mins, plus chilling   15 mins

SPECIAL EQUIPMENT
electric hand-held mixer

MAKES 18–20

7 tbsp unsalted butter, softened

⅓ cup light brown sugar

¼ cup granulated sugar

½ tsp vanilla extract

1 large egg yolk

1¼ cups all-purpose flour, sifted, plus extra for dusting

2½oz (75g) pecans, chopped

1 Preheat the oven to 350°F (180°C). In a large bowl, cream together the butter and sugars with an electric hand-held mixer until light and fluffy. Add the vanilla extract and the egg yolk and mix well to combine. Fold in the flour and then the pecans. Bring it together to form a rough dough.

2 Turn the dough onto a lightly floured work surface and knead it to form a smooth dough. Roll into a log about 8in (20cm) long. If the dough seems too soft to cut, chill it for 30 minutes to allow it to firm up.

3 Slice ½in (1cm) disks from the log, and place them spaced apart on 2 baking sheets lined with parchment paper. Bake in the top of the oven for 15 minutes, until golden at the edges. Leave on the sheets for a few minutes, then transfer to a wire rack to cool.

CALORIES: 111kcals/468kJ

CARBOHYDRATE: 10g
  sugar: 5g

FAT: 7g
  saturated: 3g

SALT: 0g

FIBER: 0.5g

HOW TO FREEZE

There's nothing better than the aroma and flavor of just-baked cookies. At the end of step 2, freeze the dough for up to 12 weeks. Now you can have fresh-baked cookies at any time.

Slice and bake butter cookies

These cookies are so convenient, as the dough can be stored uncooked in the fridge or freezer to bake when needed.

20 mins   10–12 mins

SPECIAL EQUIPMENT
electric hand-held mixer

MAKES 20

14 tbsp butter, softened

½ cup granulated sugar, plus extra for dusting

1 tsp vanilla extract

2¼ cups all-purpose flour, sifted

1 Put the butter and sugar in a large bowl and cream them with an electric hand-held mixer until light and fluffy. Beat in the vanilla. Mix in the flour to form a stiff dough.

2 Divide the mixture into 2, and roll each piece out to make a fat log about 2½in (6cm) in diameter and 8in (20cm) long. Sprinkle a work surface with sugar and roll the cookie log in it, to coat the outside in sugar.

3 Wrap the dough logs in plastic wrap and refrigerate for at least 2 hours, and up to 3 days.

4 When ready to bake, preheat the oven to 350°F (180°C). Cut off as much of the log as you need, then slice the hardened dough into ½in- (1cm-) thick disks.

5 Place on a lined baking sheet and bake for 10–12 minutes, until golden brown at the edges. Let cool for 5 minutes before transferring to a wire rack to cool.

HOW TO FREEZE

This dough can be frozen for up to 12 weeks. Cut off what you need with a serrated knife, defrost for 30 minutes, then slice and bake as usual.

CALORIES: 145kcals/607kJ
CARBOHYDRATE: 16g
  sugar: 5g
FAT: 8g
  saturated: 5g
SALT: 0.2g
FIBER: 0.5g

Peanut butter cookies

These sweet, salty cookies are perfect for anyone who loves peanut butter... and cookies!

10 mins   10–12 mins

SPECIAL EQUIPMENT
electric hand-held mixer

MAKES 20–24

14 tbsp butter, softened

¾ cup light brown sugar

2 large eggs, lightly beaten

1 tsp vanilla extract

¾ cup crunchy peanut butter

1¾ cups all-purpose flour, sifted

½ tsp salt

1 Preheat the oven to 350°F (180°C). Put the butter and sugar in a bowl and cream together with an electric hand-held mixer until fluffy. Add the eggs and vanilla and beat well. Beat in the peanut butter, then fold in the flour and salt just until the mixture is well combined.

2 Place tablespoonfuls of the mixture onto non-stick baking sheets, spaced well apart, and press down with the back of a fork in a criss-cross pattern. Dip the fork in water between each cookie, to keep it from sticking. This decorates the cookiess and helps them to spread when cooking. Bake for 10–12 minutes, until lightly colored.

3 Remove from the oven and cool for 5 minutes on the baking sheets before transferring to a wire rack to cool completely.

HOW TO FREEZE
The baked cookies can be frozen in an airtight container. Defrost thoroughly and eat within 12 weeks.

CALORIES: 222kcals/927kJ
CARBOHYDRATE: 19g
  sugar: 8g
FAT: 14g
  saturated: 7g
SALT: 0.4g
FIBER: 0.5g

Marbled millionaire's shortbread

A modern classic, this is extremely sweet and rich, just as it should be.

45 mins   30–45 mins

SPECIAL EQUIPMENT
8in (20cm) square cake pan

MAKES 16 SQUARES

FOR THE SHORTBREAD

12 tbsp unsalted butter, softened, plus extra for greasing

1½ cups all-purpose flour

½ cup granulated sugar

FOR THE CARAMEL FILLING

4 tbsp unsalted butter

⅓ cup light brown sugar

1 x 14oz (400g) can of condensed milk

FOR THE CHOCOLATE TOPPING

7oz (200g) milk chocolate

2 tbsp unsalted butter

1¾oz (50g) dark chocolate

1 Preheat the oven to 325°F (160°C). Grease an 8in (20cm) square cake pan and line with parchment paper. For the shortbread, put the flour, butter, and sugar in a bowl and rub together to make crumbs. Press into the pan. Bake for 35–40 minutes until golden brown. Let cool.

2 For the caramel, melt the butter and sugar in a heavy-bottomed saucepan over medium heat. Add the condensed milk and bring to a boil, stirring. Reduce the heat and stir for 5 minutes until it thickens and is a light caramel color. Pour over the shortbread and let cool.

3 To make the topping, place the milk chocolate and butter in a heatproof bowl over simmering water, until just melted. Melt the dark chocolate in another bowl.

4 Spread the milk chocolate over the caramel. Pour the dark chocolate over in a zigzag and drag a skewer through for a marbled effect. Let cool before cutting into 16 squares. These keep in an airtight container for up to 5 days.

CALORIES: 363kcals/1521kJ
CARBOHYDRATE: 40g
  sugar: 31g
FAT: 20g
  saturated: 12.5g
SALT: 0.4g
FIBER: 0.8g

Shortbread

This is the classic Scottish shortbread, which should be pale in color and crumbly with a light buttery flavor.

15 mins, plus chilling   30–40 mins

SPECIAL EQUIPMENT

7in (18cm) loose-bottomed round cake pan

electric hand-held mixer

MAKES 8 WEDGES

11 tbsp unsalted butter, softened, plus extra for greasing

⅓ cup granulated sugar, plus extra for sprinkling

1¼ cups all-purpose flour

5 tbsp cornstarch

1 Preheat the oven to 325°F (160°C). Grease a 7in (18cm) loose-bottomed round cake pan and line with parchment. Place the softened butter and sugar in a large bowl. Cream together with an electric hand-held mixer until light and fluffy.

2 Stir in the flour and cornstarch very gently, stopping as soon as the flours are mixed in. Bring together with your hands to form a very rough, crumbly dough. Transfer to the cake pan and firmly push the dough down with your hands to form a compact and even layer.

3 With a sharp knife, lightly score the shortbread into 8 wedges. Prick it all over with a fork to make a decorative pattern. Cover with plastic wrap and chill for 1 hour.

4 Bake in the center of the oven for 30–40 minutes. Cover with foil if it browns quickly. Take it out of the oven and re-score the wedges with a sharp knife. While it is still warm, sprinkle a thin layer of granulated sugar evenly over the top. When completely cool, turn it gently out of its pan and break or cut it into wedges along the scored lines. This shortbread keeps in an airtight container for up to 5 days.

COOK'S TIP

The best shortbread is made when all the ingredients are kept as cool as possible. Cool hands and a cool kitchen are a great help in achieving the "short," crumbly texture of the best shortbread.

CALORIES: 273kcals/1142kJ

CARBOHYDRATE: 30g
  sugar: 10g

FAT: 16g
  saturated: 10g

SALT: 0.3g

FIBER: 1g

Buttermilk scones

Homemade, these are one of the simplest and best breakfast treats. Buttermilk makes the lightest scones.

15-20 mins   12-15 mins

SPECIAL EQUIPMENT
2¾in (7cm) round cookie cutter

MAKES 6-8

4 tbsp unsalted butter, chilled, and cut into pieces, plus extra for greasing

2 cups white bread flour, plus extra for dusting

2 tsp baking powder

½ tsp salt

¾ cup buttermilk, plus extra if needed

butter, jam, and heavy cream, to serve

1 Preheat the oven to 425°F (220°C). Line a baking sheet with parchment paper and grease it. Sift the flour, baking powder, and salt into a large chilled bowl. Put the butter in the bowl, keeping everything cold.

2 Rub with your fingertips until the mixture forms fine crumbs, working quickly. Make a well in the center and, in a steady stream, pour in the buttermilk. Quickly toss with a fork. Do not over-mix.

3 Stir the mixture until the crumbs form a dough. Add a little more buttermilk if it seems dry. Turn onto a floured surface and knead for a few seconds; keep it rough, not smooth. Pat the dough out to a round ¾in (2cm) thick.

4 Cut out with a 2¾in (7cm) round cookie cutter. Pat out the trimmings and cut additional rounds until all the dough has been used. Arrange the scones so they are about 2in (5cm) apart on the prepared baking sheet. Bake in the hot oven for 12–15 minutes until lightly browned and risen. Scones should be eaten on the day they are baked, ideally warm from the oven. Spread with butter, jam, and thick heavy cream.

CALORIES: 172kcals/729kJ

CARBOHYDRATE: 24g
sugar: 1.5g

FAT: 6.7g
saturated: 4.2g

SALT: 0.6g

FIBER: 1g

Double chocolate chip muffins

These muffins make a quick after-school snack, or a great treat at any time of day.

10 mins   15 mins

SPECIAL EQUIPMENT
12 muffin liners

12-hole muffin pan

MAKES 12

2 cups self-rising flour

1 tsp baking powder

½ cup cocoa powder

¼ tsp salt

½ cup granulated sugar

¾ cup whole milk

⅓ cup sunflower or vegetable oil

1 large egg, lightly beaten

1 tsp vanilla extract

2½oz (75g) chocolate chips

1 Preheat the oven to 400°F (200°C). Sift the flour, baking powder, cocoa powder, and salt into a large bowl. Use a balloon whisk to mix in the sugar.

2 Measure the milk and sunflower oil into a bowl, then add the egg and vanilla extract and beat it all together thoroughly.

3 Pour the liquid into the center of the dry ingredients and mix with a wooden spoon until just combined. Be careful not to over-mix. Fold in the chocolate chips.

4 Put 12 muffin liners into a 12-hole muffin pan, then divide the mixture equally between the liners. Bake in the middle of the preheated oven for 15 minutes, until well risen. Remove from the oven and allow the muffins to cool in the pan for 5 minutes beforetransferring to a wire rack to cool completely.

CALORIES: 208kcals/875kJ

CARBOHYDRATE: 28g
sugar: 15g

FAT: 9g
saturated: 3g

SALT: 0.5g

FIBER: 2g

HOW TO FREEZE

The cooked muffins can be frozen in an airtight container for up to 12 weeks. Remove as many as you need and defrost thoroughly before serving.

Strawberry shortcakes

These make a perfect summer dessert. A classic when strawberries are juicy and sweet.

15 mins   15–17 mins

SPECIAL EQUIPMENT
3in (8cm) cookie cutter

SERVES 4

9oz (250g) strawberries

2 tbsp confectioners' sugar

2¼ cups self-rising flour,
  sifted, plus extra for dusting

1 tsp baking powder

2 tbsp granulated sugar

7 tbsp butter, cut into cubes

1 egg, beaten, plus extra for glazing

½ cup whole milk

⅔ cup heavy cream

1 Preheat the oven to 375°F (190°C). Prepare the strawberries by slicing them ¼in (5mm) thick and tossing them in 1 tbsp of the confectioners' sugar. Let them macerate at room temperature.

2 Rub the flour, baking powder, granulated sugar, and butter together until the mixture resembles fine bread crumbs.

3 Beat the egg and milk together. Make a well in the center of the flour mixture and pour the liquid into the center. Slowly incorporate the flour to make a soft dough, using a fork first and then your fingertips, but do not over-mix, or the mixture will become tough.

4 Turn the dough onto a floured work surface and knead it just long enough to bring it together. Pat it into a 1in- (3cm-) thick piece and cut out 4 rounds with an 3in (8cm) cookie cutter.

5 Place the shortcakes onto a baking sheet lined with parchment paper, and brush them with a little beaten egg. Bake them in the center of the hot oven for 15–17 minutes until well-risen and golden brown.

6 Remove from the oven and cool on a wire rack. Meanwhile, whisk the cream until billowing.

7 To serve the shortcakes, split them in half. Fill each with the cream, dividing it evenly, then top with some sliced strawberries, including some juice. Put the tops on and dust with the remaining 1 tbsp of confectioners' sugar to serve.

HOW TO FREEZE

The cooked shortcakes can be open-frozen on the day they are made, then transferred to a freezer bag for up to 12 weeks. Defrost thoroughly, fill, and eat within 1 day.

CALORIES: 740kcals/3096kJ

CARBOHYDRATE: 73g
sugar: 21g

FAT: 45g
saturated: 27g

SALT: 1.5g

FIBER: 4g

Madeleines

Light and incredibly addictive, buttery madeleines make an elegant afternoon treat.

15-20 mins   10 mins

SPECIAL EQUIPMENT

madeleine pan, or small 12-hole mini-muffin pan

electric hand-held mixer

MAKES 12

4 tbsp unsalted butter, melted and cooled, plus extra for greasing

½ cup self-rising flour, sifted, plus extra for dusting

¼ cup granulated sugar

2 large eggs, lightly beaten

1 tsp vanilla extract

confectioners' sugar, for dusting

1 Preheat the oven to 350°F (180°C). Carefully brush a madeleine pan, or small 12-hole bun pan, with melted butter and dust with a little flour. Invert the pan and tap to remove excess flour.

2 Put the sugar, eggs, and vanilla into a mixing bowl. Using an electric hand-held mixer, mix for 5 minutes until the mixture is pale, thick, and holds a trail (this is known as the "ribbon stage").

3 Sift the flour over the top and pour the melted butter down the side of the mixture. Using a large rubber spatula, fold them in carefully and quickly, being careful not to knock out too much air.

4 Fill the hollows in the pans evenly with the batter and bake for 10 minutes. Remove from the oven and transfer to a wire rack to cool. Dust with confectioners' sugar to serve.

CALORIES: 88kcals/371kJ
CARBOHYDRATE: 8.5g
  sugar: 5g
FAT: 5g
  saturated: 3g
SALT: trace
FIBER: 0.2g

Blueberry muffins with streusel topping

These muffins make a quick and easy anytime treat. Use frozen blueberries if you have them.

20 mins   15-20 mins

SPECIAL EQUIPMENT

12-hole muffin pan

12 paper muffin liners

MAKES 12

FOR THE STREUSEL TOPPING

⅓ cup light brown sugar

½ cup all-purpose flour

1 tsp ground cinnamon

2 tbsp butter

FOR THE MUFFINS

2 cups self-rising flour

1 tsp baking powder

¼ tsp salt

½ cup granulated sugar

½ cup whole milk

½ cup (4oz) plain yogurt

¼ cup sunflower or vegetable oil

1 large egg, lightly beaten

1 tsp vanilla extract

3½oz (100g) blueberries

1 Preheat the oven to 400°F (200°C) and line a 12-hole muffin pan with paper muffin liners. Make the topping: rub together the sugar, flour, cinnamon, and butter.

2 Sift the flour, baking powder, and salt into a bowl. Add the sugar. Measure the milk, yogurt, and oil into a bowl and beat in the egg and vanilla. Stir the wet ingredients into the dry, then mix in the berries. Spoon into the cups and top evenly with the streusel.

3 Bake for 15–20 minutes, cool in the pan for 5 minutes, then transfer to a wire rack to cool.

HOW TO FREEZE

The cooked muffins can be frozen in an airtight container for up to 6 months. Defrost thoroughly before serving.

CALORIES: 224kcals/945kJ
CARBOHYDRATE: 36g
  sugar: 19g
FAT: 6.5g
  saturated: 2g
SALT: 0.4g
FIBER: 1g

Lemon and poppy seed muffins

These light and lemony muffins make a pleasant, refreshing change when baked for weekend breakfast or brunch.

10 mins   15 mins

SPECIAL EQUIPMENT

12-hole muffin pan

12 paper muffin liners

MAKES 12

2 cups self-rising flour

1 tsp baking powder

¼ tsp salt

½ cup granulated sugar

finely grated zest of 1 lemon

1 heaping tsp poppy seeds

½ cup whole milk

½ cup (4oz) plain yogurt

¼ cup sunflower or vegetable oil

1 large egg, lightly beaten

2 tbsp lemon juice

FOR THE GLAZE

2 tbsp lemon juice

1¼ cups confectioners' sugar

finely grated zest of 1 lemon

1 Preheat the oven to 400°F (200°C) and line a 12-hole muffin pan with paper muffin liners. Sift the flour, baking powder, and salt into a large bowl. Use a balloon whisk to mix through the sugar, lemon zest, and poppy seeds.

2 Measure the milk, yogurt, and oil into a bowl, then add the egg and lemon juice and beat it all together thoroughly. Pour the liquid into the center of the dry ingredients and mix with a wooden spoon until just combined. Be careful not to over-mix.

3 Divide the mixture equally between the muffin liners and bake in the middle of the preheated oven for 15 minutes until the muffins are lightly brown and well risen. Remove from the oven and let cool in the pan for 5 minutes before transferring to a wire rack to cool completely.

4 For the glaze, mix the lemon juice and confectioners' sugar to a thin icing, drizzle it over the muffins, and sprinkle them with lemon zest.

HOW TO FREEZE

The cooked muffins can be frozen in an airtight container for up to 6 months. Defrost thoroughly before serving.

CALORIES: 209kcals/886kJ

CARBOHYDRATE: 38g
  sugar: 24g

FAT: 5g
  saturated: 1g

SALT: 0.4g

FIBER: 1g

Vanilla cupcakes with vanilla frosting

Cupcakes are an easy treat to bake, and are fabulous when freshly made. They're easy to whip up in a hurry, too.

25 mins   16–18 mins

SPECIAL EQUIPMENT

electric hand-held mixer

12-hole muffin pan

12 cupcake liners

piping bag and star nozzle (optional)

MAKES 12

7 tbsp butter, softened

⅔ cup granulated sugar

3 large eggs, lightly beaten

1 tsp vanilla extract

1½ cups self-rising flour

1 tsp baking powder

3½ tbsp milk, plus 1 tbsp if needed

FOR THE BUTTERCREAM

1⅔ cups confectioners' sugar

7 tbsp butter, softened

1 tsp vanilla extract

1 Preheat the oven to 350°F (180°C). Place the butter and sugar in a large bowl and use an electric hand-held mixer to cream them together until the mixture is very light and fluffy. Whisk in the eggs and vanilla extract until they are well combined.

2 Sift together the flour and baking powder. Add one-third of the flour to the cake batter and whisk it in well. Add half of the milk and whisk it again, then another one-third of the flour, the rest of the milk, and finally the last one-third of the flour, making sure to whisk well between each addition.

3 Place 12 cupcake liners in a deep 12-hole muffin pan (this will help the cupcakes keep their shape while cooking). Carefully spoon the cake mixture into the liners, filling each two-thirds full.

4 Bake for 16–18 minutes, until lightly colored, firm, and springy to the touch, and a toothpick inserted into the center of a cupcake comes out clean. Do not be tempted to open the oven until at least 15 minutes baking time has passed. Transfer the cupcakes to a wire rack to cool.

5 To make the buttercream, beat the confectioners' sugar, butter, and vanilla until smooth, light, and creamy, adding up to 1 tbsp milk, if needed, for a piping consistency, and transfer it to a piping bag fitted with a star-shaped nozzle (if using).

6 When the cakes are completely cold, they are ready to ice. Ice them by hand using the back of a spoon dipped in warm water to smooth the surface of the frosting, or pipe the buttercream onto the cupcakes.

VARIATION

You can make chocolate cupcakes using the same basic recipe. Simply replace ½ cup of the all-purpose flour in the cakes with cocoa powder. For the buttercream, replace 2 tbsp of the confectioners' sugar with cocoa powder, omit the vanilla, and add 1 tbsp whole milk instead, to make it easy to pipe or spread on the cakes.

PREPARE AHEAD

The cakes can be made 1 day ahead and stored, un-iced, in an airtight container, or frozen for up to 12 weeks. Defrost, then ice on the day they are to be used.

CALORIES: 319kcals/1340kJ

CARBOHYDRATE: 41g
    sugar: 29.5g

FAT: 16g
    saturated: 9g

SALT: 0.6g

FIBER: 0.7g

Red velvet cupcakes with cream cheese icing

These fashionable cupcakes taste as good as they look, with red-toned cake against pale buttery icing.

25 mins   22–25 mins

SPECIAL EQUIPMENT
electric hand-held mixer
18–20 cupcake liners
2 x 12-hole muffin pans
piping bag and star nozzle (optional)

MAKES 18–20

8 tbsp butter, softened
1 cup granulated sugar
2 large eggs, lightly beaten
2 tsp red food coloring
1 tsp vanilla extract
2 cups self-rising flour
¼ cup cocoa powder
¾ cup buttermilk
1 tsp cider vinegar
1 tsp baking soda

FOR THE ICING
¼ cup cream cheese, softened
4 tbsp butter, softened
1⅔ cups confectioners' sugar
1 tsp vanilla extract

1 Preheat the oven to 350°F (180°C). Place the butter and sugar in a large bowl and use an electric hand-held mixer to cream them together until the mixture is very light and fluffy. Whisk in the eggs, food coloring, and vanilla extract until they are well combined.

2 Sift together the flour and cocoa powder. Add one-third of the flour to the cake batter and whisk it in well. Add half of the buttermilk and whisk it again, then another one-third of the flour, the rest of the buttermilk, and the final one-third of the flour, making sure to whisk well between additions.

Mix together the cider vinegar and baking soda and fold quickly into the batter.

3 Place 18–20 cupcake liners in 2 deep 12-hole muffin pans (they will help the cupcakes keep their shape). Spoon the batter into the liners, filling each two-thirds full. Bake for 22–25 minutes, until springy to the touch. Do not open the oven until at least 20 minutes of baking time has passed. Transfer to a wire rack to cool.

4 To make the icing, beat the cream cheese, butter, confectioners' sugar, and vanilla extract until light and creamy and transfer to a piping bag fitted with a star-shaped nozzle (if using).

5 When the cakes are completely cold, they are ready to ice. Ice them by hand using the back of a spoon dipped in warm water to smooth the surface, or pipe the icing onto the cupcakes.

PREPARE AHEAD

The cupcakes can be made up to 1 day ahead and stored, un-iced, in an airtight container. They are best iced on the day they are to be eaten.

HOW TO FREEZE

The un-iced cupcakes can be frozen in an airtight container for up to 12 weeks. Defrost thoroughly before icing.

CALORIES: 228kcals/958kJ
CARBOHYDRATE: 32g
  sugar: 23g
FAT: 10g
  saturated: 6g
SALT: 0.5g
FIBER: 1g

Chocolate and hazelnut brownies

A classic recipe, these brownies are moist and soft in the center and filled with toasted nuts.

25 mins   12–15 mins

SPECIAL EQUIPMENT
9 x 12in (23 x 30cm) brownie pan, or similar

MAKES 24

12 tbsp unsalted butter, cut into cubes

10oz (300g) good-quality dark chocolate, broken into pieces

1¼ cups granulated sugar

4 large eggs, lightly beaten

1½ cups all-purpose flour, sifted

3 tbsp cocoa powder, sifted, plus extra for dusting

3½oz (100g) hazelnuts, toasted and chopped

1 Preheat the oven to 400°F (200°C). Line the bottom and sides of a 9 x 12in (23 x 30cm) brownie pan, or similar, with parchment paper. Some should hang over the sides. Place the butter and chocolate in a heatproof bowl over a pan of simmering water. The bowl should not touch the water.

2 Melt the butter and chocolate, stirring until smooth. Remove and let cool. Once the mixture has cooled, mix in the sugar. Now add the eggs, a little at a time, mixing well between additions.

3 Fold in the flour and cocoa until the batter is smooth. Stir in the nuts to distribute them evenly; the batter should be thick.

4 Pour into the prepared pan and spread so the mixture fills the corners. Smooth the top. Bake for 12–15 minutes, or until just firm to the touch but still soft underneath. A skewer inserted should come out coated with a little batter. Remove from the oven.

5 Let the brownies cool completely in the pan to maintain the soft center. Lift the brownie from the pan using the edges of the parchment to get a good grip. Using a long, sharp, or serrated knife, score the surface of the brownie into 24 even pieces.

6 Cut the brownie into 24 pieces, dipping the knife in hot water between cuts and wiping it dry. Sift cocoa powder over the brownies. These will store in an airtight container for up to 3 days.

CALORIES: 243kcals/1021kJ
CARBOHYDRATE: 26g
  sugar: 20g
FAT: 14g
  saturated: 7g
SALT: trace
FIBER: 1g

Sour cherry and chocolate brownies

The sharp flavor and chewy texture of the cherries contrast wonderfully with the rich, dark chocolate.

15 mins   20–25 mins

SPECIAL EQUIPMENT
9 x 12in (23 x 30cm) brownie pan, or similar

MAKES 16

11 tbsp unsalted butter, cut into cubes

5½oz (150g) good-quality dark chocolate, broken into pieces

1¼ cups llight brown muscovado sugar

3 large eggs, lightly beaten

1 tsp vanilla extract

1¼ cups self-rising flour, sifted

3½oz (100g) dried sour cherries

3½oz (100g) dark chocolate chunks

1 Preheat the oven to 350°F (180°C). Line a 9 x 12in (23 x 30cm) brownie pan, or similar, with parchment paper. Melt the butter and chocolate in a heatproof bowl over simmering water (the bowl should not touch the water). Stir in the sugar and cool slightly.

2 Mix the eggs and vanilla extract into the chocolate mixture. Pour the wet mix into the sifted flour and fold together, being careful not to over-mix. Fold in the sour cherries and chocolate chunks.

3 Pour the brownie mixture into the pan and bake in the center of the oven for 20–25 minutes. It is ready when the edges are firm, but the middle is soft to the touch.

4 Let the brownies cool in the pan for 5 minutes. Remove from the pan and cut into 16 squares, then transfer to a wire rack to cool. These will store in an airtight container for up to 3 days.

VARIATION

To make brownies so soft that they fall apart easily, reduce the cooking time by 5 minutes.

CALORIES: 273kcals/1146kJ
CARBOHYDRATE: 35g
  sugar: 29g
FAT: 13.5g
  saturated: 8g
SALT: 0.3g
FIBER: 1.5g

Strawberries and cream whoopie pies

Best served immediately, these strawberry layered pies make a lovely addition to any party.

40 mins   12 mins

MAKES 10

12 tbsp unsalted butter, softened

¾ cup light brown sugar

1 large egg, lightly beaten

1 tsp vanilla extract

2 cups self-rising flour

⅔ cup cocoa powder

1 tsp baking powder

⅔ cup whole milk

2 tbsp Greek yogurt or thick plain yogurt

⅔ cup heavy cream, whipped

9oz (250g) strawberries, thinly sliced

confectioners' sugar, for dusting

1 Preheat the oven to 350°F (180°C) and line several baking sheets with parchment paper. Cream the butter and sugar until fluffy, then beat in the egg and vanilla. In a bowl, sift the flour, cocoa, and baking powder. Mix the dry ingredients and the milk into the batter alternately, a spoonful at a time. Fold in the yogurt.

2 Put 20 heaping tablespoons of the batter onto the baking sheets, spaced well apart. Dip a spoon in warm water and use the back to smooth their surfaces.

3 Bake for 12 minutes, until well risen. Cool for a few minutes, then transfer to a wire rack to cool.

4 Spread the cream onto half the cakes. Top with a layer of strawberries and a second cake. Dust with confectioners' sugar and serve. These do not store and should be eaten on the day they are made.

CALORIES: 388kcals/1629kJ

CARBOHYDRATE: 33g
  sugar: 17g

FAT: 26g
  saturated: 16g

SALT: 0.6g

FIBER: 2.5g

VARIATION

For a coffee and pecan version, omit the cocoa and add 1 tsp instant coffee, dissolved in 1 tsp boiling water. Omit the strawberries and layer with 5½oz (150g) toasted pecans instead.

Black and white whoopie pies

Fast becoming a modern classic, whoopie pies are a quick and easy way to please a crowd.

40 mins   12 mins

MAKES 10

12 tbsp unsalted butter, softened

¾ cup light brown sugar

1 large egg, lightly beaten

1 tsp vanilla extract

2 cups self-rising flour

⅔ cup cocoa powder

1 tsp baking powder

⅔ cup whole milk

2 tbsp Greek yogurt or thick plain yogurt

FOR THE BUTTERCREAM

7 tbsp unsalted butter, softened

1⅔ cups confectioners' sugar

2 tsp vanilla extract

2 tsp milk, plus extra if needed

TO DECORATE

a little white and dark chocolate

1⅔ cups confectioners' sugar

CALORIES: 540kcals/2281kJ

CARBOHYDRATE: 71g
  sugar: 55g

FAT: 26g
  saturated: 17g

SALT: 0.6g

FIBER: 2g

1 Preheat the oven to 350°F (180°C). Line several baking sheets with parchment paper. With a whisk, cream together the butter and brown sugar until light and fluffy, then beat in the egg and vanilla extract.

2 In a separate bowl, sift together the flour, cocoa, and baking powder. Gently fold the flour mixture and milk, alternately, into the egg mixture. Fold in the yogurt. Place 20 heaping tbsp of this mixture on the baking sheets. Leave space for it to spread out. Dip a spoon in warm water and use the back to smooth the pies.

3 Bake for around 12 minutes, until a skewer comes out clean. Cool on a wire rack.

4 Using a wooden spoon, mix together the buttercream ingredients, except the milk. Add the milk and beat for 5 minutes. Spread 1 tbsp onto the flat side of half of the cakes, and sandwich together with the other half.

5 With a vegetable peeler, make white and dark chocolate shavings. Put the confectioners' sugar in a bowl and add enough water to make a thick icing. Spread the icing over the pies, and sprinkle with chocolate shavings.

Angel food cake

This classic is named for its pure white, light-as-air fat-free texture. It is best eaten on the day it is made.

30 mins   35-45 mins

SPECIAL EQUIPMENT
10in (24cm) tube pan

sugar thermometer (optional)

SERVES 8-12

large pat of butter, for greasing

1¼ cups all-purpose flour, sifted

¾ cup confectioners' sugar, sifted, plus extra for dusting

8 large egg whites (keep the yolks for custards and tart fillings)

pinch of cream of tartar

1 cup granulated sugar

few drops of almond or vanilla extract

FOR THE FROSTING

⅔ cup granulated sugar

2 large egg whites

strawberries (halved), blueberries, and raspberries, to decorate

1 Preheat the oven to 350°F (180°C). Melt the butter in a small pan and use generously to brush the inside of a 10in (24cm) tube pan. Sift the flour and confectioners' sugar, again, into a bowl.

2 Whisk the egg whites and cream of tartar until stiff, then whisk in the granulated sugar, 1 tbsp at a time. Sift the flour mixture into the egg white mixture and fold it in with a rubber spatula, then fold in the almond or vanilla extract.

3 Spoon the mixture gently into the tube pan, filling it, and level the surface with a palette knife. Place the mold on a baking sheet and bake for 35–45 minutes, or until just firm to the touch.

4 Carefully remove the cake from the oven and invert the mold onto a wire rack. Let the cake cool, then ease it out of the mold.

5 To make the frosting, place the granulated sugar in a saucepan with ¼ cup of water. Heat gently, stirring, until the sugar dissolves. Now increase the heat and boil until the syrup reaches "soft-ball" stage (238–245°F/ 114–118°C) on a sugar thermometer, or until a little of the syrup forms a soft ball when dropped into very cold water.

6 Meanwhile, whisk the egg whites until stiff. As soon as the sugar syrup reaches the correct temperature, plunge the bottom of the pan into a sink of cold water to stop the syrup from getting any hotter. Pour the syrup into the egg whites, whisking constantly, in a slow, steady stream into the center of the bowl. Keep whisking for 5 minutes, or until stiff peaks form.

7 Working quickly, because the frosting will set, spread it thinly all over the inside and outside of the cake with a palette knife, swirling the surface to create texture. Top with strawberries, blueberries, and raspberries, and sift over confectioners' sugar to serve.

COOK'S TIP

Sifting the flour and confectioners' sugar 2 or 3 times may seem strange, but it produces a super-light cake. For best results, lift the sieve high above the bowl before sifting, allowing the flour and confectioners' sugar to aerate as much as possible.

CALORIES: 299kcals/1273kJ

CARBOHYDRATE: 70g
sugar: 62g

FAT: 0.2g
saturated: 0g

SALT: 0.1g

FIBER: 0.5g

Rich fruit cake

A wonderfully moist, rich cake. For large celebrations, bake in a square pan for easy portioning.

25 mins, plus soaking   2 hrs 30 mins

SPECIAL EQUIPMENT

10in (25cm) deep round cake pan

electric hand-held mixer

SERVES 16

7oz (200g) golden raisins

14oz (400g) raisins

12oz (350g) prunes, chopped

12oz (350g) glacé cherries

2 apples, peeled, cored, and diced

2 cups hard cider

4 tsp pumpkin pie spice

14 tbsp unsalted butter, softened

1 cup dark brown sugar

3 large eggs, lightly beaten

1⅓ cups ground almonds

2¼ cups all-purpose flour, plus extra for dusting

2 tsp baking powder

14oz (400g) store-bought marzipan

2–3 tbsp apricot jam

3 large egg whites

4 cups (1lb box) confectioners' sugar

1 Place the golden raisins, raisins, prunes, cherries, apples, cider, and spice in a saucepan. Bring to a simmer over medium-low heat, then cover for 20 minutes until most of the liquid is absorbed. Cover and leave overnight at room temperature so that the fruits absorb the remaining liquid.

2 Preheat the oven to 325°F (160°C). Double-line a 10in (25cm) deep round cake pan with parchment paper. With an electric hand-held mixer, cream the butter and sugar in a large bowl until fluffy. Add the eggs, a little at a time, beating very well after each addition to avoid curdling.

3 Gently fold in the fruit mix and ground almonds, trying to keep volume in the batter. Sift the flour and baking powder into the bowl, then gently fold into the mixture. Spoon the batter into the prepared pan, cover with foil, and bake for 2½ hours.

4 Test to see if the cake is ready: a skewer inserted into the center should come out clean. Let cool, then turn onto a wire rack to cool completely. Remove the parchment paper. Trim the cake to level it. Transfer to a stand and hold it in place with a small ball of marzipan.

5 Warm the jam and brush thickly over the whole cake. This will help the marzipan stick. On a lightly floured surface, knead the remaining marzipan until softened. Roll out the softened marzipan until wide enough to cover the cake top and sides.

6 Drape the marzipan over the rolling pin and lift it over the cake. With your hands, gently ease the marzipan into place, smoothing out any bumps. With a small, sharp knife, cut away any excess marzipan from the bottom of the cake.

7 Place the egg whites in a bowl and sift in the confectioners' sugar, stirring well to combine. With an electric hand-held mixer, beat for 10 minutes until stiff. Spread the icing neatly over the cake with a palette knife. Wipe the cake stand clean and let the icing set overnight before serving.

CALORIES: 704kcals/2982kJ

CARBOHYDRATE: 119g
sugar: 108g

FAT: 20g
saturated: 8g

SALT: 0.3g

FIBER: 4g

Stollen

This rich, fruity German bread is served at Christmas. Traditionally it contains marzipan, but this version is simpler.

30 mins, plus rising **50 mins**

SERVES 12

7oz (200g) raisins

3½oz (100g) currants

½ cup rum

14oz (400g) strong white bread flour, plus extra for dusting

2 tsp dried yeast

¼ cup granulated sugar

½ cup whole milk

½ tsp vanilla extract

pinch of salt

½ tsp pumpkin pie spice

2 large eggs, lightly beaten

12 tbsp unsalted butter, softened and cut into cubes

7oz (200g) mixed candied citrus peel

3½oz (100g) ground almonds

confectioners' sugar, for dusting

1 Put the raisins and currants into a large bowl, pour in the rum, and let soak overnight. The following day, sift the flour into a large bowl. Make a well in the center, sprinkle in the yeast, and add a teaspoon of the sugar. Gently heat the milk until lukewarm and pour on top of the yeast. Let stand at room temperature for 15 minutes or until it turns frothy.

2 Add the rest of the sugar, the vanilla, salt, pumpkin pie spice, eggs, and butter. Mix everything together with a wooden spoon. Knead for 5 minutes until smooth.

3 Transfer to a lightly floured surface. Add the mixed peel, raisins, currants, and almonds, kneading for a few minutes until mixed. Return to the bowl, cover loosely with plastic wrap, and let rise in a warm place for 1–1½ hours until doubled in size.

4 Preheat the oven to 325°F (160°C). Line a baking sheet with parchment paper. On a floured surface, roll out the dough to make a 12 x 10in (30 x 25cm) rectangle. Fold one long side over, just beyond the middle, then fold over the other long side to overlap the first, curving it slightly on top to create the stollen shape.

5 Transfer to the baking sheet and set aside in a warm place, without drafts, for 1–1½ hours to proof once more, until doubled in size again.

6 Bake in the oven for 50 minutes or until the stollen has risen and is pale golden. Check after 30–35 minutes and, if it seems to be browning too much, cover the loaf loosely with foil. Carefully transfer to a wire rack to cool completely, then dust generously with confectioners' sugar to serve.

PREPARE AHEAD

If it is more convenient, cover the baking sheet and put the stollen in the fridge overnight in step 5, for the second proving. The loaf can then be baked fresh in the morning.

CLEVER WITH LEFTOVERS

Leftover stollen is great toasted for breakfast, or used to make a version of Classic bread and butter pudding (see p348) or even Brioche French toast (see p266).

CALORIES: 440kcals/1855kJ

CARBOHYDRATE: 55g
  sugar: 32g

FAT: 19g
  saturated: 9g

SALT: 0.3g

FIBER: 3g

Lemon drizzle cake

The gloriously tangy lemon topping poured over the light sponge cake produces a moist and mouthwatering cake.

20 mins   30 mins

SPECIAL EQUIPMENT

electric hand-held mixer

7in (18cm) round cake pan

SERVES 8

11 tbsp butter, softened

⅔ cup granulated sugar

3 large eggs

finely grated zest of 1 lemon

1¼ cups self-rising flour, sifted

FOR THE TOPPING

3 tbsp lemon juice

¼ cup granulated sugar

confectioners' sugar, for dusting

1 Preheat the oven to 350°F (180°C). In a large bowl, cream together the butter and sugar with an electric hand-held mixer until light and fluffy. Whisk in the eggs one at a time, then add the zest.

2 Fold in the flour until just incorporated and pour the batter into a lined 7in (18cm) round cake pan. Bake in the center of the preheated oven for 30 minutes until well risen and a skewer comes out clean.

3 To make the topping, gently heat the lemon juice and sugar in a small pan until the sugar has dissolved. Prick the cake all over with a thin wooden skewer and, leaving it in the pan, carefully pour the sugary mixture all over the top, a little at a time, until it has been absorbed. Allow the topping to cool before serving the cake, dusted with confectioners' sugar.

VARIATION

Try replacing the lemon zest and juice with clementine or orange zest and juice. This version is especially welcome at Christmas.

CALORIES: 345kcals/1448kJ

CARBOHYDRATE: 41g
  sugar: 28g

FAT: 18g
  saturated: 10g

SALT: 0.6g

FIBER: 0.8g

Genoise cake with raspberries and cream

This delicate cake makes an impressive dessert, and is also perfect as the centerpiece for a party.

30 mins 25–30 mins

SPECIAL EQUIPMENT

8in (20cm) round springform cake pan
electric hand-held mixer

SERVES 8–10

3 tbsp unsalted butter, melted and cooled, plus extra for greasing

4 large eggs, lightly beaten

½ cup granulated sugar

1 cup all-purpose flour

1 tsp vanilla extract

finely grated zest of 1 lemon

FOR THE FILLING

2 cups heavy whipping cream

11oz (325g) raspberries, plus 2½oz (75g) extra, to decorate (optional)

1 tbsp confectioners' sugar, plus extra for dusting

1 Preheat the oven to 350°F (180°C). Lightly grease an 8in (20cm) round springform cake pan and line the bottom only with parchment paper.

2 Bring a pan of water to a boil, remove from the heat, and stand a heatproof bowl over the top. Add the eggs and sugar and whisk, using an electric hand-held whisk, for 5 minutes, until the whisk leaves a trail when lifted; the mixture will expand up to 5 times its original volume. Remove the bowl from the pan and whisk for another minute to cool.

3 Sift in the flour and carefully fold it into the mixture. Fold in the vanilla, lemon zest, and melted butter.

4 Pour the batter into the prepared pan and bake for 25–30 minutes, or until the top is springy and light golden brown. A skewer should come out clean.

5 Let the cake cool in its pan for a few minutes, then turn onto a wire rack and cool completely. Remove the parchment.

6 When the cake is cold, carefully cut it horizontally into 3 equal pieces, using a serrated bread knife.

7 For the filling, in a large bowl, whip the cream until stiff. Lightly crush the raspberries with the confectioners' sugar and fold into the cream roughly, leaving behind any juice so the cream is not too wet; some pieces should look rippled.

8 Place the bottom slice of cake on a serving plate and spread with half the cream mixture. Top with the second slice, press down gently, spread with the remaining cream, and then place the final slice on top. Decorate with the raspberries (if using) and dust the cake with confectioners' sugar. Serve the cake immediately.

PREPARE AHEAD

The cake will keep in an airtight container for up to 1 day before being cut and filled.

COOK'S TIP

This is a classic Italian cake that uses only a little melted butter for flavoring. These cakes are infinitely adaptable, and can be filled with anything you like, but should ideally be eaten within 24 hours of baking, since the lack of fat means they do not store as well as other cakes.

HOW TO FREEZE

The cake can be kept frozen for up to 12 weeks, unfilled. Defrost thoroughly before filling and serving.

CALORIES: 410kcals/1711kJ

CARBOHYDRATE: 27g
 sugar: 18g

FAT: 31g
 saturated: 18g

SALT: 0.14g

FIBER: 2g

Victoria sponge cake

Probably the most iconic British cake, a good Victoria cake should be well-risen, moist, and as light as air.

30 mins   20-25 mins

SPECIAL EQUIPMENT

2 x 7in (18cm) round cake pans

SERVES 6-8

12 tbsp unsalted butter, softened, plus extra for greasing

¾ cup granulated sugar

3 large eggs

1 tsp vanilla extract

1½ cups self-rising flour

1 tsp baking powder

FOR THE FILLING

4 tbsp unsalted butter, softened

¾ cup confectioners' sugar, plus extra for dusting

1 tsp vanilla extract

4oz (115g) good-quality seedless raspberry jam

1 Preheat the oven to 350°F (180°C). Grease two 7in (18cm) round cake pans and line with parchment paper. Whisk the butter and sugar in a bowl for 2 minutes, or until pale, light, and fluffy. Add the eggs 1 at a time, mixing well between additions to avoid curdling.

2 Add the vanilla extract and whisk briefly until it is well-blended through the batter. Whisk the mixture for another 2 minutes until bubbles appear on the surface. Remove the whisk, then sift the flour and baking powder into the bowl.

3 With a rubber spatula, gently fold in the flour until just smooth; try to keep the mixture light. Divide the mixture evenly between the pans and smooth the tops with a palette knife. Cook for 20–25 minutes, or until golden brown and springy to the touch.

4 Test the cakes by inserting a metal skewer into the center of both cakes. If it comes out clean, the cakes are cooked. Remove from the oven and leave them for a few minutes in the pans. Turn, good sides up, onto a wire rack to cool completely.

5 For the filling, beat together the butter, confectioners' sugar, and vanilla extract until smooth. Continue to beat for up to 5 minutes until the buttercream is very light, cloud-like, and fluffy in texture.

6 Spread the buttercream evenly onto the flat side of a cooled cake with a palette knife. Gently spread the jam on top of the buttercream using a table knife. Top with the second cake, so that the flat sides are together. Serve as soon as possible, dusted with sifted confectioners' sugar.

PREPARE AHEAD

Unfilled, the cakes will keep for up to 3 days in an airtight container. Separate with sheets of waxed paper, to keep them from sticking together, and keep away from heat and light.

HOW TO FREEZE

The just-cooled cakes can be wrapped in plastic wrap, sealed with foil, and kept frozen for up to 12 weeks. Defrost thoroughly before filling and serving.

CALORIES: 488kcals/2063kJ

CARBOHYDRATE: 58g
  sugar: 44g

FAT: 26g
  saturated: 16g

SALT: 0.5g

FIBER: 1g

Lemon curd cake

For a light and tasty alternative to buttercream filling, try this mix of mascarpone cheese with lemon curd instead.

25 mins   20-25 mins

SPECIAL EQUIPMENT

2 x 7in (18cm) cake pans
electric hand-held mixer

SERVES 8

12 tbsp butter, softened, plus extra
  for greasing
¾ cup granulated sugar
3 large eggs, lightly beaten
1½ cups self-rising flour, sifted
1 tsp baking powder, sifted
finely grated zest and juice of 1 lemon

6 tbsp lemon curd
9oz (250g) mascarpone cheese
confectioners' sugar, sifted, for dusting

1 Preheat the oven to 325°F (160°C). Grease two 7in (18cm) cake pans and line the bottoms with parchment paper.

2 Place the butter and sugar in a mixing bowl and cream them together using an electric hand-held mixer until pale and fluffy.

3 Gradually whisk in the eggs. Fold in the flour and baking powder, then the lemon zest and juice and 2 tbsp of the lemon curd.

4 Divide the mixture between the pans and level the surfaces with the back of a metal spoon.

5 Bake for 20–25 minutes, or until a skewer comes out clean. Leave in the pans for 10 minutes, then turn onto a wire rack, remove the parchment paper, and allow to cool completely.

6 Place the mascarpone and remaining 4 tbsp of lemon curd in a bowl and stir together.

7 Place a cake on a serving plate and spread the filling over. Top with the remaining cake and dust evenly with confectioners' sugar.

HOW TO FREEZE

Freeze the just-cooled cakes before filling, individually wrapped in plastic wrap and sealed with foil, for up to 12 weeks. Defrost thoroughly, then fill the cakes from the start of step 6.

CALORIES: 515kcals/2156kJ
CARBOHYDRATE: 45g
  sugar: 28g
FAT: 34g
  saturated: 21g
SALT: 0.8g
FIBER: 1g

Layered carrot cake

This rich, heavily iced cake is multi-layered, and makes a really impressive centerpiece at any special occasion.

30 mins | 45 mins

SPECIAL EQUIPMENT
2 x 8½in (22cm) springform cake pans
electric hand-held mixer

SERVES 10

5½oz (150g) walnuts

2 cups sunflower or vegetable oil, plus extra for greasing

6 large eggs, lightly beaten

2 tsp vanilla extract

2¼ cups light brown sugar

12oz (350g) finely grated carrots

5½oz (150g) golden raisins

3¾ cups self-rising flour, sifted

½ tsp salt

2 tsp ground cinnamon

2 tsp ground ginger

finely grated zest of 1 large orange

FOR THE ICING
11 tbsp butter, softened

5½oz (150g) cream cheese, softened

4¾ cups confectioners' sugar, sifted

finely grated zest of 2 oranges

2 tsp vanilla extract

1 Preheat the oven to 350°F (180°C). Grease two 8½in (22cm) springform cake pans and line the bottoms with parchment paper. Spread the walnuts on a baking sheet and toast in the oven for about 5 minutes, until lightly browned, watching carefully that they don't burn. Put the nuts into a clean kitchen towel, rub them to get rid of excess skin, then set aside to cool.

2 In a large bowl, whisk together the oil, eggs, vanilla extract, and sugar with an electric hand-held mixer until light, fluffy, and thickened. Put the grated carrot in a clean kitchen towel and squeeze out any excess liquid, then fold it into the cake batter until evenly mixed through.

3 Roughly chop the cooled walnuts and fold them into the mixture with the golden raisins. Finally fold in the flour, salt, spices, and orange zest and mix to combine.

4 Divide the mixture between the pans and bake in the center of the oven for 45 minutes, or until springy to the touch and a skewer inserted into the middle comes out clean from both cakes.

5 Let the cakes cool for 5 minutes in their pans, then turn them to cool completely on a wire rack. Once cool, halve each cake horizontally using a serrated knife to give you 4 layers of cake, keeping the layers an even thickness.

6 To make the icing, cream together the butter, cream cheese, confectioners' sugar, orange zest, and vanilla extract. Sandwich each layer of the cake together with a scant one-fifth of the icing and cover the top and sides of the cake with the remaining icing.

HOW TO FREEZE

The just-cooked, un-iced cakes can be wrapped individually in plastic wrap, sealed with foil, and frozen for up to 12 weeks. Defrost thoroughly before splitting and icing as in steps 5 and 6.

CALORIES: 1285kcals/5389kJ
CARBOHYDRATE: 154g
    sugar: 117g
FAT: 68g
    saturated: 19g
SALT: 1.2g
FIBER: 4.5g

Cherry and almond cake

The classic combination of flavors in this cake is always popular with guests.

20 mins   1½–1¾ hrs

SPECIAL EQUIPMENT
8in (20cm) deep round springform cake pan

electric hand-held mixer

SERVES 8–10

11 tbsp unsalted butter, softened, plus extra for greasing

⅔ cup granulated sugar

2 large eggs

2 cups self-rising flour, sifted

1 tsp baking powder

1⅓ cups ground almonds

1 tsp vanilla extract or almond extract

⅓ cup whole milk

14oz (400g) pitted cherries

scant 1oz (25g) blanched almonds, chopped

1 Preheat the oven to 350°F (180°C). Grease an 8in (20cm) deep round springform cake pan and line the bottom with parchment paper. Beat the butter and sugar with an electric hand-held mixer until creamy. Beat in the eggs 1 at a time, adding 1 tbsp of flour before the second egg.

2 Mix in the remaining flour, baking powder, ground almonds, vanilla extract, and milk. Mix in half the cherries, then spoon the mixture into the pan and smooth the top. Scatter the remaining cherries and the almonds over the surface.

3 Bake for 1½–1¾ hours, or until golden brown and firm to the touch. A skewer inserted into the cake should come out clean. If the surface of the cake starts to brown before it is fully cooked, cover with foil. When cooked, let cool in the pan for a few minutes, then remove the foil and parchment paper, and transfer to a wire rack to cool completely before serving.

VARIATION

This recipe has classic flavors, but, for a modern twist, use 3½oz (100g) of dried sour cherries instead of fresh.

CALORIES: 409kcals/1719kJ

CARBOHYDRATE: 38g
    sugar: 21g

FAT: 25g
    saturated: 10g

SALT: 0.4g

FIBER: 1.5g

Apple, raisin, and pecan cake

A healthier option, this cake contains only a little fat and is stuffed with fruit and nuts.

25 mins   30–35 mins

SPECIAL EQUIPMENT
9in (23cm) springform cake pan

SERVES 10–12

butter, for greasing

1¾oz (50g) shelled pecan nuts

7oz (200g) apples, peeled, cored, and cut into small cubes

5½oz (150g) brown sugar

9oz (250g) self-rising flour

1 tsp baking powder

2 tsp ground cinnamon

pinch of salt

3½ tbsp sunflower or vegetable oil

3½ tbsp milk, plus extra if necessary

2 large eggs, lightly beaten

1 tsp vanilla extract

1¾oz (50g) golden raisins

whipped cream or confectioners' sugar, to serve (optional)

CALORIES: 198kcals/835kJ

CARBOHYDRATE: 31.5g
    sugar: 17g

FAT: 7g
    saturated: 1g

SALT: 0.4g

FIBER: 1.5g

1 Preheat the oven to 350°F (180°C). Grease a 9in (23cm) springform cake pan and line the bottom with parchment paper. Place the nuts on a baking sheet and toast them in the oven for 5 minutes until golden. Cool and roughly chop.

2 In a large bowl, mix the apples and sugar together. Sift over the flour, baking powder, cinnamon, and salt, and fold them in. In a bowl, whisk together the oil, milk, eggs, and vanilla extract.

3 Pour the milk mixture into the flour mixture and stir until well combined. Fold in the pecans and golden raisins, then pour the batter into the prepared pan.

4 Bake in the center of the oven for 30–35 minutes, until a skewer comes out clean. Let cool for a few minutes in the pan, then turn onto a wire rack. Remove the parchment paper. Serve warm with whipped cream as a dessert, or cooled and dusted with sifted confectioners' sugar.

PREPARE AHEAD
The cake will keep in an airtight container for up to 3 days. The lack of fat means it isn't wise to keep it for longer because it will dry out.

Orange and rosemary polenta cake

Wonderfully moist, this is one of the few wheat-free cakes that work just as well as those made from wheat flour.

30 mins   50 mins–1 hr

SPECIAL EQUIPMENT

9in (23cm) round springform cake pan
electric hand-held mixer

SERVES 6–8

juice and finely grated zest of
  1 large orange

¾ cup granulated sugar

sprig of rosemary

12 tbsp unsalted butter, softened,
  plus extra for greasing

3 large eggs, lightly beaten

½ cup coarse or fine polenta

1¾ cups ground almonds

1 tsp gluten-free baking powder

crème fraîche, to serve (optional)

1 Put the orange juice and scant 1oz (25g) of the sugar in a small pan. Heat over medium heat, stirring from time to time, until the sugar has dissolved. Add the rosemary, remove from the heat, and let infuse.

2 Preheat the oven to 325°F (160°C). Grease a 9in (23cm) round springform cake pan and line the bottom with parchment paper. With an electric hand-held mixer, cream the butter and remaining sugar until fluffy. Gradually add the eggs, a little at a time, whisking well after each addition. Add the polenta and almonds, and gently fold in with a rubber spatula. Finally, fold in the orange zest and baking powder. The batter will seem quite stiff.

3 Scrape the mixture into the prepared pan and smooth the surface with a palette knife. Bake the cake for 50–60 minutes; it will not rise much. Check that the cake is cooked by inserting a skewer; it should come out clean. Leave the cake in the pan and reheat the orange and rosemary syrup over medium heat until hot. Remove and discard the rosemary.

4 While the cake and syrup are both still hot, poke holes in the cake using a thin skewer or toothpick. Pour the syrup a little at a time over the cake. Pour more on only once the syrup has soaked into the cake, until it is all used up. Once cooled, carefully remove the cake from the pan, remove the parchment paper, and serve at

room temperature, with crème fraîche (if using). It will keep in an airtight container for up to 3 days.

HOW TO FREEZE

Wrap the just-cooled cake in parchment paper, then seal with foil. Freeze for up to 12 weeks. Defrost thoroughly before eating. If it has been previously frozen, this cake may benefit from reheating at 350°F (180°C) for 15 minutes before serving.

CALORIES: 475kcals/1990kJ
CARBOHYDRATE: 34g
  sugar: 27g
FAT: 34g
  saturated: 13.5g
SALT: 0.3g
FIBER: 0.5g

Toffee apple cake

Caramelizing the apples and soaking the cake in the cooking juices after baking make it flavorful and moist.

40 mins **40-45 mins**

SPECIAL EQUIPMENT

9in (22cm) round springform cake pan

electric hand-held mixer

SERVES 8–10

14 tbsp unsalted butter, softened, plus extra for greasing

¼ cup granulated sugar

9oz (250g) apples, peeled, cored, and cut into cubes

¾ cup light brown sugar

3 large eggs

1¼ cups self-rising flour

1 heaping tsp baking powder

whipped cream or confectioners' sugar, to serve (optional)

1 Preheat the oven to 350°F (180°C). Grease a 9in (22cm) round springform cake pan and line the bottom with parchment paper. In a large frying pan, gently heat 4 tbsp of the butter and the granulated sugar until melted and golden brown. Add the chopped apples and cook gently for 7–8 minutes until they start to soften and caramelize.

2 Meanwhile, with an electric hand-held mixer, cream together the remaining 10 tbsp of butter and brown sugar in a bowl until light and fluffy. Beat in the eggs one at a time. Sift the flour and baking powder together and gently fold into the mixture.

3 Remove the apples from the pan with a slotted spoon and set aside the pan with the juices

to use later. Scatter the apples over the bottom of the prepared pan. Spoon the batter evenly over, smoothing the top, then place the pan on a baking sheet with deep sides to catch any drips and bake in the center of the hot oven for 40–45 minutes. Let cool for a few minutes, then turn onto a plate and replace into the pan, apple-side up.

4 Put the frying pan with the leftover juices back over low heat and heat gently until warmed through. With a fine skewer or wooden toothpick, make holes evenly all over the surface of the cake, through the layer of apples. Pour the apple syrup evenly over the cake in its pan, letting it soak into the cake. Serve the cake warm with whipped cream, or cooled and dusted with confectioners' sugar.

CLEVER WITH LEFTOVERS

Peel the wrinkly skin from apples buried at the bottom of the fruit bowl and past their best, to make this delicious cake.

CALORIES: 396kcals/1669kJ

CARBOHYDRATE: 41g
 sugar: 28g

FAT: 23g
 saturated: 14g

SALT: 0.6g

FIBER: 1.6g

Espresso cake

This is the perfect accompaniment to morning coffee. Here the cake is made in small pans to give it extra height.

20 mins | **20–25 mins**

SPECIAL EQUIPMENT

2 x 6¾in (17cm) round cake pans
electric hand-held mixer

SERVES 8

12 tbsp unsalted butter, softened, plus extra for greasing

¾ cup light brown sugar

3 large eggs

1 tsp vanilla extract

1½ cups self-rising flour

1 tsp baking powder

1 tbsp instant espresso powder, mixed with 2 tbsp boiling water and cooled

FOR THE ICING

7 tbsp unsalted butter, softened

1⅔ cups confectioners' sugar

9 walnut halves

1 Preheat the oven to 350°F (180°C). Grease two 6¾in (17cm) round cake pans and line the bottoms with parchment paper. Cream together the butter and sugar in a bowl, using an electric hand-held mixer, until the mixture is light and fluffy.

2 Add the eggs one at a time, beating well between additions. Add the vanilla and beat for 2 minutes until bubbles appear on the surface. Sift in the flour and baking powder.

3 Gently fold in the flour, followed by half the espresso powder. Divide the batter evenly between the prepared pans and smooth the tops with a palette knife.

4 Cook for 20–25 minutes, or until golden brown and springy to the touch. Test by inserting a skewer: if it comes out clean, the cakes are cooked. Leave for a few minutes, then turn onto a wire rack to cool completely.

5 To make the icing, beat the butter and confectioners' sugar together for 5 minutes until smooth and fluffy. Beat in the remaining coffee. Spread half the buttercream evenly over the flat side of the least good-looking of the cakes.

6 Top with the second cake, flat sides together, and spread with the remaining buttercream. Decorate with the walnut halves.

HOW TO FREEZE

Freeze the freshly baked, just-cooled cakes separately wrapped in a layer of waxed paper and sealed with foil. Defrost thoroughly within 6 months of freezing, ice, and serve.

CALORIES: 557kcals/2350kJ

CARBOHYDRATE: 61g
  sugar: 46g

FAT: 33g
  saturated: 19g

SALT: 0.5g

FIBER: 1g

White chocolate macadamia blondies

A white chocolate version of the ever-popular brownie, studded with indulgent macadamia nuts.

15 mins   20 mins

SPECIAL EQUIPMENT
9 x 12in (23 x 30cm) brownie pan, or similar

MAKES 24

10oz (300g) white chocolate, broken into pieces

12 tbsp unsalted butter, cut into cubes

1¼ cups granulated sugar

4 large eggs, lightly beaten

2 cups all-purpose flour

3½oz (100g) macadamia nuts, roughly chopped

1 Preheat the oven to 400°F (200°C). Line the bottom and sides of a 9 x 12in (23 x 30cm) brownie pan, or similar, with parchment paper. In a heatproof bowl set over simmering water, melt the chocolate and butter. Do not let the bowl touch the water. Remove and let cool for 20 minutes.

2 Once the chocolate has melted, mix in the sugar (the mixture may become thick and grainy, but the eggs will loosen it). Using a balloon whisk, beat in the eggs a little at a time, making sure each is well mixed in before you add the next. Sift in the flour, gently fold it in, then stir in the nuts.

3 Pour the mixture into the pan and gently spread it out into the corners. Bake for 20 minutes or until just firm to the touch on top, but still soft underneath. Let cool completely in the pan, then cut into 24 squares, or fewer rectangles for bigger blondies.

CALORIES: 249kcals/1049kJ
CARBOHYDRATE: 26g
  sugar: 20g
FAT: 14.5g
  saturated: 7g
SALT: trace
FIBER: 0.5g

HOW TO STORE
The blondies will keep in an airtight container for 5 days, and will become more moist and dense in texture.

Ginger cake

If you can't find stem ginger for this delicious cake, substitute extra corn syrup and crystallized ginger.

20 mins   35-45 mins

SPECIAL EQUIPMENT
7in (18cm) square cake pan

SERVES 12

7 tbsp unsalted butter, softened, plus extra for greasing

1 cup corn syrup

¾ cup dark brown sugar

¾ cup whole milk

4 tbsp syrup from preserved ginger jar or corn syrup

finely grated zest of 1 orange

2 cups self-rising flour

1 tsp baking soda

1 tsp pumpkin pie spice

1 tsp ground cinnamon

2 tsp ground ginger

4 pieces of preserved stem ginger, finely chopped, and tossed in 1 tbsp all-purpose flour

1 large egg, lightly beaten

1 Preheat the oven to 350°F (180°C). Grease a 7in (18cm) square cake pan and line the bottom with parchment paper.

2 In a saucepan, gently heat the butter, corn syrup, sugar, milk, and ginger syrup until the butter has melted. Add the orange zest and let cool for 5 minutes.

3 In a large mixing bowl, sift together the flour, baking soda, and ground spices. Pour the warm syrup mixture into the dry ingredients and beat them well, using a balloon whisk. Stir in the preserved ginger and egg.

4 Pour the batter into the pan and cook for 35–45 minutes, until a skewer inserted into the middle of the cake comes out clean. Let cool in the pan for at least 1 hour before turning onto a wire rack. Remove the parchment paper before serving.

CALORIES: 251kcals/1063kJ
CARBOHYDRATE: 41g
  sugar: 28g
FAT: 8.5g
  saturated: 5g
SALT: 0.6g
FIBER: 0.5g

COOK'S TIP
The use of corn syrup and dark brown sugar here gives a dense, moist cake that keeps very well. If the cake is beginning to get a little dry with age, try slicing it and spreading with soft butter as a breakfast snack, or even turning it into a rich gingery version of Classic bread and butter pudding (see p348).

German apple cake

This simple apple cake is transformed into something special with a warmly spiced, crumbly streusel topping.

30 mins, plus chilling • 45-50 mins

SPECIAL EQUIPMENT
8in (20cm) loose-bottomed cake pan

SERVES 6–8

12 tbsp unsalted butter, softened, plus extra for greasing

1 cup light muscovado sugar

finely grated zest of 1 lemon

3 large eggs, lightly beaten

1½ cups self-rising flour

3 tbsp milk

2 tart apples, peeled, cored, and cut into even, slim wedges

FOR THE STREUSEL TOPPING

1 cup all-purpose flour

⅓ cup light muscovado sugar

2 tsp ground cinnamon

6 tbsp unsalted butter, in pieces

1 To make the topping, put the flour, sugar, and cinnamon in a mixing bowl. Rub in the butter gently with your fingertips to form a crumbly ball of dough. Wrap the streusel dough in plastic wrap and chill in the fridge for 30 minutes.

2 Preheat the oven to 375°F (190°C). Grease an 8in (20cm) loose-bottomed cake pan and line with parchment paper. Put the butter and sugar in a bowl and whisk until pale and creamy. Add the lemon zest, and whisk slowly until well dispersed through the batter.

3 Beat in the eggs, a little at a time, mixing well after each addition to avoid curdling. Sift the flour into the batter and gently fold it in with a rubber spatula, trying not to lose any air from the mixture. Finally, add the milk and gently and evenly mix it in.

4 Spread half the mixture in the prepared pan and smooth the surface with a palette knife. Arrange half the apple wedges over the batter, reserving the best pieces for the top. Spread the rest of the mixture over the apples. Smooth once more with a palette knife.

5 Arrange the remaining apple wedges on top of the cake. Remove the streusel dough from the fridge and coarsely grate it. Sprinkle the grated streusel evenly over the top of the cake.

6 Bake the cake in the center of the oven for 45 minutes. Insert a skewer into the center of the cake. If the skewer emerges coated in batter, cook for a few minutes more and test again. Leave the cake in the pan for 10 minutes to cool slightly. Keeping the streusel on top, remove the cake from the pan and cool on a wire rack. Serve warm.

VARIATION
This cake works well with the same amount of sliced pears, or pitted and sliced plums, instead of the apples.

Fruit baked into a sweet cake crumb and topped with a crumbly streusel topping, makes it hard to resist, even by fussy eaters who don't like fruit.

Fussy eaters!

CALORIES: 535kcals/2258kJ

CARBOHYDRATE: 61g
  sugar: 36g

FAT: 30g
  saturated: 18g

SALT: 0.4g

FIBER: 2.5g

Hummingbird cake

The bananas and crushed pineapple in this cake make it extremely moist and help it last for days.

20 mins   45-50 mins

SPECIAL EQUIPMENT

9in (23cm) square cake pan
electric hand-held mixer

MAKES 25 SQUARES

butter, for greasing

½ cup all-purpose flour

1 cup self-rising flour

½ tsp baking soda

1 tsp ground cinnamon

1 cup light brown sugar

½ cup sunflower or vegetable oil

3 large eggs, lightly beaten

3 bananas, approx. 11oz (320g)
   in total, mashed

1 x 14oz (440g) can crushed
   pineapple, drained

FOR THE TOPPING

2 tbsp unsalted butter, softened

3oz cream cheese, softened

1¼ cups confectioners' sugar

1. Preheat the oven to 350°F (180°C). Grease a 9in (23cm) square cake pan and line the bottom with parchment paper.

2. Sift the flours, baking soda, and cinnamon into a large bowl. Stir in the sugar.

3. Place the oil and eggs in a bowl and whisk well. Pour into the dry ingredients. Stir in the bananas and pineapple. Transfer to the pan. Bake for 45–50 minutes, or until a skewer comes out clean.

4. Meanwhile, prepare the topping. Place the butter and cream cheese in a bowl and beat together using an electric hand-held mixer. Sift the confectioners' sugar and beat it into the mixture.

5. Leave the cake in the pan for 10 minutes, then turn onto a wire rack and cool completely. Place on a serving plate, spread with the icing, and cut into squares to serve.

CALORIES: 171kcals/722kJ

CARBOHYDRATE: 24g
   sugar: 18g

FAT: 8g
   saturated: 3g

SALT: 0.2g

FIBER: 0.7g

Apricot and almond bars

This delicious bars are equally good served warm with Creamy custard (see p360), or cold as a quick snack.

20 mins   35-40 mins

SPECIAL EQUIPMENT

9in (23cm) square baking pan
electric hand-held mixer

MAKES 25 SQUARES

14 tbsp butter, softened, plus extra for
   greasing

¾ cup granulated sugar

2 large eggs, lightly beaten

2 tbsp milk

1 cup self-rising flour

1 cup ground almonds

3½oz (100g) dried apricots, finely
   chopped

1¾oz (50g) toasted sliced almonds

CALORIES: 159kcals/665kJ

CARBOHYDRATE: 13.5g
   sugar: 10g

FAT: 10g
   saturated: 5g

SALT: 0.2g

FIBER: 0.5g

1. Preheat the oven to 325°F (160°C). Grease a 9in (23cm) square baking pan and line the bottom with parchment paper.

2. Place the butter and sugar in a bowl and cream together using an electric hand-held mixer, until pale and fluffy. Beat in the eggs and milk. Sift the flour into the bowl and fold into the mixture with the ground almonds.

3. Stir in the apricots and transfer to the prepared pan. Level the surface with the back of a metal serving spoon and sprinkle in the sliced almonds, pressing any loose nuts into the mixture. Bake for 35–40 minutes, or until a skewer comes out clean.

4. Remove from the oven and let cool in the pan for 10 minutes. Transfer to a wire rack to cool completely. Cut into 25 squares to serve.

Devil's food cake

In this classic, coffee enhances the richness of the chocolate, adding a lovely depth of flavor to the cake.

30 mins   30–35 mins

SPECIAL EQUIPMENT
2 x 8in (20cm) round cake pans
electric hand-held mixer

SERVES 8–10

7 tbsp unsalted butter, softened, plus extra for greasing

1¼ cups granulated sugar

2 large eggs

1½ cups self-rising flour

⅔ cup cocoa powder

1 tsp baking powder

1 tbsp instant espresso powder mixed with ½ cup boiling water, or ½ cup cooled espresso

½ cup whole milk

1 tsp vanilla extract

FOR THE ICING
8 tbsp unsalted butter, cut into cubes

3 tbsp cocoa powder

1 cup confectioners' sugar, sifted

2–3 tbsp whole milk

dark or milk chocolate, for shaving

1 Preheat the oven to 350°F (180°C). Grease two 8in (20cm) round cake pans and line the bottoms with parchment paper. Using an electric hand-held mixer, cream together the butter and sugar until light and fluffy.

2 Beat in the eggs one at a time, whisking well after each addition. In a separate bowl, sift together the flour, cocoa powder, and baking powder. In another bowl, mix together the cooled coffee, milk, and vanilla extract.

3 Beat alternate spoonfuls of the dry and liquid ingredients into the cake batter. Once well blended, divide between the pans.

4 Bake for 30–35 minutes until the cakes are springy to the touch and a skewer comes out clean. Let cool in the pans for a few minutes, then turn onto a wire rack to cool completely.

5 For the icing, melt the butter in a pan over low heat. Add the cocoa powder and continue to cook for a minute or two, stirring frequently. Allow to cool slightly.

6 Sift in the confectioners' sugar, beating thoroughly to combine. Blend in the milk, 1 tbsp at a time, until smooth and glossy. Allow to cool (it will thicken), then use half to sandwich the cakes together and the remainder to decorate the top and sides of the cake. Finally, use a vegetable peeler to create chocolate shavings and scatter them evenly over the top of the cake.

HOW TO FREEZE

Freeze the just-baked, cooled, and un-iced cakes, wrapped separately in waxed paper and sealed with foil, for up to 6 months, then defrost, ice, and serve.

CALORIES: 556kcals/2350kJ
CARBOHYDRATE: 68g
  sugar: 50g
FAT: 28g
  saturated: 17g
SALT: 0.8g
FIBER: 3g

Chocolate fudge cake

Everyone loves a good fudge cake, and this is a winner. The oil and syrup keep it moist, and the icing is a classic.

40 mins   30 mins

SPECIAL EQUIPMENT
2 x 8in (20cm) round cake pans
electric hand-held mixer

SERVES 6–8

⅔ cup sunflower or vegetable oil, plus extra for greasing

1½ cups self-rising flour

3 tbsp cocoa powder

1 tsp baking powder

¾ cup light brown sugar

3 tbsp corn syrup

2 large eggs, lightly beaten

⅔ cup whole milk

FOR THE ICING

8 tbsp unsalted butter

3 tbsp cocoa powder

1 cup confectioners' sugar

2 tbsp whole milk, if necessary

1 Preheat the oven to 350°F (180°C). Grease two 8in (20cm) round cake pans and line the bottoms with parchment paper. In a large bowl, sift together the flour, cocoa, and baking powder. Mix in the sugar.

2 Gently heat the corn syrup until runny and let cool. In a separate bowl, beat the eggs, oil, and milk together using an electric hand-held mixer. Whisk the egg mixture into the flour mixture until well combined, but don't over-mix. Gently fold in the syrup, being careful not to knock out any air, and divide the batter evenly between the cake pans.

3 Bake the cakes in the middle of the oven for 30 minutes, or until springy to the touch and a skewer comes out clean. Let cool slightly in the pans, then turn onto a wire rack to cool completely.

4 To make the icing, melt the butter over low heat. Stir in the cocoa powder and cook gently for 1–2 minutes, then let cool completely. Sift the confectioners' sugar into a bowl.

5 Pour the melted butter and cocoa into the confectioners' sugar and beat together to combine. If the mixture seems a little dry, add the milk, 1 tbsp at a time, until the icing is smooth and glossy. Let cool for up to 30 minutes; it will thicken as it cools. When thick, use half the icing to fill the cake and the other half to top it.

COOK'S TIP

This firm, very tempting cake is a great base for all sorts of novelty children's birthday cakes. Chill it, then carve into shapes, or simply smother with icing and stick their favorite sweets all over the top and sides to make a show-stopping centerpiece.

CLEVER WITH LEFTOVERS

Heat leftover cake for 30 seconds in a microwave. The icing will melt into a rich, fudgy sauce, and you can serve it with vanilla ice cream for a delicious and speedy dessert.

CALORIES: 669kcals/2808kJ
CARBOHYDRATE: 68g
  sugar: 47g
FAT: 41g
  saturated: 16g
SALT: 0.8g
FIBER: 3g

Pound cake

This cake is so called because the original recipe used a pound of each ingredient. Try this scaled-down version.

10 mins   50 mins-1 hr

SPECIAL EQUIPMENT

6 x 10in (15 x 25cm) loaf pan

electric hand-held mixer

MAKES 1

14 tbsp butter, softened, plus extra for greasing

¾ cup granulated sugar

1 tsp vanilla extract

4 large eggs

1½ cups all-purpose flour, sifted

1 Preheat the oven to 325°F (160°C). Grease a 6 x 10in (15 x 25cm) loaf pan with butter.

2 In a bowl, whisk the butter and sugar with an electric hand-held mixer, until light and fluffy. Whisk in the vanilla extract. Whisk in the eggs one at a time, making sure to incorporate as much air as possible.

3 Fold the flour into the egg mixture until just blended in, and pour the batter into the pan.

4 Bake in the center of the hot oven for 50 minutes to 1 hour until the cake is well risen and a skewer comes out clean. Allow the cake to cool in the pan for 5 minutes before turning it to cool on a wire rack.

VARIATION

These cakes can be flavored as you like with lemon or orange zest, or with almond extract.

HOW TO FREEZE

Freeze the cooked, cooled cake by wrapping it in waxed paper and sealing with foil for up to 6 months.

CALORIES: 3307kcals/13832kJ

CARBOHYDRATE: 341g
  sugar: 204g

FAT: 194g
  saturated: 112g

SALT: 4g

FIBER: 8g

Orange and marmalade loaf cake

The aroma of cinnamon, oranges, and marmalade fills the kitchen while this cake is in the oven.

15 mins   45-50 mins

SPECIAL EQUIPMENT

9 x 5in (23 x 12cm) loaf pan

food processor

SERVES 8-10

7 tbsp butter, cut into cubes, plus extra for greasing

1¾ cups self-rising flour, sifted

1 tsp ground cinnamon

½ cup granulated sugar

finely grated zest of 2 oranges, plus juice of 1 orange

½ cup marmalade

½ cup whole milk

1 cup confectioners' sugar, sifted

1 Preheat the oven to 350°F (180°C). Grease a 9 x 5in (23 x 12cm) loaf pan and line it with parchment paper.

2 Place the flour and cinnamon into a food processor with the butter. Process until the mixture resembles coarse bread crumbs. Stir in the granulated sugar.

3 Stir in the zest of 1 orange and all but 2 tbsp of the orange juice. Stir in all the marmalade and milk. Spoon the mixture into the prepared pan and bake for 45–50 minutes, or until a skewer comes out clean. Remove from the oven and cool in the pan for 5 minutes.

4 Turn the cake onto a wire rack, remove the parchment paper, and allow to cool completely.

5 Mix the reserved orange juice into the confectioners' sugar 1 tbsp at a time; you probably won't need it all. When it has reached a consistency you like, drizzle it over the cake. Sprinkle with the reserved orange zest (this looks more attractive if you use a zesting tool, rather than a box grater), and set aside for the icing to set.

CALORIES: 358kcals/1512kJ

CARBOHYDRATE: 61g
  sugar: 42g

FAT: 11g
  saturated: 7g

SALT: 0.5g

FIBER: 1g

Banana cake

Leftover bananas deteriorate rapidly. Use them up in this lovely moist cake that keeps for a couple of days.

20 mins   30 mins, plus resting

SPECIAL EQUIPMENT

7in (18cm) square cake pan
electric hand-held mixer

SERVES 8

11 tbsp unsalted butter, at room temperature, plus extra for greasing

⅔ cup granulated sugar

3 large eggs

1 tsp vanilla extract

2 overripe bananas, peeled, and mashed

1¼ cups self-rising flour

½ tsp ground cinnamon

CALORIES: 332kcals/1401kJ

CARBOHYDRATE: 37g
  sugar: 24g

FAT: 18g
  saturated: 11g

SALT: 0.3g

FIBER: 1g

---

1 Preheat the oven to 350°F (180°C). Grease a 7in (18cm) square cake pan and line the bottom with parchment paper.

2 In a large bowl, beat the butter and sugar together with an electric hand-held mixer until light and fluffy. Beat in the eggs, one at a time, until they are well mixed. Beat in the vanilla extract.

3 Fold the mashed banana into the mixture until it is well combined. Sift the flour and cinnamon into the mixture and gently fold in.

4 Pour the batter into the pan and bake in the center of the hot oven for 30 minutes. Remove the cake from the oven and allow it to rest in the pan for 5 minutes before removing it and allowing it to cool completely on a wire rack.

HOW TO FREEZE

The just-cooked and cooled cake can be wrapped well and frozen on the day it is made, for up to 12 weeks.

Banana, date, and walnut loaf

This classic combination of flavors is the perfect mix of sweet and mellow. Just right for breakfast or a snack.

20 mins   1–1¼ hrs

SPECIAL EQUIPMENT

9 x 5in (23 x 12cm) loaf pan
electric hand-held mixer

SERVES 8–10

7 tbsp butter, softened

½ cup granulated sugar

2 large eggs

1⅓ cups self-rising flour, sifted

2 bananas, approx. 10oz (300g) in total

3½oz (100g) pitted dates (medjool are best), chopped

1¾oz (50g) walnut pieces, roughly chopped

1 tsp baking powder

CALORIES: 284kcals/1192kJ

CARBOHYDRATE: 35g
  sugar: 19g

FAT: 13g
  saturated: 6g

SALT: 0.6g

FIBER: 2g

---

1 Preheat the oven to 350°F (180°C). Line a 9 x 5in (23 x 12cm) loaf pan with parchment paper. In a bowl, beat the butter and sugar with an electric hand-held mixer until pale, light, and fluffy. Add the eggs one at a time, beating well as you do so, and adding 1 tbsp of the flour after each to prevent the mixture from curdling.

2 Peel and mash the bananas in a small bowl with a fork, then stir into the loaf mixture, along with the chopped dates and walnuts. Fold in the remaining flour and the baking powder, then spoon the mixture into the pan. Smooth the top, pressing well into the corners.

3 Bake for 1–1¼ hours, or until risen and firm to the touch. If the top of the cake starts to brown too much before it is fully cooked, cover with foil. Let cool in the pan, then cut into slices.

CLEVER WITH LEFTOVERS

For maximum sweetness, use up your overripe bananas with brown speckled skins in this recipe.

Coconut and lime drizzle loaf

Add a tropical twist to your baking with this zesty coconut and lime cake.

15 mins, plus cooling · 45–50 mins

SPECIAL EQUIPMENT

9 x 5in (23 x 12cm) loaf pan
electric hand-held mixer

SERVES 8–10

FOR THE CAKE

14 tbsp unsalted butter, softened, plus extra for greasing

¾ cup granulated sugar

4 large eggs

1⅓ cups self-rising flour, sifted

2½oz (75g) shredded coconut

finely grated zest of 2 limes, plus juice of 1 lime

FOR THE TOPPING

juice of 2 limes

⅓ cup granulated sugar

1 tbsp shredded coconut

CALORIES: 415kcals/1746kJ
CARBOHYDRATE: 42g
    sugar: 29g
FAT: 25g
    saturated: 16g
SALT: 0.3g
FIBER: 2.5g

---

1 Preheat the oven to 325°F (160°C). Grease a 9 x 5in (23 x 12cm) loaf pan and line the bottom with parchment paper.

2 Place the butter and sugar in a bowl and cream together using an electric hand-held mixer until fluffy. Beat in the eggs, one at a time. Fold in the flour, coconut, lime zest, and juice.

3 Transfer to the pan and level the surface with the back of a spoon. Bake for 45–50 minutes, or until a skewer comes out clean.

4 Meanwhile, for the topping, stir the lime juice and golden granulated sugar in a small bowl.

5 Remove the cake from the oven and place it, in the pan, on a wire rack. With a skewer, make holes in the cake and pour the lime mixture over the top. Sprinkle with the coconut. Leave until completely cold. Remove from the pan, peel off the parchment, and serve.

HOW TO FREEZE

Before the topping is added, wrap the loaf well and freeze for up to 12 weeks. Defrost thoroughly, replace the cake in the loaf pan, then follow the recipe from the start of step 4.

Pecan and cranberry loaf

Dried cranberries are a novel alternative to the more usual raisins, adding sweet, sharp notes to this cake.

30 mins · 50–60 mins

SPECIAL EQUIPMENT

9 x 5in (23 x 12cm) loaf pan

SERVES 8–10

7 tbsp unsalted butter, plus extra for greasing

½ cup light brown sugar

2½oz (75g) dried cranberries, roughly chopped

1¾oz (50g) pecans, roughly chopped

finely grated zest of 2 oranges and juice of up to 1 orange

2 large eggs, lightly beaten

½ cup whole milk

1⅓ cups self-rising flour

½ tsp baking powder

½ tsp ground cinnamon

¾ cup confectioners' sugar, sifted

CALORIES: 313kcals/1322kJ
CARBOHYDRATE: 43g
    sugar: 27g
FAT: 14g
    saturated: 6g
SALT: 0.3g
FIBER: 1.5g

---

1 Preheat the oven to 350°F (180°C). Grease a 9 x 5in (23 x 12cm) loaf pan and line with parchment paper. In a pan, melt the butter. Let cool slightly, then stir in the sugar, cranberries, pecans, and zest of 1 orange. Whisk together the eggs and milk, then stir them in.

2 In a separate bowl, sift together the flour, baking powder, and cinnamon. Fold into the batter, mixing well. Pour into the pan. Bake in the center of the oven for 50–60 minutes. Let cool slightly, then turn out.

3 Mix the confectioners' sugar and remaining orange zest. Add enough orange juice for a drizzling consistency. Drizzle over the cooled cake and let dry before slicing. This cake will store in an airtight container for up to 3 days.

HOW TO FREEZE

Wrap the un-iced loaf cake in plastic wrap and seal with foil. Freeze it for up to 12 weeks, then defrost thoroughly and ice as in step 3.

Picky kids and teenagers

Once children are out of the toddler stages, we often expect them to happily join in with family mealtimes. Yet for a variety of reasons, children will often continue to reject certain things. It is important to remember that many adults dislike some foods, too, and that you should not put too much emphasis on forcing children to eat things that they genuinely dislike. Having regular family mealtimes can set a good example for picky children, as they see the rest of the family enjoying a varied diet. Try not to offer alternatives to rejected meals, or you will soon be preparing several different meals at a time.

A developing diet

It is very easy to start worrying when your children seem to start excluding things from their diet. You worry that they are not getting all the nutrients and energy they need to fuel their growing bodies. Yet children will often eat more during a growth spurt and less at other times. Teenagers will start taking an interest in a healthy diet, and may cut back on previously favorite foods. It is important not to worry unduly, but do take advice from a health professional if you are concerned about your child's diet over a period of months rather than weeks.

Healthy dishes made easy

Granola breakfast bars (pp474–475) are great when children are out the door for school with little time for breakfast.

Take the time to slow down at the weekend with some indulgent **huevos rancheros (p255)** or a **breakfast burrito (p259)** for a chance to spend some family time around the breakfast table.

Hungry teens need to eat a lot, and quickly. Try easy pasta dishes such as **easy carbonara (p197)** or **pasta with peas and pancetta (p205)** for a healthy way to fill them up that won't blow the budget.

A quick fix for a sweet tooth could be some good-quality store-bought **vanilla ice cream with butterscotch sauce (p291)** or **soft fruit bruschetta with mascarpone (p324)**

Meet the challenge!

The easiest way to get kids to eat what's good for them is to use their preferences to inform your cooking. With a bit of creative thinking, you can come up with something that keeps the whole family happy.

"I hate vegetables!"

It's all about presentation This creamy, root vegetable Gratin (see p173) contains a vegetable medley of potatoes, carrots, and parsnips, and is a great source of vitamins and minerals for children who are resistant to vegetables.

"I only drink juice"

Delicious smoothies To ensure that children get calcium in their diets, make up some fruity Tropical smoothies (p268) as a healthy alternative to milkshake–the yogurt is low in fat, while the honey and fruit make the drink a delicious sweet treat.

"Give me low fat."

Feeling full For a low-fat meal that still provides carbohydates, a Shrimp, sweet chili, and Greek yogurt wrap (see p385) is a delicious treat, and contains none of the unhealthy additives found in a store-bought version.

"Meat-free, please!"

Quick and nutritious A quick and easy standby for those who don't eat meat is a delicious Cheesy soufflé omelet (see p248). The eggs are a good source of protein, and when combined with tasty cheese and a salad, makes for well-rounded comfort food.

Ideas for budding chefs

Tomato and mascarpone pasta (p193) is a quick and simple pasta dish that is easy to prepare. Peeling the fresh tomatoes is as difficult as this gets, and the sauce can be prepared in the time it takes to cook the pasta.

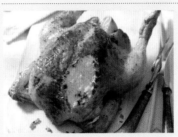

Everybody likes roast chicken, so learning to make a **classic roast chicken (p294)** should be one of the cornerstones of your teens' culinary adventures. If timing all the accompanying vegetables is too difficult, try making **roast chicken and vegetables (p302)**

Soup can be a quick, healthy and delicious way to enjoy your five a day. Encourage your teens to try making this **harvest vegetable soup (p157)** where they can add their choice of vegetables and blend it all to a smooth, even texture.

Most children learn to cook by learning to bake. Encourage your teens to move on to desserts with dishes such as summer fruits with **easy brulee topping (p327)** or **clafoutis (p326)** and get some fruit into their diet, too.

Budgeting

Feeding hungry teens can be expensive, especially when they invite their friends over. Buy basic pizzas and decorate them with extra toppings for a movie night, along with a big bowl of homemade popcorn.

Getting involved

Teenagers expect a fair amount of self-regulation, so allow them to exert some of that in the kitchen. Buy them the ingredients they need and encourage them to prepare their favorite dishes.

Cheese straws

A great way of using up any leftover bits of hard cheese that may be lurking in the fridge.

10 mins, plus chilling   15 mins, plus cooling

SPECIAL EQUIPMENT
food processor

MAKES 15–20

½ cup all-purpose flour, sifted, plus extra for dusting

pinch of salt

4 tbsp butter, softened and cut into cubes

1oz (30g) finely grated aged Cheddar or Gruyère cheese

1 large egg yolk, lightly beaten, plus 1 large egg, lightly beaten, for brushing

1 tsp Dijon mustard

| CALORIES: 45kcals/189kJ |
| CARBOHYDRATE: 3g |
| sugar: 0.1g |
| FAT: 3.5g |
| saturated: 1.8g |
| SALT: 0.15g |
| FIBER: 0.2g |

1 Place the flour, salt, and butter in a food processor. Pulse-blend until the mixture resembles crumbs. Mix in the cheese. Whisk the egg yolk with 1 tbsp of water and the mustard. Mix it into the crumbs.

2 Turn onto a floured surface and knead briefly. Wrap in plastic wrap and chill for 1 hour. Preheat the oven to 400°F (200°C).

3 Roll the dough out to a 12 x 6in (30 x 15cm) rectangle. Cut ½in- (1cm-) wide strips along the shorter side. Brush with a little egg. Holding the top of each, twist the bottom a few times to form spirals.

4 Place the straws on non-stick baking sheets, pressing down the ends. Bake at the top of the oven for 15 minutes. Cool on the pans for 5 minutes, then transfer to a wire rack. These keep in an airtight container for up to 3 days.

HOW TO FREEZE
Freeze for up to 12 weeks. Defrost and warm for 5 minutes in an oven preheated to 350°F (180°C) to serve.

Three-cheese scones

These tasty scones make a great addition to a picnic, lunch box, or just as a savory afternoon treat.

5 mins   10-15 mins, plus cooling

SPECIAL EQUIPMENT
2½in (6cm) round cutter

SERVES 6

2 tbsp butter, cut into cubes, plus extra for greasing

1½ cups self-rising flour, sifted, plus extra for dusting

½ tsp mustard powder

salt and freshly ground black pepper

1¾oz (50g) grated Cheddar cheese

scant 1oz (25g) finely grated Parmesan cheese

1 large egg, lightly beaten

3-4 tbsp milk, plus extra for brushing

scant 1oz (25g) grated Gruyère cheese

butter, or cream cheese with garlic and herbs, to serve

| CALORIES: 257kcals/1076kJ |
| CARBOHYDRATE: 21g |
| sugar: 0.8g |
| FAT: 14g |
| saturated: 8g |
| SALT: 0.9g |
| FIBER: 1g |

1 Preheat the oven to 400°F (200°C). Grease a baking sheet with butter. Place the flour and mustard powder in a medium mixing bowl and season well. Add the butter to the bowl and rub it in with your fingertips until the mixture resembles bread crumbs.

2 Stir in the Cheddar and Parmesan cheeses and the egg. Add enough of the milk to form a soft scone dough.

3 Roll out the dough on a well-floured surface to a thickness of about ¾in (2cm). Cut out 6 scones, using a 2½in (6cm) round cutter, re-rolling the dough as necessary.

4 Place the scones on the prepared baking sheet. Brush them with milk and sprinkle over the Gruyère cheese.

5 Bake for 10–15 minutes. Remove from the oven, transfer to a wire cooling rack, and allow to cool for 10–15 minutes.

6 Split the scones in half and serve warm, spread with butter, or cream cheese with garlic and herbs.

Parmesan and rosemary thins

These crackers are light and elegant, and are equally good served as an appetizer or after dinner with cheese.

10 mins, plus chilling   15 mins, plus cooling

SPECIAL EQUIPMENT
food processor (optional)
2½in (6cm) round cutter

SERVES 15–20

4 tbsp unsalted butter, softened and cut into cubes

½ cup all-purpose flour, plus extra for dusting

2oz (60g) finely grated Parmesan cheese

freshly ground black pepper

1 tbsp chopped rosemary, thyme, or basil leaves

1 Place the butter and flour in a bowl, or a food processor. Rub with your fingertips, or pulse-blend, until the mixture resembles crumbs. Mix in the Parmesan, pepper, and herbs. Bring together to a dough.

2 Turn onto a floured surface and briefly knead. Wrap in plastic wrap and chill for 1 hour.

3 Preheat the oven to 350°F (180°C). Turn the dough onto a floured surface.

4 Roll the dough out to ⅟₁₂in (2mm) thick and cut out crackers with a 2½in (6cm) round cutter. Place on non-stick baking sheets and bake for 10 minutes. Turn and bake for another 5 minutes.

5 Remove from the oven and leave on the pans for 5 minutes before transferring to a wire rack to cool completely. These keep in an airtight container for up to 3 days.

HOW TO FREEZE

Open-freeze the unbaked crackers, then transfer to a large freezer bag for up to 12 weeks.

CALORIES: 48kcals/189kJ
CARBOHYDRATE: 3g
  sugar: 0.1g
FAT: 3.5g
  saturated: 2g
SALT: 0.1g
FIBER: 0.2g

Multi-seed crackers

These can be adapted using a mixture of the seeds you like. Be sure to use the larger seeds for decorating.

20 mins   12-15 mins

SPECIAL EQUIPMENT
food processor (optional)

MAKES 45–50

1 cup whole wheat flour

½ cup all-purpose flour, plus extra for dusting

4 tbsp butter, in pieces, softened

½ tsp fine salt

2 tbsp sesame seeds

2 tbsp flaxseeds

2 tbsp pumpkin seeds, plus extra for decorating

2 tbsp sunflower seeds, plus extra for decorating

1 tbsp honey

1 large egg white

1 Preheat the oven to 400°F (200°C). In a large bowl with your fingertips, or in a food processor using the pulse-blend setting, blend the flours, butter, and salt until the mixture resembles fine crumbs. Mix in all the seeds.

2 Dissolve the honey in ½ cup of warm water. Make a well in the flour and mix in the water to form a soft dough.

3 Turn the dough onto a floured surface and knead it briefly. Roll out as thinly as possible—aim for ⅟₂₄–⅟₁₂in (1–2mm) thick.

4 Cut the dough into 1½ x 2½in (4 x 6cm) crackers. Leave on the work surface.

5 Whisk the egg white with ½ tbsp of water and brush the crackers. Scatter with the additional pumpkin and sunflower seeds and gently press in.

6 Transfer to 2 baking sheets using a metal spatula, and bake for 12–15 minutes, turning carefully halfway, or until both sides are crisp and golden brown. Let cool on their pans. Store in an airtight container for up to 2 weeks.

CALORIES: 38kcals/157kJ
CARBOHYDRATE: 3g
  sugar: 0.4g
FAT: 2g
  saturated: 0.8g
SALT: trace
FIBER: 0.7g

Savory breakfast muffins

These unusual muffins add a savory twist to a weekend breakfast or brunch.

10 mins   25 mins

SPECIAL EQUIPMENT
12-hole muffin pan
12 paper muffin liners

MAKES 12

2½ cups self-rising flour, sifted

1 tsp baking powder

7oz (200g) grated Cheddar cheese

3½oz (100g) thick-cut ham, finely diced

4 scallions, finely sliced

1 tsp smoked paprika

freshly ground black pepper

1½ cups whole milk

1 large egg, lightly beaten

1 Preheat the oven to 350°F (180°C). In a large bowl, mix together all the dry ingredients until they are well combined.

2 Mix together the milk and egg. Make a well in the center of the dry ingredients and pour the milk mixture in, incorporating it gradually to make a thick batter.

3 Line a 12-hole muffin pan with paper muffin liners, then divide the batter between them.

4 Bake in the middle of the oven for 25 minutes until the muffins are well risen and a skewer comes out clean. Transfer to a wire rack to cool for 5 minutes. Serve warm.

CLEVER WITH LEFTOVERS
If you have ham left over from the Whole glazed ham (see p320), this is an ideal time to use it up.

HOW TO FREEZE
Open-freeze the muffins, then transfer to a freezer bag for up to 3 months. Defrost, then reheat to serve warm.

CALORIES: 200kcals/835kJ
CARBOHYDRATE: 22g
   sugar: 2g
FAT: 8g
   saturated: 4g
SALT: 0.9g
FIBER: 1g

Quick cheese pastries

These pastries make appetizing canapés for a party in minutes. Make more than you think you'll need!

15 mins   10-15 mins, plus cooling

MAKES 8

7½oz (215g) sheet ready-rolled puff pastry, approx. 8 x 10in (20 x 25cm)

4 tsp pesto (see p194)

4 tsp tapenade

1oz (30g) grated mozzarella cheese

scant 1oz (25g) goat cheese

1 large egg, lightly beaten

1 Preheat the oven to 400°F (200°C). Line 2 baking sheets with parchment paper.

2 Unroll the pastry and divide it into 4 equal strips. Cut each strip into 4 equal pieces to give 16 equal-sized rectangles.

3 Place 8 rectangles on the sheets. Top 4 of them with 1 tsp green pesto each, and 4 of them with 1 tsp tapenade each.

4 Sprinkle the mozzarella over the pesto-topped squares and divide the goat cheese between the tapenade-topped squares.

5 Brush the edges of the topped squares with beaten egg and place one of the reserved pastry pieces on top of each one. Carefully but firmly press the edges of the pastry together with a fork to seal.

6 Brush each parcel with beaten egg and bake for 10–15 minutes, or until golden. If baking on two oven shelves, swap the positions of the baking sheets halfway through, to give all the pastries time at the top of the oven. Transfer to a wire rack to cool slightly for 5 minutes and serve warm.

CALORIES: 147kcals/615kJ
CARBOHYDRATE: 9.5g
   sugar: 0.5g
FAT: 10.5g
   saturated: 4.5g
SALT: 0.4g
FIBER: 0g

Stuffed parathas

These stuffed flatbreads are easy to make. Double the quantities and freeze half, wrapped in waxed paper.

20 mins, plus resting   15–20 mins

MAKES 4

FOR THE DOUGH

2 cups chapati flour

½ tsp fine salt

4 tbsp unsalted butter, melted and cooled

FOR THE STUFFING

9oz (250g) sweet potatoes, cut into cubes

1 tbsp sunflower or vegetable oil, plus extra for brushing

½ red onion, finely chopped

2 garlic cloves, crushed

1 tbsp finely chopped red chile, or to taste

1 tbsp finely chopped fresh ginger

2 heaping tbsp chopped cilantro

½ tsp garam masala

sea salt

1 To make the dough, sift the flour and salt together. Add the butter and ⅔ cup of water, and bring the mixture together to form a soft dough. Knead it for 5 minutes, then let the dough rest, covered, for 1 hour.

2 To make the stuffing, boil or steam the sweet potato for about 7 minutes until tender. Drain it well. In a frying pan, heat the oil over medium heat and cook the red onion for 3–5 minutes until soft, but not golden. Add the garlic, chile, and ginger, and continue to cook for 1–2 minutes.

3 Add the cooked onion mixture to the sweet potato and mash well. You should not need extra liquid as the potato is quite moist and the oil from the onion mixture will help, too. Add the cilantro, garam masala, and a good seasoning of salt and beat until reasonably smooth, with no large lumps. Set aside to cool.

4 When the dough has rested, divide it into 4 pieces. Knead each piece and roll it out into a circle, around 4in (10cm) in diameter. Put one-quarter of the stuffing in the middle. Pull the edges up around to form a "purse."

5 Pinch the edges together to seal, turn the dough over, and roll it out into a circle about 7in (18cm) in diameter, making sure not to roll too hard. If the filling bursts out, wipe it off and pinch the dough together to reseal the hole.

6 Heat a large, cast-iron frying pan or grill pan (big enough to take the parathas) over medium heat. Cook the parathas for 2 minutes on each side, turning to make sure they are well cooked and browning in places. Once they have cooked on each side once, brush the surface with a little oil and turn them again. Serve immediately with a curry, or as a light lunch dish with a green salad.

VARIATION

These are made with chapati flour but, if you cannot find it easily, use whole wheat flour instead. Try a variety of fillings, including leftover vegetable curry; just make sure the ingredients are diced small so the stuffing is easily contained and that it is not too wet.

PREPARE AHEAD

These can be stored overnight, wrapped in plastic wrap. To reheat (from fresh or frozen), scrunch up a piece of waxed paper and soak it in water. Squeeze out the excess water and wrap a paratha in the paper. Place in an oven preheated to 350°F (180°C) for 10 minutes, or until warm and soft throughout.

CALORIES: 451kcals/1909kJ

CARBOHYDRATE: 65g
sugar: 6g

FAT: 17g
saturated: 7.5g

SALT: 0.6g

FIBER: 12.5g

Grissini

Tradition has it that breadsticks should be pulled to the length of the baker's arm... these are more manageable!

40-45 mins, plus rising 15-18 mins

MAKES 32

2½ tsp dried yeast

3⅓ cups white bread flour, plus extra for dusting

1 tbsp granulated sugar

2 tsp salt

2 tbsp extra virgin olive oil

1½oz (45g) sesame seeds

1 Sprinkle the yeast over ¼ cup of warm water. Leave for 5 minutes, stirring once. Put the flour, sugar, and salt in a bowl. Add the yeast, 1 cup of warm water, and the oil. Mix to make a sticky dough.

2 Knead on a floured surface for 5–7 minutes until very smooth and elastic. Let rest for 5 minutes.

3 Roll the dough out to 16 x 6in (40 x 15cm). Cover with a damp kitchen towel. Leave in a warm place for 1½ hours, until doubled in size.

4 Preheat the oven to 425°F (220°C). Dust 3 baking sheets with flour. Brush the dough with water and sprinkle with the sesame seeds.

5 With a sharp knife, cut the dough into 32 strips, each ½in (1cm) wide. Stretch 1 strip to the width of a baking sheet. Set it on the baking sheet. Repeat with the remaining strips, arranging them ¾in (2cm) apart. Bake for 15–18 minutes until golden and crisp. These keep in an airtight container for up to 2 days.

PREPARE AHEAD

In step 3 the rectangle of dough can be left to rise slowly overnight in the fridge, if it is more convenient. Shape and bake the grissini the next day.

CALORIES: 63kcals/266kJ

CARBOHYDRATE: 10g
    sugar: 1g

FAT: 2g
    saturated: 0.5g

SALT: 0.2g

FIBER: 0.5g

Pretzels

These German breads are great fun to make, and the two-stage glazing method gives an authentic chewy result.

50 mins, plus proofing | 20 mins

MAKES 16

3 cups white bread flour, plus extra for dusting

1¼ cups all-purpose flour

1 tsp salt

2 tbsp granulated sugar

2 tsp dried yeast

1 tbsp sunflower or vegetable oil, plus extra for greasing

FOR THE GLAZE

¼ tsp baking soda

2 tbsp coarse sea salt or sesame seeds

1 large egg, lightly beaten, for glazing

1 Put the 2 types of flour, salt, and sugar into a bowl. Sprinkle the yeast over 1¼ cups of warm water. Stir, leave for 5 minutes, then add the oil. Gradually pour into the flour, stirring to form a soft dough.

2 Knead for 10 minutes until soft and pliable. Put in an oiled bowl. Cover loosely with plastic wrap and leave in a warm place for 1–2 hours until nearly doubled in size. Turn onto a floured work surface, and gently knock it back.

3 With a sharp knife, cut the dough into 16 equal pieces. Take each piece and roll it to make a log shape. Continue to roll the dough toward each end, until it is 18in (45cm) long.

4 Take each end of the dough and cross it over the other, forming a heart shape. Now twist the ends around each other as though they had linked arms.

5 Secure the ends to the sides of the pretzel. Repeat to make 16, placing them on baking sheets lined with parchment. Cover with plastic wrap and a kitchen towel. Leave in a warm place for 30 minutes to puff.

6 Preheat the oven to 400°F (200°C). Mix the baking soda in 2 tbsp boiling water. Brush the pretzels with the mixture. This gives them a dark color and chewy exterior. Scatter flakes of sea salt or sesame seeds over the brushed pretzels. Bake for 15 minutes.

7 Remove from the oven and brush with beaten egg. Bake for 5 minutes. Remove from the oven; they should be shiny. Let cool on a wire rack for at least 5 minutes before serving.

HOW TO FREEZE

Open-freeze the raw, shaped pretzels at the end of step 5. Transfer to a freezer bag. Defrost and bake within 12 weeks.

CALORIES: 129kcals/546kJ

CARBOHYDRATE: 25g
  sugar: 2.5g

FAT: 1.5g
  saturated: 0.5g

SALT: 0.7g

FIBER: 1.5g

Brazilian cheese rolls

Crisp on the outside and chewy within, these *pão de queijo* are a popular street food in their native land.

10 mins   30 mins

SPECIAL EQUIPMENT
food processor

MAKES 16

½ cup whole milk

3–4 tbsp sunflower or vegetable oil

1 tsp salt

1¾ cups tapioca (manioc or cassava) flour, plus extra for dusting

2 eggs, beaten, plus extra for glazing

4½oz (125g) Parmesan cheese, grated

1 Put the milk, oil, ½ cup of water, and the salt in a small saucepan and bring to a boil. Put the flour into a large bowl and quickly mix in the hot liquid. The mixture will be very shaggy and stick together. Set aside to cool.

2 Preheat the oven to 375°F (190°C). Once the tapioca mixture has cooled, put it into a food processor with a blade attachment. Add the eggs and process until the lumps disappear and it is a smooth paste. Add the cheese and process until the mixture is sticky and elastic.

3 Turn the mixture onto a well-floured work surface and knead for 2–3 minutes until smooth and pliable. Divide into 16 equal pieces. Roll each into golf ball-sized balls and place, spaced well apart, on a baking sheet lined with parchment paper.

4 Brush the balls with a little beaten egg and bake in the middle of the oven for 30 minutes until well risen and golden brown. Remove from the oven and cool for a few minutes before eating. These are best eaten the same day they are made, preferably still warm.

HOW TO FREEZE

These can be open-frozen on the baking sheet at the end of step 3, transferred to freezer bags, and frozen for up to 6 months. Simply defrost for 30 minutes and bake as in step 4.

CALORIES: 121kcals/510kJ
CARBOHYDRATE: 12g
  sugar: 0.6g
FAT: 6g
  saturated: 2g
SALT: 0.4g
FIBER: trace

Rosemary focaccia

This is a good-tempered dough that can be left in the fridge to rise overnight. Return to room temperature to bake.

30–35 mins, plus rising and proofing

15–20 mins

SPECIAL EQUIPMENT
15 x 9in (38 x 23cm) Swiss roll pan

SERVES 6–8

1 tbsp dried yeast

3⅓ cups white bread flour, plus extra for dusting

2 tsp salt

leaves from 5–7 rosemary sprigs, two-thirds finely chopped

6 tbsp olive oil, plus extra for greasing

¼ tsp freshly ground black pepper

sea salt flakes

1 Sprinkle the yeast over ¼ cup of warm water. Leave it for 5 minutes, stirring once. In a large bowl, mix the flour with the salt and make a well in the center. Add the chopped rosemary, 4 tbsp of the oil, the yeast mixture, pepper, and 1 cup of warm water.

2 Gradually draw in the flour and work it into the other ingredients to form a smooth dough. It should be soft and sticky, so do not be tempted to add more flour to dry it out. Sprinkle the dough lightly with flour and knead it for 5–7 minutes on a floured work surface.

3 When ready, the dough will be very smooth and elastic. Place in an oiled bowl. Cover with a damp kitchen towel. Let rise in a warm place for 1–1½ hours until doubled in size. Put the dough on a floured work surface and knock out the air. Cover with a dry kitchen towel and let it rest for about 5 minutes.

4 Brush a 15 x 9in (38 x 23cm) Swiss roll pan with oil. Transfer the dough to the pan. With your hands, flatten the dough to fill the pan evenly. Cover with a kitchen towel and let rise in a warm place for 35–45 minutes until it is puffed up.

5 Preheat the oven to 400°F (200°C). Scatter the reserved rosemary leaves on top. With your fingers, poke the dough all over to make deep dimples. Pour the remaining 2 tbsp of oil all over the dough and sprinkle with sea salt flakes. Bake on the top shelf of the oven for 15–20 minutes until browned. Transfer to a wire rack to cool.

VARIATION

For a roast garlic and sage version, omit the rosemary. Instead, add the chopped leaves from 3–5 sage sprigs, and incorporate 5–10 whole roast garlic cloves at the same time, to taste.

CALORIES: 231kcals/978kJ
CARBOHYDRATE: 40g
  sugar: 1g
FAT: 6g
  saturated: 1g
SALT: 1g
FIBER: 2g

Stuffed ciabatta

One of the simplest breads to master, a good ciabatta should be well risen and crusty, with large air pockets.

40 mins, plus proofing   50 mins–1 hr 5 mins

MAKES 2 LOAVES

2 tsp dried yeast

6 tbsp olive oil, plus extra for greasing

2½ cups white bread flour, plus extra for dusting

1 tsp sea salt

1 red bell pepper, chopped into ½in (1cm) cubes

1 yellow bell pepper, chopped into ½in (1cm) cubes

1 red onion, chopped into ½in (1cm) cubes

1 eggplant, chopped into ½in (1cm) cubes

freshly ground black pepper

2 heaping tbsp pesto

CALORIES: 1217kcals/5125kJ
CARBOHYDRATE: 176g
  sugar: 14g
FAT: 45g
  saturated: 5.5g
SALT: 4g
FIBER: 16g

1 Dissolve the yeast in 1½ cups of warm water, then add 4 tbsp of the oil. Put the flour and salt in a bowl. Stir in the yeast mixture to form a dough. Knead for 10 minutes, put in an oiled bowl, cover, and leave in a warm place for 2 hours, or until doubled in size.

2 Preheat the oven to 450°F (230°C). Mix the vegetables and remaining oil and season. Bake for 30–40 minutes, until crisp, then let cool.

3 Turn the dough onto a floured surface and knock it back. Form it into two 12 x 8in (30 x 20cm) rectangles. Top each with half the pesto and vegetables, then roll the loaves up like Swiss rolls.

4 Place, seam-side down, on floured baking sheets and tuck the ends under. Cover loosely with plastic wrap and a towel. Leave for 1 hour, or until doubled in size.

5 Preheat the oven again to 450°F (230°C). Spray the loaves with water. Bake for 20–25 minutes until hollow-sounding when tapped. Cool on wire racks.

Southern-style cornbread

This sweetish, rich loaf is traditionally served as an accompaniment for a barbecue, soup, or stew.

10-15 mins   25-35 mins

SPECIAL EQUIPMENT

7in (18cm) loose-bottomed round cake pan or similar-sized flameproof, cast-iron frying pan

SERVES 8

4 tbsp unsalted butter or bacon dripping, melted, and cooled, plus extra for greasing

2 cups fine cornmeal or polenta, (authentically white cornmeal, if you can find it)

2 tsp baking powder

½ tsp fine salt

2 large eggs, lightly beaten

1 cup buttermilk

1 tbsp honey (optional)

CALORIES: 207kcals/867kJ
CARBOHYDRATE: 25g
  sugar: 3g
FAT: 8g
  saturated: 4g
SALT: 0.7g
FIBER: 1g

1 Preheat the oven to 425°F (220°C). Grease a 7in (18cm) loose-bottomed round cake pan or a similar-sized flameproof, cast-iron frying pan and heat it in the oven. In a bowl, mix the cornmeal, baking powder, and salt. In another bowl, whisk the eggs and buttermilk.

2 Make a well in the cornmeal and stir in the buttermilk mixture. Stir in the butter or bacon dripping, and honey (if using).

3 Remove the cake pan or frying pan from the oven and pour in the mixture. It should sizzle; this is what gives the distinctive crust.

4 Bake in the middle of the oven for 20–25 minutes until it has risen and is browning at the edges. Let cool for 5 minutes before turning out and slicing.

VARIATION

Add 1 red chile, seeded and finely chopped, and ¼ cup finely chopped cilantro with the honey.

Pane di patate

Bread made with mashed potatoes have a soft crust and moist center. Here, the dough is coated in butter and baked.

50-55 mins, plus rising and proofing **40-45 mins**

SPECIAL EQUIPMENT

10in (25cm) tube pan, or 10in (25cm) round cake pan and 1-cup ramekin

MAKES 1 LOAF

9oz (250g) potatoes, peeled, and each cut into 2–3 pieces

2½ tsp dried yeast

8 tbsp butter, plus extra for greasing

1 large bunch of chives, snipped

2 tbsp granulated sugar

2 tsp salt

3⅓ cups strong white bread flour, plus extra for dusting

1 Simmer the potatoes in water until tender. Drain, reserving 1 cup of the liquid. Mash with a potato masher. Let them cool.

2 In a small bowl, sprinkle the yeast over ¼ cup of warm water. Stir it once and leave for 5 minutes until dissolved. Melt half the butter in a pan. Put the reserved potato liquid, mashed potatoes, dissolved yeast, and melted butter into a bowl. Mix in the chives, sugar, and salt.

3 Stir in half the flour and mix well. Add the remaining flour, ¼ cup at a time, mixing well after each addition, until the dough pulls away from the sides of the bowl. It should be soft and slightly sticky. Knead the dough on a floured work surface for 5–7 minutes, until smooth and elastic.

4 Put the dough in a greased bowl, cover with a damp kitchen towel, and leave in a warm place for 1–1½ hours, until doubled.

5 Grease a 10in (25cm) tube pan or 10in (25cm) round cake pan. If using a pan, grease the outside of a 1-cup ramekin and place it upside down in the center. Melt the remaining butter. Turn the dough out and knock back. Cover and let rest for 5 minutes. Pinch off about 30 walnut-sized pieces. Roll each piece into a smooth ball.

6 Put a few balls into the dish of melted butter and turn to coat. Transfer to the mold or pan. Repeat with the remaining dough. Cover with a dry kitchen towel, and leave in a warm place for about 40 minutes, until the dough has risen to fill the mold or pan.

7 Preheat the oven to 375°F (190°C). Bake the bread for 40–45 minutes until it is golden brown. Let it cool slightly, then carefully unmold. Serve, pulling the bread apart, while still warm.

PREPARE AHEAD

The dough can be made, kneaded, and left to rise in the fridge overnight. Shape the dough, allow it to return to room temperature, then bake as directed. You can also freeze it for up to 12 weeks.

CALORIES: 2730kcals/11545kJ

CARBOHYDRATE: 381g
sugar: 38g

FAT: 110g
saturated: 68g

SALT: 8g

FIBER: 22g

Brown soda bread

This Irish bread has a light, cake-like texture. It requires no kneading, so is a wonderfully effort-free loaf to make.

10-15 mins   35-40 mins

MAKES 1 LOAF

unsalted butter, for greasing

2¾ cups stone-ground whole wheat flour, plus extra for dusting

1½ tsp baking soda

1½ tsp salt

2 cups buttermilk, plus extra if needed

1 Preheat the oven to 400°F (200°C). Grease a baking sheet with butter. Sift the flour, baking soda, and salt into a large bowl, pouring in any bran left in the sieve. Mix thoroughly and make a well in the center.

2 Gradually pour the buttermilk into the center of the well. With your hands, quickly draw in the flour to make a soft, slightly sticky dough. Do not overwork the dough. Add a little more buttermilk if it seems dry.

3 Turn the dough onto a floured surface, and quickly shape into a round loaf. Put the loaf on the baking sheet and pat it down into a round, about 2in (5cm) high. Make a cross ½in (1cm) deep in the top of the loaf with a very sharp knife or scalpel.

4 Bake the loaf in the preheated oven for 35–40 minutes, until golden brown. Turn it over and tap the bottom; it should sound hollow when cooked. Transfer to a wire rack and let it cool slightly. It is best served warm from the oven, or the next day as very good toast.

Children who don't like brown bread will often eat something they have made themselves. This is an easy starter loaf for budding chefs with no yeast, rising, or proofing. *Fussy eaters!*

CALORIES: 1772kcals/7531kJ

CARBOHYDRATE: 320g
sugar: 34g

FAT: 18g
saturated: 6g

SALT: 11g

FIBER: 60g

Dinner rolls

You can shape these rolls however you prefer; an assortment of shapes looks attractive in a basket.

45-55 mins, plus rising and proofing   15-18 mins

MAKES 16

⅔ cup whole milk

3 tsp dried yeast

4 tbsp unsalted butter, cut into cubes, plus extra for greasing

2 tbsp granulated sugar

2 whole eggs, plus 1 yolk for glazing

2 tsp salt

3¾ cups white bread flour, plus extra for dusting

poppy seeds, for sprinkling (optional)

1 Bring the milk to a boil. Put ¼ cup into a small bowl and sprinkle in the yeast. Leave for 5 minutes to dissolve, stirring once. Add the butter and sugar to the remaining milk in the pan until melted. Cool to warm.

2 In a bowl, lightly beat the eggs. Add the sweetened milk, salt, and dissolved yeast. Gradually stir in the flour to get a soft, slightly sticky dough. Knead on a floured surface for 5–7 minutes until elastic.

3 Put in a greased bowl, cover, and leave in a warm place for 1–1½ hours until doubled in size. Grease 2 baking sheets. Put the dough on a floured surface and knock it back. Cut into 16 pieces.

4 For round rolls, roll a piece to form a smooth ball. For a knot, roll into a rope, then shape into an "8." For a "snail," wind into a spiral.

5 Put on the baking sheets. Leave in a warm place for 30 minutes. Preheat the oven to 425°F (220°C). Beat the yolk with 1 tbsp of water, brush the rolls, and sprinkle with poppy seeds (if using). Bake for 15–18 minutes. Serve warm.

HOW TO FREEZE

These rolls can be frozen at the shaping stage for up to 12 weeks, defrosted thoroughly, then glazed and baked.

CALORIES: 173kcals/734kJ

CARBOHYDRATE: 27g
sugar: 3g

FAT: 5g
saturated: 2.5g

SALT: 0.5g

FIBER: 1.4g

Walnut and rosemary loaf

A perfect combination of flavors; the texture of the nuts is fabulous here. It is very good eaten with goat cheese.

20 mins, plus proofing 30-40 mins

MAKES 2 LOAVES

3 tsp dried yeast

1 tsp granulated sugar

2½ cups white bread flour, plus extra for dusting

1 tsp salt

3 tbsp olive oil, plus 2 tsp extra for oiling and glazing

6oz (175g) walnuts, roughly chopped

3 tbsp finely chopped rosemary leaves

1 Mix the yeast and sugar in a small bowl, then stir in ½ cup of warm water. Leave for 10–15 minutes, or until the mixture becomes creamy.

2 Put the flour in a bowl with the salt and the oil, then add the yeast mixture and ¾ cup of warm water. Mix until it comes together to form a dough. Knead on a floured surface for 15 minutes. Knead in the nuts and rosemary, then put in an oiled bowl. Cover with a kitchen towel. Leave in a warm place for 1½ hours until doubled.

3 Knock the air out of the dough and knead for a few more minutes. Halve it, and shape each half into a 6in (15cm) round loaf. Cover with a towel and leave for

30 minutes to rise. Preheat the oven to 450°F (230°C) and oil a large baking sheet.

4 When the dough has doubled, brush with oil and place on the baking sheet. Bake on the middle shelf of the oven for 30–40 minutes until the loaves sound hollow when tapped on the bottom. Cool on a wire rack.

COOKING FOR A CROWD

If you are entertaining, try forming the proofed dough into individual-sized rolls for easy portion control. Let them rise, well spaced out on a baking sheet, as in step 2, then bake for 20-25 minutes, until well risen and golden brown.

Flavored loaves are a great way to let young children experiment with new flavors while eating an item that is familiar to them.

Fussy eaters!

CALORIES: 175kcals/741kJ

CARBOHYDRATE: 27g
sugar: 3g

FAT: 5.5g
saturated: 3g

SALT: 0.5g

FIBER: 1.5g

Quick pumpkin bread

Grated pumpkin keeps this bread moist for up to 3 days. Wrap in waxed paper and store in the fridge.

20 mins   50 mins

MAKES 1 LOAF

1¾ cups all-purpose flour, plus extra for dusting

¾ cup whole wheat flour, plus 1 tsp baking powder

1 tsp baking soda

1 tsp fine salt

4¼oz (125g) pumpkin or butternut squash, peeled, seeded, and roughly grated

1oz (30g) pumpkin seeds

1¼ cups buttermilk

1 Preheat the oven to 425°F (220°C). In a bowl, mix the flours, baking soda, and salt. Add the pumpkin and seeds and stir. Pour in the buttermilk to form a dough.

2 Knead the dough on a floured surface for 2 minutes until it forms a smooth mass. You may need to add more flour. Shape the dough into a 6in (15cm) round. Place on a lined baking sheet.

3 Use a sharp knife to slash a cross into the top. This helps the bread rise when baking. Cook for 30 minutes in the center of the oven until risen. Reduce the oven temperature to 400°F (200°C). Cook for another 20 minutes. The bottom should sound hollow when tapped. Cool on a wire rack for at least 20 minutes before serving.

CLEVER WITH LEFTOVERS

You can also use same amount of any summer or winter squash, such as zucchini, to use up a glut.

CALORIES:	1658cals/7033kJ
CARBOHYDRATE: 304g	
sugar: 26g	
FAT: 21g	
saturated: 4g	
SALT: 7g	
FIBER: 29g	

Sweet potato and rosemary rolls

The gentle, aromatic scent of rosemary makes these rolls something special. Eat them warm, with butter.

20 mins   20-25 mins

MAKES 8

1¾ cups all-purpose flour, plus extra for dusting

¾ cup whole wheat flour, plus 1 tsp baking powder

1 tsp baking soda

1 tsp fine salt

freshly ground black pepper

5oz (140g) sweet potato, finely grated

1 tsp finely chopped rosemary leaves

1 cup buttermilk

CALORIES:	195cals/829kJ
CARBOHYDRATE: 39g	
sugar: 3.5g	
FAT: 1g	
saturated: 0.5g	
SALT: 1.1g	
FIBER: 3.5g	

1 Preheat the oven to 425°F (220°C). Line a baking sheet with parchment paper. In a bowl, mix the flours, baking powder, baking soda, salt, and pepper. Mix in the sweet potato and rosemary.

2 Stir in the buttermilk, bringing the mixture together to form a loose dough. Turn onto a floured surface and knead for 2 minutes to form a smooth dough. You may need a little more flour.

3 Divide into 8 equal pieces and shape each into a tight round. Flatten the tops and cut a cross in the centers with a sharp knife to help them rise in the oven.

4 Place the rolls on the lined baking sheet. Cook in the middle of the oven for 20–25 minutes until the rolls are well risen and golden brown. Transfer to a wire rack and allow to cool for at least 10 minutes before serving.

Zucchini and feta loaf

This simple, savory loaf is the perfect, piquant accompaniment to a bowl of homemade soup on a cold day.

20 mins   40–45 mins

MAKES 1 LOAF

½ cup sunflower or vegetable oil

9oz (250g) zucchini, finely grated

½ tsp salt

1 cup all-purpose flour

½ cup whole wheat flour

1½ tsp baking powder

3 large eggs, lightly beaten

3–4 tbsp whole milk

2 heaping tbsp chopped parsley leaves

3½oz (100g) feta cheese, chopped

1 Preheat the oven to 350°F (180°C). Oil a 1lb (450g) loaf pan and line the bottom with parchment paper. Put the grated zucchini into a colander and toss them in the salt.

2 Sift the flours and baking powder into a large bowl and season well. Whisk the eggs, oil, and milk and mix into the flour.

3 Rinse the zucchini under cold water and press them down well in the colander to remove as much water as possible. Fold the zucchini, parsley, and feta into the loaf mixture.

4 Pour the mixture into the prepared loaf pan and bake in the center of the hot oven for 40–45 minutes, until a skewer inserted into the center comes out clean.

5 Remove the loaf from the oven and turn onto a wire rack. Allow it to cool for at least 10 minutes before cutting into it to serve warm; alternatively, allow it to cool completely before serving. If keeping the loaf for more than 1 day, wrap in plastic wrap and store in the fridge for up to 3 days, or freeze for up to 12 weeks.

CLEVER WITH LEFTOVERS

Although best served warm the same day, this bread is also great toasted, spread with cream cheese, and topped with sliced cucumber and freshly ground black pepper for a quick, healthy lunch.

CALORIES: 1911kcals/7978kJ

CARBOHYDRATE: 145g
sugar: 11g

FAT: 119g
saturated: 30g

SALT: 8g

FIBER: 17g

Zwiebelkuchen

The combination of sour cream and caraway seeds contrast well with the sweet, melting onions in this recipe.

30 mins, plus proving | 1 hr–1 hr 5 mins | ❄

SPECIAL EQUIPMENT
10 x 13in (26 x 32cm) baking sheet
with raised edges

SERVES 8

FOR THE CRUST

4 tsp dried yeast

3 tbsp olive oil, plus extra for greasing

3 cups white bread flour,
plus extra for dusting

1 tsp salt

FOR THE FILLING

4 tbsp unsalted butter

2 tbsp olive oil

1lb 5oz (600g) onions, finely sliced

½ tsp caraway seeds

salt and freshly ground black pepper

⅔ cup (5oz) sour cream

⅔ cup (5oz) crème fraîche

3 large eggs, lightly beaten

1 tbsp all-purpose flour

2½oz (75g) thick-cut bacon, chopped

1 To make the crust, dissolve the yeast in 1 cup of warm water. Add the oil. Sift the flour and salt into a large bowl. Make a well and pour in the wet ingredients. Use your hands to form a soft dough. Turn onto a floured work surface and knead for 10 minutes until elastic.

2 Place the dough in an oiled bowl, cover with plastic wrap, and leave in a warm place for 1–2 hours until doubled in size.

3 For the filling, heat the butter and oil in a large, heavy-bottomed saucepan. Put in the onions and caraway seeds, and season. Cover and cook gently for 20 minutes until soft. Remove the lid and cook for 5 minutes until excess liquid evaporates.

4 In a separate bowl, whisk together the sour cream, crème fraîche, eggs, and all-purpose flour and season well. Mix in the cooked onions and set aside to cool.

5 When the dough has risen, turn it onto a floured work surface and knock it back. Lightly oil a 10 x 13in (26 x 32cm) baking sheet with raised edges. Roll the dough out to roughly the size of the sheet and line the sheet with it. Cover with lightly oiled plastic wrap and leave in a warm place for 30 minutes until puffy.

6 Preheat the oven to 400°F (200°C). Gently push down the dough. Spread the filling over and sprinkle the bacon on top.

7 Place on the top rack of the oven and bake for 35–40 minutes until golden. Remove and let cool for 5 minutes before serving warm or cold.

CALORIES: 480kcals/2008kJ
CARBOHYDRATE: 44g
  sugar: 6g
FAT: 29g
  saturated: 13g
SALT: 0.9g
FIBER: 3.5g

Anadama bread

This dark, sweet cornbread originally hails from New England. It is curiously sweet and savory at the same time.

25 mins, plus proving | 45–50 mins

SERVES 4

½ cup whole milk

½ cup polenta or fine yellow cornmeal

4 tbsp unsalted butter, softened

½ cup blackstrap molasses

2 tsp dried yeast

2½ cups all-purpose flour, plus extra for dusting

1 tsp salt

vegetable oil, for greasing

1 large egg, lightly beaten, for glazing

CALORIES: 653kcals/2761kJ

CARBOHYDRATE: 111g
 sugar: 19g

FAT: 15g
 saturated: 8g

SALT: 1.2g

FIBER: 5g

1 Heat the milk and ½ cup of water in a small saucepan. Bring to a boil and add the polenta. Cook for 1–2 minutes or until it thickens, then remove from the heat. Stir in the butter until well mixed. Beat in the molasses, then set aside to cool.

2 Dissolve the yeast in ½ cup of warm water and stir well. Sift the flour and salt into a bowl and make a well. Gradually stir in the polenta mixture, then add the yeast mixture to make a soft, sticky dough.

3 Turn the dough onto a lightly floured work surface. Knead for about 10 minutes until soft and elastic. It will remain fairly sticky, but should not stick to your hands. Knead in a little flour if it seems too wet. Put the dough in a lightly oiled bowl, cover loosely with plastic wrap, and let rise in a warm place for up to 2 hours. The dough will not double in size, but should be very soft and pliable when well-risen.

4 Turn the dough onto a lightly floured work surface and gently knock it back. Knead it briefly and shape it into a flattened oval, tucking the sides underneath the center of the dough to get a tight, even shape. Place on a large baking sheet and cover loosely with plastic wrap and a clean kitchen towel. Let it rise in a warm place for about 2 hours. The dough is ready to bake when it is tight and well risen, and a finger gently poked into the dough leaves a dent that springs back quickly.

5 Preheat the oven to 350°F (180°C). Place one oven rack in the middle of the oven and another below it, close to the bottom. Boil a pot of water. Brush the loaf with a little beaten egg and slash the top 2 or 3 times with a sharp knife on a diagonal. Dust the top with flour, if desired, and place it on the middle rack. Place a roasting pan on the bottom rack, then quickly pour the boiling water into it and shut the door.

6 Bake for 45–50 minutes until the crust is nicely darkened and the bottom sounds hollow when tapped. Remove from the oven and let cool on a wire rack. Serve with Emmental or Gruyère cheese, or buttered and topped with ham and mustard.

COOK'S TIP

Slashing the loaf allows the bread to continue rising in the oven, and so does the steam from the pan of boiling water. They also help to give the bread a good crust.

Cooking with kids

Cooking with kids

One of the easiest ways to encourage children to eat a healthy, balanced diet is to involve them in preparing their food from as young an age as possible. Tiny toddlers can watch the adults cook from the safety of their highchairs, older children can cook alongside you, and teenagers can be taught to prepare healthy snacks or even meals by themselves. Allowing a child to help in the kitchen may sometimes be messy and time consuming, but try to encourage any interest they show. Teaching children to cook equips them with an appreciation of good healthy food, as well as providing vital skills they will need in adulthood, and it can be the one of the most rewarding things you do for, and with, them.

Safety first

Sharp knives, hot pans, ovens, oven doors, high work surfaces, and a potentially slippery mess on the floor all pose hazards for children. Smaller children should be supervised at all times, and you will need to step in to do the more hazardous jobs, such as chopping and dealing with hot objects. A small step can help children to reach a high work surface safely so they can see what you are doing and where things are. Have strict rules as to which knives are available for their use, and teach them simple lessons like moving handles away from the edge of the stove top to prevent accidents.

Keep it clean

Wiping up spills and messy work surfaces as you go is not just a good rule for safety, but also for food hygiene. Keeping a clean kitchen shows children that hygiene is an important part of preparing food. Remind children to tie back long hair, put on an apron, and wash their hands before they begin—and also after they have touched raw meat, fish, poultry, or eggs. Stress the importance of washing fruit and vegetables before using them, and also of keeping separate, clean cutting boards and knives for raw and cooked foods, and meat and vegetables.

Keep it simple

When you are choosing what to cook with your children, select recipes that they will like to eat and that are not too complicated. Producing a dish that is successful will make them feel proud of their achievement and enjoying the results will encourage them to cook again. Older children, or those with more experience, could try preparing a simple supper for the whole family and deciding on the menu. For teenagers who are about to leave home, it would be useful to get them involved in the budgeting and shopping too.

Slicing vegetables is a job for older children. Show them how to keep their fingers well clear of the blade while they hold the item steady. Be on hand to supervise when sharp knives are in use.

Cooking a family supper such as Chili con came (p470-1) provides more experienced children with a challenge. They will need to think about timings and how to serve it too.

Making your own pizzas (p460-1) is a great way for children to get messy while they knead dough and spread out topping. Step back and let it happen—they are developing their motor skills!

Have fun

If you want to get your children interested in food and cooking, time spent in the kitchen has to be fun and not a chore. Younger children will get messy (probably very messy!), and so will your work surfaces, but the important thing is not to curb their enthusiasm. Unless they are in danger, try not to discourage play, within reason. Children are very tactile, and will want to prod, touch, and squeeze whatever they can. As long as they have clean hands, let them do this, and make sure you involve them with the clearing up too—you can get them into good habits right from the start! Spending a rainy afternoon making Pizza (pp460-1) or Crunchy muffins (pp476-7) is a great way to entertain stir-crazy toddlers or school-age chefs, and you may even get something edible out of it, too!

Try something new

Getting kids involved in cooking also teaches them a lot about food—where it comes from, its seasonality, and its nutritional value. It's a great opportunity to experiment with different textures and flavors, and perhaps try new ingredients that they can choose while out shopping with you. Even the pickiest eaters can be encouraged to try something new when they have been involved in its preparation—and who knows, maybe they will find a food that they love in the process and one that they might want to try again another day!

Tips for success

A little planning while cooking with children will make a big difference. Follow these golden rules to make it (almost) stress-free.

Allow yourself plenty of time for cooking–you can't rush children in the kitchen.

Make sure everyone washes their hands and rolls up their sleeves before they start.

Get ahold of several child-sized aprons to get them in the mood, although it's probably wise to cook in old clothes!

Tie back long hair, and use something to keep any stray strands back, or their hair will be full of food by the time they finish–and the dish full of hair!

Check the children's toy box for child-sized rolling pins.

Place a damp kitchen towel, folded, under cutting boards to keep them from slipping.

Clean up spills as you go, especially from the floor.

For younger children, use small kitchen scissors to chop where possible.

Keep boiling saucepans at the back of the stove top, where they are less likely to be knocked over.

Children love cracking eggs, but if they break them into a small bowl first it will make it easier to extract any stray eggshell before they add them to other ingredients. Use the empty shell to pick out any small bits, as they will stick more easily to this than to anything else.

Teach children to keep raw meat separate from everything else and wash fruit and vegetables before cooking with them.

Mushroom and mozzarella pizza

All children love pizza, and it is one of the most enjoyable things to learn to make. Kneading dough, watching it rise, and the artistry involved in arranging toppings all make this a good project for first-time chefs. The fact that they can choose their own toppings means it is far more likely that they will enjoy the results of their labors, too.

1¼ hrs, plus rising   10 mins

MAKES 4

2¾ cups white bread flour, plus extra for dusting

1 x ¼oz package fast-acting yeast

pinch of salt

¼ cup olive oil, plus extra for greasing

FOR THE MUSHROOM AND MOZZARELLA TOPPING

1 tbsp olive oil

4½oz (125g) mushrooms, sliced

2-3 tbsp tomato paste or sauce

5½oz (150g) mozzarella, torn into pieces

VARIATION

The tomato and olive pizza (see right) is made without cheese, which is great for those who don't want mozzarella, or who are lactose intolerant. If you really love cheese on your pizza, add 2 handfuls of grated mozzarella before you put on the tomatoes and olives.

Cook's tip

The dough must be well kneaded, until it is springy and easy to stretch thinly without breaking. If your children find it difficult to do by hand, using a food processor with a dough hook will help.

CALORIES: 659kcals/2775kJ

CARBOHYDRATE: 91g
  sugar: 3g

FAT: 23g
  saturated: 7g

SALT: 0.7g

FIBER: 6g

1 Sift the flour into a bowl and add the yeast and salt. Make a well in the center, then slowly add 1½ cups of warm water. Mix until it comes together. Add the oil and mix until it forms a soft dough.

3 Now put the dough in an oiled bowl and cover the bowl with plastic wrap. Leave it in a warm place for 30–40 minutes, or until the dough mixture has about doubled in size.

5 On a floured surface, knead the dough with your knuckles to knock out the air. Then roll it out thinly, rolling away from you and turning it as you go. The pizza base needs to be about 8in (20cm) wide.

2 Place the dough on a lightly floured work surface. Knead firmly using the heel of your hand, folding the dough over as you go. Do this until the dough becomes soft and spongy.

4 Meanwhile, for the topping, heat the oil in a pan over low heat and cook the mushrooms for 2 minutes. When the dough has risen, preheat the oven to 475°F (240°C). Place a baking sheet inside to get hot.

6 Spread the tomato paste or passata over the pizza base and smooth it out evenly. Top evenly with the mushrooms, then the cheese. Bake for 10 minutes until the crust is golden and the cheese is bubbling.

Play with flavors!

Here are three other toppings to put on your pizza. Why not make up more of your own?

PEPPER AND PEPPERONI

Top with 2–3 tbsp tomato paste or sauce; 10 small slices of pepperoni; ½ a yellow bell pepper, sliced; and 5½oz (150g) mozzarella, torn into pieces.

HAM AND PINEAPPLE

Top with 2–3 tbsp tomato paste or sauce; 3 slices of ham, cut into strips; 1 small can of pineapple pieces, drained; and 5½oz (150g) mozzarella, torn into pieces.

TOMATO AND OLIVE

Top with 2–3 tbsp tomato paste or sauce; 3 tomatoes, sliced; a handful of pitted black olives, sliced; and fresh basil leaves, to serve.

Pepper and pepperoni

Ham and pineapple

Mushroom and mozzarella

Tomato and olive

Tortillas

Making tortillas is a great way to get children involved in cooking because they are so quick and easy to make. While the dough is rising, the child can help you prepare healthy fillings such as lettuce, shredded carrots, and grilled chicken. Make an easy Guacamole or Salsa (see p290 and 288) and you have a family-friendly feast.

10 mins, plus resting   15–20 mins

MAKES 8

1¾ cups all-purpose flour, plus extra for dusting

1 scant tsp salt

½ tsp baking powder

¼ cup lard or white vegetable fat, chilled and cut into cubes, plus extra for greasing

PREPARE AHEAD

Cooled tortillas can be stored overnight, wrapped in plastic wrap, and chilled in the fridge; or you can freeze them for up to 12 weeks. To reheat tortillas from fresh or frozen, scrunch up a large piece of waxed paper and soak it in water. Squeeze out the excess water, use the paper to wrap the tortillas, and bake in an oven preheated to 350°F (180°C) for 10 minutes.

Cook's tip

Be careful when frying the tortillas, as the pan can get very hot. Reduce the temperature to low after cooking the first few, so that they don't burn, or cook too quickly for children to be able to turn them easily.

CALORIES: 184kcals/774kJ

CARBOHYDRATE: 27g
 sugar: 0.5g

FAT: 7g
 saturated: 2.5g

SALT: 0.7g

FIBER: 1.5g

1 Put the flour, salt, and baking powder into a large bowl. Add the lard or vegetable fat. Lightly rub in the lard with your fingertips until the mixture looks like fine crumbs and there are no larger lumps of fat.

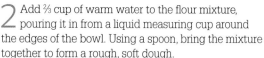

2 Add ⅔ cup of warm water to the flour mixture, pouring it in from a liquid measuring cup around the edges of the bowl. Using a spoon, bring the mixture together to form a rough, soft dough.

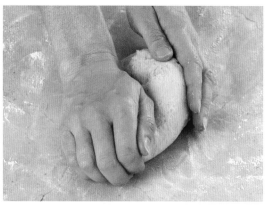

3 Turn it out onto a lightly floured work surface and knead for a few minutes until smooth. Put the dough in a greased bowl and cover with plastic wrap. Rest in a warm place for 1 hour, until puffed up.

4 Turn the dough onto a floured work surface and divide it into 8 equal portions with a sharp knife. Take one piece and leave the others covered with plastic wrap to prevent them from drying out.

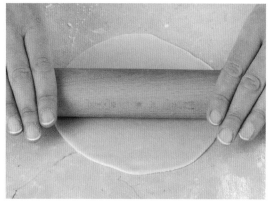

5 Roll each piece of dough out on a floured work surface to a circle 8–10in (20–25cm) in diameter. Stack the rolled tortillas with a piece of plastic wrap between each. Heat a frying pan over medium heat.

6 Take a tortilla and dry fry for 1 minute. Turn it over and continue to fry until both sides are cooked and browned in places. Transfer to a wire rack and repeat to cook all the remaining tortillas. Serve warm or cool.

Cornbread

While bread is satisfying to make, it is a lengthy process and can be quite difficult. Cornbread rises with baking powder, not yeast, so is quicker to prepare and easier to produce. Young bakers should start out with easy recipes such as this. Adding corn to the batter is another thing guaranteed to please children and adults alike.

15–20 mins · 10 mins, plus cooling

SPECIAL EQUIPMENT

9in (23cm) flameproof cast-iron frying pan or similar-sized loose-bottomed round cake pan

SERVES 8

4 tbsp unsalted butter or bacon dripping, melted and cooled, plus extra for greasing

2 corn cobs, approx. 7oz (200g) weight of kernels

1 cup fine yellow cornmeal or polenta

¾ cup white bread flour

¼ cup granulated sugar

1 tbsp baking powder

1 tsp salt

2 large eggs

1 cup milk

VARIATION

Try adding scraps of fried bacon, scallions, or grilled red bell peppers to the batter. A handful of grated cheese, some fresh herbs, chopped chiles, or even some smoked paprika would also work well.

Cook's tip

Cornbread is delicious eaten when it's still warm, but it doesn't keep well. It is easy to prepare, so try and make it on the day you want to eat it. Any leftovers work really well used as part of a stuffing for a roast chicken.

CALORIES: 272kcals/1143kJ

CARBOHYDRATE: 36g
 sugar: 8g

FAT: 10.5g
 saturated: 5.5g

SALT: 1.1g

FIBER: 2g

1 Preheat the oven to 425°F (220°C) Grease a 9in (23cm) flameproof cast-iron pan, or similar-sized loose-bottomed cake pan, and place it in the oven. Cut away the kernels from the cobs.

3 Pour three-quarters of the milk mixture into the flour mixture and stir until well combined. Add the remaining milk mixture and stir just until blended, with no patches of flour remaining.

5 Quickly brush the top with butter or bacon dripping. Be as even as possible so that the surface of the cornbread is protected from the fierce heat of the oven. Bake for 20–25 minutes.

2 Sift the cornmeal or polenta, flour, sugar, baking powder, and salt into a bowl. Add the corn and stir until evenly blended. In another bowl, mix together the eggs, butter or dripping, and milk.

4 Carefully take the hot pan out of the oven and pour in the batter, using a spatula to help you get it all into the pan, and working quickly so as not to lose too much heat; the fat in the pan should sizzle.

6 When it is ready, the bread should shrink from the sides of the pan and a skewer inserted into the center should emerge clean. Let the cornbread cool slightly. Serve, in wedges, with soup.

Tuna patties

These simple fishcakes are so easy to make, and kids will love mashing and shaping the patties.

15 mins, plus cooling • 10 mins

MAKES 8

1 x 7oz (200g) can tuna in spring water, drained

1lb (450g) cooked, cooled mashed potatoes

6 scallions, very finely chopped

2 tbsp chopped flat-leaf parsley leaves

salt and freshly ground black pepper

1–2 tbsp olive oil

green beans and lemon wedges, to serve

CALORIES: 97kcals/407kJ

CARBOHYDRATE: 8g
    sugar: 0.7g

FAT: 4g
    saturated: 1.5g

SALT: 0.1g

FIBER: 1g

---

1 Place all the ingredients, except the oil, in a bowl and stir well to combine. Divide into 8 portions. Shape each portion into a 3in (8cm) round patty.

2 Heat the oil in a large, non-stick frying pan over medium heat and cook the patties for 5 minutes on each side. (You may need to do this in batches; if so, keep them warm while you cook the rest, adding more oil if needed.) Transfer to warmed plates and serve with green beans and lemon wedges.

VARIATION

Older children might like to spice these up a bit by adding ½–1 tsp of chile powder to the ingredients at the start.

CLEVER WITH LEFTOVERS

If you have leftover mashed potatoes and a few items in your pantry, this recipe will make good use of them.

Chicken yakitori

With a little grown-up help, these skewers can be cooked under the broiler or even on a barbecue.

15 mins, plus cooling, and marinating • 10–12 mins

SPECIAL EQUIPMENT

8 bamboo skewers

MAKES 8

2 tbsp light soy sauce

¼ cup rice wine

1 tbsp granulated sugar

1 tsp cornstarch

1 tsp sunflower or vegetable oil

1 tsp fresh ginger, very finely chopped or grated

1 garlic clove, crushed

14oz (400g) boneless, skinless chicken thighs, cut into ½in (1cm) strips

---

CALORIES: 74kcals/312kJ

CARBOHYDRATE: 3g
    sugar: 2g

FAT: 2g
    saturated: 0.5g

SALT: 0.8g

FIBER: 0g

---

1 Put all the ingredients, except the chicken, into a saucepan with 2 tbsp of cold water and whisk to dissolve the cornstarch. Bring to a boil, reduce the heat to a low simmer, and cook for 2 minutes until it thickens. Cool completely. Pour the sauce over the chicken, and mix. Cover and chill for 1 hour, or up to 4 hours. Meanwhile, soak 8 bamboo skewers in water.

2 Preheat the broiler to its highest setting and line a baking sheet with foil, allowing the foil to overlap the edge. Thread the chicken onto the skewers and lay in a line along the pan, farthest away from the foil overlap. Fold the overlapping foil over the exposed handles to keep them from burning.

3 Broil for 5–6 minutes on each side, brushing with leftover marinade occasionally, until well cooked and caramelized in places.

COOK'S TIP

It is wise to snip off the ends of the skewers after threading on the chicken, to avoid any injuries.

Ham, cheese, and broccoli crépe cannelloni

Using store-bought crépes makes this recipe simple and achievable even for young children in the kitchen.

15 mins   **30 mins**

MAKES 8

butter, for greasing

4¼oz (125g) small broccoli florets

7oz (200g) low-fat cream cheese
  with garlic and herbs

⅔ cup half-and-half

5½oz (150g) ham, finely chopped

scant 1oz (25g) finely grated
  Parmesan cheese

8 store-bought crépes

freshly ground black pepper

2oz (60g) grated mozzarella cheese

½ cup fresh bread crumbs

green salad, to serve

1 Preheat the oven to 350°F (180°C). Grease a baking sheet. Cook the broccoli in boiling water for 5 minutes. Drain.

2 Place the cream cheese and half-and-half in a pan over medium heat. Warm through, stirring, until the cream cheese has melted and the mixture is smooth. Stir in the broccoli, ham, and Parmesan.

3 Place a crépe on a work surface and spread one-eighth of the filling on top, seasoning with black pepper. Roll up and place on the baking sheet. Repeat with the remaining crépes and filling.

4 Sprinkle with mozzarella and bread crumbs. Bake in the oven for 20 minutes. Serve the cannelloni hot with a green salad.

VARIATION

If your family avoids pork or red meat, use canned, drained tuna, or finely chopped chicken, instead of the ham in this recipe.

CALORIES: 270kcals/1130kJ

CARBOHYDRATE: 24g
  sugar: 3g

FAT: 13g
  saturated: 7g

SALT: 1.6g

FIBER: 0.5g

Cheesy fish parcels

Fish is very good for you, but it can be a bit boring. Try these tasty parcels for a fun, super-quick meal.

10 mins   15–20 mins

SERVES 4

4 thick fillets of skinless white fish, approx. 4–5½oz (115–150g) each

1 tbsp olive oil

salt and freshly ground black pepper

8 slices wafer-thin ham

8 slices pre-sliced sharp cheese, such as aged Cheddar

1 Preheat the oven to 400°F (200°C). Brush each piece of fish on both sides with a little olive oil and season well.

2 Wrap a piece of ham over a piece of fish and turn the fish over, using the oil to help the ham stick to the fish. Place a slice of cheese on top of the fish (you may need to trim the cheese to fit the shape of the fish).

3 Cover the cheese with another piece of ham, tucking the sides under to make a ham-wrapped fish

and cheese parcel. Place the fish on a non-stick baking sheet and top with another piece of cheese. Do the same with the remaining fish, ham, and cheese, to make 4 parcels.

4 Bake the fish in the hot oven for 15–20 minutes, until the cheese is golden and melted and the fish is cooked through.

VARIATION

This family dish can be smartened up for a dinner party by using prosciutto instead of cooked ham, and fontina cheese instead of Cheddar.

CALORIES: 305kcals/1269kJ

CARBOHYDRATE: 0.2g
  sugar: 0.2g

FAT: 18g
  saturated: 9g

SALT: 1.5g

FIBER: 0g

Stuffed baked potatoes

Turn a baked potato into a complete, balanced meal with this simple, tasty stuffing.

20 mins,   1 hr 20 mins
plus cooling

MAKES 8

4 baking potatoes

2 tbsp butter, softened

salt and freshly ground black pepper

2 tomatoes, seeded and finely chopped (see p191)

3½oz (100g) ham, finely chopped

2 scallions, finely chopped (optional)

3½oz (100g) grated cheese, such as Cheddar

green salad or garlic bread, to serve

1 Preheat the oven to 400°F (200°C). Prick each potato and bake on an oven rack for 1 hour. Let cool. Cut each in half lengthwise and use a spoon to scoop out the middles. Put the scooped-out potato in a bowl and mash with the butter and seasoning.

2 Mix the tomato into the potato with the ham, scallions (if using), and half the cheese.

3 Stuff back inside the skins. Place on a baking sheet and scatter with the remaining cheese.

4 Bake for 20 minutes, until brown, crispy, and hot through. Cool for 5 minutes before serving with a green salad or garlic bread.

VARIATION

If your family does not eat meat, these are great made with tuna and canned, drained corn, instead of ham.

PREPARE AHEAD

To make the most of your oven, and to save money, bake the potatoes a day or two in advance, while you are using the oven for something else.

CALORIES: 187kcals/786kJ

CARBOHYDRATE: 21g
  sugar: 2g

FAT: 8g
  saturated: 4.5g

SALT: 0.7g

FIBER: 2.5g

Chicken quesadillas

This Mexican dish makes a filling snack, or a delicious main meal when served with red rice (see p225) and salad.

30 mins | 20-25 mins

MAKES 4

3 skinless chicken breasts, approx. 14oz (400g) in total

2 tbsp olive oil, plus extra for cooking

salt and freshly ground black pepper

1 red bell pepper, cut into ¾in (2cm) cubes

4 scallions, finely chopped

½ cup canned corn, drained

1 tsp smoked paprika (optional)

8 x 8in (20cm) soft flour tortillas

4½oz (125g) grated cheese, such as Cheddar

1 Preheat the broiler to its highest setting, or heat a grill pan over medium heat. Rub the chicken breasts with 1 tbsp of the olive oil and season them well on both sides. Cook them either on the pan or under the broiler for 12–15 minutes, turning occasionally, until cooked through. Set aside to cool.

2 In a large, heavy-bottomed frying pan, heat the remaining 1 tbsp of olive oil and cook the pepper over medium heat for 5 minutes until it softens but only colors slightly. Add the scallion and cook for another 2 minutes. Remove the vegetables from the pan and put them in a large bowl. Wipe the frying pan carefully with paper towels.

3 Once the chicken is cooled, cut it into small pieces and mix it into the vegetables, with the corn, smoked paprika (if using), and some extra seasoning.

4 Heat a little oil in the pan over medium-low heat and place a tortilla in it. After a minute turn it over. Take it off the heat and spread one-quarter of the chicken and vegetable mixture over the surface of the tortilla. Cover it with one-quarter of the cheese, then put another tortilla on top, pressing it down well. Return the frying pan to the heat and cook for 2 minutes on each side, turning it when the underneath is golden brown and crispy and the cheese is melting.

Remove from the pan and cut into quarters to serve. Repeat to cook the other 3 quesadillas.

VARIATION

If you would like a spicier quesadilla, try adding some chopped red chile to the pan with the scallions, and sprinkle in a little freshly chopped cilantro with the grated cheese.

CALORIES: 585kcals/2463kJ

CARBOHYDRATE: 63g
sugar: 5g

FAT: 19g
saturated: 8g

SALT: 1.6g

FIBER: 4.5g

Chili con carne

Most children start to cook by learning a few simple baking recipes. Progressing to a main meal can be daunting, but this simple recipe is a good place to start. It is adaptable, and hard to overcook. Plus you can serve it with child-friendly side dishes, such as tortilla chips and Guacamole (see p290), which always go down well.

30 mins   40 mins

SERVES 6

1½ large onions, finely chopped

1 tbsp olive oil

9oz (250g) lean ground beef

1 garlic clove, finely chopped

½ green chile, finely chopped

¼ tsp chile powder

¼ tsp paprika

1 x 14oz (400g) can red kidney beans, drained, and rinsed

1 bay leaf

1 x 14oz (400g) can of chopped tomatoes

½ tsp dried oregano

freshly ground black pepper

basmati rice, to serve

tortilla chips, to serve

salsa, to serve

VARIATION

If your children don't like kidney beans, try using smaller navy or cannellini beans, which are easier to eat.

> Ask an adult to cut up the chile. It can sting your eyes if you accidentally touch them with your fingers.

Cook's tip

If your children do not like spicy food, you can cut down on the amount of chile, or omit it. Also try serving small bowls of sour cream and grated cheese in addition to the other toppings.

CALORIES: 153kcals/644kJ

CARBOHYDRATE: 11g
  sugar: 5g

FAT: 6g
  saturated: 2g

SALT: 0.6g

FIBER: 4.5g

1 Cook the onions in the oil in a pan over medium heat for 5 minutes, until softened. Add the beef and turn to brown all over. Stir in the garlic, chile, chile powder, and paprika, and cook for another 5 minutes.

2 When the spices in the beef mixture start to smell fragrant, add the kidney beans and bay leaf to the pan and cook the mixture for another 2 minutes, until the beans are just heated through.

3 Add the tomatoes and oregano and stir to mix them evenly into the mixture. Bring to a boil, season with pepper, then reduce the heat and simmer over low heat for 40 minutes, stirring occasionally.

4 Ask an adult to cook enough rice to serve everyone, using the cooking method on the rice package. Drain it in a colander. Take the bay leaf out of the chili. Serve the chili with the rice, tortilla chips, and salsa.

Shrimp and vegetable kebabs

Children really like to eat things on sticks, perhaps because it allows them to eat with their fingers. Compiling skewers of their own mean children can add their favorite flavors, and maybe try a few new ones, too. These kebabs are crammed full of healthy vegetables and low-fat protein, and make a fun option at a summer barbecue.

25 mins, plus marinating   15 mins

SPECIAL EQUIPMENT
4 bamboo skewers
rectangular dish that will fit the length of the skewers

SERVES 4

FOR THE MARINADE
juice of 1 lemon
juice of 1 lime
2 tbsp reduced-salt soy sauce
1 garlic clove, crushed or finely chopped
1 tsp light brown sugar

FOR THE KEBABS
½ red bell pepper
½ yellow bell pepper
½ red onion
1 small zucchini
8 cherry tomatoes
5½oz (150g) cooked, shelled, and deveined large shrimp
salad, to serve (optional)

! Use scissors to snip the sharp end off the skewers before eating, to avoid accidents.

Cook's tip

If you are using wooden skewers under a gas grill or on a barbecue they can burn. To avoid this, soak the skewers for at least 30 minutes in cold water before using.

CALORIES: 70kcals/292kJ
CARBOHYDRATE: 7.5g
  sugar: 6.5g
FAT: 0.5g
  saturated: 0.1g
SALT: 1.2g
FIBER: 2g

1 Soak 4 bamboo skewers in water for 30 minutes. Make the marinade by mixing the ingredients together in a glass container. Carefully cut the peppers and red onion into chunks. Slice the zucchini.

2 Thread the vegetables and shrimp onto the skewers, being sure that each kebab gets a piece of everything. Place the kebabs into a rectangular dish long enough to fit them.

3 Pour the marinade over the kebabs, then turn to coat, so that all sides of the kebabs are coated in marinade. Cover, and put the kebabs into the fridge for 1 hour. Turn them over again after 30 minutes.

4 Ask an adult to preheat a broiler to its highest setting, and to broil the kebabs for 15 minutes, turning to cook all sides evenly. Baste the shrimp every 5 minutes with the marinade (discard any leftover marinade).

Granola breakfast bars

Most children love to bake, but eating the results of their efforts may not always be the healthiest thing. Try baking this modern take on an old-fashioned favorite—oatmeal cookies. Granola breakfast bars make a perfect breakfast-on-the-go for hurried teens, or a lunch-box treat for children of all ages.

15 mins | 30 mins, plus cooling

SPECIAL EQUIPMENT
12 x 9 x 1½in (30 x 23 x 4cm) baking pan

MAKES 12

8 tbsp butter, plus extra for greasing

½ cup light brown sugar

½ cup corn syrup or honey

3⅓ cups rolled oats

3½oz (100g) raisins

1¾oz (50g) mixed nuts, chopped

VARIATION

This basic recipe can be varied to suit the tastes and ages of your children. Kids can add any combination of dried fruit, nuts, and seeds they like, as long as the overall weight remains the same. A handful of chocolate chips would also be fun.

Cook's tip

A potato masher will help little hands to get the breakfast bars well compressed in the baking pan and evenly spread the mix around before cooking.

CALORIES: 266kcals/1113kJ

CARBOHYDRATE: 36g
  sugar: 21g

FAT: 12g
  saturated: 6g

SALT: 0.17g

FIBER: 2.3g

1 Ask an adult to preheat the oven to 300°F (150°C). Grease your baking pan. Ask an adult to melt the butter, sugar, and corn syrup or honey in a saucepan over low heat.

2 Measure out the rolled oats, raisins, and mixed nuts and place them into a large mixing bowl. Mix in the melted ingredients from the saucepan, using a wooden spoon to combine them evenly.

3 Spread the mixture evenly in a 12 x 9 x 1½in (30 x 23 x 4cm) baking pan, using a potato masher to help compress the mixture well down in the pan. Bake for 20–30 minutes, or until golden brown.

4 When the mixture is baked, let it cool slightly. When cool enough to handle, cut it into 12 squares with a knife, holding the warm pan with a cloth. Take the squares out when they're cold.

Crunchy muffins

Muffins are a good alternative to a whole cake when it comes to baking with children. They are easy to make, and quick to cook. In addition, they come in individual portions, and impatient young cooks do not have to wait until they are cold to fill or ice them. The method for muffins is very forgiving, and allows for a few lumps in the batter.

30–35 mins   25 mins, plus cooling

SPECIAL EQUIPMENT

12 paper muffin liners

12-hole muffin pan

MAKES 12

1¾ cups all-purpose flour

1 tbsp baking powder

½ tsp salt

½ cup granulated sugar

1 large egg

2 tbsp vegetable oil

1 cup whole milk

4½oz (125g) raspberries

5½oz (150g) white chocolate, finely chopped

3oz (85g) crunchy oat cereal

VARIATION

Frozen raspberries would be fine for this recipe, as long as you thaw them completely. Try using other fresh or frozen fruits, such as strawberries, blueberries, or blackberries. Nuts, dried fruits, or chocolate chips would also taste great!

Cook's tip

The good thing about muffins is that it doesn't matter if the batter is a little lumpy. In fact, an over-whisked batter will result in heavy, dense muffins, so this a perfect recipe to try with young children.

CALORIES: 271kcals/1141kJ

CARBOHYDRATE: 37g
  sugar: 21g

FAT: 9g
  saturated: 3.5g

SALT: 0.7g

FIBER: 1.5g

1 Ask an adult to preheat the oven to 400°F (200°C). Sift the all-purpose flour, baking powder, and salt into a mixing bowl, tapping the edges to encourage it to slip through. Stir in the sugar.

2 Crack the egg into a glass measuring cup and add the oil. Beat the egg and oil together with a whisk until they are light and fluffy. Add the milk and then whisk the mixture until well combined.

3 Fold the egg mixture into the flour mixture. The mixture will be lumpy but, when you have finished mixing, no flour should be visible in the batter. Now fold in the raspberries and chocolate.

4 Put 12 paper muffin liners into a 12-hole muffin pan and spoon the mixture into them, being sure to divide it equally between the liners. The easiest way is to use two teaspoons.

5 Sprinkle some of the crunchy oat cereal on top of each muffin, dividing it equally between them. Bake the muffins in the center of the hot oven for 25 minutes, or until risen and golden.

6 Remove the muffins from the oven and allow them to cool for 5 minutes in the muffin pan, or until cool enough to handle. Now carefully and gently transfer each one to a wire rack to cool completely.

Easy crust apple pies

Some pastry can be hard to work with, but not filo. Even younger kids will find it easy to make these tasty treats.

15 mins   25 mins

SERVES 4

2 red apples, unpeeled, cored, each cut into 8 pieces

1 tsp ground cinnamon

2 tbsp light brown sugar

4 sheets of filo pastry, each approx. 10 x 18in (25 x 46cm)

3 tbsp unsalted butter, melted

vanilla ice cream, to serve

1 Preheat the oven to 400°F (200°C). Line a large baking sheet with parchment paper. Place the apple wedges, cinnamon, and sugar in a bowl and mix well to coat.

2 Cut each sheet of pastry in half widthwise. Place one piece of pastry on the work surface and brush with melted butter. Top with a second piece, perpendicular to the first, to form a fat cross and brush with butter.

3 Place 4 of the apple wedges in the center of the pastry and pull the edges of the pastry toward the center, scrunching them to form an open crust for the apple. The apple should be poking out of the middle. Place on the lined baking sheet. Repeat with the remaining pastry and apple.

4 Brush the pies with the remaining butter and bake for 20–25 minutes, or until the apples are tender. Serve warm or at room temperature with vanilla ice cream.

CALORIES: 249kcals/1040kJ

CARBOHYDRATE: 34g
  sugar: 16g

FAT: 10g
  saturated: 5.5g

SALT: 0.7g

FIBER: 2g

Marshmallow crispy "cakes"

These perennial favorites take just minutes to make. Decorate them with colorful sprinkles, if you like.

5 mins,   5 mins
plus cooling

SPECIAL EQUIPMENT

7in (18cm) square non-stick cake pan

MAKES 16

4 tbsp unsalted butter, plus extra for greasing

2 cups mini white marshmallows

3 cups crispy rice cereal

sprinkles, to decorate (optional)

1 Grease a 7in (18cm) square non-stick cake pan. In a large, heavy-bottomed saucepan, melt the butter over low heat until it has just melted. Stir in the marshmallows and cook over very low heat, stirring constantly, until they melt. The mixture will be very thick.

2 Take the pan off the heat and stir in the cereal. Mix until the mixture comes away from the sides of the pan. Pour into the cake pan and use the back of a large spoon that has been dipped in water to press down as firmly as possible.

3 Sprinkle with a thin layer of sprinkles (if using) and press down again with the damp spoon to secure them in place. Set aside at room temperature for at least 1 hour, then turn out onto a board and cut into 16 equal-sized cubes with a very sharp knife.

COOK'S TIP

These are very sweet, which is why they should be quite small. If you would like them to be more substantial, or for older children, just double the amount of ingredients to make a deeper "cake."

CALORIES: 62kcals/261kJ

CARBOHYDRATE: 9g
  sugar: 4g

FAT: 2.5g
  saturated: 2g

SALT: trace

FIBER: trace

Churros

These cinnamon- and sugar-sprinkled Spanish snacks take minutes to make and will be devoured just as quickly.

10 mins, plus resting   **5–10 mins**

SPECIAL EQUIPMENT
oil thermometer

piping bag with ¾in (2cm) nozzle

SERVES 4

2 tbsp unsalted butter

1½ cups all-purpose flour

¼ cup granulated sugar

1 tsp baking powder

3½ cups sunflower or vegetable oil, for deep-frying

1 tsp ground cinnamon

1 Measure 1 cup of boiling water into a bowl. Add the butter and stir to melt. Sift together the flour, half the sugar, and the baking powder into a bowl. Make a well in the center and slowly pour in the hot butter liquid, beating, until you have a thick paste; you may not need all the liquid. Let cool for 5 minutes.

2 Pour the oil into a large, heavy-bottomed saucepan to a depth of at least 4in (10cm) and heat it to 340–350°F (170–180°C). Keep the saucepan lid nearby and never leave the hot oil unattended. Make sure the temperature remains even, or the churros will burn.

3 Place the mixture into a piping bag with a ¾in (2cm) nozzle. Pipe 2¾in (7cm) lengths of dough into the hot oil, using scissors to snip off the ends. Do not crowd the pan, or the temperature of the oil will reduce. Cook the churros for 1–2 minutes on each side, turning when golden brown. Remove the churros from the oil with a slotted spoon and drain on paper towels.

4 Mix the remaining sugar and cinnamon on a plate and toss the churros in the mixture while hot. Let cool for 5–10 minutes before serving warm. These keep in an airtight container for 1 day.

VARIATION

For richer churros, add egg yolk, more butter, or milk to the batter, but the basic quantities of liquid to dry ingredients should be maintained. Thinner batter gives lighter results, but frying with a more liquid batter takes practice.

CALORIES: 416kcals/1747kJ

CARBOHYDRATE: 49g
  sugar: 13g

FAT: 22g
  saturated: 5.5g

SALT: 0.3g

FIBER: 2g

Chocolate truffles

These make a perfect homemade gift. Some children may prefer them made with milk chocolate.

20 mins, plus chilling   5 mins

SPECIAL EQUIPMENT
electric hand-held mixer
melon baller (optional)

MAKES 12–15

5½oz (150g) good-quality dark chocolate chips

½ cup heavy cream

1 tbsp granulated sugar

1 tsp butter

¼ tsp vanilla extract

pinch of salt

2 tbsp cocoa powder or confectioners' sugar, for dusting

1 Place the chocolate chips in a heatproof bowl. Heat the cream, sugar, butter, vanilla, and salt over low heat until it just begins to boil. Pour it over the chocolate and leave to melt for 2 minutes.

2 With an electric hand-held mixer, beat it to form a thick, smooth "ganache." If it does not completely melt, heat the bowl gently over a pan of simmering water, making sure the bowl does not touch the water, and stir until the chocolate is melted. Place in the fridge to cool and harden for at least 3 hours.

3 When you're ready to make the truffles, set up a bowl of water for your hands, a wide, shallow bowl containing the cocoa, and a plate. Use a melon baller or teaspoon to scoop out small balls of ganache. Dampen your hands and briefly roll the balls until smooth (be prepared for this to get messy). If it is too hard, leave at room temperature for 30 minutes. Place the truffles on the plate and continue until you have used up all the chocolate mixture.

4 Briefly roll the truffles in the cocoa powder to cover, return them to the plate, then cover and chill for at least 2 hours. These will keep in an airtight container in the fridge for up to 5 days.

CALORIES: 93kcals/385kJ
CARBOHYDRATE: 7g
  sugar: 7g
FAT: 7g
  saturated: 4g
SALT: trace
FIBER: 0.4g

No-cook vanilla fudge

This is perfect for younger children to make because it involves no high temperatures and is easy to handle.

15 mins, plus chilling

SPECIAL EQUIPMENT
electric hand-held mixer
1in (3cm) shaped cutter

MAKES 30

4 tbsp unsalted butter, softened

3 heaping tbsp condensed milk, or 1¾oz (50g) by weight

½ tsp vanilla extract

1¾ cups confectioners' sugar, plus extra for dusting

1 In a large bowl, beat the softened butter until very smooth using an electric hand-held mixer. Add the condensed milk and vanilla extract and beat again until smooth.

2 Beat in the confectioners' sugar a little at a time until it has all combined to form a lumpy dough.

3 Using clean hands, press the mixture together to form a ball, then place it on a work surface that has been dusted with confectioners' sugar and knead it gently to form a smooth dough.

4 Lightly dust a rolling pin with confectioners' sugar and roll out the fudge dough to about ¾in (2cm) thick. Use a 1in (3cm) shaped cutter to cut out the sweets. Dip the cutter in a small pile of confectioners' sugar between cuts to ensure that the fudge does not stick to it. You will need to re-roll the fudge to cut all the pieces.

5 Use a metal spatula to move the fudge pieces carefully to a plate. Let them harden, uncovered, in the fridge for at least 3 hours. Store in an airtight container in the fridge for up to 1 week.

VARIATION
Each piece of fudge can be half-dipped into a bowl of melted milk or dark chocolate. You will need 3½oz (100g) of chocolate to half-coat this recipe.

CALORIES: 47kcals/200kJ
CARBOHYDRATE: 8g
  sugar: 8g
FAT: 1.5g
  saturated: 1g
SALT: trace
FIBER: 0g

White chocolate bark

This very easy treat uses dried fruits and nuts to make a snack that is a little more nutritious than most chocolate.

10 mins,
plus cooling

MAKES 14OZ (400G)

10oz (300g) good-quality white chocolate, broken into squares

4½oz (125g) mixed dried fruits and nuts, such as dried cranberries, dried apricots, sliced almonds, or shelled unsalted pistachios

CALORIES: 140kcals/583kJ
CARBOHYDRATE: 12g
  sugar: 12g
FAT: 9g
  saturated: 4g
SALT: trace
FIBER: 0.5g

1 Put the white chocolate in a heatproof bowl and melt it gently over a saucepan of simmering water, stirring occasionally. Make sure that the bowl does not touch the water. Be very careful that no water splashes into the chocolate, as this will make it harden.

2 When the chocolate has melted, remove it from the heat and allow it to cool slightly. On a cutting board, cut up your selection of dried fruits and nuts as small as you can. Set aside 2 tbsp of this mixture, then mix the rest into the chocolate.

3 Brush a small baking sheet with water (to help the waxed paper stay in place), and line it with a piece of waced paper, cut to fit. Pour the chocolate mixture onto the paper and spread it out as thinly as you can, using the back of a damp spoon, making sure there are no gaps. It may not cover the whole pan, but aim for a square measuring 11in (28cm). Scatter the reserved pieces of fruits and nuts over the top and gently press them into the surface with the spoon.

4 Put the chocolate in the fridge for 15 minutes. Now remove the half-set bark and carefully lift it, including the waxed paper, onto a cutting board. Cut the chocolate into squares, leaving it on the paper, then put it back on the pan and return it to the fridge until it hardens. This should take at least 30 minutes. Once it has hardened, break it into squares along the pre-cut lines. These will keep in an airtight container in the fridge for up to 5 days.

VARIATION

For a special, though less nutritious, treat you can use colored sweets and small chocolate treats, instead of the fruits and nuts, for a double chocolate delight.

Chocolate is a great way to introduce nuts into the diet of a child who is otherwise not keen on them. Remember it is vital to check first for nut allergies before offering these to anyone.

Fussy eaters!

Gingerbread men

Making gingerbread men is practically a rite of passage for children. They are quick and easy to make, and the decorating is definitely the most fun a child can have in the kitchen. Get creative with colored icing and even small sweets. This dough is also quite tough, and will withstand several rollings, unlike other cookie doughs.

20 mins | 10–12 mins, plus cooling

SPECIAL EQUIPMENT

4½in (11cm) gingerbread man cutter

piping bag with thin nozzle (optional)

MAKES 16

1¾ cups all-purpose flour, plus extra for dusting

1 tsp baking soda

1½ tsp ground ginger

1½ tsp pumpkin pie spice

7 tbsp unsalted butter, softened and cut into cubes

¾ cup dark brown sugar

¼ cup molasses

1 large egg, lightly beaten

raisins, to decorate

confectioners' sugar, sifted (optional)

PREPARE AHEAD

If you plan to make these with very young children, and want to get to the fun part, prepare the dough ahead of time and chill for up to 2 days, well wrapped in plastic wrap. Bring it back to room temperature before rolling it out.

Cook's tip

For home-made Christmas presents or party bag treats, get your children to make personalised gingerbread men for their guests and wrap them in individual bags, decorated with a pretty ribbon, for a simple gift.

CALORIES: 165kcals/698kJ

CARBOHYDRATE: 26g
  sugar: 13g

FAT: 6g
  saturated: 2.5g

SALT: 0.3g

FIBER: 0.8g

1 Preheat the oven to 375°F (190°C). Sift the flour, baking soda, and spices into a bowl. Rub in the butter with your fingers until it looks like crumbs. Mix in the sugar.

2 Beat the egg into the molasses. Make a well in the flour mixture, pour in the molasses, and bring into a dough. Knead on a floured work surface until smooth. Flour the dough and roll it out to ¼in (5mm) thick.

3 Using a 4½in (11cm) cutter, cut out as many shapes as possible. Transfer to non-stick baking sheets. Mix the scraps of dough, re-roll, and cut out more shapes until all the dough is used.

4 Decorate the men with raisins, giving them eyes, a nose, and buttons down the front. Bake for 10–12 minutes until golden. Transfer carefully to a wire rack with a palette knife to cool completely.

5 If using, mix a little confectioners' sugar in a bowl with enough water to form a thin icing. Transfer the icing into a piping bag with a thin nozzle; placing the bag into a bowl to catch the drips first will help.

6 Decorate the men with the piped icing to resemble clothes, hair, or whatever you prefer; use your imagination (you can also use the icing to stick on other decorations). Let set completely before serving.

Raspberry cream meringues

These pretty little confections are the perfect thing to make for a summer party. If you are entertaining, try getting the kids to prepare them. Meringues are fairly easy to cook (especially small ones), as long as the humidity is not too high where you live. Make sure they are well whisked and cooked long and low and you can't go wrong.

10 mins   1 hr, plus cooling

SPECIAL EQUIPMENT

piping bag with plain nozzle (optional)

MAKES 6–8

4 egg whites, at room temperature (each medium egg white should weigh about 1oz/30g)

about 1 cup granulated sugar (you will need exactly double the weight of sugar to egg whites)

FOR THE FILLING

1¼ cups heavy cream

3½oz (100g) raspberries

1 tbsp confectioners' sugar, sifted

VARIATION

For sweet canapés, pipe smaller meringues and cook for 45 minutes; this makes about 20 filled meringues.

PREPARE AHEAD

The unfilled meringues can be kept in an airtight container for up to 3 days before filling and serving.

Cook's tip

Any crushed soft fruit can be used in the filling, such as strawberries or blueberries. If it seems too liquid once mashed, leave it in a sieve to drip over a bowl for 5 minutes before adding to the cream, to stop the filling from being too runny.

CALORIES: 320kcals/1337kJ

CARBOHYDRATE: 32g
  sugar: 32g

FAT: 8g
  saturated: 4.5g

SALT: trace

FIBER: 0.15g

1 Ask an adult to preheat the oven to around 250°F (130°C). Line a baking sheet with parchment paper. Whisk the egg whites in a metal bowl until they are stiff and form strong peaks.

2 Gradually add half the sugar, 2 tbsp at a time, whisking in between additions. Gently fold the remaining sugar into the egg whites, trying to lose as little air as possible.

3 Put tablespoons on the baking sheet, leaving 2in (5cm) gaps between; or use a piping bag with a plain nozzle. Bake in the center of the oven for 1 hour, until they lift easily and sound hollow when tapped.

4 Turn off the oven and let the meringues cool inside. Remove to a wire rack until cold. Next, in a bowl, whisk up the heavy cream until billowing and firm, but not stiff.

5 Put the raspberries in a separate bowl and crush them with the back of a fork, so they break up. Then gently fold together the cream and crushed raspberries, and combine with the confectioners' sugar.

6 Spread a little of the raspberry mixture onto the flat bases of half the meringues. Top each with one of the remaining meringue halves and gently press them together to form sandwiches.

Chocolate fudge cake balls

A really great recipe for children. The soft, gooey interior contrasts wonderfully with the crisp casing. Not only do these taste good, but they are also really fun to make. Rolling the balls and dipping them in chocolate is messy, but highly enjoyable. They will make an attractive addition to a children's birthday party.

35 mins   25 mins

SPECIAL EQUIPMENT
electric hand-held mixer
7in (18cm) round cake pan
food processor with blade attachment

MAKES 20–25

7 tbsp unsalted butter,
  softened, or soft margarine,
  plus extra for greasing

½ cup granulated sugar

2 large eggs

⅔ cup self-rising flour, sifted

¼ cup cocoa powder, sifted

1 tsp baking powder

1 tbsp milk

5½oz (150g) store-bought chocolate
  fudge frosting

9oz (250g) dark chocolate
  coating bark

1¾oz (50g) white chocolate

VARIATION

Try varying these by using a plain vanilla cake and butter icing. Coat them in white chocolate and dip in shredded coconut for some pretty white "snowballs" at Christmas.

Cook's tip

If time is short, or your children very young, packaged or leftover cake can be used, and even store-bought frosting will work here.

CALORIES: 136kcals/570kJ
CARBOHYDRATE: 15g
  sugar: 12g
FAT: 8g
  saturated: 4.5g
SALT: 0.15g
FIBER: 0.5g

1 Ask an adult to preheat the oven to 350°F (180°C). With an electric hand-held mixer, cream the butter and sugar. Beat in the eggs one at a time. Fold in the flour, cocoa, and baking powder. Mix in the milk.

2 Grease a 7in (18cm) round cake pan and line it with parchment paper. Spoon in the batter and bake for 25 minutes until springy to the touch. Get an adult to turn it onto a wire rack to cool completely.

3 Pulse the cake in a food processor fitted with a blade attachment until it looks like breadcrumbs. Add the frosting and blend together to a smooth, uniform mix.

4 Using dry hands, roll the cake mix into balls, each the size of a walnut. Put the balls on a plate, cover, and refrigerate for 3 hours, or freeze for 30 minutes until firm. Line 2 baking sheets with parchment paper.

5 Melt the cake covering according to the package instructions. Using 2 forks, coat the balls in chocolate one at a time. Remove, allowing excess to drip. Transfer the balls to the baking sheets to dry.

6 Ask an adult to melt the white chocolate in a bowl placed over a pan of boiling water. Drizzle it over the balls with a spoon. Let them dry completely before transferring to a serving plate.

Index

About the author

Caroline Bretherton is a busy working mom of two boys and knows the challenges of feeding a growing family only too well. Her love of cooking healthy, fresh food has helped her immensely. Caroline has worked in the food industry for almost 20 years. Her enthusiasm and skills helped her start her own catering company, which soon led to the establishment of an eatery in the heart of London's Notting Hill—Manna Café. Over the years she has worked consistently in television, presenting a wide range of food programs, as well as in print media, contributing to *The Times* as their family food writer. She has already published three books with DK Publishing: *The Kitchen Garden Cookbook*, *Illustrated Step-by-Step Baking*, and *Pies: Sweet and Savory*. Caroline is married and currently living in South Carolina.

The author would like to thank

Peggy Vance, Dawn Henderson, and Scarlett O'Hara at Dorling Kindersley for all their help and encouragement with this massive task. Borra Garson and all at Deborah McKenna for their work on my behalf. Jane Bamforth for her much valued help and recipe contribution and Lucy Bannell for her work as recipe editor. Finally, I would like to thank my family—Luke, Gabriel, and Isaac, whose critical palates and tireless consumption of far too much food helped to shape this book.

DK would like to thank

New photography: Lis Parsons, William Reavell, Stuart West **Photography art direction:** Susan Downing, Geoff Fennell, Lisa Pettibone, Penny Stock **Food styling:** Emma-Jane Frost, Paul Jackman, Jane Lawrie, Rosie Reynolds, Penny Stephens **Prop styling:** Susan Downing, Liz Hippisley, Wei Tang **Photography shoot manager:** Anne Fisher **Design assistance:** Mandy Earey, Kate Fenton, Vanessa Hamilton, Heather Matthews **Editorial assistance:** Priyanka Chatterjee, Christopher Mooney Elizabeth Yeates **Consultant for Babies and Toddlers chapter:** Rosan Meyer **Proofreading:** Claire Cross **Nutritionist:** Fiona Hunter **Indexer:** Liz Cook **Recipe testers:** Jane Bamforth, Ramona Andrews, Anna Burges-Lumsden, Amy Carter, Sue Davie, Francesca Dennis, Hulya Erdal, Georgina Fuggle, Jan Fullwood, Anne Harnan, Richard Harris, Sue Harris, Jo Kerr, Sarah King, Emma Lahaye, Bren Parkins-Knight, Ann Reynolds, Cathy Seward, Rachel Wood, and Amanda Wright.

KERALA

a magical odyssey

KERALA

a magical odyssey

Photographs by **Sudhir Ramchandran**

Text by **Anita Nair**

TIMES EDITIONS

Photography, introduction and caption text © Sudhir Ramchandran (2004)
Body text © Anita Nair (2004)

Research head   : **Dr. Sulekha Randhir**
Research coordinator : **Neha Diddee**
Caption writer   : **Sonya Thimmaiah**
Project Editor   : **Nafisah Ismail**
Designer   : **Lynn Chin Nyuk Ling**

© **2004 Marshall Cavendish International (Asia) Private Limited**

Published by Times Editions – Marshall Cavendish
An imprint of Marshall Cavendish International (Asia) Private Limited
A member of Times Publishing Limited
Times Centre, 1 New Industrial Road, Singapore 536196
Tel: (65) 6213 9288   Fax: (65) 6285 4871
E-mail: te@tpl.com.sg
Online Bookstore: http://www.timesone.com.sg/te

Malaysian Office:
Federal Publications Sdn Berhad (General & Reference Publishing) (3024-D)
Times Subang
Lot 46, Persiaran Teknologi Subang
Subang Hi-Tech Industrial Park
Batu Tiga, 40000 Shah Alam
Selangor Darul Ehsan, Malaysia
Tel: (603) 5635 2191   Fax: (603) 5635 2706
E-mail: cchong@tpg.com.my

National Library Board (Singapore) Cataloguing-in-Publication Data
Ramchandran, Sudhir, 1949-
Kerala: A Magical Odyssey/photographs by Sudhir Ramchandran; text by Anita Nair. – Singapore: Times Editions, c2003.
p. cm.
ISBN: 981-232-208-6
1. Kerala (India) – Social life and customs. 2. Kerala (India) –
Civilization. 3. Kerala (India) – Pictorial works. I. Nair, Anita. II. Title.
DS485.K44
954.83 — dc21   SLS2002016232

Printed in Malaysia by Bagan Printers Sdn Bhd

To my mother, Mrs. Vimala Ramchandran,

who I adore and whose values I deeply respect,

and my sister Dr Sulekha Randhir, the purity of whose love

I was fortunate to have experienced

Acknowledgements

Several individuals put together this production on Kerala. I thank each one of them for what has emerged in this collection of images that in some way represents my feelings for this wonderful state.

My first and profoundest thanks to my beloved wife, Sandhya, and my gorgeous children, Sapna, Sheetal and Snehal, who stoically tolerated my abrupt and long absences during the photography phase of this project and were my greatest critics.

When in a flux on the flow and structure of the book I could always call on my mother, Vimala Ramchandran, and be assured of receiving sane advice. She had a deep understanding of Keralan culture and traditional values, and I was often the grateful recipient of her sagacity.

My eternal gratitude to my late father Manjerikandy Ramchandran, whose simple truths on life and living guide me to this day. His role was taken over by my late stepfather M.

Chandramouli, who brought us up with understanding and love as though we were his natural-born children.

My fond appreciation to my sister, Dr. Sulekha Randhir, whose work has provided the impetus and core reference material for every image that was shot. She had to pass on during the making of this book. Yet through the difficult final phases of the book I could sense her soothing guidance that made this ten year odyssey a reality. Also to my sister,

9

Sushma, who was the bulwark that steadied my workplace during my long absences.

I thank all my Keralan relatives for welcoming and taking care of me especially Sithaunty, Uncle Mukundan, Uncle Chandran, Radhaunty, Remachi, Uncle Valsan, Bina, Aunty Vani and Uncle Ram. Also, Uncle Balan, Aunty Shanta, Uncle Bhaskar, Premachi, Leilachi, Raviattan, Joyattan, Kausaunty, Rajuattan and Pushpachi.

An endearing couple I could always count on for insights into the project are Ashok Koshy and his wonderful wife Tilotamma.

My deepest thanks go to my good friend and every photographer's dream, Vasanthi Devagnanam. Despite her frenetic schedule as the director of a leading international corporation, Vasanthi made her editorial and business instincts available to me at various phases of this production. I thank the Devagnanam family, especially Vasanthi's husband, Theo, for facilitating all these interactions with his encouragement.

To my team goes my heartfelt gratitude for their support and friendship through the years it took to create this book. In the beginning there was Parul Shah. An artist par excellence, Parul helped me develop the creative structure of the initial visual content. Subsequently I was assisted by Sanjay Ramachandran and Neha Diddee. They were my inspiration and strength and we formed a dream team. Post photography, Neha kept the editorial continuity flowing with remarkable discipline and innate intuition. Others in my team who provided emotional support and technical photography help were G. Kumaran, Senthil Kumar, Nevil Chitayagam, Srinivas Murthy, Renuka, K. Madhavan, Sunita Philip, Tashina Singh, Soshna Sood and Sudeep Choudhary. I know well how they suffered my idiosyncrasies over this period of time, and I thank them for their patience, in particular M.K. Haridas, who has been an invaluable support for so long and Amanda Tetrault who helped coordinate the intricacies of the prepress stage.

My sincere thanks to Anita Nair, an extremely gifted writer and a well-known novelist of international stature, for having agreed to write the body text for this book.

The captions in the book faithfully communicate both the emotional and historical information of each scene as well as the feelings of the photographer. I thank Sonya Thimmaiah for her indispensable part in telling the story of Kerala as fully as was possible.

The Tourism Director of Kerala during the making of this book, Dr. Venu V. IAS, provided his unstinting support and enthusiasm for the project. Emotions well within me whenever I remember the offer of unlimited free stay for me and my team at the Casino Group of Hotels by George and Jose, the wonderful Dominic brothers, and Mr. Suresh Iyer, vice-president of Kodak, who gifted me with film material that eased some of the fiscal burden of this venture.

I am also indebted to Bipin Shah of Mapin Publications and Edward Booth Clibborn of Clibborn Publications, who counselled me often. As did my close friends Brian and Margaret, Shova Loh, Paul Rozario and Leela Vengaldasam.

The gene of a high quality print production is always a great scan. The A.SANI KW Pre-Press Specialists led by Tony Ooi Kok Pin and his highly skilled professional team of Albert Ooi Chin Choon, Loo Yeok Yeng and Lim Eng Geok rendered plates of high technical excellence and immense tonal values.

The ultimate showcase is the print. Interpreting the mood of a picture and orchestrating the color channels of a high end Heildelberg transcends the craft of printmaking into the realm of fine art. Boon Eow's superlative print effort has breathed life into this body of work.

Lynn Chin of Times Editions has designed a platform for my story that is remarkably simple in its concept and yet extremely effective. I couldn't have asked for more.

I owe my deep appreciation to K.R. Bilimoria, my friend for over three decades, for pictorial guidance and creative insights; Honnappa Jayadeva, my sagacious sounding board and good friend; and D. Radhakrishnan, my most consistent friend and guide with whom I indulged in photographic banters over the years. My thanks to Tarun Jung Rawat for creating the first complete book design that got me noticed by my publisher.

The seed of the book was sown when my late uncle M. Gopalan, a well-known industrialist from Dar es Salaam, Tanzania, talked to me when I was a child about this beautiful state and the potential of its people. I deeply respect his wife, Aunty Shakuntala, and have fond memories of a childhood spent with his children, mostly with Venu and Neena.

Over several interactions I developed a deep respect for David Yip, my publisher. He was always encouraging and obliging to the wildly fluctuating demands of an unpredictable artist like myself. Nafisah Ismail, my editor, was always a pleasure to talk to, and is owed my thanks for her diligence and the eagle-eyed care she devoted to the progress of the book.

Everyone I met along the way to creating Kerala: A Magical Odyssey is responsible in some way or other for my vision of Kerala. Most of all I thank Kerala and her people for providing the ceaseless inspiration.

Introduction

I am one of those Indians who was born and brought up outside the country in an environment that was alien to Indian culture. My parents are from Kerala, a tiny state in southwestern India. My only initiation into Malayalam, the Keralan language, was a few words that I learnt at a local club in Dar es Salaam when I was very little. Through stories my mother told us we learnt of the characters in the *Ramayana*, the sacred Indian epic, and of how the Hindu religious book, the Bhagavad-Gita, came about.

I sailed into India at the age of 16 in the bottom deck of an ocean liner, fearful of a country that I did not know, and was completely overawed by the vast Indian Ocean at night. We docked at the beautiful, sparsely populated island of Seychelles, and I remember thinking to myself that if this is what I was going to see halfway to India, the Indian experience couldn't be so frightful after all. Docking in Bombay was a shocking experience as I disembarked into a wall of babbling humanity. I simply did not know what had hit me. A week later I landed in Kerala, a beautiful green and quiet state, where life lazily passed by people, animals and nature.

I spent two years in Kozhikode in the north of Kerala and another three years in Trivandrum, the capital of Kerala, in the south. During this period

I graduated in the Sciences and in my understanding of the state and its people. Kerala is a literate state, and I was often amazed at the knowledge of past and current events that even an octogenarian priestess or little children of the fisherfolk possessed. I joined groups that discussed politics fiercely and had an opinion on almost everything. I realised that often in Kerala a person is measured based on his level of knowledge, wit and sarcasm.

Equality between men and women is intrinsic in the character of every Keralan. The Mannarasala Temple in the south of Kerala is one of the only temples in India that is headed by a priestess. Kerala has a matriarchal system, and often in a household of joint families it is the women who make most of the crucial decisions and guide children along their career paths. However, parents strictly forbid young boys and girls talking to each other, and this prudery has resulted in overt sexuality in Malayalam literature and films.

Every Keralan household strives to be self-sufficient. Affluence is measured by the number of coconut trees in one's compound. Apartments that have begun to sprout recently were a rarity even five years ago. Everyone had individual homes with sufficient land to grow coconuts. The ubiquitous coconut has been put to ingenious use in Kerala and is used in food and home furnishings. It is understood that a girl from a household with more coconut trees could be reasonably certain of securing a well-to-do husband.

My love for the verdant nature of the state grew incrementally as I stayed on. When I returned to Kerala after a stint outside the country, I decided to photograph the state, to capture on film one of the few remaining areas in India where the bounty of nature lay unblemished. I love the clean air that signalled the crossing over of the borders into Kerala. Often my assistants, Neha and Sanjay, and I would lie on our backs in the deep forests of the Western Ghats, refreshing ourselves and cleansing momentarily the pollutants we had gathered from our urban existence.

The entire state, including the cities, has a rural feel about it. The beauty of the gushing Athirapally Falls during the monsoon is to be felt rather than seen. I can still hear the sound of its falling waters across the round grey rocks at its base, still see the golden sun's rays streaking across the greens of the river bank backlighting the leaves with a rich translucence and still feel the soft wind caressing us while the splendid azure sky fought to retain its colours against the vivid setting sun. The scene is so alive in me and is one of many memorable experiences of my ten-year photographic sojourn in Kerala. Sometimes the camera was an obstruction to the feelings that I had, and the glory of a fabulous sunset or the majesty of a towering elephant was sacrificed to my obsession with capturing the scene on film.

I have always lost myself in the spice jungles and tea estates of Munnar. On every occasion I have felt how true the ancient legend of Lord Parasurama creating Kerala with a throw of his axe into the sea and the rising of this virgin land is. Thekkady is as Eden must have been. Elephants swimming in groups, large numbers of herbivores, such as socked bison and wild boar, moving in mixed herds, and flocks of migratory birds from Eurasia and other distant places dot the Periyar basin. We sighted the shy Nilgiri tahr, and the iridescent feathers of peacocks often brushed our vehicles as we passed by. Trees of every description and rare plants, including a huge reservoir of orchid species, exist here.

I was hardly seven when I saw my first stage drama. There was a fearsome, multicoloured, horrific-looking individual prancing around the stage with a female counterpart, enacted by a man. Over the years, as I watched these complex performances across the globe, my understanding of the Kathakali art form deepened. Today I watch with pride the unfolding of the *Ramayana* epic as colours clash along with cymbals, gestures stab the air and feet stamp the footboards to staccato chanting in the wild frenzy of a Kathakali dance drama.

With my African background I could never envisage a man atop an elephant. It is amazing how the gentle counterparts to the fierce African pachyderms have become almost a part of everyday Keralan life. Elephants and their attendant mahouts are everywhere, from the ritualistic ceremonies of a temple festival to the less honourable task of moving logs in wood depots. Elephants are even used to capture and train other elephants. Most Indian elephants are trained by Keralan mahouts and come from the deep jungles of the Western and Southern Ghats. In Kerala, the mere sight of this large creature is believed to portend good fortune.

To truly experience Kerala, I think one has to do what I did: travel the *edavazhi*, or narrow pathways, on a motorbike, smell the tea in the early morning at the Munnar mountainside, savour the tapioca and fish curry at a wayside shack, feel the cold, sparkling flow of the backwaters, breathe in the pristine air of a sleepy fishing village and interact with her warm and opinionated people. No wonder National Geographic Traveler Magazine declared Kerala one of the world's 10 natural paradises.

For me, Kerala will always be my own paradise on earth. Through my pictures I hope to share some of her beauty and intricacies of character with the world.

Contents

Traditions *78–109*   Gods *110–133*   Living *134–153*

Paradise

At 1,600 metres above sea level, the idyllic slopes of Munnar in Idukki were a favourite colonial summer escape in pre-independence India. Its profusion of tea gardens are among the highest in the world and imparts to the hill station its vivid greens. Once every 12 years these wonted greens are rivalled by the flowering of the Neelakurinji, a rare plant that bestows upon these mountains an uncommon blue cast.

It is said that thousands of years ago the world was tyrannised by the Kshatriyas, and everyday thousands of innocent men, women and children were killed, maimed or punished for no fault. Kartavirya, their king, had obtained the boon of invincibility, a thousand arms and a golden chariot that went wherever he willed it to go. He would meet his death only at the hands of a man known to the whole world. In grief, the people turned to

Lord Vishnu and pleaded for help. And so Vishnu was born to a sage called Jamadagni. Even as a young lad, Vishnu performed such severe austerities that Lord Shiva, the god of death and destruction, appeared before him and taught him the use of arms. As his personal weapon, Shiva gave him an axe that once raised, would rest only when it had destroyed his opponent. And thus Vishnu came to be known as Parasurama, or Rama with the Axe.

One day Parasurama, his brothers and their father were away from the hermitage they lived in when Kartavirya visited. The villagers welcomed the king and entertained him well. But the king repaid their hospitality by taking away the sacrificial calf. Parasurama returned to find his mother in tears. So he went looking for Kartavirya. "Your tenure has come to an end," Parasurama hollered. "Never again will you oppress harmless folk. Never again will you rule the world with fear."

With his axe, Parasurama cut off all the thousand arms of Kartavirya and then killed him.

Parasurama, whose anger had the power to reduce the world to ashes, then retired to a forest to meditate and calm his mind. While he was in the forest, however, Kartavirya's sons came to the hermitage and killed Jamadagni to avenge their father's death.

Now Parasurama's anger could no longer be checked and he took an oath to cleanse the world of the demonic Kshatriyas. He went around the world 21 times to kill all the Kshatriyas and filled five large lakes with their blood.

Content that his work had been done, Parasurama went to the western coast of the land and flung his axe into the ocean.[1] From the waters emerged a thin strip of land where rivers flowed, elephants and deer roamed, birds sang, rare flowers bloomed, and pepper, cardamom and sandalwood scented the air. This was a land where all was green, lush and serene. A resting place born out of restlessness. God's own country raised by the hands of a man. Kerala.

If this is the mythical genesis of Kerala, geology claims that there were at least two stages of land rise from the sea. Seismological movements or volcanic actions created the first mass of land, and rivers depositing large quantities of silt and mud from the mountains created the second land mass. At the same time ocean currents caused sand to pile on the shore.[2]

In this narrow ribbon of land flanked by mountains on one side and the Arabian Sea on the other are customs, traditions, manners and practices that have no bearing with the rest of the country. Almost as if it has remained insular to all that was happening elsewhere and as if it had risen from the sea as a fully-formed independent being. It is this that makes the ancient Parasurama legend almost believable.

It is said that Parasurama, having raised the land from the sea, decided to populate it with 64 Brahmin families. But the Brahmins disputed

Lotuses flourish in Pookot Lake, a freshwater lake in Wayanad. The lake is surrounded by lush hills on three sides and is a popular picnic spot made more attractive by the absence of human habitation or industry.

Elephants mimic synchronised swimmers with surprising grace at the Periyar Wildlife Sanctuary. Lake tours allow thrilling proximity to the animals and laudable government efforts have replaced the small, polluting diesel boats with battery-operated, non-intrusive tourist vessels. The sanctuary is home to approximately 800 elephants, which make for fascinating herd dynamics.

Left: Paddy fields ribbon across Kerala's landscape and are significant contributors to the lush appeal of the state.

Preceding page: The graceful and magnificent Athirapally Falls near Thrissur, like a mystical lady dressed in white, plunge from a height of 80 feet to the delight of visitors from all over the country. The existence of these breathtaking falls is being threatened by a power generation project.

among themselves, and in sheer desperation to prevent anarchy and chaos they decided to invite rulers from across the mountains. The Brahmins decided that these rulers would each preside only for 12 years to avoid monarchies or dictatorships. Ironically enough these rulers were Kshatriyas and came to be known as Perumals. The first Perumal was called a Keralan.[3]

But just as one begins to shake one's head in disbelief and starts dismissing the story as a mere legend, history rears its head. The first reference to Kerala is in an edict engraved on a rock by Emperor Asoka between 272 B.C. and 232 B.C.[3] Kerala owes its origins to the word Keralaputra, which means Land of the Sons of Cheras. The Cheras were the first large empire to take roots in this state.[4]

A dawn still life in the placid backwaters of Malabar in northern Kerala. Fishing boats, palms and backwaters are perhaps the words that are most evocative of the striking landscapes of rural Kerala.

However, artefacts dating back to 4000 B.C. point to the existence of a highly developed ancient culture in Kerala.[3] There are burial stones and urns, microliths, stone records and copper plates. Ancient Keralans used stone or copper to record data till the end of the 14th century. Palm leaves took over as the medium of records until the 19th century, though paper was already in use as early as in the 16th century.[3]

The origin of this state and its name might hover in that uncertain terrain between myth and reality, but what is undisputed is the sheer natural magnificence of Kerala. From the majestic heights of the Western Ghats,

the land undulates westward towards the Arabian Sea and creates a landscape of valleys draped in varied shades of green. Many rivers weave their way through these hills to merge their waters with the sea. Along the coast there are lagoons and backwaters sheltered by sand dunes. The quiet of this enchanted world is broken only by the coos of koels, the rasping cries of Indian tree magpies and the fluttering wings of cranes. It is as if nature knew no limits when it decided to bequeath its bounty to this land. And it is one of nature's gifts that charted the course of Kerala's vivid but checkered history.

We need to step back in time to understand this. There is the legend of how the Queen of Sheba, when she decided to go to Jerusalem and present herself, carried in her train "spices, gold, precious stones and the wood of the almug tree", or sandalwood, from Ophir. Historians claim that Ophir

Untouched by human hands, the pristine Kunthipuzha River gurgles through Silent Valley National Park. It is the only river in South India with a course exceeding 20 km that does not pass through a single human settlement.

could be the ancient, submerged town of Puhar in Kerala.[5]

It is to the same period of history that the temples and palaces of the Babylonian king Nebuchadnezzar belong. Remnants of the buildings that have surfaced as a result of archaeological digs show these to be hardwoods that perhaps came from the tropical forests of Kerala.

The first reference to pepper appears in Roman history and can be dated to the first century when Pliny the Elder remarked that "the Roman nobility were depleting the treasury with their greed for pepper."[5] It is this greed for pepper that brought ships into the ports of Malabar. More interestingly

it is this trade in pepper and other spices that provide the first hints of the political history of the region that later became known by such names as Venad, Kochi, Malabar, Travancore-Cochin and finally as Kerala state.

While trade between India and the Western world had existed for many centuries, what made Malabar so tradeworthy, apart from it being a cornucopia of spices, was the discovery of the monsoon winds by Greek sailors in A.D. 45. The sailors discovered that by harnessing the monsoon winds from the Horn of Plenty in Africa, it was possible to sail to Malabar in just 45 days. Soon Muziris, which stood at the mouth of the Periyar river and whose location was where Kodungalloor stands today, became a busy port and facilitated trade with the Greeks, Arabs, Europeans and Chinese.

Vasco da Gama's landing at Kappad on the Malabar Coast in 1498 started a rash of colonialisation by the

Dutch, Portuguese, French and British. Meanwhile the peppercorn once more triggered off events in Europe that changed the course of Kerala's history and to some extent India's. The British East India Company came into being in 1599 when the Dutch hiked the price of pepper by one shilling.

The British East India Company annexed Kerala as a British colony by signing a strategic treaty with King Marthanda Varma in 1723. British rule lasted almost two centuries and ended in 1947.[5]

Kerala in its present form came into existence only in 1956 when new states were formed based on the geographical distribution of languages in India. The regions of Travancore, Kochi and Malabar were combined into one to be called Kerala.

Who would imagine that a tiny peppercorn could determine the shaping of a land's past triumphs and failures?

The peppercorn still thrives. So does cardamom, rubber, coconut, coffee, tea, paddy and tapioca. An abundance that lures the world now as it did then.

In fact if one of the ancient travellers were to return to Kerala, he would discover that while much has changed, the essence of Kerala continues to be the same. That of a race that is a conundrum by itself. A race that is defined by the language it speaks: Malayalam. And so a person from Kerala is called a Malayali.

On the one hand the Malayali finds contentment in little things: his daily splash in a river or pond, laundered white clothes, a bowl of rice and fish curry and the ownership of his own patch of land with its grove of coconut trees.

Yet this is also a voluble vocal race that lets no industry thrive, for everyone knows their rights and demands that they be met. Communism lives alongside capitalism. Marx is read by the same man who swears by the Bible or the Bhagavad-Gita. Animist practices coexist with organised religion. Ancient art forms such as Kalaripayattu and Kathakali enjoy pride of place with experimental theatre and parody shows.

Jaded and weary a traveller arrives at Kerala and finds a haven. In its valleys and backwaters, dreams are spun as coir is.

In the span of a few days the traveller is introduced to a world that is unique and perhaps unreal. The acquaintance that follows is based on a smattering of carefully packaged experiences. "This is Kerala," they think. This abundance, this many-hued green, this land with its rich folklore and caparisoned elephants.

But the real Kerala remains undiscovered. Untouched and unvoiced, it waits for you to seek it and find it....

Above: A white sari, a thick braid of hair interlocked with a string of jasmine flowers, a chain around the neck and a welcoming charm characterise the typical Keralan girl. Kerala has the highest literacy levels in all of India for both men and women. Many women have capitalised on this privilege by launching careers for themselves in industries such as information technology and hospitality.

Right: People from the backwaters of Palazhi village in Kozhikode reveal their contemplative sides in the shade of coconut palms. The agrarian life is typically exhausting with dawn-to-dusk days spent labouring in the fields.

LAND

Sahadevan, a rubber tapper at the Kalarickal estate in Kottayam, makes an expert half-spiral incision into the bark of a rubber tree. The milky sap that oozes from the incision, commonly called latex, is collected in a receptacle tied to the trunk of the tree. Kottayam is commonly known as the Land of Letters, Lakes and Latex owing to its numerous educational institutions and 100 percent literacy rate; the presence of Vembanad Lake, the largest lake in Kerala; and its production of 95 percent of India's rubber yield.

Perhaps understanding Kerala ought to begin with understanding the lay of its land. Hemmed in by the Western Ghats on its eastern side and flanked by the Arabian Sea on the other side, Kerala runs 580 kilometres along the western coast, is 121 km at its widest and a mere 32 km at its narrowest. The tall mountains made Kerala almost inaccessible by land until the 15-km-wide Palakkad gap in the Western Ghats was discovered.

Geographically Kerala can be divided into three regions: mountains, laterite hills and coastal plains. The highlands are home to tea, coffee, rubber and cardamom plantations. In the hills and valleys, crops such as cashew, coconut and pepper are intensively cultivated. The coastal area consists of river deltas and backwaters, where the people depend on fishing and the cultivation of coconuts and rice for their livelihood.[6]

There are 24 million people living on 38,863 square kilometres of Keralan land. One-sixth of this land is forested and is where mahogany, sandalwood, teak and rosewood still grow.[7] Before the birth of Christianity teak wood from Kerala was used for the construction of buildings in places such as Ur in Mesopotamia (present-day Iraq) and later in the construction of British ships used by Admiral Horatio Nelson in the battle of Trafalgar against Napoleon Bonaparte in 1805.

Of the rest of the land, most of it is cultivated and with maximum efficiency. Away from the plains and laterite hills where rice, coconut and rubber reign is the planting country. It is a land where jungle trails and footpaths through cultivated areas still outnumber roads. It is a land of few roads, and almost each one of them is a winding, twisting climb to nowhere. It is a land of breathtaking splendour.

There is a strange clear beauty of form about the mountains. They are large, imposing and grimly handsome. They stand set back and shrouded in a clear, frosty air as if each one of them would isolate itself further and forever from the landscape. Giant shadows hold the damp blue mountains in their grip. The mountainous land that is Kerala's plantation country was once inaccessible tracts of tall grass, thick jungles and malaria-infested marshes. The early planters cleared them to create the first plantations.

Elephants, it has been recorded, are the finest roadmakers in the world,

Groups of women sow paddy in Kuttanad, Alappuzha. Kuttanad is often referred to as the rice bowl of Kerala. In rural India, arduous field labour is often the responsibility of the female members of the family. Rice is the staple food of the state, and swathes of sun-burnished paddy emblazon the landscape of Kerala.

Above: In a ginger warehouse in Jew Town, Fort Kochi, mounds of ginger are gunnysacked and auctioned off as they have been for hundreds of years. Little has changed in this part of Jew Town where beguiling aromas negate the need for warehouse addresses. With Kochi a major port, spices from all over Kerala linger briefly in the warehouses before being snapped up by the lucrative export market.

Left: Women pick cardamom on one of many plantations in Kerala. Cardamom is exported to various parts of the world for sparing use in cuisine, perfumery, medicines and beverages. Vandanmedu town in Thekkady holds one of the largest cardamom auctions in the world.

Above: The weathered foreman of the ginger warehouse takes a brief respite on a hectic day.

and the early planters followed the trails made by the elephants. They built grass huts to live in, shot a variety of small game to live on, brought in labour from the plains and tried to keep them from running away from the bone-chilling damp and the almost palpable fear all around when even the moon had a devilish cast to it. There was a sense of momentariness and expectation. As though some dramatic occurrence was about to take place. An upheaval, an explosion, a furrowing of the horizon...all they knew was that they were glad to be part of it. It is from such efforts that many of today's giant estates came into being.

Misty, lush-green and nearly 1,600 metres above sea level in the Annamalai range of Kerala is Munnar, a tea plantation centre. It stands at the confluence of three rivers. *Moonu* and *aar* mean three and river in Tamil respectively. Hence the name Munnar.

Tea gardens, some of the highest in the world, stretch up the sides of the hills and are interspersed with pockets of forest rich in wildlife. Munnar from above spreads like a vast bonsai garden stretching to the end of the horizon and provides a vivid contrast to coastal, palm-fringed Kerala. Since the 30-odd tea gardens around Munnar are all privately owned, the colonial town itself is beautifully maintained and has its own charm.

While the tropical forests are inhabited by elephants, tigers, deer and gaurs, the hills surrounding Munnar are home to one of the world's rarest mountain goats, the Nilgiri tahr.

Rather like the koel's call, one of the constants of life in Kerala is the

in size, the state produced 25 percent of India's coffee in 1997 and 1998.

Right: The clouds subside with the rise of the sun and a spectacular morning unfurls over a Munnar tea plantation. Although tea plants grow to heights of up to 30 feet, regular pruning maintains them at between 4 and 5 feet, which is the ideal height for tea pickers. Trees are often planted between the tea plants for microclimatic benefits and soil improvement.

Top: The smell of fragrant coffee blossoms in Wayanad fill the air after the mid-year showers. Coffee is the second largest traded commodity in the world after oil. Although most coffee plantations in Kerala are less than two hectares

sound of the cicadas. And yet there is a place where the cicadas do not sing: Silent Valley, so named by the British for the absence of the cicadas.

The local name for the park is Sairandhrivanam, or the Forest in the Valley. This and the fact that the Kunthipuzha River drains into it give the valley a mythological dimension.

Silent Valley is located in the Kundali Hills of the Western Ghats and is a national park that has an astonishing array of rare plants and herbs. More importantly, this is the last virgin tract of tropical evergreen forest in India. Though smaller in size compared to the other national parks in India, what makes it unique is its green belt.

This green belt almost never came to be because the Kerala State Electricity Board wanted to build a project in the area in the 1970s. As this project would have caused much damage to the ecosystem of the national park, political lobbies and environmentalists

rallied together and the plan was set aside. In 1984 Silent Valley, which includes the project area, was proclaimed a national park. Finally in 1986 the park became the core area in the Nilgiri Biosphere Reserve.[8]

Though the cicadas do not sing here, Silent Valley is full of other species of wildlife and their sounds. From peninsular mammals to over a hundred species of butterflies, Silent Valley is home to many yet-to-be-classified species of flora and fauna.[9]

It is almost impossible to think of Kerala without thinking of elephants. In fact, there is a saying that when the last descendant of the Travancore family dies, so will the elephant in Kerala. Such is its link with the land, the people and traditions that an elephant has many a role to play in the everyday life of Kerala. There is the temple elephant whose domain is the temple and streets. There is also the working elephant used in logging camps and by the forest

department as employees entitled to salaries in the form of feeds and pensions after a certain age.

Nevertheless elephants in the wild

Right: A bull elephant contemplates the jungle in solitude. Bull elephants break from their herds upon attaining sexual maturity to travel either on their own or in groups of bachelors called bull bands. Elephant herds are matriarchal with the oldest and most experienced female assuming the role of leader. Among Asian elephants, only the males grow tusks, unlike African elephants whose tusks are gender-independent.

Preceding page: A hammer slung over his shoulder in place of his usual school bag, a young boy heads off into the tea plantations in Munnar. Life in the mountains often involves youngsters working on the plantations with their families and simultaneously pursuing educations that will provide them with a greater variety of career options in the future.

Left: The Nilgiri tahr is an endangered species of mountain goat found in South India. Rampant poaching had reduced the numbers of this shy animal to below a hundred at the start of the 20th century. Concerted conservation efforts brought their numbers in India up to around 2,500 in the year 2000. The Eravikulam National Park in Idukki was established in 1978 as a sanctuary for the Nilgiri tahr.

Above: The Periyar Wildlife Sanctuary in Thekkady, Idukki, extends across 777 km² and nurtures over 1,965 flowering species. Wildlife enthusiasts from all parts of the world, who are drawn to Periyar on the promise of herds of wild elephants cavorting in Periyar Lake, rarely leave disappointed. Sambar, flying squirrels and gaurs, or Indian bison, are commonly spotted at the sanctuary.

continue to be threatened by poachers. To preserve the wild elephant and other species of wildlife, the government has established numerous wildlife sanctuaries all over Kerala. The Eravikulam National Park was established specially for the preservation of the Nilgiri tahr, one of the most endangered animals on the planet. Now the number of tahrs in Eravikulam National Park has increased and makes up the largest-known population of tahrs existing in the world.

The entire district of Wayanad is a wildlife sanctuary and its hills throng with elephant stories. Here one can encounter Andy Warhol's theory of 15 minutes of fame. In Wayanad the road to celebrityville begins with the elephant. Almost everyone has an elephant tale to tell, elephant wisdom to disseminate, elephant theories to propound and at least one I-don't-know-how-I-lived-to-tell-you-this encounter with an elephant.

Sultan Bathery, the last outpost of the district, is just another small town in Kerala. Its uniqueness does not extend beyond the *kinnath appam*, which is a steamed pudding made of rice flour, jaggery and coconut milk.

However, Sultan Bathery has plenty of everything else: plastic buckets, duck eggs, jewellery, cast iron skillets and purple seedless grapes from Sangli. Add to this the knowledge that the shops are just a façade. Behind it is the jungle, a dark slumbering beast. During the day monkeys dart through its leafy limbs. At night, it comes alive with a certain stealthiness. A jackal yowls.... [1]

Despite the government's efforts, some species of wildlife have become extinct and many others are endangered. The animals' only serious enemy is man and his need to encroach into their territory. And yet, it isn't as if the average Malayali is a landlocked being. If land is the terra firma of life, it is water that determines the course of progress.

Tribal men in the Periyar settlement work in the forests and agricultural fields as daily wage earners, while the women are responsible for domestic duties such as the pounding of grain, their staple food.

WATER

Distinctive Chinese nets line the waterfront at Kochi in Ernakulam. The nets lining the harbour are called *cheena vallam* and have been in use for over 600 years, but now they yield a meagre catch because of overfishing. The graceful dropping in and lifting out of the nets from the water when they are in operation suggests a paying of respects to the sea for each catch.

Imagine a land, its people, its economy and its everyday harnessed to the rise and fall of tides...this then is Kerala. A place made up of 40 percent water and 60 percent land. Crisscrossed by many rivers and over a thousand canals. Most are almost entirely monsoon-fed, which means the rivers and canals fluctuate in size and power from season to season.

The monsoon, perhaps even more than politics, has a way of taking over daily life in Kerala. Such is its omnipresence that it hijacks even conversation. So that all that is discussed is its time and manner of arrival—with a big bang that drenches anything and everything in its path, its intensity or sometimes the lack of it.

The monsoon first arrived in India

Above: A German couple enjoys a deserted expanse of private beach at Somatheeram Ayurvedic Beach Resort in Thiruvananthapuram. The award-winning resort is a magnet for European tourists seeking a restorative holiday.

Above: The sky and sea hurl temper tantrums at each other in the period that marks the arrival of the monsoon. Even the Kovalam Beach lighthouse, perched at its elevated level, seems vulnerable to the twin furies.

Above and right: A monsoon begins at Varkala Beach. A brow of menacing clouds in an amber sky gives way to a downpour and veritable merging of sky and sea. Kerala is the first state in India to receive the southwesterly monsoon.

during the Miocene epoch between five million and 24 million years ago. The cause seems to have been the mighty uplift of the Himalayas and the Tibetan plateau. Owing to its proximity to the Arabian Sea, Kerala is the first state each season to receive the monsoon rains, which contribute significantly to its 118 inches of annual rainfall. The onset of monsoon in Kerala is eagerly awaited by the rest of India, which is baking under the heat of summer.

What scientific data will not reveal and is part of local folklore is the capricious nature of the southwest monsoon. Of how it almost always breaks on the day schools reopen after the summer vacations. So that children, in their new uniforms, carrying new bags and holding aloft new umbrellas, have to negotiate the puddles on the roads. Of rain that waits for clothes to be hung out on lines to dry, or for people to leave their homes without umbrellas before it

comes hurtling down, persisting vigorously till everything is wet and sodden before it stops with the same abruptness with which it began.

Every year the monsoon breaks at Kovalam, the much-celebrated beach 12 km away from Thiruvananthapuram. From there the monsoon begins its journey northwards. To Varkala Beach, Kollam, Alleppey, Kochi and moving up the coast rapidly, leaving a trail of wetness behind.

While much of Kerala's life

Above: Kovalam is one of Kerala's most popular beaches and draws the crowds during peak seasons. The first outsiders to discover the beach in the 1970s were hippies, but today it attracts more mainstream visitors. The restaurants that line the bay are packed owing to their dual lure of fresh seafood and live traditional dance performances.

Left: The placidity of the beach in the morning is not indicative of the throb of daily life at work. Mornings are the busiest part of a fisherman's day, when the catch is secured.

Preceding page: Coconut kernel is dried to copra for use in Keralan cuisine. The abundance of coconuts in Kerala has engendered uses for each and every part of the coconut—from the use of its leaves in thatching and handicrafts to the fermentation of its sap to brew toddy.

Below: Fishermen begin their day early and are seen hauling in their catches at dawn.

revolves around its freshwater trails, its coast is no less important. In fact, Kerala has some of India's finest beaches. Take Kovalam, a small fishing village named for its grove of coconut trees. Today it has sun worshippers from all over the world seeking its spread of surf and sand. Kovalam's most popular beach is Lighthouse Beach. It is from the middle beach called Hawah that local fishermen set sail every morning. Samudra, the quietest of these, is speckled with a few boats and fewer people. However, Kovalam also has its ugly sides. Erosion has eaten away at the beach, and the ugliness of drugs and sex trafficking, at its ambience.[10]

Kovalam is not the only beach to cast a spell. While there are many beaches, the most important ones owe their prominence to historic and religious reasons. There is Varkala Beach, which is considered to be holy. It is also known as Papanashini, meaning that which destroys sins.[11] Then there is Alleppey Beach, a spectacular stretch of sand rimmed with dense coconut groves.

The beach of historical importance is Kappad, where Portuguese navigator Vasco da Gama landed in 1498 and subsequently changed the course of Indian history. About 16 km away from Kozhikode, the pleasant and calm beach, locally known as Kappakadavu, is dotted with rocks and caressed by gentle waves.[11]

Further north is Bekal Beach, where Bekal Fort, one of the largest forts in Kerala, is located.

While the beaches alone were enchanting enough to lure travellers, what brought forth visitors increasingly was trade. Kerala's seafront was studded with port cities

Women sort shrimps brought ashore by the men according to size. A book by the name *Chemmeen*, or *The Shrimps*, written by Thakazhi Sivasankara Pillai, is one of the masterpieces of Keralan literature. The book was adapted into an award-winning film of the same title. The story tells a tragic tale of the lives of fishing folk intertwined with the wrath of the sea.

that even to this day continue to be trade zones.

Kollam was a port used by travellers such as Ibn Batuta and by the Phoenicians, Romans and Chinese. The Portuguese, Dutch and British also set up trading centres here.[12]

When the sea retreated from Kottayam and Tripunitura and the ancient port of Muziris became silted up in 1341, a great deal of the trade shifted to Kochi.

Facing the backwaters is Ernakulam, the district headquarters and an important commercial and residential area. Kochi Shipyard, the biggest shipbuilding yard in India, is situated in the southern part of Ernakulam near Willingdon Island.

Further north is Kozhikode, a city that has always conjured images of exotica. Calico, a fine variety of handwoven cotton cloth said to have originated from this place, is derived from the old city's name, Calicut.[13]

Apart from being trading centres, the coastline of Kerala has spawned other occupations. While fishing and the production of coconut oil and pressed oil cakes from coconut seeds were a thriving industry, the most significant one was boatbuilding.

There is a curious sound that reverberates through the alleys of Beypore, which is 8 km from Kozhikode. A rhythm that is hard to place. A resonance that is both familiar and strange. You think you know it. And then you think you don't. In the end when you see the source of that

pagan beat for yourself, you wonder why it never occurred to you that this music that had teased and taunted you was the note of wood on wood.

Alongside the Chaliyam river estuary that flows into the Arabian Sea lies the secret history of Beypore: its ancient boatyard.

According to Captain Iwata, founder member of the Association of Sumerian ships in Japan, Beypore had direct links with Mesopotamia and was probably a major stop in the maritime Silk Route. In fact he believes that Sumerian ships might have been built in Beypore. So when Captain Iwata set out to prove that a maritime trade link did exist between Mesopotamia and other countries, it is to Beypore he came to build his dream ship some years ago. The ship in which he would trace the famed Silk Route.

Built according to a design recorded on a Sumerian cuneiform tablet preserved at the Louvre museum, the 3,000-tonner is made entirely of wood. Its planks are held together by wooden nails and coir yarn. A special glue made of fruit and tree resins is used for additional bonding, and the anchor is hewn out of granite. While there was some

Above left: A lone ferry represents the only sign of marine activity in an otherwise bustling Kochi seafront. Red-tiled roofs, undulating palms and frenetic waterfront activities typify the cityscape of Kochi. Many theories abound on the name, the most literal being that it is a derivative of *kaci*, which means harbour in Tamil.

Above right: A dipping sun heightens the romance of a serene pool paralleling the swirling sea. The Brunton Boatyard in Fort Kochi is an intimate resort hotel that was once a fully functional boatyard.

Left: An *uru* awaits the finishing touches that precede its departure.

Above: The launch of the *uru* is an arduous process and extends into the night when the tide is high. It is time for the *uru* to prove its credentials and sail perfectly balanced into the sea after months of painstaking labour.

Left: In Beypore, a goat is sacrificed before the launch of the *Al Khalafi*, an *uru* bound for the Middle East. The meat will go into *biryani*, a dish made with rice and spices cooked along with the meat, and will be served to the community.

amount of interest in Beypore around the project, to most of its population the ship Ki-en-gi (Sumerian for Land of the Master of Reeds) was just another one of the ships constructed.

What to them seems commonplace is in truth a phenomenon. Millions of rupees exchange hands as a matter of daily activity here, for Beypore is one among the last few places in the world where boats are still being fashioned out of wood. There are orders from all parts of the world for all types of vessels: cargo ships, ketches, yachts, barges and even a ship that was meant to be a floating restaurant. The most common vessel that comes out of Beypore is a cargo ship modelled according to grain clipper ships of 18th-century Europe. The modern version, however, runs on engine power in spite of its sails.

Though the master artisans use certain Sanskrit *shlokas*, or prayers and invocations, to guide them, none of it

is on paper. The art of boatbuilding remains a closely guarded secret handed down from father to son. Only a handful of such master craftsmen are left. Four to be precise.

Just as Kerala has its seafaring people, it has its backwater people too. A great part of Kerala lives along these backwaters, which stretch over 1,900 km long. They snake over the land, bequeathing paddy fields with good harvests and linking remote, isolated villages with crowded town pockets.[14]

The backwaters become the cynosure of the eyes of the world from August to September every year, when

Above: The backwaters are large inland lakes that ribbon across Kerala. They cover an area of over 1,900 km via a network of lagoons, lakes and 44 rivers and are a lifeline of irrigation and drinking water.

Right: Sunlight streams into a narrow stretch of the backwaters as part of the daily tide of the rising and setting sun.

the celebrated Snake Boat Races, a water regatta unique to Kerala, takes place. Every year thousands of people crowd the water's edge to cheer the huge black crafts as they slice through the waters to a spectacular finish. Not all of them know what the origin of the tradition is. Or why it came to be. Nevertheless in their exuberance for the sport, the sanctity of a tradition is preserved. Perhaps that is what makes Kerala unique. Its traditions and the irrepressible need in a Malayali to follow some of these traditions, if not all of them.

Above and far left: The cacophony of sellers marketing their catch and buyers haggling resounds through and beyond the immediate environs of this fish market in Alappuzha.

Left: "How about a fight, a sword fight?", jests the fisherman as he thrusts his fish back and forth in response to the photographer, who is moving forward and backward to get the right composition. Mornings are an especially busy time at fish markets across Kerala as the newly-arrived catch is up for sale.

Above and right: Duck farming in Kottayam. Duck farming is a common sight in Kerala's backwaters. The ducks are usually fenced in but are let out to feed and also serve as playmates to children larking about in the waters. Dried shrimps are scattered into the waters as bait for fish that are quickly devoured by the ducks. The ducks are reared both for their eggs, which are larger than chickens' eggs, and their meat.

Preceding page, left: At Fort Kochi in Ernakulam, crows compete with fishermen for the catch and are often triumphant. The catch is heaved into baskets and sold in no time at markets adjacent to the fishing area.

Preceding page, right: Chinese fishing nets were introduced to Kerala between 1350 and 1450 by traders from the court of Kublai Khan, who became the first emperor of China's Mongol dynasty in 1260 and was the grandson of warrior-ruler Genghis Khan. More than 600 years after they were first used in Kerala, the nets are still a source of livelihood to hundreds of fishermen here.

Above and right: Families living along the backwaters are dependent on itinerant vendors, whose boats are often piled temptingly with wares, for their day-to-day needs.

Preceding page: A boat sits idle next to a house in the backwaters of Kumarakom in Kottayam. The number of coconut trees growing on the house premises often measures the wealth of a Keralan family. The mode of transport for

backwater families is boats, and it is a matter of great pride for a family to own one. Simple ambitions and simple lives characterise the backwater residents.

Next page, left: A houseboat lingers on the stillness of Vembanad Lake. Docked near the Taj Garden Retreat in Kumarakom, the houseboat is known locally as *kettuvallam* and is an attractive accommodation option.

Next page, right: In Alappuzha, two boats are ingeniously combined using a wooden plank to transport a car across the backwaters. In a land crisscrossed by rivers, ferries are mandatory in many parts of Kerala where road access is unavailable, and they are often used to transport heavier vehicles such as trucks and buses.

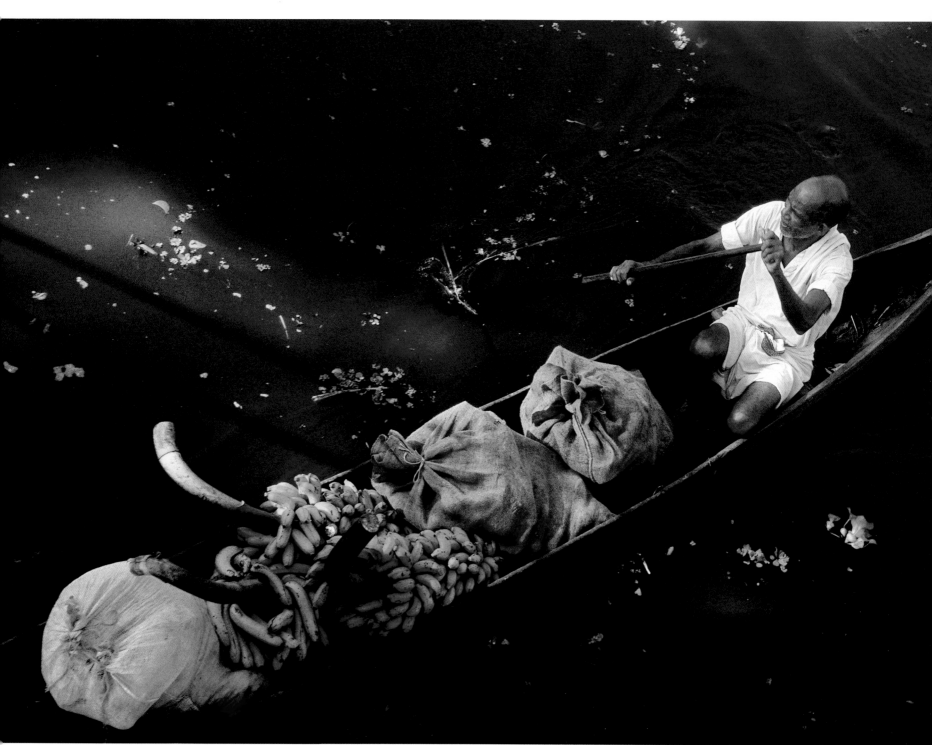

TRADITIONS

Left: A Kathakali performer replete with costume, make-up and headdress.

Given the various foreign influences that pervade Kerala, it would be natural to assume that the Malayali is a cultural mongrel. Instead one discovers a people who, despite the comings and goings of the world into their shores, are sticklers for tradition. Family reunions, festivals and weddings all have their own mores just as the everyday has its. A visit to the tea shop in villages is as customary as the daily newspaper. A ramble through the streets is as habitual as a quick discussion on world politics and local affairs. As for food, most Malayalis think of themselves as gourmands and will insist that there is nothing as delicious as Malayali food cooked the traditional way.

Ayurveda, which means the science of life, took shape in India in the second millennium B.C. It is a holistic approach to a person's health and offers not only remedies to ailments, but also to their prevention. For thousands of years Kerala has preserved this ancient tradition in its most authentic form through a long lineage of traditional practitioners and vast natural resources of medicinal herbs.[15]

Yet another tradition originates from Ayurveda: the ancient martial art of Kalaripayattu. *Kalari* means venue of training and *payattu*, martial arts. Though its exact origin is obscure,

Kalaripayattu is acknowledged as one of the oldest martial arts in the world. There is a legend about a Buddhist monk who studied Kalaripayattu in India during one of his travels and passed on his skills upon returning to Shaolin in China. Hence Kalaripayattu is said to be the originator of all other forms of martial arts. Kalaripayattu equips its practitioners not only with the skill to fight, but also the skill to heal, linking the art with Ayurveda.[16]

Kerala's two most famous dance forms are Kathakali and Mohiniattam. Kathakali, literally meaning story-play, is a dance drama that Kerala conceived in the 17th century. Kathakali combines five forms of fine art: literature, music, painting, acting and dance.[17] As much as Kathakali is an art performed exclusively by men, Mohiniattam is an art reserved for women. Mohiniattam is a classical solo dance of sheer enchantment with a very sensual undertone. In Hindu mythology Lord Vishnu took the form of Mohini, the divine enchantress, to divert the attention of havoc-wreaking demons. The dance derives its name from this divine character.[18]

Just as its dance forms, painting too had its genius and impact that percolated into the everyday life of the Malayali. Raja Ravi Varma, Kerala's most renowned painter who lived between 1848 and 1906, illustrated enchantresses, maidens, kings, scholars, gods and goddesses. In fact in a lot of Hindu homes in Kerala it is the renditions of Ravi Varma's gods and goddesses that are worshipped.

And it is this then that we must ask: in a land so steeped in tradition and so exposed to change, who are the gods and goddesses?

Left: A group of labourers in Alappuzha indulge in an extended break. Two activities are emblematic of Keralan streetlife: men engrossed in the day's newspapers and groups of men casually observing the advance of life around them.

Far left: Posing proudly in front of his teashop, this typical Keralan is content to tend his shop and observe the intricacies of day-to-day life across his shop counter.

Next page: The Panchavadyam musical performance is unique to Kerala. It involves five percussion instruments and a conch. Pictured here are Edappan Appunni and Group.

Above: Leela Cletus, a beaming Christian bride in Alappuzha is flanked by her equally exultant parents just moments before her wedding ceremony. Santosh Mani, her husband-to-be, works and lives in the Middle East. The incidence of arranged marriages like this one, once the norm in Kerala as in India, is gradually on the decline.

Right: The photographer enjoys a lighthearted moment with silk-swathed relatives at his ancestral house in Kozhikode and revisits memories of many late nights spent in this room as an eager, young photography student. The Kanchipuram silk saris of southern India are a measure of wealth and status in Kerala. From left to right: The photographer, Sudhir Ramchandran; his mother, Vimala Ramachandran; aunt, Rema Valsan; uncle, Valsan; cousin, Bina Valsan; and aunt, Seetha.

Above: Traditionally cooked in cylindrical bamboo shoot steamers, *puttu*, made from coarse rice powder and coconut, is a typical breakfast food and usually eaten with a spicy *kadala*, or chickpea, curry. For the sweet-toothed, the chickpea curry is replaced with bananas and generous sprinklings of sugar.

Right: Idiappam, or string hoppers, are steamed bunches of fluffy rice noodles that are eaten smothered in a rich potato or meat stew.

Preceding page: Kerala *paratha* are layered pancakes made from kneaded and rolled flour that is thinned by tossing it in the air. Several layers are then combined and browned on a sizzling griddle. They are most often dipped into a keenly-spiced meat curry.

Left: Not for the faint-tongued, these prawns are dusted liberally with chili powder and sautéed to a delicious crisp.

Above: The *sadya* is a smorgasbord of vegetarian delights. It is a traditional Keralan meal served on banana leaves at weddings and festival celebrations and can consist of up to 23 dishes. The positioning of the banana leaf and the order of serving the *sadya* dishes are precise. The *sadya*, like most Indian food, is eaten with one's right hand.

Ayurveda is a revered Indian healing tradition that dates back to the second millennium B.C. The words *ayur* and *veda* mean life and knowledge of respectively, and Ayurveda is essentially a treatise on the science of healthy living. Ayurveda was scoffed at by the British during their occupation of India but has now gained considerable popularity both domestically and internationally. The tradition has spawned the burgeoning industry of Ayurveda tourism.

Above left: An Ayurvedic massage in progress at Spice Village, a resort in Thekkady.

Above centre: Treatments are gleaned from palm-leaf inscriptions that are a few thousand years old.

Above right: Gigantic vats are used to prepare Ayurvedic medicines at scorching temperatures in a pharmacy.

Left: A selection of Ayurvedic herbs.

Ayurvedic treatment is much more effective during the monsoon season, when the body is cool and more responsive. Treatments are broadly divided into the rejuvenation, prevention and restoration categories. These treatments use natural herbs with each person meriting a different treatment based on his or her *prakruthi*, or unique genetic code.

Above: Ancient porcelain urns are used to mature the concoctions for Ayurvedic treatments at a traditional pharmacy.

Left: Staff pack Ayurvedic medicine at a traditional pharmacy near Kozhikode city.

Left: Between 10 and 12 hours go into the application of the intricate make-up and donning of the elaborate costumes for a Kathakali performance. The make-up is all-natural and is created from powdered minerals, spices, coconut oil and the saps and barks of certain trees and fruits. Eggplant flower seeds are inserted under the performers' eyelids to make their eyes appear bloodshot and provide a vivid contrast to the green make-up.

Far left: Kathakali artists perform at the Brunton Boatyard in Fort Kochi. Kathakali is a bewitching synergy of five forms of art: *sahithyam* (literature), *sangeetham* (music), *chithram* (painting), *natyam* (acting) and *nritham* (dance). Kathakali is usually performed in temple precincts and a single performance can extend over 10 days—one act is played out every night from dusk till daybreak.

Left: Kathakali artists apply their own make-up before a performance.

Kathakali themes are drawn from the wealth of Indian mythology and delineate the intrigues of interactions between the three worlds of gods, humans and demons. The entire story is told through the language of hand gestures and body and eye movements to the accompaniment of a vocal and instrumental score. There are five types of costumes and make-up that define the characters in any Kathakali performance. They are *pacha* (green), *kathi* (knife), *thadi* (beard), *kari* (black) and *minukku* (polished). The *chokanna thadi* (black beard) make-up, for example, represents aggressive and demonical characters. Kathakali is performed only by men.

Left and above: Mohiniattam is a classical solo dance form, performed above by Aruna Marar, that combines the grace of Bharathanatyam (a dance form native to the neighbouring state of Tamil Nadu) and the dynamism of Kathakali. Performed only by women, it originated as a temple dance performed by Devadasis—young girls whose parents betrothed them to temple deities. The dance depicts the different incarnations of feminine love and carries an air of eroticism. Temple festivals are the usual occasions for a Mohiniattam performance.

Preceding page: A whirling dance tableau by the Daksha Sheth Dance Company. The company is considered one of the most daring and contemporary troupes in India. In a land where artists rarely veer away from traditional dance forms, Daksha Sheth, a renowned exponent of the northern Indian classical dance form, Kathak, has experimented with Kalaripayattu and Chhau, a dance of eastern India. Like Kathakali, Chhau dancers remain silent and are accompanied by instruments.

All pictures: Kalaripayattu exponents in Nettoor spurn gravity in airborne face-offs. Kalaripayattu is considered as one the oldest martial arts in the world. Legend has it that Kalaripayattu was developed by Parasurama, the founder of Kerala, who taught the art to 21 disciples for the protection of the newborn territory. Kalaripayattu has a deep spiritual core with an emphasis on protection as opposed to aggression. Influences of Kalaripayattu have been borrowed and integrated into traditional dance forms such as Kathakali.

Next page: Narayanan Embranthiri dazzles the eye with his stupefying demonstration of the Kalaripayattu technique of keeping predators away from cattle. Narayanan has taken over from his father as the *gurukkal* or head teacher at the ENS Kalari Centre in Ernakulam.

Left: Brilliantly caparisoned elephants are anchored in an adoring sea of humanity at the Thrissur Pooram Festival, the largest annual Festival in India with almost a million attendees. The festival, which takes place in April, is a lighthearted duel between two temples, the Thiruvambady Krishna Temple and the Paramekavu Devi Temple, to determine which one can parade the best-looking elephants. Each temple fields 15 elephants decorated with glittering frontlets, regal parasols, peacock plume fans and yak-tail whisks. There are families in Thrissur that for generations have dedicated themselves to producing the various adornments for this particular festival. The highlight of the festival is the Kudamattam, during which the parasols are raised in turn over the elephants on either side to the thunderous roaring of the crowds. A dazzling display of fireworks and street shows forms part of the weeklong buildup to the Thrissur Pooram Festival.

Above: Tempers and temperatures cohere into the annual exhilaration that is the Aranmula Boat Race. The spectacle consists of around 26 *palliyodam,* or snake boats, thrusting down the Pamba River. Each boat is over 30 feet in length and accommodates four helmsmen, 100 rowers and 25 singers whose exhortational rhythm is echoed by the thousands of spectators. More a celebration than a competition, the Aranmula Boat Race marks the Onam festival.

Above: Raja Ravi Varma was a Keralan artist best known for his renditions of Hindu religious icons and scenes from Indian epics. His paintings of Indian women idealised the female form and were, for many years, the definitive Indian standard for feminine beauty.

Left: A Raja Ravi Varma mural of scenes from the *Mahabharata* animates a wall at the Kudira Malika Palace in Thiruvananthapuram.

GODS

Left: Krishna Jayanthi celebrations take place in Kozhikode. A 4-km-long procession of boys dressed as Lord Krishna, called a *Shoba Yatra*, winds its way to a Lord Krishna temple. Part of the celebrations depict scenes from the life of Krishna, including his mischievous exploits of breaking mud pots to treat himself to handfuls of his favourite snack of warm butter.

In Kerala, god assumes many forms. Over the years, all faiths of the world have come to Kerala and in its richness found a resting place and a haven, making it possible for all these faiths to be amalgamated with the existing forms of worship without losing their religious character. Perhaps that is the reason why in Kerala so many religions coexist in peace.

One of the foreign religions that arrived in Kerala was Judaism. The Kochi Jews claim that 10,000 Jews fled to Kerala after the Second Temple of Jerusalem was destroyed in A.D. 70. The Jewish community was ravaged by the Portuguese but left alone by the Dutch and British.

When the State of Israel was established in 1948, most of the Jews in Kochi left. Only a few hundred remained. Today the number of Jews has dwindled even further and most of them are elderly people.[19]

Christianity, in contrast, found a true home in Kerala. The Christians of Kerala today are divided into several branches: the Latin Catholic Church, the Syro-Malabar Catholic Church, the Jacobite Syrian Church, the Nestorian Church, the Anglican Church, which is now part of the Church of South India, the Marthoma Syrian Church and the Syro-Malankara Catholic Church. In addition, there are also a number of minor churches and missions. The Syrian Christians of Kerala firmly believe that St. Thomas the Apostle is the father of Christianity in India. It is said that he landed at Maliankara near Kodungalloor in A.D. 52. He preached Christianity first to the Jews and then converted 12 Brahmin families.[20]

But it is Islam that had the strongest impact in Kerala. There was much trade between India and Arabia even before Prophet Muhammad's time. Ibn Dinar came to spread the word of Islam in Kerala and set up mosques across the state. From the 15th to the 17th centuries the Muslim population flourished. This undermined the traditional Hindu caste system, negated the social superiority of the Brahmins and the Nairs and helped increase the self-esteem of the lower classes.[21]

Jainism took root in Kerala through Emperor Chandragupta Maurya, who reigned from 321 to 297 B.C. Buddhism was born in India in the sixth century B.C. and propagated by Emperor Asoka's missionaries during his lifetime between 273 and 232 B.C.[22] The religion faded after Vedic Brahmins, who arrived in Kerala between A.D. 700 and A.D. 800, proved the intellectual superiority of Hinduism over Buddhism.[23]

Today there are more than 10,000 temples in Kerala, and each has its own festivities called *pooram*. Though many of these festivals are religious, there are secular ones such as Onam, the harvest festival held in honour of the legendary King Bali.

King Bali was a noble and pious ruler. He ruled the asuras well and tried to curb their violent behaviour. Unlike his ancestors, King Bali sought supremacy over heaven and earth by non-violent means. He undertook rigorous penance instead of going to battle with the gods. By the strength of his dedication and virtue, he wrested heaven away from Indra, the king of gods. Soon Bali was king of the earth, heaven and netherworld, and everyone on earth loved him dearly. There never had been such a noble king as Bali, it was said.

Left: A small doorway belies the tunnelled potential of this dust-laden antique shop in Jew Town, Fort Kochi. Traditional masks, lamps, urns and engraved spice boxes are among some of the delights awaiting discovery.

Right: An avenue of antique shops populates the street leading to the Paradesi Synagogue. These shops are mandatory stops for both international and domestic tourists, who scour their premises for tempting bargains.

The gods soon grew jealous of King Bali and feared that they would lose their standing if he continued to reign. "The people don't turn to us in times of trouble because Bali takes such good care of them. Soon they will forget that we exist. As long as he continues to accrue such blessings, he'll be lord of the three worlds forever," the gods complained to Lord Vishnu, who was the protector and preserver of the world and restorer of moral order.

As if to convince Lord Vishnu, they added, "Bali is a good king but his children might not be such noble rulers. What then? They will destroy this universe if they inherit such enormous power!"

So Vishnu decided to step in and save the gods from further humiliation. He entered the world as Vamana, a child born to Sage Kasyapa and Aditi. Even as an adult, Vamana remained diminutive, and it was as a little man that he went to King Bali's

court asking for alms. King Bali received Vamana as though he were a very important guest and asked, "What can I do for you? How can I be of service to you?"

Vamana looked up at the king and simply said, "All I need is three feet of land!"

"Is that all?" the king asked Vamana in surprise. "Don't you need anything more?"

"Three feet of land will do," Vamana said.

"Then it shall be yours. Do take it from wherever you want," the king said, feeling curious and amused by the little man's request.

Then as the king watched, the little man began to grow and soon he was as tall as the sky. With his left foot, he covered the earth. "This is the first foot of land," Vamana said.

With his right foot, he covered the heavens. "This is the second foot. What is left, O King? Where shall I take my third foot of land from?"

King Bali realised that this was none other than Lord Vishnu and that the third foot of land had to be found. So he fell on his knees and bent his head, "All I have left is my head. Take

Left: The traditional Keralan architecture of the Munchunthi Palli Mosque in Kozhikode is indicative of the seamless assimilation of Islam into the ethos of Kerala.

Above: The Cheraman Juma Masjid in Kodungalloor was built by Hindu carpenters and masons in A.D. 629 upon the decree of the king of Kodungalloor. The very first mosques in Kerala were devoid of minarets and their gables were exquisitely carved in the fashion of Hindu temples. However, very few of these original structures remain as most were rebuilt to look like mosques in the Middle East.

Right: K.M. Haji Saidu Mohammed is a *mukri*, or muezzin, at the Cheraman Juma Masjid. He has dedicated his life to the mosque, having served there from a very young age.

Left: Muslim womenfolk pose with unusual candour outside an ancestral house in Malappuram. The Mappilas, or Malabar Muslims of Kerala, constitute 20 percent of the state's population and are one of the oldest Islamic communities in South Asia. They owe their origins to Arab traders and sailors. Unlike in North India, Islam was integrated peacefully into the fabric of Kerala as it arrived through trade and not conquest. Ibn Dinar was the man credited for first bringing Islam to Kerala.

Above: A priestess presides at the Mannarasala Sree Nagaraja Temple in Alappuzha. Amma, or Great Mother, the priestess, blesses devotees by cupping her hands in the shape of a cobra's hood. This ancient shrine is set in a serene jungle and is a renowned pilgrim centre dedicated to Nagaraja, the serpent god. A woman priestess with the exalted powers of Amma is a rarity in Kerala. She is known to cure infertility in women and leprosy, among other diseases. Any person bitten by a snake is rushed to the Amma's side for treatment inspired by her as-yet-unblemished success rate. Generations of Ammas have passed on the divine mantle to their successors since the first Amma was born in 1079.

Above: Snake worshippers lose themselves to the serpent god Nagaraja at a Hindu temple.

Right: Amma rests quietly after a frenzied ritual wherein she was supposedly possessed by the serpent deity of this temple in Kozhikode. When in this state she slithered about the temple grounds as a serpent would and leapt up frequently to spout prophecies to her ardent devotees, who stood by with bated breath.

At the Ganapathy Temple in Palakkad, freshly-
bathed priests and devotees proceed before
the crack of dawn into the misty inner rooms
where the idols reside to perform *pujas*,
or Hindu prayers. The Ganapathy Temple
 is dedicated to Lord Ganesha, considered
to be the remover of all obstacles.

All pictures and next page, left: Millions of devotees from all over India perform arduous pilgrimage rites to pay homage to Lord Ayappa at the Ayappa Temple in Sabarimala, Pathanamthitta, every year. Lord Ayappa is said to be born as the result of a union between Lord Vishnu and Lord Shiva. A 40-mile trek completes six weeks of austere living modelled on the life of an ascetic. Pilgrims observe a regimen of strict vegetarianism, celibacy and abstinence from alcohol. They are required to sleep on the floor and shun the use of footwear. Lord Ayappa was a bachelor and the confines of his temple are forbidden to all women except those yet to attain puberty and those past menopause.

Above left: An Annaprasam ceremony at Guruvayoor Temple in Thrissur. The ceremony introduces babies to their first morsels of solid food. During this highly auspicious ceremony a Brahmin priest gives the children sips of holy water and smears their little foreheads with sandal paste. The parents then feed the children with mouthfuls of rice and *payasam*, a dessert often made with rice or lentils. It is believed that performing this ceremony will ensure that the children will never want for food in later life. The Guruvayoor Temple is Kerala's most important Hindu temple.

Above right: A priest balances a baby's weight in endowments to the Guruvayoor Temple as part of Thulabharam, a special ceremony conducted by Hindus that involves a donation of fruit, sugar, coconuts or sandalwood in accordance with one's weight to the deity of the temple. In ancient India maharajahs often weighed themselves against gold or silver coins to win the deity's favour. It is also possible for non-Hindus to perform Thulabharams.

Left: Hordes of schoolboys delight in the excitement of playing Lord Krishna for a day during Krishna Jayanthi celebrations. The festival is extremely popular in India and celebrates Krishna's birthday in August. Krishna is one of the most beloved Hindu gods.

Above: The chief Theyyam performer commands the hypnotic gaze of onlookers at the Sri Muthappan Temple in Kannur. There are hundreds of different types of Theyyam, a ritualistic folk dance exclusive to northern Kerala that has a tradition going back a thousand years. The headgear of the Theyyam performer can ascend to between 9 and 12 metres and the make-up has a base colour of striking orange with the eyes banded in black and the lips a savage red. The chief performer goes into a prophetic trance and answers questions put to him from the gathered crowd about their past, present and future. This temple is the only one in Kerala that conducts daily rituals of Theyyam performances. Unique to the Sri Muthappan Temple is the non-vegetarian and alcoholic offering, which is usually dried fish and a local liquor called toddy, made to the deity.

LIVING

Left: Workers roll beedies at the Sadhoo Beedi factory in Kannur. A beedi is an indigenous, filterless cigarette produced by rolling tobacco in a tendu leaf obtained from a tree that grows wild in central India. Around 55 percent of the tobacco smoked in India is consumed via beedis as they are considerably cheaper than cigarettes, which are more prevalent in cities. A growing export market for beedis has engendered a spectrum of foreign flavours that range from black liquorice and mandarin orange to lemon-lime and wild cherry.

Life in Kerala, as in everything else about it, is composed of a texture unlike anywhere else in India. And the greatest testimony to this is the houses in the state. From spartan concrete boxes to garishly ornate mansions, from ecofriendly Laurie Baker homes to the traditional tile, wood and laterite *tharavad*, the Malayali's abode shows a discrepancy in the composition of the society. And yet each Malayali is made of the same matter within.

This eclectic range of houses is matched by an equally confounding mix of statistics: Kerala has a 90 percent literacy rate, the highest per capita consumption of newspapers in India, a fertility rate of just 1.7 births per woman and a life expectancy of 72 years, which is much higher than the life expectancy of 61 years in the rest of India. Yet Kerala also has a per capita income that is lower than Cambodia's or Sudan's and an unemployment rate

Left: Classical Keralan architecture and serene surroundings characterise Kerala Kalamandalam, which is an august academy of the arts responsible for the preservation of traditional folk art in Kerala. Students may be trained over a period of up to six years and can join performing groups that go on regular national and international cultural tours. The academy was founded in 1930 and is located in Cheruthuruthy, a small village in Thrissur.

Right: A *pathinarukettu* is a traditional house with 16 blocks built around a courtyard. Smaller variations are the *nallukettu*, or four-blocked house, and the *ettukettu*, or eight-blocked house. In the days when the caste system and untouchability were rife in Kerala, the upper castes communicated with the lower castes through the bars encircling the room.

that is one of the highest in India.[24]

In short, though Kerala is very poor, it manages to maintain a decent standard of living. This can be largely attributed to Communist policies implemented in 1957 when Communists won the elections in Kerala. The state was the first in the world to form a democratically elected communist government.[24]

For years, Kerala has survived on meagre income from the agricultural sector and cottage industries, which range from its legendary handlooms to terracotta tiles, from making beedis to banana chips and from the manufacture of rubber to coconut-based products. In fact, among the many tags Kerala has earned for itself, the most pertinent one is the money order economy. Most of the money reaching Kerala is sent from outside the state and specifically from its workers in the Middle East.[24]

Unlike the rest of India, Kerala has resisted industrialisation. This may prove untenable in the long run, and the state might have to accept some degree of industrialisation eventually. The challenge is to do so without eroding the natural splendour or quality of everyday life, which in many ways is still idyllic. All one needs to do is to take a walk through a village in Kerala to understand just why the state defies description or pigeonholing of any kind.

Let's begin with the outskirts. At a house by the fields and in the

distance are shadowy peaks. The earth is black and moist, and all day a cool breeze blows and lifts worries and anxieties away. The lushness of the vegetation, both wild and cultivated, adds to the tranquillity of the place.

Midway is the village *kavu*, or sacred grove. In the winter months, just as the moon shines with a particular brilliance, so does the Velluchapad's, or oracle's, fortunes. An offering is made every night, and the Velluchapad is a busy man. Meanwhile the RSS Pracharaks go about their drill in the temple grounds.

At the other end of the village is the *vayanashala*, or reading room. There are rows of books—some tattered and old, while others are still fragrant with printer's ink. Adolf Hitler's *Mein Kampf* sits cheek by jowl with Mahatma Gandhi's *The Story of My Experiments with Truth*. There are at least a thousand books in this little reading room, and all it costs a person to use the library is 29 rupees a year.

And then appears the first contradiction. The noise. Pure rant is the resonance of Kerala. Its chief instrument is the trumpet-shaped loudspeaker, or *kolambi*, as the villagers refer to it.

Long before even the birds wake up, the *kolambi* spews out devotional songs from the village *kavu*. Then there is a long silence that is broken by a riot of birdcalls. This is soon followed by sounds that signal the commencement of the day's activities. Jeeps begin to prowl hither and thither to advertise new shops, political meetings, a film release, lottery tickets, eye camps and so on. Everyday there is something to blare about!

Then arrive the vendors. The fish vendor has a cry that is a hoot turned into a call, and he is ably supported by an air horn. As the day wears out, the sounds of faith take their turn at commanding the airwaves. The *kolambi* hisses and splutters. In most villages, this has become the equivalent of a factory siren. Workers put down their hoes, ploughs, knives and spades and begin to walk home as the songs drown all noise, natural and otherwise. A short while later sermons begin in a mosque at the other end of the village and continue into the night.

Then rant dwindles to quiet. The cicadas begin their shrill song, and in the sky Sirius glows brighter than ever. These are the only invariables in a state where the only thing constant about life is change.[1]

The Kudira Malika Palace, or Horse Palace, was named for the line of prancing horses that support the roof of the top floor. The palace has been restored and converted into a museum displaying traditional artefacts and a collection of royal family paintings.

Left: Siblings Sujeesh and Radhika are quizzed by their mother, M.K. Sumathi, on what they have learnt in school that day as part of a daily routine. This maternal concern is a vital part of Kerala's tradition of education.

Right: Schoolchildren in Alappuzha on a break from class. Tourists, greeted with persistent cries of "Pen, miss!" from hordes of schoolchildren in Kerala as opposed to demands for money or food in other parts of the country, will vouch for the triumph of the state's education system.

Below right: Reading the daily newspaper is almost a religious activity in Kerala among the young and old. Kerala is the most literate state in India with an overall literacy level of 90 percent. Unique to the state are government-owned and privately-run reading rooms, where people retire to read and discuss matters of interest— politics being a favourite topic.

tourism industry have been quick to capitalise on its new-found international appeal.

Right: The owner of a roadside tea stall in Kottayam performs his rendition of the famed four-foot tea with typical nonchalance. The four-foot tea involves the dual tasks of mixing the tea, sugar and milk as well as cooling it to prevent scalded tongues. Exponents of the four-foot tea can be found across Kerala. Tea is one of the most popular beverages in the state.

Above: The myriad foreign occupations of Kerala are evident along a walk down Fort Kochi's streets in Ernakulam. Buildings reflect in turn the influences of the Dutch, Portuguese, British and Chinese presence in Kochi and imbue the street with a multicultural appeal.

Top: Windy palms preside over a yoga session at the Marari Beach Resort in the village of Mararikulam. Yoga is an ancient Indian practice aimed at uniting the body, mind and soul. In recent years yoga has attracted a considerable following in the West, and players in Kerala's

Preceding page: Children out on a school picnic on Kappad beach climb to an elevated point to view the Arabian Sea.

Left: The photographer's favourite aunt, Seetha Teacher as she was known to all, was wedded to her profession. She taught for almost 50 years. Many of her students are now successfully employed in different parts of the world. The photographer remembers many happy days spent studying photography by the window of this room with his aunt absorbed in religious reading in the foreground.

Above: Long-time Kannur resident Mrs. Balagopal cherishes rare moments with her holidaying daughter-in-law Sulekha and grandchildren Premalatha and Partha.

Dr. Sulekha Randhir, a first-generation immigrant to Kuwait, is one of the millions of Indians in the Persian Gulf. Kerala alone has exported about two million members of her workforce to the Middle East. Signs of Gulf money are evident in the sprawling houses and affluent lifestyle of Gulf returnees.

Above: Handloom fabrics are shipped to all over the world from the modest interiors of Commonwealth Trust (India) Ltd, or ComTrust, in Kozhikode. The pioneering ComTrust fabrics are internationally prized for their quality and variety. The word calico is derived from the old name for the city of Kozhikode, which was Calicut.

Left: The coir industry provides employment to half a million people in Kerala. Coir is a fibre produced from the husk of the coconut. The husk is separated from the coconut, soaked in water for a period of up to 10 months, beaten with a mallet and spun on a loom to produce a variety of household and personal utilities, from doormats and carpets to wall hangings and footwear. India is the third-largest coconut-producing country in the world.

Far left: Bell metal is fired in Alappuzha to produce artefacts ranging from the religious to the quotidian—from temple or church bells and lamps to cooking utensils and serving plates. Brass, tin and copper form an alloy from which the different products are fashioned. Bell metal crafting is another of Kerala's family-centred professions, passed on practically and orally from generation to generation. The younger generation's pursuit of more lucrative professions poses a grave threat to the survival of the art.

Above: PNC Menon with his wife. Founder of a conglomerate synonymous with state-of-the-art construction, PNC Menon is a Malayali who has come back to pay tribute to his roots. His Middle Eastern corporation, the Services and Trade Company, incarnated in India as Sobha Developers and has revolutionised the construction industry with its world-class standards.

Left: The much-feted Captain C.P. Krishnan Nair, chairman of Leela Palaces and Resorts, is a pioneer nonpareil in both the garment and hospitality industries.

Preceding page, left: Painter and sculptor Yusuf Arakkal meditates on a roller-coaster life that saw him go from pounding the pavements of Bangalore to being one of the most revered Indian artists of the 20th century. He has held solo exhibitions all over the world and credits his success to hard work and self-belief.

Preceding page, right: Balan Nambiar's art is fed by the deep roots of his tradition, particularly the ritual art form of Theyyam. Balan's creative energy finds expression in sculpture, painting and photography. His art resides in museums and private collections across the globe.

Body Text Bibliography

1 *Magical Indian Myths*. Anita Nair, Puffin Books, India.

2 www. shelterbelt.com/KJ/khprasuram.html

3 kerala-history.nrksite.com

4 traveltoindianet.com/history-of-kerala.html

5 members.tripod.com/anil_varghese/hland.html

6 www.kerala.com/kera/travel.htm

7 www.kerala.cc/keralahistory/index6.htm

8 www.kerala.indianvisit.com/wildlife/silent_valley

9 www.keralaonline.com/travelindex.asp?cap=thwild

10 kerala.indianvisit.com/beaches/index.html

11 www.theindiatravel.com/cityguide/state/kerala/beaches.html

12 www.kerala.indianvisit.com/destinations/quilon

13 www.bartleby.com/65/ca/calico.html

14 kerala.indianvisit.com/backwaters/index.html

15 www.healthlibrary.com/news/1-6jan2001/times-ayurveda1.htm

16 www.kalaripayattu.org/history.htm

17 www.sholay.com/culture

18 www.indianest.com/dances/00108.htm

19 www.kerala.cc/keralahistory/index35.htm

20 www.kerala.cc/keralahistory/index36.htm

21 www.kerala.cc/keralahistory/index37.htm

22 search.eb.com

23 www.kerala.cc/keralahistory/index34.htm

24 www.theatlantic.com/issues/98sep/kerala.htm

Caption Bibliography

WEBSITES

ayurveda.indianvisit.com

campus.northpark.edu

coconutboard.nic.in

elephant.elehost.com

in.biz.yahoo.com

krpcds.org

skepdic.com

teacher.scholastic.com

travel.indiamart.com

us.rediff.com

www.acorn-deepika.com

www.alappuzha.com

www.all-india-tour-
    travel.com

www.allkeralatours.com

www.american.edu

www.ayurveda-herbs.com

www.ayurvedic.org

www.ayyappan-ldc.com

www.balannambiar.com

www.bigshots.com.au

www.bismicoir.com

www.blonnet.com

www.capitalmarket.com

www.cardamomcityindia.com

www.casinogroup.com

www.censusindia.net

www.cmicongregation.org

www.cochin.org

www.dailyexcelsior.com

www.eindiatourism.com

www.evesindia.com

www.financialexpress.com

www.flonnet.com

www.freethechildren.org

www.hinduonnet.com

www.humnri.com

www.idukki.net

www.indiaagronet.com

www.indiainfoline.com

www.indianchristianity.com

www.indianembassy.org

www.indianmirror.com

www.indianspices.com

www.indiantravelinfo.com

www.indianvisit.com

www.indiaprofile.com

www.indiatravelinfo.com

www.indiatravelite.com

www.indiavarta.com

www.inika.com/arakkal

www.iyengar-yoga.com

www.kanjirappally.com

www.kannurtourism.org

www.kau.edu

www.kerala.com

www.kerala-hub.com

www.keralaeverything.com

www.klresort.com

www.kumarakom.com

www.midastreads.com

www.qjada.com

www.rediff.com

www.rubbermark.com

www.saranamayyappa.org

www.shelterbelt.com

www.smokeshopmag.com

www.sobhadevelopers.com

www.sundaykaumudi.com

www.tajhotels.com

www.thehorizons.com

www.thekkady.com

www.theleela.com

www.tribuneindia.com

www.trichurpooram.com

www.unep-wcmc.org

www.veesquare.com

www.webindia123.com

www1.cs.columbia.edu

Publications

Dance (Classic India Series). Ashish Khokar, Rupa & Co., 1994.

Dasha Avatar. India Book House Private Limited, 2001.

Discover Wayanad 'The Green Paradise'. District Tourism Promotion Council Wayanad, 1995.

Dravidian Kinship. Thomas R. Trautmann, Cambridge University Press, 1981.

Explore Kerala Travel Guide. Explore & Travel, 1998.

Facets of a Hundred Years Planting. Amita Baig and William Henderson, Tata Finley Limited, 1978.

Festivals of Kerala. P.J. Varghese, K.R. Ramachandran and P.S. Kurian, Tourist Desk, Cochin, 1993.

Important Birds of Periyar. Forestry Information Bureau, Kerala Forestry Department, 1995.

Kerala. The Guidebook Company Limited, 1993.

Kerala—Colours, Culture & Lifestyle. Salim Pushpanath and Ajay Marar, DEE BEE Info Publications, 2000.

Kerala Festivals. Salim Pushpanath and Ajay Marar, DEE BEE Info Publications, 1997.

Kerala—The Green Miracle. Salim Pushpanath & Ajay Marar, DEE BEE Info Publications.

Kerala: The Spice Coast of India. Raghubir Singh, Thames & Hudson, 1986.

Kerala—Tourists' Handbook. DEE BEE Info Publications, 1994.

Malabar Manual Volumes I & II. William Logan, Asian Educational Services, 1951.

Mattancherry Palace. Shivananda Venkatarao and Raman Namboodri, Archaeological Survey of India, Government of India, 1997.

Our Progress—A Bird's Eye View: 1902-1994. The Arya Vaidya Sala, Kottakkal.

Performing Arts of Kerala. Pankaj Shah & Mallika Sarabhai, Mapin Publishing Private Limited, 1994.

Seven Sacred Rivers. Bill Aitken, Penguin Books, 2003.

The Great Mother. Manasa Publications, 1991.

Theyyam Guide. District Tourism Promotion Council Kannur, 2000.

Tourism Directory of Kerala. Priyan C. Ooman, Global Communications, 1995.

Tourism Travel Directory of Kerala. United Communications, 1996.

These books provide valuable additional information on Kerala. However, most of them were produced in India and may not be available in other countries.

Index

Sudhir Ramchandran

is an advertising and editorial

photographer of international standing.

Photo Credits
Above : Neha Diddee
Left : M.K. Haridas
Pages 9 and 13 : On location photos by Sanjay Ramachandran,
Neha Diddee, M.K. Haridas, G. Kumaran and Tony Ooi Kok Pin.

Biography

Sudhir Ramchandran was born in Tanzania and migrated to India in his youth, and for the past three decades these multicultural roots have influenced his photography of the world.

A ceaseless innovator and tenacious perfectionist in the field of imaging, Sudhir has conceptualised and executed pioneering imaging projects all over the world. Since 1983 he has created hugely successful holistic workshops, the Compression Curve and NewSchool series, which saw expositions of some of the world's keenest creative minds in the fields of fashion, advertising, writing, design, photography and the digital arts. He is a popular lecturer on the photography circuit and holds regular workshops and seminars at various universities. He has nurtured interns from New York University, New York; Parsons School of Design, New York; and the National Institute of Design, Ahmedabad, among others.

He works with formats ranging from 8"x10"s to 35 mms and has been involved in numerous commercial and personal projects, many of which have won national and international awards including the FAO Gold Medal from the United Nations Educational, Scientific and Cultural Organisation (UNESCO). He was president of the Advertising and Industrial Photographers Association (AIPA) of India and Ambassador to the World Council of Professional Photographers (WCPP).

Sudhir's personal work consists primarily of beautiful international landscapes and people. His work has appeared in several leading international publications including *National Geographic Magazine*, premier books on India such as *Spectacular India* by Mapin Publishing Pvt. Ltd., and the prestigious Christie's London publication, *Costumes and Textiles of Royal India*. He is a frequent contributor to various magazines including Newsweek, *Architectural Digest, Interiors, Society, Asian Photography* and *India Today*.

Apart from commissioned projects that include the large format Mysore Palace publication and an upcoming book on the World Heritage Site of the Vijayanagar Empire, Sudhir has produced a series of pictorial essays on the Nilgiris that have been commissioned by Needle Industries India Pvt. Ltd. and reproduced as calendars. These calendars are a visual homage to the vanishing lifestyles and landscapes of the Nilgiris in South India. His love for spaces and people has ensured long-standing clients in the architectural and advertising fields including the Sheraton, the Taj and the Leela Group of Palaces and Resorts , and the Singapore Tourism Board.

Sudhir's work is a kinetic mix of images of surreal beauty and editorial immediacy. He is currently developing a body of work that arrests the swirl and spirit of India in eloquently composed panoramic format images.

Sudhir lives in Bangalore, India, with his wife and three children. He works out of offices in Singapore, Bangalore and London.

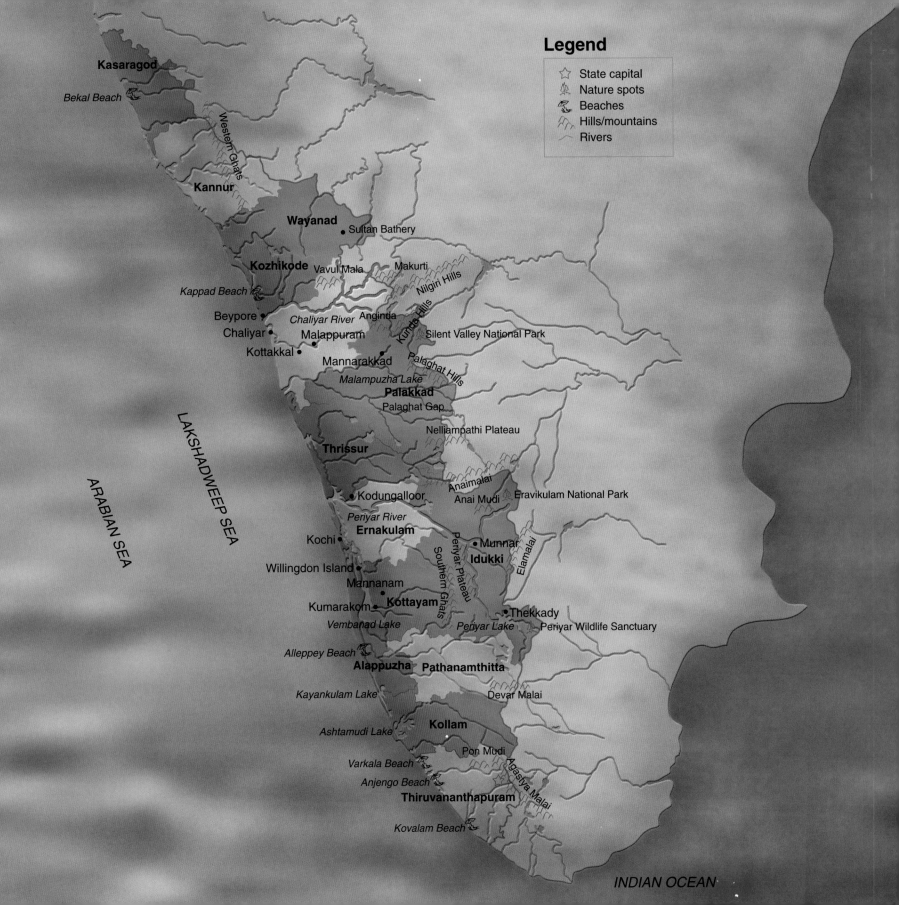

Legend

- ☆ State capital
- 🌲 Nature spots
- 🏄 Beaches
- ⛰ Hills/mountains
- 〰 Rivers

Kasaragod

Bekal Beach

Kannur

Western Ghats

Wayanad

• Sultan Bathery

Kozhikode

Vavul Mala   Makurti

Nilgiri Hills

Kappad Beach

Beypore •   *Chaliyar River*   Anginda

Chaliyar •   Malappuram   *Kunda Hills*

Kottakkal •   Silent Valley National Park

Mannarakkad   *Palaghat Hills*

Malampuzha Lake

Palakkad

Palaghat Gap

Nelliampathi Plateau

Thrissur

Anaimalai

Kodungalloor   Anai Mudi   Eravikulam National Park

Periyar River

Ernakulam

Kochi •   • Munnar

Idukki

Willingdon Island •   *Elamalai*

Mannanam   *Southern Plateau*

Kumarakom •   Kottayam

• Thekkady

Vembanad Lake   *Periyar Lake*   Periyar Wildlife Sanctuary

Alleppey Beach

Alappuzha   Pathanamthitta

Kayankulam Lake   Devar Malai

Kollam

Ashtamudi Lake

Pon Mudi

Varkala Beach   *Agastya Malai*

Anjengo Beach

Thiruvananthapuram

Kovalam Beach

ARABIAN SEA

LAKSHADWEEP SEA

Southern Ghats

Periyar Plateau

INDIAN OCEAN